POWER OF PERSUASION

Over the years of the developing judicial review of ministerial and governmental decisions, Louis Blom-Cooper was a leading advocate who grew up with the advent of a distinctive brand of public law. His range of public activities, both in and outwith the courtroom, saw him dubbed by his colleagues as a polymath practitioner. It included chairmanship of plural public inquiries in child abuse and mental health, media contributions in the broadsheet press and in broadcasting, and innovation in penal reform, as an ardent campaigner for the abolition of capital punishment and a plea for a modern Homicide Act. He styled himself as a modern, reconstructed liberal – a man before his time.

This collection of essays is uniquely prefaced by a self-examination of his unorthodox philosophy towards the law in action. It covers a variety of socio-legal topics that expresses his ambition to inform a poorly-educated public on the workings of the legal system. This aim involves a discussion of the constitutional history of Britain, unwritten and insufficiently interpreted; it reflects a commitment to the European Convention on Human Rights and portrays its international origins. The collection opines on crime and punishment; in the functioning of the courts and elsewhere the political shift from the penal optimism of the 1970s to the reactionary punitiveness of the post-1990s. The essays conclude with a miscellany of affairs, reflecting on professional practices and their product of judicial heroes in Lord Reid and Lord Bingham.

Power of Persuasion

Essays by a Very Public Lawyer

Sir Louis Blom-Cooper QC

·HART·
PUBLISHING

OXFORD AND PORTLAND, OREGON
2015

Published in the United Kingdom by Hart Publishing Ltd
16C Worcester Place, Oxford, OX1 2JW
Telephone: +44 (0)1865 517530
Fax: +44 (0)1865 510710
E-mail: mail@hartpub.co.uk
Website: http://www.hartpub.co.uk

Published in North America (US and Canada) by
Hart Publishing
c/o International Specialized Book Services
920 NE 58th Avenue, Suite 300
Portland, OR 97213-3786
USA
Tel: +1 503 287 3093 or toll-free: (1) 800 944 6190
Fax: +1 503 280 8832
E-mail: orders@isbs.com
Website: http://www.isbs.com

Hart Publishing is an imprint of Bloomsbury Publishing plc.

British Library Cataloguing in Publication Data
Data Available

ISBN: 978-1-84946-816-9

Typeset by Hope Services Ltd, Abingdon
Printed and bound in Great Britain by
CPI Group (UK) Ltd, Croydon CR0 4YY

Foreword

I have known Sir Louis Blom-Cooper QC for most of my professional life. He has always been radical in his views. He was an early advocate of human rights, long before it was fashionable to be one. His intelligence has shone through everything that he has done. Perhaps above all, his enthusiasm for and love of the law has been a hallmark of his life and remains undimmed even in old age. He continues to test and challenge received wisdom and has a knack of asking awkward questions. It is remarkable that he is still questioning and writing with vigour and insight.

My first experience of him was when he was a civil practitioner. But he was then, as he has been throughout his long and distinguished career, very much more than that. If three words could describe the expansive nature of his contribution to the law and society, '*peace, order, and good government*', Lord Mansfield's words from his seminal decision in *R v Barker* (1762) 3 Burr. 1264 come to mind. They are words that resonate throughout this majestic work and the essays collected within it. They are words that underpin this very public lawyer's life and work. Whether the subject is the development of separation of powers, consideration of reform to the law of homicide, the role of jury trial in our justice system, or the proper development of media law and regulation, his writings demonstrate his keen search for answers to the broad question of how the law can help frame a good and just society. That this is a question that continues to face us only emphasises the importance and relevance of this collection. Each essay demonstrates a depth of analysis that is matched by the breadth of sources on which he has drawn. These include personal accounts derived from conversations and discussions with past Lord Chief Justices, personal experience drawn, for example, from his work as chair of the Howard League for Penal Reform or as chair of various public inquiries, or an examination of the work of Thomas Carlyle or Alexander Hamilton. All of this is as much a testament to Sir Louis' intellectual and practical engagement over the course of a long and fruitful career as it is of benefit to the reader. Perhaps most importantly for an advocate who seeks to persuade, the essays are immediately engaging. I cannot commend this collection more highly.

The Right Honourable Lord Dyson, Master of the Rolls

Contents

Introduction

T HIS COLLECTION OF essays possesses two curiosities: first, the essays derive their origin from a multi-faceted practice as a lawyer in public fora; second, the author's aim to influence the reader on law and moral issues. First, if the essays are not, strictly speaking, polymathic, some come from a professional career that extended to activities outside the legal system, such as public inquiries and scribblings on public administration and media activities. From 1987 until retirement from practising law in 2004, I never appeared as an advocate in the courtroom, but was engaged in a range of public inquiries, ending with the needlessly expensive inquiry into Bloody Sunday. By then I had encompassed a career of rare extent – journalist, lawyer, penal reformer and public inquirer and broadcaster, never without the wig and pen.

My range of activities, by any standards, was expansive. I began practice at the Bar in 1952, a civil law practitioner of modest aims; it lacked any venture into the criminal courts, yet I made their nodding acquaintance through my lobbying for the abolition of capital punishment in 1965 and indulging in penal affairs through the Howard League for Penal Reform. This led to my first public appointment, as a member of the Home Secretary's Advisory Council on the Penal System (1966–78). The emerging vision of a civilised penal system was accompanied by an interest in criminology and a post lecturing to aspiring social workers at Bedford College, University of London (1961–81).

The judicial element was not prominent, although it emerged occasionally, if only to taste its habits. Quite exceptionally for a practising lawyer I opted to be part of the lay magistracy. When the City of London Magistrates' Court was transformed into a Bench that was fully occupied by non-aldermanic members in 1969, I sought to be appointed and remained so until 1981 (a reference to my participation in adjudication on lesser crimes is alluded to in an essay). That was not enough of a sample of higher judiciary. In 1988 I became a member (part-time) of the two Courts of Appeal for Jersey and

Guernsey; apt disqualification came in 1996 after a useful taste of appellate work. Finally, from 1992 until 1996 I sat occasionally as a deputy High Court judge, mainly dealing with judicial review cases on homelessness administered by local government. Thus, both ends of the forensic tussle – Bench and Bar – were well-sampled.

My association with academia remained a constant theme in my blossoming practice, only entering into criminal practice after I took silk in 1970. It was in the late 1960s and thereafter that I developed a growing practice in judicial review and administrative law. The fracture in legal practice thereafter was unexpected. In 1984 the London Borough of Brent invited me to lead the team inquiring into the abuse of Jasmine Beckford at the hands of her ambitious stepfather. Public inquiries became a staple diet for the next 20 years, mostly in the capacity of chairman-led inquiries. Interspersed was a part-time chairmanship, from 1987–94, of the Mental Health Act Commission, a watchdog body for the detention of mental patients, but without any executive powers of release from mental hospitals. Only a short sojourn as the chairman of the Press Council (1989–90), the newspaper industry's self-regulatory system, intervened as a continuing participant in media activities.

The beginning of the twenty-first century beckoned a retreat from professional work. The years since 2004 prompted thoughts of recollection and reminiscences of legal and other practice. Hence this collection. But why do I want to put on record what I had done, or not done? I began to contemplate explaining myself. Here it is. Whatever may be the profession's judgment on my forensic efforts, often on behalf of clients who appeared to be less deserving of justice than their fellow citizens, my motivation, in and out of the courtroom, has always been dictated by a passionate desire to effect change through persuasion, and not by any executive power that might be invested in me. What follows are my attempts, both successful and failed, to persuade.

John Stuart Mill wrote that the only purpose for which power can be rightly exercised over any member of a civilised community against his will, is to prevent harm to others. His own good, either physical or moral, is not a sufficient warrant. He cannot rightfully be compelled to do, or to forebear to act, because it will be better for him to do so; or because it will make him happier or contented. In the opinion of other reasonable persons, to do otherwise, or even simply be right, is unsustainable. It is absolutely right to say that Mill's 'Harmful Principle' is a moral argument, and does not encompass its pragmatic application. Many people – and I am one of them

– choose freely not to get themselves into trouble by espousing the application of harm to others. But nevertheless those that encounter potential trouble can be applauded for their non- utilitarian defence of the Harmful Principle of John Stuart Mill. Power is necessarily or justifiably exercisable, but only at risk to others, and under official regulation or recognised authority. An official position involves the exercise of implied power, with all its concomitants.

While I never aspired to engage in political life, I was keen to influence those constructing issues of social and legal policy. The art of persuasion is for the persuader, by the use of freedom of expression, to induce in his listener a cogent argument, and to engage in negotiation and discussion towards the translation of an idea, concept or other issue requiring administrative or legislative action. The fully fledged public intellectual, like the ancient rhetorician, for whom argument was a public act of persuasion, merged the disciplines of the politician and the intellectual. Argumentativeness, I suspect, would be the characteristic most swiftly affixed to my public image (and probably by my family, in the domestic scene). The characteristic appropriately attached to me is as a casuist.

If I have to describe myself temperamentally as a public lawyer, I instinctively recall an instance in my career on acceptance from the Secretary of State for Northern Ireland in August 1992, Lord Mayhew of Twysden, of the office of Independent Commissioner for the Holding Centres, a system of detention of terrorist suspects in the Province. On taking up the appointment in 1993 (until 2000) I was escorted around one of the three centres, Strand Road, Derry. My escort was a superintendent of the Royal Ulster Constabulary (the predecessor of the Police Service of Northern Ireland), who asked me questions in a desire to pigeonhole me politically in terms of the tribal division of the populace of the Province. Was I a Catholic Jew or a Protestant Jew? I responded instantly that my interests were entirely catholic and I had spent my whole life protesting against authority. His cheerful acknowledgement of my professional suitability initiated a sound relationship with the police force in Northern Ireland, which had endured a stream of complaints of ill-treatment, mainly from the United States: these stopped on my appointment.

I think that I am a modern exponent of the post-war atheistic principle of casuistry, which I imbibed from Hugo Bedau's *Making Mortal Choices: three exercises in moral casuistry.*[1] I had earlier

---

[1] H Bedau, *Making Mortal Choices: three exercises in moral casuistry* (Oxford, OUP, 1997).

resolved to reject, throughout my life, any concept of exercising power over fellow human beings. I would agree with Sir Colin Davis, who said that 'power is a beastly ingredient in our society'. It is the end of my journey in public life in which it is the best I can do for explaining myself. Let me shortly explain how I arrived at the decision to select the choices reflected hereinafter.

Throughout the years after the Second World War, casuistry has had a bad time at the hands of philosophical commentators. It seemed also, to all the contemporary practitioners, that I had in the formative years of my professional life pointed out that many of us were much too ready to justify what we wanted to do about moral choice; that everything depended on whatever we want is a principle that one had in mind to do. We were essentially pragmatists in a world search for some inner meaning. Not until I had been in practice for some years did I realise that this was religiously argued, and failed to meet any ruling principle. Casuistry, so aptly described by Bedau in an appendix to his three exercises, was demonstrated by Aristotle, in his *Nichomachean Ethics* around 330 BC, and also much later in Cicero's *De Officiis* in around 44 BC as the systematic approach to ethical problems derived from Ciceronian rhetoric. Rabbinic *pilpul* and Roman common law also influenced modern casuistry independently of classical rhetoric of later ages. Bedau explains it thus:[2]

> The term 'casuistry' is derived from *casus*, Latin for 'case', and refers to the study of individual 'cases of conscience' in which more than one settled moral principle (or perhaps none) applies. More broadly, casuistry is the use of the 'method of cases' in the attempt to bring ethical reflections to bear on problems requiring the decision and action of some moral agent. A casuist is thus one who is trained to provide such counsel. Accordingly, casuistry is a branch of applied ethics. Since the seventeenth century, however, the term has often been used in a derogatory sense, as though casuistry were a species of sophistical reasoning by means of which almost any conduct could apparently be deemed permissible, provided only that one is ingenious enough in exploiting exceptions and special circumstances.
>
> For the casuist, the solution to a morally problematic case is obtained by comparing and contrasting its features with various paradigm cases whose moral status is settled. Solutions to the problem cases rely both on moral principles or maxims that express the received wisdom concerning such paradigms and on analogies to them. The plurality of principles is a source of their actual or potential conflict, but their general

---

[2] *Making Mortal Choices*, Appendix 101–102.

reliability otherwise is taken for granted. Hence, casuistry as a method of practical reasoning tends to rely on some form of intuitionism as well as on some set of moral norms more or less beyond dispute.

The governing idea of casuistry is expressed in the second-order maxim that 'circumstances alter cases'. As Thomas Aquinas wrote (1275): 'The human act ought to vary according to diverse conditions of persons, time and other circumstances: this is the entire matter or morality'. The method of cases is designed to take these 'diverse conditions' into account. This is to be contrasted both with mechanical application of rigid rules of conduct and with the attempt to ground moral decision making in some grand theory of the good or the right.

The casuistic method since the 1970s is a way to investigate any case whose several moral problems 'turn out to be nested and intertwined with each other', avoiding any singular independent principle about how they would be resolved to form a part of a general conclusion. No one doubts the methodology, but different people arrive at different verdicts. They do not invalidate the several outcomes, but they evaluate them and assess them in the general context. The casuistic method questions them independently; they merely delegate their batting order. As such, the casuistic method, properly understood, survives.

What brand of casuistry – particularly as one possessed of a fertile mind[3] – would I subscribe to? I would concede, for example, that moral principles would support the comment on the propriety of self-destruction, that the physically disabled should be allowed to determine their moment of dying, and to that end lawfully seek the assistance of another: section 2(1) of the Suicide Act 1961 should be amended so as to decriminalise assisted killing. The ground of lawfulness would be that to maintain criminality in those circumstances would be disproportionate or discriminatory under public law principles. This contemporary example of legalising an issue of social policy would satisfy the casuist who implicitly accepts two strategies. These two supply the reasoning for pronouncing and evaluating the right to life (and the limited right to die as an aspect of living). As Albert Hirschmann once wrote, the reformist motivation for deciding to end one's own life, with appropriate assistance, can qualify as either 'exit', or 'voice' for dealing with institutions of civilised society. 'Exit', which is legally passive, connotes voting with one's feet and ticking the relevant box. 'Voice' expresses one's displeasure or dissent at governance; it operates to plead for change.

Reflecting on my fundamental approach to life I would describe myself as creatively inclined, but always fuelled with doubt and the

---

[3] Lord Wilberforce so referred to me in his judgment in *Zamir* [1980] AC 930.

prospect of failure. That attitude may come across as a propensity to self-subversion, because it blunders regardless of the ability to contemplate the consequence. It is as if no distinction is drawn between the sequence of events and its consequence: *post hoc, propter hoc*. Given their different impact of cause and effect, the author should have stopped to think before indulging the casuist's motive. It avoids the functional uses of negative emotions – frustration, aggression or inherent anxiety, such as failing to listen to the entreaties of others who exhibit concern for their fellow human beings. It is that which I describe as the power of persuasion that ignores or disregards the power of failure. I should explain.

Late in life I underwent major surgery – I am glad to say, successfully – to remove a malignant tumour from the cavity in my lower brain. When I first emerged from the effects of the anaesthesia, I asked the surgeon, amidst my stream of unintelligible mutterings, 'Why are bananas bent?' (I must have been referring to my inheritance during youth of the Covent Garden fruit market (and the import of Fyffes bananas). Perplexed by my asinine question, the surgeon shrugged his shoulders. Irrespective of an answer to my rhetorical question, I had already mentally answered the conundrum, with the remark that nobody had bothered to go to the jungle to adjust the bananas and make them straight. Somebody who had perceived the apparent fault in the physical appearance of a valuable fruit would have bothered to take some action, economic or administrative, to predict the outcome of marketing the banana. One would have guessed that turning a blind eye to an envisaged wrong would have avoided potential failure.

So it has been with me. I have tried to influence without foresight of influential effect. The proposition follows, that the power of persuasion is always accompanied by the product of failure. The modern casuist who neglects the proposition employs the latter reasoning of Hirschmann's two strategies – 'the voice' – and must accept the duality of the process. An outspoken project will end in success or failure, or perhaps over time, a bit of both.

I was struck recently by the primary status accorded to persuasive argument. Michael Ignatieff in his illuminating book *Fire and Ashes*[4] claimed that failure in political thought is built-in to moments of success. Success, however, matters less than the simple fact that persuasion is attempted.

---

[4] M Ignatieff, *Fire and Ashes* (Cambridge MA, Harvard University Press, 2013) 174–75 and 183.

Part I

Public Law:
Judicial and Judicious Review

1

The Scope of Judicial Review and the Rule of Law: Between Judicial Restraint and Judicial Creativity

AN ESSAY ON THE BRITISH CONSTITUTION

It is of course true that the judges in this country are not elected and are not answerable to Parliament. It is also of course true . . . that Parliament, the executive and the courts have different functions. But the function of independent judges charged to interpret and apply the law is universally recognised as a cardinal feature of the modern democratic state, a cornerstone of the rule of law itself.[1]

WALTER BAGEHOT IN *The English Constitution*[2] has explained the issue pithily: 'there are two great objects which every constitution must attain to be successful . . . every constitution must first gain authority [the Crown], and then use authority'; it must first win the authority and confidence of mankind, and then apply that homage in the work of government. First, the authority, then government. Thus, when Britain joined the European Economic Community in 1972 (the precursor to the European Union), the British Government had no difficulty in recognising that the Luxembourg Compromise of 1966 formed part of the European jurisprudence it would have to (indeed, was eager to) endorse. The British Constitution was, after all, set out in unwritten rules, conventions and customs. The Luxembourg Compromise was a 'constitutional convention', in the sense of being an unwritten rule that supports 'a political order' that underwrote, sharing roughly, the same values of government, of which there are three arms –

---

[1] *A v Home Secretary* [2004] UKHL 56, [2005] 2 WLR 87 [42] (Lord Bingham of Cornhill). All Western liberal democracies, with their commitment to the rule of law, are based on similar constitutions, whether these are written or uncodified. There is nothing untoward in a constitution being unwritten, so long as it is composed of fundamental rules.

[2] W Bagehot, *The English Constitution* (ed RH Crossman, London, Fontana, 1963) 61.

legislature, executive and judicature. The constitution was outstandingly proclaimed in the first judgment of the European Court of Justice at Luxembourg, in *Van Gend en Loos* in February 1963, as expanded in *Costa/ENEL* in June 1964. These cases conferred on litigants the right to protect themselves from the violations of the EEC.

Ever since the early 1740s, when Montesquieu devoted a whole chapter in his *De L'esprit des Loix* – misunderstandingly – to the English constitution, commentators have universally adopted, without sufficient analysis, the phrase 'the separation of powers'. This then was an unhelpful and enduring exaggeration. Governmental powers are always shared, if originally, by modern standards, disappointingly (or disproportionately) between the three arms, and are infinitely more widespread and overlapping now. The revised analysis of separation has always been, not of powers but institutional. In his collection of essays on *The Business of Judging*,[3] Lord Bingham concludes that our constitutional arrangements 'reflect no slavish adherence to the doctrine of the separation of powers. But there are some clear and generally accepted lines of functional demarcation.' Therein lies the distinction. By 2014 it could be said that the doctrine of the 'separation of powers' is only of historical interest; a more accurate word for 'functional' would be 'institutional'. All three institutions express their powers of government distributed among the three, all aiming at the ultimate goal of good government. The distribution of governmental powers was never 'separate'; but varies from time to time according to legislative action and relevant case law.

In the development of the prerogative writs in the seventeenth century, there emerged in court proceedings a distinct wish of the judiciary cautiously to exercise governmental powers. In the middle of the eighteenth century, Lord Mansfield asserted that mandamus 'ought to be used for all occasions where the law has established no specific remedy, and where in justice and good government there ought to be one'. It was in *R v Barker* in 1762[4] that he explained that these writs were collectively prerogative writs (later called orders) because of their intimate connections with the rights of the Crown, by which time each prerogative writ had developed its own charac-

---

[3] Lord Bingham, *The Business of Judging* (Oxford, OUP, 2000) 342.
[4] 3 Burr 1265. Norman S Posner, *Lord Mansfield: Justice in the Age of Reason* (McGill-Queen's University Press, London, 2013) states at p5: 'While a judge, he remained an active politician, the notion of separation of powers not being part of the unwritten English Constitution.'

teristic to establish judicial review of administrative actions. And Lord Mansfield added (at p 1268): 'Within the last century [the prerogative writ] has been liberally interpreted for the benefit of the subject and advancement of justice'. Thus the creation of Order 53 of the Rules of the Supreme Court in 1883 carried over the court's powers to control governmental action.

This constitutional structure was not interrupted in England; it became entrenched in 1986 in a judgment of Lord Scarman in *Nottinghamshire County Council v Secretary of State for the Environment*:[5] 'Judicial review is a great weapon in the hands of the judges; but the judges must observe the constitutional limits set by our parliamentary system upon this exercise of their beneficent power'. It found its written counterpart in the constitutions of British colonial territories, which give overriding powers for 'peace, order and good government'. It was judicially recognised in two twentieth-century cases in the Judicial Committee of the Privy Council.

The institutional separation was best espoused by Lord Diplock in *R v Hinds*,[6] a majority decision in the Privy Council in an appeal from the Jamaican courts. He held that that country's constitution prevented its legislature from establishing a special court to try certain firearms offences, called a Gun Court, which could exercise powers during the pleasure of the Governor-General on the advice of a Review Board of whom only the chairman was a member of the judiciary. He said that 'whatever is implicit in the very structures of a constitution in the Westminster model . . . is that judicial power is to continue to be visited in persons appointed to hold judicial office in the manner and on the terms laid down in the chapter dealing with the judicature, even though this is not expressly stated in the Constitution'. This statement, never seriously questioned, had been firmly endorsed by Lord Pearce in *Liyanage v The Queen*,[7] cited by Lord Diplock at the end of the passage in *Hinds*.

The Ceylon Act of 1962 – the colony of Ceylon achieved independence as Sri Lanka in 1971 – contained substantial modification of the Criminal Procedure Code, by purporting to legislate *ex post facto* the 60-day detention of persons for offences against the State by indicating classes of offence for which jury trial could ordinarily be ordered; the issue was whether the 1962 legislation was an unconstitutional law for Ceylon. The presiding judge, Lord

---

[5] [1986] AC 240.
[6] [1977] AC 195, 215.
[7] [1967] 1 AC 259.

McDermott (later the Lord Chief Justice of Northern Ireland) had stated, unchallenged in *arguendo*, that 'judicial functions were intended to be vested in the judiciary'. Lord Pearce demonstrated that, in the Board's opinion, the power to make legislation was given 'for peace, order and good government'.[8] This was based on all the pre-independence British colonies which were empowered to enact laws. He discussed the use of the doctrine of the separation of powers, and added: 'but there was a recognised separation of functions'; and that 'the Act involved usurpation and infringement by the legislature of judicial powers inconsistent with the written constitution of Ceylon. The judicial system, therefore, was untouched'. It has been untouched ever since.

If such Acts of Parliament are ever to be held unconstitutional, or declared incompatible, the judicial power could be effectively absorbed by the legislature by reversal of the judicial decision, thereby being taken out of the hands of judges. The Rule of Law exceptionally demands no less. The Human Rights Act 1998 confirms the constitutional infrastructure of modern democracy. Whatever Westminster ordained constitutionally, the innate doctrine of incompatibility in the 1998 Act established the primacy of the judicature as a governing institution. The judicial function is thus entrenched.

A contemporary twin model of the separation of functional government and the powers of government in a modern democracy is exemplified by the legislative powers in the UK in 2000 of access to policy-making. The Freedom of Information Act 2000 – a constitutional act of legislation – makes elaborate provisions for enabling certain citizens. The legislative provisions qualify the topics of accessible information that are exempt from disclosure at the instance of ministerial declaration, which may be challengeable (and have already given rise to judicial review; a case law has emerged). Even though the courts are apportioned powers by Parliament to determine the ultimate outcome of the powers to disclose public policy-making, the Government is finally accorded, by virtue of section 35 of the Act, the right of veto over the order to supply access to information – yet that veto itself is reviewable by the courts. That this specific veto is reviewable judicially has not been determined by the Act, and there was recently a legal challenge to the Government's refusal to allow the disclosure of correspondence between the Prince of Wales (as the presumptive heir to the throne) and cabinet ministers. This forensic

---

[8] ibid 284.

forage into the freedom of information system emphatically enhances the role of the rule of law; moreover, it examines the relationship between administrative and judicial decision-making. The judgment of the Master of the Rolls in *R (Evans) v Attorney-General*[9] admirably underlines the judicial function in its contribution towards democratic judgment, and it demonstrates constitutionally the distributive powers among the three arms of government. The Court of Appeal held, moreover, that a government department, which statutorily is entitled to refuse a request for disclosure of information, may do so as long as it establishes it reasonably, and articulates its decision. Mere disagreement with a legal decision is no more than a difference of opinion, and cannot thereby trump it judicially in the final analysis.

The modern democracy encompasses not just obligations and powers, but establishes institutions to give effect to them; they are organisations with their own independent authority and the ability to share powers intrinsic in other institutions of government. Lord Bingham put it pithily in *Pretty*:[10] a court of law is not a legislative body, but is institutionally judicial. The court cannot create a legislative act, but in terms of the distribution of powers among arms of government, it can make law.

PARLIAMENTARY SOVEREIGNTY AND THE SEPARATION OF POWERS

It has been my experience as a practising barrister from the 1960s onwards that the academic discussion about parliamentary sovereignty and its doctrine of the separation of powers has never fallen from the lips of the judiciary. Even the most recent commentary in *Public Law* (the December issue of 2012), discussing the famous *GCHQ* case, did no more than reveal three of the Law Lords agreeing that the Government's exercise of its prerogative power was judicially reviewable by the courts, while the other two thought that the power, by virtue of its notice, was not reviewable. This was not a rehearsal of the separation of powers, but the correct distribution of that power. I was personally involved in that case – appearing as counsel for the trade unions – and I do not recall any of the academic literature being cited in the relevant quotes by their Lordships in the various judgments. I had invariably based my own

---

[9] [2014] EWCA Civ 254. An appeal to the Supreme Court will be heard on 24 November 2014, with a reserved judgment delivered in the new year of 2015.
[10] [2002] 1 AC 800.

point of view, from my earliest days at the Bar, on the apt remarks made by O'Brien J in the Irish Supreme Court in *Buckley and others (Sinn Fein) v Attorney-General and another*:

> the manifest object of this Article [Article 6 of the Irish Constitution of 1937] was to recognise and ordain that, in this State [which followed the Westminster model] all powers of government should be exercised in accordance with the well-recognised principle of the distribution of powers between the legislative, executive and judicial organs of the State and to require that those powers should not be exercised other-wise.[11]

So it was thought throughout my career, until Lord Sumption, in the FA Mann lecture for 2011, asked the contrariwise argument, whether it is 'a fundamental question about the relations between the judiciary and the two political arms of the State, the executive and the legislature', and answered rhetorically, 'how far can judicial review go before it *trespasses* [italics supplied] on the proper function of government and the legislature in a democracy?' It is the first time that the separation of powers has been thus articulated in the form of an institutional divide among the three organs of government. Distribution of governmental powers (as I shall show) has never rested upon the institutional separation of the arms of government. The unanswered question is what that distribution of powers should pertain at any time. Has there ever been a dividing line between the organs of government in which it could be said that the ownership of powers could not be trespassed upon?

The Courts' Law-making Powers

Even before the advent of a distinct English administrative law via judicial review in the 1960s, and the establishment of the Human Rights Act 1998, there was in practice no effective separation of powers, in three separate legal developments. It is trite law to say that Parliament makes the law, and the courts give effect to that law. In practice, law-making is a shared occupation in a number of ways. The courts do not simply enforce the laws on the statute book, but are actively involved in their interpretation. Where, as is often the case, a statute is ambiguous or obscure in its parliamentary language, the courts will seek to find the intention of Parliament by interpreting the statute, sometimes (often) years after the statute has

---

[11] [1950] 1 IR 67, 81.

first appeared. Time alone requires protective action in the courts, while Parliament fiddles. Any statute must, by definition, be ambulatory and require replenishment meanwhile. It will be conditioned by both time and space. Here the courts are recognisably the secondary legislators. That quite apart, any decision of the courts 'makes law'. As Lord Reid stated extracurricularly at the SPTL conference in 1972, no one nowadays believes that judges do not make the law; such a thought is like Alice in Wonderland. Similarly Lord Radcliffe pooh-poohed the notion that judges do not make the law. They palpably do. No one suggests otherwise. The common law of England, moreover, proceeds upon the assumption that, barring increasing statutory intervention, it can act like a legislature. When in the case of *Shaw* in 1962 the House of Lords established the right to create a law of morals, and many years later affirmed Lord Lane CJ's decision to render husbands liable of rape against their wives, the judges were engaged in making new laws. And anyone reading the speeches of the Law Lords in *R (Jackson) v Attorney-General*[12] cannot avoid the contemplation of the common law in action at a future date. The judicature alone cannot be expected to bear the whole burden; as the late Arthur Chaskalson, Chief Justice of South Africa, said:

> Courts cannot be expected to carry the full burden of what might be required. In a democracy parliament and civil society [the legislature and the executive] are also defenders of the rule of law and it is essential that they should play their part in its protection.[13]

Lord Bingham in his *Rule of Law* claimed that that was what makes the difference between good and bad government.

The development of an English style of administrative law in the 1960s marked a clear case of judicial creativity. By amendment to Order 53 of the Supreme Court Rules – written incidentally by the legal profession through its Rules Committee – the courts were able, English-style, to fashion the ancient prerogative writs (later, orders) into an application for judicial review. Since then the judges, with no assistance from the legislature, have developed the greatest growth industry in our legal system. This was achieved by the exercise of legalistic growth of the common law. If judicial review has not transformed the legal landscape, the Human Rights Act 1998 gave further impetus to the judicial power to exercise extensive

---

[12] [2005] UKHL 56.
[13] *The Widening Gyre: Counter-Terrorism, Human Rights and the Rule of Law*, the 7th annual Sir David Williams Lecture at Cambridge University, given on 11 May 2007.

powers over civil authorities. After 2000 the courts were empowered to declare any acts or decisions by Ministers and civil servants incompatible with Articles of the European Convention on Human Rights and Fundamental Freedoms. Incompatibility was an open invitation to the legislature to reform the violation into legislation that would render the law compatible. The compromise with parliamentary supremacy in legislation was ingenious. It affirmed the constitutional arrangement of apportion of powers, not their separation.

The courts' powers to engage in law-making were not limited to activity as a secondary legislature, as indicated. A deluge of litigation, delegated by Parliament to respective Ministers, rendered such delegation supervised by the courts. Judges were able to declare the statutory instrument, drafted by ministerial officialdom, as ultra vires the primary legislation, thus conferring a further control by the courts over the scope of parliamentary legislation.

None of this answers the question: what then are the limitations on the power of the courts over acts of government? Is there such a thing as a judicial restraint that operates to restrict the ambit of judicial power over executive and (in certain circumstances) legislative actions? If so, where is the boundary line to be drawn? The question is often asked, yet never given a definitive answer. It was first discussed in the House of Lords in the *Fire Brigade* case in 1987 – most informatively in the dissenting judgment of Lord Mustill.

The judgment of Lord Mustill in 1984 (the date is important) in *R v Home Secretary, ex parte Fire Brigades Union*[14] – the fact that it is a dissenting judgment is of no consequence, since it accords with judicial expression of the need to observe the precise nature of our constitution – is of immense significance. If, on the face of it, it discloses a traditional approach to our constitutionality, on close analysis it bears usefully in the present-day view of the constitution. His opinion (actually it is a peroration) suffices to explain the purpose that lay behind 300 years of developing democratic rule.

I quote the words of Lord Mustill:

> It is a feature of the peculiarly British conception of the separation of powers that Parliament, the executive and the courts have each their distinct and largely exclusive domain.[15]

While the phrase 'sovereignty of powers' is the familiar expression of the lawyer and the constitutionalist, the use of the final word 'domain' is instructive. The separation is of all three. It is thus insti-

---

[14] [1985] 2 AC 513.
[15] ibid, 567D.

tutional, not a matter of their functioning. The word does not purport to express any operational or functional activity of the institutions. It is heritable property held in possession, lands or dominion. It is an institution, an area of influence or rule. The meaning of the sentence is that all three parts of the constitution are separate institutions, while their powers (as I will demonstrate) are shared and not distinct or discrete. No dissociation of the two 'political' arms from the judicature (presumably, but inaccurately described as non-political). They are all three concerned with 'good government'; the fact that the trio are complementary in membership (parliamentary and executive officers) and the third unelected is of no significance in terms of their functioning. The three are institutionally separate: their powers are complementary. What those powers constitute was the subject of professional discussion in 2014.

Lord Mustill then explains the separate functions of the three institutions in familiar traditional form, and adds that

> it requires the courts on occasion to step into the territory which belongs to the executive [institution], to verify not only that the powers asserted accord with the substantive law created by Parliament but also that the manner in which they are exercised conforms with the standards of fairness which Parliament must have intended [fairness or proportionality being a power shared by all the branches].

He ends the paragraph with the words

> it is the task of Parliament and the executive in tandem, not the courts, to govern the country. In recent years, however, the employment in practice of these specifically Parliamentary remedies has on occasion been perceived as falling short, and sometimes well short, of what was needed to bring the performance of the executive into line with the law, and with the minimum standards of fairness implicit in every Parliamentary delegation of a decision-making function.

And then there is added:

> To avoid a vacuum in which the citizen would be left without protection against a misuse of executive powers the courts have had no option but to occupy the dead ground in a manner, and in areas of public life, which could not have been foreseen 30 years ago.

– a description of the residual powers in the common law. That clear allusion to the development of administrative law by Lord Reid and his colleagues in the 1960s demonstrates the pre-existing separate institutions, but their separate powers lay fallow and uncultivated, if not actively dormant in the previous years. The need now (as we shall develop) is some guidance as to the proper distribution of the powers of government as properly allocated to the three institutions.

Absent a written constitution that marks out the boundary line between executive action and court intervention in the exercise of the powers of government, the distribution of powers must be clear. Lord Mustill concludes his observation of the unwritten constitution by stating – pre-Human Rights Act 1998 and devolutionary powers – that the political and social landscape has changed beyond recognition, but the boundaries [note the plural] remain; 'they are of crucial importance.' What then are the boundaries of power that are not separate but complementary in 2014?

ACTIVISM OR CREATIVITY?

The best reason for the development of the common law, acting as a secondary legislature, is the case of *Jones v Kaney*.[16] It is as good an illustration as any of the duty of a judge (particularly an appellate judge). As Benjamin Cardozo explained graphically in the 1930s, a judge must be both sensitive of precedent and be creative. (I much prefer the term 'creativism' to 'activism' – who wants a judge to be inactive?) At least Lord Cooke (the distinguished New Zealander who sat in the judicial House of Lords) said that he had a positive distaste for 'activism', which he described as 'a term of dubious import but often having a connotation of remedy'.

I have cited *in extenso* the remarks of Lord Dyson MR on his observation in the Supreme Court in two separate judgments, simply because of his willingness (with others) to alter the law of immunity for legal liability of expert witnesses before the courts, without more ado. The two out of seven dissenters in *Jones v Kaney* – Lord Hope and Lady Hale – were disposed to the change in the law, but only after acceptance by Parliament of the immunity of witnesses, often orally, in the courtroom. Lord Dyson was absolutely right in his mild and decorous denial of such a judicial function of deference to Parliament. Good government of these domestic issues demands a trilogy of powers that includes a principle of parliamentary primacy in law-making which, properly constituted, leaves certain policy issues to Parliament to decide. But the mere incantation of parliamentary supremacy in law-making is far from abso-

---

[16] [2011] 2 AC 398.

lute. It requires a judicial reasoning for forgoing the parliamentary powers – at common law at least – to override the activities of higher judiciary. What are the distinctions of these powers of law-making? I deal here only with the question of delay that accompanies actions from Parliament.

Ever since 1554 in *Buckley v Rice-Thomas*,[17] English judges have treated the expert who gives advice only on technological or scientific matters as witnesses *per se*, and alike for immunity from suit for what they say in the witness box (and probably preparatory to such testimony). Whether this was historically correct has been doubted. Whether relevant today, the fact has been that for four or more centuries experts have been treated the same as witnesses. Throughout that period Parliament has not pronounced upon the matter. It took 30 years even for the courts themselves to reverse the rule in *Rondel v Worsley*,[18] in which I unsuccessfully sought to remove the immunity of barristers for what they said in the course of legal proceedings, although Lord Lowry in 1994 in *Spring v Guardian Mutual Assurance*[19] said that he could not understand why my argument had not been accepted. The fact is that the immunity for those acting in the courtroom had not been the subject of parliamentary activity over a number of years.

I gave examples of how the activities (or inactivities) of Parliament, often prompted by political decisions, should not, in themselves, constitute deferment to parliamentary discussion, debate and decision-making. The reasons, good or bad, for non-activity of Parliament should never be regarded as good government. The courts themselves, in considering passing the buck to Parliament, must take account of the passage of time that is the inevitable consequence of legislative action at primary instance. The two examples I give are to the point. Barbara Wootton once wisely remarked that one should give at least two examples for any generalisation – so here goes!

The first example is that of *Jones v Kaney*. For some years now – quite apart from its origins in the sixteenth century – Parliament has been made aware of the deficiency in the expert witness system. Both the bodies of the Academy of Experts and the Expert Witness Institute since the 1980s have pointed up the problems of expert witnesses. Yet Parliament chose not to adjudicate upon the matter, until *Jones v Kaney* came on the scene. Even then the Supreme Court seemed nervous of the activities that were going on.

---

[17] 1554 Plowden 118.
[18] [1969] 1 AC 1.
[19] [1995] 2 AC 296.

Without expatiating on its origins, the subject of the admissibility of expert evidence in criminal proceedings in England and Wales arose in a consultation paper (No 190) from the Law Commission in 2009 and its final report (No 325) together with a draft Bill of some 11 clauses and one Schedule to the House of Commons on 21 March 2011. The closing date for agreement on the report was 20 February 2011. The judgments in *Jones v Kaney* (amounting to 190 paragraphs) before the UK Supreme Court were delivered in January 2011.

The draft Criminal Evidence (Experts) Bill would give authority to enforce principal recommendations. The relevant department, the Ministry of Justice, has declined, so far, to recommend to Ministers that primary legislation is required: instead they insist that the recommendations can be implemented administratively. The Law Commission view is that nothing short of primary legislation will suffice. The dissenters in *Jones v Kaney* seemed unaware of these promptings from the Government's chief law reform agency. Had they been aware of these administrative talks they would have been in a better position to judge whether the simple legislation dealing with the admissibility of expert evidence in criminal trials should be legislatively enacted, before concluding that Parliament should first consider the policy issues posed by *Jones v Kaney*.[20]

The Supreme Court, in *Jones v Kaney*, had to decide whether to abolish the rule that a witness could not be sued in negligence by his client. The case was a classic instance of rival views about judicial restraint on non-governmental legislation. The justification for the immunity accorded to lay witnesses is long-standing and is based on policy considerations which are well understood. The immunity enjoyed by expert witnesses from liability to their clients had also been established, although it was a less well entrenched principle, even if its origins were misunderstood historically. The majority of the Supreme Court held that the immunity could no longer be justified in the public interest. It was absurd to think that the courts should await protracted action by Parliament. They were not persuaded that, if experts were liable to be sued for breach of duty, they would be discouraged from providing their services at all; or that immunity was necessary to ensure that expert witnesses give full and frank evidence to the court; or that diligent expert wit-

---

[20] The question whether the laying down of a modern statement about the enhanced liability for an expert witness should be achieved by primary or secondary legislation has been rendered unnecessary, since the reform has been achieved at common law by a direction from the Lord Chief Justice expanding Rule 33A of the Criminal Practice Directions, which came into effect on 6 October 2014: [2014] EWCA Crim 1569.

nesses would be harassed by vexatious claims for breach of duty; or that the removal of the immunity would engender a risk of multiplicity of suits.

The dissenters took the cautious and 'non-activist' line. Lord Hope said that the lack of a secure principled basis for removing the immunity from expert witnesses; the lack of a clear dividing line between what is to be affected by the removal and what is not; the uncertainties that this would cause; and the lack of reliable evidence to indicate what the effects might be, all suggested that the wiser course would be to leave matters as they stood. Lady Hale saw the proposed abolition of immunity as an exception to the general rule that witnesses enjoy immunity from suit. She asked rhetorically how far the exception should go. Did it cover all classes of litigation? In particular, how far beyond ordinary civil litigation did it go, and did it cover all or only some of the witness's evidence? It was impossible to say what effect the removal of immunity would have, either on the care with which the experts give their evidence, or on their willingness to do so. It was not self-evident that the policy considerations in favour of introducing the exception to the general rule were so strong that the court should depart from previous authority to make it. It was 'irresponsible' to make such a change on an experimental basis. Issues that affect the process of litigation call for judicial action, and not to await policy issues that are politically neutral.

There is another, essentially human, factor at work. That is judicial temperament. It is an inescapable fact that some judges are more traditional in their approach than others. As Lord Dyson MR said on 6 November 2012 in the annual lecture for ALBA,

> some are cautious and prefer to paddle in the warm and safe shallows of clear precedent. Others are more adventurous and are prepared to give it a go in the more treacherous waters of the open sea . . . But history has shown that the product of today's buccaneer sometimes becomes tomorrow's orthodoxy.

We need both varieties, but must not spurn the advocate who displays a vision of better government tomorrow.

The second example is the more telling, and socially important. It involves the basis of our law on homicide. As long as 30 years ago, Lord Mustill began his judgment referring to the English law as 'a conspicuous anomaly' and went on to explain that the law was 'permeated by anomaly, fiction, misnomer and obsolete reasoning'. But he looked to Parliament to remedy the situation. 'I am willing to follow old laws until they are overturned, but not to make a new

law on a basis for which there is no principle'. Lord Mustill reaf-
firmed his statement five years later when he said: 'Only Parliament
has the powers, if it will choose to exercise them. It may not be a
popular choice, but surely it is justice that counts'. He might have
added the words extracurially uttered by Lord Devlin, who once
said in an essay entitled *Judges as Lawmakers*[21] that 'it is for
Parliament to change the law. But these protestations ring hollow
when Parliament has said, as loudly as total silence [and even with
expression] can say it, that it intends to do nothing at all', and even
says it by proclaiming that nothing will be done.

What happened then? The Government, no doubt spurred on by
such demands for legislation, referred the partial defences to the
charge of murder to the Law Commission in 2003. The report ultimately provided the answer, but stated that the legislation could be
complete only if the whole of murder and manslaughter were
referred for legal reform. After much prevarication, the Law
Commission was, very restrictively, given terms of reference, including no question reviewing the vital distinction between murder and
manslaughter; nor was the penalty to be discussed. Given these
restrictions, the Law Commission produced a valuable legal document which prompted a limited reform of the law. Despite a viable
form of appeal, which attracted some assents and some dissents, the
Government dithered, and ultimately rejected the limited response,
after any other reply. Instead in the legislation of 2009 – the Coroners
and Justice Act of that Year – it half-heartedly amended the partial
defences to murder, those of diminished responsibility and provocation. The former made modern sense, the latter was a convoluted
alternative of 'loss of control' to replace the outdated version of
provocation. But what of the substantive law, which represented
publicly a 'mess'? Since then the rest has been anything but silent.
Lord McNally in the House of Lords on 10 March 2012 announced
that the Coalition Government has no present intention of responding to the Law Commission, or of proposing changes in the law of
homicide. And in its 11th report in 2012 the Law Commission itself
abandoned any immediate proposal to look at the subject again.

JUDICIAL RESTRAINT

Judicial restraint is one of those familiar phrases that is full of meaning but in practice determines too little substance. It has its place,

---

[21] Lord Devlin, 'Judges as Lawmakers' (1976) 37 *Modern Law Review* 1.

but needs to be used wisely. It depends on the emanation of the precise sense: does it come from a judge to explain his attitude to parliamentary or governmental action? Or is it implicit in a historical attitude towards judicial adjudication on a statutory provision or executive action that insists on the essence of social policy? Commonly enough there is a recognition of the task of Parliament and the Executives in tandem with the courts, to govern the country. To do otherwise is to proceed to a state of unwarrantable intrusion by the courts into the political field, and thereby a usurpation of the function of Parliament. But the popularism of that eminence is, I venture to think, no longer the proper view of their relationship. Nowadays, increasingly frequently, the emphasis is on 'the relative institutional competence', a phrase that has more creative possibilities than the 'separation of powers'. It has been best described by Lord Bingham in *A v Secretary of the State for the Home Department*:

> The more purely political (in a broad or narrow sense) a question is, the more appropriate it will be for political resolution and the less likely it is to be an appropriate matter for judicial decision. The smaller, therefore, will be the potential role of the court. It is the function of political and not judicial bodies to resolve political questions. Conversely, the greater the legal content of any issue, the greater the potential role of the court, because under our constitution and subject to the sovereign power of Parliament it is the function of the courts and not of political bodies to resolve legal questions.[22]

It has the great merit of being based on an articulated awareness of the contribution each of the institutions of good government can make to constitutional checks and balances. To close one's eyes to the frequent inactivity, not to say impotence, to the activities of Parliament (often dictated by political whimsy and motivation that does not induce good government) is not an adequate response of the judge. The instant case in the court of law must always operate; it defends initially the individual against the State. It depends for its constitutional effectiveness on the existence of the restraints within Parliament. Absent parliamentary restraint, judges operate a constitutional logic for a rule that intrudes on behalf of the individual. And the citizen expects that the powers of the State are shared among the constitutional institutions according to the nature of the exercisable powers.

---

[22] [2005] 2 AC 68, 102.

What should be the principles of judicial restraint? Nothing generally should be barred from judicial restraint, if only because any remedy against the legislature or the executive would be simply 'think again'. Such was confirmed by section 2 of the Human Rights Act 1998. Judicial restraint, however, may be properly exercisable so long as the judiciary acts upon empirical evidence that is prescribed to it. Too much recent judicial action is based, not upon empirical evidence, but on opinions of public attitude that are insufficiently fact-based. An example comes from one High Court judge in June 2012, who ruled in a case testing a privileged occasion of a defence to a libel action.[23] The judge expressed as his reason the view that there was a publicly espoused confidence in the criminal justice system; and added, without any factual evidence at all, that a prosecutor's statement diminished (as opposed to enhanced) public respect for that instrument of criminal investigations. Courts of law are decision-makers on factual material and are not formers of opinions or attitudes. These are matters for politicians and the rest of us to express through democratic institutions. Financial aspects of policy and other administrative decisions are made on the basis of finite funds and a proper distribution of funds; courts are generally not a party to issues over financial matters. But other policy issues are not aptly described as 'political' matters unsuitable for courts of law where the latter have sufficient evidence to make decisions. Courts, if adequately informed, are as much political as are other institutions in society. Decision-makers (whoever they may be in the process of the legal system or public administration) must always justify what they are doing by giving good reasons, by effecting good government. Judges should not construe statutes of Parliament or ministerial actions which are said to confer power to interfere with such rights any differently from the way they would value a clause said to oust or modify their own jurisdiction. Such an attempt by the Government is simply a manifestation of one fundamental right. That is the nature of what I call judicial and judicious review.

A comparatively early example involved a challenge to the Ministerial obligation to establish and maintain the National Health Service. In *R v Secretary of State for Social Services, West Midlands Regional Health Authority and Birmingham Area Health Authority, ex parte Hincks and others*,[24] an orthopaedic surgeon and several

---

[23] Bean J in *Bento v Chief Constable of Bedfordshire Police* [2012] EWHC 1525.
[24] [1980] 1 BMLR 93.

patients awaiting hip replacement operations claimed, understandably, that they should not have to wait for additional surgical resources to be made available. Their counsel argued hopefully[25] that the Minister for the Health Service had failed to provide a reasonable remedy for the citizens in the Good Hope Hospital in Sutton Coldfield. The National Health Service Act 1977 provided that it was 'the Secretary of State's duty to provide throughout England and Wales to such extent as he considers necessary to meet all reasonable requirements' hospital accommodation and medical services. It was pleaded by way of defence that the additional services could not be provided within the money available to the Minister. More specifically, the lack of resources defeated the claim, since the duty could not be absolute; the supply of funds for the NHS was for Parliament to maintain. If finance is quintessentially a matter for executive government, that pre-determined the judicial review, unless there was sufficient evidence to negate the duty. So it would be today. But even if financial policy preceded judicial review, the defence of imperfect duty would be a legal safeguard from judicial intervention.

JUDICIAL INTERVENTION

Fairness (or what used to be called 'natural justice', and may be equated with disproportionality) now seems to dominate the scene of judicial intervention, although so far the courts have not yet fully grappled with a concept that has eluded adequate analysis. It was best described by Lord Nicholls in *Miller v Miller*:

> Fairness is an elusive concept. It is an instinctive response to a given set of facts. Ultimately it is grounded in social and moral values. These values, or attitudes, can be stated. But they cannot be justified, or refuted, by any objective process of logical reasoning. Moreover, they change from one generation to the next. [26]

Much of the problem focuses on the construction of the statutory power of parliamentary language. Until 2000 the rule of statutory construction was the literal rule, that if the words used by Parliament were quite clear they must be applied, even though the result would be absurd or undesirable. The result of the application of this literal

---

[25] I can safely describe the argument as hopeful, or even boldly ambitious, if only because I was counsel for the appellants, although I did not appear on the judicial review or advise on an appeal.

[26] [2006] UKHL 24 [4].

rule was that judges tended to look for the intention of Parliament, as if the parliamentarians put their heads together to form an overall state of mind. A classic example of this approach came in 1985 (a pointer to the last two decades of the century) in *R v Hillingdon Borough Council, ex parte Puhlhofer*,[27] which concerned specifically the local authority's duty to house the unintentionally homeless under the Housing (Homeless Persons) Act 1977, the first personal housing legislation. The question was: does the ordinary (intended) meaning of the word 'accommodation' apply, even though the place which he is thereby compelled to occupy is so lacking in cooking and washing facilities that he is compelled to eat out and to use a locally provided launderette for washing his clothes? The 'accommodation' may not be, by reason of its size, capable of accommodating a person, together with others who normally reside with him as members of his family; such a place would not usually be described as 'accommodation' in any meaningful sense. The Court of Appeal (three judges gave lengthy separate judgments arriving at the same conclusion) and the House of Lords, in which a single Law Lord gave the acceptable answer, held that Parliament's intention could not be for 'appropriate' or 'reasonable' accommodation to be provided, as Parliament had deliberately not used those words. The trial judge – Mr Justice Hodgson, a wise and humane judge who took a purposive view that a sensible legislature would seek to apply good grammar and government – had held otherwise. The reversal of his ruling by eight judges stuck firmly to the literal rule and held that 'accommodation' could not be qualified by the use of 'reasonable' or 'acceptable' accommodation such as to impute a single, meaningful word to 'accommodation', because it might in certain circumstances pertaining to the applicant be unfit for habitation. It might be a misuse of language to describe Diogenes as having occupied accommodation within the meaning of the 1977 Act. Yet a tub was good enough, according to the Law Lords, for someone to live in by the civilised standards of the twentieth century.

It is difficult, if not impossible, to be critical of the eight superior intellects, if the starting point for the exercise required in the interpretation of statutory language is the primacy, if not superiority, of parliamentary language. Apart from one critical observation (made hereafter), the higher court judgments (all models of their existing genre) sought by logical reasoning to find that Parliament could not

---

[27] [1986] AC 484.

have meant to exclude the personal qualification. If it had, would it not have inserted the qualification? They stressed, not unnaturally, that this was the first occasion on which the elected Government had engaged in housing legislation, a factor of novelty in the search for modern intervention by the State in personal affairs.

But if the approach was not that of an interpreter of the legislation, without regard to the rule of law which imparted a sense of humanity towards the public's need for reasonable housing, then the Law Lords could not be faulted. There was some satisfaction from the proponents of Mr Justice Hodgson, that in the Housing and Planning Acts 1986 – the year after *Puhlhofer* – Parliament promptly disclosed its true hand by reversing the Law Lords' conclusion. So much for parliamentary intention, or the literal rule of statutory construction of the 1977 legislation!

What particularly disturbed the commentators of that period was the Law Lords' dampener of the concept of judicial review. Put aside the present Lord Chancellor's desire to curb the use of judicial review by the instrument of limiting the time for applying and reducing the scope of the remedy, now (in October 2014) passing through Parliament in the Criminal Justice and Courts Bill, by filtering out of the system of access the cases that are insufficiently arguable. Through Lord Brightman's single judgment they said, with vigorous endorsements, that they were 'troubled by the prolific use of judicial review for the purpose of challenging the performance of local authorities in their function', and no doubt (for the time immediately thereafter) they would have included central government activities in their injunction. But all that changed in the twenty-first century, with the arrival of the Human Rights Act 1998. Not only did that Act reinforce the use of judicial review, it also encouraged the judiciary to view its new-found functions of elevating human rights and fundamental freedoms from its international law perspective by determining 'as near as possible' the compatibility of those rights with English legislation. Events were thereafter (if not before) assumed to share, in dialogue with executive government and legislature, the burden of good government. Lord Bingham's 2011 book *The Rule of Law* was the first declaration of a shared judicial responsibility.

In the 1990s, as a deputy High Court judge, I heard a number of judicial reviews in the homeless persons legislation, which was overtaken by the Housing Act 1996. In the course of these reviews I attempted – not always successfully, in the view of the Court of Appeal – to encourage improvements in the quality of administration of some local authorities towards the homeless population. I did not experience the problem of excessive jurisdiction of this aspect of judicial review, although I suspect that the legislation of 1996 was partly due to the demands of local authorities that they should fight their housing battles in a more inspectorial role, and less cumbersome and less access to justice provided by the legal procedure before the High Court. Judicial review, otherwise, had begun to flourish.

When the UK Supreme Court decided in *Jones v Kaney* to end the 400-year-old rule that conferred on expert witnesses an immunity from suit for professional negligence, it did so by a majority verdict. No longer were those who gave opinion evidence on scientific or technological issues to be treated as if they were ordinary witnesses of fact. But two of the Justices – Lord Hope and Lady Hale – would have dismissed the appeal, while at the same time agreeing that the reform was necessary; they concluded that the common law rule for witnesses should not be overruled unless and until the subject of expert witnesses had been reviewed by the Law Commission and Parliament. To allow the appeal pending statutory reform was regarded by the two justices as judicially irresponsible. The case presented a kind of dilemma for the Court – the rule should no longer apply, but not yet awhile.

The case demonstrates the respect the courts have for the sovereignty of Parliament; that body alone should alter the law. This attitude confuses the role of the appeal court (or indeed any court in the hierarchy of courts) to decide cases and its effect as law-maker. One need only remind judges that their function is to adjudicate on disputes between rival disputants and not to indulge in any exegesis on the legal topic in issue. Even if it is permissible for a judge in the course of his written judgment to pronounce upon some aspect of the law, he or she indulges an appetite for some exposition of law. It is mere obiter dicta and does not represent any part of the ratio decidendi of the judgment. It may be found as acceptable or discombobulation to the parties, but it is an excrescence on development of the law. It should be a golden rule, Judge Learned Hand wrote in a letter to his friend, the Chief Justice of Nebraska, that a judge's duty is to adjudicate a dispute between the parties, 'not write for eternity'.

It is a dilemma exceptionally facing the judiciary in its search for constitutionality. If there is a desire for reform of the law, should that task be left to Parliament and the Law Commission? If defence is deferred in favour of the supremacy of Parliament, any litigant is defeated by the preferment of the legislature. Is obsolescent the same as extinct? Where there is clear evidence that parliamentary action is in the offing, there is every reason for a deferment by the judiciary to the supreme law-making of Parliament. Hence the decision by the Supreme Court on 25 June 2014 to call upon Parliament to consider the pressing social problem of assistance to terminally ill suicides could not be faulted. But five of the nine justices assumed that the courts stood aside only while Parliament indicated the direction of reform (if any). At least that was a signal that law reform may properly be a shared occupation. For the time being, at least, the judges wait to see what Parliament decides should be the future of the Suicide Act 1961 – they have endorsed current legal opinion that it is a criminal offence to assist someone in committing suicide, even though suicide is, since 1961, no longer a crime. As a judicial authority told the House of Lords on the second reading of the Suicide Bill, on 2 March 1961, you cannot logically aid and abet a crime which no longer is criminal. Parliament in the event seemed to decide that assisted suicide should nevertheless be made a crime with a maximum sentence of 14 years' imprisonment. Logic was overcome by social reality, or at the least a curiosity in legislation. At the time of the Bill, the Bishop of Carlisle told the House of Lords that while he wanted to support the Bill on compassionate grounds and not on punishment, he wanted the law 'to be dissuasive against the unnatural act of taking one's own life'. Would that ecclesiastical view prevail today, or did Parliament listen? If so, what did the parliamentarians intend in maintaining a curiosity? Lord Neuberger's leading judgment affirmed the criminality of assisted suicide, but did it intend to criminalise the offence? May the true intention have been to mark the future conduct as unlawful, but to do no more: just de-criminalise the offence of assisting the suicide? It might have decided not to go that far in any reform. Criminologically speaking, Parliament has often opted to make the conduct criminal, but to de-criminalise the offence and leave it to the courts to decide on a non-custodial penalty, either a suspended prison sentence or some monetary or community penalty. It is the duty of our courts to interpret the meaning of the language used in the dated context of a statute; there is also a leaning towards the less punitive punishment.

All this can be determined quite apart from the duty under human rights legislation to ensure the compatibility of English law (as far as possible) with the right to life and the right to private life. If suicide is still unlawful (although no longer criminal), an assisted suicide does not escape the civil liability of aiding and abetting an unlawful act; it is simply taken out of the criminal justice system. Whatever, however, the penalty for assisting suicide may fairly be, a 14-year maximum seems grossly disproportionate to the giving of sympathetic help to an act which is no longer criminal. In 1961 Lady Wootton expressed doubt about some aspects of the Bill, in particular the maximum of 14 years in prison for aiding and abetting.

No doubt the present penalty (unreformed since 1961) has some symmetry with the penalty system for all aiders and abettors, but that does not debar an argument that sentencing policy dictates changes in penalty structure. Only in 1978 was the Home Secretary's Advisory Council on the Penal System asked to review all maximum penalties. It recommended a reduction in all maxima, according to a rational scheme reflecting what the courts were in fact handing down. The report has, unhappily, never been implemented. Parliamentary consideration hereafter provides an opportunity for studying maximum and minimum penalties.

Perhaps the lasting significance of the Supreme Court's judgment is the judicial urge for urgent parliamentary review of a law that has a growing social impact on the humanity and dignity of the distressed dying. Five of the nine justices called on Parliament to consider the law; two dissenters would have found the present state of English law incompatible with human rights. Change may come, in parliamentary and further judicial dialogue working in harmony, if – since the Constitutional Reform Act 2005 – no longer in institutional harness within the legal system.

What lesson(s) should we today learn from the eloquent words of Lord Mansfield – uttered in brilliant, clear and concise English 250 years ago – spelling out the basis of the prerogative writs and establishing thereby the boundary lines of government committed to a constitution? This author's historical account of Lord Mansfield's judgment must be treated as under-researched and speculative. Yet if it invites the reader to remain suspicious, it seeks to accept that throughout the centuries there is a record of *communis error*; there has been a confusion, if not a conflation of events, of the distribution of the powers of government with a separation of the function of those shared powers. We can recall the modern constitutionalism of Lord Bingham in *Purdy,* who described the position as follows: 'The final court of appeal is not a legislative body, but a judicial institution. Institutionally, the court cannot create a legislative act, *but in terms of the distribution of power among arms of government*, it can make law.' Is there a more resonant expression today of the duty of the courts to peace, order and good government that Lord Mansfield propagated? A separation of the three arms of government means that they share the overlapping powers of government. To make good the author's assertion, the full report of *R v Barker* is annexed below.

ANNEX

3 BURR. 1264. REX *v.* BARKER 823

[1265] HILARY TERM, 2 GEO. 3, B. R. 1762. *1434. A.C. 395:*

REX *versus* BARKER, ET AL'. Saturday, 23d Jan. 1762. [S. C. 1 Bl. 300, 352.]
  Mandamus lies to trustees to admit a dissenting teacher.

On Wednesday 10th of June 1761, Mr. Norton moved for a mandamus to be directed to the surviving trustees under a deed of release made by one Charles Vinson to John Enty a dissenting minister at Plymouth, and other trustees, settling a then new-built meeting-house, garden, &c. upon the said trustees in trust (amongst other things) "to suffer the meeting-house to be for the public worship of God by such congregation of Protestant Dissenters commonly called Presbyterians, as should sit under and attend the ministry of the said Mr. John Enty or such other Presbyterian minister or ministers as should in his and their room successively, in all times then

---

* The fact was, that two died, two were acquitted, and two convicted.

coming, be, by the members in fellowship of the said or such like congregation or congregations, regularly and fairly chosen and appointed to be the minister, preacher or pastor, to preach in the said meeting;" requiring them to admit Christopher Mends to the use of the pulpit thereof, as pastor, minister, or preacher there; he the said Christopher Mends being duly elected thereto.

He produced an affidavit of the facts, and of Mr. Mend's election: and of demand and refusal of the use of the meeting-house; and he cited the * case of *Rex v. Bloore*, P. and Tr. 1760, which was a mandamus to restore William Langly to the office of curate of a chapel; and the rule was made absolute upon this principle, that where there is a temporal right, this "Court will assist by mandamus."

Lord Mansfield took this opportunity of declaring, that the Court had thought of that case of the curate of the chapel of Calton, since the determination of it, as well as before; and they were [1266] thoroughly satisfied with the grounds and principles upon which that mandamus was granted.

Where there is a right to execute an office, perform a service, or exercise a franchise; (more especially, if it be in a matter of public concern, or attended with profit;) and a person is kept out of possession, or dispossessed of such right, and has no other specific legal remedy; this Court ought to assist by a mandamus; upon reasons of justice, as the writ expresses—Nos A. B. debitam et festinam justitiam in hac parte fieri volentes, ut est justum;" and upon reasons of public policy, to preserve peace, order, and good government.

The interposing this writ where there is no other specific remedy, is greatly for the benefit of the subject and the advancement of justice. The speedy decision of the question, in that case which has been mentioned, by an immediate trial in a feigned issue shews it.

This case is not indeed quite the same as that was; but still it is reasonable to grant a rule to shew cause.

On Monday, 23d November 1761, Mr. Thurlow and Mr. Dunning shewed cause against the mandamus.

They controverted, by affidavit, the election of Mends; and endeavoured to support the election of Mr. Hanmer, whom the trustees had put into possession.

The majority of the congregation seemed to be on the side of Mends: the trustees espoused Hanmer, and meant to maintain him with a high hand.

There was no colour for the election of Hanmer: and that of Mends was liable to objections.

This contest had raised great animosity, spirit, and obstinacy; especially in those who were for Hanmer; and as they thought their strength lay in throwing obstacles in the way of any (more especially a speedy) redress, as Hanmer was upholden and maintained in possession by the trustees; their counsel, with great earnestness and ability, argued against making the rule absolute for a mandamus; and contended that it could not be "to admit," where another was in possession.

A mandamus "to admit" goes no further (they said) than to give a legal possession where otherwise the [1267] party would be without remedy. And to prove the distinction between a mandamus to admit and a mandamus to restore to a former possession—they cited the case of *Rex v. Dean and Chapter of Dublin*, 1 Sir J. S. p. 538, per Pratt. "A mandamus to admit is only to give a legal, not an actual possession; though in a mandamus to restore, the Court will go further."

But here is another person (Mr. Hanmer) is in possession: and Mr. Mends never has been so. Here is no legal right: and this Court can not take notice of trusts, so as to give relief, upon an equitable title only. Nor is this gentleman the cestuy qui trust: at most, his title is only equitable.

Lord Mansfield—A mandamus is a prerogative writ; to the aid of which the subject is intitled, upon a proper case previously shewn, to the satisfaction of the Court. The original nature of the writ, and the end for which it was framed, direct upon what occasions it should be used. It was introduced, to prevent disorder from a failure of justice, and defect of police. Therefore it ought to be used upon all

---

* Vide ante, p. 1043 to 1046. [And qu. if there ought not to have been an affidavit that the prosecutor was qualified, and the meeting house registered according to the Toleration Act 1 W. & M. c. 18. See also 1 Durn. 398, 399. 2 Durn. 180, 259. 3 Durn. 577, 649.]

occasions where the law has established no specific remedy, and where in justice and good government there ought to be one.

Within the last century, it has been liberally interposed for the benefit of the subject and advancement of justice.

The value of the matter, or the degree of its importance to the public police, is not scrupulously weighed. If there be a right, and no other specific remedy, this should not be denied.

Writs of mandamus have been granted, to admit lecturers, clerks, sextons, and scavengers, &c. to restore an alderman to precedency, an attorney to practice in an Inferior Court, &c.

Since the Act of Toleration, it ought to be extended to protect an endowed pastor of Protestant Dissenters; from analogy and the reason of the thing.

The right itself being recent, there can be no direct ancient precedent: but every case of a lecturer, preacher, schoolmaster, curate, chaplain, is in point.

The deed is the foundation or endowment of the pastorship. The form of the instrument is necessarily by way of trust: for, the meeting-house, and the land upon [1268] which it stands, could not be limited to Enty and his successors. Many lectureships and other offices are endowed by trust-deeds. The right to the function is the substance, and draws after it every thing else as appurtenant thereto. The power of the trustees is merely in the nature of an authority to admit. The use of the meeting-house and pulpit, in this case, follows, by necessary consequence, the right to the function of minister, preacher, or pastor; as much as the insignia do the office of a mayor: or the custody of the books, that of a town-clerk.

Mr. Just. Wilmot—It has been granted in the case of scavengers. It is a prerogative writ, and shall be granted to ampliate justice, and to preserve a right; where there is no specific, legal remedy; where no assize will lie.

Mr. Just. Foster—Here is a legal right. Their ministers are tolerated and allowed: their right is established, therefore is a legal right, and as much as any other legal right.

The Court proposed an issue to try "whether Mr. Hanmer * was or was not duly elected;" as the cheapest and best way to put it in.

It was then adjourned to the first day of this present Hilary term, in order that the parties might give an answer, "whether they would agree to this issue;" or "whether they would agree to proceed to a new election:" and the parties themselves to be consulted, and make their election.

But afterwards, (on Tuesday 24th November 1761,) Lord Mansfield proposed and made an alteration in the rule to be drawn up in this case: which alteration he judged to be necessary, as Mr. Hanmer himself was no party to this litigation about the mandamus.

He therefore directed it to be drawn up to the following effect, (and indeed gave the very words;) viz.

It is ordered, that the first day of next term be given to Pentecost Barker, Richard Dunning, Philip Cockey, and Elias Lang, to shew cause why a writ of mandamus should not issue, directed to them, requiring them to admit Christopher Mends to the use of the pulpit in a certain meeting-house appointed for the religious worship of Protestant Dissenters commonly called Presbyterians, in Plymouth in the county of Devon, as pastor, minister, or preacher there. And it is further ordered, that they [1269] the said Pentecost Barker, Richard Dunning, Philip Cockey, and Elias Lang, do at the same time acquaint this Court "whether they insist upon the validity of the election of John Hanmer;" and if not, "whether they are willing to proceed to a new election of a minister, pastor, or preacher there;" the prosecutor of this rule having declared his consent "to wave his claim, in order to a new election." And it is further ordered, that notice of this rule be given to the said John Hanmer; to the intent that he may be heard, as he shall he advised; and that he may acquaint this Court "whether he insists upon the validity of his election," and "whether he is willing to have it tried in a feigned issue."

Mr. Thurlow and Mr. Dunning now give an answer, by direction of their clients, "that Pentecost Barker, Richard Dunning, Philip Cockey, and Elias Lang, do insist

---

* N.B. This Mr. Hanmer was in possession, and claimed to be duly elected to the same ministry or pastorship.

826

upon the validity of the election of John Hanmer ; and that they are not willing to proceed to a new election, &c. and that the said John Hanmer does insist upon the validity of his election, and is not willing to have it tried in a feigned issue."

After which Mr. Thurlow and Mr Dunning were heard again, in general ; and argued strenuously against granting a mandamus. They knew, the election of Hanmer could not be supported upon a trial. The election of Mends seemed liable to objection as irregular. But, if the matter was proper for a mandamus, they were aware that in case neither was elected, the Court would issue a mandamus "to proceed to an election ;" in which case, the majority of the congregation were inclined to Mends. The trustees therefore obstinately persisted in opposing a mandamus and refusing a trial.

Lord Mansfield—Every reason concurs here, for granting a mandamus. We have considered the matter fully : and we are all clearly for granting it. I have made a collection of cases on this subject, since the last argument : but I have it not here, at present.

Here is a function, with emoluments ; and no specific legal remedy. The right depends upon election : which interests all the voters. The question is of a nature to inflame men's passions. The refusal to try the election in a feigned issue, or proceed to a new election, proves a determined purpose of violence. Should the Court deny this remedy, the congregation may be tempted to resist violence by force : a dispute "who shall preach Christian charity," may raise implacable feuds and animosities ; [1270] in breach of the public peace, to the reproach of Government, and the scandal of religion. To deny this writ, would be putting Protestant Dissenters and their religious worship, out of the protection of the law. This case is intitled to that protection ; and can not have it in any other mode, than by granting this writ.

The defendants have refused either to go to a new election, or to try it in a feigned issue.

We were, all of opinion, when a trial was proposed to them, that a mandamus ought to issue, in case of a refusal. Their answer ought to be put into the rule, as prefatory to it : and I do this, with a view that their refusal may be authentically given in evidence to the jury, upon a trial.

Many cases have gone as far as this, or farther.

Mr. Justice Denison, Mr. Justice Foster, and Mr. Justice Wilmot, all declared themselves of the same opinion.

The Court ordered a mandamus to issue.

V. post, pa. 1379, 1380, 28th April 1763.

2

Judicial Review: its Genesis and Growth Post-1977

I CLAIM, NOT over-modestly, to have grown up professionally in the 1970s with the beginnings of judicial overseeship of ministerial and administrative action taken by the State against the citizen. In the latter part of the twentieth century it had become imperative in modern democratic societies that governments should be answerable and accountable to the institutions which constitutionally safeguarded the rights of the citizen against public authorities. The late Professor Stanley de Smith, in the early (1960s) edition of his classic work, *Judicial Review of Administrative Action*, wrote, in his fluid and distinctive literary style with meticulous accuracy and thorough scholarship, that 'departmental administration may bring in a political storm'. If he was depicting a legal tsunami, he was accurately predicting the permanent system of English administrative law. Politicians did not relish this judicial function.

It is not that this country wished its government to go unchecked. Lord Devlin aptly observed that the British had no more wish to be governed by judges than they had to be judged by politicians and administrators. Given that attitude by a citizenry which espoused individual freedom, it is little wonder that the judiciary initially limited its tentacles to controlling inferior tribunals via the exercise of the prerogative procedure on behalf of the sovereign royalty. But the huge gap of control over ministerial and administrative action had sooner or later to be filled. This happened in two post-Second World War stages, enhancing the remedy for complaints against public officials. The first came in 1967 with the passing of legislation providing for the Parliamentary Commissioner for Administration, exemplifying the public stirrings on the subject of governmental administration. An informed and increasingly informative public led to a Scandinavian creature called the Ombudsman ('grievance man'). In typical Englishness, it took time for the title of Parliamentary Commissioner for Administration to be known, first colloquially and then officially via the Oxford English Dictionary, by its Scandinavian title.

In 1958 Professor Stefan Hurwitz, a distinguished criminologist at the University of Copenhagen, who had in 1954 become the first Danish Ombudsman, gave a lecture tour of this country describing the duties of surveillance over administration. His visit had stimulated interest in Denmark (and in 1959 simultaneously in Norway) of the first Ombudsman in the style of the Swedish mode which originated obscurely, in the Swedish constitution of 1809, but had been studiously ignored outside Sweden and Finland. As the *Observer*'s legal correspondent, I was an early stimulant. In the spring of 1959 I visited both Denmark and Norway and observed the nascent development. What I found there I described in detail in two articles in the Sunday newspaper in May and June 1959. The follow-up was a committee of JUSTICE under Sir John Whyatt, a former Attorney-General in Kenya during the Mau Mau troubles. It recommended the appointment, which was promptly taken up by both of the main political parties without much fuss or bother. I can do no better than quote part of the leader article published by the *Observer* on 7 June 1959. It reads as follows:

> For some time we have looked towards the Scandinavian countries as models of what a democratic State should be. In town planning and architecture, in social and industrial relations, in physical education and penal reform, they are often in advance of this country. Can it be that they have, in the Ombudsman or grievance man, another institution which Britain should try to copy?
>
> That there is a need for something of this kind is certain. The growing power of the State has given Government departments and bureaucrats of all kinds enormous powers over the affairs of ordinary citizens. In most cases these powers are used carefully and with restraint but when a department or a bureaucrat oversteps the limits and acts tyrannically, it is extremely difficult, if not impossible, for the ordinary citizen to obtain redress.
>
> In Scandinavia both these cases would have gone to the Ombudsman. There any citizen who has a complaint to make against a department or an institution, may have it investigated, free of charge, by this official, who is appointed by Parliament for the purpose. Unlike anyone else outside the Government, he has the power to pry into all Government documents and can hear witnesses. The Ombudsman has no executive power, but he is so trusted and respected both by citizens and Governments that his recommendations are almost always accepted.
>
> The natural place to look is to our judiciary. In Britain, the judges have traditionally been the protectors of the citizen's rights against incursion

by the executive agents of the State. Indeed, it was the alliance of the Common Law with Parliament which won for Parliament its legal supremacy over the Crown. But the Common Law has grown old and stiff; it no longer has the youth and suppleness to combat the new invasion of the citizen's rights by administrative power.

The idea originated in Sweden. An Ombudsman would have come quite naturally to the Swedes even in 1809. Ever since 1766 the Swedish citizen has had the right – it was lost temporarily between 1772 and 1809 – of free access to official documents. The citizen could walk into any government department and ask to see any document, except for specific documents vital to the safety of the State. The Ombudsman, in his access to official documents, was therefore merely exercising the collective rights of every citizen.

Since 1967 there have been nine appointments, and the system was extended to local government in 1973. The appointees have generally been retired civil servants of senior rank, reporting regularly to Parliament. In 1972 the system was extended to local authorities, without the necessity of the citizen having to process the claim through an elected councillor. But neither system possessed any executive power to enforce the remedy: a recommendation to compensate sufficed. The appetite for complaints systems did not abate. It spread throughout the system, with a clamour for legal remedies.

Judicially, it mushroomed in the growing field of public administration. In the 1970s there was a regular pattern of forensic action by way of the High Court, under the presidency of the Lord Chief Justice hearing applications for leave to grant one or more of the prerogative writs. No doubt stimulated by the arrival of Ombudsmanry, applications for leave multiplied – I have always preferred the good Anglo-Saxon word 'leave', to the Woolfian introduction in 1998 of the Latinism of 'permission' (the two are now permanently interchangeable). With the waning capacity of Lord Widgery, the court portfolio became unmanageable by the administrators. Lord Justice Donaldson (later, as Master of the Rolls in succession to Lord Denning in 1982, given the title of Lord Donaldson) was drafted in to clear the Augean stables of this specialist jurisdiction. This was achieved successfully and swiftly, giving rise to the advent of Order 53 of the Rules of the Supreme Court.

3

Judges in Public Inquiries, Redivivus

T HE EVER-POPULAR USE of members of the higher judiciary (either alone, or with assessors) to conduct public inquiries into major social scandals or serious human disasters
remains fashionable, even if it is labelled euphemistically as a
'quasi-judicial forum'. Governments are still inclined to employ
judge-led inquiries, despite a professional debate about their utility
following legislation in 2005 and the formidable lecture delivered
in Jerusalem in 2004 by Lord Justice Beatson.[1] He alluded to the fact
that appointments of senior judges should be made sparingly, and
that judges should be hermetically sealed off from inquiries that
were politically sensitive, or which might be susceptible to hostile
criticism regarding the independence of the judiciary. Ministers
should heed the warning against an urge to respond too readily to
the popular clamour for a '*judicial* inquiry'. The report of the Select
Committee of the House of Lords on the Inquiries Act 2005 in March
2014,[2] however hesitantly, endorsed the popularity of judge-led
inquiries. The early effect of legislative action is a distinct move
towards treating investigation under the Inquiries Act 2005 as an
endorsement of the public inquiry as an emanation of ministerial
power by a Commission of Inquiry, rather than as an outcrop of
legal proceedings. Is the inquiry rather an act of public administration?

THE INQUIRY SYSTEM

The starting point in assessing the status of any public authority is
whether it is a tribunal or body exercising the judicial power of the

---

[1] 51st Lionel Cohen Lecture at the Hebrew University, Jerusalem, 1 June 2004.
[2] *The Inquiries Act 2005: post-legislative scrutiny* (HL paper 143, 11 March 2014).

State;[3] if it is not such a tribunal or court of law, then what is it? The public body springs from the declared provisions in the scope of the statute and its principal procedures, now the Inquiries Act 2005. It is the nature of the beast – its legal labelling – that has tended to dictate the essence of the process. When, in 1974, Lord Scarman classically declared that a public inquiry was decidedly *not* a species of litigation, and to be conducted inquisitorially, he did not elaborate upon the procedures of other inquiries; he assumed that other methods of eliciting evidence could prevail. And little (if anything) was said about discarding the forensic habits of legal practitioners, beyond stating the limits of questioning of witnesses by advocates. Not for another two decades (until Sir Richard Scott's assault in the *Arms for Iraq* inquiry in 1996) did the procedures of public inquiries come into conflict, both within the inquiry and extracurially. The chairman of a public inquiry asks himself initially what procedure is to be adopted, both statutorily and by way of the chairman's discretion, to dictate the manner of investigation. Overall, one will want to know the basic principles that lie behind the inquiry's process. Until 7 June 2005 (when the Inquiries Act came into force) the practice was variable until the Royal Commission of Tribunals of Inquiry (the Salmon Commission) reported in 1966, very much by then under the influence of legal habits adopted in legal proceedings. Thus a dose of legalism was injected into the practice, although the recommendations, generally acceptable, did not induce any legislation. But the legal profession neatly converted the procedure: it avidly adopted its habit of conducting inquiries 'adversarially', rather than 'inquisitorially'. Legalism played a distinct role in the conduct of the inquiry; it hijacked the process as if it were a trial. It adopted the euphemism of 'semi-judicial', whatever that meant precisely.

Traditionally and historically, the common law of England, in contrast with Continental systems of western Europe, established a litigious process whereby the plaintiff in civil litigation and the prosecution in the criminal court engaged in an adversarial role: the claimant (or prosecution) has to prove his claim, in a civil court on the balance of probabilities, and in criminal proceedings to a higher standard of proof, that of being 'beyond reasonable doubt'. The system of trial by jury in civil cases was almost entirely abolished in 1934; trial by jury for serious crime continues to this day in 95 per cent of criminal cases. But the standard of proof remains

---

[3] Compare also an inquiry conducted privately by a public authority: see *Kennedy v The Charity Commission* [2014] UKSC 20 [115], [120] and [128].

distinctively higher, conveying the message of the severe onus of this mode of trial.

By contrast, the rival European civil systems of a single judge (or a mixture of professional and lay members) adopted the more logical process of ensuring a true verdict, as opposed to the jury system of legally admissible proof, failure to attain which had the effect of acquittal of crime. The systems are based on opposing modes of trial, although the European Court of Human Rights has declined to differentiate between the two modes of trial. The verdict must rest on a 'fair trial' by either system. So in 2010 in *Taxquet v Belgium* (a country which had until than adopted the system of trial by jury), the case turned on whether extracurial, untestified statements by an accused violated the Convention. But if the adversarial versus inquisitorial modes of trial remains rooted in the two systems, it is no longer sensible to regard the binary systems of trial as poles apart: over the years, much more borrowing between the systems has been displayed.

The scene, if not the landscape of the judiciary in public inquiries, has perceptibly changed as a result of a House of Lords Select Committee report (*The Inquiries Act 2005: post-legislative scrutiny*),[4] which generally endorses the workings of the Inquiries Act 2005, although the report wishes to sweep away some procedural rules affecting freedom of speech. The report awaits parliamentary debate and public discussion. What follows from the report about judge-led public inquiries?

The basic role in the civil courts imposed on the legal system a duty of active case management. Historically, litigation had been fundamentally adversarial, in the sense that evidence was proffered by the rival disputants to support their claim or defence, rather than by the court itself through witnesses, although increasingly it is forced to adopt the inquisitorial process, as, for example, with family law cases. Truth, if it emerges, does so only inferentially, as a by-product of evidential proof. But the Inquiries Act specifically debars the inquiry from the exercise of any 'power to find or determine any person's civil or criminal liability'. It goes on to provide that the inquiry is not to be inhibited in the discharge of its investigative function by any likelihood of liability being inferred from the facts that the inquiry finds, or the determinations that it makes.

An inquiry, therefore, is not part of, nor does it emulate, the adversarial process (and does not ape the legal system): what then

---

[4] HL Paper 143, published on 11 March 2014

is there left of the rival attributes of adversarial versus inquisitorial? Is the ban on affixing liability merely procedural in the conduct of an inquiry; or is it fundamental to the institution established administratively, by statute, on Ministers? And if so, how should the role of the judge-led inquiry be regarded?

Nothing should prevent an inquiry panel from seeking evidence which will allow it to perform the central task of eliciting the truth. What the witnesses want to say is not necessarily what the inquiry needs to know, but it is not debarred from ferreting out whatever relevant information it desires. In the sense that the inquiry is uninhibited in the search for truth, it is decidedly inquisitorial. As the House of Lords Select Committee observed (para 213, p 66), most of the Committee's witnesses agreed that inquiries were best served by an inquisitorial rather than an adversarial procedure. The report cited approvingly Jason Beer, QC, prime author of a text-book on *Public Inquiries*, who told the Select Committee that an inquisitorial model best serves its task of investigation. It

> allows the inquiry to remain focused on its terms of reference . . . It allows the inquiry to focus on the issues that are of concern to it, to the chairman or the panel members, because an inquisitorial method has the inquisitor at the centre. Lastly, it allows often contentious and difficult issues to be examined and determined in a relatively dispassionate environment.[5]

The Committee recommended adoption of an inquisitorial method. It stated (para 215, p 67):

> We agree with our witnesses that an inquisitorial procedure for inquiries is greatly to be preferred to an adversarial procedure, and we conclude that the Act provides the right procedural framework for both the chairman and counsel to the inquiry to conduct an inquiry efficiently, effectively and above all fairly.

But it fell short of abandoning the rival procedures, while recognising that both can be accommodated readily by the overall obligation to conduct the inquiry fairly. Insofar as the inquiry finds a technique of procedure taken from the courtroom (adversarial type) congenial, it can freely adopt that technique of acquiring evidence under its overriding duty to conduct the inquiry with fairness. Section 17 of the Inquiries Act explicitly treats 'fairness' as a prerequisite of the inquiry. Yet the House of Lords Select Committee surprisingly seems impliedly to single out the judge-led inquiry, in

---

[5] Ibid, para 213, p 66.

contrast to any inquiry being led by a non-judicial chairman. The chairman is treated without distinction, save for one matter. It states (para 270, p 81) that 'we consider that a serving judge who has chaired an inquiry not concerned with the practice or procedure of the courts should play no further part after submitting his report, leaving this to Ministers, others to whom the recommendations are addressed, or Parliament'. This recommendation was part of a wider responsibility on the chairman to follow up his own recommendations if he desires to do so. Should that responsibility (exercisable at the chairman's discretion, whether to participate in public discussion of the inquiry) include the judge-chairman? The Committee stressed this point, whereas Lord Justice Beatson had encapsulated it as a vital aspect of contrast between the judge-led inquiry and one with any other chairman:

> Unless an inquiry directly concerns the administration of justice, or where there has been prior agreement about this (normally when the terms of reference are settled), a judge should not be asked to comment on the recommendations in his report or to take part in its implementation. This is the position of judges in relation to their decisions in legal proceedings over which they have presided. There are three principal reasons for the same principle governing judge-led inquiries:
>
> (i)   the judge may be asked to give an opinion without hearing evidence;
> (ii) the judge may be drawn into political debate, with accompanying risks to the perception of impartiality, as discussed above; and
> (iii) implementation is the responsibility and the domain of the executive.[6]

Apart from the purported relationship between two of the three arms of government, there is no formal relationship between the judiciary and members of executive government. More pertinently, the rule (or convention) which excludes the serving judge from any external consideration of his/her recommendations as a chairman of inquiry applies only to a judge in the exercise of his traditional occupation within the legal system. And it does so only for the purpose of giving the rival disputants to the litigation of their issue a guarantee against potential bias in the subject under inquiry. Where, in a public inquiry, there is no discrete issue to 'find and determine' any civil or criminal liability, and, where the witnesses at the inquiry are not witnesses to anything other than to questioning administered by the inquiry without legal effect, the rule has no application. Judges, like all other inquiry chairmen, are treated stat-

[6] ibid, para 268, p 80.

utorily on the same footing. Both are Commissioners of Inquiry; the chairman of an inquiry under the Inquiries Act 2005 is colloquially the long arm of the Minister, carrying out an investigation on his behalf. In every respect, the judge-led public inquiry is in no different position from that of any other chairman. It is the history of no definition to the public inquiry that leads the traditionalist to label it as 'judicial' in form.

Recently, in the inquiry into the standards and ethics of the press, this fact was misinterpreted. The problem started with an appellation, and not just a case of a terminological inexactitude. Every public pronouncement called the chairman of that inquiry 'Lord Justice Leveson'. But Sir Brian Leveson was sitting to conduct a public inquiry, not as one of Her Majesty's judges sitting regularly as a member of the Court of Appeal with fellow Lords Justices of Appeal. He was a Commissioner of Inquiry, pursuing an investigation as a part of a process of public administration, acting under terms of reference dictated by a Minister or Ministers. What then was Sir Brian's function, if he was not determining issues of criminal or civil liabilities of anybody? A public inquiry is palpably not a court of law. Legalism must play no part in its process, a process that has no legal effect. The conduct of the inquiry is flexible enough to allow the maximum amount of evidential material to be adduced and evaluated, and reported to Ministers.

The exclusive initiator of a public inquiry is a Minister (or Ministers) of the Crown, and it is an act of public administration outwith the legal system (there is now not even a requirement to obtain the authority of a parliamentary resolution and there is no appeal). The 2005 Act provides for Ministers to set Terms of Reference. The Minister appoints an inquiry chair, including specifically a judge as the chair. If the Minister thinks that the chair should be a serving judge, he is obliged to consult the head of the relevant judiciary. The inquiry is not permitted to determine civil or criminal liability of those appearing before it, but in the course of the finding of facts the inquiry is not inhibited from stating matters from which civil or criminal liability may be inferred. It is distinctly not a court of law and its recommendations cannot, and do not have any legal effect. At most, they may lead to other action such as a claim or a prosecution. The aim of an inquiry is to restore public confidence in systems or services by investigating the facts and making recommendations designed to prevent recurrence. Blameworthiness is not precluded, but it is a subsidiary function. Sections 17 to 23 of the 2005 Act regulate the conduct of inquiries, including the express requirement that the chairman must act fairly throughout the inquiry. There is no reference to the chairman acting judicially as if he were conducting a piece of litigation. The only legal control is by way of judicial review of any decision of the inquiry and imposes a time limit of 14 days for bringing an application for judicial review. Of the 13 inquiries conducted under the Act by October 2010, nine were conducted by retired English, Scottish or Northern Irish judges (although one of those nine retired during the course of the inquiry), and three were conducted by others not qualified; the other was chaired by a leading Queen's Counsel expert in mental health cases. In July 2011 Sir Brian Leveson, a serving Lord Justice of Appeal, was appointed as the sole chairman of the Inquiry into the Culture, Practices and Ethics of the Press, and he reported on 29 November 2012. In none of the 13 earlier inquiries did the chairman elaborate on his or her function under the Act.

Anyone conducting a public inquiry under the 2005 Act is a Commissioner of Inquiry, who may properly in his professional life be a serving judge functioning under a judicial oath to determine issues between rival disputants in litigation. Apart from Sir Brian Leveson, none of the inquiry chairmen was a serving judge and was then not referred to publicly by other than his or her daily title. There is, of course, nothing improper in a Minister of the Crown appointing a serving judge as the inquiry chairman. But if he does, the judge is merely a Commissioner of Inquiry. Sir Brian purported throughout the inquiry that he was performing a judicial-like act. He was not.

PUBLIC ADMINISTRATION

When analysed, the public inquiry is part of the development of resolving public issues that are not or could not be encompassed in a system of law that is costly to the litigating public. Stripped statutorily of any judicial function of adjudicating on rival disputes and enforcing its orders, the inquiry's chairman has a primary role of fact-finding and evidentiary decision-making. These roles are exemplified by those administering the assessment and evaluation of evidential material, as well as the credibility and reliability of witnesses. As such, they require the attributes of practising lawyers and other regular decision-makers. They do not exhibit more lawyerly than qualification. Additionally, they should be equipped with good judgment and common sense. Wisely, the Inquiries Act 2005 makes no distinction among potential Commissioners of Inquiry. The skills sought are to be found in the selection of persons qualified both legally and otherwise; Ministers will select those deemed suitable, whether judicially qualified or not. The statutory requirement then is that, in proposing to invite a judge to be chairman, there should be consultation with the judge's superior office-holder directed to the availability of members of the judiciary; it is a sensible precaution against the misuse of available talent, and not just selection preference. There is deliberately no requirement that inquiries should be judge-led, in contrast to Israel and some other jurisdictions. But it is noteworthy that the public demand latches on to its membership. They regularly call for a 'judicial inquiry'; 'elliptically' in more senses than 'judicial'.

There are two distinct occasions where the choice of a judge as chairman should instinctively be preferred, primarily for his or her expertise in cases calling for objective adjudication. First, the Minister of the Crown sponsoring the membership (a chairman, with or without assessors) must decide whether the subject matter calls for a public function, well covered in the media, for such an inquiry. The underlying question is whether the inquiry will depend on a fact-finding exercise, a test of a witness's credibility and reliability. This is an exercise for which the elements of justiciability prevail. If, on the other hand, the topic to be inquired into evokes issues of social policy, or even requires a study of the systems and services at play, then the judge, unqualified on the topic, may not be a preferred choice, but will sit with assessors. The next stage is to define the powers of the chairman, as a Commissioner of Inquiry, exercising his procedure and conduct of the inquiry by virtue of the discretionary power in section 17(3) of the Inquiries Act 2005. Fairness is universal in decision-makers. The fairness of the inquiry procedure is as between the rival disputants; the public is simply a watchdog, observing critically. Equally, the latter is imbued with a sense of being considered fairly, not just collectively but personally.

If the background to the establishment of an inquiry is a matter of public concern, the appointed chairman is, willy-nilly, embroiled in a matter of controversy, certainly less publicly articulated than the active politician or the engaged citizen. The enterprise of resolving disputes through the legal system, familiar to a judge, must not be injected into the inquiry system: section 2, which excludes any finding or determination of guilt by the inquiry, but endorses otherwise by comment any inference of blameworthiness on any person, means essentially that the judge is for that purpose not a judge. He is under no judicial oath, but is an extension of public administration, and carries out the statutory duty to carry out the inquiry on the terms of reference given to him by the Minister, and reports on his findings. The evidence binds no one. The Minister may decline to act upon the report and any recommendations. Chairmanship is an art, not always found in judges in the exercise of coercive powers. The chairman of the inquiry, whatever his normal occupation may be, is a Commissioner of Inquiry. It is one thing that proceedings are conducted well in the matrix of factual evidence, but what if the conclusions fail to convince? There have been two examples which demonstrate the public reaction to the particular inquiry.

The first example is the inquiry which Lord Hutton (immediately on retirement from the judicial House of Lords) conducted into one of the events leading up to Britain's involvement in the invasion of Iraq in March 2003. A propos of the conduct of the sessions held to elicit the evidence, Lord Hutton was hailed as the essence of impeccable conduct, and the analysis in his report of the events surrounding the disclosure of the government's approach to Iraq's alleged weapons of mass destruction (WMD) was masterly. Otherwise, it was considered as faulty. Lord Hutton's report concluded with the question of whether the Government had misled the public in its report into the relevant weaponry in the hands of Saddam Hussein, and whether the early morning unscripted broadcast by Andrew Gilligan on the intelligence gathering of the WMD report was the result of defective management by the BBC. On the two rival issues of palpable blameworthiness, Lord Hutton unwisely exonerated the Government, and strongly criticised the governors of the BBC. The public reception was in both respects unfavourable. Lord Hutton was denounced by some commentators as a lackey of whichever authority the reader of the report did not agree with. The judiciary was predictably regaled as expressing a politically controversial judgment, an impairment of the constitutional guarantee of judicial independence.

Whenever the projected inquiry presents within itself a host of political controversy, the judiciary may nevertheless be favoured, but only if on the panel of inquiry, the judge-chairman sits with assessors, to provide that element of expert knowledge of the topic under inquiry. There are within our society people well-versed in matters of procedural fair play – due process, if you will – to make suitable candidates for chairmanship. It may be sensible to select as an assessor someone with legal expertise, such as a practising member of the Bar. That precedent was present in the inquiry into Legionnaires' disease at Staffordshire Hospital in 1980 by Sir James Badenoch, a prominent physician, as chairman of a panel that included a leading Queen's Counsel.

For very different reasons, it was appropriate for a judge (with two Commonwealth judges sitting as assessors) to hold the second public inquiry into Bloody Sunday, which took 12 years to conclude and cost the public purse approximately £250 million. Among the legal profession at least, the subject-matter of the inquiry by Lord Saville into the tragic events of 30 January 1972 was very properly overseen by a very senior judge. The conduct of the case was a typical example of a public (lawyerlike) inquiry that was popularly described as a judicial inquiry – namely that it had the value-added quality of judiciality that endorsed public confidence in impartiality and judicial independence. In terms of cost and delay, it was a disaster, universally dubbed as 'never again'. It prompted, nay compelled, the Government to introduce the Inquiries Act 2005. The Government had asked the Law Commission to consider its proposals, long before Lord Saville presented his report in June 2010.

Public inquiries today should no longer be described as judicial inquiries: they are acts of public administration, conducted on behalf of, but independent in their conduct from, the sponsoring Minister. The House of Commons Public Administration Select Committee, in a 2005 paper contemporaneous to the enactment of the Inquiries Act 2005, gave as its reasons to support the frequency of judge-led inquiries that they were, arguably, 'a quasi-judicial forum'. After the 2005 Act the public inquiry ceased to have such a judicial quality. The point is made clear in a passage in the judgment of the Supreme Court in *Kennedy v The Charity Commission*:[7] if the Minister can decide whether to accept or not the findings of the Commissioner of Inquiry [under section 19 of the Inquiries Act] (whether it is judge-led or not), it becomes an administrative decision, not a judicial or quasi-judicial act. Section 18(3) of the Inquiries Act 2005 requires, as with the Freedom of Information Act, disclosure of documents to be left to the Minister; that too renders it outside the route of being judicial or quasi-judicial.

The day-to-day occupation of its chairman as a judge is, if at all relevant, purely formulistic. As with every appointee as chairman,

---

[7] [2014] UKSC 20.

the judge in the chair is properly described and functions as a Commissioner of Inquiry in pursuance of public administration. We must not accord a member of the judiciary any greater status by placing him on a pedestal that promotes civilly a special role.

4

The Road to Rome and Strasbourg via San Francisco: the Genesis of Human Rights

(a) A statement in concise form of the fundamental personal rights and the right to free political elections, based mainly upon the Universal Declaration of Human Rights.

Memorandum produced in Paris in February 1949 of a committee meeting to plan for a convention on human rights, cited by AWB Simpson, *Human Rights and the End of Empire* (Oxford, OUP, 2010) 650.[1]

O N 4 JULY 2014 (auspiciously anniversarial), the *Guardian's* leader-writer, extolling the virtues of the European Convention on Human Rights and Fundamental Freedoms (to give it its full title, indicating, more than titulary, the distinction between human (natural) rights and civil liberties), asserted that its origins lay in British constitutional history dating back to Magna Carta in 1215. He writes that the Convention's contents were 'written by English jurists in the mid-20th century at a time when all these things were violated in Europe'. Not so. That assumption, widely held, is both historically inaccurate, and internationally geographically misguided. The events of the Second World War and the horrors of the Holocaust provided a strong impetus to the nascent human rights movement, emanating internationally after the League of Nations in 1919 had considered a universal declaration of human rights but rejected its inclusion, above all, for further activity in both the USA and elsewhere in the world. The Convention, signed in Rome in 1950 as the outstanding establishment of the Council of Europe, opted for the city of Strasbourg as the site of the Commission and Court, and was well-founded in the internationalism engendered by the creation of the United Nations in San Francisco.

---

[1] The essence of this essay is based upon an article by Jan Herman Burgers, 'The Road to San Francisco: The Revival of the Human Rights Idea in the Twentieth Century' (1992) 14 *Human Rights Quarterly* 447.

The crowning of the universal declaration of the rights of man came on 26 June 1945. The author was none other than General Jan Smuts, the archetype of internationalism, who declared in his draft preamble to the Charter of the United Nations of 1 May 1945 that the Charter was 'achieving cooperation in promoting and encouraging respect for human rights and fundamental freedoms for all without distinction as to race, language or religion', one of the very purposes of the United Nations. It called on the international community 'to reaffirm faith in fundamental human rights, in the equal rights of men and women . . .'. Of course, there is a link to the horrors perpetrated by the Nazis during the war; these were breaches of human rights, but no emphasis could be placed on human rights in the San Francisco conference for the Charter of the United Nations. At most, some of the events before 1945 were still percolating into the public domain, but the full extent of the horrendous Holocaust was yet to emerge; much later, it provided further impetus to the human rights movement.

The existence of an international instrument, a universal declaration of human rights (which was declared on 10 December 1948 without direct legal enforcement) was novel (in the sense that it was the first document establishing the rights of man), and was 'based mainly on the Universal Declaration of Human Rights'.[2] The European Convention on Human Rights in April 1950 was the first international treaty additionally to establish the enforcement of the right to individual petition. Therein lies the origin of legal enforcement of the international law of human rights. Its role was separate and distinct from individual rights accrued by nation-states, in which the US was prominent.

Before I allude to the activity of international human rights law, it is important to observe its nature. Strictly speaking, only Articles 2 and 3 of the Convention are a reflection of human rights. Other rights, such as the universal franchise, are conferred on citizens by democratic countries. The former are rights from which member States cannot derogate under Article 15 of the Convention. The rest (effectively Articles 4–12) are civil liberties conferred constitutionally on citizens, all of which are declared to be 'necessary in a democratic society' and are qualified serially as matters of public interest. 'Human rights' is a catchphrase that has an emotional ring in the public eyes and ears. They are fundamental rights which are

---

[2] ibid, 18, and *cf* Hoffmann, 'Human Rights and the House of Lords' (1999) 62 *Modern Law Review* 159, 166 and Hoffmann, 'The Universality of Human Rights', Judicial Studies Board Lecture, March 2009.

automatically acknowledged by national legislatures. The rest are acquired qualifiedly.

Even before the Human Rights Act 1998 became part of UK law and the decisions of the European Court of Human Rights were, by section 2(1) of the Act, to be 'taken into account' in deciding cases in the municipal courts of the UK, it was plausibly argued that having regard to decisions of the Strasbourg Court as a test to inform the content of the common law was no less legitimate than referring to cases decided in other jurisdictions. In fact there were additional reasons why the Strasbourg Court should be regarded differently from other international tribunals. For a good many years – at least since the right of individual petition was granted in 1966 – significance was given to human rights issues; they contained values derived from that lowest of common denominators, human dignity and humanity, reflected in the unbroken custom whereby civilised nations adhered to constitutional norms. International human rights norms are intrinsically of higher value in the eyes of domestic courts if there is evidence of consistent state practice indicating the binding nature of such norms. If the concept of equality (now enshrined in statutory form) had become our law before the Human Rights Act, judgments such as Lord Scarman's dissent in *Ahmad v ILEA*[3] would not then have been regarded as an exception; he would have treated the development of the common law in the light of not only international standards but also the positive domestic law enacted to implement the principle of equality, including the anti-discrimination legislation. In terms of the development of common law principles, there is surely less, not more in 2014, than any regard to a replacement of the jurisprudence of the Strasbourg Court by a municipal Bill of Rights. The majority in the Coalition's Commission on a Bill of Rights put far too much emphasis, misguidedly, on the practice of the law before the incorporation of the Convention. They reflected the belief that Britain had uniquely invented effective protection of personal rights ('it was the land of the free') going back to Magna Carta, which was the author of the 'rule of law'. The explanation for the Human Rights Act 1998 is

---

[3] [1978] QB 36. The best exposition of the relevant principle is that set out by Dame Rosalyn Higgins, then a judge of the International Court of Justice (and later to become President of the Court), in an essay in 2002 where she observed that the European Court of Human Rights (including the Convention so far as possible) is part of international law; it must on the one hand be mindful of the Convention's special character as a human rights treaty while also taking the relevant rules of international law into account (for which proposition she cites the case of *Fogarty v United Kingdom* (2002) 34 EHRR 302) – see R Higgins, *Themes and Theories*, vol 2 (Oxford, OUP, 2002) 948.

quite otherwise. How did the English courts apply the law after the Human Rights Act 1998 came into force on 2 October 2000?

Time, the historians tell us, moves in only one direction, and legislation is part of historical development that takes us forward and replaces past attitudes. During the passage through Parliament of the Human Rights Bill there was clear warning from the Conservative opposition (which did not object to the principles in the Bill), through its Lord Chancellor-in-waiting, Lord Kingsland, that the provision for interpretation of the Convention into UK law, namely the direction to the courts, was insufficiently clear in its language and unhelpful to English judges. 'Taking into account' the Strasbourg jurisprudence and decisions has proved to be the source of a plethora of appellate judgments and academic debate after the famous statement of Lord Bingham in *Ullah v Special Adjudicator*[4] that the duty of national courts is to keep pace with the Strasbourg jurisprudence as it evolves over time: 'no more, but certainly no less'. What followed the epigrammatic phrase that Lord Brown cunningly rephrased as 'certainly no less, but no more', indicating what Lord Bingham had said, that it was of course open to a judge in the UK to provide rights more generous than those guaranteed by the Convention as interpreted by the Court at Strasbourg. Better to recall the words of the poet George Herbert: the best mirror is an old friend. Whether the phrase could be said to be a 'mirror' or a 'ceiling' provided the forensic disputation. But did it resolve the question, where on the spectrum did the UK judge's duty lie?

But Lord Kingsland's warning was not heeded. So what to do? The hearty dislike, even distaste, among Ministers and other politicians, for the jurisprudence emanating from the Court at Strasbourg and strongly differing from the values of the UK, is signalling a parliamentary re-run of the Human Rights Act, even if the Coalition Government appears to contemplate replacing the wording of section 2(1) of the Act.

The criticism about the proper approach to the Strasbourg jurisprudence has a respectable solution in practice and judicial intercourse, by a judicial dialogue between the two judiciaries. It is a dialogue which happily has a recent example. 'Taking into account' a Strasbourg judicial pronouncement (backed by political activity in the Council of Europe) should include a discretion to the courts in the UK to engage in any unresolved point of human rights law in the Convention. After all, the UK judiciary is obliged by section 3 of

---

[4] [2004] UKHL 26.

the Human Rights Act 1998 to treat any human rights issue, as nearly as possible, as making UK law compatible with the rights in the Convention.

THE NATURE OF THE EUROPEAN COURT OF HUMAN RIGHTS

The public dislike (or distaste, if you will) of the European Court of Human Rights is misconceived. It is not at heart anything to do exclusively with western liberal democracies, although its cradle in 1950 was the Council of Europe (and, of course, the environs of its main institutions, the Commission and Court, are Strasbourg). The Council of Europe's outstanding achievement was initiated in 1949 at Strasbourg University under the guidance of the European Parliament's deputy Secretary-General, a distinguished English naval hero, Dunstan Curtis, a solicitor and civil servant in post-war Europe.[5] Those procedural beginnings and the cultural (European) heritage of the institution, as largely promulgated domestically in the schedule to the Human Rights Act, are international in character – neither English nor French, domestically-speaking, or of the British Foreign Office which played a pivotal role in the development of the origin of the various Articles. Above all, it has to be remembered that the Court is only supervisory; it is supranational in that sense, and it is there to observe that the domestic courts – that is, the courts of the Member States – are primarily under a duty to comply with the Convention. It neither dictates nor overrides the national courts. It endorses no religion, race or creed; its purpose is to envelop mankind. Article 19 states that it is there 'to ensure the observance of the engagements undertaken' by the parties to the Convention and its Protocols. To adapt the soubriquet used by Judge Learned Hand, they are Platonic guardians of our universal humanity. The UK Supreme Court has shown that the 1998 Act provides for and gives expression to a dialogue between the UK Government and Strasbourg. The Articles of the Convention (let alone the various Protocols, some of which the UK has undertaken to implement) are written in a language (English) which can be readily understood by the British public.

Since 2000 the Court at Strasbourg has supervised the operation of these rights. A supranational court – it has 47 justices, one from

---

[5] Dunstan Curtis was my next-door neighbour at my second home in Montgomery, Powys in the late 1990s: we spoke frequently of his work at the Council of Europe in the immediate post-war years.

each member State – it seeks to rationalise the various rights between different legal systems. It is the guardian (not the determiner, which is the role of the Convention) of those rights. It has no other constituency of the 800 million people of Western Europe. It reflects the cultural heritage of the region of 47 countries, not just the British Isles or the original 12 states that initially signed the Convention. The Court is not international but supranational, in that it supervises all courts of last resort, not just Britain's. As Sir Nicolas Bratza, Britain's representative in the Court until October 2012, stated in 2011:

> The Strasbourg Court does in my perception pay close regard to the particular requirements of the society in question when examining complaints that a law or practice in that society violates the Convention.

Jonathan Sumption QC (now Lord Sumption, a Justice of the UK Supreme Court) makes the point – even if his solution favours a detachment from government, the contemporary equivalent of 'judicial restraint', or its opposite, 'judicial activism' (but either way, who wants the judiciary to be 'inactive'?) – that:

> Even where the case for recognising a Europe-wide human right is strong, the varying political and constitutional arrangements of different countries will mean that the same rights and the same derogations are *not equally necessary or desirable in all places*, and will not always require the same measures to make them effective.

It is important to remember that each member State has freely decided to ratify the ECHR and to become bound by each of its standards. Further, both the ECHR and the Committee of Ministers (in fulfilling its role of supervising the execution of the ECHR's judgments) have consistently refrained from imposing particular measures on member States that are required to be implemented in order to comply with a judgment of the Court. A much more sophisticated approach to the problem facing the judiciary in England has usefully come from a judgment in the Supreme Court, in the 2013 case of *Osborne v The Parole Board*,[6] where Lord Reed described the situation:

> 55. The guarantees set out in the substantive articles of the Convention, like other guarantees of human rights in international law, are mostly expressed at a very high level of generality. They have to be fulfilled at national level through a substantial body of much more specific domestic law. That is true in the United Kingdom as in other contracting states.

[6] [2013] UKSC 61.

For example, the guarantee of a fair trial, under article 6, is fulfilled primarily through detailed rules and principles to be found in several areas of domestic law, including the law of evidence and procedure, administrative law, and the law relating to legal aid. The guarantee of a right to respect for private and family life, under article 8, is fulfilled primarily through rules and principles found in such areas of domestic law as the law of tort, family law and constitutional law. Many other examples could be given. Article 5, in particular, is implemented through several areas of the law, including criminal procedure, the law relating to sentencing, mental health law and administrative law: indeed, article 5(4) is said to have been inspired by the English law of habeas corpus (*Sanchez-Reisse v Switzerland* (1986) 9 EHRR 71, 88). As these examples indicate, the protection of human rights is not a distinct area of the law, based on the case law of the European Court of Human Rights, but permeates our legal system.

Lord Reed explained this analysis to the treatment of prisoners fairly in granting parole licences:

> 59. When the House of Lords considered in *R (West) v Parole Board* [2005] UKHL 1; [2005] 1 WLR 350 the circumstances in which determinate sentence prisoners recalled to prison were entitled to an oral hearing before the board, it took the common law as its starting point, and considered judgments of the European court, together with judgments from a number of common law jurisdictions, in deciding what the common law required. It went on to hold that the board's review of the prisoner's case would satisfy the requirements of article 5(4) provided it was conducted in a manner that met the common law requirements of procedural fairness.[7]

DIALOGUE

In the case of *Horncastle*,[8] the UK Supreme Court's unnecessarily lengthy judgments dealt with reference to hearsay evidence from witnesses. The case involved absentee witnesses who had died before trial or who were absent through fear of giving open testimony. The decision was that there is no requirement in English law that a conviction cannot be based on the sole or decisive evidence of an absent witness. In England a conviction based on that sole or decisive evidence is available as for any other absent witness. Lord

---

[7] By describing the protection of human rights in the Convention as 'permeating' the English legal system, Lord Reed might more aptly have talked of the Convention as 'entrenching' its protection, simply because the imagery is familiar to constitutional lawyers.

[8] *R v Horncastle and others* [2009] UKSC 14.

Phillips and his colleagues seemed to make their decision in conflict with the case of *Davis*,[9] in which Lord Bingham had acted upon the presumption that there cannot be a fair trial within Article 6 of the European Convention with an anonymous witness providing written testimony which is the sole or decisive evidence. *Horncastle* was directly in conflict with the Strasbourg jurisprudence. The Supreme Court was conscious that it was making a plea for a re-examination by the Grand Chamber of the European Court of Justice, which did so, modifying its earlier application of the 'sole and decisive' test. A qualification of that ruling could be departed from in a suitable case. Strasbourg's second thoughts were found acceptable. Judicial dialogue appeared to succeed. But should it have offered a sensible compromise between the two systems upholding a right to a fair trial? Here then was the nub of the problem – a difference in attitude between the binary modes of criminal trial, both judiciaries talking at cross-purposes. The UK Supreme Court based itself on the reliability thesis, which encompassed the criminal justice philosophy of the criminal justice process actively assisting in the general aim of crime control. Given the absence of the witness, the jury could properly look to other evidence to feel confident that the account of the witness is in fact reliable, having regard to the safeguards in the Criminal Justice Act 2003 about anonymous witnesses. By contrast with the English system, which is geared to the courts exercising the public interest in controlling crime, the mode of trial in most of Western Europe is linked to the overriding principle of due process in Article 6 of the Convention. The procedural rule of fairness in the criminal trial overrides, if it does not exclude, any other purpose than the trial. Public policy on criminality is the function of the enforcement agencies outwith the courtroom.

Each mode of criminal trial reasonably functions to legitimise the difference in principle towards anonymous witnesses. The European qualification to the UK Supreme Court's plea for a re-think may bring the binary systems closer. But we shall have to await the outcome of criminal justice cases. If the European Court of Human Rights can be said to have abandoned the full effect (if any effect) of the 'sole and decisive' rule, it may be argued that it too proceeds upon the principle of reliability of testing. In which case, has 'due process' taken a step towards a unified system of criminal justice within the Council of Europe? The relationship between due process and the test of overall reliability of testimony may still have

---

[9] *R v Davis* [2008] UKHL 36.

to be fought out. In which case, there is much to be debated in the administration of criminal justice within the European Union. The present difficulty is not lessened, because in many of the concurring judgments in *Horncastle* and in other cases since the modified pronouncement in the modification at Strasbourg, there is the respectable opinion that what is said in Strasbourg can properly be ignored in London. To 'take account' of Strasbourg, because that court speaks the last word (except for special circumstances), simply perpetuates conflict: hardly a recipe for dialogue and compatibility.

CONCLUSION

The respective manifestos of the political parties for the General Election on 7 May 2015 will inform the public. Did the United Kingdom explain signing the European Convention on Human Rights in 1950 as part of the long history of English constitutional law (as the majority asserts in the report of the Commission on a Bill of Rights), or did it rationally justify its signing of the Convention in the general political history which had manifested itself in a much longer-standing factor of the development of international human rights law, which began as early as the League of Nations in 1919? No doubt the parties' manifestos which threaten the debate on the future parliamentary attitude to the Human Rights Act 1998 will emerge unscathed. Or will there be a desire for textual reform?

One of the most striking differences between the Covenant of the League of Nations in 1919 and the Charter of the United Nations in June 1945 has been that human rights found no place in the conference report. Apart from some references in Article 23 to 'fair and human conditions of labour' for everyone, and to 'just treatment' of the native inhabitants of dependent territories, there was no mention of human rights during the drafting of the Covenant. Yet there was a good deal of debate about the obligations of all League members to respect religious freedom and to refrain from discrimination on the basis of religion. This is not to say that human rights had not been raised during drafting sessions. The concept of international human rights was at least embryonic. By the time of the Second World War, there were angry pronouncements that activated the delegates at the conference at Dumbarton Oaks, a mansion belonging to Harvard University, between August and October 1944, prior to the establishment of the United Nations at San Francisco.

Significantly, American involvement was evident. As regards an international status for human rights, the proposals for a new world organisation came from the United States, the Soviet Union, China and the United Kingdom, although an American proposal to insert into the Charter a statement of principle about respecting human rights did not meet expectations. Far stronger language on human rights had to await the Charter at San Francisco. Far from the two events dictating the status of human rights – the ending of the war and the revelation of the horrendous Holocaust – the founders of the United Nations at the Conference in San Francisco established internationally the promotion of human rights as an important part of the new world organisation.

Whereas before the Second World War the idea of giving human rights a positive political response was advocated by a few commentators, it was itself stimulated through the mainstream of public discussion. A flood of publications emerged, of which the most significant was President Roosevelt's peroration on the Four Freedoms, when addressing the US Congress on 6 January 1941. The opening passage in his speech is telling: 'In the future days, which we seek to make secure, we look forward to a world founded upon four essential freedoms', after which he set out as the freedom of speech and expression, freedom of worship, the freedom from want and the freedom from fear. That was not entirely novel, even if until then it had not been publicly pronounced. It reflected a determination of the US Government to avoid a repetition of the failure after the First World War when the Senate had withheld its approval to the Covenant of the League of Nations, for which President Woodrow Wilson had advocated at the Paris Peace Conference. But behind the political pronouncements, the scene had been set in the 1930s.

On 23 October 1939, HG Wells wrote a letter to *The Times* in which he referred to 'the extensive demand for a statement of war aims on the part of young and old, who want to know more precisely what we are fighting for', but also to the practical responsibility of making any statement in terms of business, federations and political ramifications at the present time. The letter included the text of a draft 'Declaration of Rights' consisting of a short preamble and 10 articles. Soon thereafter, a Penguin Special appeared, *The Rights of Man, or What we are Fighting For*, containing the draft from October 1939. The book also reproduced the text of a declaration of rights emanating from the University of Dijon. This was the International Law Institute, set up in Paris in 1921 to study the protection of universities and of human rights in general.

This burgeoning of scholarship in the international law of human rights was promoted by two eminent émigrés, the first of whom was Professor Mandelstam, a Russian jurist who had been a diplomat in the Tsarist government. He fled the Bolshevik revolution and devoted his studies to international law in Paris, as did another émigré, Professor Frangulis, a Greek jurist who had represented the Greek government at the League of Nations from 1920 to 1922. In 1926 he founded the International Diplomatic Academy which organised conferences and published in the field. One of the first actions of the Academy was to set up the study of the protection of human rights. The safeguarding of human rights was always a feature of Frangulis' activities.

HG Wells' *Rights of Man* was a huge publishing success. It achieved widespread recognition and support. The human rights movement of the period between the two world wars undoubtedly influenced events both during and after the Second World War. Did these events directly or indirectly lead to the establishing of the Council of Europe in 1948 and its judicial creation of a Commission and Court of Human Rights? Professor AW Brian Simpson, in his massive work *Human Rights and the End of Empire*,[10] concludes thus:

> The explanation why the United Kingdom promoted and ratified the convention must be sought *not in the history of English constitutional thought*, but in *the general political history of the period*. It was a product of British foreign policy, not of the British legal tradition, much less of British domestic policy. The belief in governmental circles that it was in Britain's interests to take the most prominent part of any of the major powers in the human rights movement, both in Europe and in the United Nations, arose as an aspect of the conduct of international affairs (italics supplied).

Professor Simpson notes that, unrelated to international affairs, there was another, much more long-standing factor emanating from the domestic politics of the pre-war years. This is that Britain was a country that protected its citizenry under the rubric of the rule of law. This tradition was founded in part on the habit of avoiding any written document guaranteeing any rights or duties. It is an attitude that prevails in limiting the extent of international activity. But the rights and duties safeguarding citizens in legal form are separate and distinct, ever in harmony, never in harness.

---

[10] AWB Simpson, *Human Rights and the End of Empire* (Oxford, OUP, 2001) 18.

5

Towards a Legal Forum of the Isles

SEPARATION AND DEVOLUTION

UNDER THE AGREEMENT reached in the Multi-Party Negotiations in Belfast on Good Friday, 10 April 1998 (the Good Friday Agreement) the parties established the British-Irish Council with the aim of promoting the harmonious and mutually beneficial development of the totality of relationships among the peoples of the Islands. The members of the Council are the Irish and British Governments, together with representatives of the devolved institutions in Northern Ireland, Scotland and Wales; and representatives of Jersey and Guernsey and of the Isle of Man. The British-Irish Council is a forum for Ministers to consult and exchange information with a view to co-operating on issues of mutual interest within the respective competences. So far, the British-Irish Council has met at least once per year, and has issued a number of reports.

The idea of a legal forum to consult and exchange information among the judges and lawyers of the Isles, with a view to airing issues of mutual interest and seeking to promote harmony and parallel development of the legal systems of the respective jurisdictions, would appear to provide an independent but useful auxiliary to the British-Irish Council. To that end, there should be set up by the heads of the judiciaries a Legal Forum of the Isles, to match the representation of the British-Irish Council, including the Channel Islands and Isle of Man judiciary and leading legal practitioners in the four jurisdictions.

To date, members of the British-Irish Council have agreed practical co- operation in areas as diverse as the misuse of drugs; environmental issues; indigenous, minority and lesser-used languages; social inclusion; and knowledge economy issues, with work continuing in other sections, including tourism and transport. In two of these areas, on the misuse of drugs and transport, the Council has been considering issues of particular practical importance – namely, the confiscation of criminal assets, and mutual recognition of driving disqualifications (in February 2006 there was an exchange of letters between Ireland and Britain on a proposed bilateral agreement on the mutual recognition of driving disqualifications).

At its first summit meeting in 1999 the British-Irish Council had added a number of topics, including specifically prison and probation issues. At its eighth summit meeting on 2 June 2006 the Council approved the proposal to add demography as a new work area, concentrating initially on ageing and migration. Some at least of these topics currently under review involve issues of legal topicality, even of potential law reform. But there is a host of topics which lend themselves to comparative study within the four jurisdictional systems. One that immediately springs to mind is the review of the law of murder; the Law Commission has completed the review by a report to the Home Office.[1] Since 2007 the Ministry of Justice has stated that there is no prospect of any review of the law and penalty for murder. The topic was discussed at the meeting in Northern Ireland (at which judges and lawyers from each of the four jurisdictions attended on May 12–14, 2006). Other topics for that weekend were substantive legitimate expectation and the prosecution of sex offenders. That meeting provided some indication of what might be expected of a permanent body overseeing contemporary legal issues. Other issues that could usefully be considered are asylum and immigration; anti-terrorist legislation; litigants in person; modes of criminal trial; judicial standards, training and discipline; and judicial independence.

The suggestion is that the secretariat for the Legal Forum of the Isles should not be based in England but in one or other of the three jurisdictions. The venue should be determined at the first inaugural meeting of the four Chief Justices.

It might be wise, initially at least, to limit the membership of the Forum to the higher judiciary of the four jurisdictions and possibly the chairmen of the respective Bar Associations, and/or treasurers of the Inns of Court, the Dean of the Faculty of Advocates and the representative of King's Inn, Dublin. While recognising the heritage of the English common law, the promoters of the Legal Forum of the Isles will wish to demonstrate that the fissiparous development that has taken place in the separate jurisdictions over the last hundred years has been left behind as archival interest, and to foresee a future of harmonious development of the legal systems of these Islands. The referendum in Scotland in September 2014 might be

---

[1] Law Commission, *Murder, Manslaughter and Infanticide* (Law Com No 304, 2006).

an occasion for examining the peripheral issue of legal relationships in the UK. With the prospect of developing devolved powers
within the UK, the legal implications begin to evolve, perhaps even
to federalism. Law, even constitutionally, never stands still.

Postscript:

In the wake of the referendum on Scottish independence on 18
September 2014, the idea of a legal forum should become part of
any future extension of devolved powers. What about a third
Scottish judge as a permanent Justice of the UK Supreme Court?

Part II

Crime and Justice

6

A Calendar of Murder: the Causes of Unjustifiable Homicide

MUCH, PERHAPS TOO much, for the sake of preserving any sensible restriction on information overload, saturated the public zone of instinctive attitudes towards retaining the death penalty for murder, which was finally abolished in 1965. (At that time it was estimated that probably 80 per cent of the electorate favoured the ultimate penalty for murder. Today (2014) there are probably 65 per cent in favour.) A great deal of the debate in the modern movement towards abolition focused on the morals of hanging the guilty murderer; some feared the uncertainty of the conviction, and miscarriages of justice. But overall there remained the rival claims of revenge, rehabilitation, the facility for remorse and the argument of the penalty's deterrent effect. Matters of life and death were argued out in contemporary literature, the most significant of which was the completion of the script in October 1955 of *Reflections on Hanging* by Arthur Koestler, enhanced by the author's personal experience of undergoing the threat of execution. The book was seen initially by the publisher Victor Gollancz, and a fellow campaigner of Gerald Gardiner, an outstanding Queen's Counsel (and Lord Chancellor in the Labour administration that won the election of October 1964). Gardiner had written to Koestler: 'I thought that I knew pretty well anything there was to be known on the subject, but I find that I have learned a lot from it.' Gardiner worried that Koestler's uninhibited attack on, among others, Her Majesty's judges (notably the previous Lord Chief Justice, Lord Goddard) were too libellous for print, and pointed to passages that needed to be toned down. The ultimate publication pitchforked Koestler into the public campaign, but in November 1955 it was followed by the first mass rally of the National Campaign for the Abolition of Capital Punishment, which took place in Central Hall, Westminster. Koestler was on the platform but did not speak. He explained to his colleagues on the committee that 'a foreign accent and a foreign name would be an added liability in a campaign basically directed at irrational, emotional prejudice'. Nevertheless, he was publicly acknowledged as the principal initiator of the campaign.

Koestler's book was serialised in five lengthy instalments in the *Observer*, 'scoring a huge success with readers', according to his biographer, Michael Scammell.[1] That journalistic venture was only the first step towards Koestler's undoubted entitlement to be acknowledged, by his authorship and subsequent purveying of the evidence on homicide, as the most influential proponent of abolition. That entitlement needs to be expounded by the events of the late 1950s until the General Election of October 1964, when public opinion for the first time became aware of the evidence of the relationship, in many cases, between the killer and victim of murder. The extent of the true relation between the parties to homicide had never been authoritatively assessed; it could only be conjectured. The evidence, imputed by Koestler and others, points strongly to some influence, even if only to retract some of the retentionists' claims and to reduce the incidence of retentionism. The publicity of the campaign to abolish the death penalty in the early 1960s led to the revelation of some empirical evidence of the nature of homicidal events; hitherto, the debate had all been about moral issues.

Prior to the publication of *Reflections on Hanging*, the public had responded to individual murderers who suffered the death penalty, but suspicions of miscarriages of justice were episodic and infrequent (some of them were only acknowledged as such much later). A trilogy of cases in the 1950s – Timothy Evans (1950), Derek Bentley (1952) and Ruth Ellis (1953) aroused hostility to the criminal justice system that was accompanied by initial success in Parliament in the course of an amendment to the Criminal Justice Bill of 1947; that had led to the establishment of a Royal Commission on Capital Punishment to determine the means (if any) of limiting the incidence of the death penalty for murder. It reported in 1953 that it was chimerical for any system to differentiate between unlawful killings, implying that the only way forward was abolition. The movement towards such a reform was interrupted by the loss of governmental power by Labour, and the passing of the much-disliked Homicide Act 1957.[2] The legislation quelled any further

---

[1] M Scammell, *Koestler: The Indispensable Intellectual* (London, Faber and Faber, 2004) 444.

[2] This calls for a separate discussion of the Royal Commission on Capital Punishment in 1953, the political reaction and the judicial hostility to the act, which has been written

parliamentary action; the campaign continued to lobby without immediate success from the persistent activities of penal reformers. The outstanding evidence stemmed directly from Arthur Koestler's authorship demonstrating existing patterns of murder.

To revert to the events post-November 1955, the rift between Gollancz and Koestler – two hugely energetic figures with oversized egos that dominated any relationship – was complete. Effectively, it drove Koestler to approach David Astor (a totally different, emollient man and a brilliant editor) with a view to perpetuating the idea of painting a vivid picture of the homicidal event, the relationship of the sufferings of victims, often instigated by the victim's killer, to any provocative and other controversial behaviour. The tone of the article was set in a preface that recalled Koestler's memories of prisoners executed in Seville. He wrote:

> These three months left me with a vested interest in capital punishment – rather like 'half-hanged Smith', who was cut down after fifteen minutes and lived on. Each time a man's or a woman's neck is broken in this peaceful country, memory starts to fester like a badly healed wound.

The temporary victory in the Criminal Justice Bill in favour of abolition in 1947 nearly dissolved the campaign, but with the inevitable opposition to the Commons debate in the House of Lords, and the impending general election, it was rescued by Koestler resigning, with the footnote that he would continue to 'write and work for abolition' but would not attend meetings. Koestler only wrote the occasional article under the name of 'Vigil'; his last column was published as a pamphlet entitled *Patterns of Murder*. Until then, the National Campaign continued to meet under the auspices of Cannon John Collins, then the Dean of St Paul's Cathedral, together with his organisation called Christian Action, which was actively engaged in opposition to the apartheid regime in South Africa. The committee met at the Dean's official residence at Amen Court. David Astor was a member of the committee, and when Koestler discontinued his articles for the *Observer*, Terence Morris, an outstanding criminologist at the London School of Economics, and I (then the *Observer*'s legal correspondent) were asked to take on the function of 'Vigil'. We did so, producing in 1961 a pamphlet called *Murder in Microcosm*, much in the same vein as Koestler's earlier work. That led inevitably to a fuller, updated version of every case of a

about extensively elsewhere. See Morris and Blom-Cooper, *The Penalty for murder: a Myth Exploded* (1996) Crim LR 707.

defendant who stood indicted with murder from March 1957 (the start of the Homicide Act 1957) until 1962, some 762 cases.

Each entry gave a pen-portrait of the victim and his accused killer, and gave information of the judicial proceedings. The hard detail revealed, unsurprisingly but unexpectedly to a thoughtless public, that in about 70 per cent of all homicides the parties had been related to each other before the homicidal event, and in an overwhelming number of cases the killing was the product of domestic violence. Rarely was the victim a total stranger to the killer; the main exception was the result of the abuse of children in the early days after their birth. The public was made aware that murder was anything but the result of the violence of young robbers on elderly women in post offices. Killer and victim were often related, sometimes closely.

The volume of 762 cases was published as *A Calendar of Murder* in 1964, and was prominently referred to in the course of the debates on the Murder (Abolition of Death Penalty) Bill during 1964/65. To demonstrate the kind of information, gleaned from court records and newspaper cuttings, studied at the British Library's store at Colindale, I produce an extract from *A Calendar of Murder*:[3]

Accused	*Victim*
Joseph Martin	Pamela Masterson

Martin (27), unemployed, visited the house where his mistress (22) lived, but, finding her to be not at home, went to bed with her friend who lived in the same house. In the morning, while showing her the working of a Luger pistol which he was carrying with him (because 'there was someone looking for him with a gun'), the gun went off and Mrs Masterson was killed instantly.

Martin was acquitted at the Old Bailey, 24.5.1960, of capital murder but convicted of manslaughter (i.e. accident with gross negligence). He was sentenced to 6 years' imprisonment.

* * *

Lilian Medd	Denise Kay Medd (4)
	Michael Medd (1)

Mrs Medd (28), a widow, who was in part-time employment, became very depressed and worried about her financial prospects and about the prospects for the children, so she turned on the gas tap in the room in which they were all sleeping. Mrs Medd was found unconscious but survived.

[3] T Morris and L Blom-Cooper, *A Calendar of Murder* (London, Michael Joseph, 1964) 150–51

Defence pleaded diminished responsibility on account of acute melancholia and Mrs Medd was convicted of manslaughter under Section 2 at York Assizes, 12.2.1960. Sentencing her to 2 years' imprisonment, Mr Justice Salmon said: 'This is one of the most terribly sad cases which I have ever had to deal with.'

* * *

Philip Morris   Matilda Morris

Morris (59), an unemployed sheet metal worker, was found guilty, on grounds of diminished responsibility, of the manslaughter of his invalid wife (72) – a 'mercy killing'; he was sentenced to life imprisonment by Mr Justice Austin Jones at Glamorgan Assizes, 6.12.1960. During the trial two doctors gave evidence that Morris was suffering from depression superimposed on a chronic anxiety state. Mr Justice Austin Jones refused to allow the prosecution to raise the issue of insanity although the prosecution's medical evidence showed an even greater degree of mental abnormality than the defence doctors (cf. Price 1962). The Court of Criminal Appeal, [1961] 2 QB 237 at pp 240–1, had this point argued but declined to rule on the question as not being directly in issue. It upheld the life sentence because the provisions of the Mental Health Act gave a wide discretion to the judge. But it laid down that, normally where punishment is not intended, it was better to make a hospital order and not leave it to the Secretary of State to transfer the person from prison to a mental institution (see Duke (1961)).

* * *

James Lawrence Nash, steeplejack   Selwyn Keith Cooney
James Alexander Read, unemployed
Joseph Henry Pyle, street trader

Nash (28), Read (28) and Pyle (25) were accused of murdering Soho club-owner Selwyn Cooney (31) in the Pen Club in Stepney. Cooney was shot as an act of revenge during a gang feud, and all three faced charges of capital murder, though it was alleged that it was Nash who had carried and used the revolver.

At their trial at the Old Bailey, there was evidence that witnesses were being intimidated and others were remaining in hiding, and that jurors were being tampered with. Mr Justice Gorman stopped the trial and dismissed the jury.

At the re-trial before Mr Justice Diplock, objections were made by counsel to 9 of the 12 people called for the jury before the prosecution announced that it was offering no evidence against Read and Pyle on the capital murder charge; they were formally found not guilty. During Nash's trial, there were further intimations of false evidence and witnesses disappearing before Nash was acquitted of capital murder,

4.5.1960, owing to lack of sufficient evidence, the principal prosecution witness having deliberately failed to attend the trial. All three were then tried on charges of causing actual bodily harm to Cooney. Nash was sentenced to 5 years' imprisonment, and Read and Pyle to lesser terms.

[Authors' note: The events surrounding this trial suggest there may be times when the power of the criminal underworld defeats the ends of justice. It might be argued that where Crown witnesses, themselves embroiled in associated criminal activities, are likely to be intimidated, there is a case for key witnesses also being placed under automatic police protection or house arrest pending the trial.]

7

Towards a New Homicide Act

O N RUMMAGING THROUGH the debris of voluminous papers in which the late Professor Terence Morris and I had ventured to articulate reasons for a statutory revision of the law of murder (constructed 400 years ago by Sir Edward Coke and still operative by the common law), I came across a document which together we submitted to the Law Commission in March 2006. The submission we made was in direct response to the Law Commission's Consultation Paper No 177 in which the Commission politely countered our argument in favour of a radical reform of the law of homicide, an argument which we had advanced in a book, *With Malice Aforethought*, in 2004. Our response to the Law Commission's rejection of our proposal in favour of a single homicide offence suitably redefined the offence.[1] We received an official acknowledgment from Professor Jeremy Horder, then a Law Commissioner, who wrote in manuscript on 28 March 2006, thanking us for our response 'which will actually be very helpful to us in finalising the Report'. The final report of the Law Commission was published on 29 November 2006. Its restricted recommendations were rejected by the Government. The report contained no reference to our alternative proposal; nor did it allude to the matters raised in paragraphs 2.32–2.38 of the Consultation Paper. Against public announcements that no reform of the law of murder (apart from amendments to the partial defences to a charge of murder – provocation and diminished responsibility – in the Coroners and Justice Act 2009) is contemplated by Government, the rest has been an ominous silence, except for a tangential issue that reflects the earlier thoughts of change.

In the Criminal Justice and Courts Bill, which had a second reading on 30 June 2014,[2] the starting point for sentencing the murderer of a police or prison officer in the course of their duty has been raised to the status of 'whole life'. The singling out of the two law

---

[1] I annex paras 2.32–2.38, on pp 32–33 of Consultation Paper No 177 of November 2005 at pp 80–81, below.

[2] *Hansard* HL Deb, 30 June 2014, cols 1538–39.

enforcement officers as candidates for the potential sentencing order of 'life without benefit of parole' revives the rationale of the inviolability of life on the grounds of 'sanctity', in order to support the ultimate penal sanction for murder, as argued for in the Law Commission Consultation Paper No 177. The chairman of the Law Commission from 2002 to 2006 was Sir Roger Toulson, now Lord Toulson, a Justice of the Supreme Court of the United Kingdom. Professor Jeremy Horder, a fellow Commissioner, is the Professor of Criminal Law at King's College, London. The text of our response to the Consultation Paper is reproduced below.

Introductory

We are grateful to the Law Commission for its comments on the proposal in our book, *With Malice Aforethought: A Study of the Crime and Punishment for Homicide*[3] for a single criminal homicide offence to replace the crimes of murder and manslaughter, even though our proposal does not fall within the restricted terms of reference given to the Law Commission by the Home Secretary. Accordingly, we have taken it upon ourselves in the following submission to answer the Law Commission's rejection of our proposal. We trust that the Law Commission will, in the light of this response, feel able to include in its final report to the Home Secretary a further comment on our proposal.

This document, therefore, deals with three topics only:

(a) the reliance of the Law Commission on the notion of the sanctity of life to sustain a contemporary law of murder and manslaughter;

(b) a rejoinder to the Law Commission's rejection of a single criminal homicide in the manner of the Kilbrandon formula; and

(c) the persistence of the Government to retain the mandatory penalty for murder.

The concept of the 'sanctity of life' in the context of law

1. Consultation Paper No 177 refers at paragraph 2.20 to the concept of the 'sanctity of life', a term used in the context of the law of murder by the Criminal Law Revision Committee (CLRC) in its report of 1980.[4] The word 'sanctity' derives from the Latin *sanctus*, generally translated as 'holy', and the term 'sanctity of life' has therefore strong religious connotations. Thirty years ago, when the CLRC was deliberating, there was probably less awareness of the fact that society was changing signifi-

---

[3] L Blom-Cooper and T Morris, *With Malice Aforethought: A Study of the Crime and Punishment for Homicide* (Oxford, Hart Publishing, 2004).

[4] Criminal Law Revision Committee 14th Report, *Offences Against the Person* (Cmnd 7844, 1980) para 15.

cantly in its ethnic and confessional characteristics, and it would have been accepted that ideas drawn from the Judaeo-Christian tradition were dominant; this notwithstanding that it had been long established that Christianity formed no part of the law of England.[5] This is not the case today, when other religious faiths are now recognised as a major feature of the social landscape. While it is certainly the case that there is still a widespread religious belief in the unique quality of human life, it may be expressed in different ways. No less important, however, is the fact that our society is nevertheless predominantly secular, a fact which is reflected in the character of its institutions, including law. Their function is to provide a lingua franca, in which those ethical principles that are consonant with wide cultural diversity can be both expressed and approved without dissent or ambiguity.

2. We would argue strongly, therefore, that terminology which employs concepts such as 'sanctity' is unhelpful and ought to form no part of the jurisprudence of homicide, not least since the matter of the inviolability of life is better accommodated by reference to Article 2(1) of the European Convention of Human Rights which is now incorporated within domestic law. Article 2 initially provided that the right of everyone to life shall be protected by law and that none shall be deprived of it intentionally save in the execution of sentence of a court following conviction for a crime for which death is the penalty prescribed by law. Effectively this is no longer applicable since capital punishment has been abolished within the various jurisdictions of the Convention signatories as a consequence of the Sixth and Thirteenth Protocols. Article 2, however, sets out the conditions in which deprivation of life constitutes a contravention of the Article with the proviso that this was, ab initio, a limited as distinct from an absolute right. Nevertheless, it has been judicially identified as one of the most fundamental provisions in the Convention from which there can be no derogation under Article 15. Consequent upon the Protocols excluding capital punishment, it has to all intents and purposes acquired a character that is difficult to distinguish from an absolute right.

3. The obligation of the State under Article 2(1) extends beyond its primary duty to secure the individual's right to life, by requiring the State to put in place effective provision in criminal law to deter the commission of offences against the person.[6] It further includes the establishment of a criminal justice system which provides for the trial and punishment of those who take life. The nature and extent of the provisions of the criminal law are left to be determined by the individual State.[7]

---

[5] *Bowman v The National Secular Society Ltd* [1917] AC 406.
[6] *Osman v UK* (1988) 29 EHRR 245.
[7] See: R Clayton and H Tomlinson, *The Law of Human Rights* (Oxford, OUP, 2000) 341 para 7.08 and 354 para 7.35; J Rowe and D Hoffman, *Human Rights in the UK* (Harlow, Pearson Longman, 2009) 105; N Jayawickrama, *The Judicial Application of Human Rights Law* (Cambridge, CUP, 2002); *R v Weir* [2001] 1 WLR 421, 427 [18].

4. We would strongly argue that the term 'sanctity of life' be no longer employed in discussion of reform of the law of homicide, and the term 'right to life' be substituted: it has a pragmatic (as distinct from theological) character that can be accepted and readily understood by any reasonable participant in the debate.[8] For this purpose it can be regarded as an absolute right identified in proactive terms that contrast with 'sanctity of life' which at best is no more than ambiguously descriptive.

5. There are further arguments against the use of the term 'sanctity of life' in the context of the law of homicide. In paragraph 2.23 the Consultation Paper makes reference to the distinction to be drawn between intentional and accidental or careless killing. In our view, while it is entirely logical to recognise that homicidal events encompass a very wide range of culpability and intention, the outcome of such events is that a life has been lost, whether by intent, accident or failure of duty to care. It is a simple and incontrovertible matter of fact that the dead are dead, however death may have come about.

6. It is this which is central in the minds of those who have been bereaved, and upon which the culpability or intention of the person responsible can have only a bearing, usually to accentuate it in proportion to the degree of recklessness, irresponsibility or evidently malicious intent. It would be difficult to maintain that the grief of a parent whose child has died under the wheels of a drunken driver is generically distinct from that of a parent whose child has been killed by a paedophile. Whatever the circumstances, the inalienable right to life has been violated, or, to employ the term that the authors of the document would evidently prefer, the sanctity of that life has been profaned. The quality of the life that has been lost is entirely sui generis, and is no way contingent upon the nature of the killing by which it has been prematurely terminated, although doubtless the circumstance attending the event may aggravate or mitigate the sense of grief. One ought not to overlook the variable response of forgiveness – or lack of it – by secondary victims.

7. In this context we note that paragraph 2.26 cites Exodus 20:2–17 as 'Do no murder'. The Authorised ('King James') Version of the Bible published in 1611 does not use the word 'murder', but the broader term 'kill', as does the Douai Version of 1609 which is a direct translation of the Latin Vulgate. In Latin there is no word corresponding 'to murder'

---

[8] In this context we would consider the term 'inalienable' to be the corollary of 'right'. It is, however, important to note that the right defined in Art 2 is not entirely consonant with the idea of 'sanctity of life': indeed, recalling that for centuries religious believers have been content to put to death not only offenders against the criminal law but those who have been defined as heretics and unbelievers, it can be said to go well beyond it by way of positive guarantee.

that is distinct from the word 'to kill'.[9] 'Kill' is also used by the Revised Standard Version in all its three editions of 1881-5, 1901 and 1952. The Ecumenical Edition of the RSV, published in 1973 and accepted by Roman Catholic scholars, similarly uses the word 'kill'. The New International Version published in Chicago in 1973 appears alone in employing the term 'murder' in this text from Exodus. Given that by the end of the 16th century the term 'murder' as distinct from manslaughter had emerged within the Common Law,[10] it is not unimportant to note that Biblical scholarship, both Anglican[11] and Roman Catholic, remained consistent with the approach of the mediaeval jurists for whom the distinction was much less apparent.

8. Although in paragraph 2.28 there is a quotation from Finnis, Boyle and Grisez[12] in which the Law Commission cite Exodus 20:13 as 'Do no murder', they go on with their analysis of its meaning by reference not to the word 'murder', but 'kill' or 'killing', no fewer than four times in a single paragraph. One must conclude either that this is simply a case of terminological inexactitude, or that they acknowledge murder to be no more than a synonym for unlawful killing. It is significant that they also, within this same passage, refer to 'reckless homicide'. The essence of their argument, however, would seem to be to draw a distinction between recklessness, however blameworthy, and the deliberate killing of the innocent.

9. Again, this raises problems, for if we are to pursue the argument that the worst kind of homicide consists of deliberate killing, that must extend beyond situations involving innocent victims to those where that label cannot possibly be attached. Let us suppose that an armed police officer, called to a house, finds a man who has just killed his wife and is standing over her body holding a golf club. The officer shoots the suspect through the head, killing him instantly.[13] The circumstantial evidence points to the shooting having been deliberate, and in

[9] All forms of killing are understood by the general term *interficere*, to 'do away with' or 'put an end to' and by *caedere*, literally to 'cut down' or 'beat' from which the word *homicida* derives: literally 'cutting a man down'. What is not without interest is that Latin, while not attempting to distinguish killings in terms specific to categories of culpability, is nevertheless the source of words that identify the victims of homicidal events in concepts such as 'patricide', 'matricide', 'fratricide', 'infanticide' and 'regicide'.

[10] The term 'murder' first appears in Statute in 1532 (23 Hen. VIII. Ch. 1). Although it might be seen as a term to describe what is essentially deliberate killing, our view that Coke's subsequently highly idiosyncratic interpretation of the law of homicide has been a legacy of dubious value, (set out in *With Malice Aforethought: A Study of the Crime and Punishment for Homicide*, at pp 15–32) remains unaltered.

[11] The *Book of Common Prayer* of 1662 in using the term 'murder' in its text is, no doubt, representing the usage that had developed in the 130 years since the term appeared in the Tudor statute and the 30 years following the publication of Coke's Institutes.

[12] J Finnis, JM Boyle and G Grisez, *Nuclear Deterrence, Morality and Realism* (Oxford, OUP, 1986) 78.

[13] If this example seems bizarre, we would pray in aid a practice of forensic exaggeration for academic purposes of which Professor Kenny was a noted exponent.

circumstances in which the disparity in weaponry was self-evidently extreme.[14] While it could not be said that the suspect so killed was innocent, since he had evidently just killed his wife, the police officer would have had no licence to take the suspect's life and could, as the law presently stands, be properly charged with murder. The life thus taken could certainly not be described as that of an innocent man, since he had shortly before clubbed his wife to death and one would need to stretch the concept of 'sanctity of life' to reason that, notwithstanding the evidence of deliberate homicide, that 'sanctity' was in no way compromised.

10. The central issue here is not the 'sanctity', or otherwise, of the life of the uxoricide, but the violation of his inalienable right to life that his conduct, unlawful and morally reprehensible though it may have been, has in no way affected. Not only is this association of the concept of deliberation with that of innocence a non sequitur, it is also highly misleading. 'Innocence', or indeed any specific characteristic of the victim, is not a necessary element in establishing the criminal guilt of the offender, although such factors are likely to be highly relevant in establishing culpability for the purposes of sentencing.

11. Our fictional example is a clear case in which the right to life, underwritten by Article 2, must be the paramount consideration, notwithstanding that in the circumstances the moral desert of the husband might be regarded as negligible. A right is either violated, or it is not. In the 19th century trial of Dudley and Stephens the defendants, who, cast adrift for days after shipwreck and without food or water, had chosen to eat and kill the cabin boy, unsuccessfully ran the defence of 'necessity'.[15] It is instructive in its demonstration that even in a situation as grave as theirs, the right to life enjoyed by the cabin boy was inalienable.[16] (Under the Law Commission's proposal Dudley and Stephens would be guilty of first degree murder.)

12. In 2.30 it is stated that the provisional view of the Law Commission is that the connection between the law of murder and the view that life is sacrosanct is best expressed through the creation of the crime of 'first degree murder'. The proposition that 'life is sacrosanct' needs to be more

---

[14] Apart, perhaps, from a highly contrived argument in support of a plea of diminished responsibility, it is difficult to think of a plausible defence against the charge. At the same time, there is no certainty how a jury might find, no matter how clearly and impeccably the judge may have summed up the facts and the law!

[15] Here 'necessity' can be distinguished from the defence of 'self-defence'. The cabin boy Richard Parker was not a threat to the lives of his killers. Aquinas, who in the *Summa* argues a case for necessity by which it is licit for a starving man to steal food to preserve his life, does not extend this to a situation in which the 'food' supply arises directly from a homicide.

[16] (1884) 14 QBD 273. See: AWB Simpson, *Cannibalism and the Common Law* (London and Chicago, University of Chicago Press, 1984).

closely examined in the ways in which the law has considered the taking of human life. The mediaeval notion of what were termed the 'petty treasons' is instructive in demonstrating that the lives of some members of society were regarded as more important than those of others. The essence of such treasons consisted of a failure of duty owed to one deemed a social superior, primarily within the framework of feudal obligation.[17] This graduated hierarchy of superiority among homicide victims is reflected in Coke's analysis of what he terms 'malice implied'. Thus: 'As if a magistrate or known officer, or any other that hath lawful warrant, and doing or offering to do his office, or to execute his warrant, is slain, this is murder, by malice implied by law.'[18] The notion of there being special categories of homicide victims, largely concentrated among those responsible for law enforcement, was much in evidence in the various proposals for amending the law of homicide in the latter part of the 19th century and was very much in evidence in the Homicide Act 1957 in which the killing of a police or prison officer was a specific instance of a capital murder.[19] Why fire service and ambulance personnel were considered unworthy of such putative protection has never been satisfactorily explained.

13. Nor is it the case that in the workplace human life has always been regarded as sacrosanct. Throughout the 19th century the mortality of those employed in the construction industry – mining, quarrying, fishing and shipping – was extremely high. In the merchant shipping industry it was not unknown before 1874[20] for unscrupulous owners to send vessels to sea that were known to be unseaworthy, risking the lives of their crews which were regarded as expendable, while in the knowledge that their cargoes were insured. 19th century Blue Books are replete with evidence that the lives of workers were frequently regarded as of little account, not least when the supply of labour was plentiful. The practice subsequently initiated after fatal industrial incidents, of bringing criminal prosecutions under the Factory Acts rather than for manslaughter, continued throughout the 20th century and remains essentially unchanged. The reason for this is undoubtedly the extreme difficulty in prosecuting corporate manslaughter, but the penalties are manifestly less onerous, both in quantum and social stigma, than those possible on conviction for a homicidal offence. The effect is to send a signal that no matter what the magnitude of failure in respect of a duty of care, the loss of life is not so great a matter as it would have been had the penalty been one imposed upon a conviction for murder or manslaughter.

[17] See: T Plucknett, *A Concise History of the Common Law*, 4th edn (London, Butterworth, 1948) 418.

[18] Coke, *Institutes* vol 3, 51–52.

[19] One might note that the slaying of judges and magistrates in the execution of their office was no longer a capital matter such as Coke would have most certainly regarded as an instance of 'malice implied by law'.

[20] The Act piloted by Samuel Plimsoll MP.

14. By the same token, the hiving-off of the offence of causing death by dangerous driving by the Road Traffic Act 1956, providing substantially lesser penalties than those available following conviction for manslaughter, has sent a signal that to kill a person with a mechanically propelled vehicle upon a public road is not as serious as killing a passenger by driving a train through a signal set at danger, or, indeed, in the course of any other system of public carriage.

15. Our point, therefore, is a very simple one. If human life is regarded as 'sacrosanct', the evidence both of history and the patterns of prosecution suggest that, to adapt Orwell's phrase, the law regards the lives of some people as more sacrosanct than those of others. That, in our view, is a consequential defect of the disarray in the present law, which we maintain is remediable by returning to a single crime of criminal homicide.[21]

The argument for a return to a single offence of criminal homicide: our rejoinder to its rejection

16. Admitting that murder, though co-extensive with deliberate killing, has not hitherto been confined to it is a recognition of what we have elsewhere defined as the 'penal premium', deriving from Coke's notion of constructive malice.[22] The anxiety of the Criminal Law Revision Committee three decades ago that to abolish the separate crime of murder and with it the mandatory sentence of life imprisonment would be to give a public signal that murder was no longer a 'specially or uniquely grave crime' was understandable, given the circumstances of the time when capital punishment had only recently been abolished.

17. In its Fourteenth Report CLRC noted that, in response to its Working Paper of September 1976 in which it invited attention to the Kilbrandon proposal, the Law Commission alone supported it.[23] The criticism of the present Consultation Paper is directed towards our advocacy of it. While it is, of course, accepted that the present Law Commissioners cannot be bound by the conclusions of their predecessors, we cannot fail to note that in rejecting our advocacy of the Kilbrandon Formula, no mention is

[21] Unless it is suggested that some violations of Art 2 be treated as matters intrinsically for the civil jurisdiction we see no reason why they should not be dealt with by the criminal law since, as we have argued in terms of right, one instance of homicide cannot be treated differently from any other.

[22] See: Blom-Cooper and Morris, *With Malice Aforethought: A Study of the Crime and Punishment of Homicide* (Oxford, Hart Publishing, 2004) 25–27.

[23] While sympathetic to the Kilbrandon proposal, the Law Commission recognised the possibility that it might result in the public perception of what was generally understood to be the gravest crime, namely murder, appearing to be in some way diminished in its gravity, that is not, in our view, a conclusive case against Kilbrandon. What the public perceives is not the arcane manifestation of the substantive law, but rather the penalties that may be imposed upon conviction.

made of the fact that at the time the CLRC was rejecting the Kilbrandon Formula, the Law Commission was supporting the idea. Nevertheless, having now had the opportunity of reading the comments of the Law Commission in 1978[24] upon the Criminal Law Revision Committee's Working Paper on Offences Against the Person (which run to some 24 pages) we are somewhat puzzled as to why the present Consultation Paper, in rejecting the Kilbrandon Formula, makes no reference to its support by the Law Commission of the time.

18. Nevertheless, that the disappearance of 'murder' as a discrete category of homicide might be interpreted as a 'signal' that the deliberate killing of another is no longer to be considered the gravest of crimes is a point that cannot be ignored. But, as an argument against what we term the Kilbrandon Formula, we consider it defective. By what reasoning can deliberation be demonstrated to be the source of the 'unique gravity' of the crime of deliberate killing? As the law currently stands, to prove murder the prosecution needs to prove intention to cause serious harm, notwithstanding that the defendant may stoutly maintain that he had no intention to exceed that objective and that that outcome was one he would bitterly regret for the rest of his life. Deliberation can be shown to be present in other homicides where death was not the outcome sought by the defendant, including those now charged as murder, though the intention extends no further than to do serious harm and which the Commissioners propose should be defined as murders in the second degree. Deliberation is undoubtedly indicative of a high degree of moral culpability and such killings can give rise to feelings of the greatest revulsion. But what of instances of reckless disregard for the welfare of others such as the terrorist who plants a bomb in a public building, whether a specific duty of care is owed to them or not? What of the conduct of the aggressive drunken driver who forces an oncoming vehicle off the road after having deliberately overtaken other traffic, with the result that its occupants are killed? While it cannot be said that he deliberately killed them, not least since he had no foreknowledge of their presence, their right to life has been violated by his unlawful conduct. To drive whilst intoxicated is to invite moral opprobrium and, when combined with reckless irresponsibility and aggression behind the wheel, must surely invite substantial amplification of that opprobrium. If, on conviction, the offender demonstrates remorse, a wish that he had never become the author of his own penal misfortune, rather than genuine contrition manifested in a desire to express a sincere regret at the enormity of the consequences of his conduct, then surely the crime merits the description of substantially grave, if it is not uniquely so.

---

[24] We are grateful to the Law Commission for having furnished us with material upon our request. The Law Commission's response to the CLRC was almost certainly drafted by Mr Derek Hodgson QC (later Mr Justice Hodgson). The Chairman of the Law Commission at the time was Mr Justice Cooke.

19. We would underscore this point by saying that it was the statutory separation of killing by the drivers of mechanically propelled vehicles from that part of the general corpus of homicide known as manslaughter by the Road Traffic Act 1956 and its (initial) maximum penalty of 5 years' imprisonment that has led to this category of crime being reduced in its perceived social importance. By no means all road deaths result in this being charged at all. Indeed, in some instances it is now largely a matter for determining damages in tort, with the element of criminality being marginalised to what the relatives of the dead frequently perceive to be derisory penalties.

20. In referring to unlawful deaths arising from what we would term road crimes[25] we recognise that the offence of causing death encompassed in road traffic legislation is outwith the present remit of the Law Commission. That, in our view, is an arbitrary exclusion for which the Law Commission bears no responsibility but which is most unhelpful to the development of an intellectually credible law of homicide.[26] The number of deaths arising from road crimes is not negligible and exceeds those deaths that are presently prosecuted as murder or manslaughter. Nor is there any evidence to suggest that the social consequences of such deaths are less for those who are bereaved, other than that relatives frequently believe that both the substantive law and its penal outcome marginalise both their suffering and the value of the lives that have been lost.

21. Therefore, though Government has excluded certain categories of homicide from the present review, we maintain that it is important to demonstrate how such exclusion must inevitably distort the outcome of the debate. The deliberate exception of the issue of abolition from the terms of reference of the Royal Commission on Capital Punishment (1949-1953) introduced a not dissimilar element of unrealism into its deliberations. We make no apology, therefore, in underscoring our argument that to pursue the notion that a new Homicide Act cannot ignore a whole range of homicidal events without reinforcing that condition which Lord Mustill described as 'permeated by anomaly, fiction, misnomer and obsolete reasoning'.[27]

---

[25] Our use of this term is deliberate, since in our view the use of the term road 'accident' can be misleading in that such incidents are very often nothing of the sort. That offences identified by the Road Traffic Act are crimes, some of them very serious, can be otherwise undeservedly sanitised.

[26] Both to exclude consideration of homicides other than those currently identified as murder and manslaughter *and* the mandatory life sentence for murder, would seem to hope for a production of *Hamlet* not only minus the Prince but Ophelia too.

[27] *Attorney General's Reference No 3 of 1994* [1998] AC 2455, 2502F.

22. The conduct of the aggressive drunken driver[28] described above surely exemplifies the variety of reckless indifference as to causing death[29] that the Law Commission's proposals have in mind. What is crucial is that the essence of the offence resides in the 'reckless indifference', not the fact that the instrument of death was a motor vehicle – a potentially lethal weapon – or that the result came about as a consequence of either intoxication or the manner of the driving. These are circumstantially descriptive of the criminal event. Other kinds of aggressive driving, such as 'tailgating' and 'undertaking' on motorways when vehicles are travelling at high speed, may equally demonstrate a 'reckless indifference' to causing death. On what basis would such conduct, when it resulted in death, continue to be charged as causing death by dangerous driving when it patently meets the criteria for the new offence of second degree murder?

23. We find additional difficulty in instances in which the killing has come about '. . . through gross negligence as to causing death, or through a criminal act intended to cause injury, or where there was recklessness as to causing injury'.[30] The Law Commission proposes that the offence in these circumstances should be that of manslaughter. Let us consider the following example which demonstrates the complexities involved. D, who is driving a large white van in lane 3 of a busy 3 lane motorway and at a speed in excess of 70mph, comes up behind a small saloon car driven by V who is observing the speed limit whilst legitimately and safely overtaking slower moving goods vehicles in lanes 2 and 1 on his near side. D flashes his vehicle headlights on the rear of V's car, and when V does not increase speed D approaches to within a few feet of V's car such that no safety gap remains. D then notices a gap between the goods vehicles in lane 2 and, cutting in to the left, drives alongside V and attempts to overtake from the inside by then cutting in front of V. Misjudging the manoeuvre, he collides with V's car, forcing it against the central barrier from which it ricochets into the path of following traffic. In the resulting series of multiple collisions three drivers die and a number of others sustain a range of injuries. The van driver is not seriously injured.

24. Presently, a charge of causing death by dangerous driving would seem a likely choice for the prosecution, but manslaughter would not necessarily be excluded. Would these circumstances support a charge of manslaughter per the Law Commission's proposals? While gross negligence would not appear relevant, do the facts nevertheless disclose

---

[28] Since intoxication is, in the overwhelming majority of instances, the outcome of a voluntary act, it cannot be a defence to the driver's later conduct: additionally, he will have elected to drive and, once behind the wheel, will have chosen to drive in a manner that had a potential for causing serious harm to others, including death.

[29] Law Commission Consultation Paper No 177 para 3.3(3).

[30] ibid, 3.2(4).

evidence of 'a criminal act intended to cause injury'? D's conduct as a driver is entirely criminal, (i) lacking in reasonable consideration for other road users, (ii) driving in excess of the speed limit, (iii) driving dangerously close to the vehicle in front, and additionally so in the course of overtaking on the nearside. It would not, moreover, be unreasonable to view his 'tailgating' as threatening behaviour intended to coerce V into moving out of his path and employing his vehicle as a weapon.[31] Did D's conduct amount to an assault,[32] in that V was put in fear, and did that fear, no doubt of being run down from behind, constitute an injury? Such would constitute the apprehension of immediate and unlawful violence.[33] In 1984 Goff LJ (later Lord Goff of Chievely)[34] in considering the notion of 'violence' quoted Blackstone:

> The law cannot draw the line between different degrees of violence, and therefore prohibits the first and lowest stage of it; every man's person being sacred, and no other having a right to meddle with it, in any the slightest manner.[35]

It might be noted that while Blackstone clearly subscribes to the idea of 'sanctity of life' he might also be said to acknowledge something of the indivisibility of the principle enshrined in Article 2, namely that no other has 'a right to meddle with it'. But again, it is difficult to anticipate the nature of the prosecution. Would the van driver, as presently, confidently expect the likely charge to be one under the Road Traffic Act, or might he be at risk of being prosecuted for manslaughter under a new Homicide Act for England and Wales?

25. No less important is the general perception that it is the severity of the penalty that is the benchmark against which the gravity of the offence is measured, not the label by which the offence is identified. This is demonstrated across the whole spectrum of statute law and exemplified in the varying level of maximum penalties attaching to particular offences. If, in our lexicon, a criminal homicide is proved and the circumstances of the criminal event disclose not only deliberation but also other aggravating circumstances of the gravest kind, then there would be absolutely no reason why a sentence reflecting those facts would not be available to the court, up to and including imprisonment for life or any other order the court considered necessary in the public interest. The assumption of what is now termed murder into the generic offence of criminal homicide would have no bearing upon the penalty, save to provide the court with the flexibility – and thereby the ability better to serve

---

[31] The analogy might be made with the man who forces his way to the head of a bus queue by brandishing a knife.

[32] See *Fagan v Commissioner of Police for the Metropolis* [1969] 1 QB 439.

[33] As in *Fagan* above.

[34] *Collins v Wilcock* [1984] 3 All ER 374 at 378. The matter is discussed by Smith and Hogan in *Criminal Law*, 7th edn (London, Butterworths, 1992).

[35] *Commentaries* 3.20.

the public interest – that it is presently denied by the existence of the mandatory penalty of life imprisonment on conviction of murder. Moreover, a strict liability offence, which we are proposing, emits as strong if not a stronger message than liability that requires a   specific intent.

26. We turn now to paragraphs 2.32–2.38 in which the document considers our argument for what we term the Kilbrandon Formula. We suggest the following:

a. in important respects our argument has been misunderstood;
b. the fact that what we would consider a return to the single offence of criminal homicide is a proposal that has discernible support within the constituency of judicial opinion places an obligation upon the Commission to expand its contrary argument beyond the seven paragraphs in which it is rejected.

27. We consider that the approval of Victim Support for what is in effect the Kilbrandon Formula in their response to Consultation Paper 173,[36] Partial Defences, is important, in that it would reduce the adversarial dimension of the criminal trial generated by attempts by the defence to achieve a reduction in the outcome from murder to manslaughter. In our view the defences which seek to reallocate the homicidal event from the category of murder to that of manslaughter are the source of much of the 'mess' which presently characterises the law of murder. Not least are they a source of difficulty in that such technical reallocation inevitably redefines the character of the conduct in ways which may be an additional source of distress to those who have been bereaved.[37] Would not the same ingenuity be employed to escape first degree murder in favour of second degree murder, and to escape second degree murder in favour of manslaughter?

28. To be convicted of manslaughter is to suffer less moral opprobrium than to be convicted of murder. To be convicted of causing death by dangerous or drunk driving, with its lower statutory maximum penalty, serves to diminish the mark of opprobrium still further. Indeed, to employ the argument of the CLRC, the effect of the Road Traffic Act 1956, in hiving-off road killing from the general body of manslaughter, notwithstanding a subsequent increase in the maximum penalty, has been to send out a signal that he or she who kills with a mechanically propelled vehicle on a public road commits a crime less serious than a train driver who goes through a signal set at danger or one who kills with a broken glass in a public house brawl. Such offenders remain at risk of

---

[36] Law Com CP No 173 (October 2003).

[37] It is astonishing that one effect of the proposals will be to elevate the partial defences of provocation and diminished responsibility, which, if sustained, are currently able to reduce murder to manslaughter, to inclusion among the criteria of second degree murder – see Consultation Paper 1.39(3) and 2.7(2)(c).

receiving a discretionary life sentence. Not only is the law of homicide in a 'mess'; at the supposed periphery its apparently capricious allocation of penalties of varying severity and social opprobrium to homicides that occur in particular situations such as these serves to diminish public confidence in the objectivity of the criminal justice system..

29. Thus, *pace* the argument of the CLRC, which the Law Commission clearly approves in 2.30, if it is indeed the available penalty which signals the degree of opprobrium attaching to the offence, it must by the same token give an indication of the degree of 'sanctity' attaching to the life that has been lost. Yet it is difficult to accept that the life of one who dies as the outcome of a road crime is somehow less sacred than that of one whose throat is severed with a broken beer glass or one who is shot to death in a gangland killing, simply as a result of the circumstances of the criminal event. 'Innocence', whether demonstrable or merely putative, is not even an issue. We return, therefore, to underscore our earlier argument, namely, that by defining unlawful homicide as a violation of the right to life enshrined in Article 2, in this respect every life taken in the course of unlawful conduct is, by definition, of equal value.

30. It is stated by the Law Commission in 2.34 that:

If, for Blom-Cooper and Morris, fault is merely a factor to reflect in sentence then that could logically be said to be true of the outcome (the victim's death) as well. Why single out unlawful killing for separate treatment, when it may purely have been chance that the victim died and the result could have been more or less serious bodily harm done?

31. We confess to some difficulty in following this line of reasoning. In this context we understand 'fault' as a neutral term to describe no more than liability arising from the conduct of D. The right to life enshrined in Article 2 places an obligation upon State and citizen alike, analogous to a general duty of care, in that the duty to preserve life involves both a range of positive conduct as well as inaction. What happens in criminal homicide is that D has taken the life of V. The nature and circumstances of the criminal event will inevitably vary, but what will remain invariable is the fact that V's right to life has been violated by the conduct of D. By the same token, the circumstances of that conduct will vary in respect of the blameworthiness of the action.

32. Fault is not 'merely a factor to reflect in sentence'. That is not our contention. It may indeed be the case that it was by chance that the victim died and had this not been so, homicide would not have been at issue. But in homicide, death, by definition, will have occurred. A lesser outcome is irrelevant, save where D is charged with an attempt to kill. The task of the prosecution, in our view, ought to be focused on proof that the death was unlawful and that it was the outcome of the intrinsi-

cally unlawful conduct of the offender. Such unlawfulness may consist in a failure of duty to care, recklessness or deliberation – whether merely to inflict harm or cause death. The experience of many trials is that hours, even days or weeks, may be spent in an attempt to determine what was or might have been in the defendant's mind at the time; whether there was provocation, and if so what tests of its magnitude or expected effect might be applied, whether D was suffering from diminished responsibility and if so, in what did it consist and over what period. The burden placed, not only upon juries in interpreting what may often be a confusing plethora of evidence from expert witnesses brought by the defence and the prosecution, but also upon judges in guiding juries through these forensic thickets, cannot be underestimated. How much time and expenditure of resources might be saved by simplifying the task remains to be calculated, but it cannot be inconsiderable.

33. We have considered Professor Robinson's material in detail,[38] and in particular his point that the rule that is violated in homicide can be said to be the rule prohibiting unjustifiably harming someone simpliciter. It appears to us that he is affirming the inclusive nature of the prohibition of unjustifiable harm.[39] The consequence of that infliction of harm will vary from physical injury to death. But it is at the point at which harm is inflicted that the threshold of criminal liability is crossed. Conduct is either criminal or it is not, and the relative seriousness of the act, as defined by its consequences, cannot affect its primary, criminal character. It would be unjustifiable for a householder to use excessive force against an intruder; likewise, it would be unjustifiable for the householder to kill him. Once the boundary between the force necessary to restrain or expel the intruder has been exceeded, the harm becomes unjustifiable. It would be as 'unjustifiable' to break a burglar's leg as to break his neck.[40]

34. We re-affirm our argument that in criminal homicide it is the right to life that is infringed; a right which is the corollary of membership of civil society and which cannot be modified or qualified, since it is enjoyed by every citizen irrespective of the circumstances in which it has been infringed.

35. Footnote 20 to paragraph 2.34 refers to our definition of criminal homicide in which it is suggested that we distinguish between 'simply causing serious physical harm to another person in which the various fault elements . . . are relevant and the crucial fatal result, to which they

---

[38] In para 2.35 the Commissioners quote Professor Robinson as arguing that causing death, can, like the more culpable of the mental elements (intention/recklessness), be regarded as simply a matter of grading.

[39] Upon which point Blackstone would appear in agreement – see fn 35 above.

[40] Which further point Blackstone would presumably also approve.

are not'. Again, we believe this to misunderstand our position.

36. In employing a definition that encompasses an act or omission – an intention to cause serious harm, or the manifestation of recklessness, gross negligence, or failure of corporate management – we seek to identify the necessary circumstances which must be proved to have existed before a death can result in a conviction for criminal homicide. The essence of Professor Robinson's argument, as we understand it, is that as the law presently stands mens rea and actus reus, far from being conceptually distinct as necessary elements that must be established before criminal guilt is determined, are unhelpfully confused. Attempting to assess the intention of the offender, whether by subjective or objective criteria, in order to determine criminal guilt (for example whether murder or manslaughter, or in the application of partial defences, such as provocation or diminished responsibility), gives rise to not inconsiderable difficulty.

37. The Law Commission at 2.36 states:

> If the fact that death has been caused can provide sufficient justification for the creation of a distinct offence worthy of special categorisation, so can the mental element with which it was caused.

We agree that it may be logical to equate the existence of the mental element with the actus reus of criminal homicide, but it is just as logical to exclude the mental element from criminal responsibility, as is done in crimes of strict liability.

38. In his classic work *The Common Law*, the great American jurist Oliver Wendell Holmes Jr (Mr Justice Holmes of Supreme Court fame) had taken pains to emphasise in his chapter on criminal law[41] that the tests of liability are external and independent of the degree of evil in the particular person's motives or intentions. As his biographer Edward White wrote, 'his championing an external standard of liability was to strip the common law, like other legal subjects, of the baggage of morals . . . he was interested in converting terms such as 'malice' or 'intent' from subjective to objective concepts'.[42]

39. If the mental element is to be properly preserved in a civilised system of criminal justice as envisaged in Article 2 of the ECHR, its proper place is assessment of the degree of moral culpability for the unlawful killing, rather than constituting an element in criminal responsibility. In other words, English law has consistently put mens rea in the wrong place. Motive, intent, or premeditation, all belong to the stage of sentencing the offender as the penalty for breaking the criminal law. That is

---

[41]   OW Holmes Jr, *The Common Law* (Boston, Little, Brown & Co, 1880) 50.
[42]   E White, *Justice Oliver Wendell Holmes: Law and the Inner Self* (Oxford, OUP, 1993) 259.

the purport of Lord Kilbrandon's formula; once rid of the arcane distinctions between different categories of homicide – notably murder and manslaughter – the offender can be sentenced in the most appropriate way and proportionate manner.

40. We suspect that within some of the objections to the notion of a single crime of criminal homicide there resides an anxiety that with the removal both of the term 'murder' and the mandatory penalty of life imprisonment the judges will take the opportunity to impose sentences of lesser severity, even for crimes which appear to be among the gravest and most socially repellent in character. In short, there exists a distrust of the judiciary – in our view wholly groundless and manifestly ill-deserved – encouraging support of the status quo. This ought not, in our view, to be a fatal objection since sentencing in criminal matters generally discloses little evidence, either of random inconsistency or undue lenity.

41. The abolition of the mandatory penalty for murder, which would be the automatic consequence of a single offence of criminal homicide, would permit a greater degree of 'fine tuning' of sentencing by the appellate process, which would in turn be strengthened by giving the Crown wider opportunities for appeal.[43] Our argument is that, given the problems of balancing mens rea and actus reus at the trial stage, it is better to ask the prosecution to establish its case on an altogether simpler basis. Was the death the result of an act or omission by the defendant? Can it be demonstrated that the defendant caused[44] the harm? Was there evidence of failure of corporate management? Did such conduct cause harm, even though not intended? Was the death the result of such harm? Did this conduct manifest recklessness or 'gross' negligence? It is not, moreover, easy to distinguish the criteria whereby a negligent act may be defined as grossly so. Baron Rolfe in 1843 said that he 'could see no difference between negligence and gross negligence . . . [it was] the same thing, with the addition of a vituperative epithet.'[45] A more helpful way of describing such conduct which attracts criminal responsibility is that the accused demonstrated a serious failure to achieve the standard of care objectively to be expected of a reasonable person.

42. In short, we would approve proof of guilt in criminal homicide to approach more closely to the norm of strict liability. While it might be

---

[43] There is an argument for establishing equality of arms between prosecution and defence in the appellate process, not least where juries may have found verdicts that the defence would certainly challenge as not being 'true'.

[44] Causation is the crucial issue for the jury: nothing more complicated than that.

[45] *Wilson v Brett* [1843] 11 M&W At 113, 115-16. To similar effect see Lynskey J in *Pentecost v London District Auditor* [1951] 2 KB 759, 764. Hodgson J in *Dietman v Brent London Borough Council* [1987] 1 CR 737 at 748H added: 'And, in the field of criminal law, the use of the phrase as a quasi-term of art has been unhelpful'.

immediately suggested that we are doing that which the late Professor Glanville Williams criticised in the House of Lords judgment in *Smith*,[46] namely, that it would henceforward be possible to commit murder (or criminal homicide) by accident, that criticism is only valid if the consequence of conviction is the imposition of what Lord Reid in *Sweet v Parsley*[47] described as a 'disgraceful penalty', by which he had in mind imprisonment. It is our argument that some of the evidence presently adduced for the purpose of establishing a partial defence, together with other evidence neither relevant nor necessarily admissible in the course of trial, should be presented after a finding of guilt but before sentence. There is no reason why a court cannot perfectly well take such matters into account, not least since modern sentencing is reliant upon the preparation of expert reports, in addition to hearing mitigation. It is at this stage that the moral dimensions of personable accountability and desert may be properly accommodated within the sentencing process. The circumstances of the criminal event might be at the very margins of blameworthiness, as in a so-called 'mercy' killing. Alternatively, they might be such as to attract a condign penalty, as in a so-called 'contract' killing.

Degrees of murder and the mandatory penalty

43. At the heart of all the difficulty in reforming the law of homicide in England, whether the concern is specifically with murder or with the entire corpus of homicide law, is the mandatory penalty of life imprisonment. The tenacity with which it is defended as if it were some axiomatic proposition underpinning the whole law of homicide has caused it to become an unreasoning and unreasonable impediment to any attempt at applying reason in the process of reform. The Law Commission proposal to limit its application to what would be first degree murder would, without doubt, limit the extent of its applicability but this would do no more than did the Homicide Act 1957 to limit capital punishment by restricting the offences which fell within the capital category.

44. The introduction of two categories of murder that is proposed by the Law Commission differs from such earlier proposals only in that the basis of distinction consists not in the identity of the victim but in the deliberation or otherwise of the offender. In one sense, that is an undoubted improvement upon all the suggestions for degrees of murder that have been proposed and deservedly foundered in the past 150 years. But it is not, in our view, the way forward. It is, at best, only a partial remedy for the 'mess'. Every past attempt to construct a list of victims whose killers deserve the most condign punishments has been guided

---

[46] *DPP v Smith* [1961] AC 290.
[47] [1969] 2 WLR 470.

by the same ignis fatuus, and to employ the putative mental element in the offender, as distinct from the social identity of the victim, can scarcely hope for better success.

45. As the distinction is presently proposed, we see it is having an effect no different from the distinction in the Homicide Act 1957 between capital and non-capital murder. It would provide the court with the opportunity of passing the sentence of its own choice as distinct from the mandatory sentence which would still apply to first degree murder, irrespective of any mitigating circumstances. Just as the 1957 Act produced some quite absurd anomalies,[48] the present proposal would undoubtedly be vulnerable to the sometimes capricious decision-making of juries.

Conclusion

46. We have not attempted to comment upon every part of the Consultation Paper, a scholarly excursus of the law of murder today valuably demonstrating many aspects of the current 'mess'. Rather, we have concentrated upon particular issues which include the comments made by the Law Commission on our own position as set out in our book *With Malice Aforethought*. We should point out that in the period of almost two years since publication, while we have reflected upon the comments of critics we have at the same time been able to consider other writings on the subject. While our belief that the Kilbrandon formula offers the simplest and most effective way of resolving the 'mess' of the present law has, if anything, been reinforced, where the establishment of criminal guilt is concerned we are now firmly inclined to favour a move towards a model approximating more closely to one of strict liability. In combination with the Kilbrandon formula, this would lead to a perceptible strengthening of the law; not, as some critics might suggest, to a weakening of it.

47. To do so would be to simplify a trial process that has become ever more complicated, not least by the use of defences that, while they may be readily transparent in their possession of little intrinsic merit, have a great instrumental value to defendants when they are employed to persuade a jury to bring in a manslaughter and not a murder verdict. Just as defending advocates once employed their every art to turn the M'Naghten Rules (and later, between 1957 and 1965, diminished responsibility) to advantage, thereby protecting their clients from the gallows, so today, essentially the same practice is used to ensure that neither the mandatory life sentence, nor its attendant Schedule 21,[49] render them immediately liable

---

[48] A man who shot his wife with a gun committed capital murder, but if, having run out of ammunition, he had still failed to kill her and finished the task by battering her with the butt end he could only be indicted for non-capital murder.

[49] Criminal Justice Act 2003.

to long periods of incarceration and subsequent liability to it for the remainder of their lives. A simplified approach to prosecution has additional merits, not least in terms of court time and legal resources generally.

48. To permit judicial discretion across the entire spectrum of homicide convictions would, in our view, lead to a more rational pattern of sentencing. By its nature, this would more accurately reflect both the opprobrium in which some offences are quite properly held, as well as the sensitivity and compassion appropriate to those other offences arising out of the often tragic circumstances of the human condition. Such possibilities ought to be embodied in a law of homicide that recognises both justice and mercy, and without distinction.

ANNEX: EXTRACT FROM LAW COMMISSION CONSULTATION
PAPER NO 177

The Argument of Sir Louis Blom-Cooper and Professor Terence Morris

2.32 Sir Louis Blom-Cooper and Professor Terence Morris have recently argued in favour of the abolition of the crime of murder.[50] The importance of their argument, and the influence that it has had, warrants special attention here. In their view, there should be a single offence of 'criminal homicide'. Matters such as provocation, diminished responsibility, and other mitigating factors, should be dealt with through the nature and degree of severity of the sentence given, not through a rigid structure of grades of offence and discrete (partial) defences, with all their complex restricting conditions.

2.33 There is powerful force in this argument. An argument for a single offence of unlawful homicide is also put forward by Victim Support.[51] They see virtue in ridding the law of the adversarial dimension to trials generated by the natural desire of defendants to see their crime reduced from murder to manslaughter. This, says Victim Support, often entails blaming the victim as part of the defence to the murder charge, a feature of trials they would like to reduce or eliminate. It may be, however, that reform of the doctrine of provocation as a partial defence to murder will address these concerns to some degree.[52]

2.34 Even if it were within our terms of reference to consider it, however, we do not agree that it is the right course to recommend the creation of a single offence of unlawful killing. If, for Blom-Cooper and Morris, fault is

[50] L Blom-Cooper and T Morris, *With Malice Aforethought: A Study of the Crime and Punishment for Homicide* (Oxford, Hart Publishing, 2004).
[51] *Response to Partial Defences to Murder* (Consultation Paper No 173, 2003).
[52] See *Partial Defences to Murder* (Law Com No 290, 2004); see also Part 6.

merely a factor to reflect in sentence, then that could logically be said to be true of the outcome (the victim's death) as well. Why single out unlawful *killing* for separate treatment, when it may purely have been chance that the victim died, and the result could have been more or less serious bodily harm done?[53] Let us consider this point further.

2.35 Professor Paul Robinson, has argued that causing death can, like the more culpable of the mental elements (intention/recklessness), be regarded as simply a matter of grading.[54] On his account, the rule one violates in homicide cases can be said to be a rule prohibiting unjustifiably harming someone *simpliciter*. On this view, the fact that one caused death is simply an aggravating factor, a possible ground for increasing the sentence.[55] It is not the basis for a separate offence.

2.36 We take it that Blom-Cooper and Morris would not wish to endorse this line of argument, if it led to the conclusion that there should be no separate offence focused on the fact that the defendant has committed 'homicide'.[56] In our view, though, if the fact that death has been caused can provide sufficient justification for the creation of a distinct offence worthy of special categorisation, so can the mental element with which it was caused.

2.37 All Consultation Papers must have some fixed points, if consultation is to be focused and meaningful. Virtually all jurisdictions have a special category of homicide approximating to murder, whether or not they impose the mandatory life sentence for that offence. Accordingly, it is not proposed that such a category should cease to be a part of the law of England and Wales.

2.38 Further, our provisional proposal is that to maintain a firm and clear connection between the sanctity of life and the structure of the law of homicide, intentional killing should be made into a unique offence: 'first degree murder'. Intended killing is rightly regarded as specially grave species of wrong, because it involves a successful attack on the most basic of values, life, through the deliberate destruction of human being born alive.

---

[53] This point seems especially pertinent in the light of the fact that in Blom-Cooper and Morris's definition of 'criminal homicide' a distinction is drawn between simply causing serious physical harm to another person, to which the various fault elements – such as intention and recklessness – are relevant, and the crucial fatal result, to which they are not: L Blom-Cooper and T Morris, *With Malice Aforethought: A Study of the Crime and Punishment for Homicide* (Oxford, Hart Publishing, 2004) 175.

[54] See P Robinson, 'Should the Criminal Law Abandon the Actus Reus-Mens Rea Distinction?' in S Shute, J Gardner and J Horder (eds), *Action and Value in Criminal Law* (Oxford, Clarendon Press, 1993) 211.

[55] See, in the driving context, *Boswell* (1984) 6 Cr App R (S) 257.

[56] It should be noted that this is not Robinson's conclusion: P Robinson, 'Should the Criminal Law Abandon the Actus Reus-Mens Rea Distinction?' in S Shute, J Gardner and J Horder (eds), *Action and Value in Criminal Law* (Oxford, Clarendon Press, 1993) 211.

8

The Penalty for Murder: Life after Death

INTRODUCTION

ON THE ENDING of capital punishment for the crime of murder in 1965, it became the duty of the court to pass a mandatory sentence of life imprisonment on anyone found guilty of murder. This mandatory sentence has always entailed the murderer losing his or her liberty for the rest of his or her life, instead of being executed by hanging. However, the 'lifer' could expect a review of his or her sentence and a possibility of release from custody at some point in his lifetime (subject to supervision in the community, and to recall to prison if considered to be a danger to the public). The sentence for murder is still (in 2015) mandatory life imprisonment. The average (mean) time spent in custody for a murderer convicted in 1965 was nine years.

Who would have predicted that half a century later the 'lifer' population would expect to receive a review of its sentence *only* after, on average, twice the time spent in custody, given the overall comparative liability (even a recent reduction) in the murder rate? The speculative answer would have depended on the declared approach by bipartisan politicians spouting the phrase 'tough on crime, and tough on the causes of crime (with the Prime Minister's version of a peculiarly punitive penal policy). It reflected the country's desire for punishment; an insistence on revenge to balance the traditional policy of rehabilitation.

The sentence of the court originally related solely to the loss of liberty; the decision on how long should be spent in custody was originally left to the Home Secretary, advised by the prison administration, and after considering a letter sent by the judge and Lord Chief Justice with a suggestion of what the minimum period should be. After several challenges and changes to this procedure, the Criminal Justice Act of 2003 finally set out minimum periods for which the 'starting points' for an adult are normally 30, 25 and 15 years, depending on the gravity of the offence, which the judge determines when sentencing the offender. On completion of the minimum period, set to reflect the presumed need for punishment and deterrence, the prisoner is now reviewed by the Parole Board to determine if he/she can safely be released under supervision.

Schedule 21 of the Act states, however, that if the murder is 'so grave that the offender should spend the rest of their life in prison, a 'whole-life order' is the appropriate starting point'. If this is imposed, there is no period fixed for review by the Parole Board. The schedule emphasises that 'such an order should only be specified where the court considers that the seriousness of the offence is exceptionally high. Such cases include:

(a) the murder of two or more persons where each murder involves a substantial degree of premeditation, the abduction of the victim, or sexual or sadistic conduct;
(b) the murder of a child if involving the abduction of the child or sexual or sadistic motivation;
(c) a murder done for the purpose of advancing a political, religious or ideological cause; or
(d) a murder by an offender previously convicted of murder.

Although a prisoner might always have died in prison – and some did – before being considered worthy of release, the 'whole-life order' is entirely different because it forecloses the possibility of review by the Parole Board at the time of sentence. The situation is completely different from what had been the former practice. As Sir Ernest Gowers (Chairman of the Royal Commission on Capital Punishment, 1949–53) said in his book *A Life for a Life?* in 1968, there was then no recorded case of any lifer having been told at the time of sentencing (or later) that he would never be granted release on licence, although he might die in prison. Like the death penalty, the whole-life order is an inhumane act of revenge by society, which can be described as depriving the prisoner of the 'right to hope'. It is rarely (if at all) a proportional punishment, because it is arbitrary; it may be measured in days or decades, according to how long the murderer has to live. It is an excessive infliction of human suffering.[1] The concept of proportionality goes to the heart of the question of whether punishment is inhuman or degrading, especially so

---

[1] See *R v Ralston Wellington* [2007] EWHC 1109 (Admin) [39] (Laws LJ), cited approvingly by Lord Bingham in *Boucherville v State of Mauritius* [2008] UKPC 37 but disapprovingly by Lord Hoffmann and his colleagues in the appeal to the House of Lords in the *Wellington* case.

where it is related to the length of time for which the offender is sentenced.

THE POLITICS OF ABOLITION

History is likely to record that the abolition of the death penalty for murder in 1965 was brought about, not so much as a result of any perceived inefficiency in the ultimate penal sanction as a means of keeping down the homicide rate, but by a growing moral revulsion at the practice of hanging a human being by the deliberate act of Government. The final stages of the successful campaign to abolish the death penalty for murder in Britain were achieved in a comparatively short period of time by no more than a handful of ardent penal reformers, pertinacious in their lobbying and propaganda, in the face of majority opinion favouring retention of an admittedly barbaric but, to that majority, necessary penal instrument. Even though the final debates were rather protracted – Mr Silverman's private members' Bill (with invaluable legislative time given by the Government) was introduced on 4 December 1964, and reached the Statute Book only on 4 November 1965 – the history of the campaign is a remarkable testament to British democracy, which can convert convinced minority opinion into progressive legislative action. The legislature which caters for such minority views deserves some commendation in the face of almost continuous opprobrium for the clogging it undergoes nowadays from the political machine.

While the degrading influence of the trappings of the gallows was met with fierce crusading from the nineteenth-century penal reformers, few countenanced abandoning the ultimate sanction for the ultimate crime. Not until a young Quaker, E Roy Calvert, wrote the first really dispassionate and scientific argument for total abolition in 1925 (*Capital Punishment in the 20th Century*) was the modern campaign brought on to the stage of public discussion. And even then, the debate rarely touched the grass roots of public opinion. The debate in fact was conducted in the rarefied atmosphere of parliamentary corridors, over coffee cups in clubs and in public halls before largely converted audiences. At no time was a referendum advocated; had the public's view been taken, many parliamentarians would have been most gravely embarrassed in filing through the abolitionist lobby. Given the modern fashion for a referendum, what now would the electorate decide? Perhaps there is still a majority in favour of hanging or other killing device for an unjustified homicide.[2]

Accompanied by such moralistic instincts of a civilised society committed to a welfare state not to put its murderers to death, a trilogy of murder convictions and executions in Britain in the 1950s heralded the nascent desire to rid the justice system of miscarriages and a failure to take account of strong mitigating circumstances, both of which had enhanced moral revulsion.

Timothy Evans (March 1950) was the first of the three suspicious cases of wrongful conviction, recognised 50 years later as perhaps the most notorious miscarriage of justice in contemporary legal history. His neighbour at the infamous house in Rillington Place (a street now appropriately demolished from the area of West London) was former part-time policeman John Christie, a serial killer who was the main prosecution witness against Evans. Three years later he confessed to having killed a number of women, including Evans' wife (but not their child). The notion that an innocent man may have been obliterated by the hangman percolated the public conscience.

Derek Bentley's conviction in 1953 for murdering a police officer created its own dubiety. At the time of his co-accused fatally shooting a police officer, Bentley was in the physical custody of another policeman. If there was a query about his criminal responsibility, there was little quarrel at the time that the Home Secretary acted wrongly in 'allowing the law to take its course'. Bentley's conviction was later shown to be demonstrably flawed when, in a reference in 1997 from the Criminal Cases Review Commission, the Court of Appeal (Criminal Division), under the presidency of Lord Bingham of Cornhill (then Lord Chief Justice) comprehensively and convincingly quashed the conviction as an unfair trial in an impressive judgment that enforced today's standards of criminal justice on the lower standards of the past.

Ruth Ellis's conviction in 1955 touched the emotional aspects of public opinion. Her *crime passionelle* of a former lover went virtually undefended at her trial. Her supposed wish to die did not detract from the public's hearty dislike that a woman should suffer the hangman's noose. The British public in the 1950s was thus

---

[2] The polls show about 50% in favour, but considerably less support among the generation that has grown up since the death penalty was abolished. Public opinion about the mandatory sentence is much less supportive of Government policy: see Mitchell and Roberts, *Exploring the Mandatory Life Sentence for Murder* (Oxford, Hart Publishing, 2012).

beginning to accept that the death penalty by hanging (or any less inhumane method of execution) was at most 'a cruel necessity'.[3]

These cases undoubtedly emboldened the abolitionists in the national campaign for the abolition of the death penalty that had been formed in the 1930s, and revitalised after the Second World War when the House of Commons had voted in favour of abolition during the passage of the Criminal Justice Bill in 1947, only to be severely defeated in the House of Lords.[4] Undoubtedly, the three miscarriages of justice in the 1950s also aroused public opinion. The publication of the Royal Commission's report in 1953 impliedly favouring the ending of capital punishment as well as the composition of MPs after the 1951 General Election combined to produce the necessary impetus to reform.

If these various factors presented political imponderables, what precisely were the grounds upon which the political and legislative process ran its course up to 1965? Had the Labour Party not lost power in 1951, it is very likely that abolition would have come a decade earlier than it did. Although the parliamentary Labour Party had not committed itself electorally to abolition, the Commons vote in 1948 in favour of suspending capital punishment for a period of five years indicated ultimate acceptance of the inevitable, although it would have meant a tussle with the House of Lords, which was at that time obdurately hostile to change, to a large extent influenced by the pronouncement from the Lord Chief Justice, Lord Goddard, that all the High Court judges wished to keep the ultimate deterrent for murder. (Subsequently it turned out that a sizeable minority was beginning to favour abolition, a fact to which Lord Goddard had to admit. His successor as Chief Justice, Lord Parker, as noted below became a crucial proponent for change.)

By long convention, Members of Parliament have invariably been entitled to vote on any issue involving the death penalty according to their individual conscience. Unwhipped, the membership of the House of Commons in the post-war period favoured abolition, to some extent stimulated by the report of the Royal Commission on

---

[3] I refer here to an utterance by Oliver Cromwell as he stood at the side of the coffin of Charles I, although Morley asserts in his biography of Cromwell that the incident was pretty certainly apocryphal, since the phrase did not reflect the dialect of Cromwell's philosophy. If only the Bill of Rights of 1689, which contained language identical to that of the Eighth Amendment of the US Constitution (and was the apparent precursor of similar provisions in most state constitutions of the United States) had been construed in the Cromwellian sense, instead of being treated as a conjunction of cruel and unusual, banning only excessive or illegal punishments, the jurisprudence of the US Supreme Court might have been very different.

[4] See Radzinowicz's impressive account of this in his *Adventures in Criminology.*

Capital Punishment (the Gowers Commission) in 1953. It is inter-esting to observe that the convention has always been adhered to. When the Council of Europe passed the Sixth Protocol to the European Convention on Human Rights in 1986, the UK declined to ratify the Convention, on the ground that the question was not for Her Majesty's Government but could be enacted only by the indi-vidual votes of MPs. Again, in 1998 when the Government was 'bringing human rights home' in the form of the Human Rights Act 1998, the Sixth Protocol was originally omitted from the Schedule to the Act on the same ground. But individual members ultimately persuaded the Foreign Secretary, Jack Straw, to yield to the demands of Labour MPs who were devoted abolitionists. With individual voting the order of the day, final, complete abolition was bound to arrive. In accordance with the convention on the free vote of MPs, the Bill in 1965 to abolish capital punishment for murder, as well as that abolishing it for all remaining crimes in 1998, were strictly pri-vate members' Bills or Amendments, although (certainly in the case of the 1965 Act) orchestrated by the Labour administration.

By the mid-1950s there was evident support from an actual major-ity in the House of Commons for total abolition. For a century before that there had been successive Parliamentary assaults on the death penalty. As far back as 1866, only four years after the abolition of the death penalty for a wide range of criminal offences in 1861, a Select Committee of 12 MPs considered its abolition for the offence of murder; five members of the Committee voted for abolition. The following year the Howard Association (a year after its formation) began its long campaign for the abolition of capital punishment. Its successor, the Howard League for Penal Reform (a merger of the Howard Association and the League for Penal Reform, formed in 1922 by Brockway and Hobhouse, both First World War conscien-tious objectors who had spent time in Brixton Prison) was a vigor-ous proponent of abolition.

In 1930 a Select Committee of the House of Commons reported in favour of suspension of the death penalty for murder in cases tried by civil courts for an experimental period of five years. (Six mem-bers of the Committee of 15 withdrew from the Committee; the rec-ommendations were those of the majority of nine: seven Labour and two Liberal.) The report was never debated in Parliament. In the immediate aftermath of the Second World War there were no fewer than three attempts to provide for suspension. In 1948 the House of Commons did vote for a five-year suspension, but (as mentioned previously) this provision was defeated in the Lords. In 1955 a similar motion was defeated in the Commons by 245 votes to 214. In February 1956 the House of Commons under a Conservative administration passed a resolution calling for the abolition or suspension of the death penalty by a vote of 292 to 246.

This resolution marked a watershed in the history of the English treatment of the crime of murder and its single penalty. Convinced that public opinion did not support abolition (a Gallup poll of 1953 disclosed 73 per cent in favour of the death penalty), the Tory Government was content to rely upon a hostile House of Lords to curb the reformist zeal of opposition MPs and others. Yet it sensed that there was public disquiet about the inequality of treatment as between those convicted murderers who were reprieved and those who did not escape the hangman's noose. The search for categories of murder had long since occupied the legal profession and politicians. The Gowers Commission, in a passage that should be on every penal reformer's agenda, stated:

> Our examination of the law and procedure of other countries lends no support to the view that the objections to degrees of murder . . . are only theoretical and academic and may be disproved by the practical experience of those countries where such a system is in force. We began our inquiry with the determination to make every effort to see whether we could succeed where so many have failed, and discover some effective method of classifying murders so as to confine the death penalty to the more heinous. Where degrees of murder have been introduced, they have undoubtedly resulted in the limiting of the application of capital punishment and for this reason they have commended themselves to public opinion, but in our view their advantages are far outweighed by the theoretical and practical objections which we have described. We conclude *with regret* that the object of our quest is chimerical and must be abandoned.[5]

The Government's response was to enact the Homicide Act 1957, which followed the Scottish experience by introducing the new partial defence of diminished responsibility, but directly rejected the view of the Gowers Commission as regards creating a category of 'capital murder'. The 1957 Act eliminated the death penalty except for five categories of murder. Capital murder was retained for murder committed in the course or furtherance of theft; murders by shooting or causing an explosion; murder of a police officer acting in the course of his duties; murder in the course of or for the purpose of preventing lawful arrest or of effecting or assisting in an

---

[5] Gowers, *Royal Commission on Capital Punishment 1949–1953, Report* (London, HMSO, 1953) para 534.

escape from legal custody; and murder of a prison officer by a prisoner. Double (or repeated) murders were added as a sixth form of capital murder. All other kinds of murder became non-capital, automatically attracting the sentence of life imprisonment.

The effect of the Homicide Act 1957 was instantly counterproductive and proved to be a potent reason for many parliamentarians becoming, even reluctantly, abolitionist. But I venture to think that the Act was misunderstood in its governmental and hence legislative purpose. It was widely stated that the Act in defiance of the Gowers Commission was a failed attempt to distinguish between 'heinous' killing and 'less serious' (mostly domestic violence) killing. For example, murder by poisoning was always thought to be the most premeditated and quintessentially wicked (and as such, traditionally prosecuted in court by the Attorney-General in person). Yet in 1957 it became a case of non-capital murder. But the *raison d'etre* of the five categories in fact was not to single out the most *serious* of murders. The particular classes chosen were not an attempt to distinguish between murders according to heinousness and horrendous nature, or even their moral depravity. The five categories were designed to opt for the death penalty for those 'rational' types of murder for which its deterrent effect was thought to be the more powerful. As is now tolerably clear, however, it was impossible to determine whether capital punishment was a unique deterrent.

When the legislation to abolish first emerged in the form of a Bill, it aimed exclusively at ridding the country of the death penalty. The instinctive and appropriate substitute was life imprisonment – a kind of civil death – as understood within the Home Office regime for lifers. Apart from the significant change from 'death' to 'life', which was definitive and symbolic, the 1965 Act was implicitly unconcerned with the question, how long is life? The prime instigators of the Act – led notably by the Lord Chancellor, Lord Gardiner (a lifelong protagonist among the abolitionists) – were intent at all costs to get rid of the death penalty. They were more than content to let the sentence of life imprisonment follow the established pattern of executive release from prison. The Bill made no reference or allusion to the process of discharge, recall or parole, the latter becoming a feature of the penal system only in the Criminal Justice Act 1967. And then it was only an afterthought; there had been no intention within the Home Office to give up its power of granting release and alter the established practice. The Home Secretary of the day, Roy Jenkins, acceded, however, to a powerful lobby of penal reformers who were keen to regularise the early release of all prisoners, both 'lifers' and those serving determinate terms of imprisonment for all crimes. As a footnote, Roy Jenkins was insistent that the chairmanship of the Parole Board should not be given to someone with a judicial qualification. Lord Hunt of Everest fame was an outstanding first (lay) chairman. Only in 2009 with the part-time appointment of Sir David Latham (a retired Lord Justice of Appeal) was the tradition from 1967 finally broken. A review of the Parole Board is overdue.

There was not even an inclination generally to tamper with the existing process of a mandatory sentence, reflecting a uniform sentence for all convicted murderers. The refusal to contemplate perpetuating degrees of murder, especially after the debacle of the 1957 Act, was accompanied by an even greater reluctance to confer a discretion on the court as to the penalty in murder cases and, above all, the insistent opinion that such a discretion should not be imparted to a jury. Mr Justice Frankfurter of the US Supreme Court had given authoritative evidence to the Gowers Commission of the various American states, which presented then, as now, a crazy quilt pattern of sentencing which combined degrees of murder and the device of reposing in juries a discretion as to the penalty to be inflicted, except for certain cases where the death penalty was then (and until 1976) mandatory for first degree murder. The complexities of that system are reflected in the exasperating array of case law from the Supreme Court of the United States in application of that country's death penalty system.

The Gowers Commission had felt that the removal of the main evil of the law (a grotesque continuation of a solemn sentence of death, passed at the court of trial by a judge donning a black cap and intoning the death sentence, followed in at least half of the cases – by the 1950s it was even higher – by a reprieve via the Prerogative of Mercy) was needed to achieve a morally acceptable result. This clumsy process led the Gowers Commission to suggest tentatively that, if capital punishment were to continue for certain types of murder, the only solution might be to entrust the decision to the jury to determine the appropriate penalty. But that suggestion never attracted any real support in Britain, and the American experience was happily rejected. Discretion to juries has never been considered expedient for determining punishment. In a debate in the House of Lords in 1954 on the scheme for 'jury discretion', all the legal members present condemned it as 'completely unworkable' and the Lord Chief Justice, Lord Goddard, said, 'rather than take part in such a performance as that, I would resign the offices I hold, for I think it would be destructive of everything in British [*sic*] law'. If the language was predictable, it was still somewhat hyperbolic, affirming that sentencing was a judicial function of a discretionary nature – except, of course, for murder. 'Jury discretion' could never be a viable option. Indeed, the Bill in 1965 did not consider any option to the immediate alternative – another mandatory penalty, a life sentence rather than death. Unlike the debate being vigorously undertaken in respect of those countries that still retain the death penalty, where the viable alternative penalty is fully aired, no such debate took place in 1965. The current debate internationally about capital punishment is increasingly focused on whether the sentence should be indeterminate or determinate and, if the former, whether it should be a parolable or – for some cases at least – a non-parolable life sentence (some countries have not accepted indeterminate sentences at all).

Thus, in abolishing the death penalty for murder, Parliament in 1965 left a piece of business unfinished. To transpose life for death made no significant difference to what constituted, in practice, the sentence of life imprisonment for the individual murderer.

Contrary to a popular and sedulously much-fostered myth over the last five decades, there never was a bargain, express or implied, that the retentionists would concede the ending of the death penalty as a quid pro quo for much longer periods of custody for 'lifers'. Together with Professor Terence Morris, I have described elsewhere how this myth originated in the minds of contemporary Home Secretaries from Howard, through Straw and Blunkett to Charles Clarke and beyond. There is every indication that, far from any such political deal between the rival parties on the penalty for murder, there was a strong desire to transfer the executive power of sentencing to a judicial function. Most significant (because the judges had to carry out the sentencing) was the change in judicial attitudes. At that time the judges were publicly silent outside the courtroom. Their private opinions were discoverable only much later.

THE ROLE OF THE JUDICIARY

At no stage in the movement towards the abolition of the death penalty were the courts of England involved. Although Article 2(1) of the European Convention on Human Rights of 1950 allowed for the death penalty as an exception to the right to life, Article 3 embodied the modern version of the seventeenth-century proscription of cruel and unusual punishment; the wording is more modern – inhuman or degrading treatment or punishment. The Sixth Protocol, abolishing the death penalty in peacetime, was still two or three decades away. No convicted murderer in England and Wales ever sought to challenge the legality of the death penalty, although many years after the abolition of capital punishment in the UK, the English judiciary in the Judicial Committee of the Privy Council in appeals from the Caribbean countries belatedly appreciated the complexities of the argument of unconstitutionality of capital punishment, if only because of the delay in carrying out the execution. Contrariwise, abolitionists in America have spent large resources in attempts to have the death penalty declared unconstitutional under the Eighth Amendment – 'cruel and unusual punishment'. Only the Supreme Court of California in 1972, in *People v Anderson,*[6] was able to prohibit the death penalty by alighting on the interchangeable term, 'cruel *or* unusual punishment'[7] which was the language of Article 1, section 6 of the California Constitution. The disjunctive cruel *or* unusual punishment led the majority of the Court to find that the Bill of Rights 1689, which was adopted in the Eighth Amendment and which was the precursor of most of the constitutions of the various states, prohibited cruel penalties. That Californian court, uniquely in the annals of American jurisprudence, found that capital punishment was impermissibly cruel. It was later reinstated under the new, more restrictive provisions approved by the Supreme Court in 1976.

A moratorium during the 1960s culminated in a concerted challenge in the US courts. But the classic decision in 1972 in *Furman v Georgia*[8] found only two dissenters among the nine justices in favour of outright unconstitutionality. The majority opinion struck down state laws on the grounds that the death penalty operated discriminately, primarily against black defendants, particularly those whose victims were white. The Supreme Court's failure to align itself with almost all the rest of the civilised world in fact provided an impetus to state legislatures perversely to revise their death penalty laws in *Gregg v Georgia*[9] and other cases in 1976, in order to meet the objections raised in *Furman v Georgia*. This led to the so-

---

[6] 63 Cal 2d 351. In a referendum in November 2012 53% of Californians voted to keep the death penalty, endorsing the death row phenomenon.

[7] My italics.

[8] 408 US 238 (1972).

[9] 428 US 153 (1976).

called death row phenomenon, as the death row population expanded with each succeeding conviction for first degree murder in a handful of the 37 states that kept the death penalty.[10] For the 30 years following *Furman v Georgia* the Supreme Court of the United States based its criteria for the perpetuation of the death penalty for murder in all its attendant aspects on the doctrine of 'evolving standards of decency'. Whether those standards were attained depended on the Court concluding that there was a national consensus that aspects of homicide did not decently require the death penalty. Thus in 2003, 'mentally retarded' offenders became an exempted category from execution (by now almost always by lethal injection, rather than hanging or the electric chair). In March 2005 in *Roper v Simmons*,[11] by a majority of 5:4, the Court, reversing its decision five years earlier, held that there now existed a national consensus which dictated exempting from the death penalty anyone under the age of 18 at the time of the commission of the crime. The majority of the Supreme Court, notably, prayed in aid the influence of international law and practice as supportive of a general distaste for executing young offenders. Three of the dissenters, in a judgment written by Justice Scalia, emphatically disavowed the application of international human rights norms; the other, Justice Sandra Day O'Connor, disclaimed any alliance to such a jingoistic approach to the penalty for murder, but thought it was too early for the Court to exempt young offenders from the death penalty – too often, she said, their crimes were indistinguishable from those of their adult counterparts.

The conclusion must be that the United States is still some way off abolition, either by judicial process or legislative action in most, if not all, of the state legislatures which retain capital punishment.[12] At best the Supreme Court is inching towards standards of decency. And there is no sign of legislation in the US Congress; none of the candidates for the two parties, Republican or Democrat, has espoused abolition in Presidential elections this century (in 1988

[10] Under the 'super due process' provisions of the new legislation, longer and longer periods were spent between the offender's sentence and eventual execution (if it occurred at all). Today, 2.3 million are in prison in the US, of whom just over 3,000 are on Death Row.

[11] 543 US 551 (2005).

[12] In recent years six states have abandoned capital punishment: New Jersey, New York, Illinois, New Mexico, Maryland and Connecticut; and several states have a moratorium on executions. Very few now regularly carry out capital punishment. Professor Roger Hood is altogether more optimistic. He argues persuasively that abolition in those six states indicates a mood among US legislators to adopt the growing international move to end the death penalty for murder.

Senator Michael Dukakis favoured abolition; he disastrously failed to be elected President). But the outlawing of capital punishment as being unnecessary to any legitimate goal of the modern civilised state, and thus incompatible with the dignity of man and the rational judicial process does not appear to be other than on the horizons of the American landscape. The movement towards abolition is due more to economic factors than to rational morality; the same economic influences are shaping criminal justice in England, with swathing cuts in publicly funded legal aid.

Until the Homicide Act 1957 it was possible to say that the Queen's Bench judges of the High Court (at that time, only they were entrusted to try offenders charged on indictment for murder) were predominantly in favour of capital punishment. Under the influence of the Lord Chief Justice, Lord Goddard (a scholar indeed, but a traditional relic of stern Victorian moral values) the view of the higher judiciary would have been pronounced publicly only by their actions as dictated by the law, or extrajudicially by the Lord Chief Justice. Even the Law Lords in the House of Lords in their legislative capacity did not incline (to put it mildly) towards the minority view. The 1957 Act and a change of Chief Justice, however, dramatically altered the judicial complexion on the issue. As early as 1959 Lord Parker, only a year or so after becoming Lord Chief Justice, publicly declared his hearty dislike for the perceived defects in the categorisation of murder into capital and non-capital. He was to repeat his opposition to the Act when he addressed the National Association of Probation Officers in 1961, combining his hostility with a desire hopefully for the return of corporal punishment, no doubt designed to demonstrate that he was no 'softy' on crime and punishment. The overriding feature that determined the outcome was the extrajudicial attitude of the judges. The attitude of the Lord Chief Justice and the judges of the Queen's Bench after the Homicide Act 1957 demonstrated a powerful, if publicly unnoticed, shift in judicial attitudes to crime and punishment. Homicide was no exception.

This judicial outburst was ill-received by the Home Secretary (RA Butler), who protested to the Lord Chancellor about such extrajudicial pronouncement in a public forum. Unlike a successor 40 years later, 'Rab' Butler, himself privately an abolitionist, quietly fumed and continued to exercise the Prerogative of Mercy at much the same rate as his predecessors. Nowadays such tension between Ministers and judges is articulated in a digital world.

Lord Parker's outburst was later, however, to have a hugely effective legislative airing, by which time many of the High Court judges had come to share their chief's hatred of the 1957 Homicide Act; some were abolitionist even by general inclination. By the time of the 1965 Bill, there was certainly no judicial opposition to the reform. Moreover, it became clear that not merely did the judiciary accept, without demur, the ending of capital punishment, but there was a positive desire that trial judges should have the exclusive task of selecting the appropriate term of imprisonment (or even a non-custodial sentence for mercy killings), up to a maximum of life imprisonment when it was considered at the time of conviction that it was not possible to decide when it would be safe to discharge the prisoner from custody. All this was manifest in the parliamentary events at the end of July 1965.

But an event, covered by Chatham House Rules about disclosing the contents of a private meeting without named attribution, took place in 1961. I quote the account of a meeting between the Lord Chief Justice and the Parliamentary press lobby in the Palace of Westminster. Here it is: it bears out my assertion that MPs were quietly aware, via the parliamentary journalists, of judicial approval of abolition. A note to file reported that:

> Lord Parker gave his views on capital punishment to a group of Lobby and Press Gallery correspondents. The talk was off the record but it was clear that correspondents could use the information given so long as the views were not attributed to Lord Parker. In essence he said that although he was once against abolition he had become over the last three years an abolitionist himself. Not for sentimental, social or religious reasons but because of the anomalies of the present law. He gave examples of this. He felt, however, that some kind of deterrent was necessary to take the place of hanging, which, in his opinion, is a deterrent at present. Further, he felt that public opinion regarded it as a deterrent and would not be happy if it were abolished and not replaced with something else. He dismissed the possibility of going back to the position before the Homicide Act with the phrase 'we must go forward and not back' . . . The solution which he favours, and which he thinks would be acceptable to the police and to public opinion, is to abolish capital punishment but to allow judges to place restrictive conditions on the life sentences which they must by law impose. These restrictions would not interfere with the Home Secretary's functions but he would have regard to them when life sentences came up for review. I understand that in private conversation Lord Parker left the impression that this solution would be acceptable to 'more than half the judges in England'.

The only concession to particularity in the sentence of life imprisonment was section 1(2) of the Murder (Abolition of Death Penalty) Act 1965, which stated that

The Court may at the same time [as passing the sentence] declare the period which it recommends to the Secretary of State as the minimum period which in its view should elapse before the Secretary of State orders the release of that person on licence.

In practice, the recommendation was little used – in less than 10 per cent of cases – and the appellate court pronounced in 1972 that the minimum recommendation should not be less than 12 years, indicating that the judges thought that the minimum recommendation was designed to cater only for the dangerous prisoner, and did not permit short minima for cases of extreme mitigation, like mercy killings (Lord Parker in 1965 had said that judges were quite capable and willing to be merciful as well as severe). A specific minimum recommended at trial was abolished in 2003. The future law and practice of sentencing murderers has thus provided Parliament's unfinished business. The mandatory sentence of life imprisonment became for the next 40 years the battlefield of penal reform.

The argument against the mandatory element continued unabated, accompanied by a bland, if even deafening, silence to meet the deficiency in prescribing any judicial discretion in the sentence of life imprisonment. The mandatory sentence reduces the court's normal sentencing function to the level of a rubber stamp; it negates the idea of individualism in the sentencing of an offender. The morally just and the morally reprehensible are similarly treated for their culpability in crime. Extenuating and aggravating circumstances count for nothing at the time of sentencing, although they are recognised if and when the prisoner's case is reviewed with a prospect of release, often many years into the serving of the sentence. No consideration, no matter how valid or compelling, can affect the question of the sentence. The mandatory sentence cannot consider even the harsh and inequitable result that might flow from such a situation. Judicial policy is opposed to mandatory sentences; indeed a separate function, even a distribution of power, should debar this legislative interference with judicial control. The sound administration of justice and its social image determines abolition in favour of a discretionary sentence. In terms of human rights law, human rights are not commodities; they are creatures inherently endowed with qualities that are ends in themselves, and not merely means to an end. One of the elements of the dignity of the individual is the 'right to hope' that an indeterminate sentence is always subject to a 'dedicated review mechanism' at the time of sentence.

When the Government announced its official review of the law of murder on 27 October 2004, and on 21 July 2005 the terms of reference for the review, it assigned the first stage of the review to the Law Commission. The Government was insistent that the crime of murder would remain to be penalised by the mandatory sentence of life imprisonment. The categories of murder, including both the more heinous and the less morally culpable cases of murder, would be visited by the mandatory life sentence. This specific restriction on the terms of reference was *absurd*. How could the country's legal reform agency – demonstrably independent – not consider at any stage the law and penalty for a crime? It was the same device that directed the Royal Commission on Capital Punishment in 1949 *not* to review the death penalty, but only how to reduce the mandate of the death penalty.

The Government intended to legislate on the law of murder before the 2010 General Election. The outcome became uncertain about the consequential shape of the law covering all unlawful killings. The prospect is, however, that the law of homicide, acknowledged to be a 'mess', will remain an unremedied mess well into the twenty-first century. No doubt public debate on the substantive law of murder will be lively, hopefully well-informed and intellectually based, as well as taking full cognisance of public opinion which must be fully tested, not by reliable pollsters, but the empirical evidence of social researchers. About the penalty, one must be less circumspect if the Government's only intention is to keep the penalty in as 'messy' a state as it is.

If the Government adheres faithfully to the convention that Members of Parliament are free to vote according to their individual consciences, unwhipped by party officials and unaccountable to other constituencies, it may, however, not win the day. Prediction is always a matter of guesswork, however informed and persuasive. The history of the politics of abolition of the death penalty suggests a vote for common sense, and a sensible alternative. A rational sentencing framework set by the legislature, with maxima penalties for crime and a discretion to trial judges, acting under the guidance of the Sentencing Guidelines Council and controlled by the appellate courts in their guidance decisions, should doubtless be properly informed by considerations of penal policy. The unfinished business of almost 50 years ago is due for completion. Will the parliamentarians of tomorrow subscribe to sound penal philosophy, recalling the wise words of the philosopher George Santayana that 'those who cannot remember the past are condemned to repeat it'?

LIFE AFTER DEATH

The official (i.e. Government) response to provide a statutory sentence of life imprisonment in place of the death penalty was not slow in coming. After the affirmative motion in December 1969 to extend the life of the Murder (Abolition of Death Penalty) Act 1965, the Home Secretary (Mr James Callaghan) gave the Criminal Law Revision Committee (CLRC, a body exclusively composed of judges and lawyers) the task of reviewing all offences against the person; the terms of reference specifically said that the review should include homicide in the light of, and subject to, 'the recent decision of Parliament to make permanent the statutory provisions abolishing the death penalty for murder'. In an interim report in 1973 the Committee concluded that the mandatory sentence should be left undisturbed. There was a powerful dissent from the doyen of academic criminal lawyers, Professor Glanville Williams, who neatly set out the rival arguments. When it came to its Fourteenth Report on Offences Against the Person in March 1980, the CLRC (never formally abolished thereafter) had shifted its stance. Almost evenly divided, the Committee made no recommendation. Thereafter for 20 more years almost all official and unofficial reports (of which there were many) opted in favour of abolition of the mandatory sentence. The most compelling voice for the removal of the mandatory element was Lord Bingham, then the Lord Chief Justice. His lecture to the Police Staff College in March 1998 is reproduced in *The Business of Judging*.[13] It was unhappily ignored by the Labour administration (through the Home Secretary, Mr David Blunkett), which promoted the relevant provision of the Criminal Justice Act 2003. Significantly, because at the time – February 1978[14] – it was unpublished, the Law Commission, responding to a restricted questionnaire from the Criminal Law Revision Committee, issued a memorandum on the question of offences against the person which strongly favoured the abolition of the mandatory life sentence. The rest was statutory silence, even when the subject was raised by leading politicians in the Conservative and Labour administrations. The 2003 Act was an aspect of the rhetorical statement of 'tough on crime, tough on the criminal' – interpreted by the Prime Minister as being rationally applied.

---

[13] Tom Bingham, *The Business of Judging* (Oxford, OUP, 2010) 329–43.
[14] It was revealed in the course of the Law Commission's report on murder, in 2005.

The sole conversation on the topic of what has become known as 'whole-life' crept into public awareness when the Home Secretary (Mr Leon Brittan) announced a series of changes that brought sole control over decision-making on the length of time to be served to the Home Office, even to the extent that not even the Lord Chief Justice was notified of changes (normally an increase on a judicially recommended minimum term). By 1994 another Home Secretary, Michael (now Lord) Howard, said that he intended to impose 'whole-life' tariffs (which he invented) on some 20 notorious killers (the number of prisoners serving 'whole-life' sentences is now in excess of 50) and in 1995, in a letter to the Home Affairs Committee, reminded members of what Leon Brittan had said in 1983, and spelt out future statements as to what it meant. The review after 25 years, which those who had been marked out for whole-life terms had enjoyed, was administratively taken away by Michael Howard, a move endorsed in the legislation of 2003.

WHOLE-LIFE ORDERS: ECHR AND UK

Three prisoners serving life sentences together with 'whole-life' orders, imposed by the judiciary at the time of sentence, applied in 2010 to Strasbourg, alleging violation of their human rights. The 'tariff' of whole-life was the result of a judicial calculation of the culpability for murder: the so-called 'exceptionally grave' or the 'worst of the worst' should be sentenced to life imprisonment, with no minimum period of incarceration, but committal for their 'whole-life'. Should this mean, literally, the whole of the murderer's natural life, thus denying them at any time a review so as to mitigate the essence of 'whole-life'? It was at this point in the penological numbers game that the question was raised by prisoners, whether imprisonment for the rest of a murderer's natural life violates Article 3 of the European Convention on Human Rights as being 'inhuman or degrading treatment or punishment'.

Without dilating on a veritable overload of legal reasoning from both the English and the Strasbourg courts, the following timetable of court hearings assists in understanding the issues and the outcome (so far, in 2015).

On 17 January 2012 a seven-judge panel in the European Court of Human Rights, by four votes to three, held that there was no violation. The dissenters were the presiding judge, Judge Garlicki, with Judges David Thor Bjorgvinsson and Nicalaou.

On 9 July 2013, the Grand Chamber of 17 judges, by 16 votes to one, allowed the appeals. Notably, the Irish member, Judge Ann Power, delivering a short concurring opinion, said that what tipped the scale in favour of the prisoners was the acceptance of a 'right to hope' being encompassed in the right to humane punishment.

On 24 January 2014, the five-judge English Court of Appeal, presided over by the Lord Chief Justice, Lord Thomas, agreed with the Strasbourg Court that a literal 'whole-life' order would be a violation of the Convention, but that the law in this country did not necessarily mean that the whole life of the prisoner would be spent in custody, because the Secretary of State has the legal power to review a 'whole-life' order. This ruling depended upon a construction of section 30 of the Crime (Sentences) Act 1997 which gives the Secretary of State the power to release a 'lifer' *if he is satisfied that exceptional circumstances exist which justify the prisoner's release on compassionate grounds.*[15] The English judges concluded that on the narrower issue, there is present in English law a 'dedicated review mechanism' so as to comply with the Article in the Convention on the validity of a whole-life order for murder. The European Court of Human Rights thought that the legislation in section 30 was lacking in certainty and that the whole-life order was a violation. Lord Thomas said simply: 'We disagree.' If that sounds too confrontational, even juristically so, one should remember that the legal maxim decrees that two reasonable decision-makers can reasonably come to two different conclusions.[16] Technically there is only one winner. Since the applicants seek a remedy under the Human Rights Act 1998, the English court is the sole governor of its law. Strasbourg's finding in interpreting the Convention has to be taken into account by the UK court, which it has done. Strasbourg's jurisprudence does not bind the English court. But one may indulge a lawyer's appetite for having independent views of Parliament's meaning in a statute. The problem in the instant case is that when

[15] Italics supplied. Section 30 of the 1997 Act reads as follows:

'30 Power to release life prisoners on compassionate grounds.

(1) The Secretary of State may at any time release a life prisoner on licence if he is satisfied that exceptional circumstances exist which justify the prisoner's release on compassionate grounds.

(2) Before releasing a life prisoner under subsection (1) above, the Secretary of State shall consult the Parole Board, unless the circumstances are such as to render such consultation impracticable.'

[16] The maxim is based on a statement by Lord Hailsham LC in the case of *Re W (An Infant)* [1971] AC 682, 700, where he said: 'Two reasonable parents can perfectly reasonably come to opposite conclusions on the same set of facts without forfeiting their title to be regarded as reasonable.'

reading of section 30 of the 1997 Act one must see it in context. While it specifically covers every sentence of life imprisonment (which definitionally includes life imprisonment without benefit of parole), the statutory order of whole-life in Schedule 21 to the 2003 Act was not then in existence, even though at that time it was functional in administrative terms. It seems to me that the whole-life sentence was not part of 'a dedicated review *mechanism*'. The section conferred a power, 'in exceptional circumstances', to a Minister to release a life prisoner on licence. As regards those given a whole-life order, nothing is explicitly said about a 'review' after the service of a minimum (or tariff) term; nor does it specify that the possibility of a review or discharge should be given expression to at the point of the trial judge passing sentence.

It is an intriguing situation between a municipal court and a supranational court which is the guardian of specific human rights; ideally, a case for mutual respect and judicial dialogue. Perhaps the Council of Europe will consider conferring such a power on judges to powwow.[17]

THE FUTURE PENALTY

What prospect is there for ridding the sentence for murder of its mandatory nature? Is there a parliamentary disposition to complete the business omitted from the abolition of capital punishment? Parliament in 1965 wanted to consign the death penalty to the museum of penal history. It did that, and no more – sentences were left to be settled.

The evidence for today's parliamentarians to respect the views of their predecessors points this way. On 28 October 1965[18] the House of Commons debated finally the Bill on the death penalty, simply to consider the motion of its sponsor (Mr Sydney Silverman) to accept the House of Lords' amendment. The amendment had provided for the trial judge to pass a minimum recommendation (without legal effect), which became section 1(2) of the Murder (Abolition of Death Penalty) Act 1965, a section which was little used and ultimately repealed in the Criminal Justice Act 2003. That provision – incidentally, a minimum term could not legally endorse a 'whole-life' order – was required under parliamentary procedure affecting the legislative powers of the two chambers.

---

[17] New Shorter Oxford English Dictionary, 2316.
[18] *Hansard* HC Deb, vol 718, col 90.

All the speakers on that day strongly favoured the option promoted successfully by 80 votes to 78 in the Lords on 27 July 1965[19]
that the sentence of life imprisonment should be discretionary. No
one demurred; only Henry (later Lord) Brooke, the former Home
Secretary, hesitated to join the chorus of the (later withdrawn)
amendment floated expectantly by the Lord Chief Justice, Lord
Parker. The Conservative spokesman on home affairs, Mr Mark
Carlisle (later a Home Office Minister for Education in 1979, and
who became Lord Carlisle), described an amendment of the minimum recommendation that was proposed to be inserted in the Bill
as 'a dismal compromise' to the discretionary sentence, advanced
but withdrawn by Lord Parker. Mr Carlisle strongly favoured the
sentencing judiciary treating all murderers alike at the discretion of
the trial judge. Mark Carlisle's view was seconded by Sir John
Hobson QC, a former Conservative Attorney-General, Mr Reginald
Paget, a Labour member known for expressing independent views,
and Sir Richard Glyn, a non-lawyer Conservative member. But most
notable among the speakers in the truncated chamber was Mr Peter
Thornycroft, a former Conservative Chancellor of the Exchequer. He
declared that the amendment to the Bill 'had not a friend in the
House except for the [Labour Home] Secretary' (referring to Sir
Frank Soskice).[20] He (Mr Thornycroft) added the reason for not voting against the preferred mandatory element; that 'it would not be
proper to lose the Bill over some muddle concerning a Lords'
amendment'. Given the lateness in the parliamentary agenda – the
Bill received the Royal Assent on 4 November 1965 – and the
expected, not to say overwhelming commitment to being rid of
the death penalty for good, these words are unsurprising. Lord
Gardiner, the Lord Chancellor and the progenitor for abolition,
had himself orchestrated the legislation by, inter alia, ensuring that
the Government should devote time in processing what in fact was
a private members' Bill. A mandatory life sentence for murder was
the inevitable replacement for the death penalty.

Is a mandatory penalty for any offence ever an acceptable part of
a civilised penal philosophy? It is one thing to sentence a convicted
murderer to imprisonment for life; it is altogether another matter for
society to ensure a lifetime in custody to mark the severity of punishment for the crime. We do not subscribe to the biblical doctrine
of 'an eye for an eye' – retribution must always be qualified. Locking

[19] *Hansard* HL Deb, vol 268, col 1241.
[20] *Hansard* HC Deb, vol 718, col 380–81.

someone up and throwing away the key, without the benefit of parole at the time of sentencing, is another matter. As a matter of humanity there are powerful arguments which suggest that there is a risk of a whole-life sentence that is predetermined at the time of sentence being inhumane; a sentence of life imprisonment with no chance of release, which is to destroy any hope of seeing freedom again, can be seen as unmitigated, revengeful punishment. The existence of a parole system inserts the possibility of release at some stage of custody and the probability of review avoids the destruction of all hope. But the law established in 1965 with the abolition of the death penalty omitted to differentiate the sentence of life imprisonment from the time to be served as the proportionate punishment. Abolition of the death penalty was statutorily effected. The sentence of life imprisonment did no more, and left unanswered the substance of any indeterminate period of imprisonment. The provision in section 269 of the 2003 Act (especially in subsection 4, which provides for the appropriate starting point of a whole-life order, where the seriousness of the offence is exceptionally high) could not amend the whole-life sentence, since a 'whole-life' order could never be a minimum period. It cannot be assumed that the combination of a whole-life sentence with a whole-life order achieves an amendment of the penalty for murder which is the sentence.

Penal philosophy dictates a resolution of the confusion over the penalty for murder that acknowledges the possibility of the rehabilitation of the 'lifer' who, on review, no longer constitutes a risk, if discharged from custody.

Earlier, Lord Bingham had indicated in the law prior to the Criminal Justice Act 2003 how the confusion should be resolved:

> One can readily accept that in requiring a sentence of imprisonment for life on all those convicted of murder Parliament did not intend 'sentence' to mean what it said in all or even a majority of cases, but there is nothing to suggest that Parliament intended that it should never (even leaving considerations of risk aside) mean what it said.[21]

But after the legislation in 2003, doubts crept into the forensic scene. Lord Justice Laws in 2003 described the English law as the *lex talionis*, if there was no proportionate punishment. But some Law Lords on appeal did not agree with Lord Justice Laws that a revengeful penalty was impermissible. To the extent that the law

---

[21] *R v Secretary of State for the Home Department, ex p Hindley* [1998] QB 751, 769 B-C.

can exact revenge, it seems from the latest pronouncement from the Court of Appeal that it can do so, if the penal administration grants a power of release 'in exceptional circumstances'. But the 'highly restrictive power' is, however, not an integral part of the sentence of the court. Its purport to determine the penalty by a whole-life fulfilment of the sentence is legally insufficient.

The array of parliamentary unanimity, demonstrated in the House of Commons in 1965, deserves to be revived. Fifty years is a long enough period to cogitate over the legislative intent, particularly since Parliament has not since then taken the opportunity – indeed, it has actively refused – to reconsider its proposed stance, implicitly telegraphed by a favourable vote in the House of Lords on 6 March 2010[22] in favour of abolition of the mandatory element.

The mental condition of a prisoner at the time of his trial for murder may raise, and fail to establish evidentially, a partial defence of diminished responsibility. Nevertheless the psychiatric evidence, called by the defendant, may be sufficient to conclude that the murder was not to be dubbed one of 'the worst of the worst'. But the diagnosis may be that the defendant is treatable in prison. The jury's rejection of a defence plea of diminished responsibility is relevant only to the issue of proof beyond a reasonable doubt. It is not a factor that should be taken into account subsequently on questions relating to the prisoner's mental condition at the time of the homicidal event or at trial. A subsisting mental disorder will always have a bearing on the degree of culpability for murder.

Quite apart from assessing the prisoner's mental condition at the time of sentence for murder, the Grand Chamber in the case of *Vinter and others v United Kingdom*[23] on 9 July 2013 correctly observed[24] that there may arise a circumstance (such as a psychiatric disorder) or a fresh condition which becomes relevant to any review or release; and for that purpose examination should be conducted within a wholly judicial framework, rather than by the Executive, even if subject to judicial control. It is one's experience, admittedly impressionistic, that many of the worst homicides are committed in circumstances that disclose a culpability induced by a mental disorder. As such, it is nigh-on impossible to categorise such a murder as more or less heinous than other murders. Even if

---

[22] *Hansard* HL Deb, vol 713, cols 1008–1109. The vote was 113 in favour of the proposal to the Coroners and Justice Bill and 155 against. See T Morris and L Blom-Cooper, *Fine Lines and Distinctions* (Hook, Waterside Press, 2011) 375.

[23] (2013) 34 BHRC 605.

[24] At paras 122–24.

mentally disordered murderers are the most dangerous offenders from whom society needs to be protected by a long period in custody, their need for constant review is all the more necessary. 'Worst' is the superlative of bad or evil, itself the worst case of murders. What evidence can a trial court adduce to clarify the instant case as compared with, on the face of it, another that seems just as heinous?

The Grand Chamber's assessment[25] demonstrates persuasively that, acknowledging the scope of each country's margin of appreciation that allows for different whole-life sentences to be effected, most Member States of the Council of Europe regard the unreviewability of the sentence of life imprisonment as grossly disproportionate treatment, and inhumane. In Chapter 11 of *The Death Penalty*,[26] Professors Roger Hood and Carolyn Hoyle, in considering the challenge of a suitable replacement to the death penalty for murder, conclude as follows:

> Those who campaign for the humane treatment of prisoners will need to refocus their attention on creating for life-sentenced prisoners a humane prison environment, accompanied by an effective and judicious system for reviewing suitability for release that adequately protects the public while respecting the humanity of the prisoner. In our opinion, sentences of life imprisonment which preclude any possibility of parole are not only inhumane, they are unnecessary and counter-productive. They raise many of the human rights issues that have been at the heart of the attack on the death penalty itself. They too should be abolished. [27]

The public punitiveness of today has no place in the penal system of a civilised country. It too should be abolished and consigned to a museum of penal history.

---

[25] Paras 102–22.
[26] R Hood and C Hoyle, *The Death Penalty*, 4th edn (Oxford, OUP, 2008).
[27] ibid 403.

9

The Apotheosis of Amateurism
Trial by Jury

THOSE WHO MOST vocally proclaim the supreme virtue of the system of trial by jury (strictly speaking, in the English system, it is trial by judge and jury, the two in harness functioning in an unspoken alliance to pronounce the verdict) rely heavily on the famous aphorism of Lord Devlin in the Hamlyn Lectures of 1956. He wrote: 'Each jury is a little Parliament . . . it is more than an instrument of justice and more than one wheel of the constitution: it is the lamp that shows that freedom lives'. It is the last nine words that most frequently come trippingly off the advocate's tongue. Putting on one side its allusion to parliamentary practice, if Lord Devlin's classical view of trial by jury is the starting point for any valuable assessment of the system, what did the words encompass? Was it meaningful rhetoric, or a monumental myth? Do his words encapsulate a constitutional element, even if they are unwritten? Clearly, the illuminating phrase purported to claim for the jury the unauthorised power to do three things: first, to reject the relevant law (common law or statutory provision) that criminalises the wrong for which the defendant is being tried. Second, to reject, not the criminalisation of the act, but the level of sanction attached to it, displaying a distaste for penal sanction. And third, while jurors may accept the relevant law and the concomitant sanction, nevertheless they simply have no desire to see them applied to the particular defendant on trial. All three situations are said in their differing ways to justify what is called 'jury nullification' – in other words, the power of the jury (with or without help from the judge) to negate their oath to try the case according to the evidence heard in the courtroom and not including any extraneous material. Constitutionally, jurors are entitled (so it is proclaimed) to exercise their vote in defiance of their oath of office. At best, these matters are conventionally asserted.

Jury nullification has been the subject of academic study for some time, seeking to justify an expression of popular opinion. The advocacy of juristic independence finds its statutory basis in the oath administered to each juror. It overlooks or ignores that the juror's expressed duty is to deliver a unanimous verdict (only after 1967 could there be a majority vote of 10-2) on the evidence admissible in the proceedings. Jurors were encouraged to ensure that they did not look to any extraneous material for the purpose of its statutory duty. Therein lies the growing problem of information technology.

The proponents of jury trial unthinkingly assert that it is a right – even a fundamental freedom – that belongs to every person charged with an indictable offence. But this is not so. There is no option. If charged, the defendant is under an obligation to undergo a trial before the established criminal tribunal. A constitutional *right* must be the subject of choice. Yet there remains stout opposition from supporters of jury trial for any waiver, in favour of a professional tribunal. Some Anglo-Saxon systems have a limited right to 'bench trial', and occasionally extreme considerations have led Parliament to approve the removal of trial by jury (such as manifest nobbling of witnesses or jurors). In the cause of anti-terrorism in Northern Ireland, for 30 years the 'Diplock courts' (trial by a single judge) operated a system that was acceptable to all in terms of criminal responsibility for terrorism in the Province.

The mode of a fair trial is the test under the common law of England, as complying with Article 6 of the European Convention on Human Rights, which is not more specific. In the case of *Taxquet v Belgium*,[1] in November 2011 the Grand Chamber declined to favour any established mode of trial. So long as the system produced a 'reasoned verdict', it would comply. Jury trial in any case remains intact.

Devlin attributes to the jury an element over and above the 'instrument of justice', but it is difficult to discern what that element is, if it means more than that the juror's verdict is unaccountable and unanswerable (subject to the limitations of the appellate process). A verdict of acquittal is inviolable; no public system can declare it other than an end of the trial. Even the recommendation from Sir Robin Auld in 2001 in his survey of *Criminal Justice*, that a perverse verdict of the jury should become reviewable, has so far been rejected. The legal profession maintained the purity of jury decision, if otherwise directed correctly on the law and the admissibility of the evidence. Proportionality in the decision in relation to the criminal offence plays no part in the process.

---

[1] (2012) 54 EHRR 26.

The jury's duty is two-fold: first to apply the relevant law as directed by the trial judge, and secondly to evaluate the available evidence after a proper direction from the judge. Strictly speaking, the jury must apply the law as it is told to them; factual judgment is entirely for the jury collectively. Their verdict is unarticulated and unreasoned. Whether the absence of a reasoned verdict invalidates the process of a 'fair trial' has been held by Strasbourg to constitute a violation, but the essence of jury trial (if it procedurally exhibits a fair trial) has not been declared a breach of a modern mode of criminal trial. Each conviction must nevertheless contain a procedure whereby some reasoned issue can be discerned. It may be that the courts will begin to develop a method whereby the trial judge administers to the jury a questionnaire, to which answers supply sufficient reasons for the verdict. We have yet to witness the ambit of a jury's verdict as a mode of trial compatible with the Convention. Better than mouth Lord Devlin's hyperbolic label as a constitutional constituent of right for serious crime, the proponents should examine how the system can be modified, and whether trial by jury should not be a matter of choice rather than imposed by the prosecuting authority. If the value of the verdict is the criterion, that is one thing. The quality of the criminal process is the crucial element.

SOME CRITICISMS OF THE JURY SYSTEM

If the sole test for evaluating the mode of serious criminal trial is the outcome of the legal process – that is, the correctness of the decision-maker, be the court of trial a professional judge(s) or a number of unqualified jurors – the exercise causes little social difficulty. The empirical evidence posits little difference in comparing the two modes; nothing is broken to warrant political mending. Leave the system of trial by jury (or, strictly speaking in the English court, trial by judge and jury) alone. If, on the other hand, the reasonable citizen thinks that the quality of service provides a substantially different, and better, criminal proceeding leading up to a verdict, the issue is more difficult. If the disparity is wider than a tiny percentage (as the evidence suggests at present) some assessment of the modes of trial must be made. We should evaluate the merits of trial by professionals or trial by ordinary members of the public. Political reality dictates that democratic society must select which system it prefers to adopt. The European Court of Human Rights makes no choice. It merely states, by Article 6, that everyone is entitled to a mode of criminal trial which is fair and is conducted by an independent and impartial tribunal in public and within a reasonable time.

When, in the early 1950s, I came to the English Bar I had resolved to become a civil practitioner, with no aspiration of conducting criminal cases. Although I had an academic interest in criminology and penology, I abstained from joining my professional colleagues in appearing in the criminal courts. During my two decades as a junior counsel I had formed an opinion against the jury system (which was abolished almost entirely in the civil courts by 1934). My reasoning was prompted by an intellectual study of the literature about modes of trial. In the 1960s I had begun to teach criminology, part-time, in the University of London, and by 1966 I had, unusually, joined the ranks of the London magistracy that tried 98 per cent of the lesser criminal offences. When I was granted the upgrading to senior counsel in April 1970, I was encouraged to engage in some criminal work; it was a time when the generosity of the legal aid system fashioned on Queen's Counsel the confetti of legal aid certificates. Like many others, I grasped at the opportunity, and for a number of years I practised within the criminal courts, a practice which unexpectedly took me frequently into the courts of criminal appeal. The unique experience confirmed my extracurial dislike for the criminal justice system, and my distrust of the jury system. But that is another story. Here I am concerned to say why I took up the cudgels of jury trial. The academic discussion of the system is certainly not one-way. Many of the thoughtful comments among practitioners and some academic lawyers strongly favour the present system. Hitherto, I will record the rival opinions given down the ages. But at this point, I must confess that I take the modern system as it exists, if only because before the Criminal Justice Act 1972, only property-owners qualified to serve as jurors. I would assume that the proponents of the jury system would willingly support such a limitation on the juror. A change in the Criminal Justice Act 2003, for broadening the qualification, with some exceptions, was popularly proclaimed by the legislature.

Given the hypothesis that the proper criterion for evaluating the system is the quality of criminal justice that dictates the process of a fair trial, I must state my reasons for thinking that it is defective, such that we should contemplate change, if only to introduce either the mixed tribunal (judge and jury together at all stages) or at least the accused's right to choose a waiver of the system of jury trial to be tried by a court of professionals alone.

No modern system of a fair trial can deny both prosecution and defence knowing the reasons for a verdict of guilty or not guilty; that is quite irrespective of the limited recommendation (which was rejected by the Government) of Sir Robin Auld in his *Review of the Criminal Courts* in 2001 to abolish any perverse adjudication by a jury. The court at Strasbourg has only partially, in *Taxquet v Belgium* in November 2011,[2] said that, without in any way condemning jury trial, in principle any court must supply the wherefore, if it is to rule that the verdict is the result of a fair trial. This ruling opens up the question whether the answers by any jury to questions posed by a questionnaire will suffice to satisfy the court's requirement for a fair trial. Answers to specific questions may suffice, but at the moment it has not been decided that they will do so, or whether they cannot displace the need for a jury to state its full reasons, without any judicial aid, save assistance in the summing-up of the evidence adduced and direction as to the relevant law. That is a matter to which future development in criminal procedure will call for discussion and decision at appellate level. Subject to that inevitable movement, the jury is not required to include the whys and wherefores of the criminal event under scrutiny. When considering the utility of administering a questionnaire to jurors, the judge needs to remember what Mr Justice Maule said in 1841:[3] 'The trial by jury is not founded upon an absurd supposition that all twelve will reason infallibly from the premises to the conclusion.' With the vast experience of information technology, acquired outside the courtroom, the warning is even more relevant today.

The jury is inarticulate, monosyllabic and secret, without any answerability or accountability to another institution. It cannot be asked to disclose the process of deliberation in the jury room (although misbehaviour by a jury may be investigated thereafter). No reasons, however, is the watchword for juries. No civil court could today avoid complying with that edict. The giving of reasons is axiomatic in the modern age, even though historically, when society was a good deal less literate, it complied with the requirements of a fair trial. The constitutional reason for opposing the jury system is that the inviolacy of the jury's denial of its reasons for the verdict renders this country defective in establishing a fully appellate system. I must explain why this is so.

---

[2] (2012) 54 EHRR 26.
[3] *Smith v Dobson* (1841) 3 Man + G 59, 62.

Literary allusions are repeatedly mentioned to justify or negative the jury system, proclaimed as a great British innovation. The quotations are boundless – both for and against. Judging them in their historical context, they still deserve to be quoted. Here they are.

Sir William Blackstone, the eighteenth-century expositor of the English common law, whose writings found instant acceptance and subsequent acclaim in the United States of America, called the jury, variously, 'the glory of the English law; the benchmark of liberty; the palladium of justice'. Thomas Jefferson, who detested Blackstone as an arch Tory, agreed with him at least on that one subject. Encomia of the jury today still abound on both sides of the Atlantic and, as in the past, they resonate across the political spectrum. Baroness Kennedy of the Shaws QC, an articulate New Labour politician and skilled criminal law practitioner, stated eloquently the overriding populist aspect of trial by jury in a Lords' debate on 28 September 2000 on the Criminal Justice (Mode of Trial) No 2 Bill:

> jury tradition is not only about the right of the citizen to elect trial but also about the juror's duty of citizenship. It gives people an important role as jurors – as stakeholders – in the criminal justice system. Seeing the courts in action and participating in that process maintains public trust and confidence in the law.

This assumes that public participation in the administration of criminal justice is enshrined in a collective right. The reverse is true. For centuries the criminal justice system has functioned as a mechanism of social control which enabled those with wealth and power to maintain their propertied, social superiority. The property qualification for jury service only disappeared under the Criminal Justice Act 1972. Until then, indisputably undeniable.

Baroness Kennedy repeated her rhetoric in the Lords' debate on the Criminal Justice Bill on 15 July 2003, saying that the exceptional cost of our criminal justice system 'is a legitimate price to pay for the *wonder* that is the jury' (italics supplied; her word). She, with other devotees of the jury system as involving the citizen directly in the criminal process, should be reminded of James Madison's maxim: 'Populism is a slippery concept in a politician's hands'.

Lord Hunt of Wirral, a former Conservative Minister, who on 15 July 2003 successfully moved the amendments to remove all traces of restricting jury trials from the Criminal Justice Bill, by implication endorsed the claims of fundamentalism in the jury system.[4]

---

[4] *Hansard*, HL Deb vol. 651, cols 768–74.

Lord Thomas of Gresford QC, a Liberal Democrat spokesman on legal affairs, described the jury as a 'mini-parliament – a democracy in itself – and which has always acted as a buffer against repressive regimes and against repressive laws'.[5] Lord Hooson QC, a fellow Liberal Democrat peer, described the jury 'as one of the great bulwarks of freedom in this country'.[6] Lord Brennan QC, a Labour peer and a former Chairman of the Bar Council was even more specific in this display of adulation for the jury. He said: 'A jury trial exquisitely and democratically combines those two aspects of citizenship – *one's right to be tried by one's fellow men* and one's duty to participate in that process when called upon to do so.'[7] This duality of function was encapsulated by another former chairman of the Bar Council, Lord Alexander of Weedon QC, who proclaimed that 'such an important right [was] vested in the defendant'.[8]

None of these 'counsel learned in the law' appears to acknowledge the true legal position of the jury as stated by Lord Justice Auld in his *Review of the Criminal Courts in England*, as follows:

> In England and Wales there is no constitutional, nor indeed any form of general right to judge and jury, only a general obligation to submit to it in indictable cases. [9]

As Lord Cooke of Thorndon, a former President of the Court of Appeal in New Zealand and occasional member of the House of Lords in its judicial capacity, reminded the House, international law required only an independent and impartial tribunal; it is silent as to any mode of trial. That is apparent from the Universal Declaration of Human Rights, the International Covenant on Civil and Political Rights and the European Convention of Human Rights.

Public pronouncements on the criminal justice system tend to echo the same sentiment of devotion to the jury system which, in the eyes of the ordinary citizen, accommodates far more than the tiny percentage of cases tried in the Crown Court. In so doing, the crude mixture of myth and emotion, infused by exaggerated language, is perpetuated.

That august journal, the *Economist*, wrote in its issue for 11–17 March 2000, that 'trial by jury has long been a cornerstone of British justice'. The *Economist*'s mural imagery (a fair reflection of intelligent public opinion) is only slightly less laudatory of the jury as an

---

[5] ibid, col. 774.
[6] ibid, col. 789.
[7] ibid, col. 799 (italics supplied).
[8] ibid, col. 801.
[9] Para 5.7, p 137 of the report in October 2002.

indispensable mode of criminal trial, than those views uttered by even distinguished jurists. The most frequently quoted praise for the jury is Lord Devlin's 'lamp that shows that freedom lives' – a forerunner of Lord Thomas of Gresford's 'mini-Parliament'. Yet it is worth citing the passage from which that illuminating expression comes, in order to demonstrate how the jury in contemporary society is impermissibly perceived to be, not just an adjudicator or umpire between prosecutor and prosecuted providing a fair trial, but as the linchpin of a modern parliamentary system of government (and not just an example of Athenian democracy). Lord Devlin wrote:

> Each jury is a little Parliament. The jury sense is the parliamentary sense. I cannot see the one dying and the other surviving. The first object of any tyrant in Whitehall would be to make Parliament utterly subservient to his will; and the next to overthrow or diminish trial by jury, for no tyrant could afford to have a subject's freedom in the hands of twelve of his countrymen. [10]

He concluded:

> So that trial by jury is more than an instrument of justice and more than the wheel of the constitution: it is the lamp that shows that freedom lives. [Which Lord Lane, a great Chief Justice, once described to me privately as 'hyperbolic crap', while maintaining a stout advocacy of the system.]

Here Lord Devlin is clearly not confining his remarks to the requirement of a fair trial; he, above all, would not have made the mistake of linking his remarks to the strictly legal position, both nationally and internationally. He was attributing to trial by jury in England an import of constitutional significance that reaches beyond the framework of adjudication of undiluted criminal liability, based upon the evidence elicited admissibly in the courtroom.

Lord Devlin's view of the jury, when stripped of its dramatic language, cannot lightly be dismissed. The essence of his statement is that the strength of the jury lies in the fact that it is not circumscribed by legal rules; and that it has the power, in practice, to do what it thinks is the justice of the case, and not do just what is technically required by the legal process, to try the case according to the admissible evidence, which is what the jurors' oath requires. The jury thus evaluates the evidence with both a non-legal eye and a non-professional approach. Mr Justice Holmes, speaking in 1920 for

[10] In his Hamlyn Lectures in 1956, p 104.

the majority of the US Supreme Court in *Horning v District of Columbia*,[11] said: 'The jury has the power to bring in a verdict in the teeth of both law and facts.' While it must be conceded that the power in its proper exercise represents the jury in a favourable (in the sense of popular) light, its occasional perversity (which its advocates concede happens) is an abuse of power, bearable only because of its instant ephemerality. Lord Justice Auld's recommendation to outlaw perverse acquittals has not been universally accepted.

Thus the oddity of an institution, politically unaccountable in an age insistent upon audit and answerability, remains. But what in fact is this curious institution, which decides the guilt of an accused by way of an unarticulated verdict proclaimed in never more than three syllables? It is, in essence, an oracular utterance devoid of any overt ratiocination. Lord Devlin's view of the jury as a mini-parliament is of immense historical interest, but must now be consigned to the archives of constitutional history, if only because the extra dimension of a constitutional element cannot be part of a 'fair trial'.

The nearest example of the dual roles of judge and jury in assessing the quality of admissible evidence is to be found in the former's ability to halt the trial prematurely. The decision whether a properly directed jury, acting reasonably, could convict on any count or counts in an indictment with which the defendant is charged, is made following submissions from defence counsel and in the absence of the jury, usually but not necessarily at the close of the prosecution's case. The test for deciding whether to remove the case from the jury was authoritatively stated by Lord Lane CJ in *R v Galbraith*:[12]

(1) If there is no evidence that the crime alleged has been committed by the defendant there is no difficulty – the judge will stop the case.
(2) The difficulty arises where there is some evidence but it is of tenuous character, for example, because of inherent weakness or vagueness or because it is inconsistent with other evidence.

    (a) Where the judge concludes that the prosecution evidence, taken at its highest, is such that a jury properly directed could not properly convict on it, it is his duty, on submission being made, to stop the case.
    (b) Where, however, the prosecution evidence is such that its strength or weakness depends on the view to be taken of a witness's reliability, or other matters which are generally speaking

---

[11]   254 US 135 (1920).
[12]   [1981] 1 WLR 1039.

> within the province of the jury, and where on one possible view
> of the facts there is evidence on which the jury could properly
> come to the conclusion that the defendant is guilty, then the
> judge should allow the matter to be tried by the jury.

If the judge's function is, as one robust member of the judiciary
described it, 'making sure the jury brought in the right verdict', a
judicial view of the accused's innocence could be effected by exercising the power to stop the trial. But that, in contemporary conditions, might be said to fall foul of Article 6. A fair trial must be fair
to both sides, defence and prosecution. If the judicial view is of the
accused's guilt, the judge will hope to steer the jury in the right
direction. But leading the jury by the nose is a hazardous practice
which, the advocates of the jury system would say, is one of the
reasons for having the jury!

As such, the system, the functioning of which we are only dimly
aware (due to the secrecy of the process) is fondly thought to be
supported by the public and the majority of the legal profession.
But the jury has always had its detractors, both ancient and
modern, as well as its loud proponents. In 1844, Gilbert à Becket,
soi-disant descendant of the ill-fated, legally qualified, Archbishop
of Canterbury, and author of the *Comic History of England* (à Becket
was both a lawyer and regular contributor to *Punch* magazine), said
of the jury that it was 'difficult to see the British bosom with a
sufficiently tranquil state to discuss this great subject, for every
Englishman's heart will begin bounding like a tremendous bonce at
its bare mention'. Fifty years earlier, the views of Jeremy Bentham,
a notable iconoclast of English legal institutions, finds an echo in
the provisions for jury waiver. He wrote:

> I give it to those who choose to have it, in cases in which they choose to
> have it and not unless they insist upon having it: looking upon it as an
> institution admissible in barbarous times, not fit for enlightened times,
> necessary as matters stand in England.[13]

Bentham today is the accepted libertarian, and my comment is: A
monument to unassertive sanity!

If the jury is perceived as the protector of civil liberties, rather
than just as an appropriate mode of trial of an individual accused,
the English view would be that, at best, it has provided protection
for small minorities, such as the fascists of the 1930s, the protesters
at the deployment of British troops in Northern Ireland in the 1970s,

---

[13] J Bentham, 'Draft of a Code for the Organisation of the Judicial Establishment in
France', *Works*, vol IV (first published 1770, Bowring ed, London, 1843) 314.

the opponents of genetically modified crops in the 1990s, and leakers of official secrets in the twenty-first century. Professor Glanville Williams, probably the most outstanding academic criminal lawyer in post-war Britain, did not support the general view of the jury as the great protector of our liberties. He argued that most of the great pronouncements on constitutional liberty from the eighteenth century onwards have been the work of judges, either sitting in appellate courts or giving directions to juries, and the assumption that political liberty at the present day (he was speaking in 1955) depends upon the jury is 'merely folk lore'. (One might cite Lord Mansfield in *Sommersett's Case* (1772),[14] that if a slave were brought to England he must be treated in all respects as a free man.) Professor Plucknett, Professor of Legal History at the University of London, wrote in 1929:

> Ever since the seventeenth century when juries began to express sentiments against the government, there has been a tendency for the jury to become, at least in popular thought, a safeguard of political liberty. It is only natural, therefore, that its history should have been idealised and traced back for patriotic reasons to the supposed golden age of Anglo-Saxon institutions.[15]

Given the significance of his continental European origins, education and training, Professor Sir Leon Radzinowicz, the eminent criminologist, unequivocally rejected the basis of the non-jury systems of Western Europe:

> The longer I live and cast my eyes on what is going on in the world at large, I firmly endorse the saying of W.L. Birbeck that the jury and the law of evidence are an Englishman's two great safeguards against the worst of all oppressions – that oppression which hides itself under the mask of justice![16]

And one could go on, *ad infinitum*, quoting both the pros and cons of this very English institution.

But will it last in an age of austerity? A citizen charged today with an indictable offence is obliged to undergo trial by judge and jury. Pronouncements against the jury system from authoritative voices cannot, therefore, hope to unlock the iron-fast equation between serious criminal offences and trial by jury. For some of its loudest proponents, the jury is simply an article of faith: not much room for

---

[14] 98 ER 499.

[15] Plucknett, *A Concise History of the Common Law*, 5th ed (Boston, Little, Brown & Co, 1956).

[16] L Radzinowicz, *Adventures in Criminology* (London, Routledge, 1998).

debate there. But sober and rational debate must accompany the Government's legislative attempts to unlock the equation.

Even those in Government, driven by considerations of cost, are also quick to declare their faith in the jury system. But, as Lord Justice Auld in his *Review of the Criminal Courts in England and Wales* reminded us, it is doubtful whether the various metaphors are apt as a principle or a practical justification for the institution in contemporary society. The jury can hardly be said to be representative of the community as a whole, notwithstanding the enlargement of jury qualification, matching the right of the adult citizen to vote, and randomly chosen without reference to their individual capacity for effective participation in the trial process – decisions, incidentally, for which they are publicly unaccountable and unanswerable. The jury cannot even properly claim to be a democratic institution. It cannot claim to confer a right on the citizen, since for the most serious crimes it is inflicted on the accused, willy-nilly, or on the merciful approach of the prosecutor, who can downgrade the crime on which the charge is framed. As Lord Justice Auld states, it is 'not some ancient, constitutional, fundamental or even broad right of the citizen'. As an absolute obligation, moreover, it can hardly be dubbed a 'right'.

THE HISTORY OF THE JURY

Let us look for a moment – even if superficially – at the history. The Greeks had a jury system, but ours did not derive from it. Although not all historians today are in accord on this topic, some say that the germ of the modern English jury is to be found in ninth-century France, a by-product of feudalism which took root in a different complexion in the Anglo-Saxon world. When, in the ninth century, the feudal system of social control was called into question, 12 men of the neighbourhood were recruited to seek the facts on oath. The jury then consisted, in effect, of witnesses to the crime. And so it remained, as a feudal tool of social control, when it was modified in England, after 1066. If this be correct history, it has its amusing aspect: the jury, prized by many today who mistrust administrative agencies, began its life as an agent of government. Jurors with knowledge of the criminal case today would be automatically disqualified from jury service. Article 6 of ECHR would see to that.

At any rate, in England, it spread as a mode of trial, competing with the ordeals which were ecclesiastically outlawed in the thirteenth century. According to Maitland, the jury was not imme-diately popular. He states that, at first, trial by ordeal was generally considered more desirable, more safe. (Parenthetically, we might add 'satisfactory', the phrase used in the Criminal Appeal Act 1968, but unwisely jettisoned in the Criminal Appeal Act 1995.) But the jury later superseded trial by ordeal. By the end of the fifteenth cen-tury in England the jury began to develop into what it is today – no longer a body of witnesses, but a body of persons randomly selected who hear the witnesses and who are not privy to the events under scrutiny. In the seventeenth century, the jury came to be highly regarded, popularly, as a check on Royal judges doing the bidding of the Crown. One thing is clear. Magna Carta, traditionally but erroneously regarded as the foundation of English liberties, clearly did not establish a right to trial by jury. (The essence of Magna Carta has been aptly summed up as 'One Baron, one vote'.) Pollock and Maitland in their *History of English Law*, talking of a period before the time of Edward I, contended that 'this palladium of our liber-ties' is in its origin not English but Frankish, not popular but Royal.[17]

Furthermore, it cannot claim to be a constitutional entitlement. Those who too readily point to Article 6 of the European Convention on Human Rights as requiring 'a fair trial before an independent and impartial tribunal' would get short shrift at Strasbourg if they claimed that denial of jury trial was a violation of the Convention.

To return briefly to the historical development of the jury system. In the American colonies (as elsewhere in the British Empire) juries often stood up to judges controlled by a hostile British Government. Little wonder, then, the adoption by the US and state constitutions, after the American revolution began, of provisions entrenching jury trial. Later, in the period when the Jeffersonians were pitted against Federal judges, juries were often anti-judge. So, in the US, the jury was considered a champion of the popular cause, cherished as a bulwark against oppressive government, acclaimed as essential to individual liberty and democracy. While it is appropriate to regard the modern jury as essentially an Anglo-American institution – the more so, since the US is truly trial by jury, whereas in England it is trial by judge and jury – other systems combine the legal and non-legal as the decision-maker *after* the facts are found by the *juge d'instruction* in the form of a dossier for the court of trial. The inter-action of the English judge's summing-up of the evidence and direc-

---

[17] Sir F Pollock and FW Maitland, *History of English Law* vol I, 2nd ed (Cambridge, CUP, 1898) 142.

tion on the law is in sharp contrast to America, where the judge is debarred from relaying the factual evidence with the jury, and commenting on it – neutrally, of course – to the jury. It is unsurprising that Americans are even more wedded to the jury system than anyone else among the Anglo-Saxon systems of law, although many jurisdictions within the Commonwealth have abandoned jury trial.

Trial by judge and jury for the most serious crimes – less than 1 per cent of all prosecuted crimes – supposedly retains public confidence. But I suspect that that confidence is waning, and is not universal. Yet it is likely to be the mode of trial, perhaps even at the election of the accused, for some time to come. It is incumbent on a civilised system, however, to pose the crucial question, as the Morris Committee on Jury Service in 1965 did. Stripped of all the rhetorical response that comes trippingly off the protagonist's tongue, does the jury, as a mode of criminal trial, provide as good, if not a better quality of justice than other modes, primarily trial by professional(s)? That is the question: not whether trial by judge and jury is a fundamental freedom or God-given right to the English. Lord Brennan QC, in the Lords' debate, at least conceded that, if the value attached to trial by judge and jury is to be altered, it must be justified by serious, intelligent and convincing evidence and argument.

A circuit judge, Judge Andrew Geddes, wrote in the *Guardian*[18] severely questioning whether juries were delivering justice. I suspect that his critique on the efficiency and effectiveness, not to say fairness of jury trial would be echoed by many of his colleagues on the Circuit Bench and many High Court judges today – but perhaps only in private!

No contemporary study has been possible in England, because since 1981 there has been a statutory ban on jury research. Even before 1981 it was thought improper – even a contempt of court – for jurors to reveal what happened in the secrecy of the jury room, although on occasions articles appeared in journals and elsewhere. Research has hence been meagre, effectively confined to countries outside the UK. In America, Kalven and Zeisel, in their work on the jury system in 1966, found that juries were reckoned to be less lenient than the judge in a small but significant proportion – 3 per cent – of the cases analysed. In 1979 Baldwin and McConville, in their study of jury trials in England, also found evidence of strong disagreement between professionals and juries over certain convictions.

[18] 27 March 2001, p 20.

More than 5 per cent of those found guilty by a jury were considered by professionals to have been convicted in questionable circumstances, a statistic which the authors regarded as the most disturbing arising from their study. Criticisms of the Baldwin and McConville study were founded on the thesis that juries were being assessed according to the standards of professional lawyers, whereas a prominent feature of jury trial is precisely its unlawyerly and layman-like perspective. That is no basis for criticism; it is a self-defeating argument, since jurors do not attain – they could in fact be said to evade – professional standards. At least the Baldwin and McConville study laid low the myth that juries are universally more disposed to favour defence lines of argument than professional judges. But such a small percentage difference might lead one to think that the system works – for the time being.

Since the legislative ban of 1981 there has been a deafening silence about the workings of the jury system. The Royal Commission on Criminal Justice (the Runciman Commission) in 1993, in a study conducted in the Crown Courts, revealed that judges and prosecuting counsel thought that jury convictions ran contrary to the evidence or the law in 2 per cent of cases. Professor Zander, a member of the Commission who organised the study, predicted uncritically in his recent Hamlyn lectures that jury trial will remain with us for the foreseeable future – a self-fulfilling prophecy, no doubt! Other thoughtful commentators on the legal scene and practitioners in the Crown Courts of England and Wales will echo the sentiment of GK Chesterton that our civilisation has decided, and very justly decided, that determining the guilt or innocence of men is a task too important to be trusted to trained men. But must it be an absolute requirement for all indictable offences?

We should not forget who is ultimately responsible for wrong verdicts. The Runciman Commission in 1993 reminded us that the convictions of the 'innocent' and acquittals of the 'guilty' – the 'miscarriages of justice' – are exclusively decisions of the jury. No one can anticipate the jury's verdict, the only body that can declare anyone innocent or guilty of the crime charged. The police may have fudged or even concocted the evidence; the prosecutor may have incompetently prosecuted the case; the defence counsel may have done a botched job for his client; the judge may have misdirected or over-persuaded the jury in a way that does not fall foul of the Court of Appeal, or inappropriately excluded relevant evidence; the appeal court may feel that it cannot interfere because the jury is exclusively the fact-finder, a matter which in principle must be respected. But the jury is the exclusive decision-maker, adjudicating on the evidence elicited before it. Has the jury the equipment and ability to see through all the potential defects of the criminal process? Its failure to discriminate between the correct and incorrect result must constitute an ever-present worry to the administrators of criminal justice.

The courts have often said that juries cannot be expected to give coherent reasons for their decisions, and regularly do not do so. There could be no better illustration of the enormity of the task they might face in doing so. The trial judge in *Boreman*[19] in 2000 found it necessary to instruct the jury in the law relating to murder, causation, self-defence, provocation, the effect of intoxication on the specific intent in murder, and the 'all important matter of joint enterprise', to say nothing of standard directions on the burden and standard of proof – at least half a term's course for an undergraduate studying criminal law! In addition, the judge ought to have directed them as to the need for unanimity on the basis of each defendant's guilt. The judge would deal only with those aspects of the law which were relevant to the present case; but this was a formidable task for him, and much more so for the jury. And what about the assessment and evaluation of the facts, on which the judge was bound in his summing-up to assist the jury? The jury could never reasonably have been expected to give coherent reasons for its decision on each of these matters. Indeed, they would probably not be able to produce composite reasons this side of Doomsday!

But if the giving of reasons is an essential feature of due process and of justice, and if it is impracticable to require juries to give reasons, where does that leave the jury system in an English trial, now dressed up in European garb?

THE FUTURE OF TRIAL BY JURY

Jury trial in England and Wales, as I have already noted, is in fact trial by judge and jury. The former has the duty to direct the jury on the law and to sum up the relevant facts. Judge and jury, in performing their discrete functions, have a symbiotic relationship, even if symbiosis stops short of direct communication in the deliberative process. The most the jury can do is to return to court and ask for further directions on the law and guidance on relevant factual

---

[19] [1999] All ER (D) 1350.

issues. But we have no idea about the chemistry of that relationship. Juries are presumed to do what they are told is the law. But there is evidence, almost entirely anecdotal, that juries will occasionally, even perversely, defy the judge who indicates a conviction, and will acquit. Conversely, a judge who leans toward an acquittal will sometimes be rebuffed by a convicting jury. Given the opacity of the problem, what will the courts say about jury trial and the right to a fair trial which involves essentially a reasoned verdict of the decision-maker?

A possible approach will be to say that the complementary role of the judge and jury adequately satisfies the requirement of the reasoned decision. Assuming that the jury loyally follows the judge's directions on the law, and is fully apprised of all the relevant facts, the standard of a fair trial would be adequately met. But it will mean that trial judges will have to tailor their recitation of the facts in a way that supplies, by a process of forensic interaction, the requirement of reasons. It will mean that the Court of Appeal (Criminal Division) will have to be more insistent on a high-quality summing-up. No latitude, along the lines that the jury will have listened carefully to all the evidence without careful exposition of the relevant evidence, will be permitted, although there are few judicial advocates in favour of abolishing the summing-up of the facts to the jury. An additional requirement will be for the judge at the conclusion of the summing-up to formulate specific questions, to which the jury will be required to provide yes-or-no answers. Some judges already do provide short questionnaires. Directions on the law should likewise invariably be reduced to writing and shown in advance to advocates.

The future survival of the jury system is nevertheless clearly under threat from the new legal order of the Human Rights Act 1998 and the necessity to provide reasons as an ingredient of a fair trial. The alert has been given by the European Court in *Taxquet v Belgium* in 2011,[20] without taking sides on the precise meaning of 'mode of trial'. For now, trial by jury survives, so long as it provides a 'fair trial'.

The jury is the highpoint, the apotheosis, of amateurism. As such, it is potentially a recipe for incompetence and unbridled bias. Civilised systems of criminal justice increasingly demand professionalism from those operating the trial process. I do not mean to be contemptuous of the amateur's ability to judge human conduct. It is only that the task of evaluating evidence in the courtroom is a job

---

[20] (2012) 54 EHRR 26.

for professionals, not for occasional amateurs. It is the insistence on judiciality (behaving as a judge).

Any change to trial by judge without jury, if it comes at all, will inevitably be slow in its advent. Already it can be substituted if there is evidence of 'jury tampering'. The British are likely for years ahead to remain wedded to the institution, but the cornerstone of jury trial is being gradually chipped away. The masonry is gradually losing its angularity, to the point where the new surface will uncover optional modes of criminal trial. We need to start educating the British public that the gradual dismantling, or even ultimate disappearance, of its cherished institution will not be disastrous. It will in fact bring clarity and purpose to a civilised process of ensuring justice to both prosecutor and prosecuted. True justice must be even-handed.

Since Government has no specific interest in the prosecution of crime, other than to bring offenders to justice on behalf of victims and society generally, the judge cannot properly be seen as favouring the Crown rather than the accused in the dock. There is no basis for imputing perceived bias, one way or another. Individual prejudice and preconception is readily avoidable by the precepts of judiciality. It may be that where the offence charged is one of the crimes against the State (e.g. the Official Secrets Act), civil liberties might at least dictate a choice of trial by judge alone or a jury of 12 lay persons. That apart, we should begin to modify the system of jury trial, at least by developing the waiver, giving a choice to the accused of the mode of his or her trial. Another modification should be the change to trial by special tribunal for serious fraud cases for reasons of economy of resources and time, as well as to remove the strain on jurors; they will at least serve to demonstrate the validity of professionalism in criminal justice. And if the police evidence of intimidation and harassment of jurors and witness is valid, is not the example of the Diplock courts sufficient to justify trial by judge alone?

Trial by judge alone, in restricted classes of case, may establish whether the lay element in the judge/jury system does provide added value to criminal justice. If so, there may be room, particularly in complex fraud cases, for a tribunal composed of judge and specialist assessors as the joint decision-makers. Other modes of trial, compliant with Article 6, ECHR, might also merit consideration.

These modifications of trial by judge and jury for indictable offences are modest inroads to the system. Far from the introduction of a 'two-tier', discriminatory procedure, the comparison might be highly informative and evocative, even in the absence of any social research into the inner (secretive) workings of juries; at least judge-alone trials cannot be excluded from research. Rhetorical statements, from Sir William Blackstone to Baroness Kennedy of the Shaws QC, should, at long last, be put on trial, not by counter-rhetoric but by empiricism alone.

The jury is an essential part of the trial. As such, it is subject to the rules of contempt of court that govern us all, in particular those whose job it is to observe and comment. If, argumentatively, the jury represents the public in the democratic process that notionally gives the public a stake in the serious (95 per cent) criminal trial, how does it work? Recent research has uncovered evidence that some jurors need a good deal more guidance and assistance in the forensic role. There is a growing experience about how the jury should govern its role and the method used by jurors to deliberate their decision-making with their colleagues (strangers, but at least temporarily thrown together in concentrated association). Commentators have loosely described their conduct as a 'perfect storm' for committing contempt of court. The advent of the internet and associated devices for taking account of information from sources other than those strictly advised within the confines of the unusual ethos of the institutional courtroom must also be taken into account. It all adds up to a potential distortion of the trial, anathema to the student of the trial process.

If, but only if, there was some method whereby the jury's verdict could be assessed by the articulated process of stating the reasons for its decision, the aspect of amateurism would be largely addressed, or at least sufficiently rectified as an instrument of a 'fair trial'. But without the means of assessing the validity or reliability of the jury, the principles of accountability and responsibility remain uncertain, even unpredictable. Their absence is crucial towards only value judgment. That is why the existence for over 30 years of the practice of terrorist-style trial in Northern Ireland (the Diplock Courts, a system of trial by judge alone) is so valuable as a research tool to the purposes of the jury. The inability to acknowledge, let alone study, the Diplock Courts is a serious omission. The elite selection of judges in that provincial territory of the United Kingdom suggests that juryless trials, albeit in a limited area of criminality, have proved a satisfactory mode of trial. A review and comparative study are desperately needed.

Until society engages seriously in comparative studies – not just with Northern Ireland, but with other countries of Europe, subject to the universal rule in Article 6 of the European Convention of Human Rights – we are depriving ourselves of much valuable material to adjudicate reasonably on the future of the mode of trial in criminal justice. We must not remain a country that functions without any official accountability or responsibility that all other public institutions correctly submit to.

One might add that a jury in the European system is a denial[21] – true, this is very theoretical – of the independence of the trial judges. By abdicating the ultimate verdict of an otherwise fair trial, the judge negates the essence of his function – to pass judgment on the individual facing the criminal charge.

At heart there is a problem for the modern democrat. What mode of criminal trial is constructed by a civilised country to constitute a fair trial? It has quintessentially to be conducted by an independent and impartial member of an established judiciary. He or she (with or without assessors) must decide the case 'according to the evidence admissible in the courtroom' and not otherwise. The overwhelming difference is the contrasting attitude to the formal setting. The professional lawyer is imbued with the sense of judiciality by legal training and education. The juror lacks such a skill and encounters the forensic function only exceptionally: he or she cannot be expected to imbibe the ethos of testing the credibility and reliability of witnesses to the same judicial standard. The professional opposes the populist; the latter is the amateur *par excellence*.

---

[21] Perhaps the trial in South Africa of Oscar Pistorius by Judge Thokozile Masipa as a judge alone is not theoretical and may explain why many lawyers have been critical of her reasoned articulated decision. See the article by Frances Gibb, a prominent correspondent and reliable reporter on legal affairs, in the *Times*, 18 September 2014.

10

English Juries on Trial

TRIAL BY JURY in the United Kingdom, embedded in the
culture of criminal justice, is unlikely to implode in the near
future. The populace is devoted to the process, despite some
unceasing questioning of its validity. But the problem of a civilised
system of sustaining the society's criminality frequently misses an
essential element of the jury process which is essentially English.
The verdict of the trial is demonstrably that of the jurors, but unlike
the American system, the jurors' decision is arrived at unanimously
(but with a potential verdict of 10 votes to two, if unanimity is
impossible to reach), and is a composition exercise. The fact-
finding process is subject to two conditions. First, the jurors are
bound to take their instructions on the relevant law from the judge.
Since we do not know whether juries faithfully accept this legal
direction, we cannot say that they perform their duty.

There has long been a suspicion that the jury can, and occasionally
does, reject the law; it acts perversely. Never mind the jury acting
independently of their legal duty, many proponents of the jury system regard this wayward function as a positive aspect. It is claimed
as a distinct impression of the public's will that its lay representatives should defy the rule of authority. So much is claimed for the
return of a perverse verdict that there has grown up a respectable
doctrine of 'jury nullification'. Somehow there is a constitutional
principle that endorses the verdict of the jury, even if it appears that
it totally rejects the law, or indeed defies the effect of inevitable reasoning of the evidence. A proposal by Sir Robin Auld in his *Review
of the Criminal Courts* in 2001 recommended that there should be a
right of appeal against a perverse ruling by a jury. It failed to persuade
the Government of the day, and there was a sigh of relief from the
devotees of the system.

Even if the jury loyally applies the relevant law, it is still not alone
in evaluating the facts. The second condition of the fact-finding process is that the jury is required to listen and inwardly assess the
views expressed by the judge in the summing-up of the evidence.

While the summing-up should be neutral, there is nothing to deter the judge from expressing a view that might strike a chord with all or some of the jurors. The decision-making process is therefore a mixture of views from the Bench and the jury room, but achieved by an unknown process. The alchemy of judicial evaluation and juror assessment is achieved in separate roles. Over the years, the judges in the appeal court have focused further on the direction given to jurors. This has led to the development of supplying the jury with a questionnaire that is designed to assist the route towards sound reasoning. Simple answers to questions are given in aid of the monosyllabic verdict. The problem is, how can the court otherwise discern the combined effect of eliciting the evidential material? Access to the internet, seeking information beyond the evidence adduced in the courtroom to the trial process, has brought in complications. Courts are exercising contempt powers if jurors are known to have acted unlawfully. The ambit of information permissible to the confines of the evidence at trial is a continuing concern. It exercises the judges in administering a fair trial for both the accused and the prosecutor.

It is the duty of Government, subject to the Human Rights Act 1998, enacting Article 6 of the European Convention on Human Rights, that it does no more than generally require a mode of trial that is fair. So far, Strasbourg has interpreted that the trial is fair without deciding on the particular mode of trial. If all it requires is that every aspect of the process must accommodate the principle of a reasoned verdict, the fact that the English jury is not required to deliver expressly a reasoned verdict does not invalidate its one-word verdict. Each case has to be tested according to its own facts. Hence implicit reasoning can supply the absence of an explicit verdict that is unreasoned.

The European Court of Human Rights has left the door open on the prescribed mode of trial. It says that there is no stated requirement in the Convention that jurors should give their reasons for the verdict, and that trials by non-professionals who decide cases unreasonably are valid. Reasoned decisions form part of the guarantee of a fair trial. Nevertheless, the requirements of a fair trial must be maintained; the public must be able to understand that the decision has been safeguarded from any condition that betokens unfairness. The result is thus essentially episodic. Fairness must be assessed, on a case-by-case basis, on the peculiarities of the system that allows verdicts to be unaccompanied and unarticulated from the totality of the proceedings. The reasoned verdict can thus be inferred. The absence of a definitive ruling on the mode of trial thus prompts the question, what next? The jury system is left unquestioned, but it cannot be inviolate. Reform instinctively and increasingly beckons the case for some mixture, reciprocated by a separate process of reform, of the binary systems of criminal justice within the European Union. If nothing else, the practice of extradition within the European Union, backed by the European Warrant of Arrest, has signalled a desire for reciprocity.

The desire to produce a fair trial for every accused continues to encounter problems in the world of modern technology. In March 2014 at the annual meeting of JUSTICE, the incoming Lord Chief Justice, Lord Thomas, in his *Reshaping Justice*,[1] alluded to the need for revising the use of juries in serious fraud cases. If the judicial alert to such change does not resonate with traditional voices, the move towards modification has led to official studies on the issue of mixed tribunals.

[1] http://www.judiciary.gov.uk/wp-content/uploads/JCO/Documents/Speeches/lcj-speech-reshaping-justice.pdf.

11

The Ambit of Innocence

THE PRESUMPTION OF INNOCENCE

C LICHÉ HAS IT that you are 'innocent until proven guilty'.
Unfortunately (or perhaps not) the maxim is only legally, not
factually true, as one utters it in social terms. It is better to
reserve the phrase for use in the criminal law, and to understand
how civilised society describes allegations of suspicious behaviour.
As Roy Hattersley wrote so engagingly, listening to what people say
is important, but it provides no answer to a problem that the law
prescribes. To explain the law, one must lapse into legal language.
The law regards a person as innocent only from the moment the
accused faces trial; it ends with the conclusion of the court proceedings.

The conclusion of a criminal trial is that an acquittal of a criminal
offence, whether by the trial jury or by the Court of Appeal in quashing a jury conviction, is of no value whatsoever in English law,
except as the result of a prosecution by the Crown; it is as lawful to
assert that an acquitted person was guilty of the offence of which he
has been acquitted as it is to make any other assertion which would
reflect on the person's reputation. In any such case, a statement
about a person's reputation – 'innocent until he is proved guilty' –
is legally meaningless. The maker of such a statement can be sued
for libel, and has the same burden of proving the truth of the assertion; the fact of the acquittal is irrelevant. The only qualification is
that, by section 4 of the Defamation Act 2013, Parliament has now
added a public interest defence, primarily but not exclusively in
respect of responsible journalism. How the law comes to such a
result has the consequence that the phrase is only evidential; it
applies only within the system of criminal justice on the question
of a presumption of innocence until proven guilty.

The Criminal Appeal Act 1968, by section 2(3), provides that 'an
order of the Court of Appeal quashing a conviction shall, except
when under section 7 below the appellant is ordered to be retried,

operate as a direction to the court of trial to enter, instead of the
record of conviction, a judgment and order of acquittal'. The successful applicant is therefore in the same position as if he had been
acquitted by a jury, no more and no less. The acquitted person
cannot be tried for the offence of which he has been acquitted, or
for any offence of which a jury could have convicted him on that
indicted. This is known as the double jeopardy rule, which can now
be inapplicable in the limited and unusual case where the Crown
has fresh evidence of which it could not have had any knowledge at
the time of the acquittal.

The law as stated is taken from a controversial passage from Lord
MacDermott in *Sambasivan v Public Prosecutor, Malaya:*[1]

> The verdict of an acquittal . . . is not completely stated by saying that the
> person cannot be tried again for the same offence. To that it must be
> added that the verdict is binding and conclusive in all subsequent
> proceedings between the parties to the adjudication. The maxim '*res
> judicata pro veritate accipitur*' is no less applicable to criminal and civil
> proceedings.

There are difficulties in reconciling this extension of the effect of an
acquittal with the decision of the House of Lords in *DPP v
Humphreys,*[2] but assuming it to be correct, it marks the limit of the
effect of an acquittal: the acquittal is binding and *conclusive
between the parties to the adjudication*, that is between the Crown
and the acquitted person. It is not binding and conclusive between
the acquitted person and anyone else, or between the Crown and
anyone else. If A has been acquitted of an offence, the Crown may
subsequently indict B for aiding and abetting, counselling or pro-
curing to commit that offence and, at the trial of B, adduce evidence
that proves that A was in fact guilty of the offence of which he has
been acquitted. A's acquittal is not admissible in the evidence at the
trial of B: *Hui Chi-Ming v R.*[3] Where A and B are alleged to have
conspired together to commit an offence, and there is evidence
against B (e.g. a confession) which is inadmissible against A, the
jury may properly convict B of conspiring with A, while acquitting
A of conspiring with B: *DPP v Shannon.*[4] This is so whether A and
B are tried together, or B is tried after A's acquittal. This all appears
to be gobbledegook, but is now entrenched. It establishes the ambit
of innocence; the law establishes it conclusively – the decision to

[1] [1950] AC 458, 474 (PC).
[2] [1977] AC 1.
[3] [1992] 1 AC 34 (PC).
[4] [1975] AC 717 (HL).

acquit has no 'after-life', unless and until there is some indicated development under Article 6 of the European Convention on Human Rights at Strasbourg.[5]

Since jurors are always directed that the jury must not convict unless they are sure of the accused's guilt, the only safe deduction from a verdict of acquittal is that the jury were not 'sure', or that they retained a reasonable doubt (the traditional formula as the test for a not-guilty verdict). A jury which is satisfied only that it is more probable than not that the accused is guilty, or even that it is highly probable that he is guilty, will acquit if, as one assumes, they follow the direction of the judge. Thus the Lord Chancellor's Law Reform Committee in 1967 on whether acquittals should be admissible in evidence rightly concluded: 'So the acquittal, if admitted for "what it is worth", would be worth nothing: not only would it have no effect on the onus of proof but it would be without any probative value'.[6] The Committee recommended that, on the grounds of public policy, defamation proceedings should be treated differently, and that proof of an acquittal should be conclusive proof of innocence. Parliament at that time did not accept the recommendation, and so the law remained the same: in *Loughams v Oldham Press Ltd*[7] the defendant in the libel action successfully pleaded the defence of justification, proving on the balance of probabilities that the claimant had committed the offence of murder. It is the same when the Court of Appeal quashes a conviction, as when a jury acquits.

FACTUAL AND LEGAL INNOCENCE

Since a change in the law in 1995 the Court of Appeal has been required to quash a conviction if it concluded that it was 'unsafe' (it had been 'unsafe or unsatisfactory'), and in any other case to dismiss the appeal. The fact that the Court quashed a conviction did not mean that they necessarily thought that the appellant was innocent of the crime. Quite the contrary: the Court may have been quite sure that he was guilty, but for some good reason have thought the conviction was 'unsafe'. That has been repeatedly stated and was best illustrated by the case of *R v Algor*,[8] when the Court quashed

---

[5] See *Allen v UK* App no 25424/09.
[6] Fifteenth Report (Cmnd 3391, 1967) para 15.
[7] [1963] CLY 2007 (QBD)
[8] [1954] 1 QB 279.

the conviction because inadmissible (yet relevant and reasonable) evidence had been admitted at trial. The Lord Chief Justice, Lord Goddard, was reported in the Times Law Report for 16 November 1953 to have said to the appellant, who was present in court: 'Do not think we are doing this because we think you are an innocent man. We do not. We think you are a scoundrel.'

The phrase is adopted historically from the English common law and today finds its declaration in Article 6 of the European Convention on Human Rights and Fundamental Freedoms, and all other international declarations of civil liberties. This states categorically that 'everyone is innocent until proved guilty': all too readily it comes tripping off the tongue. In practice it functions only evidentially. Only as and when you are charged with a criminal offence – and not before the criminal process begins to run – does it come into play. Then and only then, legal innocence is appropriately assigned to the criminal defendant. There is nothing to indicate factual innocence or non-involvement in crime. To underline the point, it is necessary to quote the opinion of our leading jurists. Most concisely and with utter clarity, the late Lord Rodger of Earlsferry said in a Scottish judgment in February 2010:[9]

> It is, of course, trite that an individual charged with a crime is presumed to be innocent until proved guilty. But that is not to say that he has to be treated in all respects as if he were an innocent person against whom no charge has been brought.

The Scots are not alone in stating the truism.

A modern description comes from Lord Justice Mantell in July 2000. Three men were freed by the Court of Appeal (Criminal Division), ruling that there had been a 'profoundly disturbing' conspiracy between police officers investigating the crimes of murder and robbery to give perjured evidence at the accused's Old Bailey trial. The Lord Justice, at the end of his judgment quashing the convictions as unsafe verdicts, said he and his colleagues were doing so 'not as a finding of innocence; far from it.' What he was saying clearly was that a criminal trial does not address the question of 'factual innocence'. It is there to determine whether the Crown has proved its case beyond a reasonable doubt. If so, the accused is found guilty – if not, the accused is found not guilty; the court makes no finding of factual innocence, since it would not fall within the ambit of purpose of the criminal law. More recently (in 2011) the judiciary similarly endorsed these sentiments. In an appeal to

---

[9] *Allison v HM Advocate* [2010] UKSC 6 [9].

the UK Supreme Court in *R (on the application of Adams) v The Secretary of State for Justice*[10] they repeated those sentiments in a case involving the payment of compensation for miscarriages of justice to anyone who had been wrongly convicted as a result of such a miscarriage, whether acquitted thereafter or not. Lord Phillips, the Court's President (although the dissidents disagreed as to whether the courts were entitled to express their views) added: 'While we are entitled to express our reasons for the result in clear and strong terms, as we have done, we cannot make a formal legal declaration of the appellant's factual innocence.' Lady Hale, in the same case, added that 'innocence as such is not a concept known to our criminal justice system. We distinguish between the guilty and the not guilty . . . irrespective of whether he is in fact innocent.' The two dissenters, Lord Brown and Lord Judge, then Lord Chief Justice, in drawing the same, vital distinction between 'factual' and 'legal' innocence, nevertheless thought that judges were restricted to deal only with the presumption of innocence in the criminal – an evidential safeguard to the accused facing a criminal charge. Lord Judge said he disagreed, and that the court is not 'entitled' to state that an appellant is 'innocent': 'The processes of the Court of Appeal do not allow for a formal declaration of factual innocence, any more than the trial process recognises a verdict of "innocent".' Lord Brown (with whom Lord Rodger agreed) added pithily that 'of course, innocence as such (factual as opposed to presumptively) is not a concept known to the criminal law . . . the criminal law deals only with the safety of convictions'. He endorsed what Lord Justice Lloyd said in 1991 when freeing the Birmingham Six after their 16 years in prison. The Birmingham Six specifically ignored the words of the Court of Appeal, that it was neither obliged nor entitled to state that an appellant was innocent. The task was simply to say whether the jury's decision at their trial should stand. The six men frequently thereafter claimed that they had been found innocent of the bombings; and they persisted in this assertion by suing or threatening to sue in libel proceedings anyone who thought differently.

The most difficulty arises where the accused successfully appeals against his conviction. Can he or she publicly pronounce to the world at large (including, persistently, the media) that he or she is innocent, factually as well as legally? Strictly speaking, the answer is no. The factual innocence is still at large, and debatable. It was

---

[10] [2011] UKSC 18.

this issue that directly engaged me personally when I wrote in 1997 about the case of the Birmingham Six. Suffice it to say, the social or public question of any citizen claiming his or her innocence, whatever the courts may have ruled, is very much up for discussion. I deal with it at the end of this chapter.

The presumption of innocence which arises when a person is charged with a criminal offence is a sacrosanct principle of criminal procedure, enshrined in the language of the Convention. Taken alone, however, Article 6(2) is susceptible to different conclusions. It provides simply that 'everyone charged with a criminal offence shall be presumed innocent until proved guilty according to law'. What does 'everyone' mean? Or does it mean everyone when charged, or likely to be charged in the future, with a criminal offence and for as long as such charges are pending? Is the presumption something that is triggered, that only becomes legally meaningful when events occur through which he is, in reality, facing or likely to face a criminal charge which has not as yet been determined? If these are more than neat philosophical questions, how they are answered is critical to any case. The free-standing, post-acquittal (thus eternally live) model of interpretation of Article 6(2) is appealing and attractive; there is some arguable support for this mode, at least where a sufficient link exists between the observations of the court after they have acquitted on the ground of the conviction being unsafe, and the criminal responsibility of the accused. Even if one adopts the overall 'fair trial' context, it reinforces the argument that, for the rest of us (not connected even indirectly with the criminal proceedings), we are not envisaged as either factually or otherwise not factually innocent. The legal (and social) reality is that there is neutrality. We are neither innocent of complicity in crime, nor guilty. What then is our status?

Our model of criminal trial is unconcerned with activities beyond the criminal process. Even if one adopts a more compelling reach, which is that the criminal court is involved in the general canon of control, there are questions as to the court's assistance to the other institutions of our society concerned with maintaining law and order. Encompassing the totality of citizenry have the courts implicitly treated us as potential offenders, and therefore not innocents? While we might like to treat ourselves as personally unaffected by the criminality among our neighbours, it is wiser not to affix labels which confer an unwanted status. For those who, inadvertently, become affected by the criminal process, there may be a case for compensation by the State. But that is a different question.

This chapter merits a footnote. On 12 July 2013 the Grand Chamber of the European Court of Human Rights, in a decision in *Allen v United Kingdom*,[11] decided that a claim to compensation for a miscarriage of justice is not covered by Article 6. But the majority of the 16 to one voters did touch on the potential for a future jurisprudence, giving a claimant some claim. It contemplated developing an 'after-life' to the concept of the presumption of innocence. If such a posthumous jurisprudence can exist, it has no logical place in the English system. Compensation for miscarriages of justice must be calculated on some other basis, and not following some obiter dicta of judges as a possible test for defects in the criminal justice system; a number of current applications are pending before the Strasbourg Court, so the story is far from being over. Innocence of crime may have a legal label beyond the evidential ambit. But how to define its breadth?

I ought simply to state why I favour strong support for the single concurring opinion of Judge de Gaetano (the Maltese representative) in the *Allen* judgment. He takes his decision on the traditional (if you like, the narrow) interpretation of the presumption of innocence. If 'innocence' – a human concept, without legal content – were at stake, a different matter would arise. A presumption of something happening does not exist alone; it is not self-standing as a principle; it depends upon the existence of a substantive rule in criminal justice; to adopt the language of the law, it is strictly evidential and depends for its life on the continued existence of a criminal charge. Once the criminal proceedings are concluded, the presumption lapses; the evidence supporting it lapses as well. There is nothing formal that revives it. Innocence is not and cannot be a legal concept, unless and until Parliament decides that it does have some effect post-acquittal.

---

[11] (2010) 51 EHRR 22.

12

'Consuming Your Own Smoke'

T O GUARANTEE A citizen a fair trial, the criminal justice system confers on the convicted person a right of appeal. If, at the conclusion of the appeal, the conviction is set aside and an acquittal is substituted, what follows? If there is finality in the criminal process, the case cannot be reopened, save only by an extrajudicial process. Until 1995, it was possible to request that the Government should refer the case back to the Court of Appeal; thereafter the convicted person has been able to take his or her case to the Criminal Cases Review Commission (CCRC). That change followed the freeing of the Birmingham Six in 1991, when the Court of Appeal (on a second reference from the Home Secretary) had quashed the convictions but had emphatically declared that the reversal of their convictions did not mean that they were 'innocent'. But, when Parliament in 1995 established the CCRC as an independent body, it related its duty *not* to assessing whether there had been a 'miscarriage of justice', but instead to reassess the case so as to decide whether the criminal proceedings would predictably have led the court to a reversal of the conviction. It focused on the criminal trial, not on any question of criminality outwith the system of criminal justice. But it is linked to compensation for the maladministration of that system.

The Criminal Appeal Act 1995 accepted a judicial view that the two grounds of appeal, 'unsafe' and 'unsatisfactory', could conveniently be expressed under the single element, that the conviction was 'unsafe'. By coalescing the two concepts, the law obscured distinction between the case of the truly innocent person from that of the person acquitted on technical or procedural grounds. The CCRC was thereby injected into the criminal justice system, and there was no scope for any finding that says that the criminal justice system miscarried. It poses the question: is there a 'real possibility' that the claimant would have been acquitted? That the two issues are intertwined is exemplified by a recent case. The two cannot be treated separately. Failures of criminal justice should instantly arouse a claim for compensation, separately assessed. To put it specifically, can the Government refuse to compensate someone for a miscarriage of justice as a violation of the claim of legal innocence, or, going further, must the person establish his factual innocence? Alternatively, should the task of determining compensation be given, even if only advisorily, to the CCRC? That depends on the assessment of the CCRC in its work over the last two decades. The conclusion by Sir Robin Auld in his *Review of the Criminal Courts in 2001*[1] was that the general tenor of opinion was that its functioning was a success. There is nothing to qualify that sound beginning.

The distinction to be drawn between the acquittal of criminal liability by the courts and the decision as to compensation must be either that acquittal is on the merits, or that it relates to some function of the criminal procedure, irrespective of merit. The latter test must apply if, on policy terms, the administrator of criminal justice has caused the acquittal. Only an acquittal on fresh evidence (if differing from that adduced at trial) should be treated differently.

Compensation to those alleging punishment as a result of the investigation of criminality is a matter of government response for anything that it does in public law. Its obligation to provide compensation for the administration of criminal justice stems from section 133 of the Criminal Justice Act 1988, which complied with international obligations. That it enacted a limited role in Article 6 of the European Convention on Human Rights (according a fair trial) is exemplified by the failure of the UK to sign or accede to Protocol No 7 of the European Convention on Human Rights, which is replicated in Article 133. The UK has no need to compensate a person who has suffered punishment as a result of a criminal conviction.

Is there any scope left for extending the complaint to matters beyond the purview of the CCRC? The dilemma is complicated by the insertion of compensation 'for the miscarriage of justice', which divided the nine-judge Supreme Court of the UK (by five to four) in *Re Adams*.[2] The majority's finding was that there remains unresolved the question of what may or may not be provided in civil compensation arising from the same facts that gave rise to the criminal prosecution and investigation. To say that, it all depends on how you ask the question: does the question impute a lack of actual criminality (innocence of a criminal event), or is it limited to the

---

[1] *Review of the Criminal Courts of England and Wales* (London, HMSO, 2001).
[2] [2011] UKSC 18.

criminal justice system (a legal process)? The fact is that a 'fair trial' has no part to play in claims for civil compensation, whether the claim is the outcome of acquittal in criminal proceedings, or where no criminal proceedings have ever been initiated.

Following the decision of the Supreme Court in *Adams* on the ambit of 'miscarriage of justice' in section 133, the Government objected to the test at common law, whether it had been established beyond reasonable doubt that no reasonable jury would have considered awarding compensation. The ostensible reason was that the test would allow a claim for compensation to be brought by the person whose conviction had been quashed on appeal because of some failure or fault in the handling of the prosecution. When the Anti-Social Behaviour, Crime and Policing Bill was produced, a miscarriage of justice was defined as a case where a new, or newly discovered, fact shows beyond reasonable doubt that the applicant was innocent. An objection was raised by the House of Lords, on the grounds that English courts do not establish innocence. Any acquittal operates only within the confines of the criminal trial. The Government acknowledged this, replacing the offensive words 'was innocent' with the phrase 'did not commit'. From March 2014 on, the claimant for compensation has to show that he did not commit the offence with which he was charged and ultimately acquitted. But what's the difference, even though the language differs? Whatever is the test, there will always be the issue for the compensating authority (the Minister) to determine the right test to decide the entitlement. The Minister will usually not be aided by what the criminal court judges will have said. In the case of the Birmingham Six, moreover, Lord Justice Lloyd specifically said that the question of innocence was a separate constitutional question:

> Nothing in section 2 of the [Criminal Appeal Act 1968], or anywhere else obliges or entitles us to say whether we think that the appellant is innocent. This is a point of great constitutional importance. The task of deciding whether a man is guilty falls on the jury. We are concerned solely with the question whether the verdict of the jury can stand.[3]

The theory is that it has never been the function of Ministers to pronounce upon whether a person has committed a crime. Only as and when a person is prosecuted for a crime are the courts exclusively performing the task of determining whether the accused is guilty or not. For the rest, the question is only of factual innocence.

---

[3] *R v McIlkenny* [1991] 93 Cr App R 287, 311.

The European Court of Human Rights[4] has endorsed the English approach to the test for compensation for miscarriages of justice. Civilised legal systems cannot ignore the clichéd test to which I referred at the start of the last chapter. One senses that the requirement that a person charged with a criminal offence 'shall be presumed innocent until proven guilty' may possess an after-life when compared with civil proceedings where no criminal prosecution has been initiated.

---

[4] *Allen v UK* on 12 July 2013 endorsed the English test: see *R (Ali and others) v Secretary of State for Justice* [2013] EWHC 72 Admin.

13

Crime and Justice: a Shift in Perspective

T HERE IS NO such thing in England and Wales as a criminal justice system; only a series of government departments and public agencies that contribute to a process of justice in response to a variety of criminal events. Each contributor has its own budget, and vies competitively for public funding; each has its own agenda for its functioning towards declared aims of criminal justice. Inevitably, there is much overlapping of functions (if not duplication) and even helpful collaboration. Each contributor is answerable and accountable to an arm of government, and ultimately to Parliament.

In their impressive work, *Where next for Criminal Justice?*,[1] David Faulkner and Ros Burnett argue that when the criminal justice services had to be managed in accordance with the Government's Financial Management Initiative, together with policies for efficiency, economy and effectiveness in the 1980s, a system evolved. Nevertheless they recognise the view of the criminologist Lucia Zedner in her essay 'Reflections on Criminal Justice as a Social Institution',[2] that criminal justice is 'no more than a series of largely independent organisations with different cultures, professional ethos and practices which come together and interact only insofar as is necessary to pursue their respective goals'. System or no system, the independence of the judiciary and the operational independence of the criminal court of trial dictates (as I will demonstrate) a separate identity.

The aim of the present chapter is thus to examine the role and function of the criminal courts, *simpliciter*, and their relationship

---

[1] D Faulkner and R Burnett, *Where next for Criminal Justice?* (Cambridge, Policy Press, 2012) 32.
[2] L Zedner, 'Reflections on Criminal Justice as a Social Institution' in D Downes, D Hobbs and T Newburn (eds) *The Eternal Recurrence of Crime and Control* (Oxford, OUP, 2010) 69–94.

to the other agencies contributing to the overall public response to criminality. The focus is the trial of accused persons for the commission of a criminal offence. The prosecution of an offender is prescribed by Article 6 of the European Convention on Human Rights, whose language and purpose is pure English common law. Our system of trial by judge and jury is fully compliant with the Convention, as the recent decision of the Grand Chamber of the European Court of Human Rights in *Taxquet v Belgium*[3] demonstrated. The defendant is entitled to receive a fair trial in public before an independent and impartial tribunal, within a reasonable time-frame. The trial (at least, the English mode of criminal trial) has two distinct parts: determination of guilt or innocence, and sentencing. Since the sentence is dependent on a verdict of guilt (which alone legitimises the disposal of the convicted person through a selection of penal sanctions), the prime focus of this chapter is the former aspect. Prosecution of the offender with a view to conviction is all-important. Sentencing of those found guilty is ancillary to the trial process, and calls for appropriate disposal by the trial judge alone. (Strictly speaking, the jury has no role to play in determining the penal disposal of the convicted person.)

At the outset it is necessary to consider comparatively the basic models of criminal trial within the criminal processes of the Member States of the Council of Europe. It is, however, neither appropriate nor fully accurate to separate the judicial systems of the world into common law and civil law jurisdictions, any more than to divide them between those that observe, on the one hand, adversarial/accusatorial traditions (favoured by Anglo-Saxon systems) and, on the other hand, those that are organised according to the inquisitorial model which favours either a professional tribunal or a court of professional judge and lay members. Such a binary vision is gradually adapting to borrowings that increasingly have a tendency to render the two main models more like each other. But while the dissimilarities remain a stumbling block, there is, I venture to think, a consensus of principles encompassed in modern criminal justice that renders the traditional labelling of the modes of trial by practitioners and commentators unhelpful and unrewarding. Under the aegis of the European Court of Human Rights (the international judicial arm of the Council of Europe) with its explicit recognition of the margin of appreciation accorded to the criminal jurisdiction of the Member States, there is now (in the twenty-first

---

[3] [2010] ECHR 1806.

century) a discernible commonality of purpose in responding to crime. Accepting that commonality, my starting point is the jurisprudence and practice of the English criminal court.

It is a common, if not universal, claim of judges and criminal law practitioners that they are agents of crime control. To provide an example (Barbara Wootton taught us all that to make any generalisation, you need at least two examples) I rely on only one typical, lawyerly statement from the most liberal judge of our time. In *R v Powell and another*,[4] Lord Steyn declared that criminal justice 'exists to control crime'. (One should observe that New Labour upgraded crime prevention as the main purpose, as distinct from the administration of criminal justice.) Their Lordships in *Powell* were dealing, not very satisfactorily, with the case of joint criminal enterprise where a number of individuals (often organised gangs of youths) had been engaged in violent conduct that had resulted in fatal injury inflicted by one (often unidentified) individual with others participating in various degrees of culpability for the victim's death. The reach (indeed, overreach) of the criminal law to secondary liability in homicide on those participating in violent behaviour often discloses a pronounced judicial desire to affix criminalisation beyond what is either necessary or just. The assumed controlling of criminal conduct through the instant trial dictates an enlargement of criminal responsibility to secondary offenders – an undeclared claim to control of crime in society generally. It is transparently all part of the judicial attitude that reflects its purpose in deterring criminal behaviour by potential offenders.

A more recent example of judicial outreach to meet the perceived requirements of public policy is the Supreme Court decision in *R v Gnango*.[5] The facts were decidedly odd, but simple. A and B voluntarily engaged to fight out their rivalry with pistols. It was a gunfight. A fired the first shot, without effect. B retaliated; one of his bullets killed a young woman who was innocently walking home from work. B has never been found, but A was prosecuted for murder and convicted. Five senior judges in the Court of Appeal quashed the conviction, on the basis that it was impossible to hold A liable for the unlawful killing of the victim. Of the seven justices in the Supreme Court, only Lord Kerr agreed with the Court of Appeal that on orthodox principles there was no room for extended secondary liability, because any agreement that A and B may have

---

[4] [1999] 1 AC 1, 14-15. The case was refined in *R v Rehman* by the House of Lords.
[5] [2011] UKSC 59.

had did not sensibly include agreement that B should shoot at A. A could be guilty only if he aided, abetted, counselled or procured B in the killing of the victim, who was an innocent bystander. It was obvious that A was not a principal, as he did not actually kill the victim. This was not obvious to the other judges, who in a variety of legalistic principles about joint enterprises were hell-bent on extending the law, for policy reasons. In essence they thought that anyone who participates in serious public disorder runs the risk of liability for lethal consequences, whoever is the author of the killing. The net of criminal liability is thus thrown wide open.

Lord Phillips and Lord Judge, with Lord Wilson agreeing, took the extremely pragmatic approach of saying that it matters not whether A was a principal or a secondary party, he and B both acted dangerously in a public place and each should be held accountable for the death of the victim. Either could have killed someone and it was just fortuitous that the person who fired the fatal shot was B. These judges, and Lord Dyson, preferred the secondary liability route to responsibility, but they agreed with Lords Brown and Clarke that principal liability could also be used as the basis for liability. Is it right that you can just pluck somebody out of an unruly mob and say that this person could easily be the one who caused the relevant harm, and that he should therefore be held responsible for it, even if it is known that he did not actually do it himself? Can you pretend that he intentionally assisted or encouraged the commission of an offence, when there is no evidence of him meaning to help or encourage its commission? The law must further the interests of the community, but there must be a rational, formalist basis for attributing responsibility for crime. Otherwise we will have a society in which judges can simply say that we should not let a defendant off, so we will hold him liable. Once again, our highest judges are making a mess of a civilised system of criminal justice. They see themselves as instruments of crime control; their aim is chimerical.

CRIMINAL JUSTICE AND CRIME CONTROL

The rationale of English criminal justice is quite to the contrary. Crime control by courts is not, and cannot be, an instrument of criminality in the community, other than as satisfaction to the instant victim (if identifiable). The English model of criminal justice is wedded to the adversarial system of due process and does

not contemplate crime control, other than as a by-product of individual penal sanctions. Given exaggerated claims of general deterrence from sentencing (the more severe, the greater the deterrent
effect, it is rashly claimed) the criminal process has in the past
remained stubbornly unresponsive to any external considerations
of social control. The contemporary outcrop of terrorism has
implanted in the minds of criminal courts their contribution to
public safety. But social control and public safety are not, historically, features of a fair trial.

Fitzjames Stephen wrote in 1883[6] that 'the object of the lawmaker
was rather to reconcile antagonists upon established terms than to
put down crimes by the establishment of a system of common law
as we understand the term'. And so, broadly speaking, the adversarial trial procedures remain in place, despite some powerful
onslaughts from prestigious sources. Jerome Frank, a judge of the
famous US Second Circuit Court of Appeal and a prominent figure
among the American realist school of jurisprudence in the twentieth century, wrote in *Courts on Trial*[7] that the Anglo-Saxon system
subscribed to a fight theory of justice, rather than a truth theory. The
criminal process was and is distinctly not a search for the truth
about a criminal event but, far too often, a golden opportunity for
defence lawyers to conceal the truth, a method of trial that permits
the defence advocate to throw up a smokescreen in front of the jury;
what Jerome Frank epitomised as the equivalent of throwing pepper
in the eyes of a surgeon performing an operation on his patient. The
trial is to ascertain the guilt or innocence of the accused according
to a process that is fair in its procedural rules. It might (or might
not) produce the right result; the advocates do not have to prescribe
to a truthful outcome.

Students of the criminal law are familiar with the writings of
another distinguished American commentator, Professor Herbert
Packer. He suggested that society may adopt one of two models of
criminal justice – the crime control model and the due process
model – which are founded on two discrete value systems. The
crime control model places a premium on the effective and efficient
processing of criminal events so as to optimise society's efforts to
exert a dampening influence on the perceived burgeoning rate of
crime. The due process model assumes the existence of the control
functions outside the jurisdiction of the criminal courts, but it

---

[6] JF Stephen, *A History of the Criminal Law of England* vol 3 (London, Macmillan,
1883).

[7] J Frank, *Courts on Trial* (Princeton, Princeton University Press, 1949) 80–102.

focuses mainly, if not exclusively, on demanding justice for the individual offender facing loss of liberty. Justice to the instant victim and to the public, by catching criminals and punishing them, is at best relegated to an ancillary role. Increasingly, however, there is a public demand to modify the due process model so as to take account of a social policy of remedying harm done to victims and for providing protection to the vulnerable public. The pressures for criminal justice to supply satisfaction other than to the immediate contestants will, if given effect to, distort the existing mode of trial.

There are three parties to criminal proceedings – the court, the prosecution and the defence. Witnesses (including the victims of criminal events) are not parties to the trial process, providing only evidential material to the court. The essential, residual difference between the adversarial and inquisitorial systems of criminal justice lies in the role and function of the court in relation to the two other parties; prosecutor and accused remain adversaries, whichever system of criminal procedure and trial is adopted. The Royal Commission on Criminal Justice (1991–93) declined to recommend any fundamental shift away from the principles of an adversarial-based system, but it considered there was scope to widen the judicial involvement in the pre-trial process, as well as the trial process, in order to achieve greater efficiency in the disposal of the caseloads of criminal courts. Legislation implementing a scheme whereby judges are required to hold hearings before trial in order to clarify the issues at trial has been a significant development in court management. As Professor John Jackson noted in his inaugural lecture as Professor of Public Law at Queen's University Belfast on 4 February 1997, there were moves afoot to encourage judges to shed their traditional role of umpire, in favour of a greater managerial role; by the beginning of the twenty-first century, court management in criminal proceedings is emerging slowly. As such, it would be merely a shift in court management, not an inroad into the established system of trial by jury. (Recent improprieties by jurors have given rise to a questioning of the integrity of the jury system.) Given this restrictive function of criminal justice, can the civil process be used, either in substitution for, or at least in aid of, criminal justice? I defer consideration of that question.

To return to the nature of the trial process, witnesses to the criminal event and other evidence are merely the instruments for the actors in the criminal proceedings to use in pursuance of their respective, adversarial functions. Only a fraction of the victims of crime become involved in the criminal process beyond the stage of investigation by the police or some other agency of law enforcement. For the most part criminal justice bypasses the victims of crime.

The evidence about criminal activity strongly – even overwhelmingly – suggests that criminal justice policy and practice can have only, at best, marginal effects on crime levels. As Professor Robert Reiner points out,

> the police-recorded statistics are problematic, because of the so-called 'dark figure' of unrecorded crime. In the well-worn metaphor, the recorded rate represents only the tip of the iceberg of criminal activity (and, *a fortiori*, culpable harm). At issue is what we can learn about the totality from the part that is visible.[8]

Even the most reliable statistics elicited in the British Crime Survey, which are based on the incidence of crime by victims, offer only an alternative source of data capable of mapping trends in interpersonal violence. Victimless crimes, like drug trafficking offences, are not recorded – and many other crimes go publicly unnoticed. It is, therefore, unsafe if not unwise for those engaged in social policy to do more than take note of apparent trends (both upwards and downwards) in criminal activity. That criminal justice policy should be formulated on such deficient evidence violates the fundamental principle of evidence-based policies. And when it comes specifically to fashioning the role of the criminal courts, with their stated objective of punishing the guilty, even greater caution should be employed. Punishment by the State as a moral response to wrongdoing is a dubious policy. As Professor Reiner rightly observes, 'there are both pragmatic and ethical grounds for not seeing criminal justice as central to the control of crime.'[9] Just so; indeed, criminal justice is at most peripheral to the control of crime, even though the populace fondly believes that criminal justice is society's revenge for crime.

It is necessary therefore to construct proposals for the support and protection of victims beyond the bounds of criminal justice. Victims of crime are in need of comfort, aid and protection immediately consequent upon the criminal event and not delayed while the criminal process, if any, runs its unpredictable course. The broad areas of need are: receipt of information from the official agencies of crime control of their response to the criminal event; monetary compensation for injury or harm caused by the event; and

---

[8] R Reiner, *Law and Order: an Honest Citizen's Guide to Crime and Control* (Cambridge, Polity Press, 2007) 46.
[9] ibid 11.

the ongoing social support of bereaved families of homicide victims and others suffering long-term traumata. There are other issues of secondary victimisation, including financial hardship and health problems which must be addressed through social services and healthcare systems, loss of employment and housing. The due process model of the criminal court is not structured to take care of these needs for victims and for the safety and security of the community disturbed by criminal activity. Victim Support has recently (December 2010) introduced a national homicide service, supplied by Victim Support volunteers, to support secondary victims of homicide in coping with their bereavement – an example of public support in pursuance of social (*not* criminal) justice.

Given the nature of the basically unreconstructed adversarial contest, the system can never hope to deliver justice other than, in the restricted sense, to the individuals involved directly in the criminal proceedings and, conceivably, to the immediate community affected by the criminal behaviour. Indeed, it has (as I have explained) never pretended to lead to the truth about the circumstances leading up to, or even surrounding a criminal event, only a highly institutionalised truth, requiring the prosecutor to prove the case according to strict rules as to the admissibility of evidence and the imposition of a high standard of proof beyond reasonable doubt (to use the outworn formula, now to be mouthed to the jury as 'certain so that you are sure'). Ensuring justice in the widest sense would be possible only as and when the system acknowledged the existence of, and paid respect to both the interests of victims of crime and of the public generally. But a criminal trial is definitionally not a public inquiry; it has its own institutional function.

THE INTERESTS OF THE VICTIM

The need to acknowledge victimisation is beginning to dawn in quite a few jurisdictions of modern European countries. I pause only momentarily to consider why it is that in the last quarter of the twentieth century the 'victim support' movement began to impinge upon the consciences of the administrators of criminal justice, although the scheme of compensation for victims of violent crime, introduced in 1964, is traceable to the writings of Margery Fry in the late 1950s. Historically, the introduction early in the nineteenth century of organised police forces meant that the State entered into a compact with its citizens, whereby the latter agreed to forgo self-help and the former undertook to protect the citizen through policing, and to deal appropriately with the offender. According to such social contract theorists as Hobbes, men (and women) surrendered their rights to self-help in return for the sovereign's protection and by such means the State, through its laws, became the guarantor of the individual's freedom from assaults on property or person (I put the two in that order because initially the criminal law was designed to protect the propertied classes). It is not a large step further to assume that the prescriptions of the State, as embodied by law, have a legitimacy, grounded upon its authority alone. Thus by the middle of the nineteenth century the isolation of the victim from the criminal process by a male-dominated justice system was complete. Only the existence of the victim's right to bring a private prosecution has survived to give the victim any formal recognition as a party in criminal proceedings. And even today the right to a private prosecution is highly qualified and is even largely theoretical. The power of the Director of Public Prosecutions to take over a prosecution and then drop the proceedings has rendered the private citizen's right to prosecute obsolescent, if not obsolete. Even if the citizen is exceptionally permitted to pursue a criminal prosecution, it is prohibitively expensive and fraught with uncertainty in the result. The case in 1997 of Stephen Lawrence in South London was an example of such a frustrated private prosecution. Strangely, the Law Commission gave support to the continuation of private prosecutions, in recommending a rationalisation of the statutory requirements of prior consent from the Attorney-General or the Director of Public Prosecutions. The fact that the public prosecutor can nowadays judicially review any improper exercise of his discretionary or legal powers suffices to render the private prosecution redundant. It should be pensioned off by Parliament.

It cannot be gainsaid that victims of crime have to be reckoned with by the functions of the criminal process, aided by the civil law. The victim undoubtedly has interests that demand official recognition and protection. Compensation for the injury or loss caused has been with us for over 40 years now, but administered entirely outside the criminal justice system. Compensation for crimes of violence has, since 1996, been put on a statutory footing, administered by a government agency on a tariff system. But there are now efforts to encompass the victim within the criminal process. There are at present, as I see it, two solutions being proffered.

The first is prominently visible by practical reform of existing criminal justice. The point is made that there is an over-emphasis on the rights of the accused. Provisions such as limitations on the consequences of insisting on the right to silence, or the greater disclosure of the accused's defence in advance of trial are clearly attempts to redress an inequitable balance. It is claimed that society is over-protective of the offender. The shift towards easing the prosecutor's task of convicting the supposedly guilty is an essay in assuaging the victim's irritation at a system that so often fails to bring offenders to justice. The Criminal Procedure and Investigations Act 1996, moreover, has been widely thought to favour unduly the prosecution in the requirement of disclosure to the defence of relevant material. I do not wish to follow the purpose of this solution in providing an equality of arms. It proceeds, in my view, to sustain, in essence, a criminal justice system that is rightly insistent upon a single, due process model to cope with multifarious criminal events. Availability of all relevant evidential material may require discrimination according to the nature of the criminal activity. Terrorism is one example.

The other solution is to approach the problem of crime control alongside, if not distinctly outside, the due process model of criminal justice. The fundamental principle is that one would start from the position of victims' rights, while in no way forgetting the rights of offenders in jeopardy of their liberty. There is in the dichotomy of the two models a sense that, rights being in competition, the emphasis is to focus upon those areas where the interests of victims and offenders coincide. A prime example of this line of reasoning is where reparation by the offender to the victim leads to the imposition of a more lenient treatment in the labelled offence and penalty by the criminal court. More and more, the interests of victims have been reducing the retributive element in the criminal justice system, although there may be occasional notorious cases where private revenge may surface. Reconciliation and mediation are currently being proposed as devices to circumvent the divisiveness of criminal justice. Restorative justice is the favoured theory of contemporary criminologists (it is even the flavour of the month for many reformists). But does restorative justice have any (and if so, what) role to play in the criminal trial process, or even within the spectrum of the criminal process as a whole? Restorative justice, strictly applied, can operate in any event only at the stage of penal disposal, since it operates only as and when the offender has admitted at least involvement in the criminal event, if not legal guilt, in causing harm to the victim. Much as I favour the process of the victim and offender confronting each other (where appropriate), restorative justice belongs to the field of social action. Justice Sachs (Albie Sachs, the distinguished and recently retired member of South Africa's Constitutional Court) wisely observed in *S v M*[10] in 2007: 'Central to the notion of restorative justice is the recognition of the community rather than the criminal justice agencies as the prime site of crime control'. Like the case for attending to victims' needs, restorative justice fits more easily into the system of civil justice or, less formally, in social welfare and community care.

One thing, however, is tolerably clear. Criminal justice, as we know it, cannot provide (nor can it hope to cope with) the appropriate formulae for all, or indeed many, of the legitimate claims of victims and society. Where then do we go in search of a system of dealing with antisocial conduct which is currently labelled 'criminal'?

What do the following incidents have in common? A number of cars are stolen or vandalised in a leafy suburb of a provincial town; a child on a housing estate is discovered to have been sexually abused by a foster parent; a bunch of youths cause a serious disturbance in the village community centre; a bank clerk disappears with customers' deposits; a well-known financier is discovered to have defrauded the Inland Revenue over a number of years of substantial sums of money; a young woman is raped in an area of town notorious for the commission of sexual assaults; an aged couple are found dead in their home from severe injuries inflicted by stab wounds; a paedophile ring is uncovered in a residential hostel run by a charitable organisation; an area of town has been terrorised by persistent burglaries and witness-intimidation by a family of brothers; a supermarket finds that its losses are exceeding the acceptable slippage of 2 per cent of its stock . . . and so on and so on. What, if any, attributes do these disparate, daily occurrences, events, happenstances – call them what you will – share? True, they all indicate the commission of an offence within the country's criminal calendar; more relevantly, they present to an ordered society variegated social problems which call for variable responses from the agencies of social control. How should we as a society in fact respond? Apart from affixing on the convicted offenders the label of criminality to each of the criminal events, each of them automatically becomes susceptible to criminal justice, and then only at the stage of sentencing – itself a process that is not intrinsically judicial, but is rather administrative.

---

[10] [2007] ZACC 18.

There is no reason why all culprits should be selected for prosecution and hence squeezed into the single straitjacket of the criminal process, as we know it. Indeed, the burden of what I have to say is that there is everything to be said in favour of a selective process whereby variable criminality is assessed and evaluated with a view to differentially appropriate action. It is not simply a diversion from criminal justice, but a matter of constructing alternative ways of effective social control. To speak of crime suggests an analogy with disease, implying that crime, like disease, is a unitary phenomenon, whereas we are dealing with a variety of disparate crimes or, rather, criminal events. We should instantly appreciate that there is no single theory or practical response to all crimes (or criminal events) any more than there is a single theory or cure to be found to explain and treat all diseases. Lord Atkin once defined crime in the following terms:

> The domain of criminal jurisprudence can be ascertained only by examining what acts at any particular period are declared by the State to be crimes, and the only common nature they will be found to possess is they are prohibited by the State and those who commit them are punished. [11]

Just so, except that I would replace the word 'punished' by action on the part of society to reduce the risk of harm. We would do well if we invariably talked about crimes – criminal events, more accurately – and how society should respond to them. The abstraction of crime is an unhelpful deviance from sensible debate and dialogue.

Is it then axiomatic, as is so often assumed, that a criminal trial of any serious, or less serious offence – I take that to encompass all cases tried at the Crown Court – is a necessary prerequisite to social intervention in the offender's liberty? If the investigation of the event – how, when and why – took place first, without necessarily identifying the perpetrators (just as happens in a Coroner's Court to determine the cause of death), the proceedings would not need to be constrained by the strict rules of evidence in criminal cases, which the Law Commission proposed should be relaxed further to allow for the admissibility of hearsay evidence (enacted in the Criminal Justice Act 2003);[12] they would proceed on the basis of the civil standard of proof, the balance of probabilities; and in non-jury

---

[11] In the Privy Council case of *Proprietary Articles Trade Association v Attorney General of Canada* [1931] AC 310, 324.

[12] In July 1995 the Law Commission published *Evidence and Criminal Proceedings: Hearsay and Related Topics* (Law Com CP 138, 1995). Its final report appeared in 1997.

trial there would not need to be the inscrutable and inarticulate verdict of a jury. The county court judge would hear the case and deliver a reasoned judgment, indicating what happened, how it happened and (where necessary) who, if anyone, was responsible for the incident, together with an apportionment of any such responsibility among the participants. There are some logistical problems associated with the criminal jurisdiction, namely, bail or custody of the defendant, and the protection of witnesses. (The protection of vulnerable witnesses is currently accommodated by procedural safeguards; this may lead to the lessening of orality and a greater use of written statements.)

The complainants of the incident would be an agency, possibly the local authority, but specifically not the Crown Prosecution Service. The police would doubtless have to be the fact-gatherers, working to the orders of the complaining authority. Once the civil court's verdict was delivered, there would be time enough to consider what action, if any, should be taken against any identified culprits. The range of sanctions might conceivably be those currently available, but the decision-makers of what those sanctions should be would not be exclusively the judiciary, high or low, although the county court judge might be the appropriate chair. It would be a composite body, with a large element of the local community most affected by the disturbance. Systems outwith[13] criminal justice should be available, appropriate to the social conduct under scrutiny.

Even if we cannot in some instances dispense with the individualised justice of the due process model, or tailor it to some aspect of crime control, may we not sensibly use the civil process in favour of justice? There is, for example, clearly room for use by local authorities of their protective powers of the local citizenry under the Local Government Act 1972 to proceed by way of injunctive relief against offenders who manage to frustrate the process of criminal justice. In 1995 Coventry City Council was in possession for a whole year of an order from a High Court judge banning two brothers, who had terrorised a housing estate, from entering a defined restricted zone. The relief thereby afforded to the inhabitants was, if ephemeral, immense. The ASBO, set up by the Crime and Disorder Act 1998, proved ineffective, if only because it was framed in the context of the criminal courts. Its replacement by the device of civil injunc-

---

[13] I prefer this to 'outside', which conveys a meaning of exclusivity. 'Outwith' is meant to infer an aid to, but not part of, criminal justice.

tions seems a much more suitable means of dealing with public disorder. Civil (or social) justice is preferable to the heavy armoury of criminal justice.

Civil justice might also be made available in certain circumstances as a direct auxiliary to the criminal courts as part of a two-way process. A contemporary problem prompts the idea. Only half of the prosecutions for rape end up in a conviction. The victims of these forensic circuses have to undergo the ordeal of reliving the criminal event and frequently do not even have the satisfaction of knowing whether their version of events has been accepted by the jury, let alone the result of a favourable verdict.

The ordeal of the experience in the witness-box is frequently exacerbated by the tenor and temper of cross-examination, particularly aggravated if conducted by the alleged rapist himself, reviving the horrors of the criminal event, rather than by his advocate. The problem appears insoluble so long as the accused's right to defend himself subsists uncontrolled, or, at most, controlled only within narrow judicial constraints. A remedy may lie in a radical proposal. The proposal commended itself to Sir William Utting in his 1997 report to government, *People Like Us*, on the safeguards for children susceptible to abuse. The idea met a deafening silence.

Whenever the Crown Prosecution Service decides to prosecute an accused with rape or other serious sexual offence, there should be a prerequisite that a certificate to proceed to a criminal trial be applied for in the county court. The civil process would establish, according to the civil standard of proof, the responsibility of the defendant for the commission of the alleged criminal act. Civil liability would be the basis for the certificate, but the court would have to be satisfied that a criminal trial would be appropriate. On past records, many cases would end at the civil stage, the victim at least gaining the important satisfaction of having established her case in the courtroom. The court would always have the additional power to grant an injunction (where appropriate), and even to award damages. The grant of a certificate to proceed to a criminal trial ought to result in a high rate of conviction, thus remedying the present unsatisfactory state of a high acquittal rate. Pleas of guilt would be more forthcoming if the accused's version of the criminal event had been rejected by the certifying court. This proposal is, I think, workable, although it has resource implications for the county court.

ALTERNATIVE SYSTEMS OF CRIMINAL JUSTICE

There already exist other interesting examples of an alternative system to the process of criminal justice. I refer, first, to the powers of HM Revenue and Customs (HMRC) to administer monetary penalties, of up to three times the amount of back duty, on any taxpayer who defrauds HMRC. Prosecution by the HMRC of fraudulent tax evaders is rare, and then only to deal with a new or particularly prevalent form of revenue crime.[14] Second, the investigation and pursuit of white-collar crime is increasingly taking place away from criminal courts. A high proportion of cases being tried today by judges in the Chancery Division of the High Court are effectively criminal cases whose victims – companies and shareholders – have opted for the civil process for the recovery of property lost through fraud. The prediction is that expert consultants, composed of solicitors, accountants and ex-police officers, will in the future offer fraud investigation services. Victims will pay large fees in return for investigation. Whether the results land up in the civil or criminal courts must be a matter of speculation. But the development of private investigation connotes a shift away from the exclusivity of criminal justice. The development of the regulatory system for financial services is a welcome alternative to complex fraud trials.

The trouble about criminal justice today is that it is time-consuming; the outcome is always problematic, and the legitimised penal sanction of imprisonment is costly and cumbersome and, at most, does no more than inflict individualised, temporary incapacitation. As the former Secretary of State for Justice, Mr Kenneth Clarke, said, prison is a waste of public money. There will always be some criminal events which demand the full panoply and majesty of the criminal trial. If only for reasons of symbolism, there is a compelling need, in certain defined circumstances, for all the trappings of the criminal court to be in place – a judge endowed with the Olympian authority of the Crown, festooned with distinctive robes (and, foreseeable for years to come, the wig), sitting in a public building that evokes the might of the State. But the vast bulk of criminal cases, run-of-the-mill offences against property and the less serious offences against the person, do not call for such elaborate and fancy, hugely institutionalised response, a large proportion of which is properly handled by the magistrates' courts. (The future

---

[14] Compare the far greater number of benefit fraud cases that are currently brought to the criminal courts.

role and function of the English magistracy is due for a thorough review.) The criminal event which exposes unacceptable social conduct and legitimates control of the perpetrator by way of imposition of penal sanctions demands a much less solemn, more expeditious and simpler procedure than is exhibited by the adversarial process of criminal justice. It was Jeremy Bentham who aptly observed that substantive law, by which he meant the basic ingredients of the criminal offence, is never self-enforcing; it is sustainable only by the adjectival law of sound procedures and evidence. The adjectival segment of criminal justice is fraught with difficulties, engendered by the justifiable need to preserve the safeguards against a wrongful conviction.

Apply the alternative approach to the occasion of an affray in the local village. There may well be a case for eliciting, for public view, the circumstances leading up to and surrounding the incident. The civil process of fact-finding, stripped of any sentencing function, would more than adequately provide the forum and pointer for appropriate social action. If the identified miscreants must, for reasons of public protection, be deprived of their liberty, as opposed to any non-custodial sanction, there might have to be further safeguards built into the sentencing process to compensate for responsibility having been imposed by the lesser standard of proof than would ordinarily be a prerequisite to the penalty of imprisonment. The problem is that this process would merely tend to replicate the courts of criminal justice. A differential would need to be devised. We must not forget that many dangerous people are detained under mental health legislation without undergoing the criminal process; their discharge is controllable by resort to the administrative tribunals, the Mental Health Review Tribunals. The whole question of detention for the sole purpose of public protection needs to be examined.

Recent developments surrounding criminal justice are indicative of public unease – a better word would be 'dis-ease' – about its failure to cope with the problem of social disorder. The aim of injecting diversionary tactics into the criminal process is a recognition of a desire to escape the consequences, often unintended, of the pursuit of a criminal conviction. Probation itself was an expression of society's aim to break the iron equation between crime and punishment. The development of non-custodial penalties and forms of intermediate treatment has similarly reflected an attempt to escape the single-minded purpose of criminal justice, to punish the convicted offender. Mediation and conciliation are recent entrants onto the scene to effect avoidance of the treadmill of prosecution, trial, conviction and penal disposal.

Court-based psychiatric assessment should indicate the removal of mentally disordered persons from criminal justice and the penal system into the mental health system. The apparent clamour of victims of crime for a larger say in the process of decision-making, particularly in influencing the sentencing process, is a clear declaration of some (unquantifiable) public dissatisfaction with criminal justice. But victim support groups have generally remained neutral on questions of sentencing offenders.

Such developments as I have indicated that are afoot at present are peripheral to the main thrust of the criminal court. Rather than providing sensible alternative options of social response to the criminal events, they actually sustain activity within criminal justice. By mitigating the worst features of the process, they positively acknowledge the centrality of the courts and prisons as the instrument to be deployed initially for social control. We start from assuming imprisonment for all serious crimes as the core of the penal system and then work downwards in recognition of the need to avoid the worst effects of the inutility (over and above individual incapacitation) of incarceration.

It is time to review fundamentally the aims of criminal justice, a matter which the Runciman Commission on Criminal Justice left untouched in 1993, mainly for reasons of a restricted remit and a limited timescale for reporting to government. The Chief Constable of Kent in a seminar of the British Academy of Forensic Sciences in 1997 described the Commission's report as 'uneventful . . . in recommending nothing of fundamental significance which was not already inevitable [it] endorsed the status quo'; so matters remain largely untouched. What is needed is some theoretical underpinning to the system of social control, some alternative approach to criminality, with the corollary of a justice system tailored to meet particular forms of criminality. This is no wish for an epidemic outbreak of the itch for change – what Chief Justice Hale described three centuries ago as 'a certain restlessness and nauseousness of men in what they have, and a giddy humour after something that is new'.[15] It is a plea for a concerted search for something better than today's largely unreconstructed criminal process for which we pay dearly, with too little return for our money. Criminal justice pro-

---

[15] From 'Considerations touching the amendment or alteration of lawes', in Francis Hargrave (ed) *Collection of Tracts relative to the Law of England* Vol I (1787) 249.

vides naught for our general comfort. At best it provides a patch-work solution to individual cases brought to court, and on its past record too many miscarriages of justice – or should it be 'carriages of injustice'?

How then do we persuade today's politicians of the need for a more creative and less tramlined outlook on the problems of social control and criminal justice? How do we inculcate in those respon-sible for policy the need to employ more judicious and, where necessary, judicial means to provide justice for both the victims (the individual and the community) of crime and the offenders? The first step is to restore the erstwhile consensus among professionals and legislators in criminal justice and penal affairs. There is noth-ing to be gained from the contemporary attitudes that permit politi-cians to indulge unthinkingly in the rhetoric of law and order. Only when the bipartisan, authoritarian approach is abandoned will we be able to re-define the boundaries of criminal justice and look to civil justice to promote the prevention of crime, the reduction of reoffending and the public sense of community safety. We do not need to swallow the wholesale abolitionist case of Professor Louk Hulsman and his supporters. But we do need a distinct shift away from the deployment of criminal justice, if only because a minimal-ist approach is more likely to affect the honest politician's attitude to crime control.

Criminal courts should focus exclusively on their task of ensuring a fair trial for the contestants in their courtrooms – adherence to the precepts of due process under the authoritative guidance of Strasbourg – and abandon any notion that they are directly engaged in society's grappling with the problems of criminality. Where crim-inal justice is appropriately wheeled into place, the sole function of trial by judge and jury is quintessentially to ensure a fair trial. The task of crime control is for the civil authorities.

The new Lord Chief Justice, Lord Thomas of Cwmgiedd, has repeated the oft-quoted claim (or could it be a case of wish-fulfilment?) that sentences passed by the criminal courts were obliged to focus on the reduction of crime, including the demotic principle and the protection of the public's safety.[16] The adjudica-tion of a criminal offence and the consequential disposal of the offender was thus effected by the same tribunal as had given him 'a fair trial'. It fulfilled two separate functions, and meant to serve a

---

[16] *R v Monteiro* [2014] EWCA Crim 747, endorsing the mandatory system in cases of knife crime: *R v Povey* [2008] EWCA Crim 1261.

purpose of general deterrence. The penalty for the criminal offence operated as punishment, both reactively to the crime and prospectively to criminality. The criminal courts played their part in the governmental aim to control crime through the established doctrine of deterrence, as well as the symbolic majesty of the criminal and civil systems. It was a firm commitment to the penal policy of sentencing.

There is impeccable logic in combining both functions procedurally in the hands of the judiciary. But does that mean, further, that the identical court must perform both functions simultaneously? Punishment, whether inflicted for past crimes or for prospective delinquency, may properly be separately adjudicated upon; the detention, post-conviction, may properly be equated with a parole system, discharge and post-custodial care in the community.

14

The Magistracy – a Professional Court?

O
F ALL THE criminal trials that take place in the magistrates' courts of England and Wales (which constitute 95 per cent of all trials in the criminal courts), less than 10 per cent are tried by individual district judges (formerly, stipendiary magistrates), of whom, in 2010, there were 143 lawyers sitting full-time and 151 lawyers sitting part-time. As professional lawyers aspiring to judicial preferment, they are recruited and trained separately; they are culturally distinct from the 23,000 or so lay magistrates who sit in panels of three to try the 95 per cent of less-serious criminal cases. Generally speaking, there are no mixed criminal tribunals for adult offenders, composed of district judges and magistrates. Justices of the Peace (to give the lay magistrates their ancient title) are drawn from all walks of life, with little or no qualification in the processes of judicial behaviour. Nevertheless, by virtue of initial training and in-service tuition, many of them readily exhibit professionalism in their separate fields of endeavour. Yet there is no formal judicial disparity between the Justice of the Peace and the district judge.

Although not disqualified from appointment to the lay bench of the magistracy, lawyers are an uncommon sight among those sitting in judgment. Even those lawyers engaged in legal practice (including conceivably a Queen's Counsel, no less) may exceptionally be appointed; the only restriction is that they cannot appear as counsel in the courts where they might be asked to sit. That such a legally qualified magistrate might find himself or herself exceptionally adjudicating on a case conducted by a fellow practitioner could be avoided by instant disqualification from sitting. The odd occasion in which a legal practitioner would be one of three magistrates seems rarely to have aroused public (let alone specialist) interest; a suggestion for emulation on a regular basis has gone unheard, even unnoticed beyond the instant case.

I make these prefatory remarks as an introduction to a personal experience. From 1966 until 1981 I was that *rara avis* – a practising member of the English Bar, called by the Middle Temple in 1952, becoming a Queen's Counsel in 1970 practising largely in the field of public law, at a time when the concept of judicial review of ministerial decisions was developing as a major feature of litigation. But I anticipate my magisterial experience by describing the route to magisterial status. The description reveals the nature of the legal profession at that time and its resistance to change, either in the form of a unified system for solicitors and barristers or for a lessening of the marked difference in the attitudes of the legally qualified and those not versed in the ways of those fortunately imbued with the notion of the superior status of all English common lawyers.

When I began my career at the Bar, unlike my contemporaries in practice, I acquired no experience, let alone any expertise in the practice of the criminal law. I saw nothing of the daily fare of a magistrates' court, although I had an academic interest in the criminal process as it functioned forensically and in its investigatory powers. Thus, extramurally and extracurricularly, I had some pretensions towards the study of criminology, and more particularly the penal system. (In the 1950s, until the abolition in 1965 of the death penalty for murder, I was actively engaged in the campaign for its abolition. Homicide has remained a perennial interest.) It was as a part-time academic – I began teaching criminology to social science students in the Department of Social Administration at Bedford College, University of London – that I touched base with members of the Magistrates' Association. Kindly, I was invited to give talks to groups of magistrates up and down the country on topics that encompassed the field of crime and justice (including the punishment of offenders). I was quickly made aware of the fact that while I might possess some legal acumen, of a distinctly academic variety, I was hopelessly out of touch with the pressing problems of a magistracy that was involved daily in delivering justice as it was experienced in the courtroom. The oft-repeated remark – nearly always delivered in a friendly manner – was that, interesting as some of my remarks were, I saw only the magisterial dilemma of doing justice to the public interest and the individual defendant through tinted spectacles. It determined me to rectify the omission, were I to continue my lecturing activities.

There was another aspect to my desire to rectify my lopsided view of the criminal process as it unfolded in the magistrates' (and other) courts. The ambition among practitioners was generally to round off a career at the Bar (either criminal or civil) by becoming a judge, if not on the top rung of the judicial ladder, at least in what were, until 1971, the Assize Courts (now Crown Courts) or, more relevant to my career, in the civil courts, where judging, not by way of trial by judge and jury, was the process of finding the facts and applying the law. Yet the avenue of advancement into the judiciary provided, at that time at least, little experience of being a decision-maker. On the magisterial bench, the magistrate is the decision-maker of the factual matrix as well as conducting the process of determining guilt and punishment. Even today, the lawyer aspiring to a judgeship will, almost invariably, have spent time acting as a part-time assistant recorder or recorder. As such he will *not* be a decision-maker, but generally summing up the evidence to an expectant jury.

I had the good fortune and privilege to become acquainted with Gerald Gardiner, an outstanding lawyer who in 1964 became Lord Chancellor in the Labour Administration of Harold Wilson. I asked him if he would be prepared to appoint me to the London magistracy. He applauded my wish to broaden my experience of the criminal law in action. I was duly appointed in 1966 and even allowed to dispense with the requirement to undergo initial training. If that was a proper concession to a practising lawyer like me, I now regret it. It is as necessary for the untutored to undergo initial training, whencesoever he came in public or private life.

My first experience was sitting – at least in the early days – as a book-end of Greenwich and Woolwich Magistrates' Courts. I cannot vouch for any objections my legally unqualified colleagues had to my presence. If they thought that the qualified lawyer was an unwelcome injection into a system designed to reflect a popular outlook on criminal justice, they were kind enough not to express any degree of animosity. The process of deliberation in the justices' retiring room was usually uneventful, although I suspect strongly that my unorthodox views on penal affairs did not always accord with those of other magistrates. But my recollection is that only rarely did we impose immediate terms of custody for convicted offenders, so that I was never troubled, and did not cause trouble. But I was conscious then (as I will explain later) of the relationship between the magistrates and the justices' clerks who served ostensibly as the court's legal advisers and judicial amanuenses. That experience was to await my translation in 1969 to the City of London Magistrates' Court, sitting primarily in the Mansion House (the only building that combined an official residence for the Mayor, a courtroom, and prison cells in the basement). The change under the Justice of the Peace Act 1969 was truly innovative. Until then, for centuries, the elected aldermen of the City of London had administered the criminal jurisdiction of the city. The change was the formation of a bench of 72 justices, of whom 24 were the extant aldermen (no women at that time!). The arrangement of the municipally elected and the lay Justices of the Peace worked well enough. It seemed then, and appears now, to arouse little public concern, apart from the odd high-profile case.

It was not too long before I became, by virtue of seniority, the presiding magistrate for the day's working list. It was a peculiar feature of the City of London Magistrates' Court that by the manner of its composition, and the range of judicial fare, it provided an unusually high degree of professionalism in the performance of judicial duties in cases that reflected the criminality of a sparse residential population and a large daily peripatetic workforce. An example of this unique mixture was the last case in which I was involved. I sat with two magistrates – one, a leading liquidator and chairman of the Royal Opera House, the other (a woman) the head of the international section of Barclays Bank in the City of London.

The case was intrinsically unique. Under the Exchange Control Act 1947 (later repealed) there was an odd provision, that with the consent of the prosecutor and the accused, a magistrates' court could try an offence under the Act summarily. The monetary penalty on conviction could be up to five times the amount of money involved in the commission of the statutory offence. The case involved two stockbrokers who had engaged in a practice known in financial circles as a 'revolving-fund fraud'. The practice was to send monies whizzing around the world's financial markets, picking up in the process the dollar premium on the monies. The practice was criminal.

We sat for 30 working days; the case was expertly conducted by Treasury counsel, who regularly appeared at the Central Criminal Court at Old Bailey, and leading counsel for the two accused. At the end of the hearings, we reserved our judgment, later delivering a 45-page reasoned finding in support of a guilty verdict. We considered imprisonment unnecessary and fined the two offenders half a million pounds. We were told subsequently that, if the case had gone to the Old Bailey before a jury, it would have lasted anything up to six months. This instance of a mixed tribunal was cited approvingly by the Roskill Committee in 1984 on *Serious Fraud Trials* as an example of why the Committee's recommendation for a professional tribunal in serious fraud cases should be adopted. After the election in 1997 the Labour Government tried legislatively to substitute a mixed tribunal for trial by jury in serious fraud cases.[1] The provision in the Criminal Justice Act 2003 could be implemented only on positive motion of Parliament. It failed. The rest is history; the silence betokens an unwavering popular devotion to the system of trial by judge and jury. But the day must surely come when the time taken and the escalating costs will dictate a change. Will a revised magistracy play any part in such a development?

I must apologise for the one example I have given for pointing in the direction of a revamped magistracy of forging the link of the professional lawyer (the district judge) and the lay magistrate (the Justice of the Peace). The late Barbara Wootton, whose outstanding biography *A Critical Woman*[2] appeared in 2011, once proclaimed that for any generalisation you need at least two examples. To avoid dilation on the topic of mixed tribunals, I record that I actually sat on a second 'revolving-fund fraud' trial on the City of London Bench, and other multitudinous cases during my 12 years as a magistrate. I can say that I found the presence of two non-legally qualified magistrates almost invariably helpful, even on occasion a hearty corrective to my seemingly excessively liberal attitudes to criminal justice.

The one postscript for the magisterial experience I have described fortifies my plea for some development towards a mixed tribunal. At the end of the 30-day hearing I indicated to our justices' clerk (a man of huge experience and skill in managing a magistracy containing one or two mavericks and eccentrics) that we would be delivering a reasoned judgment, at which he metaphorically threw up his hands in horror, attesting a warning that that would be a recipe for disaster, because the accused (if guilty) would appeal to the Central Criminal Court (strictly, a rehearing before a circuit judge and two magistrates from the London magistracy), to which I politely pointed out that if we were wrong in our reasoned judgment, we jolly well ought to be appealed. In fact there was no appeal; the two stockbrokers were later struck off the list at the Stock Exchange.

The reaction of the justices' clerk was typical of the view at the time, that magistrates should decide cases and not open their mouths, just like the mother whale advising her young that it is only when you begin to spout, that you get harpooned. The day of

[1] See Ch 15 below.
[2] A Oakley, *A Critical Woman: Barbara Wootton, Social Science and Public Policy in the Twentieth Century* (London, Bloomsbury, 2011).

the unarticulated verdict of a magistrates' court has long since passed, although I expect that 'ticking of boxes' does not suffice to meet the need for giving reasons. It may just be possible to advance reform of the mixed criminal tribunal as an alternative to trial by jury. We should recall that Sir Robin Auld in his *Review of the Criminal Courts* in 2001 recommended that defendants should be allowed to waive jury trial if they so wished. The alternative form of criminal justice could become that alternative.

On 17 October 2012 Professor Rod Morgan delivered an impressive, but depressing, vision of the future for the lay magistracy in the Jane Blom-Cooper Lecture at Middle Temple.[3] His address included an allusion to the future of a mixed tribunal.

---

[3] Jane was my adored wife for 37 years, who died tragically, aged 67, on 30 December 2006.

15

Serious Fraud Offences: Whither Their Trial?

'We now have a battle over jury trial – an equally important component of our liberties'.

Lord Kingsland (the shadow Lord Chancellor of the Conservative Party) on 20 March 2007 on the second reading in the House of Lords of the Fraud (Trials without a Jury) Bill.[1]

FOR 30 YEARS the administrators of the mode of criminal trial for serious fraudsters aimed, in vain, at introducing a modification in criminal justice, supported throughout by the Labour Administration and opposed mainly by the proponents of the existing system of trial by jury as the thin end of the wedge in a culturally entrenched system of justice. The aim has been concluded by a single section in the Protection of Freedom Act 2012 – section 113. Section 43 of the Criminal Justice Act 2003, notorious for its inclusion of the ill-fated IPPs (imprisonment for public protection) provided (subject to an affirmative resolution of both Houses of Parliament) for applications by the prosecution on indictment for certain fraud trials to be conducted without a jury. The 2012 Act has simply removed it from the statute book. Thus ended the protracted parliamentary episode and – seemingly for the foreseeable future – any public debate over non-jury trial for serious fraud cases. Why, and how the crusade for a modest reform to jury trial for the more serious offences was sustainably opposed is a lamentable tale of action by interested pressure groups and modern representative democracy. But, first, the historical version of the affair in democratic rule of government.

---

[1] *Hansard* HL Deb vol 690, cols 1146–1202.

HISTORY

The governmental desire to bring the perpetrators of serious frauds expeditiously and effectively to book found expression in the establishment by the Lord Chancellor and the Home Secretary, Mr Douglas (later Lord) Hurd, of a committee in November 1983 to examine *Fraud Trials* under the chairmanship of Lord Roskill, a Law Lord. The Committee reported on 10 January 1986 (the report,[2] I add scholastically, lacks any index), recommending that for complex fraud cases a type of tribunal was required, as 'Fraud Trial Tribunals'. Of the eight Commissioners, there was one dissenter, Mr Walter Merricks, then secretary of the Law Society. In his note of dissent[3] Mr Merricks did not engage in any possible change in the existing mode of English criminal trial, but stated that 'if fundamental features as jury trials are to be reviewed, the review should be a comprehensive one not confined to a narrow band of cases of an indefinable class'; he added: 'such a fact-finding operation would, in my view, be an essential preparation for, and precondition of any initiative to modernise and reform more fundamental aspects of the trial process.' The opposition to the Roskill recommendation was substantially (not wholly) emotive. Significantly, Lord Mayhew (as Mr Patrick Mayhew, Solicitor-General in 1986) supported the Conservative Government's decision of the day, not to accept the recommendation of the Roskill Committee that serious and complex fraud trials should be tried by a special tribunal.[4] And so it became the Party's policy, as evinced in the debate in 2007 of the Fraud (Trials without a Jury) Bill, and was finally given its Parliamentary quietus on 10 May 2012 by section 113 of the Protection of Freedoms Act 2012.

Second, before I address other than emotional arguments for and against the change, it is worth a moment's pause to consider the parliamentary process, from 2003 to 2007, that thwarted the government's resolve to make the numerically significant but socially modest change. Section 43 of the Criminal Justice Act 2003 was passed through all the stages of the parliamentary process, with the *caveat* of an affirmative resolution. Despite private consultations and a seminar of interested parties that produced no indication of such an affirmative resolution, the Labour Government went ahead

[2] Roskill, *Fraud Trials Committee: Report* (London, HMSO, 1986).
[3] ibid 190–99, 195 line 18.
[4] *Hansard* HL Deb 20 March 2007, vol 690, col 1177.

instead with a second reading in the Lords to implement section 43, without having the need for a further motion. The Bill received a second reading in the House of Commons by a substantial majority. At the Report stage the Government secured substantial majorities and the Bill was duly read a third time. To defy the Commons, by denying the Bill a second reading in the Lords and a Committee stage (where amendments could be debated) constituted a dangerous inroad upon the Lords' capacity to adopt such action; it was – and is – a reversal of the report of the Joint Committee on Convention which was approved by both Houses of Parliament. Significantly, that report concluded that in recent years the House of Lords will usually give a second reading to any Government Bill, 'whether based on the manifesto, or not'. As Lord Tomlinson[5] expostulated in 2007 on the second reading in the Lords of the Fraud (Trials without a Jury) Bill, their Lordships were about to take (and nevertheless took) 'the step of voting against a second reading *at our peril'*. Perilous or not, the House of Lords flexed its dubious muscle in order to deny the Government its wish to limit jury trials. It is not without significance that section 44 of the Criminal Justice Act 2003 was not, likewise, executed. That section, which has been implemented on a few occasions since 2003, provided that the prosecution may apply for a trial to be conducted without a jury 'where there is a danger of jury tampering'.[6] The fate of section 43 deserves at least a reconsideration of the grounds for proposing an associated reform.

SERIOUS FRAUD OFFENCES

Quite apart from the arguments favouring the system of jury trial as the mode of a fair trial (of which there were numerous examples in the debate on 20 March 2007), two matters were advanced for advocating the change recommended by Lord Roskill and his colleagues in 1986, and repeated by Lord Justice Auld in his one-man review of the criminal courts in 2001.[7] In using a panel of experts in any frauds tribunal, Sir Robin highlighted numerous difficulties, including the precise role of expert members. Nevertheless the Government took the view that the better solution lay in section 43. It proceeded to legislate in 2007.

---

[5] ibid col 1186.
[6] See Lord Judge CJ in *R v Twomey and others* [2009] EWCA Crim 1035
[7] *Review of the Criminal Courts of England and Wales* (London, HMSO, 2001).

THE 2007 DEBATE

The Attorney-General (Lord Goldsmith) was at pains to limit the scope of non-jury trials. He explained that section 43 was not a general assault on the principle of trial by jury. Nor was it about choosing between a fair trial and an unfair trial: 'it is about choosing between modes of a fair trial', and fairness required a different process in a small number of serious and complex fraud cases involving inordinately long trials with complex evidential information that became excessively burdensome for 12 jurors. Nothing has emerged in recent years to gainsay the sensible assertion that a select few cases of fraud would enhance the quality of justice if they were conducted by professionals rather than by the cumbersome and lengthy process of trial by jury. What conceivable evidence was there (or is there) to refute this general impression gleaned by those administering the system of serious frauds? There is evidence that there are undoubtedly comparable complex cases other than in serious fraud. But does that fact invalidate the case for singling out the serious fraud trial? The answer must be that the complexities of financial transactions are peculiarly not in the experience of the average citizen, unlike other serious crimes, such as domestic violence. The composition of the mode of trial is relevant, unlike almost all other forms of criminality that come before the courts of criminal justice. The only argument surrounds the ticklish issue of admissibility. A jury is shielded from hearing certain evidence that is not excluded from trials by professionals, but that difference may need attention in investigating the process of investigation of crime, as opposed to the appropriate mode of trial. Access to information other than in the courtroom raises an issue of importance.

The most compelling – one might describe it as 'arresting' – point was in the speech by Lord Carlile of Berriew in the debate on 20 March 2007. As a Liberal Democrat peer (and at that time *not* part of any Coalition Government, but a distinct advocate of civil liberties), Lord Carlile's words are weighty, if not heavy with the expected logic of a distinguished lawyer and formerly the official surveyor of anti-terrorist legislation. I quote his words verbatim:[8]

> I agree entirely with the noble and learned Lord that, over the years, the Diplock courts [the non-jury trials in Northern Ireland which persisted from 1972–2012] have reached high standards of justice in Northern

---

[8] *Hansard* HL Deb 20 March 2007, vol 690, col 1166.

Ireland. I also agree with him entirely that there are certain classes of case in which, in this modern age, it is no longer possible to have a reliable trial by jury, but they are a very special class of case. They are not cases where the jury has to be there for a long time or has to make a difficult judgment; they are cases where the jury system is so undermined by, for example, intimidation or threats to jurors or sectarian conflict that it is simply not possible for the jury to return a reliable verdict.

So far, so good – a model exposition of the proposed reform! This dissociation from the Diplock courts in a tribally divided society did nothing to detract from the quality of judges, which is specifically mentioned. Similarly if the material is so complex and confusing to laymen in a jury, surely that tends to invalidate the mode of jury trial; it does not detract from the quality of judge alone in judicial expertise. But Lord Carlile goes on to elaborate this flawed distinction. He states – and once again I have no quarrels:

> By no stretch of the imagination do fraud cases fall into that category [presumably 'undermined . . . or intimidation of jurors']. This is an attempt at a pragmatic Bill; it is an attempt by the Government to persuade the House that, quite simply, fraud cases are too burdensome for juries. However, for reasons that I shall set out, *I disagree wholeheartedly.*

If the reasons 'set out' are criminologically a matter for serious argument (pragmatic or fundamental), it can hardly result in more absolute terms of rejection. Lord Carlile, like so many of his colleagues, relies too heavily on opinion evidence, which frequently is far removed from professionalism. If the administration of the system can reasonably argue for a different, but acceptable mode of trial, what is there to negate their modest proposal that the judiciary should decide on an application which is the preferred method of an equitable system of criminal justice 'in the modern age' (which Lord Carlile rightly adheres to) calls for an alternative mode of trial.

But how does Lord Carlile perceive this 'modern age'? In a paragraph of his reasoning he said:[9]

> Jurors' determinations of fact are based on a collective view as lay people of the conduct of the defendant. A judge's determination of fact may in some cases – I hesitate to say this in the presence of distinguished and retired judges in this House – be sometimes idiosyncratic and a great deal worse. The annals of the law reports are full of cases where judges have made serious mistakes; as I said earlier, jurors have made few.

---

[9] ibid col 1167.

Whatever may be said of Lord Carlile's perception of the processes of the law, he cannot claim any empirical – let alone speculative – evidence of the decisions of jurors, unelected and unanswerable, giving monastic, monosyllabic utterances, compared with reasoned (and reviewable by way of appeal on fact and law) decisions of judges, however idiosyncratic or eccentric they may occasionally be in the civil jurisdiction. For criminal justice the jury is the inviolable determiner of fact and disregarder of law. Perversity is their option, infrequently though it is deployed. Lord Carlile's pronouncement is no more reliable than that of the mythical visitor from Mars. Indeed, academics have ingeniously constructed the concept of what they like to call 'jury nullification'!

If the sole criterion for testing the mode of criminal trial is the verdict of the decision-maker of the accused's guilt or innocence (a rash assumption, at the best of times) then the differential is important. But empirical evidence suggests that the differential between the judge alone and the jury system is so marginal – it is judged at 1 per cent in favour of jury acquittals – that it cannot be used as the basis for a decision on whether one mode of trial is preferred to another. If, however, the criteria are the various aspects of the criminal process (including litigant satisfaction with that process) then the differentials matter. The fact is that criminologically we know little or nothing about the functioning of the system. The studies so far by Professor Cheryl Thomas are admirable, but they do no more than speculate that jurors behave responsibly.

POST-2007

It would seem politically wise not to envisage a return to section 43, although a change of administration in 2015 might influence its promoters to renew the arguments for reform. On the other hand, the composition of the upper chamber of the House of Lords might incline the law reformers not to renew the March 2007 compromise. What then? The obvious alternative is to revive the alternative of the Roskill dissenter, Mr Walter Merricks, of 30 years ago. There is now an even more pressing need for a comprehensive review 'not confined to a narrow band of an indefinable class'. Before I embark on the virtues and values of any mode of trial, there is one suggestion that addresses the 'narrow band' of serious fraud cases.

There is one persistent claim by the jury-apologists that calls for comment. Citing commentators on the system, not excluding the dramatic, and oft-quoted, remarks of Lord Devlin – 'the lamp that shows that freedom lives' – expounding the constitutional guarantees of trial by one's peers, are the claims to the citizen's right to jury trial.

In the 'battle over jury trial' – to which Lord Kingsland referred in the 2007 debate – the progenitors of the rival arguments should at least remember this: jury trial (or more specifically, the English trial by judge and jury in which the latter is the distinctive fact-finder and decision-maker) is strictly not a right at all. It is a duty upon everyone indicted before the Crown Court for a serious offence – roughly 98 per cent of all crimes. Subject to what I have to say, the defendant has no option but must subject himself to the jury's verdict – since 1967 a majority of 10 out of 12 jurors will suffice. It is at best, therefore, not a constitutional right, such as some advocates would wish, but a citizen's obligation to place his reputation before 12 good men and women who have been selected generally from among the electoral roll. (As an aside, only property owners could qualify before 1972.) The second thing to remember is that, apart from the monarch as Head of State, there is no other public institution in our democratic system of government that is unanswerable and unaccountable for its verdicts. It pronounces its decision monastically and in monosyllables. Subject only to the consequences of a fair trial under the authority of *Taxquet v Belgium* by the Grand Chamber of the ECHR, it is generally an acceptable mode of trial. And for the independence of the judiciary in the fairness of the mode of trial in England it has one distinctive disadvantage. The verdict of the jury is an exclusive interpretation of the result of a serious criminal offence, so long as the judge properly directs the jury. It is even more so for the appellate judge who must acknowledge the exclusive fact-finding role of the jury of 12 ordinary people. Trial by jury is an abdication of the judge's function; he may sum up the factual material, but he may not have any say in the jury's verdict.

The protocol of 22 March 2005, dealing with the control and management of heavy fraud cases, provided that the best handling technique for a long case is continuous management by an experienced judge nominated for the purpose. If pre-trial case management on an intensive scale is essential, what can there be against allowing a defendant at least to request trial by judge alone? The interim report of the Fraud Review Team, set up by the Attorney-General in October 2005, recommended the possibility of specialised fraud courts with specialised judges, and the final report instigated the proposed legislation of 2006/7. Choice of criminal courts has long existed for the hybrid offences whereby defendants can elect a magistrates' court or Crown Court trial. It cannot, therefore, be theoretically objectionable. Can the seriousness of criminality expel the precious element of choice? The ostensible objection is that it would be discriminatory. But all exercise of choice is just that. The only obstacle to the introduction of waiver (or bench trial) is the fear, rational or irrational, that it would be regulated properly (by which is meant 'the thin end of the wedge' – a last-ditch plea for an indefensible argument). This is an unacceptable inroad upon the jury as the prime instrument of criminal justice. So is it time now for Lord Kingsland's plea, five and a half years ago, to 'battle over jury trial'?

This is not the place to argue for or against the present system, but to point to the criteria for choice in a rational debate (we can put on one side the utterances of pleasantries in favour of or against the jury). If the sole test is the social acceptablility of trial verdicts, the topic is unanswerable. On the basis of inadequate empirical evidence of how the jury works (or not), the difference in result between judge-alone and jury verdicts is no more than 1 per cent. Parenthetically, prosecutionally, decision-making is reserved for juries in high-profile cases. But that apart, the consensus must be that in terms of result there is at most comparability. Neither of the protagonists in the debate can claim overriding virtue for one model of fair trial than another – that is, if the criterion is the verdict, without more ado.

But if one reads Article 6 of ECHR with objectivity, the test is the quality of criminal justice that determines the mode of trial as producing a quality service, and that must involve testing the process of criminal justice, including importantly the verdict, which is decidedly not decisive. That much is the outcome of the European Court's verdict in *Taxquet*, which declined to evaluate the various modes of trial operative in the Member States of the Council of Europe. But that decision, which evaluated the evidential material requisite for admissibility at trial, did point to the issue of juristic value in the criminal trial process. Clearly, though, the constitutionality of a fair trial encompasses not just the attributes of the trial process; it includes both the investigation of criminality pre-trial and the outcome of the verdict, including the appellate process and the quality of the sentencing procedure. There is also the perception of the whole process. Does the trial induce a sense of acceptance by the prosecutor and the defendant? Does the trial inspire public confidence in the system? It is assumed by criminal practitioners that the system does evoke the public's confidence. But what evidence do we have for that supposition? I sense, impressionistically speaking, that until the Second World War the British had overwhelming faith in the jury system that was then in use. I adjudge that the support is still strong, but that there is a growing disenchantment with its validity. This is not yet sufficient to indicate a change. But, given a comprehensive review of the quality of criminal justice in the twenty-first century, we might be able to determine the future of the mode of criminal trial. I stop there to say that the need for a study of the criminal justice system in its nascent European setting appears to ripen. The two systems of the Anglo-Saxon and Continental justice systems should now be viewed in their binary, and not adversarial context. There is much to be learned from both of them in a world of mobile populaces (specifically in the growth of extradition), as the Royal Commission in 1993 under Lord Runciman acknowledged, but felt constrained by the Commission's timetable to leave the matter for another day. That day has perhaps arrived. But that advent, for from distance at least not imminent, does not distract us from further debate and inaction. I would add only that the increase in extradition in Europe will lead to more comment.

WAIVER OF JURY TRIAL

The Roskill Commission of 1986 did consider the prospect of a choice by the defence (and possibly by the prosecution as well) adding an alternative tribunal of non-juries. But in the result, it opted for the nominated judge, chosen by a senior High Court judge or the Recorder of London, to choose the nature of the lay members who would be selected to sit on the Fraud Trial Tribunal. The Commission thought that trial by jury should be dispensed with only if both parties consented, and that the mode of trial should lie only with the court. And on the question of the defence alone consenting, the Commission was far from satisfied that 'many defendants would choose to be tried in this way'. Recent experience of a lack of such waiver in New South Wales and New Zealand, moreover, merely confirmed its doubts about the paucity of defendants who had so elected.

But that was 'in the early stages of our inquiry' (probably 1984–85) in the light of the experience in New South Wales (introduced in 1979 for 'long and complex cases') and in New Zealand (again in 1979, and not restricted to fraud cases). So limited an inquiry deserves to be comparatively reproduced. There appeared, moreover, to be no objection in principle to choice being elected, both by the prosecution and the defence, at the instance of ultimate decision by the court itself, whenever both parties agree. The Roskill Commission did not consider whether, if the court had to assent to the parties' 'views', the mode of trial could not be judicially negatived.

The Roskill Commission, with implicit but not specific approval, did quote a valuable instance of a jury trial by judge and lay members:

> Our attention was drawn to the fact that before 1978 the Director of Public Prosecutions could elect for summary trial in prosecutions under the Exchange Control Act 1947. These cases were usually heard in the City of London and went to summary trial in order to save costs and to secure a speedier result than trial by jury would allow. Magistrates in the City were considered to have a better understanding of the complexities involved. Two cases in particular were described to us as 'large revolving fund exchange control cases involving the defendants' ingenious and very complicated use of abstract and esoteric exchange control concepts.' In one of these cases the Chairman of the bench was an experienced lawyer, while the other two magistrates were a retired bank official who had worked on exchange control and a businessman with experience of the stock market [He was Mr Kenneth Corke, an experienced liquidator]. The case took about 30 days to hear, but the lawyers estimated that it would have taken up to three or four times that length had there been trial by jury. This was mentioned to us as a practical example of the workings of a tribunal in effect consisting of a judge and two specially qualified lay members.
>
> A judge sitting with lay members is the proposal most widely supported by those who gave evidence. Provided the lay members are well chosen, comprehension of the evidence would be at a high level. Knowledge of the background to the case, the terminology, customs and practices of the business in which the alleged fraud had been perpetrated, would be available. Provided the lay members were given an equal vote on the matter of the verdict (though not on questions of law or sentence), they could demonstrate their independence of the judge, if necessary by outvoting him. If the tribunal consists of the judge and only two lay members, the problem of assembling and maintaining a list of suitable candidates to serve would not, we think, present much difficulty. [10]

[10] Report (n 2) 146–47 paras 8.49 and 8.50.

I have to confess that the Chairman of the Bench on both occasions was none other than myself. I remember it well, and have since (in 2012) explained how it came about, in a book by the Magistrates' Association on 675 years of the lay magistracy.[11] In paragraph 8.51, at page 147, the Roskill Commission, on that evidence, concluded: 'In the light of the evidence put before us we think that a judge and two lay members would be the most appropriate tribunal to try complex fraud cases.'

The waiver issue – which essentially is the act of waiving a right – is commendably up for grabs. A prime consideration is the nature of jury trial. The protagonist of trial by jury reasserts that on a matter of serious crime (indictable, or at the sole insistence of a public prosecutor), there is the inherent obligation to criminal offences being tried by one's peers (if, only since 1967, a qualified majority of the 12 are in agreement). Strictly speaking, an obligation to undergo unequivocally (subject only to a judicial determination that there has been no abuse of the criminal prosecution in framing the case against the accused) is not a citizen's *right*. It is a duty. As such, it cannot be waived. But if it is properly (if not jurisprudentially or philosophically) regarded as a 'right', the accused must be allowed the choice of mode of trial. That much has been considered politically so in both New South Wales and New Zealand, if not also in the civilised legal world. (It exists, I think, in some jurisdictions in the USA.) (Parenthetically, it is noteworthy that Parliament has recently – in section 11 of the Defamation Act 2013 – ruled that libel cases are to be tried without a jury unless the court orders otherwise.[12])

There is, moreover, the question, raised by the Roskill Commission, that its recommendation of a Fraud Trial Tribunal would

> considerably reduce the length and cost of trials, while at the same time increasing the prospects of a sound verdict being reached. The savings of judges and court time and the greatly improved comprehension of the matters under enquiry would draw more, if not all complex fraud cases to be brought to trial and provide a further deterrent for those who seek to engage in fraudulent operations.[13]

The statement in January 2013 by the Director of Public Prosecutions, Mr (now Sir) Keir Starmer QC, of examples of invigorating pursuit of tax evaders and other fraudsters is further stimulus to such

---

[11] See Ch 14 above.

[12] For an early example of the legislation in action, see *Yeo v Times Newspapers* [2014] WLR(D) 383.

[13] Roskill, *Fraud Trials Committee: Report* (London, HMSO, 1986).

prosecutions in up-to-date charging standards – as indeed is the extended financing by the Treasury of the Serious Fraud Office. The advent of rising costs and the diminution of public funding through the legal aid scheme deserves a fresh look at the financing of public and private sources to fulfil the existing services of criminal justice. The threatened strike action by the Bar and their disinclination in December 2013 to represent eight defendants in a serious fraud trial provides a hint for a less expensive solution. I do wonder, however, whether Sir Keir was right to urge higher prison sentences for the more serious fraudulent offences. But the severity of punishment for property crimes is another subject for another debate.

CONCLUSION

What next? If for the foreseeable future the prospect of trial by jury – 'an equally important component of our liberties' – is here to stay in its purest form, there is no reason to discern ways of modifying the system. And I do not stop to consider the outcome of the decision in November 2011 of the Grand Chamber of the European Court of Human Rights in *Taxquet v Belgium*, the argument in favour of a waiver. We do not need to accept the recommendation in 2001 by Sir Robin Auld[14] that 'with the consent of the court . . . it should be able to opt for trial by judge alone in all cases now tried on indictment . . .'. Not just in serious fraud cases, but in all cases of trial by jury the defendant should be free, if the court assents, to waive the right in favour of a non-jury trial. Serious fraud offences present an opportunity to experiment, and, being essential pragmatists in good government, we should give the idea a trial.

---

[14] Review (n 7) 181, section 118.

16

James Hanratty:
a Vindicatory View

OUTSIDE THE ARCHED courtroom at Bedford Special Assizes on 22 February 1962 I stood looking admiringly at the statue of John Howard which stands in the town square opposite the public building. Little did I know that 10 years later I would become the chairman of the Howard League for Penal Reform, a pressure group formed in 1922[1] which acknowledged the great penal reformer of the eighteenth century. But on that occasion I was awaiting the return of the jury, which had asked for a further direction from the trial judge, Mr Justice Gorman, in the trial for murder in *R v James Hanratty*. After an impeccable summing-up on that Saturday, the jury had asked what was meant by 'proof beyond reasonable doubt'; they received a traditional explanation from the judge. A short time thereafter, we entered the courtroom to hear the jury pronounce the verdict of guilt.

James Hanratty was sentenced to death; his appeal was rejected and, amidst a growing campaign of a miscarriage of justice, the Home Secretary, Mr RA Butler, refused a request for a reprieve. We were still a few years away from the abolition of the death penalty for murder. Before that happened, in late 1965, I had the temerity to put pen to paper. In 1963 I wrote a Penguin Special called *The A6 Murder: R v James Hanratty: The Semblance of Truth*. It was a modest attempt to explain the English criminal justice system that had produced what I thought was the unjust verdict of guilt on the basis of the admissible evidence heard in the courtroom. The jury should not have convicted him; and he should certainly have been spared the hangman's noose. But I concluded then that the European systems of justice at that time had been designed to unravel the truth of the criminal event. Unlike the English system they were designed not to prove the prosecution's case, but to seek the truth of what

---

[1] The Howard Association was formed in 1921 by Fenner Brockway and Hobhouse, and merged with the Penal Reform Group the following year.

happened. In common parlance, the European mode of trial is, inaccurately, described as the inquisitorial method of trial, as opposed to our accusatorial system. Both types of criminal trial over the years have borrowed from each other, but their binary rights largely bear comparison. And so I recorded.

That book inspired me to develop throughout my professional career an attitude of comparative study, and led me to become a critic of the jury system. Students of criminal law and procedure in the law schools of the 1960s gave the subject some sensible judgment and academic discussion. As far as I am aware, most of the public comment came from journalistic sources, and was actively hostile. If student awareness of the book went unnoticed in publication terms, it received widespread review from the contemporary journals and noted commentators. It received a firm academic rebuke from a leading member of the Institute of Criminology at Cambridge. In a lengthy review in *New Society* of 17 January 1963, the late Professor Richard F Sparks wrote that 'a rather turgid account of that trial and the gruesome events leading up to it is not very impressive'. For the rest there was a resounding critique about its handling of the case (or its inattentiveness to past mental behaviour of 'the psychopath and the Court'). Its adverse comments at least served to promote future controversy about the case – at least until 2002. Throughout the ensuing three decades the publicity was mostly aimed at convincing the readers of the media and their authorship that there had been a serious miscarriage of justice. I took little or no part in these public utterances, save for the fact that I was interviewed from time to time on either radio or TV.

I should explain at this point what I had imbibed as my experience in 1961/2, and occasionally thereafter so far as it is relevant. During the latter part of the 1950s I had become the legal correspondent of first, the *Guardian* (still then the *Manchester Guardian*) and then the *Observer*. I also began to teach criminology to the social science students of Bedford College, University of London, for their social administration degree, although, unusually at that time, I became a lay magistrate in first, Greater London and then the City of London (from the Justice of the Peace Act 1969 until 1981). Against this background I interested myself in criminal proceedings, including the Hanratty case. I should mention also that I became friendly with a contemporary student at King's College, London, Michael Sherrard, to become junior counsel for Hanratty. Until I took silk in 1970 I had never practised in the criminal courts. For a number of years in the 1970s I acted as leading counsel for the defence. My first experience of jury trial did nothing to repair my view that any civilised mode of criminal trial had to be conducted professionally. But that is another question, treated elsewhere in this book.

The Hanratty trial covered in my book was largely academic and explanatory: the subtitle tells everything – 'the semblance of truth'. Ever since the nineteenth century the English Anglo-Saxon jury system (strictly speaking, trial by judge and 12 laymen appointed electorally) had evolved into a modern system, recognised as an acceptable mode of fair trial (in public, independently and impartially of any outside influence, by Article 6 of the European Convention on Human Rights and Fundamental Freedoms of 1950. Twelve states of Western Europe, Scandinavia and Turkey signed the Convention.) What contrasted the British method from that in Europe? Basically, the principal approach. For whatever reason, Europe had sought to seek the truth of the event through an investigation, conducted by an examining magistrate (*juge d'instruction*) to determine which suspect(s) should be tried, at which time the suspect(s) would invariably be the first to give evidence before the court of trial – usually a mixed tribunal of professionals and jury, which together rendered the verdict. By contrast, in England and Wales (and also in Scotland and Northern Ireland), any suspect who became the defendant to a serious criminal charge could remain entirely silent throughout the proceedings (much of that has changed in later years). The essence of the criminal proceedings was to require the prosecution to prove its case according to very strict standards of proof. Short of that, the defendant was acquitted, discharged without more ado (that was only slightly changed in recent legislation, when a future prosecution could be launched). Some of the differences were pointed out in November 2011 in the case of *Taxquet v Belgium,* and the debate on the future of criminal justice remains. In 1961, the basic approach was observed. My book concluded, inconclusively, with this opinion:

> If *R v Hanratty* was not one of the most significant trials in our legal history, it raised, as I have tried to show, a large number of general questions about the way in which we deal with those who are accused of crime. In particular, the judicial killing of a youth, certified as a mental defective with a long history of mental unbalance (not one word of which was heard at the trial), makes cruelly clear that the English criminal process is concerned not with the truth about the crime, but solely with the assessment of criminal responsibility. Indeed, the trial system, which is the instrument of that assessment, is contrived in such a way as

to reduce to a minimum one's knowledge of the crime; and in Hanratty's case, as I have tried to make clear, this effect was most pronounced.

Justice is not merely a process devised by lawyers for assessing the guilt or innocence of an accused. Justice is a process which allows all those concerned with the administration of the criminal law, and even those interested in society's attitude towards crime and its criminals, to see the particular malaise in society that produced the crime. Research into the causes of crime – it seems a blindingly obvious statement – should find its most fruitful material from the administration of criminal justice. Sad to relate, in England it finds little or no assistance from the legal process. [2]

There was one feature of the Hanratty case that made it unusual, and affected distinctly the reason why some of us thought he committed the crimes, but was convicted by the jury on inadmissible evidence. The first concerned a valuable piece of evidence. During the period after the criminal event, James Hanratty had stayed in a boarding house in North London; on one occasion he had left a pair of distinctive gloves that bore a close resemblance to those described, not altogether satisfactorily, by Valerie Storie, when she was the victim of rape by the killer of Michael Gregsten in a car in a Berkshire cornfield. For some reason, that piece of evidence was uncovered by the police only during the trial. After the defence had given evidence, the prosecution sought to adduce that material as rebutting evidence. Mr Justice Gorman, displaying a fondness for the admissibility of evidential material, rejected the prosecution's plea; a circumstantial piece of evidence was excluded from the trial.

The media and others attacked me persistently throughout the 1960s and onwards. The culmination was a considerable tome (approximately 450 pages) by Mr Bob Woffinden in 1997. Throughout three decades, the campaign to dissociate James Hanratty from complicity in the crime of 1961 did not desist. Paul Foot and Woffinden, in particular, disliked my reasoning for concluding that, although convicted wrongly on the admissible evidence, Hanratty was by strong implication guilty of the crime. Their unremitting advocacy, bolstered by political activity, was abruptly halted by an official requirement for the exhumation of Hanratty's body, and a further reference to the Court of Appeal to give a direction, among others, whether the admissibility of fresh evidence of the new DNA material should be upheld as being 'safe'.

The matter came before the Court in April 2002 before the Lord Chief Justice (Lord Woolf), Lord Justice Mantell and Lord Justice

² L Blom-Cooper, *The A6 Murder* (Harmondsworth, Penguin Books, 1963) 132–33.

Leveson. The Court admitted the fresh evidence. The issue was whether the DNA material, after all these years, could be taken as conclusive evidence that James Hanratty was the murderer and rapist. Counsel for the appellant accepted that if the DNA material was found to be uncontaminated, the submission, standing alone, was certain proof of James Hanratty's guilt. They held that it was uncontaminated. The conclusion of informed commentators 40 years ago had been proved accurate. The only argument remaining was the issue of contamination of the DNA. Bob Woffinden and his colleagues persisted, somewhat unrealistically, that the Court of Appeal on 10 May 2002 got it wrong.

The long saga of the Hanratty case has been closed. Yet what, if anything, has been learnt from this never-ending campaign to insinuate yet another miscarriage of justice? Apart from intrinsic factors in the instant case, it is not without significance that it took place in 1962, at the height of the public controversy over capital punishment, still then three years from abolition by Parliament. In the context it is noteworthy that there were, professionally at least, some worries about the propriety of the jury's verdict of guilt. Before considering the case in its public context, the trial, the verdict, the trial judge's approach, the professional reaction and the appellate process deserve some after-thoughts.

Many legal figures thought that the trial judge had been disposed favourably to the defence, and was even helpful to the defence in the course of the trial. Generally speaking, commentators considered that the system of trial by jury may have come to the right result, but that, evidentially speaking, the verdict was insecure. It was certainly the view of the lawyers engaged in the case. Counsel for the prosecution was Mr Graham Swanwick and his junior Mr Geoffrey Lane, then on the point of becoming a Queen's Counsel (eventually progressing to become Lord Chief Justice in 1980). Geoffrey Lane was a personal friend of mine, with whom I discussed the Hanratty case from time to time. One incident, during the Saturday evening of 17 February 1962 after a retirement of some little time, will suffice to tell the tale.

When the jury returned from its deliberations in the early evening, to ask for further guidance on the standard of proof, and received a traditional direction, Geoffrey Lane told me personally that at that moment his doubts about a conviction were resolved. He thought it, rightly indicated a jury acquittal. He did not wait for the opposite result that, surprisingly, came later. He proceeded to endorse his brief (for the non-professional, that means that his

written instructions to appear as counsel were marked by him indicating on the document the result of the prosecution). The simple
fact that junior prosecuting counsel should conclude a likely acquittal was reflective of a thoroughly professional view of all the evidence entrusted to the jurors (in fact, since day one, only 11 of
them; one juror fell sick at the outset; this happened at a time before
juries could, after a time limit, enter a majority (10-2) verdict).

The classic statement is that the appeal judges are not there to try
the case where there was evidence proper to be left to the jury upon
which the jurors could come to the conclusion at which they
arrived. If there is evidence on both sides, and it is impossible to
say that the verdict is one which the jury could not properly have
arrived at, that is that. In short, the appeal court is not a court of
appeal; the verdict of the jury is theirs and theirs alone. It is not
reviewable. Did Hanratty fit the bill? The fact that others, fully
informed, thought otherwise is neither here nor there. The fact-
finder is exclusively the inarticulate, monosyllabic jury. The appeal
judges, presided over by Lord Parker CJ, could find no reason to
interfere with the jury's decision. James Hanratty was executed on 4
April 1962. But should he have been reprieved by the exercise of
the Royal Prerogative? A 'lurking doubt' about the trial may not be
enough for the judiciary. But what about a Home Secretary? Since
abolition in 1965, the prerogative power is only of historical interest in the process of the penal system. But occurring during the
campaign for abolition of the death penalty, it is worth some
thought.

RA Butler had become Home Secretary in 1957 and there was a
suspicion, at least in liberal circles, that he was a secret abolitionist,
but his innate moderation led him to independent judgment,
although he had been a party to the retention of capital murders
under the Homicide Act 1957. The exercise of the reprieve power
was, moreover, for him a profound constitutional responsibility.
For 19 months no executions had taken place, and he adopted a
stern task, probably in isolation of the contemporary debates on
abolition. According to his biographer, Anthony Howard, Butler
concluded that 'the law must take its course'. Howard added that
'the decision did not spare him some severe journalistic criticism
but, perhaps because it coincided with the end of the parliamentary
session, it did not provoke any major political storm.'[3]

---

[3] A Howard, *RAB: The Life of RA Butler* (London, Macmillan, 1957) 254.

At that time I was deeply involved in the campaign for the abolition of capital punishment, and I do not recall that the Hanratty
case aroused much of an interest in the campaign. Much more was
focused on the cases of Ruth Ellis and Timothy Evans before the
Homicide Act of 1957, and the consequences of that flawed piece
of legislation. The activities of the early 1960s in the abolition
campaign are relayed in a separate chapter. For this chapter, my
early involvement in the Hanratty case tells its own intrinsic tale of
disputed miscarriages of justice.

My conclusion is that, in the context of a criminal trial, the
considered verdict of those educated and training in the law was
definitively trumped by the decision-making of unqualified jurors.
Was that the expectation in 1950 of the architects of Article 6 of the
European Convention on Human Rights when describing a 'fair
trial' before an independent and impartial tribunal? I think not. The
authors of contemporary civil liberties in the legal process, determining both civil and criminal obligations, preferred professionalism to populism.

17

An Advocate's Tale

AT FIRST INSTANCE

IF THE AIM of advocacy is 'to seduce, to seize the mind for a predetermined end',[1] the legal representative and the decision-maker share a fundamental role as vicarious voices in the courtroom – the advocate speaks on behalf of his client-litigant, the judge speaks on behalf of the citizenry interested in an efficient system of justice. The resultant encounter will be, in great part, dependent on harmony between judge and advocate. Disharmony may not always be avoidable, but both advocate and judge have a joint and several interest in conducting their respective roles of seducer and seduced without incidents that might disturb that alchemy of the vicarious voices. Insufficient attention is paid, however, to the incidental interchanges or sharp exchanges between judge and advocate in the course of the legal process, even if it is not possible to judge whether, and if so, how the litigious outcome is materially affected. Yet it cannot be doubted that forensic intercourse is influential, if only rarely decisive of the litigious result. Incidents may nevertheless have their intrinsic interest, quite apart from momentary disturbance of the forensic process. One's experience as an advocate would incline to the view that it is frequently the judicial intervention that triggers an unseemly incident. How the advocate handles such intervention will determine the consequence, for good or ill, of the advocate's cause. Twice in my life in the law, I encountered judicial intervention that seemed at the time unwarranted, although the result in either case was not unrewarding to the advocate and hence to the client. Paradoxically, both encounters with the judiciary were in the context of a jury trial – or rather, a trial by judge and jury.

---

[1] The phrase is an extract from the speech of Mr Justice Frankfurter, who said that the fundamental role of the advocate 'is not to enlarge the intellectual horizon. His task is to seduce, to seize the mind for a predetermined end, not to explore paths to truth'. (1955) 68 *Harvard Law Review* 937, 939.

Birmingham Crown Court in 1972 was the scene of one of the earliest trials involving Irish terrorists, that subsequently disfigured the criminal justice scene for three decades. Only a couple of years ahead lay the public house bombings in that great city and the public debate over the trial of the Birmingham Six. That miscarriage of justice overshadowed the case in which I was involved at a trial before Mr Justice Kenneth Jones and a jury. The judge had been a prominent figure in the criminal courts, primarily singled out as leading counsel for the prosecution against the Kray brothers. That notoriously adversarial, but nonetheless witty judge, Mr Justice Melford Stevenson, had been the trial judge. Once asked what was memorable about the Kray trial, he espoused the opinion that there were only two truthful statements in the whole of the trial: that he (the judge) was biased, and that Kenneth Jones was a big fat slob. If that was an unkind quip, Kenneth Jones did prove to be a formidable figure on the Bench, without exhibiting too much lenience towards defendants in the dock.

The prosecution alleged a conspiracy by two men to effect the escape of IRA prisoners housed (or warehoused?) initially at Winson Green Prison, Birmingham's local prison, which was typical of the penal institutions erected in the nineteenth century to meet the demands connected with the ending of transportation. One weekend, the prison service had got wind of suspicious activity surrounding the prison, so that the prisoners were instantly transferred to Bedford Prison, a smaller (Class B) institution famed, a decade earlier, for having imprisoned and executed James Hanratty for the A6 murder. When police officers raided my client's house they uncovered an amateur drawing distinctly replicating the exterior of Bedford Prison. This piece of circumstantial evidence justifiably prompted a separate charge of a conspiracy to effect the release of the IRA prisoners from that penal establishment of historical fame.

The prosecution was led by Mr Harry Skinner QC (a delightful opponent, and later an outstanding judge who died much too early for the good of criminal justice) and his junior, Mr Igor Judge (later the formidable Lord Chief Justice). The two Crown Counsel had indicated to me personally that they were intending to call as a witness a prison officer serving at Bedford Prison, to demonstrate that my client's drawing was precisely an amateurish depiction of the prison: QED, he was intent on an attempt to spring the prisoners from the gaol. My immediate request was to ask to be supplied with a copy of the plan of the prison so that I could be in a position to cross-examine the witness. This was politely refused, on the grounds that disclosure of the layout of the prison would be contrary to national security. Undeterred by this prosecution ploy to thwart any effective questioning of the prison officer's evidence, I instructed my instructing solicitor to issue a subpoena to the Secretary of State for the Home Department to produce the document. That was done, with the predictable riposte that the plan would not be produced: the Home Secretary would plead Crown Privilege (known today as public interest immunity). Battle was thus joined over the plan of Bedford Prison.

At the conclusion of the day's hearing, with the jury retired for the day, Harry Skinner rose and politely asked Mr Justice Kenneth Jones for guidance. The Crown, he said, was not prepared to yield to my request. The judge was anything but sympathetic to my predicament of being in a position sensibly to cross-examine the prison officer without having a sight of the actual layout of the prison. Indeed the judge was near-apoplectic, as if he had been bitten by a nasty mosquito. How dare a responsible member of the English Bar, the judge expostulated, think it right to issue a subpoena, knowing full well that there was a complete bar to disclosure of such a sensitive public document! Without providing me with an opportunity to address the judge in court, the proceedings were adjourned to the judge's private room to heap further judicial execration on defending counsel. Even then my efforts to explain my position were brushed aside. The judge would simply require an explanation from me by the next morning, after which he would decide whether to report my conduct to the Bar Council (my professional association) with a view to disciplinary action. Little did he realise that he was on the point of shooting himself in the foot; the judge's peremptory warning to me displayed not merely judicial impatience but also a failure to appreciate counsel's position.

What Mr Justice Kenneth Jones did not know was that at that time I was a member of the Home Secretary's Advisory Council on the Penal System, and in that capacity I had regular contact with the senior civil servants at the Home Office and members of the Prison Service. My remedy was close at hand. Leaving the judge's chambers, only mildly infuriated by the injudicious, not to say injudicial conduct of the judge, I immediately contacted someone in the works division of the prison service. There was no difficulty in persuading an official – indeed the willingness to help was entirely forthcoming – to come to Birmingham the next morning, along with the plan of Bedford Prison for me to have in front of me to cross-examine the prison officer. The official sat behind me, recovering the disputed document on completion of my forensic task.

The exquisite moment arrived when I rose to cross-examine the prison officer. It was immediately obvious that I was in no difficulty in conducting the questioning of the prison officer. The judge, not perceiving the foolishness of his exposed position, asked me in hostile fashion what it was I was reading from. I answered, defiantly I now assume: 'My Lord, a plan of Bedford Prison.' Judicial deflation was complete and composure distinctly ruffled. But the scene was climactic. Thereafter the exchanges between judge and defence counsel were polite, even decorous. The judge knew that I had scored a bull's eye, although judicial pomposity denied me any apology. I relished the moment and did so thereafter whenever I retold the story. The case was made even more memorable, because my client's appeal to the Court of Appeal (Criminal Division) against his conviction at Birmingham Crown Court was successful. Lord Widgery, the Lord Chief Justice, and his two judicial brethren said that Mr Justice Kenneth Jones had wrongly left to the jury the issue of conspiracy by my client with an unknown individual to effect the prisoners' escape from Bedford Prison; the two defendants had been acquitted by the jury of attempting to 'spring' the prisoners from Winson Green Prison. Since a conspiracy has to be grounded on an agreement with some other malefactor, and none could be identified as my client's co-conspirator, no criminal offence had been committed. Had the judge paused just for one moment to inquire about my predicament, I could have indicated my association with the penal system and offered to explore the possibility of controlled access to a sensitive document. But I was not afforded the opportunity owed to any defence counsel in my position. Judicial impropriety was rewarded with egg on the judge's face – well deserved, I venture to think!

The second tale also demonstrates judicial hostility unbridled by a sense of fairness to a defendant. The culprit was Mr Justice Lawson, a lawyer of academic renown but lacking in a display of humanity. The case was complicated by the existence of conflicting expert evidence from two rival forensic pathologists on the time of death of a very young child who had been brought early one morning by his mother, an intelligent Sierra Leonean, to a recently contracted carer, a West Indian woman living in Stockwell, South London with her own two young children. The child was delivered after breakfast time, wheeled into the carer's flat, wearing a floppy headgear, in a carry-cot or 'buggy'. The mother duly left for work, her child, apparently asleep, in a side room. There the child remained undisturbed until midday, when the carer went to see the child and discovered a moribund child with a head injury. The emergency services were called; the child was hospitalised and put on a life-support system where it was declared dead 72 hours later. The cause of death was a multiple fracture of the skull.

When was the fatal injury inflicted? If it was at any time after 8am, it had to be at the hands of my client. The Crown's expert, the late Dr Keith Mant, insisted that the severe blow had occurred not more than four hours before the child reached hospital at midday. My expert, Mr Iain West, (now deceased, but famous for his opinion about the death of Robert Maxwell) disagreed. Relying on the fact that some distortion of the brain resulted from the deceased having been put on artificial respiration, he calculated that the time lag between infliction and hospitalisation could be anything up to 12 hours. That raised the possibility of the skull fracture occurring before 8.00 am; that meant that either one or other of the child's parents had been the perpetrator. The child's mother was the prosecution's first witness. Had she or her husband caused the fatal injury?

Cross-examination took place after the jury had heard Dr Mant, but Iain West's contrary opinion had not been heard. The forensic situation presented a challenge. The cross-examiner was bound to throw suspicion on the witness or her husband as the only other member of the deceased child's household. A preliminary skirmish with the witness, questioning her without coming to the point of accusation, seemed the sensible course to adopt. It involved a series of meaningless questions about the movements of the child's buggy on arrival at the carer's premises, before the child was left in the side room. At this point the judge, no doubt frustrated at seemingly irrelevant questioning, intervened: 'I suppose, Mr Blom-Cooper, you will soon be suggesting that the ceiling fell on to the child's head and fractured his skull.' Without a moment's hesitation (it was a characteristic of mine that I often spoke before thinking) I answered the rhetorical question by saying 'My Lord, that is the kind of flippant remark that ill-befits a High Court judge.' The moment I uttered those words, I sensed that I had overstepped the mark of permissible advocacy. But the die was cast. Thereafter the judge and I were at hammer and tongs; it lasted throughout the trial. So much so, that when it came to the judge's summing-up, I urged him to tell the jury that it was either a verdict of guilty or an acquittal; the severity of the blow was such that it was not possible for the jury to bring in a modified verdict of manslaughter. I was very conscious that a jury, uncertain about which of the two experts to believe, might reach for the compromise – reject a verdict of murder, with its mandatory penalty of life imprisonment, and bring in a verdict of manslaughter. Disregarding my plea, Mr Justice Lawson firmly told the jury that they could find the accused guilty of manslaughter. They did as bid. The judge gave my client six years' imprisonment, a relatively light sentence for inflicting serious harm and killing the child in her trust. An appeal proved prospectively hopeful, on the basis that the judge had seriously underplayed Iain West's evidence, to the point where he had misdirected the jury. And so it proved to be the case. In front of the Court of Appeal, my task was made easier by a robust approach by Lord Lane, Lord Chief Justice at the time. When I had concluded my submissions on the expert evidence, I was about to sit down, confident that the appeal was about to succeed. But Lord Lane immediately pointed out to me that my grounds of appeal had included a submission that the trial judge had exhibited such hostility towards me that it amounted to bias, and on that ground, the conviction should be set aside. Tactically, I decided that it would not help to further my submission on the judge's behaviour, mainly because on reflection, and having read the exchange between the judge and myself on the transcript, I thought that I was at fault in my response: to which Lord Lane replied that he thought that the judge and I had traded remarks that the jury would have considered a fair battle of opposing attitudes. At that point, I responded that there was no such balanced judgment; in the eyes of the jury, there is no equality of arms as between judge and counsel. My point was immediately taken by the court. In his judgment allowing the appeal, Lord Lane found a misdirection by the judge on the expert evidence. He also heavily criticised the judge for his unseemly remarks during my cross-examination of the child's mother. A fair trial includes fairness to the accused's counsel as well as to the accused.

For the English lawyer, reared and nurtured in the adversarial mode of trial, advocacy is almost entirely an exercise in fact-finding. To the extent that there will be issues of law in applying the facts as found (or in interlocutory matters, where the facts are as pleaded) advocacy on legal issues is determined by established principles: a judge at trial is not expected to act creatively, his task being to find the law as it is. Creativity (if at all permissible) is for the appellate judge, although the development of public law since the mid-twentieth century, with its emphasis on written statements and largely without any cross-examination, does lend itself to law-making in the general sense. But apart from the process of judicial review of ministerial and administrative decisions, Justice Frankfurter's injunction to the advocate 'not to enlarge the intellectual horizon' is entirely apt for the trial lawyer. To argue the client's case successfully requires an unalloyed attention to the evidential material and the logical conclusions to be drawn from it. The advocate will always have to bear in mind the legal context into which he will steer the factual material. But to engage in urging law reform in the instant trial must be a rare adventure for the advocate. The creative advocate will have to reserve his or her leanings for law reform to the appellate stage.

ON APPEAL

An appeal court's functions are quite different from those of the court of first instance. The facts having been found at trial, the appellate judge(s) will review or revise the reasoned judgment of the trial judge. (If the appeal is in the criminal jurisdiction, the appeal process in a jury trial will be reduced to due process and a limited appeal on the merits of the jury's verdict.) The appeal court's review or revision will be concerned with an assessment of the judge's findings.

Some cases intuitively excite the practitioner-law reformer. Others are designedly brought by individuals who view the individual's right of access to justice to argue a wider public interest for their own ends, to challenge existing principles of law head-on. Both types of case are actively promoted and even assisted by pressure groups intent on pursuing their reformist agendas. Other cases induce in certain advocates the spirit of inquiry and testing of legal issues. In short, the legal system is in public perception inert, if not static; as such it invites the progressive advocate to advance the development of the system, if only in the practice and procedure of the courts.

When Norbert Rondel, a West London Rachmanite henchman, was convicted in May 1959 of grievous bodily harm to a doorkeeper of tenanted property, and sentenced to 18 months' imprisonment, no one could have imagined for one moment that in February 1965 (just within the period of limitation) the role of the advocate at the Old Bailey proceedings would re-emerge in the form of civil proceedings to question the professionally cherished immunity of barristers from suits for professional negligence. *Rondel v Worsley*,[2] a House of Lords decision in 1967 thus became an extensively discussed issue of law reform. How it got its distinctive reformist label discloses a tale of tortuous litigation, initial professional resistance to change, and reformers' failed advocacy, until ultimately (nearly four decades on) a long-established rule of English law was reversed by the House of Lords itself in 2001.

At his Old Bailey trial Rondel had been granted a dock brief, that outmoded method of legal aid for an impecunious defendant in the criminal courts, affectionately depicted in the fictional deeds of Horace Rumpole. The nominee of Rondel's dock brief was an established practitioner at the Central Criminal Court, Mr Michael Worsley. Of all the regular performers there, he was a barrister renowned for his meticulous attention to detail; his earlier experience in the field of accountancy enhanced that particular skill. Any professional colleague would have insisted that he was the last advocate to be guilty of a lack of care in representing his client. Worsley's unsuccessful attempt to persuade the Old Bailey jury in 1959 of an unattractive, even implausible defence did not deter the madness of his client. Once convicted and imprisoned, Rondel complained that Worsley had been incompetent in conducting Rondel's defence, the allegations themselves being barely plausible. Armed with the citizen's fundamental right of access to justice, Rondel nevertheless proceeded to issue a writ alleging negligence. The issue of whether Worsley had failed in his duty of care to Rondel was never put to the test; had it been, there could realistically have been only one answer. Rondel would have been given short shrift by the court. But Worsley, no doubt with supreme confidence of the result, applied to strike out Rondel's claim as disclosing no reasonable cause of action. For at least 400 years, English law had declared that barristers could not be sued for anything done or said in the course of the forensic process. The action was duly terminated at the first instance. But Rondel had a right of appeal on the interlocutory issue.

There was no legal aid in the civil proceedings for Rondel, but undaunted he forged ahead, preparing a shambles of a statement of claim. His plight attracted the attention of a self-proclaimed law reformer and academic author on the legal process who, while teaching law full-time to students at the London School of Economics, nevertheless held a practising certificate as a solicitor.

---

[2] [1969] AC 191.

Professor Zander had prepared a draft statement of claim in proper shape, but that did not overcome the legal point that a barrister could not be sued for professional negligence. The point of law was decided against Rondel by Mr Justice (later Lord Justice) Lawton. By this time, the testing of the legal professional's immunity from civil suit had aroused widespread interest, such that the Court of Appeal gave Rondel leave to appeal. After obtaining that leave Rondel was assisted voluntarily by Professor Zander, who prepared for the members of the Court of Appeal a typewritten document of 116 pages setting out all the arguments and legal authorities in support of the contention that barristers were no longer immune for action for negligence. The Court of Appeal (composed of Lord Denning and Lords Justices Danckwerts and Salmon) agreed to receive this 'brief'. While Lord Denning referred to it as a very valuable document, Lord Justice Danckwerts in his judgment deprecated the practice of a litigant proffering to the court a submission written by a lawyer assisting him. That judicial attitude would not prevail today, since the practice of intervening parties would replace the unsolicited brief from an unrepresented litigant.

Professor Zander's document was indeed not merely impressive as a piece of legal scholarship; it proved to be invaluable, since it formed the basis of counsel's legal submissions made to the House of Lords after the Law Lords had granted Rondel leave to take his case to the final court of appeal. If the legal system appeared to provide the optimum opportunity for testing an important point of law, there was little desire in the public authorities to echo the judicial initiative. The legal aid authorities rejected Rondel's application for leading and junior counsel to be briefed in the House of Lords at public expense on the ground that it appeared to the committee 'unreasonable' that Rondel should receive legal aid, in the circumstances of the case. A judicial review of the legal aid committee's decision failed. Rondel appeared, represented by junior counsel, instructed by Professor Zander, without fee.

Despite, at its outset in 1965, an unpromising prospect for change in the law, the case was propelled thereafter by the zest of the advocates for Rondel for law reform. The upholding by the Law Lords of the advocates' immunity was in practice a loosening of the established rule. Hitherto the rationale for the profession's protection against disgruntled clients took a decisive turn which envisaged ultimate abandonment of the immunity. Barristers, it was argued rather absurdly, but effectively, received payment for their services only as an honorarium and not as a contractual liability. So they could not be sued. Such a spurious and antique ground for the immunity could not survive twentieth-century judicial scrutiny. A study of Lord Reid's judgment (the lead of five separate judgments) put the basis for the immunity squarely on the grounds of transient public policy. The peculiar nature of the barrister's duty to the court was reflected in a peculiar approach to the obligations of the profession – in fact, the profession of advocacy, since the Law Lords included the solicitor-advocate, who had not, until then, shared the same protection. Moreover, public policy was not immutable. Lord Reid contemplated that changing practice in legal services to litigants might be reflected in a change in public policy. So it has proved to be.

The House of Lords' decision in 1968 had a unique consequence for me, counsel for Rondel. Some years later, in *Spring v Guardian Insurance Co*,[3] Lord Lowry said this:

> In marshalling my thoughts on public policy I have drawn freely upon the argument in *Rondel v Worsley* [1969] 1 AC 191 at 203 of Louis Blom-Cooper whose submissions, although not rewarded with success in that appeal, strike me as particularly appropriate in the context of the present case.

Can any losing advocate have received a more rewarding consolation prize than that? But even that was not the end of the *Rondel v Worsley* saga for me. When I sat as a justice of appeal in the Court of Appeal for Jersey in 1996 the issue arose whether the law of Jersey was bound by a House of Lords decision. Sir Godfray Le Quesne, the doyen among us mainland counsel who were appointed to the two Courts of Appeal for the Channel Islands, criticised my judgment assenting in the decision not to strike out the plaintiff's action in *Picot v Crills*.[4] I concluded that only a decision of the Judicial Committee of the Privy Counsel bound the courts of Jersey: the decisions of the House of Lords were only powerfully persuasive. I went on, with a hint of diffidence, to cite Lord Lowry's words of comfort and hold that *Rondel v Worsley* was no longer good law in Jersey:

> Modesty compels me to say that the compliment [paid by Lord Lowry] does no more than hint that public policy considerations today might support, in Lord Lowry's eyes, the demise of the barrister's immunity. Indeed, I may be so bold as respectfully to repay the compliment, and to draw on Lord Lowry's approach to the court's application of public

---

[3] [1995] 2 AC 296, 326.
[4] 1995 JLR 33.

policy – that unruly horse which judges ride at their peril, a particularly dangerous standard if it is employed to oust some fundamental right.

'[Public policy] is a very unruly horse, and once you get astride it you never know where it will carry you. It may lead you from sound law. It is never argued at all but when other points fail',

per Burrough J in *Richardson v Mellish* (1824) 2 Bing 229 at 252, [1824–34] All ER Rep 258 at 266. Lord Lowry [whose Chief Justiceship of Northern Ireland during the 'troubles' was distinctive in upholding the independence of that judiciary at a time of civil conflict], in the context of careless misstatements in an employer's reference said ([1994] 4 LRC 302 at 326–327, [1995] 2 AC 296 at 325–326):

'The defendants' second argument (which, in order that it may prevail, must be made to stand independently on its own feet) is that, even if one concedes foreseeability and proximity and even if it would otherwise be just and reasonable for the plaintiff to recover under the head of negligence, *public policy dictates* that the person who has been the subject of a negligent misstatement shall not recover. The argument is grounded on the proposition that the maker of the misstatement, provided he has acted in good faith, must, even if he has been negligent, be free to express his views in the kind of situation (including the giving of any reference) which is contemplated by the doctrine of qualified privilege which is part of the law of defamation. This argument falls to be considered on the assumption that, but for the overriding effect of public policy, a plaintiff who is in the necessary proximate relation to a defendant will be entitled to succeed in negligence if he proves his case. To assess the validity of the argument entails not the resolution of a point of law but a balancing of moral and practical arguments. This exercise could no doubt produce different answers but, for my own part, I come down decisively on the side of the plaintiff. On the one hand looms the probability, often amounting to a certainty, of damage to the individual, which in some cases will be serious and may indeed by irreparable. The entire future prosperity and happiness of someone who is the subject of a damaging reference which is given carelessly but in perfectly good faith may be irretrievably blighted. Against this prospect is set the possibility that some referees will be deterred from giving frank references or indeed any references. Placing full reliance here on the penetrating observations of my noble and learned friend Lord Woolf, I am inclined to view this possibility as a spectre conjured up by the defendants to frighten your Lordships into submission. I also believe that the courts in general and your Lordships' House in particular ought to think very carefully before resorting to public policy considerations which will defeat a claim that ex hypothesi is a perfectly good cause of action. It has been said that public policy should be invoked only in clear cases in which the potential harm to the public is incontestable, that whether the anticipated harm to the public will be likely to occur must be determined on tangible grounds instead of on mere generalities and that the burden of proof lies on those who assert that the court should not enforce a liability which prima facie exists. Even if one should put the matter in a more neutral way, I would say that public policy ought not to be invoked if the arguments are evenly balanced: in such a situation the ordinary rule of law, once established, should prevail.' (Lord Lowry's emphasis.)

In marshalling my thoughts on public policy in relation to the conduct of an advocate's conduct of the client's case, I begin by asserting the fundamental right of anybody to sue the professional person for negligence, without any legal hindrance to coming to court. In so reminding myself, I do not adopt a neutral stance. A citizen's right to unimpeded access to the courts can be taken away only by express enactment: see *Chester v Bateson* [1920] 1 KB 829, *R & W Paul Ltd v Wheat Commission* [1936] 2 All ER 1243, [1937] AC 139, *Raymond v Honey* [1982] 1 All ER 765 at 762, [1983] 1 AC 1 at 14 per Lord Bridge of Harwich. And here there is no 'express enactment', only judge-made law. What aspects of public policy in 1995 are so powerful as to supplant or negative this fundamental right? And can they survive the impact of art 6 of the European Convention on Human Rights (Convention for the Protection of Human Rights and Fundamental Freedoms (Rome, 4 November 1950; TS 71 (1953) Cmd 8969))?[5]

Five years later the House of Lords in *Simmonds v Hall* reversed its own decision. Their judgments made no reference to my bold departure from the law laid down in *Rondel v Worsley*, probably because counsel did not cite the Jersey case to their Lordships. I was spared any criticism from their Lordships for such forensic irreverence.

Unattractive individuals are attracted to advocacy for change. Prisoners in particular have plenty of time on their hands, and some devote their attention to pursuing claims in the courts. One of them, Steven Raymond, at one time in a life of professional crime a student of criminology, did much to advance the cause of prisoners' rights. *Raymond v Honey*,[6] which found its way straightforwardly to the House of Lords via a two-judge court in the Divisional Court of the Queen's Bench Division, established the proposition that a convicted prisoner retains all civil rights which are not taken away expressly or by necessary implication. That proposition led to a striking down of a prison rule as ultra vires, since it interfered with a prisoner's fundamental or constitutional right of access to justice. Raymond had deliberately provoked a prison governor to prevent him from lodging an application to the High Court. The decision of

---

[5] [1995] 2 LRC 247, 262.
[6] [1983] 1 AC 1.

the courts, holding the governor to be in contempt of court, was predictable, even if it came about by a prisoner's design. Raymond's case was advanced mainly by his counsel uncovering a recent decision of the Supreme Court of Canada on precisely the same point of law (it was readily conceded without demur by counsel for the governor, Mr Andrew Collins (later Mr Justice Collins)). For the last 30 years, *Raymond v Honey* has spawned a raft of cases that continues to give prisoners the entitlement to judicial review of purported justification by prison authorities for infringements of prisoners' rights. This represents a huge improvement on the days when prisoners' right issues were not even considered justiciable, although it played no part in sustaining the constitutional right of a convicted prisoner to exercise the franchise during his incarceration. Advocacy can come from unexpected quarters in unexpected ways.

18

Criminal Justice on Trial

A PERSON'S CRIMINAL liability is precluded from the findings and determination of any public inquiry. It is a matter exclusively for courts of law. The mode of trial is the term used – in Western Europe, the trial is to seek the truth surrounding the criminal event; in England it is generally not the 'truth' that matters. The question is whether on the evidence adduced in the courtroom the prosecution has proved its case beyond a reasonable doubt. The truth about the criminal event is normally inferred from a proven offence. What happened, then, if a criminal trial had produced a miscarriage of justice left uncured by the national appellate system?

Uniquely at that time, in 1975, the Home Secretary, Mr Roy Jenkins and the Attorney-General, Mr Sam Silkin QC (in differing ways, two outstanding politicians of their day) ordered an inquiry into the circumstances leading to the conviction (later quashed by the Court of Appeal) of two of three boys charged with the unlawful killing of Maxwell Confait, a transvestite homosexual living in a house in Lewisham, south London, and the arson of the premises, following the homicide. The quashing resulted from the disputable timing of the cause of death. The inquiry, which reported in December 1977, was conducted by Sir Henry ('Harry') Fisher (son of a former Archbishop of Canterbury), a lawyer of high distinction who, after a short time as a High Court judge, had resigned and, much to the overt displeasure of the legal establishment, went into investment banking in the City of London, and later became the Master of Wolfson College, Oxford.

The ensuing report[1] was a masterpiece of legal analysis of English criminal procedure that led up to the Royal Commission on Criminal Justice (the Phillips Commission) and the historic reform in the Police and Criminal Evidence Act 1984, known in legal circles,

---

[1] *Report of an Inquiry by the Hon Sir Henry Fisher into the circumstances leading to the trial of three persons on charges arising out of the death of Maxwell Confait and the fire at 27 Doggett Road, SE6* (London, HMSO, 1977).

affectionately, as PACE. (It did indeed produce outstandingly a vital reform, successful in altering police investigation.) The three boys had been found guilty as a result of confessions that they had made after extensive police questioning, without any independent person present at their interrogation. The three boys were Ronnie Leighton, then aged 15, who was clearly of limited intelligence; Colin Lattimore, then aged 18, who was mentally handicapped; and, third, a young (aged 14) Turkish-Cypriot boy called Ahmet Salih. At their trial in November 1972, Lattimore was convicted of manslaughter on the ground of diminished responsibility; Leighton was convicted of murder. All three were convicted of arson. The Fisher Report states:[2]

> I make criticisms of the way in which the boys were interrogated and the statements taken. But despite these criticisms, I conclude that the record is in all material aspects substantially accurate, and that (apart from that part of the confessions which relates to Lattimore's participation in the killing) the answers and statements are substantially true. The answers could not have been made and statements given as they were unless at least one of the boys was involved in the killing and arson. If that conclusion is correct then it is not controverted by the fact that the story told is bizarre and improbable; it could be controverted only if there were factual evidence *inconsistent* with the truth of the statements which (apart from Lattimore and the killing) there is not.

The case for the prosecution (which never wavered) was, from the outset, that Leighton and Lattimore had jointly administered a ligature to Confait's neck and killed him, while Salih had stood in the doorway to the room witnessing, but not taking part in, the homicidal act. The case at trial had been heavily dependent on the time of Confait's death. Subsequently, on a reference of the case to the Court of Appeal, it turned out that the time of death had been hopelessly misjudged by the forensic pathologist, Dr Cameron (famous for his misdiagnosis in the Chamberlain case in Australia). It was due to a failure to take account of the effect of the heat engendered in the building by the fire (allegedly started by the three) as part of testing the onset of *rigor mortis*. When the evidence at the inquiry discovered that Lattimore had a cast-iron alibi, it seemed that the consequence for any inquirer was crystal clear. Brimful of confidence – a trait to be avoided by any aspiring advocate – I argued on behalf of the boys that the explanation for the killing of Confait, which had been assiduously advanced by the prosecution, was in

----

[2] ibid 75, para 9.5.

tatters. The case against all three collapsed entirely. It was, I imagined, inconceivable that Harry Fisher could reconstruct the homicidal event such as to inculpate any of the three boys for the killing. In order not to make the reader of this essay doubt that what I say transpired, I recite verbatim what Harry wrote (unaided, and therefore unguided in the analysis, I should add, by either of his two joint secretaries, civil servants respectively in the Home Office and the Law Officers' Department).

At paragraph 2(c) at page 8 of the report of 13 December 1977 there appears this finding:

> I accept the evidence that Lattimore was at the Salvation Army Torchbearers youth club from about 7.30 pm to about 11.30 pm. I find that he was not present in the killing of Confait, and that all three boys could have taken part in setting fire to 27 Doggett Road.

and then at paragraph 2(d) – wait for it! –

> I find that Leighton and Salih could have been present at *and taken part in the killing of Confait* and that all three boys could have taken part in setting fire to 27 Doggett Road.

And, at paragraph 9.7:

> I conclude that the explanation which does least violence to the evidence is that Leighton and Salih were involved in the killing; that all three boys took part in the arson at 27 Doggett Road; and that Leighton and Salih persuaded Lattimore to confess falsely to having taken part in the killing. I so find on the balance of probabilities.

Thus, without more ado, the young Turkish-Cypriot boy was taken from his position as observer in the doorway to the room and pitchforked into the killing, thus fingered as one of the two individuals who had strangled Confait. (Before I make any comment on the extraordinary leap from factual data to absurd surmise, I should add that, a few years later, two men in prison admitted that it was they who had unlawfully killed Confait.) There could hardly be a clearer case of a total miscarriage of justice. The three boys were not just legally innocent as a result of the quashing of their original conviction and release from prison after three years in custody. They were factually innocent of any crime at 27 Doggett Road on that fatal day, including the event of arson subsequent to the homicide.

Harry Fisher's findings of who were the probable killers reminds me of the remark attributed to Professor Harold Laski when he once replied to a question how he viewed a fellow political scientist who was regarded as his adversary in academic circles: 'What I like about that man,' Laski replied, 'is that he has his feet firmly planted in mid-air'. It is my experience of a professional life in the law that, likewise among practising lawyers, let alone academics, there are some immensely clever judges and barristers who exhibit similar attributes to Professor Laski's colleague. There is a word in Yiddish – *nudnik* – which, translated, roughly means the village simpleton. A 'Phudnik' is a *nudnik* with a PhD. There were quite a few Phudniks in my day, and I am sure that there are still some who grace the top echelons of the legal profession. I venture to think that these persons were – much less so, today – the products of their education and training. Most of the judges of the twentieth century (less so in the twenty-first) had been educated at private prep schools, then at one of a number of prominent independent (misleadingly called 'public') schools, followed by Oxbridge and ultimately going to the Temple. In short, they had been reared in an environment that was singularly monastic; their links with the world, outside their socially elitist upbringing, were remote. Even when they engaged in practice at the Bar, their association with lay clients did not appear to varnish their unworldliness. I am glad to see that, for a variety of reasons, this former image of our judiciary is obsolescent, if not obsolete. Diversity as a major element in appointing the judges may still not have become other than a matter of wish-fulfilment, but it is having an impact on the social attitudes of the legal profession. The remnants of 'judge-itis' are waning.[3]

It is now 40 years since the Confait inquiry (which incidentally was conducted in private) emerged into the sunlight of public scrutiny. But at the trial in November 1972, two aspects of forensic science displayed a further failing of the legal process. The ultimate discovery of the true perpetrators of the unlawful killing of Confait, and the significant reforms of the criminal process in the legislation of 1984 should have restored public confidence in criminal justice. Alas, subsequent miscarriages of justice have not disappeared from the criminal courtrooms. Why is this? The inherent feature (I regard it as a weakness) of the Anglo-Saxon adversarial system of criminal justice is the absence of judicial control, or at least independent overseership, of the investigation of criminal events by police officers. Unlike other legal systems (which may have their own faults or deficits) the analysis of evidential material in the English system is not undertaken until the trial, often many months after the criminal event, which can lead to evidence being delayed and untested. The

---

[3] See Ch 3, 'Judges in Public Inquiries, Redivivus'.

decision-makers (judge and jury) are presented with a version of events constructed by the investigators and the prosecution. The creation of the Crown Prosecution Service (a major development in 1984) and the development of pre-trial case management by the courts have lessened the impact of deferred analysis of the evidence for and against the selected accused until tested at trial. At a time when there is a growing awareness of the influence of European systems of criminal trial, it is encumbent upon reformers to conclude that the quality of our criminal justice might benefit from refurbishing in the context of criminality in Europe in the twenty-first century. An analysis of the main features of the binary systems of criminal justice (which increasingly have borrowed from each other in some aspects of the criminal process) gains impetus from Article 6 of the European Convention on Human Rights. This Article provides simply for an unspecified mode of trial that is fair; as such, it should provide the focus for a single European system of criminal justice which incorporates the main principles of fairness to all participants in the public process.

As a psychologist of the *Confait* era, Doreen McBarnet, comments:[4] 'The weakness of civil rights lies not just in abuse of the law, but with the law itself.' If that was so some 40 years ago, it remains the case, despite some, if not all, of the abuses remedied in 1984.

An additional feature of the Confait case deserves a comment. The late Dr Barrie Irving (who died in March 2013), a distinguished forensic psychologist, gave evidence to Fisher in 1976 in which he demonstrated that the confessions of the three boys were false. He was proved to have been right all along. Sir Harry blithely commented that 'if the conclusion was correct then it is not contradicted by the fact that the story told is bizarre and improbable'.[5] It was proved by Dr Irving to be not so bizarre, but factually accurate. The fact is that while Dr Irving, who became the first and distinguished Director of the Police Foundation, is listed as one of the witnesses who gave evidence to the Inquiry,[6] at no point in the report is the contradictory evidence alluded to. His subsequent assignment (1978–81) by the Royal Commission was to carry out observation on police stations. His study included 76 suspects in a Brighton police station. He found that 35 of the suspects made self-incriminating admissions, and another four confessed after the interviews ended. He also identified 165 different tactics used by the police to obtain

---

[4] (1978) 41 *Modern Law Review* 455.
[5] Report n 1, para 9.5.
[6] ibid Appendix D p 249.

confessions. This information amply justified the reforms proposed by the Royal Commission, and adopted by the legislature in PACE. But the judicial unwillingness to accept expert evidence in the area of psychological behaviour is still lamentably suspicious.

19

Victims Adrift

PRIVATE PROSECUTIONS TODAY are obsolescent, if not obsolete. Ever since the family of Stephen Lawrence unsuccessfully raised the criminal liability of his killers (two men were later convicted by the Crown Prosecution Service of his murder), the victim's ability to prosecute had been severely truncated. The corollary is the disinclination, if not the denial of a prosecution at the insistence of anyone other than the public prosecutor.

But legislation persists to confer the right of the individual (the victim) to prosecute. To allow the public prosecutor to trump the victim's access to the courts, and then instantly to drop the criminal proceedings, is intrinsically unfair. More apposite, it would be fairer to abolish the right to prosecute individually. The state's duty to safeguard the victim is a matter of social justice. Where the Director of Public Prosecutions declines to take criminal proceedings, there is statutory recognition that he may take over the prosecution from the private prosecutor and then proceed to discontinue the suit. In effect, criminality is, by implication, a public concern, in which the victim is of course a prime concern, but only as a crucial witness.

If private prosecutions are a dead letter, there remains a desire that, if a case is not prosecuted, the Director of Public Prosecutions should be required to supply adequate and intelligible reasons for his decision. In the *Treadaway* case, however, Rose LJ dampened the hope that reasons would ordinarily be given not to prosecute.[1] In the Republic of Ireland a similar approach was made. In *H v Director of Prosecutions and the Commissioner of Gardia Síochána*,[2] O'Flaherty J, in the Supreme Court, said that 'in deciding whether to bring or not to bring a prosecution, the Director is not settling any question or dispute or reciting rights or liabilities; he is simply making a decision on whether it is appropriate to initiate a prosecution'.

---

[1] *R v Director of Public Prosecutions, ex parte Treadaway* The Times, 31 October 1997.

[2] [1994] 2 IR 589, 602.

Exceptionally, reasons are required as an aspect of the duty to act fairly. In *R v Director of Public Prosecutions, ex parte Manning and Melbourne*,[3] a prisoner had died in the course of a struggle with prison officers. Death resulted from fatal pressure to the prisoner's neck, which had been applied by one particular officer. Lord Bingham CJ, in declining to impose an absolute and unqualified obligation to give reasons for a decision not to prosecute, nevertheless decided that the death of a person in custody, followed by an inquest culminating in a verdict of unlawful killing, called for the giving of reasons why the Director of Public Prosecutions declined to act on the coroner's verdict.

The *Manning* case was treated by Gillen J (now LJ) in *Re Adams*,[4] however, as little more than a working illustration of 'that exceptional class of case where even a Director of Public Prosecutions will be required to furnish reasons to a victim for failing to prosecute'. In that case, the applicant had successfully sued for damages for injuries inflicted on him by a police officer while on reception at Castlereagh Holding Centre, Belfast. Gillen J, at the end of an exhaustive review of the case law, declined to order the giving of reasons by the DPP not to prosecute the police officer or other officers in attendance at the Holding Centre. (Paradoxically, the documentation in the judicial review proceedings effectively disclosed the reasons for not prosecuting.)

The decision to prosecute or not is, like any other administrative decision or act, susceptible to judicial review. As such, the traditional grounds should apply to uphold the administrator's decision, or otherwise. But, in upholding such action, the court ought, as a general rule, to demand some explanation, and not just exceptionally. The duty to consult can often predicate the legitimate expectation induced by the decision-maker. Reasons alone will often satisfy the public that a prosecution is not justified. Silence simply feeds suspicion of some political or ulterior motive. The recent public disquiet over the respective acquittals of media celebrities and others, such as the Deputy Speaker of the House of Commons, following the disclosure of multiple sexual offences, revealed also in the case of Jimmy Savile, has prompted a more careful scrutiny by officialdom of such sexual prosecutions with a greater degree of reasons for apparently wider use of proceedings against the victims of sexual offences.

---

[3] [2000] 3 WLR 463.
[4] Northern Ireland High Court, 7 June 2000.

The disappearance of the victim of crime from the criminal justice system reinforces the awareness of the exclusivity of Article 6 of the European Convention on Human Rights to the fairness in public of a criminal trial; the fact that the criteria for Article 6 encompass the pre-trial procedure after the defendant has been charged with a criminal offence, does not minimise the priority accorded to the trial proceedings. The human rights question remains whether the policy and practices of the public prosecutor excludes the like activity of a private prosecutor. The answer would appear to be unanimous, that it applies to public prosecutions alone. The existence of the European Arrest Warrant would seem impliedly to support a single system of prosecution policy. Like letter-writing today, it slips from view.

The trend towards greater involvement by victims in the criminal justice system is not new; in practice the victim of crime predominated until the creation of a police force in 1829 and the ultimate establishment of a public prosecutor in 1880. Even then public prosecution did not obliterate private action in the criminal courts, although such private prosecutions dwindled in the twentieth century, while legislation seeking to protect indirectly the victims of crime continued. But in providing relevant evidence for a fair trial, victims have displayed little direct interest to the court. Apart from allowing victim witness statements to be proffered in the sentencing process, there is no formula for victims to participate as witnesses in the trial other than in testifying to admissible events. An offered experiment to finance assistance to the families of murder victims was sparsely supported; it was not enacted.

The voice of the victim was freshly aired when a scheme for victim support was launched by the retiring Director of Public Prosecutions, Sir Keir Starmer QC. His analysis of insufficient concern for the plight of victims induced a national review and reform of victim issues that call for action both before and after trial. Active participation by way of evidence or advocacy is incompatible with the due process of a fair trial under Article 6 ECHR, peculiarly where the mode of criminal trial by jury adequately encompasses the populace and excludes the professional adjudicator.

At the time of my becoming in 1994 the chairman of Victim Support (the National Association of Victim Support Schemes), the publicly funded organisation (to the tune of £13m a year from central government, in addition to 20 per cent from its own income) was well established, focusing its volunteer members on assisting victims with the personal consequences of being victims of crime.

At that point the emphasis of its activities had been extended to the establishment of an ancillary system of witness service for victims only at the Crown Court. The activity perceptibly shifted its purpose from general assistance and counselling to criminal justice activity. The immediate interest became focused on the sentencing of offenders rather than with the trial process and its immediate consequences.

The primary role of Victim Support grew out of its origins in the 1970s as an adjunct of work by probation officers; as such it associated its work within the non-custodial aspect of the criminal justice system in pursuance of its aspect of criminal prosecutions. With the diminution in the early twentieth century of the private prosecution and the advent of the police force and formal prosecution in 1880, the victim of crime became increasingly irrelevant to the criminal process. But the victim's needs did not disappear; increasingly after the Second World War they involved aspects of social justice, including the important supply of information about the victim's offenders throughout the criminal justice system, emphasising the public interest in the penal solution of the criminal courts. In the latter respect English criminal justice became evidentially more lacking in transparency. As Sir Robin Auld explained in his *Review of the Criminal Courts*,[5] by far the greatest number of complaints came to him from those who had been called to give evidence in criminal trials. He emphasised proposals directed towards consultation about criminal proceedings or discontinuation of a prosecution.

Another development in the early days of the twenty-first century was the desire of the victim support movement to be involved, either directly or indirectly, with the sentencing of offenders. This was most marked on the part of the families and associates of those killed unlawfully. Victim impact statements (a phrase borrowed from the United States as victim statements) were sufficiently prolific in documentation preferred to public prosecution to require official recognition. While some victim statements were acceptable to the criminal courts, the legal profession was resistant to any official form of the statements being used in the sentencing process, although there was some judicial sympathy for the ability to rebut an accusation made by the offender's advocate that had gone unchallenged in the course of the trial. A pilot scheme of advice and assis-

---

[5] R Auld, *Review of the Criminal Courts of England and Wales* (London, HMSO, 2001) 497 para 246.

tance to the relatives of homicide victims was sponsored by the Government. But the results of the study were insufficiently adopted to warrant any reform, and no action was taken.

The role of the victim today would seem to fit much more neatly into the scope of civil justice. Advice and assistance by the social system should be less trammelled by a principle of restorative justice, and more concerned with the remedying of individual harm or hurt, less with a sense of mutuality between the wrongdoer and the injured. Just as the State has the overriding duty to safeguard its citizenry, so the corollary should be an aspect of civil justice, to supplement the safeguard by appropriate action by its social agents. In any event, its past primary role in criminal justice has long since gone. A system of justice to victims is adrift.

Part III

Penal Affairs

20

The Whys and Wherefores of Penal Policy

THERE CANNOT BE any doubt that it is the duty of an elected Government to consult widely about policies regarding its penal system. Security of the state and its populace demands nothing less. To that end it cannot abdicate its bounden duty to others. And there is a need for any Government to have available to it the best and well-informed sources of advice to inform policies, devoid of political partisanship. It must adopt policies that are socially acceptable and maintainable. But how does it arrive at those policies from within established resources? From 1944 to 1964 and again from 1966 to 1978 Government employed the device of independent corporate advice; successive administrations, obdurately, over the last 30 years have declined to look to any corporate body to supply the knowledge and expertise of penal affairs. Was that wise? I was a member throughout the 12 years (1966–78) of the Home Secretary's Advisory Council on the Penal System (ACPS). No other member of that corporate body has put pen to paper; none more survives to tell the tale. One, Sir Leon Radzinowicz, who was a member from 1966 until his retirement in 1972, and who was formerly a member of the predecessor to the ACPS, the Advisory Council on the Treatment of Offenders (ACTO) from 1950–64, had written at length on the two bodies in his autobiography, *Adventures in Criminology*,[1] a fascinating account of his life as the doyen of British criminology in the years after the Second World War. Only the intermission of the aborted Royal Commission on the Penal System, from 1964–66, separated ACTO from ACPS. In his view of the ACPS, Sir Leon said that 'in fairness a broad and dispassionate assessment' of the work accomplished by the Advisory Council on the Penal System 'it should produce nothing but high promise'.[2]

---

[1] L Radzinowicz, *Adventures in Criminology* (London, Routledge, 1998).
[2] ibid 331.

Other observers voiced similar views of overall approval.[3] So the history of Britain's formulation of post-war penal affairs needs to be told.

It was Herbert Morrison as Home Secretary in 1944 who announced his intention to establish an advisory body on the penal treatment of offenders. There was nothing untoward in this; for some time it had been the practice of administrations to set up bodies to supply expertise to Ministers. Such had been predicated ever since the Committee on the Ministry of Government in 1918 under Lord Haldane had described the role and function of government departments.

On 31 March 1998 senior judges in the House of Lords (those were the days when Law Lords sitting on the Appellate Committee could still vote in the deliberative aspect of the Upper Chamber) forced a defeat on the Government on the Crime and Disorder Bill. By 114 votes to 105 they passed an amendment setting up a standing Advisory Council on Criminal Justice and the Penal System, a body somewhat more elaborate and sweeping than its predecessor. At a later stage on 28 April 1998 in the Commons, the Government removed the amendment by 11 votes to two, the two dissenters being Liberal Democrats on the committee. There the matter has rested, parliamentary-wise at least.

After 40 years of independent corporate advice on selected topics of penal reform, why did the Governments abandon such advisory bodies? The plain argument for change was the Home Secretary's wish not to revert to old-style matters of policy-making, but to be forward-looking in seeking expeditious advice and prompt action, either administratively or legislatively. Delay in earlier processes of the ACPS dictated to central government much swifter action. The recipe for dealing with the delayed advice in the past was altogether a lame excuse for a speedier process. In 1991, when Mr Kenneth (later Lord) Baker set up the Royal Commission on Criminal Justice, following the court reversal of the conviction of the Birmingham Six, he specifically gave Lord Runciman and his colleagues two years to complete their assigned task. They duly complied; the report was published in 1993. Time limits for reporting topics to Ministers are common enough. Indeed, the Commission on a Bill of Rights was asked in March 2011 to report by the end of 2012; it submitted its report on 18 December 2012. If the ACPS had been unnecessarily dilatory in proffering its advice – and there were grounds

[3] ibid 352, fn 16.

for this complaint – the remedy was for Ministers to impose a limit – an easy enough device to import in the terms of reference. In a letter of May 1998, Mr Jack Straw wrote to me, emphasising that he had various relevant sources which he could, and did regularly consult. But they were disparate bodies in the areas of criminal justice and were not independent bodies with the specified remit to render advice on remitted topics. Jack Straw, moreover, initiated lunchtime meetings with experts on penal issues of the day. He listened attentively, but heard nothing other than what he wanted to hear. I was a consistent member of these groups. I concluded that the philosophy (if it can be called that) of 'tough on crime, and tough on the causes of crime' outbid any rival claim for evidence-based knowledge and informed views on penal issues. Penal reform was a matter for pressure groups whose voice was drowned by the politics of the Government and the Opposition alike. Since 1998, any attempts to persuade Government to take advisory opinion failed miserably to receive anything but polite rejection. It is not without note that in Mr Straw's recent (2012) autobiography of over 400 pages, penal affairs receive not even a passing reference during his period of Home Secretaryship, when prison administration often arose to cause public disquiet.

The final report of the ACPS in June 1978, *Sentences of Imprisonment*, was on maximum penalties. With the exception of the chapter on the mandatory life sentence for murder (which was foremost in the long-standing debate on the penalty for murder, still unresolved) the remainder of the report's recommendations on maximum penalties were not implemented, nor even seriously discussed publicly. The report received a hostile reception from academic criminologists and was quietly buried in Whitehall circles, and has never resurfaced. Yet it was hardly the most radical policy to come from that body.

The proposal, which was specifically only for a trial period of three to five years, sought to respond to the Home Secretary's request for guidance, since it was obvious that the maximum penalties on the statute book had grown, higgledy-piggledy, over the last hundred years. The device for new maxima was to equate the existing statutory provisions with a figure that represented 90 per cent of what the courts currently passed on offenders within the maxima provided. The result of fixing the new maxima across the statute book was to determine the 90 per cent rule for each separate offence. Thus, for example, the statutory maximum penalty for rape was life imprisonment; the 90 per cent rule reduced that to seven years. The

Council made absolutely no evaluation of the maximum for any offence; it merely applied the mechanical rule, whatever the result. But it felt compelled to deal with the exceptionally serious cases, for which the maxima would be regarded publicly as a wholly inadequate penalty for the specific crime. The Council proposed that the trial judge could exceptionally (according to prescriptive criteria) escape the new statutory maxima and impose sentences for cases of 'serious harm'.

The two criminologists – Professor Sir Leon Radzinowicz and Dr (later Professor) Roger Hood – published a letter to the editor of *The Times* (19 July 1978) severely criticising the Council, on the footing that the Council abandoned the principle of equality as introducing an unacceptable proposal of bifurcation. Their criticism was hugely influential, and led to the report lying fallow. Some of the criticism was seriously flawed and unfair. I said so, and produce, substantially, what I said at the time. I repeat the substance of my response, which was warmly applauded by a number of my colleagues. Since the argument advanced by the Council is relevant today (2014), it is worthy of repetition, even if rejected in the final analysis.

> Any contribution from two of our leading criminologists about what sentencing system this country should adopt commands instant attention from any student of this intractable social problem. The critique by Sir Leon Radzinowicz and Dr Roger Hood on July 19, 1978, of the report of the Home Secretary's Advisory Council on the Penal System, entitled *Sentences of Imprisonment*, is, however, less than the best that one is entitled to expect. The two authors, in substantial part, misunderstand the purport of the Council's proposals and disappointingly fail to proffer any alternative, practical solution. Their criticisms are long (and well-grounded) on penological theory but short (and hence unhelpful) on the hard world of realism, where penal theory has to be translated into legislation and judicial practice. [Much of what they complain about, the bifurcation of the system of sentencing serious offenders, was in fact adopted in later legislation, specifically in the fatal creation of IPPs – imprisonment for public protection – in the legislation of 2003.]
>
> First, the misapprehensions. The authors do not properly understand the application of the proposed '90% rule'. It is correct of course to state that the Council recommends that the new maximum for each offence should be calculated at the level of 90% of current sentences passed by Crown Court judges. But it is inaccurate to state that 'for the remaining 10% the Council proposes power to impose an exceptional sentence'. This suggests a demarcation rigidly fixed at the 90% level. That is simply not the case. Paragraph 170 of the Council's report states, loud and clear: 'The figure merely fixes a dividing line between the ordinary

offender and the exceptional offender . . . It does not, of course, mean that in future years a fixed 90% of those imprisoned will be ordinary offenders and a fixed 10% of the exceptional cases.' To take a concrete example, it may be that rarely, if ever, will a convicted thief satisfy the criterion for an exceptional sentence. Thus 100% (or only slightly less) of the thieves who are thought to merit imprisonment will receive sentences below the substantially reduced new maximum of three years' imprisonment. Rapists, on the other hand, might frequently qualify for the exceptional sentence, in which case perhaps more than 10% of those sent to prison might receive sentences longer than the new reduced maximum of seven years.

The definition, devised to reflect cases of serious harm for which alone an exceptional sentence would be available, is arguably defective in penological terms. What the Council had in mind to do was to propose something it thought would accommodate a wide variation of opinion on what constituted the justification for a protective sentence. It avoided the term 'dangerousness' as far as possible, for the very reason that the concept of dangerousness is ambiguous. The Council would welcome any suggestion for improving the criterion, for it acknowledges (paragraph 316) that its guiding formula might be considered insufficiently precise. It wants to ensure that only those offenders who represent a risk of serious harm would qualify for sentences in excess of the new reduced maxima. If others escape the barrier of the ordinary maximum, the formula will not have achieved the Council's purpose.

It is precisely because this is an area of obstinate difficulty and uncertainty in practice that the Council was insistent that the two-tier scheme should be subjected to an experiment – lasting 3 to 5 years – before any legislation is even contemplated. It is sad to hear Dr Hood, who has been a persistent critic of the Council for its failure in the past 12 years to pay proper regard to criminological research, failing to acknowledge the Council's insistence, on this occasion, that some scheme like the two-tier system should be put under the researcher's microscope (indeed, a *leitmotif* of the Council's report is the need for detailed research into sentencing practice). Further, it is difficult to understand – except on a superficial level – the criticism that the Council's proposal for unlimited lengths of sentences in the exceptional cases would lead to stiffer sentences. The experiment would necessarily have to be conducted within the existing legislative framework of the present maxima. Thus during the researched experiment courts could not pass sentences beyond the present statutory maxima.

The authors are unfair in saying that 'only one safeguard is proposed for the prisoner sentenced to an exceptional sentence'. In fact three safeguards (of various strength) were proposed. First, no reference is made to the significant recommendation that every offender sentenced to an exceptional sentence would be entitled to legal aid. What was intended by this proposal was that every such offender would have his case reviewed by the full Court of Appeal. The authors' conclusion that 'there seems to be no justification for giving unbridled discretion to the judiciary to sentence the exceptional cases' overlooks the fact that such discretion would almost invariably be reviewed by the Lord Chief Justice and his fellow Lords Justices of Appeal who sit regularly in the Court of Appeal (Criminal Division). The Council places more trust in that handful of senior judges than apparently do academic criminologists. Again, the Council would like to see how its system would work in practice before anyone adopts either the Council's scheme or any variation on the theme, or indeed any other viable model.

Second, the Council is further castigated for not building into the parole provisions greater safeguards for the exceptional offender. Rightly or wrongly, the Council regarded the mechanics of the parole system as way outside its terms of reference, much as Dr Hood might have liked the Council to depart from its remit and go along his path of outright hostility to the parole system. That is another subject, perhaps for another remit to a future Council. Third, the Council states (paragraph 208) that an exceptional sentence shall not be imposed without prior warning from the trial judge – a lesser, but not unimportant safeguard.

The Council is finally chastised for having averted its gaze from the intractable problems of sentencing and, in a blinkered way, pursued the safe path of a 'neat, clear-cut solution'. That is also unfair. The Council was acutely aware of the penological philosophies that adorn the subject of sentencing. The debris of disputations among penal theorists is strewn across the battlefield of social science. The Council could have discussed, at interminable length, the competing theories of deterrence, retribution, rehabilitation and social defence. It did not think that line of argument particularly profitable. Sir Leon will recall that he and his fellow Commissioners on the Royal Commission on the Penal System in 1966 came to grief over just such issues, so that, unprecedentedly, that Commission was dissolved.

The Advisory Council was asked to devise a practical and workable system of maximum penalties. It would have been only too easy to have adopted Lord Scarman's proposal of an arbitrary overall ceiling of 5 years' imprisonment; instead the Council went for a gradualist approach to maximum penalties. It put forward its proposals tentatively, with a view to a sustained period of consultation with those involved in the administration of criminal justice; and then, given a fair wind, they would be subjected to a period of experiment.

The Council hopes that both informed and uninformed opinion will contribute to the debate with suggestions for alternative proposals. Sir Leon Radzinowicz and Dr Roger Hood offered in their article no alternative scheme; they remained faithful to the facile iconoclasm of much modern criminology. Now that the debate has begun in earnest one hopes that they will return to the subject in a more constructive mood. After all, Sir Leon, during a long and distinguished professional life, has ceaselessly thought and taught upon this thorny topic.

The rest was a deafening silence from the two critics of the Advisory Council on the Penal System. It was the last report of the Council, in June 1978. Along with other unrelated quangos it was abolished, even though a distinguished former Conservative Minister, Lord Windlesham, deeply regretted its demise.

One sentence uttered by the Advisory Council is worthy of repetition, if only because it is lost in the plethora of legislation on sentencing, but is largely relevant today in the context of a rising prison population. In an interim report in 1977 on its study of maximum penalties the Council pronounced: 'A longer sentence of imprisonment is no greater deterrent than a shorter one'. How many sentencers respond favourably to that simple principle in computing their sentence lengths?

If only the current policies had been subjected to scrutiny, as was the case in 1978, the date of the Advisory Council's last report, it might have alerted the penal administrators to the folly of the exercise of the Criminal Justice Act 2003. In the last two decades legislative and administrative policies have underlined the validity of the criticisms of how we deal with dangerous offenders. The hastily-established IPP (imprisonment for public protection) orders of the 2003 legislation (over-hastily introduced in the Parliamentary process) had to be abolished nine years later after the intervention of pressure groups; there was no independent advisory body to warn the policy-makers off the unhappy experience of the IPP system. And present pronouncements from the Secretary of State for Justice do not augur well for the taking of independent advice before penal policy is passed.

21

Community Service: Penological Progress

F ROM THE BIRTH of community service orders, 40 years ago, to today's rebranding of community work as a punishment for crime, the changes witnessed in the penal system are examples of the maxim that penal reform is not necessarily penal progress. Together with the imminent transfer of the probation service (which has assiduously managed the system of rendering a difference in offenders' lives), the innovation in penal policy is for prisoners to be supervised in the private sector performing unpaid work. The intention, apart from cost-cutting, is to impose conditions of employment on prisoners. Thus a private company can make a profit on the back of the State's miscreants repaying their indebtedness, a feature these days of the privatisation of prisons. It is a far cry from the principles set up by the sub-committee (the Wootton Committee) of the Home Secretary's Advisory Council on the Penal System (1966–78). I was a member of the Wootton Committee, and record now how far we have departed from a previously distinct shift in restricting the use of imprisonment and deploying non-custodial penalties and disqualifications. Society is now abandoning, consciously or not, the trend towards reducing the prison population. That is until the Criminal Justice Act 1991, with its ambition to throw off the recent past, alas discarded thereafter.

The Community Service Order, officially sanctioned in the Criminal Justice Act 1972 which rapidly enacted the proposal, was not even as revolutionary as Wootton recommended. Apart from the general proposition that, like probation (itself an innovation at the beginning of the twentieth century), the new order was to be a condition of that sentence which was designed to replace short prison sentences. Moreover, in its aspect of social justice, the Committee hoped that the service would be extended so that offenders would work alongside non-offenders. The time prescribed for this service was limited, doubled by the legislation. The parliamentary approach to the concept was to provide a sanction for non-imprisonable offences by supplying an element that encompassed both ends of the penal spectrum: the liberal approach and the fiercer attitude by conservatives to crime. Instead it was the Wootton Committee itself that concluded its proposals were satisfactory from all shades of penal policy. In patting itself on the back, the Committee felt constrained to come up with an idea that prompted public consensus. It was, however, dismayed not to have completely won over officialdom, but acknowledged that for its public acceptance there was a need to accommodate the inherent concept of punishment for crime.

Barbara Wootton was herself an ardent reformer and no admirer of the English criminal law – she thought that many of our archaic systems of criminal justice and, in particular, the sentencing system, 'seemed incongruous in a scientific age'. Hence the idea of an offender paying the price for less serious crime with work for the community had an instant attraction. But she was not alone, although she supplied the inspiration and leadership to the members. An early example of a sentencing judge in Darmstadt, Germany in 1950 was the impetus to rendering a pragmatist's work to officialdom. Judge Karl Holzschul used his judicial power in ordering an offender, convicted of dangerous driving which had severely wounded a pedestrian, to work as an assistant to nursing staff in the accident and emergency department of the general hospital in Darmstadt for a certain period of time. The story from Germany was instantly seized upon as a sensible way of disposing of the case, and converting the individual judge's idea into a full penal sanction. If the members of the Committee readily adopted the European example, it did not attain the support initially of the officials. After a decorous dismissal of the idea as woolly and liberal (since it might not work in practice), the Home Office adopted the idea. Legislation of the 1970 report in the Criminal Justice Act 1972 was a welcome response. It reflected a groundswell of public support that expected, correctly, a dose of penal reform. It even was injected into our penal systems; thousands of offenders benefited, and still do, even under a harsher regime.

Philosophically, the original idea was that although the Committee regarded a community service order as a sentence of the trial court, it had the virtue of being a constructive penalty whereby the offender accepted the burden of some responsibility towards others. Even the judiciary took to the idea, although traditionally the view was that the offender should not be involved in the sentence imposed. When the Lord Chief Justice, Lord Parker, came to give evidence, he expressed dissent from the idea of a deferred sentence (which was also added in the 1972 legislation). His approach was that the offender ought not to be involved in his own penal treatment, such as providing some task before returning to court for the appropriate penalty. Lord Parker was pointedly told that penal policy indicated a change in the behaviour of the convicted.

The community service order dominated the report, which was given the remit of reviewing 'non-custodial and semi-custodial penalties and disabilities'. The Committee's report later that year (1970) was extensive, but not nearly exhaustive of the disposal of offenders without resort to imprisonment. The movement for avoiding prison sentences for non-violent offences is some way off. So is the tilt of the penal system in favour of treatment and control in the community. Today the aim is to inject an element of punitiveness in addition to a community service order – a sign of the times in penal affairs.

22

Prisoners' Right to Vote

A CONVICTED PRISONER retains all his civil rights, save those which are taken away expressly or by necessary impli-cation. The fundamental (or constitutional) right to vote in the franchise was expressly upheld by the House of Lords in *Raymond v Honey* in 1981;[1] strikingly, there is no mention of it in any of the various judgments on prisoners' votes by the Supreme Court in *R (on the application of Chester) v Secretary of State for Justice* in 2013.[2] The Justices had to consider whether the right to vote for prisoners had been taken away by the electoral law in the Representation of the People Act 1983 (as amended to exclude remand prisoners and dubiously resolved in debate in February 2012), which explicitly endorsed the statutory ban on votes for pris-oners. The Justices were confronted with the case law (since 2006) of the European Court of Human Rights. In *Chester,* on 16 October 2013, the Supreme Court declined to reject the violation of Article 3 of the First Protocol, but did not endorse it. If the result of the appeal was dismissed, much of the reasoning and obiter dicta of the Justices which dealt with the penal aspects of electoral policy are, at best, highly dubious, not least the absence of the right of universal suf-frage in a modern democracy; a prisoner's fundamental right to retain all his civil rights not taken away; the individualism of the sentencing process; and the application of punishment by the State. Why that was worrying is the burden of this essay. But the Court declined the Government's plea not to apply the ECHR's ruling of a violation, but likewise declined to make any further declarations of incompatibility with English law.[3]

If the legal position remains unresolved until Parliament debates the alternative sections in the draft Bill containing an optional response to the 1983 Act, what conceivable harm could there be to

---

[1] [1983] 1 AC 1.
[2] [2014] 1 AC 271.
[3] A parliamentary committee considering the draft legislation has opted to recom-mend that a convicted prisoner serving a sentence of 12 months or less may vote.

anyone in Britain today, or indeed to civilised societies, if those convicted of serious crimes, and serving prison sentences, were not automatically prevented from voting alongside the rest of us in a Parliamentary or local government election? The instinctive answer from the rational citizen is, unequivocally, none, although Lady Hale begins her judgment by proclaiming that the issue is an 'emotive subject'. Why then is it (as of now, in 2014) that the Coalition Government (and no doubt many of its supporters) argue for the blanket disenfranchisement of all convicted prisoners (but not those on remand) – that in committing criminal offences, the prisoner's loss of liberty is rightly forfeited for the period of incarceration? The answer to these two questions depends upon two principles in a civilised society. The first confuses criminality and punishment; the second depends upon whether the disenfranchisement of offenders is a matter of penalty for past wrongdoing, or is based upon harm done in the commission of a relevant offence. After six years of legal wrangling in various courts, the Grand Chamber of the European Court of Human Rights (by the resounding vote of 16 to one) declared that a blanket provision of our law – the Representation of the People Act 1983 (amended marginally in 1985 and 2000) – was a violation of human rights under the Convention. The reaction by Ministers of the Coalition Government was immediate, and disappointingly stated that the Strasbourg Court had got it wrong; although the Supreme Court endorses that stance for the time being. Strasbourg has indicated that, other than an outright ban, a compromise of a lost franchise may comply with the ECHR.

Forfeiture of the right to vote has a respectable ancestry. Parliament disenfranchised serious criminals in 1870 with the ending of transportation to the colonies. Parliament decreed that prisoners should lose the citizen's right to vote, and the High Court in 2001 did not disturb the indiscriminate exclusion of all convicted prisoners from the electorate. But the European Court of Human Rights had other ideas. In 2006 the Court ruled that there was no evidence that Parliament had ever thought to weigh the competing interests, or to assess the proportionality of a blanket ban on the right of a convicted prisoner to vote. It held in other cases that life sentences without benefit of parole were incompatible with Article 3 of the Convention. The Grand Chamber, however, would not be drawn by the UK Government into indicating what would be permissible restrictions on the right to vote. It is not the function of the European Court of Human Rights to give guidance on how Convention rights ought to be enforced. Its function is simply to assess the measures which are in force. The municipal Member State has a margin of appreciation as to what it should provide, as part of a debate which identifies, proportionally and indiscriminatorily, cases where prisoners might lose the vote.

Some years ago, the Department of Constitutional Affairs issued a consultation paper setting out a number of options, although significantly it did not include total enfranchisement. Alternative options included removing the right for the duration of a prison sentence or allowing the trial judge at the sentencing stage to decide whether a particular prisoner should retain voting rights. (I would call this loss of the right to vote a penal sanction, penologically plausible, alongside other non-custodial penalties or disabilities. As such I would doubt whether one such individualised penalty could fall foul of the Convention in much the way that the European Court of Justice at Luxembourg in the 1970s upheld the power to order a convicted person to be bound over and come up for judgment on condition that they lived outside the jurisdiction of the English courts for a number of years.)

After much procrastination by the Labour administration, which prompted the Ministers in the Council of Europe to ask for a response from the UK Government, it belatedly indicated its proposal for legislation in its draft Bill. The Government's persistence in maintaining partial disenfranchisement of prisoners rested on the premise that the more serious criminality, reflected arbitrarily in the lengthier terms of imprisonment, is an adjunct of the prisoner's removal from society and entails removal from the privileges of society, amongst which is the right to vote. This is both bad law and unsound reasoning.

In the landmark case of *Raymond v Honey*[4] the House of Lords held that prisoners retain all their civil rights save those expressly or impliedly taken away. In that case the prisoner's inalienable right of access to justice – surely a basic civil right – was upheld. In subsequent cases, the House of Lords emphasised that prisoners do not lose all the rights of citizenry.[5] The right to vote is a fundamental aspect of a democracy. I was counsel in *Raymond v Honey* (which was heard in the House of Lords in 1981);[6] nothing was said in the court proceedings to indicate that the Government was intending to affirm the lack of any right to vote in all convicted prisoners, even though the electoral legislation in the Representation of the People

---

[4] [1983] 1 AC 1.
[5] *Simms* [2000] 2 AC 115; *Daly* [2001] 2 AC 332.
[6] [1983] 1 AC 1.

Act 1983 was then in the official pipeline. And there appeared at the time none of the penal reform groups – at that time the Prison Reform Trust had only just been formed – little discussion took place until Strasbourg was invoked in the early twenty-first century. By 2011, in an entirely different context, the UK Supreme Court, through Lord Collins of Maplesbury, enunciated the fundamental freedom of the universal franchise in the constitution of the UK. It must be assumed that the rule of law is inapplicable to convicted prisoners, at least until there is an official response to the dictates of the European Convention on Human Rights.

Prisoners are, of course, treated differently from the rest of the population, since the main, if not the sole, object of imprisonment is to curtail personal liberty. Where any civil right is a necessary adjunct of the prison regime, such a right may be lost. But the right to vote is not part of any control of prisoner activity, since it is exercisable outwith the institution, and moreover relates to a fundamental freedom. The law's insistence on equal treatment must ensure that any differential treatment is based on real differences. If (as is the case) the difference in prison length relates to the criminality pre-incarceration (at different trials at different times) how can that differential possibly be an aspect of the prison regime? Apart from keeping the prisoner in custody for the prescribed period, the prison service is rightly indifferent to the imposition of the court's sentence. The Electoral Commission has indicated that the prison administration has no difficulty in arranging for the exercise of penal voting: it does so now for the unconvicted prisoner.

The rationale of disenfranchisement (total or partial) cannot logically be justified on the grounds of a prisoner losing a 'privilege' which is not part of any sanction lawfully imposed by a court or by necessary implication of the fact of lost liberty. Justification for any restriction on the right to vote must relate directly to the proper administration of the prison as it affects the regime and the individual prisoner. And once enfranchisement is conceded to the shorter-term prisoner, what element of proportionality can justify such discrimination? The right to vote is not time-fixed; it is a fundamental right that resides in the prisoner whenever the citizenry is empowered to go to the polls. Since voting is often carried out by post or other method of communication, it cannot be any impediment to the prison administration. What then can justify the Government's disinclination to opt for a reform that pertains in many (although not all) Western European countries? Twelve other

Member States of the Council of Europe grant the right with restrictions. Some, like the UK, are absolute in denying the right.

Far from being harmless, the conferring on prisoners of the unqualified right to vote has positive values. Since one of the purposes of the ban in the UK is a combined one to reduce crime, to punish offenders and to enhance civic responsibility and respect for the rule of law, what better way to incorporate peaceful co-existence in society than to remove any sense of second-class citizenry through disenfranchisement during custodial sentences? It is precisely what the Government is preaching in its Green Paper on sentencing reform – namely, greater and more vigorous efforts in the practices of prison institutions to the rehabilitation of prisoners. Since rehabilitation of prisoners calls for avoiding future misconduct, it relies on the principle that avoiding harmful action is the aim of law enforcement. The harm principle enunciated by John Stuart Mill alone justifies the argument that preventing prisoners from voting does nobody any harm.

The Justices of the Supreme Court appear not to subscribe to (but likewise not to reject) the Mill doctrine of harm, yet they display some odd views about penology. They disavow the basic principle that sentencing offenders is a judicial exercise on the individual offender, and is not a simple reflection of a class penalty. Some prisoners deserve condign punishment, while others warrant nothing other than a temporary loss of liberty. They cannot sensibly or fairly be lumped together. Moreover, mandatory penalties themselves violate a principle of individual treatment, since they do not permit the sentencing court to evaluate the degree of criminality. It is assumed that all imprisonable events automatically deprive the prisoner of a civil right. If so, on what does the deprivation derive its origin? At this point, emotion may play its part, according to Lady Hale, although the Supreme Court is asked to adjudicate with legal reasoning. Will Parliament ultimately endorse the 1983 ban? It is offered a compromise of giving the vote to some prisoners who have offended less seriously. A sentence of 12 months' imprisonment or less has been recommended by a parliamentary committee.

23

Dangerousness

ONE OF THE more useful things I did as chairman of the Howard League for Penal Reform (a post I held from 1973 to 1984) was in May 1976, when I convened a committee of independent experts to review and report on the law and practice in relation to 'dangerous' offenders. The inspired choice of Jean Floud, then Principal of Newnham College, Cambridge, meant that she and her distinguished colleagues learned a great deal more about an intractable topic as a result of the stimulus of organised discussion. Their report, *Dangerousness and Criminal Justice*, published in 1981,[1] demonstrated its value not in terms of any pressing need for change in the present arrangements (on which the members agreed to differ), but on the principles which would delimit and govern the practice of protective sentencing and on proposals for legislation which would embody them; it might prompt an improvement on present practice as and when the time came for refreshing sentencing powers to provide public protection, following the flawed legislation of IPPs (Imprisonment for Public Protection) – introduced in the Criminal Justice Act 2003, and statutorily axed in 2012.

I am unaware of the impact (if any) that the report has had on politicians, save to note that it was prophetic in recognising that change in penal philosophy was in the offing. But until the 1960s, sentencing by the courts largely reflected society's view of just punishment as the prescribed penalty for offences against the criminal law. It contained determinate periods of imprisonment for all serious offences and, apart from a tiny proportion of sentences of life imprisonment, there was no element of public protection, except impliedly in the temporary removal of the offender from the community and the lessening of the risk of future re-offending. Sentencing, broadly speaking, made a distinction only between the offender who was a social nuisance (usually the repetitious, petty

---

[1] Floud and Young, *Dangerousness and Criminal Justice* (London, Heinemann, 1981).

offender) and the social menace of the high-risk offender. Both were held to represent social dangers in the natural sense of danger, meaning an unacceptable risk of harm. Parliament had responded in Acts of 1908, 1948 and 1967 to deal with the problem of persistence and incorrigibility by means of devices of preventive detention and the extended sentence. Otherwise it was left to the courts to use ordinary determinate sentences, or alternatively the indeterminate prison sentence to provide protection against the risk of serious harm. With abolition of capital murder in 1965, life imprisonment became mandatory, with a gradual increase in the 1970s of the numbers of such prisoners, statistically insignificant but socially important in public opinion.

The devices of preventive detention and extended sentences came under sustained attack, directed mainly against the idea of combating the nuisance by draconian means. Often what was a 'danger' was little mentioned, since the index offence hardly warranted such appellation. The state and composition of the class of dangerous offenders was sufficiently small and heterogeneous not to cause official, and certainly not parliamentary, action. All this was documented in the Floud report, which I re-read in 2013; its contents are just as relevant today, as Parliament returns to the pressing issue of sentencing for public protection. The other notable events of that time were the last two reports of the Advisory Council on the Penal System, *The Length of Prison Sentences* (interim) (1977)[2] and *Sentences of Imprisonment* (1978), which had embarked on a review of maximum penalties of imprisonment to deal with the pressing question of the policy to reduce sentences for ordinary offenders. The full report, however, recommended a pilot sentence for adjusting the statutory maxima, but added a possible system for exceeding the maxima for an offence that was especially harmful. The final report was academically and otherwise attacked for introducing a bifurcatory system. If it was prematurely innovative, it was speedily buried by the penal policy of the incoming Conservative Government. The political rhetoric of 'tough on the causes of crime, and tough on the criminal' was swiftly adopted by Blair and Straw. The Labour victory in 1997 endorsed the political acceptance of punitiveness in the system; the prison population had escalated in the 1980s and thereafter. Presently it tops the league table of countries in western Europe at around 85,000.

---

[2] One of the most notable, but judicially ignored, was the statement in 1977 that 'the longer sentences of imprisonment have no greater effect than do shorter sentences'.

Dangerousness is meaningless other than in a social context; that is why the late Peter Scott, an outstanding psychiatrist, once proclaimed that dangerousness was a dangerous concept. Therein lies the difficulty. Who qualifies to be labelled 'dangerous', and how does criminal justice identify him for special treatment? The legislator's task is to provide the sentence with a definition of 'serious harm' and to prescribe for those so defined a civilised system of review and sentence extended beyond that of the normal offender detained under a determined sentence.

It is essential, if not readily to hand, to draw the distinction implicit in sentencing policy between the ordinary offender who pre-emptively receives a penalty for past criminality – call it punishment, if you will – and the exceptional offender whose criminality should be formulated so as to take account of the risk of repetitious behaviour. The legislature's motive should be to infer a substantial reduction in the length of sentences of imprisonment, while providing explicitly a necessary measure for public protection; the latter is punished for the seriousness of his or her crime and additionally is made subject to custodial control beyond the determinate sentence. Other than for the public protection provision, the indeterminate prison sentence should cease to be available for non-homicidal offences. The determinate sentence of imprisonment for public protection should be precisely prescribed as the core of the penal system. For homicidal offences, encompassing serious harm, indeterminacy would remain available discretionarily; the sentence of life imprisonment for murder would cease to be mandatory, which has been loudly proclaimed by reformists for 50 years since the abolition of capital punishment. The reform should bury the myth that the alternative penalty in 1965 meant custody for the rest of the offender's natural life. 'Whole life' sentences – sentences without the benefit of parole, or other form of review – would disappear as non-compliant with human rights. No sentence for imprisonment which inferentially contains an element of protection for the public, or notionally imports a concept of general deterrence, may be made longer than would be justified on other sound penological grounds, unless they are legally provided. The fundamental aim of the legislation would be to endorse the bifurcatory system, recognised but unimplemented in 1978 by the Advisory Council on the Penal System; the penalty system would be to draw a sharp line between the mainstream of offenders and those who represent a future danger of serious re-offending.

The modern penal system, exacerbated by the natural concern to combat terrorism, has been aware of the need for protective sentencing without clearly defining that which is to be statutorily protected. The debate has focused on what constitutes 'serious harm' or 'dangerousness'. It should encompass all unlawful killings, serious bodily harm, serious sexual assaults and other serious crimes involving prolonged pain or mental stress or permanent mental disorder. It covers the worst offences against the person. Should it be extended to property offences? The Advisory Council on the Penal System in 1978 thought that serious fraud, affecting numerous victims, should qualify, even if unaccompanied by any physical violence. Nothing that has occurred since that time should alter that judgment. A victim's deprivation by a fraudster can be just as devastating as a major wound. They both inflict serious harm.

PROTECTIVE SENTENCING

The courts should be empowered, for the protection of others against serious harm by an offender, to sentence him to imprisonment for a specific period greater than that which would ordinarily be specified, but proportional to the seriousness of the anticipated harm and the court's estimate of the duration of the risk. Such would be labelled a protective sentence. The court must be satisfied, both in fairness and proportionality, by reason of the nature of the offence, the offender's character, conduct and antecedents, that the offender is more likely to do further serious harm than other serious offenders. The court must first exclude that there is no sensible way of dealing with the offender which offers the necessary protection for the public. Then, and only then, may the court impose a protective sentence. An offender becomes eligible for a protective sentence only if he has done, attempted, threatened or conspired to do serious harm, as defined, *and* has committed an act of a similar kind on a separate occasion from the instant offence; the protective sentence should be available for a homicide offence, but only so long as the life sentence is available. An offender under the age of 18 at the time of the offence, or suffering from a mental disorder that qualifies for a hospital order under mental health legislation cannot receive a protective sentence; the mental patient can be so ordered if there is no hospital order available. A protective sentence should not be imposed without first giving the offender an opportunity to prepare his defence, together with full reports on the offender's physical and mental health condition. In cases of the imposition of protective orders, the court must state its full reasons, and the order should be reviewable as of right, by the Court of Appeal.

RELEASE ON LICENCE

A protective sentence should entail the minimum curtailment of the offender's liberty compatible with its purpose of depriving the offender of liberty, beyond punishment for criminality, because of a further risk of harm. Such a sentence will initially be served in maximum custody, but the offender should be released on licence as and when he no longer presents a real risk to the public, were he to be released, which should happen at the earliest opportunity. The condition of release should favour specific rather than general curtailments of liberty, but invariably include a power to recall on breach of any condition.

The decision to release an offender on licence and to modify or terminate the conditions of the licence should rest with the Secretary of State for Justice for the duration of the sentence imposed by the court, subject to receiving the decision to review. As soon as the offender is formally notified that his entitlement to review is due, the offender should have access to an advisory body for advice and assistance in the procedure for review. The advisory board, known as the Protective Sentence Advisory Board, shall be independent of the prison administration.

The Secretary of State shall establish an independent body, known as the Parole Board, to carry out the review, assess and evaluate the risk of the offender re-offending, and shall not engage in any exercise of re-evaluating the protective sentence, save for evaluating the index offence for the sole task of risk assessment. The Parole Board shall be an impartial and independent tribunal in compliance with Article 5(4) of the European Convention on Human Rights and equally the principles of the Common Law of England; the Parole Board's decision shall be automatically subject to judicial review, exercisable by 14 days' notice but not subject to any appellate function, save for that established within the Parole Board to consider the availability of the material relevant to the conditions of release on licence. The Parole Board shall consult the Protective Sentence Advisory Board in any case that the Parole Board thinks ought in fairness to be consulted.

A prisoner released from custody in the course of a protective sentence should be subjected to an added element, namely supervision by the Probation Service until such time as the protective sentence expires. The prisoner, on recall, shall be subject to any further conditions of the licence by the Secretary of State for Justice after consultation with the Protective Sentence Advisory Board. If so, the Secretary of State for Justice may impose fresh conditions of the licence for a further period, not exceeding three years, after the sentence imposed by the trial court has expired. But it will do so only if the Secretary of State is of the opinion that such further conditions are desirable in the offender's interest, or in the public interest.

The Parole Board shall consider the case of an offender as soon as is practicable after a protective sentence has been passed and should fix the date for review; in no case should this be later than that on which the prisoner will have served one third of the sentence imposed by the court, whichever be the less (alternatively, whatever fraction as would determine the prisoner's eligibility for parole from a non-protective (ordinary determinate) sentence).

THE MEMBERSHIP OF THE PAROLE BOARD

It has always been a practice for Home Secretaries to exercise a prerogative power to release any prisoner on licence. When in 1966 the Labour administration signalled its wish to legislate for a justice system for post-war Britain it did not, however, include any provision in the Criminal Justice Bill of that year authoritatively regulating its internal (prerogative) powers of discharge. It was envisaged that, as a result of the abolition of the death penalty in 1965, and its replacement of death by 'life' imprisonment, parole would be a consideration of the working of the Department by the new Home Secretary, Mr Roy (later Lord) Jenkins, certainly the most distinguished holder of that office since the Second World War. The subject of paroling prisoners in an expanding prison population was rife, not just among penal reform groups. But the operation of the function of parole in the days when the daily prison population was around 35,000 and when the few 'lifers' (life imprisoned offenders) served around nine years differs distinctly, particularly after the Criminal Justice Act 2003 when it became principally a decision-maker and recall agent.

I was a member of a private delegation in 1966 that sought an assurance from the Home Secretary that there should be established statutorily a parole board that would independently make recommendations to the Home Secretary (the predecessor, until 2007, of the Secretary of State for Justice (the former Minister of the Constitutional Affairs Department)), through an elaborate system of Local Review Committees at the prisons and a board of members to whom the LRCs would report after interviewing the applicant prisoners. Mr Roy Jenkins readily acceded to the request, and the Bill duly included the new authority, the Parole Board. It was made abundantly clear to the deputation that the Home Secretary insisted that the selected chairman would always be a distinguished figure who did *not* possess any legal qualification, and still more would not be a member of the judiciary. It was at that time that the judiciary did not actively support the system, mainly on the ground that the release of prisoners was a function of the court system. It was, however, commendable that from the outset it was accepted that the Board would always contain two serving High Court judges as vice-chairmen of the Board – and so it has remained until very recently.

The first chairman was Lord Hunt of Llanfair Waterdine, publicly known as the leader of the first successful expedition to reach the summit of Everest. He was an outstanding public figure who graced the early beginnings of the statutory parole system. It is no exaggeration to say that his leadership ensured the sound system that has sustained it over the years; although there had been some doubt in the early days of the viability of an independent system established by law.

What emanated from that positive ministerial decision was that the system should be regarded as a vital element in the public administration of the prison system. It would not follow a reasonable argument that any lessening of the time served in custody which exclusively was considered by a criminal court of law had to remain a part of the criminal justice system and was to be reconsidered by a judicial authority. The rival arguments are relevant today, as I shall prescribe later.

The chairmanship of the Board was in the hands of a non-judicial figure until March 2009 when Sir David Latham (a recently retired Lord Justice of Appeal) was appointed part-time, and succeeded in 2012 by Mr Justice David Calvert-Smith, a retired High Court judge who had been a former Director of Public Prosecutions after a distinguished career as a prosecuting counsel at the Old Bailey.

Those favouring a less formal and less rigorous objective procedure than that which pertains to the court of law look for something
more akin to an administrative tribunal, stripped of traditional
legalism. The essential principle for initially detaching a modern
parole system from criminal justice is that, in determining release
from custody, the tribunal must avoid any review (but not a study)
of the sentence of imprisonment, that task being essentially one of
risk assessment, with (as part of that assessment) a recognition of
the original criminality that led to imprisonment. It reflects the traditional attitude of a parole system since its statutory introduction
in the Criminal Justice Act 1967. That is not to deny the judicial
elements of adjudication and disposal that is a precursor of lost liberty, but it is a system that incorporates relevant procedural safeguards for a prisoner, akin to court procedure, familiar to judiciary,
the legal profession and administrators of the legal system. What is
needed is a hybrid tribunal, a quasi-judicial body that ensures an
equality of its members, with the legally trained among them playing an equal, but never a dominant role; the doctrine of *primus inter
pares* belongs to the chairman, not to his or her professional qualification.

There is a strong case for granting any prisoner – particularly
where custody is in the form of a protective sentence for a dangerous offender – the right of access to an independent tribunal of a
specialist kind, charged with a unique view and a duty to report on
the case to the relevant Minister in the exercise of his or her political function in the administration of a civilised penal system. This
need not entail any constraint on the ministerial discretion to permit the prisoner's release on licence without further reference to the
criminal justice process. Once a prisoner is consigned by the criminal court, subject to any appellate process which is (as now) time-
limited, to the penal administration, the only court function
thereafter is the process of judicial review of the prison system, and
that procedure is already well-developed.

The recent history of legislation protecting the public has been
demonstrably ill-judged. Only in March 2014 did Mr David Blunkett
(who, as Home Secretary in 2003, was the architect of the indeterminate sentencing of serious offenders – and some less serious)
confess that the IPPs were wrong and had induced injustices.[3] The
need now is for a parliamentary form of controlling the release of
prisoners back into the community; it should involve a review of

---

[3] *Newsnight* on BBC2, 13 March 2014.

the parole system. The task should form a part of the remit of a Royal Commission on the Penal System, advocated by Professor Séan McConville and myself in a pamphlet published on 18 November 2014.

Part IV

Media Law

24

Press (Media) Freedom: Constitutional Right or Cultural Assumption?

O N MY DESK in chambers in the Temple I used to keep a framed   cartoon depicting two gentlemen perusing the editorial pages of a broadsheet newspaper. One of them is saying to the other: 'No, I don't know the phrase, press freedom, but I know *of* it.' That sentiment neatly captures the situation for most of us. We know *of* press freedom, and no one fails to have plenty of opinions *about* it. What 'it' is somehow tends to elude us. The aim of this essay is thus more in the nature of an exploration than an exposition of a topic of immense concern for freedom of expression in a democratic society.

From those who propound the virtues and values of journalistic activity, the phrase comes trippingly off the tongue, as if we were all expected to imbibe its momentous meaning, that the press is the fourth estate of the realm. In his book *The Essential Anatomy of Britain*[1] Anthony Sampson, describing journalism and the media, wrote:

> Who as the watchdogs are to bark at abuses of power? The most obvious has been the Fourth Estate (the phrase was first used by Fielding in 1752 to describe the mob, but later by Carlyle in 1834 to describe the Press).[2]

The implication is self-evident. The evocative phrase implies a quasi- constitutional status. The provenance of the 'fourth estate' is, however, misplaced, misunderstood and muddled in thought and speech, even often with deliberate intent to ward off any statutory intervention, whatever the legislation might provide, as if 'statute' spells instantaneous danger.

---

[1] A Sampson, *The Essential Anatomy of Britain* (London, Hodder & Stoughton, 1991).
[2] ibid ch12, p 123.

At this point, I cannot resist the temptation to quote Oscar Wilde's quirkish view of the 'fourth estate', from *The Soul of Man*:

> In old days men had the rack. Now they have the press. That is an improvement certainly. But still it is very bad, and wrong, and demoralising. Somebody – was it Burke? – called journalism the fourth estate. That was true at the time, no doubt. But at the present moment it really is the only estate. It has eaten up the other three. The Lords Temporal say nothing, the Lords Spiritual have nothing to say, and the House of Commons has nothing to say and says it. We are dominated by Journalism.

I should preface this exploration of press freedom by stating that the citizen's right freely and publicly to criticise the organs of government, the conduct of public affairs (whether by executive, legislature or judiciary), and non- governmental organisations, is of supreme importance, and is not to be taken as diminished one iota from what comes hereafter. Lord Hoffmann once remarked, perhaps somewhat incautiously, that there was no question of 'balancing freedom of speech against other interests. It is a trump card which always wins.'[3] As Sir Sydney Kentridge QC noted,[4] the statement is sometimes quoted out of context. In the case (*R v Central Independent Television plc*), the Court of Appeal refused to prevent a television broadcast of a programme which would have exposed a young child to harmful publicity. Lord Justice Hoffmann (as he then was) was later at pains to explain that the desire to avoid intrusive publicity was not an interest to which English law gave protection, at least at that time. In his Goodman lecture in 1996 Lord Hoffmann sought to explain what he really meant. He said:

> Some people have read [the remark] to mean that freedom of speech always trumps other rights and values. But that is not what I said. I said only that in order to be put [in] the balance against freedom of speech, another interest must fall within some established exception which could be justified under Article 10 of the European Convention

A skilful *ex post facto* rationalisation, no doubt.

My exploration covers initially the exploitation by the media of press freedom. Do the media today enjoy a status separate and distinct from individual rights of free expression, exercising those rights collectively, and if so how and why? Or are speech rights and press rights (as reflected in some countries' constitutions, specifi-

---

[3] *R v Central Independent Television plc* [1994] 3 All ER 641, 652.

[4] In the 19th FA Mann Lecture, delivered in October 1995 (and reproduced in vol 45 *International and Comparative Law Quarterly* 253–70, esp 256).

cally the First Amendment to the US Constitution) co-extensive, in the sense that they were used interchangeably in the eighteenth century? Whatever the answers to these questions, is not now the time for re-thinking the freedom of the press (which has probably now transmuted into freedom of the media)?

THE 'FOURTH ESTATE'

It was almost certainly Thomas Babington Macaulay who first coined the phrase, when he referred to the reporters in the gallery of the two Houses of Parliament. It appears in an essay which Macaulay wrote in 1828 on Hallam's *Constitutional History*, contributed in the *Edinburgh Review* of that year. Macaulay is reported to have said that in addition to the three estates – the King, Lords and Commons – 'the gallery in which reporters sit has become the fourth estate of the realm.' The statement was later attributed to Edmund Burke, but that attribution has been taken to be false, since the lexicographers have consistently been unable to trace the remark to anything the great parliamentarian either spoke or wrote. Writing in 1829, the historian Thomas Carlyle[5] described the power which he said newspaper reporters were claiming for themselves, in the speech referred to by Anthony Sampson. Carlyle wrote:

> Or turning now to the Government of men. Witenagemote, old Parliament, was a great thing. The affairs of the nation were there deliberated and decided; what we were to *do* as a nation. But does not, though the name Parliament subsists, the parliamentary debate go on now, everywhere and at all times, in a far more comprehensive way, *out* of Parliament altogether? Burke [sic] said there were Three Estates in Parliament; but, in the Reporters' Gallery yonder, there sat a *Fourth Estate* more important far than them all. It is not a figure of speech, or a witty saying; it is a literal fact, - very momentous to us in these times. Literature is our Parliament too. Printing, which comes necessarily out of Writing, I say often, is equivalent to Democracy: invent Writing, Democracy is inevitable. Writing brings Printing; brings universal everyday extempore Printing, as we see at present. Whoever can speak, speaking now to the whole nation, becomes a power, a branch of government, with inalienable weight in law-making, in all acts of authority.

While Carlyle's interpretation of a free press led him rhetorically to question whether the nation's affairs might be conducted in a far more comprehensive way *outwith* Parliament, Macaulay's phrase

---

[5] T Carlyle, *Heroes and Hero-Worship*, vol XII (London, James Fraser, 1841) 194.

was focused on the proceedings in Parliament, the essential element being the reporting of parliamentary proceedings. In a country
which was then run by the Bishops, the aristocracy and the House
of Commons, it would seem a step too far nowadays to treat the
Macaulay statement as meaning the fourth estate of modern government as a check and counterbalance to the established three estates
of executive, legislature and judiciary. Macaulay would, however,
have been only too aware of the historical and contemporaneous
significance of the press.

The introduction of the printing press in the sixteenth century
brought about sweeping changes. The press promised an essential
element in the chemistry of what were the revolutionary new theories of self-determination in the body politic. The printed word
became an undeniably effective means of carrying speech beyond
the accustomed range of the speaker and within the grasp of the
individual as a potential electorate. Regulations grew more sweeping as established political thought, through the printing presses,
was threatening to those in power. Throughout the seventeenth century, prosecutions for seditious libels flourished in an atmosphere
that smacked of official supervision. Professor David Lange, in an
illuminating 1975 article, *The Speech and Press Clauses*, wrote:

> And yet illicit presses continued, sheet by sheet, to reinforce the English
> commoner's growing awareness of himself and his nascent political
> power. Though another two centuries (the 17th and 18th) would pass
> before the restrictions would begin to wither, the struggle itself was
> enough to assure the continued legitimacy of the concepts of free speech
> and press for the common man.[6]

The terms 'freedom of speech' and 'freedom of the Press' were used
interchangeably in the eighteenth century, particularly among persons who were interested in the terms at a conceptual level.[7] It was
in fact the heritage of the struggle that the colonists brought with
them to the New World, and finds its expression in the First
Amendment in the Constitutions of all the independent states
which established the provision. The states refused to ratify the US
Constitution without 10 amendments, the first of which was the
freedom of speech and the press. Interestingly, the original draft of
the US Constitution did not provide for the freedom of the press.
Alexander Hamilton argued against any such guarantee, supporting
the legal status in contemporary England:

---

[6] (1975) 23 *UCLA Law Review* 77–119.
[7] See ibid 77

In the first place, I observe that there is not a syllable concerning it in the constitution of this State; in the next, I contend that whatever has been said about it in that of any other State amounts to nothing. What signifies a declaration that 'the liberty of the press shall be inviolably preserved'? What is the liberty of the press? Who can give it any definition which would not leave the utmost latitude for evasion? I hold it to be impracticable.[8]

It was licensing of the press that lay at the heart of the battle to escape the shackles of governmental control. 'Freedom of the press' was the freedom of that press which had been enslaved, and that was every press, and every use of every press. The old verbiage of one of the old taxes on knowledge, under which the newspapers and other forms of printing were restricted, clearly illustrates the definition:

> Every person possessing a printing press or types for printing, and every typefounder, was ordered to give notice to the clerk of the peace. Every person selling type was ordered to give an account of all persons to whom they were sold. Every person who printed anything also had to keep a copy of the matter printed, and write on it the name and abode of the person who employed him to print.[9]

An aside is warranted: from its Royal Charter in 1557, the Stationers' Company in London kept a series of registers in which old books (including newssheets[10]) printed by members of the Company were entered, thus ensuring for the owner the exclusive right to print that book. A further element to this form of registration gave the State a degree of control over what was printed. Eventually, first by voluntary agreement with, for example, Sir Thomas Bodley's library in Oxford, and then through legislation, this was to evolve into the legal deposit system of today, whereby all new publications are deposited with the British Library and the other copyright libraries.

Macaulay would doubtlessly have been reflecting the recently acquired freedom of the press from prior restraint to report the proceedings of Parliament. In Hallam's *Constitutional History of England*, with which Macaulay was directly acquainted, the former wrote: 'We read the noble apology of Milton for the freedom of the press with admiration; but it had little influence on the Parliament

---

[8] *The Federalist Papers*, (Harmondsworth, Penguin, 1987) 476.
[9] L Salmon, *The Newspaper and Authority* (Oxford, OUP, 1923) 188.
[10] Though the first news pamphlet in England was printed around 1513, giving an eyewitness account of the battle of Flodden, the first regular newsbooks began only a century later, published by Thomas Archer and followed by Nicholas Bourne and Nathaniel Butler.

to which it was addressed.'[11] The issue for the press was to be unshackled and independent, with absolute freedom to publish. As Hallam further stated: 'the liberty of the press consists, in a strict sense, merely in an exemption from the superintendence of a licensor' – hardly the concept of a constitutional status within government, merely an assertion to everyone's freedom of speech not to be restrained by the prior intervention of officialdom.

Macaulay's phrase, even assuming that it could claim to be authoritative, was to accord its function as a chronicler of parliamentary proceedings, and nothing more. It reflects only a fraction of the freedom that one finds in Article 10 of the European Convention on Human Rights and Fundamental Freedoms. And Macaulay's dictum addresses directly another freedom, the openness of the parliamentary process and, by analogy, the right to open justice. Where the public has access, so do the agencies of the media. There is a tendency, as I will observe later in the context of Family Courts, to fudge the two concepts, of transparency for proceedings conducted in public and freedom of expression. A leading case in the US Supreme Court neatly illustrates the point. In *Richmond Newspapers v Virginia*[12] it was argued that the First Amendment primarily guarantees the press and the public a right of access in criminal trials. The English common law has, as expounded in 1913 in *Scott v Scott* in the House of Lords,[13] always maintained the openness of justice, and the US legal system followed suit. The Ninth Amendment to the US Constitution provides that 'the enumeration in the Constitution of certain rights shall not be construed to deny or disparage others retained by the people.' The Ninth Amendment does not *create* any rights of its own force; it contains no rights, but is a rule of interpretation. While the opinions of the justices in the *Richmond* case appeared to be based on the First Amendment, giving right of access equally to the citizen and the press is better explained on the firmer basis of the Ninth Amendment. Chief Justice Warren Burger, writing for a plurality of the Court, treated the Ninth Amendment as supporting the existence of a presumed right of public access to the courtroom.[14]

It is hard in any event to argue that freedom of speech is involved when people want to observe a criminal trial and when the speak-

---

[11] H Hallam, *Constitutional History of England*, 2nd edn (London, John Murray, 1829). Milton's apology was the *Areopagitica: a Speech of Mr John Milton for the Liberty of Unlicensed Printing to the Parliament of England in 1644*.

[12] 488 US 533 (1980).

[13] [1913] AC 417.

[14] 488 US 533 (1980), 579–80.

ers at the trial, including the prosecutor and the accused, want the trial to take place in private. Likewise in the civil courts, the claimant and respondent may wish to exclude the public from their dispute. Freedom of speech does *not* include the right to hear something a speaker does not want you to hear. Article 10, moreover, confirms the individual's right to silence, even if it also implies the journalist's right, even duty, to investigate.

The right to open justice derives, not from freedom of speech provisions, but from a right retained by the people, and by the press only derivatively of that right. I observe that Professor Jaconelli's book *Open Justice*[15] – 350 pages long – contains only one fleeting reference to freedom of the press.[16] While a defendant or the parties to criminal or civil proceedings have the right under Article 6, the openness of the court proceedings is a common law right vested in the public. Public means the citizenry, including representatives of the press. The confusion between two distinct freedoms seems not to have been appreciated in the recent controversy over Family Courts, a familiar failure of English lawyers to conceptualise.[17] Observation is the primary purpose of open justice. As Mr Justice Walsh in the Supreme Court of Ireland observed,[18] 'the actual presence of the public [and the press][19] is not necessary, but the doors of the courts must be open to satisfy the requirement that justice must be administered in public.'

FAMILY COURTS

Representatives of newspapers and news agencies have a right under section 69(2)(c) of the Magistrates' Courts Act 1980 to attend hearings of the Family Proceedings Court, except in the case of adoption proceedings. But child care and child welfare proceedings in either the High Court or the county court are closed to both the public and the press. Parliament endorsed that situation in the Children Act 1989. As part of a growing clamour for all Family

---

[15] J Jaconelli, *Open Justice* (Oxford, OUP, 2002).

[16] ibid 27, a reference to *R v Waterfield* [1975] 1 WLR 711.

[17] Not all English lawyers have failed to appreciate that there are different interests in play, protected variously by Arts 6, 8 and 10 – see, for example, Munby J's comments in *Re Brandon Webster (a child)(No 1)* EWHC 2733 (Fam), particularly at paras 17, 76 and 80.

[18] *Re R Ltd* [1989] IR 126 and see *The Irish Times Ltd and others v His Honour Judge Anthony G Murphy* and *RTE v Ireland and others* [1998] 1 IR 359, 409 (Ronan Keane J (as he then was)) and 398 (Denham J).

[19] My insertion.

Courts to be transparent, and a desire on the part of the judiciary to accommodate this move, Mr Justice Munby (now Sir James Munby, President of the Family Division) in November 2006 acceded to an application that the media (but not members of the public) be permitted to attend a hearing in a high-profile case involving children taken into local authority care.[20] As the judge signed off a lengthy and closely reasoned judgment for this exceptional decision, he noted that 'there was no suggestion that access should be afforded to the public generally.' And he mused,

> I say nothing about how an application for public access, had it been made, would have been decided. I merely observe that . . . different issues *may* arise if it is to be suggested that the general public and not merely the media should have access.[21]

But how different? As Munby J himself stated:[22]

> What goes for the media seeking to exercise their right under Article 10 to 'impart information and ideas' to the general public, must also, in my judgment, go for the parents, as they seek to exercise their rights under Article 10 . . . to the media and, via the media to the world at large.

Dr Marjorie Jones, in her 1974 work *Justice and Journalism*, noted that in informing the public of how justice is being performed in magistrates' courts, the journalist enters the court 'as a member of the public taking notes',[23] even if he is paid to be there. If the public is excluded, whence does the journalist derive his or her personal right of access? Apart from the statutory right in family proceedings in the magistrates' court, there is no basis whatsoever for any such right. This represented a serious anomaly, now recognised by the Ministry of Justice's consultation paper *Openness in Family Courts – a New Approach*, published in July 2007. The Ministry's 'new approach' for 'openness', however, reverts to the principle of the closed doors to Family Courts. In the Government's earlier consultation, greater openness was said to be required 'so that people can understand, better scrutinise decisions and have greater confi-

---

[20] *Re Brandon Webster (a child) (No 1)* [2006] EWHC 2733 (Fam).

[21] My italics. Munby J's use of the word 'may' was intended to convey a note of scepticism. For his personal views on this point, see his Jordan's Family Law Lecture, published in [2005] *Family Law* 945.

[22] In *Re Brandon Webster (No 2)* [2006] EWHC 2898 (Fam) [49].

[23] M Jones, *Justice and Journalism* (Chichester, Rose, 1974) 24. I should perhaps declare an interest – I was one of a panel of two persons who supervised Dr Jones' PhD thesis at Birmingham University. Dr Jones was the wife of Clement Jones, the distinguished editor of the *Wolverhampton Star and Echo*. I became acquainted with her through his membership of the Press Council.

dence.' That document hence proposed that the media should be allowed, 'on behalf of, and for the benefit of the public', to attend proceedings as of right, though the court would have a discretion to exclude them if appropriate to do so in the particular circumstances. Others could apply to the court to be permitted to attend.

Once the policy is to ensure the opacity of the proceedings, as an exception to Article 6, there is a blanket exclusion on the attendees (other than parties and relevant participants).

The solution to the problem of protecting children and their families lies not in refusing access to the proceedings, but in the scope and flow of information. It was the same Marjorie Jones who urged reform to prevent injustice by unwanted and prejudicial publicity by legalising anonymity. Her plea was endorsed by the Royal Commission on the Press in its report of 1977 calling on the Government to set up a committee to consider the question of anonymity in all court proceedings. There has been a deafening silence from officialdom, gleefully endorsed by the media, which has persistently maintained its right to name those undergoing the forensic spotlight. Once there are clear restrictions (strictly enforceable) on reporting any details identifying a child or family, why is the welfare of the child at risk? The Judicial Proceedings (Regulation of Reports) Act 1926 effectively curbed the hitherto uncontrolled press reporting of unseemly aspects of some divorce litigation. Focusing on the potential harmful aspects of the court procedure will at least preserve the right of access exercisable by the citizen, whether or not he or she packs a writing pad and pen in a briefcase. The Benthamite dictum that where there is no publicity there is no justice should be strictly observed. Access is not the preserve of those occupied full-time in reporting the proceedings of a public institution. Culturally, a democratic society will facilitate the journalist's task as a means of exercising a citizen's constitutional right of access to justice. There is an important downside to any privilege accorded to the media. If representatives of newspapers or news agencies possess the right, any selection process will involve accreditation. In a paper to the conference on *Opening up the Family Courts: an open and closed case* on 30 October 2006, Lord Justice Wall (then President of the Family Division) contemplated a dialogue between the judges and the press. He envisaged that the press would reciprocate in the process of opening up the courts, and added: 'If it does not, the judiciary will have to think of the sanctions it can impose – such as the withdrawal of accreditation.' Who says which journalist is to be nominated? I will not dwell on this, save to say that the procedure will smack of a licensing system – something the media have justifiably set their face against ever since 1694. Judges cannot be censors.

THE JOURNALIST

If what I have said about the current controversy over Family Courts is a distraction from the theme of press freedom, it illustrates the thrust of this essay which reveals the issue of open justice (not a matter of free speech), as distinct from the meaning and scope of Article 10. Where then do the investigators and purveyors of information fit into that important aspect of public affairs, freedom of speech? One can do no better for a prime answer than look to the writings of Professor Harry Street. I am citing from the sixth edition of *Freedom, the Individual and the Law*, because it was the edition in 1989 first edited under the hand of Geoffrey Robertson QC (and therefore has the imprimatur of a leading authority on media law) after Professor Street's acknowledged work had gone through five editions since the first in 1963. In the chapter on 'Freedom of Expression', the occupation of journalists is neatly described in the following unambiguous terms:

> It is the exercise by occupation of the right to free expression available to every citizen. That right, being available to all, cannot in principle be withdrawn from a few by any system of licensing or professional registration, but it can be restricted and confined by rules of law which apply to all who take or are afforded the opportunity to exercise the right by speaking or writing in public.[24]

The courts have confirmed this view. In the *Spycatcher* case in 1988, the then Master of the Rolls, Sir John Donaldson, described:

> an affirmation that newspapers have a special status and special rights in relation to the disclosure of confidential information, which is not enjoyed by the public as a whole. This is not the case. I yield to no one in my belief that the existence of a free press . . . is an essential element in maintaining parliamentary democracy and the British way of life as we know it. But it is important to remember why the press occupies this crucial position. It is not because of any special wisdom, interest or status enjoyed by proprietors, editors or journalists. It is because the media are the eyes and ears of the general public. They act on behalf of the

---

[24] H Street, *Freedom, the Individual and the Law*, 6th edn (ed G Robertson, London, Penguin, 1989) 301.

general public. Their right to know and their right to publish is neither more nor less than that of the general public.[25]

In his judgment in the same case, Bingham LJ (as he then was) stated:

It is elementary that our constitution provides no entrenched guarantee of freedom of speech or of the press, and neither the press nor any other medium of public communication enjoys (save for exceptions immaterial for present purposes) any special position or privileges.

What more is there to say than that the journalist by occupation acquires nothing from the law that does not apply to anyone minded to take the opportunity to exercise the right of free speech, with the qualifications that apply likewise to the journalist and the non-journalist citizen. Freedom of speech belongs indiscriminately to all of us, including those working in the media.

Professor Street prefaced his description of the journalist's occupation by saying that 'journalism is not just a profession'. In recognising that the right of free speech cannot be withdrawn by any system of licensing or professional registration, he was using the phrase 'profession' in the loose sense of a collective of persons engaged in an enterprise of mutual interest. A profession normally implies an occupation or service that can be carried out only so long as the individual qualifies according to imposed ethical standards which can be enforced through a disciplinary system. Any such professional registration would be a negation of the basic right of freedom of expression. No one can be prevented from exercising free speech other than by a law of general applicability – libel, breach of confidence and contempt of court are complex laws that impinge more fiercely on the media, if only because of the practical impact of journalistic activity. Authors of books, which newspapers and magazines are prone to serialise and regularly review in their columns, may have special reasons for claiming better protection from legal suits, if only because of the book's specialised audience as opposed to the unknown, ephemeral reader of a newspaper. HW Fowler (the famous author of *Modern English Usage*) once wrote to his publisher at the Oxford University Press, 'Habent sua fata libri' ('Books have their own destinies'), by which he meant that authors positively invite reviewers and commentators to criticise their work, and even provide a right of reply in kind, but not by way of individual litigation. Publishers of books derive their freedom of

[25] *Attorney-General v Guardian Newspapers (No 2)* [1990] 1 AC 109, 183.

expression likewise under Article 10. It appears that the courts are at present treating authors of books, for the purpose of establishing the public interest and qualified privilege for the publication, as engaging in 'responsible journalism';[26] they have it since the passing of section 5 (4) of the Defamation Act 2013.

It might be claimed that the protection of journalists' sources of information is indicative of a special immunity. But section 10 of the Contempt of Court Act 1981 is indiscriminate in its cloak of protection: 'No court may require *a person* [my italics] to disclose . . . the source of information contained in a publication for which he is responsible.' Journalists and other regular purveyors of information may be more vulnerable to proceedings for disclosure, but the law applies without reference to the undisclosed material and the suspected source. As Laws LJ said in *Ashworth Hospital Authority v Nasse*, 'the public interest in the non-disclosure of press sources is constant, whatever the merits of the particular publication and the particular source.'[27] It is in the public interest, moreover, that the informant seeking anonymity for the journalistic information should be likewise protected – particularly if he or she happens to be a whistle-blower. A degree of special protection might be claimed by constitutionalists where the Human Rights Act 1998 afforded provision in section 12, but even then it could be seen as little more than a government acceptance of media resistance to any potential privacy law. Section 12(4) provides that a court must pay particular regard to the importance of the constitutional right to freedom of expression, and where the respondent to any proceedings claims 'journalistic, literary or artistic material' the court must have regard to the material being, or potentially being, in the public interest. 'Any relevant privacy code' is specifically recited in section 12(4)(b). But, as Professor Eric Barendt points out in his *Freedom of Speech*,[28] while the subsection might appear to give some priority to freedom of expression over competing rights, the courts have rejected that interpretation.[29] It cannot be a privilege or right for journalists themselves rather than the source (or the general public). If that were the case, the journalist could waive the

---

[26]   *Charman v Orion Publishing Group Ltd and others* [2007] All ER(D) 145.

[27]   [2001] 1 WLR 515 [101]. For a helpful analysis of the law relating to the protection afforded journalists, see R Costigan, 'Protection of Journalists' Sources' [2007] Autumn *Public Law* 464–87.

[28]   E Barendt, *Freedom of Speech*, 2nd edn (Oxford, OUP, 2005) 44.

[29]   *Douglas v Hello* [2001] QB 967 and *Campbell v MGN* [2004] 2 AC 457 [55] (Lord Hoffmann, a pronounced supporter of press freedom).

privilege or right.[30] The statutory provision places the position of journalistic (and other forms of written) material within the qualification of Article 10(2) – hardly conferring a constitutional right on journalists per se.[31]

CONCLUSION

Where has this exploration taken us? The 'fourth estate' is, at worst, a piece of linguistic trickery or, at best, a *façon de parler* expressing imperfectly a cultural asset in our society. Freedom of expression (alias press freedom) is a legal concept distinct from the right to open justice. Both rights belong separately to the citizenry. And, finally, the scope and flow of information is ours to be controlled insofar as it is necessary to protect other cultural values. Self-regulation of the press – aka the media – cannot begin to act as a protector or enhancer of these other cultural values. Something much more is needed to instil an attitude of responsibility on the part of newspaper owners, editors, journalists and all disseminators of information, whatever the medium. Regulation of the media is entirely compatible with, indeed required by, society's commitment to the values of freedom of speech. There is a need for a new watch-dog which barks authoritatively, and, where appropriate, in stentorian terms, but does not bite, except indirectly and influentially. Until we have thought through (or rather, re-thought) the freedom of the press in the twenty-first century (including the core issue of regulation), the status of the media will remain unclear and controversial. For the time being I think I have merely answered the question posed in the title to the 22nd Harry Street Lecture: press freedom is a cultural assumption, and not a constitutional right. And it certainly is not a human right, as some academic writing would seem to suggest.[32] It is a human necessity. The utterance, The Fourth Estate, is no more than journalistic rhetoric; it is at best the freedom of expression exercised invariably by the public.

---

[30] But see the US Supreme Court decision in *Cohen v Cowles Media Co* 501 US 663 (1991).

[31] For a fuller discussion see H Fenwick and G Phillipson, *Media Freedom under the Human Rights Act* (Oxford, OUP, 2006).

[32] In a lecture delivered at University College, Dublin on 25 October 2007, entitled 'Is Freedom of the Press a Human Right?', Professor Frederick Schauer persuasively argues, from a philosophical viewpoint, in the negative, although in US and Irish terms, it is a constitutional right.

25

The Jurisprudence of Privacy

WHEN THE PRESS Council was disbanded in 1990 and succeeded by the Press Complaints Commission, there was a strong plea that the new body should set about establishing a code of future adjudication on privacy; the plea repeated a recommendation in the report of the Younger Committee[1] in 1972 that the Press Council should give rather readier guidance to busy practising journalists, and the interested public, and that this should be kept up-to-date. Neither the Press Council nor the now defunct Press Complaints Commission responded in any jurisprudential sense (if at all) to the plea for codification on privacy; there was a public need for the latter to garner its own adjudications over the last 20 years, but it failed to present any form of adequately reasoned adjudications. It is vital that the new regulatory body for the newspaper industry, the Independent Press Standards Organisation (IPSO), which is to be the new regulator under the monitoring of the Royal Charter, should heed these recommendations, if only because it is vital that the new defence of 'public interest' in section 4 of the Defamation Act 2013 should be replicated as a likely form of defence to a claim for breach of confidentiality, as exemplified in privacy claims. Privacy itself should be expounded by an extension (which the Americans describe as the 'zone of privacy') which hopefully will be emulated by IPSO, which began on 15 September 2014 with Sir Alan Moses, an eminent retired Court of Appeal judge, as chairman. The courts have developed their case-law on the law dealing with breaches of confidentiality, but it is that breach of law alongside the common law that safeguards the individual's right to his private life and family.[2]

Two departmental committees, two decades apart, focused on the persistent and unresolved problem of reconciling press freedom with press responsibility, particularly as regards invasion of pri-

---

[1] (Cmnd 5012, 1972) p 52, para 193.
[2] See the judgment of Nicol J in *Ferdinand v MGN Ltd* [2011] EWHC 2454.

vacy. Responding to the Fourth Report of the National Heritage Committee on *Privacy and Media Intrusion*, the Lord Chancellor's Department and the Scottish Office sent out a consultation paper, *Infringement of Privacy*, on 30 July 1993, proposing the creation of a civil remedy against whoever infringes an individual's privacy. The consultation paper envisaged a Press Ombudsman, established by the press (and hence non- statutory), to deal with complaints from the public about press conduct, as a quicker and less formal remedy than court proceedings in privacy cases involving the press. An Ombudsman scheme, which 'would probably not be obliged to follow the procedures built up under a new law' would exist alongside the statutory remedy, as a complement to it. How should the non-statutory remedy develop, having regard to the past experience of the Press Council and its successor body, the Press Complaints Commission?

The call by the Younger Committee for codification and a developed body of case law fell on deaf ears, until the scare of legislative intervention in 1989 and the report in June 1990 of Calcutt Mark I propelled the newspaper industry to set up the Press Complaints Commission, equipped with an industry-drafted code – including an article on privacy – which the Commission was charged to interpret and apply. In spite of long-standing concerns about invasion of privacy, neither the Press Council's uncodified corpus of decisions over the 37 years of its existence (1953–90), nor the attempts of the Press Complaints Commission over the 24 years that followed have adequately addressed the problem. Comprehensive and coherent guidelines about the boundaries of the private arena of individual lives, which the press must not invade, by journalistic investigation or editorial publication, have yet to be established. Since a law of privacy is still not statutorily contemplated, and the recent jurisprudence of the courts is sparse, any non-statutory development of the principles applicable to protection of private lives from press intrusion must be welcome.

It was not until 1976 that the Press Council bowed to pressure and did at least issue a declaration of principle regarding privacy. Even then, the standard articulated was a vague one, and subsequent adjudications have done little or nothing to clarify the line over which the press should not step. The perceived failings of the Press Council generally, and in the invasion of privacy context specifically, were undoubtedly a factor that discredited it in the eyes of the public and led to its disbandment and replacement by a new body charged with adjudicating complaints under a Code of Practice framed exclusively by the industry. The decisions of the Press Complaints Commission on privacy deserved close attention and evaluation, but only as a pointer to future development. They have done little or nothing to enlighten the reader of adjudications.

It may help the reader of this essay to see the relevant article of the Press Industry's Code of Practice (and any successor code by the new regulator) on privacy as set alongside the suggested article in both Calcutt Mark I and the proposed code of practice in the report of the National Heritage Committee, and the prospective new Code of Conduct that will be annexed next year to IPSO:

THE PRESS INDUSTRY'S CODE OF PRACTICE	CALCUTT COMMITTEE'S PROPOSED CODE OF PRACTICE	THE NATIONAL HERITAGE COMMITTEE'S PROPOSED CODE OF PRACTICE
4. Privacy	4. Privacy	4. Privacy
Intrusions and inquiries into an individual's private life without his or her consent are not generally acceptable. Publication can only be justified when in the public interest.	(i) Making inquiries about the personal lives of individuals without their consent is not generally acceptable.	(i) Making inquiries about the personal lives of individuals without their consent is not generally acceptable.
This would include:	(ii) Publishing material about the personal life of individuals without their consent is not generally acceptable.	(ii) Publishing material about the personal life of individuals without their consent is not generally acceptable.
(i) Detecting or exposing crime or serious misdemeanour.		
(ii) Detecting or exposing seriously anti-social behaviour.	(iii) An intrusion into an individual's personal life can be justified only for the purpose of detecting or exposing crime, or seriously anti-social conduct, protecting public health or safety, or	(iii) An intrusion into an individual's personal life can be justified only for the purpose of detecting or exposing crime, protecting health or safety, or preventing a
(iii) Protecting public health and safety.		
(iv) Preventing the public from being misled by some statement or action of that individual.		

preventing the public being misled by some public statement or action of that individual.

(iv) An individual's personal life includes matters of health, home, personal relationships, correspondence and documents but does not include his trade or business.

harmful deception of the public.

(iv) An individual's personal life includes matters of health, home, personal relationships, correspondence and documents but does not include his trade or business.

While relatively few complaints have been brought under clause 4 of the PCC's code, several of the privacy adjudications have been among the highest profile matters considered by the Commission. The relative rarity of invasion of privacy adjudications in the early years makes it difficult to analyse the Commission's privacy jurisprudence in a systematic way. Difficulty in discerning privacy principles from the adjudications is exacerbated by the Commission's failure to draft them with any sense of juridical purpose – that is, to identify essential issues arising from a complaint and then to apply the rule of the relevant Code article to determine the proper result. The difficulty was further compounded by the fact that adjudications were not issued separately but were included in a monthly bulletin, while the short statement of the reasoning for decisions presented further difficulty to the jurist or the intelligent reader. A number of other adjudications could properly be considered as privacy cases, although clause 4 was not cited. The utility of a case law on privacy has been disappointingly sparse, if not almost absent.

Consider however this early attempt, the Clare Short matter. Because the complaint dealt with a number of issues that arose in subsequent complaints, it *might* have set precedents to influence or determine the outcomes of those matters. Nothing since has elucidated the case. And the newspaper's acceptance that it was miserably misled in its investigations of its hacking activities invalidated the ability of the Press Complaints Commission as a public regulator.

(The trial of Rachel Brookes and Colin Coulson in October 2013 reveals that there were other interests than formal adjudications on privacy; indeed its focus was the criminal offence of hacking by the *News of the World*.)

Ms Short's allegations of invasion of privacy arose from an investigation by a *News of the World* reporter and story subsequently published by that newspaper. Her complaint, enumerating a number of incidents arising from the reporter's activity and the subsequent publication, raised both clause 1 (inaccuracy) and clause 4 (privacy) issues. In brief, the chronology of events leading to Ms Short's complaint was that, in 1986, she had introduced a Bill in Parliament which would have curtailed publication of 'page 3 girl' photos, which she considers pornographic. She alleged she was subsequently the object of a 'campaign of vilification' by the *Sun* and its sister paper, the *News of the World*. Ms Short complained about two specific incidents where the latter had linked her, in quite a misleading fashion, to pornography. The Commission upheld her complaint in this regard, albeit on unspecified grounds, noting the 'inescapable suspicion' that the paper engaged in these objectionable activities with a purpose to embarrass Ms Short in retaliation for her anti-pornography stance. It is unclear whether this reprehensible motive carried over, and was relevant to other activities about which Ms Short complained.

In late 1990, Ms Short had received several reports indicating that she was being investigated by a *News of the World* reporter. The reporter had first contacted her former husband, asking him for a photo showing Ms Short topless or in a nightgown. The reporter's knowledge that the former husband was mentally unstable and had previously threatened Ms Short was undisputed. Secondly, the reporter had investigated Ms Short's friendship, during the early 1970s, with John Daniel, a man who had been convicted of various criminal offences prior to that friendship. Several years after the end of his relationship with Ms Short, Daniel had been the victim of a murder for which no one had ever been charged. Early in 1991, convinced that the *News of the World* was about to publish a story related to these investigations, Ms Short gave a speech in the House of Commons outlining these investigations into her private life and attacking the publication and its staff. The material about which she had spoken was published by the *News of the World* a few days later.

Ms Short's complaint was considered under clauses 1 and 4 of the Code of Practice. The invasion of privacy claims may have related only to the investigation, and the inaccuracy claims may have related only to the publication. This is logical, given the manner in which Ms Short presented her case. After all, any information that was 'private' was first published by her House of Commons speech which attacked the investigative tactics used by the *News of the World* reporter. Accordingly, she would have waived any right to complain of invasion of privacy over its subsequent publication in the newspaper. A complaint that the newspaper report contained inaccuracies and misrepresentations was, however, appropriate.

One issue on which the Commission correctly focused, as a determinative element of the adjudication, was Ms Short's status as a public figure – at least inasmuch as that brought the matter within the purview of 'public interest' (statutorily to be a defence to a defamation action). As both Ms Short and the *News of the World* accepted, the paper was justified in inquiring into aspects of a public figure's private life on the assumption that information discovered might be in the public interest. Still, the Commission held that such inquiries could not justify publication of the information unless the facts discovered in the course of the investigation satisfied the 'public interest' test of clause 4 of the editors' Code. Commenting on the meaning of 'public interest', the Commission stated that it is not merely 'whatever happens to interest the public'. The adjudication expressly recognised that 'circumstances in the private life of [an MP] may bear on her conduct of that office or fitness for it', but it never concluded whether the test was satisfied on the known facts. The Commission simply noted that the *News of the World* had not sought to 'suggest that information it possessed . . . would have justified an article about her which was in the public interest', implying that both parties agreed there was none on the facts revealed by the investigation. At no point was any specific part of clause 4's four-prong public interest test discussed, leading one to wonder whether the Commission considered the codified test at all.

Rather than concluding its inquiry with this finding, that 'public interest' could not justify publication of the offending statements, the Commission in its adjudication considered several other matters, stating some informative dicta, but also making several comments that served only to obscure the issues on which the decision turned – or at least should have turned. Among its more positive contributions, the Commission noted that passage of time does not necessarily diminish the relevance of justification for publishing material that otherwise meets the 'public interest' test. As with many American courts' handling of suits for publication of private facts, the Commission was also sensitive to the investigative, newsgathering techniques employed by the *News of the World* journalist. The Commission considered the reporter's knowledge of the former husband's psychiatric condition particularly damning, calling the journalist's behaviour 'indefensible'. It upheld Ms Short's complaint 'in this respect', a statement which is somewhat confusing by its implication that an independent basis for complaint arises from the investigative technique of the journalist. If the Commission considered this activity independently to give rise to a privacy complaint, it should have been explicit about that finding. Generally, under the common law of most American states, for example, deceptive or otherwise offensive newsgathering techniques do not independently give rise to a cause of action, unless they rise to the level of 'intrusion upon seclusion' – as literally into one's home. The method of obtaining information is relevant as a potentially aggravating factor, but it is not generally the subject of ultimate inquiry.

The Commission appeared to attribute more import to the investigative process. This is consistent in some ways with the Calcutt Mark I's recommendation that certain forms of physical intrusion should be criminal offences in England and Wales. Ms Short's physical privacy, however, was not invaded in any of the ways enumerated in Calcutt Mark I's recommendation, so it is surprising that the adjudication did not specifically refer to the Calcutt proposal. What the Commission ought to have recognised – and probably sought to in the Clare Short adjudication – is that one's privacy may be invaded in the investigative phase leading to an anticipated publication, not only by the publication itself. This can mean psychic or emotional privacy, not only physical privacy. Thus, Ms Short's privacy was invaded by the '[i]ntrusions and inquiries into [her] private life' – to quote the code language. The Commission considered *inquiries* into her relationship with John Daniel to be justified in the public interest, while inquiries made to her former husband, seeking a salacious photo of the MP, were not. None of the information disclosed as a result of either inquiry, however, achieved the level of public interest that would have justified its publication.

Under the laws of most American state jurisdictions, this is certainly the case. The motive of the publisher/defendant is simply not discussed. The only instance in which it is arguably relevant is when a public official or public figure is the complainant. In those cases, the rule of *New York Times*[3] and its progeny, which establish

[3] *New York Times Co v Sullivan* 376 US 254 (1964).

different standards of intent for those allegedly defaming different types of defamation plaintiffs, also apply to public official and public figure plaintiffs bringing invasion of privacy actions. The level of culpability which public figure/official defamation plaintiffs must prove is 'actual malice', further defined as 'knowledge of falsity' or publication 'with reckless disregard as to truth or falsity' of the statement.

In the 1967 case of *Time, Inc v Hill*,[4] the US Supreme Court held that the First Amendment precluded application of a New York privacy statute to redress reports of matters of public interest, even if they depicted the plaintiffs in a 'false light', absent proof that the defendant had published the report with 'knowledge of its falsity or in reckless disregard of the truth'. However, the actual malice standard defined in *New York Times* does not transfer comfortably or sensibly into any privacy context except the false light one. This is because 'knowledge of falsity' or 'reckless disregard' as to truth or falsity is irrelevant to 'private facts' cases, in which 'privacy', not 'falsity' is the key inquiry. American courts have exhibited some confusion as to how this standard should be applied in privacy cases. Some have roughly translated actual malice as knowledge that a publication would constitute an invasion of privacy or reckless disregard as to whether it would or not. Most courts have determined that the standard applies only to false light cases.

Thus, a US legal analysis of the Short complaint might have found the publisher's bad motive relevant, but it is unlikely because her allegations would be considered publication of private facts, rather than a false light type of invasion of privacy, the latter being generally necessary to trigger an 'actual malice' analysis.

The adjudication discussed at length the motives of both Ms Short and the *News of the World*. This may be because each party sought to focus on the reprehensible motive of the other. As previously noted, Ms Short alleged that the *News of the World* was pursuing a long-standing vendetta against her over her political crusade to ban 'page 3 girls' – and who could blame her now, regarding their hacking activities, televisually revealed in the Leveson Inquiry? The Commission gave credence to the relevance of this motive by acknowledging the 'inescapable suspicion' that the newspaper had sought to embarrass Ms Short in retaliation for her political stance on pornography. Motive should not necessarily be an issue with regard to invasion of privacy. Either an invasion has occurred, or it

---

[4] 385 US 374 (1967).

has not. The motive of the publishers is of no moment. Generally, a complainant's behaviour is relevant only insofar as he or she may have waived any right to action, because of previous publication of the sensitive information, or because he or she may otherwise have consented to the disclosure. With the Short complaint, the Commission apparently considered her behaviour relevant because the *News of the World* claimed that Ms Short's speech in the House of Commons in January 1991 had provoked it to publish the objectionable story. During her parliamentary speech, Ms Short strongly condemned the behaviour of the paper and its staff, including that of editor Ms Patricia Chapman, who coincidentally was the chairperson of the committee that drafted the industry's Code of Practice and who, from its inception, was a member of the Press Complaints Commission. Ms Short said she made the speech in the expectation that publication of a *News of the World* article was imminent. The *News of the World* editor resisted Ms Short's complaint, in part by claiming that it had not decided to publish a story based on its investigations until Ms Short made her speech in the House of Commons, after which the editor claimed that an article and editorial were the 'only effective way' to answer Ms Short's allegations and to correct her alleged inaccuracies. The Commission was sympathetic to this justification, but on the whole accorded far too much attention, and therefore implicitly assigned far too much importance to the motive issues.

The Press Complaints Commission appears never to have been quite able to sort through the complexity of Clare Short's complaint, and it stumbled several times because of its lack of understanding about how a privacy analysis might best proceed. For example, the initial inquiry might logically have been whether any invasion of privacy had occurred. Clause 4 asserts the basic unacceptability of 'intrusions and inquiries into an individual's private life'. But what does 'private life' mean? Does it include a person's home or private business address? Information about a person's sexual practices? About a family member's drug problem? The Commission did not, in the Short adjudication, and has not in handling any subsequent complaint, dealt with the meaning of 'privacy' or 'private life' as a term of art representing a concept on which a complaint may be based. Beyond this threshold issue, the Commission should have determined whether there has been an 'intrusion' or 'inquiry' into, or 'publication' relating to, this private sphere. If the answer is 'yes' the defences of 'consent' and 'public interest' become relevant.

The Short adjudication represents an early unsatisfactory adjudication of the Press Complaints Commission. This was not necessarily because it got the result wrong. Rather, it was because it did not proceed with such step-by-step analysis. Accordingly, very few free-standing principles about privacy can be garnered from it. The adjudication, in its construction and language, lacked a sense of juridical purpose. The Commission seemed to focus only on making a decision about a matter at hand; it was seemingly oblivious to any implications it might have for subsequent cases, and so unhappily it has been. It was similarly oblivious to its obligations to interpret in a meaningful way the Code of Practice, and to provide guidelines of acceptable press behaviour for both the media and the public. Its failure to expand the ambit of clause 4 was no doubt in part responsible for its demise. (The fact that until the last years of its existence no lawyer was a member of the Press Complaints Commission indicated the lack of legality of the Code.) Can IPSO do better?

THE MEANING OF 'PRIVACY'

Not every matter that a complainant considers an invasion of privacy actually constitutes an invasion into the private sphere of life. The Calcutt Committee discussed the meaning of 'privacy' at great length, considering the parameters set by the laws of various other countries. The Committee tentatively concluded that it is the 'right of an individual to be protected against intrusion into his personal life or affairs, or those of his family, by direct physical means or by publication of information'.

The report went on to note that the right to privacy 'could include' protection against: (a) physical intrusion; (b) publication of hurtful or embarrassing personal material (whether true or false); (c) publication of inaccurate or misleading personal material; and (d) publication of photographs or recordings of the individual taken without consent. Although the Committee did not expressly acknowledge such, three of these four categories roughly correspond to those recognised by American privacy tort jurisprudence: intrusion, publication of private facts, and false light. As regards the first 'photography' element of the fourth Calcutt category, it is similar in some instances to the American 'appropriation' type of privacy invasion which redresses the grievance of a person whose image has been exploited for commercial purposes. Despite the Calcutt Committee's apparent dalliance with American privacy concepts, these rather distinct types of privacy invasions are not reflected in the Code of Practice which was enforced by the Press Complaints Commission. As reflected in its quotation above, clause 4 of the Code speaks more generally of 'intrusions and inquiries' into an individual's private life being unacceptable. It goes on to enumerate instances when such intrusions may be justified as in the public interest, but it does not provide further guidance as to what manner or sorts of intrusions or inquiries are objectionable.

Both the National Heritage Committee of 1993 and the Government's consultation paper discussed the meaning and importance of privacy as an aspect of human personality. The Code of Practice does not reflect these categories. As noted in relation to the Clare Short case, privacy may refer to either or both of psychic privacy and physical privacy. These may be invaded either by *inquiries* into a personal matter, as in the Short case, or by *publication* of personal information.

The sort of information considered sufficiently private to be the basis of litigation is difficult to discern from its cursory litigation. Not a single adjudication of a clause 4 complaint engages in any substantive discussion of what is sufficiently 'private' to support a claim on this basis. One could deduce that the Commission deemed certain matters sufficiently private simply because complaints based on disclosure of these matters have been upheld under clause 4. Of course, if the Commission had not actually considered the privacy implications of such disclosure, this may be presumptuous and inappropriate. Still, without more explicit guidance from the Commission, it is all that the media or the public have on which to base a judgment of the Commission.

Consider the Princess Eugenie application, in which the Commission held that *The People's* publication of nude photos of the infant princess breached clause 4. In response to the newspaper's defence that the photos were 'charming' and 'natural', published 'good-naturedly and affectionately', the Commission responded that such claims were irrelevant, as was the offensiveness of the photos, because they were simply an invasion of privacy.

What the Commission failed to recognise is that issues of offensiveness and naturalness may be evidence of the ultimate issue of privacy invasion. Under the 'publication of private facts' prong of American privacy law, for example, a matter disclosed must be sufficiently private to 'violate ordinary decencies' or 'offend', in order to give rise to a cause of action. Thus, an offensiveness inquiry should not have been so summarily dismissed by the Commission. It assumed, probably correctly, that nude photos of a child, taken surreptitiously and published in a national newspaper, were sufficiently invasive of privacy to justify complaint. Even though the adjudication discounted an 'offensiveness' analysis, it perhaps implicitly engaged in one by noting the circumstances of both acquisition and publication of the photos, rather than focusing merely on their content, which, as the Commission noted, would be quite unexceptionable if only displayed in a family album. The Commission missed other opportunities to distinguish between disclosures which are of a sufficiently *personal* nature to constitute an invasion of privacy and matters which do not violate ordinary decency, even though the subject of them might prefer that they not be made public.

In adjudicating a complaint by the then leader of the Labour Party, Mr Neil Kinnock, and his daughter, who complained about an article in *Today* reporting a 'dust-up' between Mr Kinnock and four youths who were taunting him as he was 'ticking off' his daughter, the Commission held that the story did not breach the Code of Practice. No particular clause of the Code was ever cited; however, several references were made to the lack of 'intrusion into privacy', so it is fair to infer that it was decided on clause 4 principles. Though the Commission did not expressly find such, it might well have concluded simply that the matters published were not sufficiently 'private' or 'personal' as to constitute an invasion of privacy. Instead, it obscured this threshold issue by also noting that politicians seek and must expect regular exposure to the press, implying that 'public interest' had more to do with the decision than perhaps it should have.

INTRUSION UPON SECLUSION

Under American law, intrusion upon one's seclusion may give rise to a privacy action, even if no publication results from information gathered. Indeed, the Calcutt Committee recognised the seriousness of such invasion, and recommended that certain types of physical intrusion should be criminal offences in England and Wales. These included: (1) entering private property, without consent of the lawful occupant, with intent to obtain personal information with a view to its publication; (2) placing a surveillance device on private property, without consent of the lawful occupant, with the same intent; and (3) taking a photograph, or recording the voice, of an individual who is on private property, without his consent, with a view to its publication and with intent that the individual should be identifiable.

PUBLIC INTEREST TEST

The Calcutt Committee expressed unease with a 'public interest' concept, suggesting instead the concept of 'seriously anti-social conduct'. The Government's consultation paper suggested that the Calcutt Committee was right to draw attention to the vagueness of the term 'public interest', and stated that it would be preferable to indicate those matters that are of public interest, such as 'crime or seriously anti-social conduct; public health or safety; the discharge of a public function; the correction of a misleading statement'. The paper invited comments as to how the public interest definition should be formulated, and in particular whether it is preferable to define it in special terms or to be most specific. The comparable concept in US privacy jurisprudence was, until the early 1990s, 'newsworthiness', a term of art so broadly construed that it is now considered to be essentially whatever the press considers it to be, rather like Alice in Wonderland. The preferred option in the US became, anything which is of 'legitimate concern to the public'. The law provides no assistance, since the public interest defence to defamation is not amplified. IPSO's remit should give some guidance to the law.

The Code of Practice, that the Press Complaints Commission was charged with enforcing, embraces the concept of 'public interest' and employs it as a justification or defence for an invasion of privacy. In the amended Code of Practice, ratified by the Press Complaints Commission on 30 June 1993, a public interest exception could be relied on in relation to new provisions barring bugging devices and the use of long-lens cameras to photograph people on private property. Exceptions are allowed only in the public interest, which was defined as 'detecting or exposing crime or a serious misdemeanour; protecting public health and safety; protecting the public from being misled by the statement or action of an individual or organisation'. The amended Code went on to state that in any cases raising issues beyond those definitions, the Press Complaints Commission would require a full explanation by the editor, seeking to demonstrate how the public interest was served. It is not clear whether the defined exceptions were applicable to justification for a defence to an alleged breach of the privacy provisions in the Code. It is also difficult to understand the reference to 'misdemeanour', a criminal law concept abandoned by the UK legislature in 1967.

Even among the few adjudications that have assessed the 'public interest' rationale, it is difficult to discern any consistent application of the term. None has referred explicitly to the guidelines set forth in clause 4. Consider again the Clare Short adjudication, in which the Commission stated that 'public interest' is not synonymous with whatever interests the public. It emphasised that maintenance of the distinction between those two concepts is crucial, especially with respect to those people who are in public life. Contrast these comments with those responding to Neil Kinnock's complaint. Stating that '[l]eading politicians seek, experience and must expect regular exposure in the press', and that the article 'dealt largely in trivia about Mr Kinnock and his family in which *readers might be interested*', the Commission declined to uphold the complaint. Although both decisions were probably decided correctly, their language regarding what does and does not constitute 'public interest' is internally inconsistent. The adjudications send mixed messages about the sorts of justifications to which the Commission is sympathetic, one scoffing at public curiosity, the other legitimising it. If the distinction is well understood, there is as yet nothing from the newspaper industry to demonstrate that it accords the distinction any true meaning.

No doubt any adjudicator in this difficult area of regulation will be influenced by the way the courts will now interpret the 'public interest' defence in actions both for breach of confidence and in defamation cases. In a case in the former class of action, Ungoed-Thomas J, in *Beloff v Pressdram*,[5] said that justification for breach of confidentiality could be founded on

> matters carried out or contemplated in breach of the nation's security, or in breach of law, including statutory duty, fraud, or otherwise destructive of the country or its people, including matters basically dangerous to the public, and doubtless other misdeeds of similar gravity.

CONCLUSION

An essential function of any regulatory system – particularly a self-regulatory system – is to provide to the industry being regulated, as

---

[5] [1973] 1 All ER 241.

well as to the public, adjudications clarifying the precise scope and meaning of the provisions of the relevant code of conduct. That is precisely what the Younger Report asked for 40 years ago. Although the Code of Practice adopted by the Press Complaints Commission included a clause on privacy, adjudications interpreting and applying it have provided little guidance as to precisely what standards are expected of journalists and editors. The Commission's decisions are frequently only summary in analysis, thus failing to provide insight into the bases for them. Furthermore, that analysis which the adjudications do feature often missed the most obvious points, and hence obscured the issues that should have been dispositive.

The quality of output of adjudications cannot encourage anyone to conclude that the industry's 'last opportunity' (the euphemism of Mr David Mellor QC, repeated ever since) to make self-regulation work, especially self-regulation superintended by a Royal Charter, has been grasped with that degree of effectiveness which would allay disquiet about the lack of press responsibility. Indeed, Calcutt Mark II stated that 'the press has demonstrated that it is itself unwilling to put in place a regulatory system which commands [respect], not only of the press . . . but also of the public, and which fairly holds the balance between them'. Sir David Calcutt QC made no analysis of the Press Complaints Commission's case law on clause 4; yet he saw 'no realistic possibility of that [unwillingness] being changed by voluntary action'. Was he perceptive in that regard? It is an open question whether the freedom of the press is intact. Time will tell.

It is tolerably clear that there may be some private law remedy for the infringement of privacy, and we will have the benefit of case law from the courts. While the proposal is being translated into legislative action, and some statutory guidelines given to the crucial issue of the public interest defence, the industry and the public will look to the new regulator under the superintendence of the Royal Charter (or some like body) for guidance and assistance in a delicate area of social policy – the more so if the Government withdraws from its move towards a law on privacy. The basic notion of what is 'private' and the breadth of public interest defence will have more impact on privacy jurisprudence than any other sub-issue. Editors and journalists, as well as the public, must be provided with meaningful guidelines about precisely what is in the public interest, lest it be concluded that any determination of what is permissibly publishable on grounds of newsworthiness is left to the self-serving interests of the press. It is a prime function of a regulatory body that it should delineate the boundary between freedom of expression and reasonable journalism.

26

Media Freedom:
a New Concept in Free Speech

WITH THE WELCOME establishment of a public interest defence to a libel action, simultaneously abolishing the *Reynolds* (responsible journalism) defence, by the Defamation Act 2013 Parliament has brought English law into line with other democratic media laws. In effect, it has redefined the phrase, 'freedom of expression' from its personal individual base of information, to that of the public interest in information to the institution publishing that information. It ceased to be an exclusively personal right. Thus the privilege of public information took on a constitutional status which many other democratic countries' multifarious domestic and international obligations express in their constitutional documents. The unwritten constitution of England has always lagged behind in that attribute. The legal context of freedom of expression (including the concept of press freedom) becomes, in both theory and doctrine, media freedom.[1] Both Lord Hoffmann and Lady Hale had anticipated the jurisprudential label when considering the ambit in the *Reynolds* defence of responsible journalism. The constitutionalism of the freedom of expression is now firmly entrenched in modern democracies, which are pervaded by the extensive information of the internet. Based also on Article 10 of the European Convention on Human Rights, I attempted in the late 1990s to anticipate – unsuccessfully – the development of media freedom before the courts of the Republic of Ireland, in the context of the critique of criminal proceedings, including the English case of the Birmingham Six.

Crime is an event of public interest, a good deal more than just of interest to the public. A criminal trial is an essential institution of a democratic society that is held in public and reported on by the

---

[1] J Oster, 'Theory and Doctrine of "Media Freedom" as a Legal Concept' (2013) 5 *Journal of Media Law* 57.

media contemporaneously with absolute privilege in defamation law. The object was to plan that any media coverage, at the time of the criminal proceedings having concluded, or subsequently within a reasonable time, should qualify as a right that outbalances (overrides) any different claim to a defence of public interest. Such a modest judicial mood emulated the pre-2013 law of conferring a privilege on a fair and accurate report of legal proceedings. The reporting of criminal proceedings by the media accorded rights to anyone thereafter to comment. But it did not preclude action for defamation. The Defamation Act 2013 appears to change that position.

27

Censors in the Courtroom

T WICE IN THE course of my life in the law I have indulged
my literary appetite as an inveterate scribbler. I wrote two
books (strictly speaking, they were little more than pam-
phlets or booklets, since both were short in length, crisp in style
and aimed at an intelligent audience that could be persuaded by
critical commentary). Both were commentaries on English criminal
justice as seen through two high-profile cases; both were explanatory in tone, on the subject of cases described publicly as 'miscarriages of justice'. Both aroused vociferous support from detractors
of English justice; too little was heard in defence of the valued legal
institution of criminal justice. They can best be adjudged by presenting them separately.

The first case was that of James Hanratty, separately treated in
this volume, who was convicted of the murder of Michael Gregsten
and the rape of Valerie Storie, at Bedford Assizes in 1962. The incident took place in a cornfield in rural Berkshire where Hanratty
encountered the courting couple in a stationary car. At gunpoint he
made Gregsten drive the car and while on a stretch of the A6 highway he ordered the car to stop, whereupon the violence took place.
Hanratty's appeal against his conviction was refused and he was
duly executed. My book, entitled *The A6 Murder; the semblance of
truth*[1] was a critique of the English system which I explained was
conducted adversarially – the prosecution has to prove its case
beyond reasonable doubt – and was not an exercise in seeking to
establish the truth, other than inferentially, about a criminal event.
I concluded that on the *admissible* evidence, Hanratty should not
have been convicted, and he should certainly have been reprieved.
I did not conclude that Hanratty was innocent of the crime. I was
much criticised by certain left-wing journalists (eg Paul Foot, Bob
Woffinden et al) for implying that Hanratty was guilty. There were
at least two other books written about the case, arguing strongly that

---

[1] L Blom-Cooper, *The A6 Murder* (Harmondsworth, Penguin Books, 1963).

Hanratty was wrongly convicted and did not commit the crime. The controversy raged for the next 40 years, until DNA evidence pointing to Hanratty's complicity led to the Court of Appeal (Criminal Division) in May 2002 upholding the conviction in a compelling judgment. The publications were nearly all one-way, contending that the arrest and conviction of Hanratty were wrongful, as was his execution (abolition of the death penalty was still a few years away).

The second case was the Birmingham Six trial, arising out of terrorist bombs planted in a public house in the centre of Birmingham in November 1974. Six men (one other was acquitted) were convicted of the murders of 21 people at Lancaster Crown Court in August 1975. Their appeal was unsuccessful. In 1978 their case was referred back to the Court of Appeal (Criminal Division), but after an exhaustive hearing the appeal was dismissed. The judgment of 159 pages contained two passages of note. Early on in the judgment Lord Lane, the Lord Chief Justice, said that quite apart from the written admissions to the police and some forensic evidence, there was still a strong case against the Six on a mass of circumstantial evidence. This passage was not quoted in press reports, but the peroration to the judgment was widely quoted, and has remained a focus of hostility towards an outstanding Lord Chief Justice. He said that the longer the case lasted, the more convinced the court was that the jury's verdict was safe and satisfactory. In 1991 the case was again sent back to the court: this time the convictions were quashed and the Six were freed after 16 years in prison. Thereafter they loudly and persistently proclaimed their total innocence, as they were entitled to do.

My book, The Birmingham Six: Victims of Circumstance,[2] was published in 1997. Its publishers subsequently went into liquidation and did not stay to fight the libel proceedings that ensued. The book's theme was twofold. The quashing of a criminal conviction did not, in law, constitute a declaration of innocence on those whose convictions were quashed. Even an acquittal at trial does not have that effect. As Lord Rodger in the Supreme Court in *Allison v HM Advocate (Scotland)*[3] explained, the presumption of innocence (an evidential rule) is not to say that the defendant has to be treated in all respects as if he were an innocent person against whom no charge has been brought: 'More obviously, in an appropriate case, he can be remanded in custody pending trial or granted bail subject to appropriate conditions', and Lord Rodger gave other examples

---

[2] L Blom-Cooper, *The Birmingham Six: Victims of Circumstance* (London, Duckworths, 1997).
[3] [2010] UKSC 6.

where defendants are not regarded as less than trustworthy or credible persons. The second theme was to demonstrate that, contrary to popular belief, circumstantial evidence (if compelling) is preferred by the law to eye-witness testimony which is inherently fallible due to memory loss and contamination by external influences. I concluded that the only reasonable conclusion was that of agnosticism as to the complicity of the Six in the bombings. In 1998 the Six sued me for libel in the courts of the Republic of Ireland.

If you are looking for a modern example of an injustice propagated by members of the judiciary, you need look no further than the Supreme Court of Ireland. On 8 October 2009 five justices of that court, led by the Chief Justice, Mr Justice Murray, in effect burnt a modest book of legal scholarship. Without any reasoned judgment, the Supreme Court ordered that the case should be sent back to the High Court to continue the proceedings for libel. Subsequently, the case was amicably settled. Miscarriages of justice have long been a threnody among dissidents with political agendas, but their hymn sheets are often overlooked by courts – the fact is that justice can miscarry both ways. The wrongly convicted may not have been wrongly arrested and tried before a judge and jury. The dissidents are rarely accorded any acknowledgment of the rival arguments about the guilt and innocence of convicted offenders. The Irish judges did nothing to rectify the imbalance between advocates of the wrongly convicted and the supporters of the criminal justice process. My criticism, not to say invective inveigled against the Irish judges, will appear as mere assertion so long as it is not made good by a detailed account. (The use of the power of contempt of court is virtually non-existent.) If, however, in stark contrast, the author seeks to support the verdict of the criminal trial and appeal proceedings, there is no safeguard against the issue of libel proceedings. The courts have recently erected a constitutional principle of reasonable journalism; they have yet to confer the same legal status on responsible authorship.

A court trying an action for defamation should nowadays (since the passing of the Human Rights Act 1998) instantly strike a balance between freedom of expression and the protection of reputation. There is no longer any primacy in favour of the reputation of a defamed individual; it takes its place alongside a competing freedom. The case law from Strasbourg has definitively accepted a person's right to protection of his or her reputation as encompassed by Article 8 as being part of the right to respect for private life, and simultaneously balanced it against the right to freedom of expression under Article 10.[4] And in March 2012, in the decision in *Flood v Times Newspapers Ltd*,[5] the President of the UK Supreme Court, Lord Phillips of Worth Matravers, pointed out that the rights introduced into our domestic law as a consequence of the 1998 Act require that approach:

> Publication is permitted, even though this may involve publishing allegations that are clearly defamatory. The balance in respect of the reporting of such proceedings is heavily weighted in favour of freedom of speech. The public interest in favour of publication is firmly established . . . In developing the common law the courts as public authorities are obliged to have regard to the requirements of the Convention.[6]

It is noteworthy that the judgment of Bean J, in *Bento v Bedfordshire Chief Constable*,[7] proceeded upon the basis of the established framework of common law principles relating to the defence of qualified privilege. It falls short of engaging in the wider perspective of a fast-changing jurisprudence. The essential question in *Bento* was whether an impugned statement from the police (as criminal investigator) which was defamatory was made on a privileged occasion (whether absolute or qualified). I approach that question from a binary viewpoint; it is unnecessary to pigeonhole types of privileged defence, although it must be observed that the libel claim was defended on traditional, qualified privilege, rather than under the development of the law in *Reynolds v Times Newspapers Ltd*.[8]

The facts in *Bento* were straightforward, if slightly unusual. The claimant for libel had been charged with the murder of his erstwhile girlfriend with whom he had been cohabiting. At his trial at Luton Crown Court his defence was that he was innocent of any crime, and that the victim's death was the result of suicide. Her body had been recovered on 24 January 2006, after her disappearance on 13 December 2005. She had drowned in a local lake shortly after having been seen near the lake and was caught on CCTV, appearing to be carrying her familiar type of handbag. That had been a crucial piece of the circumstantial evidence that implicated the claimant, and to that fact there had been crucial evidence from a forensic video analyst. If the expert's evidence was reliable, that the bag belonged to the dead girl – 'she can be seen carrying her

---

[4] *Cumpana and Mazure v Romania* (2004) 41 EHRR 200 and *Pfeifer v Austria* (2007) 48 EHRR 175.
[5] [2012] UKSC 11.
[6] ibid [45] and [46].
[7] [2012] EWHC 1525 (QB).
[8] [2001] 2 AC 127.

favourite handbag' – the claimant was implicated because the bag was later recovered by the police in premises to which the claimant had access. The claimant was convicted by the Luton jury. He appealed to the Court of Appeal (Criminal Division). On the footing that the defence desired to call fresh evidence from an expert, to deal with the uncontradicted evidence of the Crown expert at trial, the Court of Appeal gave leave to appeal, quashed the conviction and ordered a retrial. Subsequent to the order of a retrial, the Crown's expert died; he had committed suicide. In July 2009 the Crown Prosecution Service indicated that it was discontinuing the prosecution. At a brief hearing in the Crown Court, the prosecution offered no evidence; a verdict of not guilty was entered. On 9 July 2009, following the court hearing, the Bedfordshire Police issued a statement in response to a request from the local newspaper, which was released by email to various local media. Although it did not appear to attract any national coverage, it was clearly in the public domain. It stated:

> Bedfordshire Police were told by the Crown Prosecution Service [on] Tuesday evening that the case against Nico Bento has been discontinued.
>
> We are extremely disappointed on behalf of Kamila's family, for whom this reopens a devastating chapter in their lives. The police conducted the most thorough and ethical investigation in this case and did their utmost to secure justice for the family.
>
> The role of the police in cases such as these is to assemble the available evidence and present it to the CPS. In this case the evidence initially presented resulted in a conviction at the Luton Crown Court where the decision of the jury was unanimous.
>
> The CPS have now taken the view that confusion in regard to the expert evidence in this case means there is no longer a realistic prospect of conviction.
>
> The police investigation found no evidence whatsoever that Kamila killed herself. Therefore, as with all unresolved murder investigations, this case will not be closed and will be continually kept under review in an effort to discover new evidence and build a stronger case.

The defence to the libel action was twofold: justification and traditional qualified privilege (old-style – that is pre-*Reynolds*). Mr Justice Bean's examination in detail of the circumstantial evidence that led to the conviction for murder – minus, presumably, the evidence no longer extant in the expected retrial – predictably found that it could not be substantiated. Despite the jury's verdict Mr Justice Bean concluded:[9]

---

[9] ibid [91] and [92].

Either of these scenarios is possible. But the suicide scenario is by far the more probable of the two. That far greater probability is not outweighed by the circumstantial evidence, even of the flowers incident. My conclusion is that while it is possible that Mr Bento killed Kamila, the balance of probabilities is that he did not and that she committed suicide. The defence of justification therefore fails.

On the separate issue of qualified privilege Mr Justice Bean thought that that too failed to measure up to the required standard of proof. The defendant could have limited his defence by issuing a modified statement that would have protected its own interests without implying that Bento was guilty of murder or that he probably killed her. The judge awarded Bento £125,000 damages. The Bedfordshire Police decided not to appeal the decision; apparently their insurers declined to continue the litigation.

The recent development in the jurisprudence of the English courts came in the classical judgment of Lord Nicholls in *Reynolds v Times Newspapers Ltd*, which ushered in the concept of responsible journalism as a development of the defence of qualified privilege, to the point where Lord Hoffmann and Lady Hale in the later case of *Jameel v Wall Street Journal Europe SPRL*[10] suggested that the law of defamation is now poised to adopt a new jurisprudential creature of responsible journalism. It is worth pointing out that the responsible journalism defence is not the sole preserve of the media. As Lord Phillips said in *Flood v Times Newspapers Ltd*,

> *Reynolds* privilege is not reserved for the media, but it is the media who are more likely to take advantage of it, for it is usually the media that publish to the world at large . . . The importance of the public interest in receiving the relevant information has to be weighed against the public interest in preventing the dissemination of defamatory allegations.[11]

Mr Justice Bean's judgment records the various arguments advanced by counsel for the defence, for demonstrating that the duty to publish and the interest or right to receive information was applicable to the statement made by the Bedfordshire police.[12] Strangely, throughout this detailed attempt to argue for an apparent broadening of the *Reynolds* privilege, not a word appears in the judgment about the *Flood* case, which was decided by the UK Supreme Court on 21 March 2012 (the trial of *Bento v Chief Constable of Bedfordshire Police* took place in April/May 2012; judgment was

[10] [2007] 1 AC 359.
[11] [2012] UKSC 11, 45.
[12] [2001] 2 AC 127 [94(i)]–[94(xvii)].

reserved on 9 May 2012 and delivered on 1 June). What is the more surprising is the omission of any reference to another pertinent passage in Lord Phillips' judgment in *Flood*. Referring to the nature of 'reportage' as an example of the *Reynolds* privilege, he said:

> There is a danger in putting reportage in a special box of its own. It is an example of circumstances in which the public interest justifies publication of facts that carry defamatory inferences without imposing on the journalist any obligation to verify the truth of those inferences. *These circumstances may include the fact that the police are investigating the conduct of an individual, or that he has been arrested, or that he had been charged with an offence.*[13]

In short, the police issuing, on request from a journalistic source, a press release for public information, following the decision of the Crown Prosecution Service, might well be regarded as an adjunct or auxiliary to the privilege accorded to the media, post-*Reynolds*.

The nub of Mr Justice Bean's rejection of the defence of qualified privilege (or, if you like, a defence of reportage or technique of journalistic reporting incidental to the media coverage) is contained in a single paragraph. I quote the paragraph verbatim:

> I accept that there is a high public interest in maintaining confidence in the criminal justice system. That public interest underlies much of my working life and that of any judge who sits in the criminal courts. But I do not accept that that public interest is served by encouraging the police to issue statements indicating their opinion that the decision of the CPS not to pursue a prosecution (or, for that matter, the decision of a judge that a defendant has no case to answer) is wrong because the individual concerned is or is probably guilty. On the contrary: such statements reduce confidence in the criminal justice system, as well as seriously damaging the right to reputation of the individual.[14]

What conceivable evidence is there of the nature and extent of public opinion about criminal justice? And what empirical evidence (as opposed to judicial opinion) is there that a press statement from the police in the case of *Bento* would 'reduce confidence in the criminal justice system'? Apart from pure judicial surmise, or even the informed guess of a seasoned practitioner in the criminal courts (for what this is worth as evidence of the social situation), it is an open question whether, and if so, what degree of confidence the public has in the criminal justice system – and that is assuming an overall view of criminal investigation, the powers of arrest, the charging of

---

[13] [2012] UKSC 11 [35] (italics supplied).
[14] [2012] EWHC 1525 [98]

a criminal offence and the process of a fair trial with an appropriate appellate system. The plain fact is, as criminologists point out, that as a society we know precious little about what the public thinks about crime and justice. What little we do know is gleaned almost entirely from unreliable (in the sense of extremely limited research) opinion polls and largely irresponsible media coverage of criminality. There is undoubtedly a 'high public interest' in the criminal justice system (whether it carries public confidence or not), and that is a factor properly taken into account in assessing the balance between Articles 10 and 8. But we need to be informed publicly of the functioning of criminal trials.

Whatever the constitutional status of the criminal justice system, its emanation finds ample expression in Article 6 of the European Convention on Human Rights, obliging a Member State to provide its citizenry with a fair trial in full gaze of the public. Just as Article 10 may trump any Article 8 right, so Article 6 is surely supplemental to the guaranteed 'sunlight of publicity' provided in criminal proceedings. Lady Hale in *Jameel*[15] described 'the general obligation of the press, media and other publishers to communicate important information upon matters of general public interest and the general right of the public to receive such information', and added: 'There must be some real public interest in having the information in the public domain.' Lord Phillips in *Flood* commented:[16] 'I doubt if this formulation could be bettered.'

The Bedfordshire Police press statement of 9 July 2009, by way of response to the announcement of the Crown Prosecution Service that it had decided to discontinue its prosecution of Bento in a second trial, as ordered by the Court of Appeal, was a report of a court proceeding, in that it brought to public attention the ending of the extant prosecution; it indicated that the homicidal event would be subject to any future prosecution only on the basis of fresh evidence sufficient to invoke the reversal of the rule of double jeopardy under section 76 of the Criminal Justice Act 2003. The court hearing to quash the conviction would not have indicated the state of any further criminal investigation. The public was entitled to be informed about the prosecutorial consequences of the decision of the Crown Prosecution Service.

If both the media and other public commentators have immunity (whether absolute or qualified privilege) from defamatory action,

---

[15] [2007] 1 AC 359 [146] and [147].
[16] [2012] UKSC 11 [42].

they are entitled in the exercise of that right to be wrong, just as much as the Crown Prosecution Service may have taken a wrong decision not to pursue a second trial, for which, incidentally, it was susceptible to judicial review. Together, the Bedfordshire Police as the investigators of the crime and the CPS as the prosecuting authority were subject to public scrutiny. If the Bedfordshire Police was in breach of policing ethics, it or its officers could be disciplined administratively. Mr Justice Bean further observed[17] that the Bedfordshire Police 'could perfectly well have issued a statement saying any or all of the matters short of suggesting, defamatorily, that Bento killed the victim who did not commit suicide'.

Why should it be assumed that the press statement of the Bedfordshire Police of 9 July 2009 would reduce the confidence of the community in the Bedford area – and beyond, in the country? It might actually enhance its reputation, in that the reasonable reader of the press statement might have felt that it was only the misfortune of the death of the Crown's expert that had upset the verdict of a local jury. We do not know, and cannot even sensibly guess, at the public reaction to the press statement. It might actually have been 'a very wholesome act'.[18] Judges in any event should not engage in guesswork about social responses. That requires hard evidence.

There was hard evidence directed to the issue, which of the alternative scenarios was the right answer. Mr Justice Bean was amply entitled (after a lengthy excursion through the evidence on the issue of justification) to conclude that the more probable cause of the drowning was suicide and not culpable homicide. But whatever the preferred finding – suicide or culpable homicide – might be in the libel proceedings, that in itself cannot, for the purposes of assessing public opinion, negate the findings of the jury in the earlier criminal proceedings. Public opinion might, or might not, prefer the verdict of the jury, even though it was quashed on appeal, with an order for a re-trial. The public is free to choose which of the two scenarios it is inclined to view as the more likely. And the press statement of 9 July 2009 was one piece among much other information in the public domain that could properly be taken into account. The problem for the modern democrat in assessing Bean J's decision is that one man's Article 8 right (to protect his reputation) was allowed to eclipse the Article 10 rights, not just of the Bedfordshire

---

[17] [2012] EWHC 1525 (QB) [99].

[18] As per Coleridge CJ in *Bonnard v Perryman* [1891] 2 Ch 269, 284, where he stated that 'often a very wholesome act is performed in the publication and repetition of an alleged libel'.

Police, the populace of Bedfordshire and its environs, but also of the victim's family[19] and friends, and all of us serious scribblers in England and Wales. So much for the striking of a balance!

CODA

From the point of view of social policy and free speech, the most disturbing consequence of the *Bento* decision is that the claimant in the libel proceedings may proclaim publicly and with impunity his exculpation from inflicting any harm on the victim who drowned in the lake at Bedford. No one sensibly would wish to deny Bento his desire publicly to declare his innocence of any crime; after all, the criminal justice system has declared him legally – but, it should be noted, *not* factually – innocent. It is a common misunderstanding that there is a 'presumption of innocence' for everyone at all times. The 'presumption' arises, however, only as and when a person faces a criminal charge. The 'presumption' is a rule of evidence; nothing more nor less than a valuable procedural safeguard to an accused in a criminal trial. It is inapplicable to the rest of us, even where there are public allegations of criminality. But at the same time as Bento declares his innocence – for good measure, he may even assert that his deceased cohabitee committed suicide – the rest of us are disentitled from speaking publicly on a matter of high public interest (a murder trial) to a contrary view under the threat of an action for libel. The legal system has effectively muzzled us, so long as Bento is alive. The demonstrable inequality in the rights to freedom of expression is a plain denial of such a right under Article 10 of the ECHR; it is discriminatory, if nothing else. Civil liberties demand equality of arms as between disputants, at least on matters of opinion – Bento and the police should be entitled to express rival views as to his criminality.

If the *Bento* judgment accurately reflects the result of the law, so be it. But I protest. No one (least of all this commentator) would wish to stifle anyone's claim to his or her reputation among associates and fellow citizens. But a civilised society should not perpetuate such a disparity of treatment on its citizenry. The rest of us should be free to state publicly that Bento is wrong, and why we think he is wrong, as perhaps also was the Crown Prosecution Service (which the Bedfordshire Police evidently thought). Others

---

[19] Arguably one might include the dead victim's reputation defended by the immediate family.

may argue forcibly that Bento is factually innocent. We all need to adhere – unswervingly, I assert – to the principle proclaimed a hundred years ago by Justice Oliver Wendell Holmes in *Abrams v US*[20] that 'the best itself of truth [for completeness and clarity, I would add 'on matters of public interest'] is the power of the thought to get itself accepted in the competition of the market . . . It is an experiment, as all life is an experiment.'

---

[20]   250 US 616 (1919).

28

The Historical Background to Self-Regulation of the Press

THE LEVESON REPORT ('the Report') on 29 November 2012, an inordinate 1,978 pages in length (and 46 pages of summary), was successful both publicly and politically on the issue of a self-regulatory body to replace the Press Complaints Commission – with or without statutory underpinning. One had only to read the House of Lords debate of 11 January 2013 to note that judgment; with rare diversion, the seven-hour debate focused on the system that should succeed the Press Complaints Commission as the self-regulatory body for the newspaper industry. The contents of the Coalition Government's Royal Charter (published on 12 February 2013) are covered in the next issue of Hansard. It reflected, in the ensuing months only, its core recommendation in consideration of the 'culture, practice and ethics' of the print media. The Report, on the other vital aspects of the media – tracing and culture of journalism, the ownership of the media (indeed its cross-media issues), the plurality and funding of a free press and its relationship with data protection, politicians and the police – was either largely underdiscussed or exclusively favourable to the Establishment. The Leveson Inquiry's findings, moreover, disclosed an initial failure to observe the nature of the press's public service to a public that voraciously called for an independent inquiry under the Inquiries Act 2005. But the Report in its historical background (20 pages of it, at pages 195–215) to its remit of July 2010 purports to set out the beginnings of press regulation.

The opening sentence of the historical background to the Report on 'culture, practices and ethics of the Press' states that, 'in order to understand the present position in relation to press regulation, it is necessary to examine what has happened in the past'. But for any useful purpose, the report of the Leveson Inquiry is sadly unreliable. This is why. For all its 1,978 pages, the historical background to self-regulation of the press is both short and inadequate. Its description of that single element in the Inquiry is a misstatement of elementary facts, misrepresentation of events from 1988 to 1990, and a misjudgement over the period of 37 years of the Press Council. Independence, moreover, had been a prominent feature of the Press Council, from 1966 to 1990. Was that not a prime consideration in evaluating independence and press freedom? Or rather, how much independence of the Council did it in fact portray?

The gravamen of the Leveson Report was its total failure to reverse the finding of the Calcutt Committee and therefore deal with the argument, advanced by Sir David Calcutt and his colleagues, that the two roles of the Press Council (ever since 1953) of maintenance of the freedom of the press alongside a growing system of dealing with individual complaints of press maltreatment were incompatible.[1] It followed that the Council should be replaced exclusively by a complaints body. In my written submission to Sir Brian Leveson on 6 December 2011 I urged that this reasoning was constitutionally and practically flawed. I can do no better than repeat these submissions, which I maintain were hugely relevant to the future system of self-regulation. The Report ignored this fundamental challenge.

CHAIRMANSHIP

The Report notes that the third Royal Commission on the Press (1974–77) – it omits any reference to the first and second Royal Commissions – was established 'under the chairmanship of Professor Oliver (later Lord) McGregor on 7 March 1974', an independent individual, as the Press Council's constitution provided after 1966. This was strictly inaccurate, as could have been discovered by referring to Shannon's *A Free Press and Responsible*.[2] The chairman selected by Harold Wilson's Labour Government was in fact Mr Justice Finer, a judge of the Family Division of the Supreme Court, who sadly died nine months into the working life of the Commission; he was succeeded by his deputy and close friend, Professor McGregor, who effectively led the Commission to its final report in 1977. McGregor was, truly, an academic and head of the Social Administration Department at Bedford College of the University of London – he held the chair of Social Institutions. His

---

[1] In case anyone infers that Sir David was instinctively hostile to my appointment, I would like to point out that at the English Bar we were the greatest of friends. When Sir David became Treasurer of Middle Temple in 1998 he nominated me as the Reader for the Lent Term (a kind of deputy to the Treasurer).

[2] R Shannon, *A Free Press and Responsible* (London, John Murray, 2001) 15.

speciality was as an agrarian historian of the Victorian era, and he had no medical or legal qualification, or expertise, save that he served as chairman of Reuters. The medio-social element in the department was battened on to the Social Administration Department under the separate leadership of Professor Margot Jeffreys.

Professor McGregor was, correctly, made a peer under the title of Lord McGregor of Durris and became in 1980 the chairman of the Advertising Standards Authority, a self-regulatory body for the advertising industry. As we shall see later in this chapter, but which was unnoticed in the Leveson report, he was the preferred candidate for chairmanship of the Press Council in 1988 on the announced resignation of Sir Zelman Cowen, the former Governor-General of Australia and Provost of Oriel College, Oxford. He was interviewed by the members of the Press Council in April 1988, in circumstances that will be described below.

The Report noted (para 4.4, p 204) that the third Royal Commission (1974–77) stated that to increase public confidence in the institution it should increase the number of lay representatives 'and the appointment of a *lay* chairman'. The Report omits to observe that, since 1966, the independent chairman had been exclusively a prominent lawyer – from Lord Devlin and Lord Pearce (both retired Law Lords), Lord Shawcross (the chairman of the second Royal Commission in 1964), Sir Patrick Neill QC (now Lord Neill of Bladen) and Sir Zelman Cowen[3] in 1983. This dominance was never adversely commented upon in public, but was a familiar theme within the newspaper industry. In 1990 the Newspaper Proprietors' Association appointed Lord McGregor as the Chairman of the Press Complaints Commission; no contest for its chairmanship was envisaged. It should be noted that in the initial composition of the Press Complaints Commission there was nobody selected who was legally qualified (later appointments relented in this regard). None of this important aspect of independence, stemming from judicial or legal experience, was mentioned in the Report.

THE NATIONAL UNION OF JOURNALISTS (NUJ)

Under the constitution of the Press Council, the NUJ was given two members, nominated by the newspaper industry, out of a total

---

[3] The report mentions only Lord Pearce in connection with the Press Council. An omission to identify Lord Devlin (a very distinguished judge) is startling.

membership of 36 members. The Report, correctly, states that the NUJ had withdrawn its members from the Council in 1980, as a result of a growing disenchantment with the functioning of the Press Council. What the Report omitted to state was that the NUJ resumed its membership in April 1990, thus restoring the actual arithmetical balance between the 18 independent members and the 18 newspaper members. The importance of this omission is that for a period of nearly a decade the independent members formed the majority of the Council's membership. When, therefore, a new chairman was sought in May 1988 there was a majority of independent members to select the new chairman. Ever since 1966, as a result of the second Royal Commission on the Press chaired by Lord Shawcross, the chairman was appointed by the Council, and not by the newspaper industry, as became the practice of the Press Complaints Commission from January 1991 and onwards.

THE CHAIRMANSHIP IN MAY 1988

In terms of the independence of the Press Council, the most significant event was the method of selecting the new chairman in May 1988. The Report makes no allusion to the selection of a chairman, but the circumstances with regard to independence, since 1966, had been of some general significance. The chairman had always been a distinguished lawyer. On Sir Zelman's resignation in 1988, the Council determined to seek a replacement, without any general advertisement. It did so by canvassing a number of persons familiar with the practice of self-regulation and information services, although not directly involved parties. The Newspaper Proprietors Association, under the chair of the late Sir Frank Rogers, proffered the candidature of Lord McGregor, on the grounds of his profound interest in press matters as evidenced by the report of the third Royal Commission in which was contained some strong criticism of the Press Council. While it did not contemplate the disbandment of the Council, the McGregor report of 1977 argued for reform on a number of issues, and specifically renewed the urge to compile a code of conduct for the press. For reasons which are not at first hand explicable to this writer, the Council, after interviewing Lord McGregor, declined to appoint him to succeed Sir Zelman Cowen. They evidently did not like his prescription for the future of the Press Council. It was at that point that Sir Zelman contacted me personally, to see whether I would be willing to be interviewed for the post. I was duly interviewed, and appointed to succeed Sir Zelman at the end of 1988. None of this episode is recorded in the Report, but the reaction to it in Fleet Street circles was profound. Its significance was the appointment itself, independent of the power of the newspaper industry, in the face of its own preferred candidate, and in circumstances where it did not hold the majority of the membership. It was an event that went to the heart of a perceived development of a Press Council that was destined to produce a greater public image within self-regulation. The newspaper industry knew publicly of a desire on my part, as there had been on the part of Sir Zelman Cowen, to advocate a statutory law of privacy.

I should add, parenthetically, that there is one reference in the report (para 5.6 and footnotes 47 and 48) to the two written statements by me,[4] which were a reference to my view on the suggestion that newspapers in the 1980s were declining to report adverse findings of complaints upheld by the Press Council, although I did say that findings were often traduced and undermined by articles in the pages of some newspapers. Otherwise my efforts at reviewing the Press Council were not noted in the Report.

FUNDING

The newspaper industry had throughout the history of the Press Council funded the operation of the body, levying its members for contributions to the financing. When I became chairman the budget was a paltry £650,000; almost immediately the Council asked for this to be increased for 1989 to £700,000 annually, with a desire to seek a negotiated increase in 1990. At that time the industry was establishing a Press Board of Finance (Pressbof); it refused to grant any increase. This fact of limiting the financial resources of self-regulation, although specifically noted in Calcutt I, does not appear in the Report; no note of the budgetary provision is recorded in the Report. It might have also been noted in the Report that on the establishment of the Press Complaints Commission (PCC) Pressbof announced that it (the PCC) would start life, in 1991, with a budget of £1.2 million.

---

[4] I had made a supplementary submission to that of 6 December 2011 in June 2012, and had made a separate legal submission on the construction of r 13 of the Inquiries Rules 2006.

MEMBERSHIP

This aspect of the Press Council was totally absent from the Report. At the time of its disbandment in 1990 the Council was 36 members strong – an absurdly overmanned governing body. But it was distinctively independent in its composition. The significance was enhanced by the method of appointment.

Each year there were advertisements signifying vacancies among the 18 members of the Council. In my last year, there were over a thousand applicants for membership. The selection was conducted entirely outwith the purview of the newspaper industry or of any government agency. A separate appointments commission was chaired by Lord Asa Briggs, a distinguished historian and a retired Provost of Worcester College, Oxford. There could hardly be a more open system of appointing half of the members of the self-regulatory body than this. Yet the Report makes no allusion to this important element in the control of the print media.

CODE OF CONDUCT

From the outset, the General Council of the Press was encouraged, as 'a necessary and non-negotiable element of an effective regulatory regime for the British press', to 'build up a code of conduct in accordance with its highest professional standards'.[5] For reasons that are not readily explicable, and lacking in any rationality, the Press Council did not act upon this recommendation. It was specifically urged by the third Royal Commission in 1977 to take heed of this persistent recommendation. The response was a deafening silence. As the Calcutt Committee noted at the beginning of 1989,[6] however, the Press Council announced that it was to conduct a detailed review of its role and function, as a result of which it produced a Code of Practice on 1 March 1990. The Code was noted by Calcutt I at Appendix P, pp 119–120. The Code is not substantially dissimilar to that produced as the Editors' Code of Practice issued by the Press Complaints Commission. The Report makes no reference to the review, or indeed to the production of a code of conduct. This was followed very shortly by the return in April 1990 to the membership of the Council of the NUJ, thus restoring the equality

---

[5] (Cmd 7700, 1949) p 170, para 640.
[6] (Cm 1102, 1990) p 61 para 14.16.

of lay members and newspaper representatives. The report records the withdrawal of the NUJ in 1980 but makes no mention of the return in 1990. Had the Council during the 1980s improved its image it might have persuaded the Calcutt Committee of the earnest desire of the Press Council to reform itself and prove to be more effective publicly.

THE CALCUTT COMMITTEE: THE LOSS OF PRESS FREEDOM

The Calcutt Committee on Privacy and Related Matters[7] (June 1990) was hardly expansive in its conclusion that 'the two distinct functions of defending the freedom of the press and adjudicating on complaints sit uneasily together'.[8] While the Committee grudgingly acknowledged that 'no incompatibility had been detected [*sic*] by the three Royal Commissions on the Press', and the Press Council in its internal (1989) review of its functions had strongly expressed its desire to strengthen the objectives of the Council as established by the newspaper industry founders in 1953, the Calcutt Committee stated in cavalier fashion: 'We have come to a different conclusion.' It proceeded to give as its sole explanation for such a categorical, unhistorical attitude, that 'there is insufficient interdependence between these responsibilities to make it necessary for one body to undertake both'.[9] The Committee did not deign, moreover, to refer to what the Council's first independent chairman Lord Devlin (a retired Law Lord) said in 1966 in a public speech to the Commonwealth Press Union, that he had a profound belief in the Council functioning to promote press freedom and as a complaints system. If the Calcutt Committee's conclusion was woefully inadequate as a sound reason for 'detecting' incompatibility, it is true that by the end of the 1980s (if not much earlier) the predominant work of the Press Council had been handling and adjudicating formally upon complaints of breaches of uncodified journalistic ethics in ever-growing numbers, such that its other functions played a minor role in its work. This was due not just to the increasing volume of complaints by readers of newspapers (both regional and national) and periodicals, but to the paucity of funding for the Council's operations.

---

[7] The Committee consisted of chairman Sir David Calcutt, David Eady QC (later Mr Justice Eady), John Cartwright MP, Professor John Last, John Spencer (later Professor of Law at the University of Cambridge) and journalists Simon Jenkins and Sheila Black.

[8] Para 15.2.

[9] Para 15.3.

Anyone addressing Article 10 ECHR will instantly appreciate that press freedom (everyone's freedom of expression) in Article 10.1 is qualified by an enumerated list of public concerns in Article 10.2: the two parts of Article 10 are interrelated, and entirely compatible. It was precisely what Lord Devlin had proclaimed in 1966 – the regulatory organisation was to stand up for the freedom and rights of the press as well as to censure misconduct. 'To censure misconduct effectively,' he asserted,

> it needs the support and respect of the press and it will obtain that much more readily if, in the words of its constitution, it seeks to preserve the established freedom of the British press and work as to maintain its character in accordance with the highest professional standards.

He added, prophetically, that the organisation 'must never allow itself to become mostly a tribunal which convicts or acquits'. In 1990 the newspaper industry did not desire to possess a complaints system that undermined its precious task of press freedom. Only after it was found wanting in this public task did it accept the Leveson report's urge for the new body to be solely the recipient of readers' complaints.

CONCLUSION

The Press Council was replaced, not because its procedures were largely dilatory, ineffective (which, by common consent, they were) and lacked public confidence in its function as a viable self-regulator, but because the newspaper industry disliked (not least indirectly, by curtailing its financial resources) the Council's tendency to ensure greater concern for the public through its independent element, and because some of the newspapers disliked not having control over the appointment of chairmen and lay members. It desired a complaints system solely, over which it restricted any interference on a free press. Since the degree of independence is now the litmus test of any future self-regulatory body, it is not out of place to test the credibility of the leaders of the newspaper industry in actively supporting the independence of the regulator. The events of 1988–90 (if not the paucity of independence in the functioning of the Press Complaints Commission) are surely factors to be taken into account. The history, in the Report, gives no support for the claim of independence in the new body. Independence of the members from government and from the newspaper industry is crucial.

Part V

Miscellany

29

Jan Christiaan Smuts (1870–1950): Middle Templar Extraordinary[1]

PROLOGUE

AT THE TIME that I was called to the Bar by Middle Temple in July 1952, I had paid little or no attention to the constitutional and legal problems of South Africa. But in 1958 I was asked by the newly created International Commission of Jurists to attend as an observer, together with Fred Lawton QC (then a leading practitioner in England, later to become a Lord Justice of Appeal) the forthcoming opening of the trial in Pretoria of 156 people charged with treason. I duly attended those preliminary proceedings which began on 1 August 1958 (and ultimately were aborted), and over the following years I visited South Africa as an observer of other political trials, that is, until 1965.[2]

British subjects did not require a visa to visit South Africa, but the Minister of the Interior, unsurprisingly, possessed the power to take away that privilege and render any undesirable visitor a prohibited immigrant. Accordingly, I duly received a letter from the Secretary to the Minister of the Interior depriving me of the visa privilege. It was a long letter – two full pages of A4 paper. It chronicled (very accurately) all my misdeeds over the years, writing and lecturing against apartheid and constantly consorting with defence counsel in the political trials. The letter ended as follows: 'I am instructed by my Minister to tell you that you have seen enough of South Africa, and South Africa of you – I remain your obedient servant'! (That official sentiment might rank with the remark that Smuts is reported to have made when Mahatma Gandhi (whose spiritual qualities Smuts admired) left South Africa before the First

---

[1] On the spelling of his middle name – with two 'a's – I have followed the entry in the South African Baptismal Register, as did his biographer, Professor WK Hancock, and as does the Middle Temple Bench Book.

[2] I subsequently wrote an article in the *International and Comparative Law Quarterly* on the beginnings of the trial, which appeared in the issue of January 1959, pp 59–72.

World War, in similar circumstances, to the effect that South Africa was glad to see the back of the Saint!) I have treasured that excellent piece of poetry. I thought that one day it might be my passport to revisit South Africa. Alas, I did not return until two years ago, when Middle Templars conferred delightfully with judges and lawyers there. On that occasion I was astonished to find that there was no formal celebration of the centenary of the Union of South Africa and its court system, which remains the same today, except since 1994 with the overarching power of the Constitutional Court.

SMUTS THE UNIVERSAL MAN

If you stand in Parliament Square, you will instantly observe that of the 10 statues there, three are not of Englishmen. Abraham Lincoln is one. The other two are both South African – Nelson Mandela and Jan Smuts. The former's fame is rooted in contemporary literature following the demise of apartheid in the last decade of the twentieth century. But who in England today remembers Jan Smuts? Shortly before his 80th birthday on 24 May 1950 (only weeks before he died) Smuts remarked: 'I belong to antiquity.' As Professor Antony Lentin, in his recent study of Smuts[3], said, that remark felt true in more senses than one. Smuts was a universal man ('such as might have stepped out of the pages of Plutarch's Lives'); he had touched life at many points. He was a fine soldier who fought against the British in the two Boer wars at the end of the nineteenth century, and for the British in the First World War; he was also an adroit politician in his homeland, twice becoming Prime Minister of South Africa; he was one of the British delegates at the Paris Peace Conference in 1919, and a prominent member of Lloyd George's Imperial War Cabinet; and he was an international statesman, directly involved in the formation of both the League of Nations and the United Nations. But nowadays, who appreciates that Jan Smuts was also a scholar, jurist, scientist, philosopher (he read Spinoza during lulls in the Paris Peace Conference of 1919), and the author of the classic work on holism?[4] 'Even the great', the South African writer Alan Paton wrote, 'thought he was great'.

The overriding problem that faced South Africa in the first half of the twentieth century was race. The failure to devise an enduring

[3] A Lentin, *General Smuts: South Africa (Makers of the Modern World)* (London, Haus, 2010).
[4] JC Smuts, *Holism and Evolution* (London, Macmillan & Co, 1926).

solution ensured that the problem persisted through the second half of that century. Any proper understanding of Jan Smuts' approach to the political and human rights of the non-white population has to be contrasted with the position which faced Nelson Mandela in the latter years of the century. Smuts side-stepped the problem of the native population, while Mandela, in different circumstances, confronted it and was not distracted by other political issues. RW Johnson concludes in his *South Africa's Brave New World*,[5] Smuts 'failed to concentrate sufficiently on the home front'. (That may be an exaggeration, but if related to the post- Second World War era, Smuts' primary interests were decidedly international. Prior to that his focus was on an independent South Africa, loyal to the Crown, a member of the British Commonwealth.) By way of comparison, Nelson Mandela in his inspiring leadership of the African National Congress focused starkly on the home front. Jan Smuts began his task, after the Boer War, of forging a nation out of the four colonial territories (two Boer Republics annexed as Crown colonies, and two British colonies) in promoting the constitutional framework for the Union of South Africa in 1910 and the welding of the disparate groups, which ended with his political defeat in 1948.

Smuts undoubtedly began his political life as a white suprema-cist. South Africa was to be a white man's country. But would it remain so, a half-century later? Might the establishment of an inde-pendent judiciary buttress the political status quo, or could it fash-ion a legal development that modified the inherent inequality between the races – a question rarely posed by commentators? Would the supremacy of whiteness ultimately yield to the ethical imperatives of human rights for all races? But I anticipate my theme. First, some biographical details of Jan Smuts, the lawyer.

To start with, he was a Middle Templar, admitted in 1892.[6] He had been an undergraduate at Stellenbosch, gaining a double first in the mixed literature and science degree. He was later a student at Christ's College, Cambridge, where he took both parts of the Law Tripos simultaneously (an achievement then without precedent) and headed the list of candidates with a double first, winning prizes in jurisprudence and Roman law. The legal historian FW Maitland described Jan Smuts as the most brilliant law student whom he had

---

[5] RW Johnson, *South Africa's Brave New World: The Beloved Country Since the End of Apartheid* (London, Allen Lane, 2009).
[6] He was admitted to the Middle Temple at the age of 21 on 7 May 1892 and was described as the second son of Jacobus Abraham Smuts, of Riebeek West, district of Malmesbury, Cape Colony, corn farmer.

taught and supervised: little wonder that Smuts was offered a fellowship by his college, which he turned down in favour of returning to South Africa. He was never called to the English Bar, although before returning to practise in Johannesburg and later in Pretoria, he was a pupil at 1 Paper Buildings in the chambers of John Roskill, the father of Master Eustace Roskill. In the recent publication, *History of The Middle Temple*,[7] Master Stockdale retells a delightful tale. In December 1903 the Finance Committee of the Inn received a letter from the surety of a South African student member of the Inn who had been on active service in the Boer War, actually on the enemy side. The surety paid the arrears of duty amounting to £6, adding in his covering letter that he had reason to believe the member had no intention of being called to the Bar, or indeed of recognising the Inn. The surety had misjudged the student, for in June 1904 the student sent £6 to the Inn. He was duly informed that the arrears had already been paid and that his name would be restored to the list of members on payment of the current year's duty of £1, which was immediately paid. In 1906 the student came to London to speak to the Junior Minister for the Colonies to plead for the incoming Liberal Government to grant autonomy to the two Boer republics within the British Empire; that Minister was Winston Churchill, who was sympathetic but sceptical. The student was Jan Smuts. In 1917, by then a general in the British Army (and having conquered the German colonies in what are now Namibia and Tanzania), Smuts was made an honorary Bencher on the nomination of Master Treasurer.[8] He was made Chancellor of Cambridge University in June 1948, and his portrait hangs beside Milton's at Christ's College.

UNIFICATION OF SOUTH AFRICA

Jan Smuts made a major and influential contribution to the drafting of South Africa's constitution. In 1908 he took the first steps towards realising his ambition to combine the English-speaking provinces of

---

[7] R Havery (ed), *History of The Middle Temple* (Oxford, Hart Publishing, 2011).

[8] Upon being invited up to the Bench, Smuts wrote to Lord Parmoor, the Treasurer of the Inn: 'May I thank you and the Benchers of my old Inn for the great honour they have done me? Of the many marks of distinction and regard which I have received there is none that I value more highly than that of being elected an honorary Bencher of the Middle Temple.' Smuts was called to the Bench at a dinner on 14 June 1917. Announcement of the intention to call Smuts to the Bench was made on 26 April 1917 by Master Treasurer, 'and the Lord Chancellor will second'. (In fact, in the absence of the Lord Chancellor at a Parliament on 3 May 1917, the Lord Chief Justice seconded the proposal.)

Cape Colony and Natal with the Afrikaans-speaking Transvaal and Orange Free State in a Dominion of South Africa aspiring to free itself from Imperial tutelage. He called a national convention of the four colonies. At Pretoria Smuts moved a resolution which was unanimously adopted. Smuts' legal expertise and political skill were instantly put into play. Smuts himself made the most active contribution to the formation of the union, producing a variety of draft proposals for consideration by 33 delegates to the Constitution. The proposals were duly processed through the four Parliaments and were approved by the Liberal Government of Sir Henry Campbell-Bannerman, whom Smuts had met in 1906, and ultimately by Parliament at Westminster. It was Campbell-Bannerman who acceded readily to Smuts' pleas. Might it not have been better for the indigenous population had Britain insisted on retaining Imperial rule, or even insisting on a US-style constitution protecting human rights?

What was to be the form of the constitution and the structure of the court system? Smuts' inclination was strongly conditioned by his legal training in the British tradition of Cambridge University where he had imbibed the historical, evolutionary interpretation of the British constitution, with the creation of an untrammelled legislature (call it parliamentary sovereignty, if you will) rather than a legislature subject to constitutional limitations in the mould of the US Constitution, with its power of judicial review by its Supreme Court. Smuts was not initially averse to a federal structure, but by 1907 had become convinced that a unitary constitution was preferable. On 23 June 1908 he told the Transvaal Legislative Assembly in clear form his reasons:

> The federal system is not only undesirable because it involves even more expense and means more machinery superimposed on the people of South Africa, which is already groaning under all this administration, but to my mind the great difficulty with federation is this, that it assumes that a number of independent parties come together into a compact, into an agreement, which is binding for the future . . . Is that the sort of Constitution we want for South Africa, a country in its infancy? Do we want a Constitution which will lead to civil wars as the American Constitution led to? No, we prefer to follow a different type – that of the British Constitution.

There is no recorded indication that between the two World Wars Smuts changed his stance over the South African constitution. The international distractions from domestic politics were ever-present. In 1917 Smuts was in London as a member of Lloyd George's

Imperial War Cabinet, and in 1919 as a member of the British dele-gation at the Peace Conference at Versailles. Twenty years later Smuts was actively engaged in the Allies' conduct of the war in Europe and North Africa.

THE NATIVE PROBLEM

As the nineteenth century turned into the twentieth, Jan Smuts had considered that South Africa faced two fundamental problems: first, consolidation of the white race, and secondly, white policy towards the other races (native, Asian and Cape Coloureds). The instant need was to fuse or consolidate the 'two Teutonic' peoples of South Africa, which seemed to him to be self-evident and of pressing pri-ority. As an Afrikaner by birth and English by legal disposition, he felt he was uniquely qualified and in an ideal position to be the welder together of the two white communities. Of the second prob-lem, he was in advance of most Afrikaners both in apprehending the problem and in acknowledging that it would have to wait and be grappled with in the future, but all in good time when the devel-opment of the black population reached the standards of European civilisation. An early (1906) expression of his political stance dis-closed his attitude as a supremacist:

> I sympathise profoundly with the native races of South Africa whose land it was long before we came here to force a policy of dispossession upon them. And it ought to be the policy of all parties to do justice to the natives and to take all wise and prudent measures for their civilisation and improvement. But I don't believe in politics for them. Perhaps at bot-tom I do not believe in politics at all as a means for the attainment of the highest ends; but certainly so far as the natives are concerned politics will to my mind only have an unsettling influence. I would therefore not give them the franchise, which in any case would not affect more than a negligeable [*sic*] number of them at present. When I consider the political future of the natives in SA I must say that I look into shadows and dark-ness; and then I feel inclined to shift the intolerable burden of solving that sphinx problem to the ampler shoulders and stronger brains of the future. Sufficient unto the day etc. My feeling is that strong forces are at work which will transform the Africander [*sic*] attitude to the natives.[9]

An example of Smuts' approach to the politics of South Africa throughout the first three decades of the Union is best shown in his

---

[9] A letter from Jan Smuts to John Xavier Merriman, Prime Minister of Cape Colony 1908–10, 13 March 1906.

discourses with private persons of a liberal disposition, the most notable being the author Olive Schreiner, who had a large reading public throughout the English-speaking world, and with whom he had a close relationship over many years at the beginning of the twentieth century. She was a passionate advocate for a range of socio-political issues, often exhibiting contradictory intuitions – she was anti-capitalist, pro-Boer, pro-Native, anti-Whitehall, all things at one and the same time. Some of Olive Schreiner's letters to Smuts made swingeing comments about white trade union leaders who produced white-only unions and 'protected' skilled jobs for whites only. A letter of 16 April 1911 referred to the 'little handful of oligarchic white men, who call themselves "working men" to keep down the millions of their fellow citizens'. She had written, prophetically, that

> the continual association with creatures who are not free will ultimately take from us our strength and our own freedom, and men will see in our faces the reflection of that on which we are always treading and looking down. If we raise the dark man we shall rise with him; if we kick him under our feet he will hold us fast by them.

Smuts shared that passionate feeling, but his warm-hearted approach was controlled by a cool head. He knew instinctively that the issue of the franchise was not for today, but should be left to the morrow. His political struggles with such liberal causes did not detract from the strength of his friendships, which were reciprocated.

Toni Morrison, addressing the American literati in her essays entitled *Playing in the Dark*,[10] has forcefully reminded 'all of us [that we] are bereft when criticism remains too polite or too fearful to notice a disrupting darkness before its eyes.' But those of us who have conducted public inquiries – rather akin to the task of the historian – are acutely aware of the hazard of judging human conduct from afar. Time, so far as we know, flows only in one direction, and despite our recognition of the seductive appeal of hindsight, we are prone to give it prominence. The significance of events under scrutiny, especially when viewed through that most accurate of diagnostic instruments, the 'retrospectivescope', are far removed from the hectic, demanding and fleeting days as they were lived. As the Third Priest comments in TS Eliot's *Murder in the Cathedral*:

. . . one moment

[10] T Morrison, *Playing in the Dark: Whiteness and the Literary Imagination* (Cambridge, MA/London, Harvard University Press, 1992).

Weighs like another. Only in retrospection, selection.

We say, that was the day. The critical moment.

Yet Smuts can speak for himself, as in this letter to a friend from 1942:

> What will it profit the country if justice is done to the underdog and the whole caboodle then, including the underdog, is handed over to the wreckers?

There speaks the experienced voice of pragmatism. If Smuts retained an aspiration for native representation in Parliament, he left unresolved his personal contradiction of denying the franchise to fellow citizens with fundamental human rights – as Professor Hancock, in his magisterial biography of Smuts (vol II at page 485), neatly observed: 'that expressed in a nutshell the mechanics of the struggle for power within an electorate established prominently upon the principle of racial discrimination'.[11]

During the early part of the twentieth century Smuts had provided no answers to the second problem – indeed his constitution-making of 1910 worked positively against such an immediate solution – and deliberately left it for others in the future to solve. He was generally unreceptive to theories about universal franchise and regarded himself as a pragmatist. He thought that development about voting rights would emerge in the course of political power, whereby the whole population would exhibit its responsibility and power, and not abuse that power as regards the native population. For the time being he was unsure how this approach could be reconciled with the enfranchisement of the majority. But, quintessentially, Jan Smuts believed in the rule of law and the evolving international human rights law. As the author of *Holism and Evolution,* he would have expected that human rights for all persons would evolve along 'holistic' lines. As the reputed draftsman in 1945 of the preamble to the Charter of the United Nations, he became a primary subscriber 'to re-establish faith in fundamental human rights [seven words specifically inserted in an amendment proposed by South Africa], in the sanctity and ultimate value of human personality, in the equal rights of men and women . . . and to promote social progress and better standards of life in larger freedom'.

In 1941 Smuts, having only recently (in 1939) become Prime Minister of South Africa for the second time, was directly engaged

---

[11]   WK Hancock, *Smuts: The Fields of Force* (Cambridge, CUP, 1968).

in Britain's grim resistance to Nazi Germany; it was his parliamentary stance that declared South Africa at war with Germany. In the following years he became instrumentally engaged in the establishment of the United Nations. It was at the very least a time for rethinking, if not an instant reshaping of the ever-present problem of the development of the non-white population in his own country. As one looked to the world after the ending of hostilities, Smuts did start to look beyond the political horizon, but time was short.

At the insistent invitation from Churchill, Smuts made his second wartime visit to England at the end of 1943. On 25 November 1943, Smuts addressed a private meeting of the United Kingdom branch of the Empire Parliamentary Association in the Houses of Parliament on the topic of *Thoughts on the New World* (the meeting was subsequently fully reported on the editorial page of the *Times*[12]). In short, the race and colour problem was prospectively visualised by Smuts, although predictably with persistent prevarication. He said:

> You can have no simple, straightforward approach to a problem such as the vast diversity of race and colour, culture, and levels of civilization existing in our Empire. That is the sort of problem with which we have dealt in the past, and which will face us even more in the future . . . I know it is one of the questions on which people are thinking deeply and with which they are very much concerned nowadays. Many well-meaning people think you can by short cuts arrive at a solution. But you will not. Simplification will not help you. Simplification will mean falsification of the real difficulty. It is only by a long process of experience and patient experiment that you can deal with situations such as these.

INTERNATIONALISM

Significantly, the Covenant of the League of Nations in 1919, for which Smuts took some responsibility for framing, contained no provision for human rights, apart from references in Article 23 to 'fair and humane conditions of labour' for everyone and to 'just treatment' of the native inhabitants of dependent territories. While human rights were discussed during the drafting of the Covenant, no obligations regarding human rights were incorporated into the Covenant of the League of Nations. Smuts would have been alive to

---

[12] The speech and the editorial were printed in the paper on December 3 at pp 5 and 8, with a further, explanatory, editorial on December 7, when the newspaper also printed a lengthy letter to the Editor from Dr Margery Perham (a life-long liberal friend and critic of Smuts).

the contrast between 1919 and 1945. If during the inter-war years he continued to do nothing (*niksdoen* –Afrikaans for doing nothing – as his liberal friends were wont to say) and to watch, the policy of separate development of the races gradually disintegrated. A small token of such disintegration was exhibited by Smuts being prepared to arm the non-white population, were the Germans during the First World War to have invaded South Africa. That at least infuriated the Afrikaners. By the 1940s, he had become, perhaps belatedly, convinced that the country had to tackle the Native problem. Even before his commitment in 1945 to the charter of the United Nations, he had acknowledged the need for change. Addressing the Institute of Race Relations in Cape Town in February 1942 he at least dispelled the oft-repeated criticism that he had cared chiefly for primitive Africans, to the neglect of the urgent and nascent problems of African urbanisation.

> Isolation has gone and segregation has fallen on evil days too. But there are other phenomena springing out of these conditions . . . A revolutionary change is taking place among the Native peoples of Africa through the movement from the country to the towns – the movement from the old Reserves in the Native areas to the big European centres of population. Segregation tried to stop it. It has, however, not stopped it in the least. The process has been accelerated. You might as well try to sweep the ocean back with a broom.
>
> When people ask me what the population of South Africa is I never say it is two millions. I think it is an outrage to say it is two millions. This country has a population of over ten millions, and that outlook which treats the African and Native as not counting, is making the ghastliest mistake possible. If he is not much more, he is the beast of burden; he is the worker and you need him. He is carrying this country on his back.

But by the 1940s such high-sounding expressions about racial issues came too little and too late. His plan for the forthcoming general election of 1948 included recognition of African rights in the urban areas but specifically did not envisage any immediate extension of African parliamentary representation. Therein lay the complexity of Smuts' problem. On the one hand there was his deep love of public duty as Prime Minister and on the other his countervailing liberalism. The inherent contradiction between the humanitarian in him and his South African (particularly, Afrikaner) heritage created the politician's dilemma.

If there existed in terms of *realpolitik* insufficient leeway for radical change, such as to fend off the Nationalists and to avoid the loss of power at the general election, Smuts' years of drifting on policy towards racism had already – in all likelihood, unintentionally – paved the way for the advent of apartheid. But at the brink of the electorate's decision in 1948 there occurred an event of political significance.

The event was precipitated, not by the black community under the growing strength of the African National Congress, but by the Asian population. In 1943 the Government under Smuts introduced the Trading and Occupation of Land Bill (the Pegging Bill), whose purpose was to extend severe restrictions on the freedom of the Asian population living in the Transvaal and Natal. The Indian population was, not unreasonably, outraged by the loss of rights that had existed since the 1860s. After many political vicissitudes, the Bill became law in 1946 as the Asiatic Land Tenure and Indian Representation Act. It imposed restrictions on the purchase and tenure of land, and controversially created a separate electoral register for Indians, allowing them the right to elect three white representatives. Smuts declared that the Government intended 'fair play and justice for our Indian fellow-citizens, but we do not want to change the structure of our society . . . we want to preserve the European orientation of our society'.

The Indian Government withdrew its High Commissioner, and took the issue to the first meeting of the General Assembly of the United Nations. Smuts travelled to the United States to hear Mrs Ranjit Pandit unleash an attack on Smuts and South Africa. The Charter was essentially non-discriminatory. By that standard, South Africa's racial policies were indefensible. Smuts' only plausible defence was to claim, legalistically, that the Act was exclusively the concern of South Africa's domestic jurisdiction, and not for international intervention. India won the day. As Bill Schwarz in *The White Man's World*[13] describes the event: 'the author of the Preamble to the UN Charter found himself the first to be arraigned for violating its principles.' Just so. Smuts' correspondence at the time displayed not anger, but bewilderment. (India was at the forefront of the UN non-recognition of South Africa's sovereignty over Namibia: Smuts had gone to the UN to face the music.) It is conceivable that, for Smuts, that one defining moment would have propelled him towards a realisation that the Indian victory at the UN had produced an early example of the outcrop of international human rights law which, at his life's end, was beginning to envelop the post-war world.

[13] B Schwarz, *The White Man's World* (Oxford, OUP, 2011).

It was not until Smuts had been two and a half years in his grave that the Indian Government mounted an attack on the whole front against South Africa's policies on colour. Two conspicuous landmarks were the Universal Declaration of Human Rights in 1948 and the South African Group Areas Act of 1950 – the first instalment of the unalloyed apartheid regime.

The first of the two problems identified at the outset by Smuts – the welding of the two European races – by 1950 was still unfinished business. The second problem of African integration as citizens of the Union of South Africa that Smuts had designed could only have been aspirational and required personally an unresolved contradiction. All that might lead one to conclude that he died a failure, two years after losing power. Not so, for one is entitled not only to judge him in the context of the burgeoning South Africa, but also to speculate how he would have responded to the early years of apartheid.

There has been a long-standing difference among social historians in their interpretations of the effectiveness of separate development of the races between 1910 and 1948. By different assessments of the cohesion and homogeneity of the apartheid State from 1948 onwards, one argument is that there was, generally speaking, an unbroken lineage from the first decade of the twentieth century through to the Smuts era, culminating in the advent of apartheid. An alternative view is one of a more fractured development in which segregation did not become a coherent policy until the 1920s, and even then was distinguishable from apartheid in its rigorous political form. Bill Schwarz concludes his impressive discussion of the two views and their varieties, that Smuts never had to confront the politics which was necessary to ensure that segregation continued into the 1950s, 'and we shall never know how he would have responded politically to such a situation'. My supposition is that the non-white population, increasingly urbanised and politically active, were, in Smuts' eyes at least, on the cusp of civilised behaviour in the Western European style. Forty years earlier (in 1906) Smuts had observed that 'the burden of solving' the problem of political change for the non-white population would have to be solved in the future. He added that for the time being 'strange forces' would be at work to transform Afrikaner attitudes to the non-white population. For those 40 years Smuts was that future. But, given the times in which he lived politically, he procrastinated and prevaricated on the issue of his country's policy of segregation of the races. But time and circumstances of the new world of internationalism must have forced him, ineluctably, to rethink his personal, internal contradiction. Even the most ardent apologist could not deny that Smuts was innately a supremacist and segregationist: his ancestry and cultural heritage ensured that instinctive posture. He struggled unsuccessfully to reconcile the supremacy of the white population with his commitment to liberty and democracy. The events in New York in 1946 stung Smuts too late for action or for meaningful words. Within two years he was out of office and, two years after that, he died.

The international dimension of the immediate post-war years crucially influenced the opponents of apartheid. By that time, the politics of colour had become a distinct feature of internationalised controversy. The consequences of South Africa's domestic policies inevitably became issues of that country's foreign policy. The rest is a lamentable tale of the second half of the twentieth century, until the miracle of 1994 and the end of apartheid.

At Smuts' death, the British Prime Minister, Clement Atlee, aptly remarked: 'A light has gone out from the world of free men.' So I conclude as I began, standing before the statues of Smuts and Mandela in Parliament Square. Viewed from the perspective of the entire twentieth century, the juxtaposition of the two men's statues might reasonably seem to the fiercer critics of the system of apartheid to be paradoxical. Viewed, however, from the standpoint of the two halves of the century, the statuary proximity of Jan Smuts and Nelson Mandela – the two giants of the South African nation, each in his own half of the twentieth century – is entirely apposite and congruent.

30

Intervention and Amicus Curiae

I T WAS FORMERLY a rare practice in our courts for judges to seek help from anyone other than the parties to litigation. But by the beginning of the twenty-first century, faced with unfamiliar challenges – the advent of human rights notably prompting the major challenge – an increasing number of organisations (mainly pressure groups) had entered the forensic scene, usually by way of written and sometimes oral submissions. By 2008 Lord Hoffmann was in a position to say, in *E v Chief Constable of the Royal Ulster Constabulary,* that 'the expectation is that their [the interveners'] fund of knowledge or particular point of view will enable them to provide the House [of Lords] with a more rounded picture than it would otherwise obtain', but pointedly he stressed that 'interveners must do more than reiterate points of view already made adequately by one of the parties'.[1]

But this procedural transformation in the process of intervention by third parties, although conceptually accepted as part of the legal process, was traditionally ignored or resisted, even at times declared unwelcome. The history of this change of judicial heart can be traced through instances in my professional life, as counsel and as an aspiring intervener.

My earliest experience of intervention in legal proceedings followed the unilateral declaration of independence in Southern Rhodesia on 11 November 1965, when a number of acute legal consequences called for judicial determination in the English courts. One example was the recognition in England of divorce decrees granted by the rebellion judges. Joanna Adams, who was born and brought up in England, was divorced from her Rhodesian husband, after which she returned to England and sought a declaration here that she was validly divorced by English law. She gave notice of her proceedings to the Attorney-General, and I was briefed by the

---

[1] [2008] 3 WLR 1208 [2] and [3]. Lord Brown of Eaton-under-Heywood agreed with the statement of Lord Hoffmann.

Treasury Solicitor to intervene on behalf of the Crown to argue that no recognition could be given to the orders of a Rhodesian judge who had chosen to act under the rebellious government of Mr Ian Smith and his ministerial colleagues. The matter duly came before the President of the Divorce Division (the predecessor to the Family Division of the High Court) in July 1970. Sir Jocelyn Simon (later Lord Simon of Glaisdale) held that the Attorney-General had a right of intervention in a piece of private litigation whenever the legal issue might affect the prerogatives of the Crown. He also held that the Attorney-General could intervene, at the invitation or with the permission of the court, wherever the legal proceedings raised any question of public policy on which executive government may have a view which it may desire to bring to the notice of the court. Helpfully, my opponent, Michael Havers QC (a future Lord Chancellor, whose time in office was cruelly cut short by illness and premature death) welcomed my presence as an intervener, even though his advocacy, characteristically delightful, failed to win the case for the divorced wife. Sir Jocelyn encouraged the intervention and acknowledged the Crown's contention that the Rhodesian judges appointed by the Crown under the pre-UDI constitution of 1961/1964 could cease to be Her Majesty's judges only in accordance with that constitution. He observed that the wife had been ill-used matrimonially and was the victim of political circumstances for which she had no responsibility. The judicial plea for Government to resolve the unsatisfactory basis of the divorce jurisdiction of the English court was duly heeded by the legislature. Rhodesian divorcees received English recognition of their proper status.

The exercise was repeated six years later. This time the issue was the validity of a bankruptcy order made in Rhodesia against a fraudulent solicitor whose funds were thought to have found their way into the hands of his brother in Bromley, Kent. Could the Registrar in Bankruptcy in London give effect to a Rhodesian bankruptcy order as an order of a 'British court' under the Bankruptcy Act 1914, in order to examine the bankrupt's brother? This time there was no hesitation in the court granting the Attorney-General leave to intervene when the brother appealed to the Court of Appeal against the Registrar's order recognising the Rhodesian bankruptcy order. And again I was briefed – this time to appear before the Master of the Rolls, Lord Denning, sitting together with Lords Justices Scarman and Geoffrey Lane, during six days at the end of July 1976. The intervention by me appears to me now to have been less than helpful to Lord Denning, although thankfully for me he was the dissenter when the Court gave its reserved judgment in October after the Long Vacation.

Denning began his judgment in his idiosyncratic style as a kind of popular story-teller: 'David Emlyn James is a lawyer who has gone astray', the tale trailing off into a revisitation of the details of the bankrupt's depredation of his partners' funds. My argument, which raised the constitutional issue whether any purported law in post-UDI Rhodesia could be given any recognition in England, won the day; the two other appeal court judges paid strict attention to the constitutional law. But in Denning's eyes he would have nothing of so formidable a legal obstacle as the enforcement of British obligation to a UN resolution on sanctions for Rhodesia. I recite the words in Denning's judgment:

> [It was] Mr Blom-Cooper, who launched the main attack on the Rhodesian courts. It was he who asked us to give no recognition whatever to what the Rhodesian courts had done. He said that we should give no help whatever to get in the money or the property of David James – so as to restore it to the rightful owners. It was, he said, in the interests of high policy. All I would say about that argument is this: if it be in the interests of high policy, it is not in the interests of justice. I see no justice whatever in letting David James get away with his ill-gotten gains and letting the rightful owners go away empty-handed.

The sequel to the delivery of the three judgments provided an oddity in the appellate process. My opponent, Andrew Bateson QC, naturally applied for leave to appeal to the House of Lords, no doubt with confidence, since Lord Denning's body language exhibited a desire that his dissent might find favour upstairs in the final appeal court. But his two colleagues, Lords Justices Scarman and Geoffrey Lane, demurred. The odd feature of the application was that under the existing legislation (the Bankruptcy Act 1914), the only route to the final court of appeal was by leave of the Court of Appeal. Quite unusually, Parliament had decided that in the bankruptcy system there was no free- standing leave process to go higher. Normally, if you did not get leave from the Court of Appeal, you could still chance your arm before three Law Lords sitting in the Appeal Committee of the House of Lords. When Lord Denning announced that Andrew's application was turned down, I am unsure whether the Master of the Rolls was aware of the exceptional restriction on the appellate process. Whatever his disappointment, in Lord Denning's plea for individual justice to the victims of David James' fraud, I had the pleasure of a forensic triumph. Few lawyers then (and probably none now) would adopt the disconcertingly unsubtle view of both the identification and identity of international law that there can be no international law without centralised sanctions, and therefore international law 'does not exist'. This view is sometimes regarded as a matter of *realpolitik*, but it lacks sophistication and shows ignorance of the nature and function of international law. Even if there was no centralised system of enforcement of UN sanctions, in the case of Southern Rhodesia, the British Government had issued an Order in Council enforcing sanctions against Ian Smith and his rebellious judges.

If I felt only slightly miffed about the treatment of my argument, I took away with me at least an abiding sense of how courts, when dealing with cases that raised difficult legal issues, might be materially assisted by interested observers of some (in a legal sense) high-profile cases. Twenty years later, when I was chairman of the Mental Health Act Commission, I was alerted as such an observer to intervene in the case of the sterilisation of a mentally handicapped woman.[2] Under the Mental Health Act 1983 there was an unusual provision for safeguarding the interests of mental health patients who were contemplating undergoing operations for psycho-surgery. Before the neurological system could perform the intrusive operation, permission to go ahead had to be given by the Mental Health Act Commission. The prescribed procedure was for a designated psychiatrist and an approved social worker to be nominated by the Commission to inquire into the request for psycho-surgery and proceeding to recommend (or not) the operation.

It occurred to me and my colleagues on the Commission that this unique power was highly relevant to the questions posed for the courts when faced with the medical decision whether the medical profession could go ahead and sterilise the patient. I managed to convince the civil servants at the Department of Health that the Commission should seek the leave of the House of Lords to intervene, not to advance any argument for or against either of the parties to the litigation, but directly to assist the Law Lords in their deliberations. The Department applied; the application was granted, without apparent fuss.

Mr (now Mr Justice) Duncan Ouseley was appointed as counsel to appear as an intervening party. He did so in his usual competent and expansive manner. But the presiding Law Lord, Lord Bridge, showed more than mere disinterest in what the Commission did in

---

[2] *Re sterilisation of a female patient* [2000] 2 AC 1.

performance of its task to control the medical use of lobotomy and like surgery. He treated Duncan with the worst form of judicial mis-behaviour. I think Duncan will not easily forgive me for putting him in the forensic firing line. But at least two other Law Lords referred to the Commission's submissions. One of them had inter-vened in the course of Duncan's argument, to soften the lordly blows.

Lord Bridge's hostility to our intervention focused on the func-tion of an intervener. Up to that point, intervention had been accorded (other than where the Crown was intervening as of right, as it did in the Rhodesian cases) to pressure groups which were desirous of pursuing their heavily biased agendas, almost invaria-bly to support one side or the other in the litigation. Neutral advo-cates – what the lawyer knows as an *amicus curiae* – were in the English system restricted to counsel who appeared on behalf of the Attorney-General whenever (rarely) the court itself requested assistance on some thorny legal issue. No one could offer himself or herself as an *amicus*.

I was to learn that, to my personal cost, some time later. In 1999 Myra Hindley's appeal against the Home Secretary's fixing of the tariff of her life sentence as 'whole life' was heard in the House of Lords. Much of the argument centred on a proper interpretation of the mandatory sentence of life imprisonment for murder as the sub-stitute penalty when Parliament abolished the death penalty in 1965. A friend of mine of over 40 years was the late Terence Morris, once Emeritus Professor of Criminology and Criminal Justice at the London School of Economics. We had co-authored a book in 1964 called *A Calendar of Murder*,[3] a study of every murder case in the courts of England and Wales from 1957 (on the passing of that year's Homicide Act) until 1962. Thereafter we have written frequently in law journals and elsewhere on the law and practice of homicide. We have regarded ourselves as aficionados of, if not experts in, mur-der. Not appreciating the limited view which the judiciary was tak-ing to the practice of intervention I wrote to Lord Browne-Wilkinson, the Senior Law Lord, asking whether the two of us might be permit-ted to submit a written brief to their Lordships. His reply was friendly, but presently unforthcoming. I quote from his letter of 5 March 1999:

> You are quite right in saying that we are more open to application from organisations such as JUSTICE to put in an *amicus* brief and, in excep-

[3] T Morris and L Blom-Cooper, *A Calendar of Murder* (London, Michael Joseph, 1964).

tional circumstances, to address the Committee orally. However, the new procedure is at a very early stage and is not properly worked out as yet.

Although I am sympathetic to your desire to present the materials you wish to put before the Committee yourselves, I do not feel able to encourage you to do that at this stage since I think we must learn how to deal first with the pressure groups, such as Liberty or JUSTICE, acting as an *amicus* before trying to deal with the rather different problems which I think would be raised if individuals were allowed to act as *amici.* I hope you do not think I am being unduly stodgy but I suggest that you should channel your information through JUSTICE or Liberty. Although of course I cannot give any assurance, certainly we would be likely to take such an application seriously.

In the event we decided not to channel our information through the two pressure groups mentioned, mainly because we did not wish to be seen as partisan, but rather as objective scholars on the topic under judicial scrutiny.

The role of intervener, taken on by statutory bodies and non-governmental organisations, will be likely to be partisan, more or less fiercely so. The 'assistance' they give will no doubt be potentially helpful, although the inherent bias will tend to diminish the value of the assistance. Hence, one readily understands Lord Hoffmann's injunction to such interveners to keep their submissions short, to the point and not to replicate the submissions of the litigating parties. But if the purpose of intervention is to provide help to the court, particularly when for their own litigious purposes the rival parties do not advance some relevant argument, the unbiased assistance of the expert on a specific topic should surely be welcome.

By January 2006 the House of Lords had learned how to deal with the pressure groups which had regularly been intervening. The practice was systematised in Practice Direction 37 of the Practice Directions Applicable to Civil Appeal, although the breadth of intervention in its personality was left for decision on a case-by-case basis.

In 2008 the House of Lords delivered judgment in 74 cases, in 16 of which permission to intervene was granted. The range of interveners included the Equity and Human Rights Commission (on four occasions), Liberty and JUSTICE (three occasions) and INQUEST and MIND (two occasions). A department of Government intervened on four occasions, principally to present a view on how the Human Rights Act 1998 should be applied. No individuals intervened.

The Court of Appeal (Civil Division) only took up the baton of third party intervention at the turn of the twenty-first century, but even then only to let matters flow: it neither encouraged nor discouraged intervention, according to a retired Lord Justice of Appeal, Sir Henry Brooke, in an article in *Public Law*.[4] Between January 2001 and November 2006 there were 67 formal applications to intervene, at a rate of 12 a year. Since then the practice has begun to develop.

If third-party intervention by public authorities and non-governmental organisations at the appellate stage, both final and intermediate, was embedded in the area of civil litigation, it was far from reception in the criminal jurisdiction. No distinction has been made between civil and criminal appeals in the House of Lords, although intervention in the latter cases was rare (the most notable instance being an early reference to the European Convention on Human Rights, where Liberty was permitted to intervene[5]). But in the Court of Appeal (Criminal Division) there was overt hostility to the notion, as I was to learn to my cost.

In the second appeal in the Sally Clark case in January 2003, the Expert Witness Institute (of which I was then chairman) sought to intervene. The appeal focused on the flawed expert evidence of Professor Sir Roy Meadow. Sally Clark's second appeal in this high-profile, seemingly unexplained child cot death case raised acute issues relating to expert witnesses; the case at the trial had involved no fewer than 11 medical experts – forensic pathologists, neuro-pathologists, opthalmologists and psychiatrists, including notably a distinguished professor of paediatrics and child health, Sir Roy Meadow, who gave impermissible statistical evidence – he testified that in his opinion there was only a one in 73 million chance of having two cot deaths in the same family. While the appeal focused on the cause of death of two infant boys, the case clearly exposed weaknesses in the procedures for hearing and testing expert testimony – issues which were exercising the minds of my colleagues and me in the Expert Witness Institute (EWI). We compiled a statement for the Court of Appeal (Criminal Division) suggesting that the Court might seize the opportunity in its judgment to comment on the practice and procedure for admitting and testing evidence on scientific and technological issues.

The Court convened to hear the appeal, presided over by Lord Justice John Kay, now deceased but then considered to be a strong candidate to become Lord Chief Justice in the near future. On submitting our memoranda, we received the message that the Court

[4]   H Brooke, 'Interventions in the Court of Appeal' [2007] *Public Law* 401.
[5]   *R v Khan* [1996] 3 All ER 289.

was unwilling to authorise intervention by EWI. Lord Justice Kay indicated that as EWI's chairman I would be allowed to address the Court at the opening of the appeal. This I did, standing not in counsel's row but on the bench in front of the row of leading counsel, from a position from which I, unwigged and unrobed, was unaccustomed to addressing a court. For approximately 10 minutes, after Lord Justice Kay had obtained from counsel to the parties no objection to my application to intervene, I sought to persuade the Court that intervention from interested parties had become a regular feature of court procedure, although there appeared to be no reported incident in the criminal appellate system.

Throughout my career at the Bar, I had only occasionally met with outright hostility from any member of the judiciary. This was the exception to the rule. It was obvious from the outset of my application that I had not merely failed to persuade the Court, but Lord Justice Kay in refusing to countenance any help I might have given to the Court expressed his ruling in forthright, unfriendly terms. The question of the admissibility (and the handling) of expert evidence is currently the topic of a Consultation Paper from the Law Commission.[6] Lord Justice Kay will not be one of the Law Commission's consultees: he died in office at the age of 60. I am not aware that intervenors have yet been entertained in the criminal courts, either at trial or on appeal.

In the years 2011–12 the UK Supreme Court heard seven cases out of 77 where interveners were involved, in one of which – *Rubin v Eurofinance SA*[7] – there were three interveners. But that was exceptional. In *R v Hughes*[8] on 4 January 2013 an application was initially made by two academic criminologists, but they were told that if they wished to apply without having to pay the fee of £750 it would be necessary for the applicant to be a registered charity who would be allowed to intervene without payment. The courts have yet to consider the American style of intervention by *amici curiae*.

The helpful assistance from *amici* is still not to hand. I would like to think that I have persuaded the Justices of the UK Supreme Court to adopt the practice of entertaining submissions – initially in writing, occasionally by oral advocacy – from any interested person or organisation that can help (without payment of a fee) towards a sound judgment on issues of public interest.

---

[6] Consultation Paper No 190, *The Admissibility of Expert Evidence in Criminal Proceedings in England and Wales* (2009).
[7] [2012] UKSC 46.
[8] [2013] UKSC 56.

31

Bench and Bar

NOT UNUSUALLY, OR even uniquely for someone practising at the English Bar, where judging involves an assessment of witnesses' credibility and reliability, I shared a common ambition of becoming a judge; in my case it was qualified by wishing to experience the role of a decision-maker, whether sitting as a magistrate in the lowest court within the criminal jurisdiction, or possibly taking an appointment in a higher civil court. Over my time, however, I doubted my capacity and ability for the higher reaches of the profession, at least not to espouse it as a full-time occupation. In the event, with the eccentricity of a barrister sitting as a lay Justice of the Peace, I did manage to scale the upper reaches, at least as a supernumerary. At the end of 1988 I was appointed as an additional judge in the Court of Appeal of Jersey and Guernsey. Quirkishly, the two Channel Islands, with populations of 100,000 and 65,000 respectively, declined to be separately represented, although the personnel were identical and the courts sat for a short time every three months successively in St Helier and St Peter Port respectively. They were established by legislation in 1961 to hear all appellate cases under the Judicial Committee of the Privy Council, a jurisprudence which was rarely excercised, and then too costly. It was the practice for appointments to be made from Queen's Counsel in England and Scotland. When I reached the age-limit of 70 and had to retire, I persuaded the authorities to replace me for the first time with a leading silk from Northern Ireland. Peter Smith was chosen and sat with great distinction.

The judicial experience which I gained provided me with an additional qualification to assess and evaluate the service which the English judiciary supplied. In the early years of my career, the number in the higher judiciary was quite small and, dare I say it, comparative to the population, an elitist class, made up entirely of male members with middle class backgrounds who had been successful practitioners. Much has changed over 50 years. What I describe is general and contemporary, although there are some allusions to the past, which I experienced as an advocate.

Elsewhere in this volume, Lord Denning's judicial dominance (at least in the eyes of the public) has been separately noted. But it would be a distortion to conclude from one judge's efforts that other senior judges over the period were to be regarded in a similar mould. Nothing could be further from the truth. The response among the stance of appellate colleagues of Lord Denning was variable – from faint amusement at the idiosyncrasies of their leader in civil justice, to degrees of opposition to his pyrotechnic distortions of the legal system. Few judges at appellate level exhibited forthright dislike of Denning's forays into his unique formula of law reform, even if they disapproved, but there were occasional outbursts at ostensible deviation from the traditional common law. Lords Justices of Appeal (in 2014, now 37 in number, but far fewer in Denning's days) never became book-ends in personal terms. If they were to some extent publicly unnoticed, professional rumblings from the Bench bubbled introspectively. For the rest, High Court judges, they watched from their lower status a hobbled but clever maestro; they too admired the craftsman at work, even if they were not in awe of his prodigious output. Assenting and, much less often, dissenting judgments were always permissible. They were – particularly the latter – infrequent, even if judgments were rarely composite.

To assess the quality of judicial service in the second half of the twentieth century calls for a distinction both within the hierarchy and the distribution layers of the judicial hierarchy. First, the criminal law (which was barely touched upon in Lord Denning's career almost exclusively in civil justice) was operational at two levels – a) the judges who sat regularly with juries as the decision-makers; and b) the changing nature of the criminal appellate court, from 1968 onwards. Crime touched the justice system at trial level alone until 1907, and was confined to judicial control of trial proceedings, with judges never being decision-makers, except in the sentencing of offenders. Criminal law was thus a Cinderella among legal practitioners, and then only peripheral to a form of jurisprudence within the courtroom. A few notable judges had pronounced the principles of the common law in curricular and non-curricular capacities. And until the middle of the nineteenth century, Parliament had barely invaded the statute book. Astonishingly, even today, the law of murder (supposedly the most serious crime on the calendar) is defined by the English common law, constructed single-handedly by Sir Edward Coke 400 years ago. Parliament consistently ignores the calls for statutory reform of the substantive law, despite over the years since 1965, and more particularly by the Law Commission in 2006, clamours for sensible updating of the law of homicide. On sentencing, the legislature has been forever tinkering with the system and has consistently ratcheted up the level of imprisonment.

From the establishment of a criminal appellate system in 1907 (and until 1968) the Court of Criminal Appeal exercised a restricted avenue of appeal against the guilty verdicts of 12 good men (and, since 1928, women) and true. It produced a branch of judicial function, overseen by the Lord Chief Justice and the puisne judges of the day. Selected Lords Justices who manned the civil appellate system for the first time joined in forming a criminal division of the Court of Appeal. Even then the criminal law marginally began to fashion a modern system juridically of criminal justice. I recall, around the time of the change, a distinguished practitioner from the list of Treasury Counsel at the London Bar declaring with conspicuous honesty that there was 'only a court of no criminal appeal'. Times have changed. The change post-1968 (with single Lords Justices presiding) displayed a welcome development, even though the criminal appellate system still remained an inferior brand of justice. That was – and is – the result of trial by jury, since the capacity to overturn a jury decision occurs only if the verdict is 'unsafe', and that means that normally a jury trial, if properly conducted and adequately summed-up on the facts, is inviolate. If directed properly, their verdict is always confirmed. Recent problems have been created by influences outside the courtroom – the increase in informational technology by way of the internet is beginning to impact on safe verdicts.

It is a nice question whether the Anglo-Saxon devotion to trial by jury (in England, strictly speaking, trial by judge and jury) can last the course. Professionalism in approach to problems of justice will inevitably creep in to change the system: trial by judge alone for serious fraud cases is an ever- important demand. But it will not come about for some time. The economics of jury trial will ultimately effect some, if not complete, reform.

During my lifetime of practice, I have watched a growing professionalism of the criminal law, but that has been because the subject attracted academic analysis of the law. For 50 years now, the criminal law and procedure has been graced by a trilogy (at least) of outstanding university teachers: Professors Glanville Williams, John Smith and John Spencer have conferred upon the criminal law an expertise and wisdom that has profoundly affected the law in action – academia at its very best. Each of them (and others) became highly respected by the higher judiciary. The law reports are punctuated by reference to their academic writings. Their respective pens have advanced a modern system of law, through judicial acknowledgment of their valuable contribution. A handful of judges took up the cudgels of criminal law – Lord Lane, the Lord Chief Justice from 1971–82, Lord Justice Lawton, a judge from 1951 until his retirement as a Lord Justice in 1986, and, miraculously (because he had been a civil practitioner both as a barrister and judge), Lord Bingham when he was inspirationally appointed as Lord Chief Justice, from 1996–2000. The criminal law at appellate level, however, was rooted at the stage of first appeal. The House of Lords was not given an appellate function (other than very exceptionally) until 1960, when leave to appeal became no longer the prerogative of the Attorney-General. And when they did utter their final thought, it was hardly in tune with modern thinking about crime and justice.

Their limited role on criminal matters meant that the Appellate Committee of the House of Lords was hardly ever composed of Law Lords with comparable experience of criminal law principles and practice. Even with a burgeoning involvement in criminal justice legislation – after 1963 a statute was passed every sixteen months – the criminal law in the courts was rarely accorded any systematic and principled system. Professor Spencer spoke feelingly when he wrote in 2009 that the

> academic lawyer . . . gets the feeling that the barbarians [the legislators of yesteryear] are at the gates – and prays, though perhaps with little hope, that the new Supreme Court [the successor in 2009 in its composition to the judicial House of Lords] will be strong enough to keep them at bay.

The practitioner can only endorse that sentiment. We have yet as a modern democracy to produce a codification of the criminal law, a venture launched by the Law Commission 40 years ago, but abandoned half-way through the excellent labours of John Smith and his collaborators. Our legislators decline to accommodate a nascent desire of the legal profession and others to produce the basic tool of a modern system of criminal law.

Contrary to popular belief, I never entered a criminal courtroom until I took silk in 1970. Up until then my extracurricular activities focused on criminological studies and penal affairs, about which more ado elsewhere. On my arrival at the front bench of barristers, my clerk (the first female senior clerk in the Temple) identified me as a leading counsel who was 'not a high flier' – off to the Old Bailey was her prescription. And so for half a dozen years my daily fare was as defence counsel in criminal trials. I should add that, in those palmy days in criminal practice, certificates of legal aid for accused offenders were like confetti – plentiful and profitable. The daily fare was variable and not uninteresting although I discovered that the practitioners who regularly prosecuted on behalf of the Crown, and many defence lawyers, did not relish legal practice: they were quintessentially and demonstrably able advocates: they were involved in fact-finding and had little or no time for case law other than that to be found in *Archbold's Criminal Practice* (then in its 20th edition or so). There was an early occasion that sticks in the memory, when I appeared in an eleven-handed defence in a trial which was for an affray between rival mini-cab gangs in a shoot-up on Romford High Street. I appeared for a marginal defendant who was alleged to have spirited away one of the two villains in hiding. My client was simply charged with a conspiracy to pervert the course of justice. At half-time I made a submission of 'no case to answer', based on decisions of what needed to be proved in cases of protecting an offender who was a fugitive from justice. I like to think that my submission was legally respectable. It certainly was professionally treated by one of the more distinguished, regular judges at the Central Criminal Court. He was Judge Hines, whom I later got to know (and like) as members of the Home Secretary's Advisory Council on the Penal System (1966–78). He rejected my submission, with sound reasoning. At that point my opponent, sitting immediately in front of me in the front row, a Mr Desmond Vowden QC, later to become a circuit judge in Swindon, turned round and said in a loud and not too friendly voice: 'Why don't you go back to Lincoln's Inn, where you belong?' I treated it as an impolite warning to take my law books to the chancery and common law courts in the Strand. His intervention was typical of the attitude of his fellow practitioners – with one or two outstanding exceptions. One of them was Stephen Mitchell, who became a High Court judge and edited *Archbold*. The others were Dai Tudor Evans and David Calvert-Smith, who both subsequently graced the High Court Bench. The last-named retired early in 2012 to become part-time chairman of the Parole Board, where my daughter, Martha, was one of the two full-time directors. The other outstanding practitioner was Michael Worsley, with whom I had two interesting encounters during his lengthy service as a prosecutor and defender at the Old Bailey.

Trial work in the Crown Court is carried out by the circuit judge, of whom I have no knowledge professionally. From observation and conversation they present a mixed lot. Some are excellent in managing criminal trials, and are courteous and sensitive to all participants. Others, I am told, are not so good; some frankly are failed practitioners and provide a variable quality of justice.

CIVIL APPEALS

The picture of the system and practice of the civil jurisdiction is altogether vastly different, if only for the reason that our common law system has a long history of adherence to the rule of law. But I speak only from experience of 50 years practising and surveying the forensic scene. It was not an auspicious start to my career on 1 July 1952. The Treasurer for that year was Lord Jowitt, recently retired Lord Chancellor in the Labour Government of 1945–51. He was a towering figure in the legal profession at the time, noted nowadays as a ferocious opponent in Cabinet in 1950 to this country's signing of the European Convention on Human Rights; Jowitt is remembered for little else of jurisprudential significance and politically had changed allegiance from the Liberals to Labour. I recall nothing of that momentous day other than shaking hands with the Treasurer on my being called to the English Bar. My espousal of the Convention in advocating its acceptance in the 1970s and onwards, long before incorporation into UK law in 2000, was rare but not unique. I had little success – particularly in front of Lord Denning – but retained great hopes for future litigants. The contemporary controversy over the Human Rights Act 1998 is depressingly espoused by those propagating right-wing policies of a bygone age. The issues deserve separate treatment hereafter.

Today it is not supererogatory to claim that in terms of adherence to the finest tradition of independence and impartiality we have as good a judiciary as a modern liberal democracy can expect to adopt. But in some respects judges (not the judiciary as a whole but the individual) think otherwise. Outside and outwith the courtroom, judges treat themselves as a cut above the rest of the population. They do so because we put them on a permanent pedestal. They respond alike.

I constantly remind myself about retrospective judgments, that time (for the historian, but perhaps not the scientist) goes only in one direction, and that judgments about affairs today are not exempt from that assessment. I recall specifically the wise words of Felix Frankfurter, much favoured by President Franklin Roosevelt, who nominated that outstanding academic lawyer to the US Supreme Court. On the occasion of an assessment two weeks after Roosevelt's death – the occasion was a retrospective assessment of a great man, but is applicable (at the right moment) to any notable public figure – Frankfurter said that fluctuations of historic judgment are the lot of great men: 'If the judgment of the time must be corrected by that of posterity, it is no less true that the judgment of posterity must be corrected by that of the time'. English judges of the past have rightly earned civilised praise internationally, and no doubt that can be sustained today. But judges until the Second World War, with their instinctive abstention from constitutional affairs, were treated deferentially, aloof and professionally elitist; as such they kept themselves remote from political (at least partisan) affairs, as well as the general citizenry. They responded to their image.

With national developments that brought the judiciary increasingly into open contact with politicians, in and out of governmental power, the relationship palpably altered. Where once the senior judiciary behaved grandly and considered itself, both on and off the Bench, as a class above the rest of us, that judicial attitude receded markedly, but not entirely. There is still an atmosphere among some of the judicial brethren – a display of superiority that is justified as an acceptable mode of independence (not exclusively a legal posture) and impartiality. As and when, within a decade or so, we select (elect satisfactorily) our judges from a more diverse section of the populace, judges should be regarded as our respected public servants, performing of course a judicial function of adjudication in full public view from the courtroom. Away from the arduous task of judging, they wear no exceptional garments that would distinguish them from the publicly respected among the *hoi polloi*, especially as court hearings have only recently been subjected to televisual broadcast. Mr Justice Snodgrass, away from judicial duties, is Mr Snodgrass (must he automatically be knighted, a mark of inequality which is served up with the rations?).

It all added up to a verdict that by the twenty-first century, England had a legal system that not only proclaimed a high standard of judicial quality, but evinced a good reputation from the rest of the civilised world. The historical insistence on independence and impartiality was justly endorsed in the adherence by government to it – statutorily, under the Constitutional Reform Act 2005. Complacency is not totally absent in the watchfulness of its advocacy. Vigilance demands constant comment and advancement of traditional values. What are the manifestations of the high regard for Bench and Bar: what are the factors that pertain to an independent practitioner in the courts, distinguishing him from the same individual exhibiting those valuable practices when translated careerly to judicial life, unlike the legally trained students pitch-forked from the start to life on the Bench?

The essence of the barrister or advocate is the fundamental duty to the client. Subject to an overriding duty to the court, he or she is the mouthpiece of the client. What the client instructs is the essence (even detail) of his or her case, and cannot properly be diverted by the advocate's unexpressed precondition or, more popularly, prejudices (not to be confused with bias, if any). The advocate learns to sublimate his own views for those of the person he represents. Short of issues of fraud, the word of the witness before the court always prevails. If such a criterion of an independent profession, seeking to ensure justice is done (and seen to be done) why is that not carried out when fulfilling the function of decision-maker on the Bench? The theoretical answer is that the judge is instantly stripped of his practitioner's duty to a client. Suddenly, there is no client to whom a duty, constitutional and moral, is owed. The judge's duty lies in the oath – to do justice to all without fear or favour and to serve the sovereignty of the State. Therein the member of the judiciary acquires among the country's citizenry a status that, if admired, calls for behaviour that is demonstrably wise and fair. It implicitly calls for a high standard of publicly inspired activity that undoubtedly sets the judge's task as unique. But how differently must the judge behave from any other persons performing public duties? The undeniable response, unless acknowledged and counteracted appropriately, is that the judicial culture gives way to a public sense that the task of official judging imposes upon its actors a level of class that sets him or her on some kind of pedestal, entitling them to an exalted status. There is a tendency, stronger in some than in others, to give rise to a treatment not accorded to lower folk. Yet, in reality, they are public servants, no better than the senior civil servants. The obvious example in today's society is the use to which the government uses judges to undertake public duties away from the Bench. It is acceptably normal that those judicially qualified are asked to conduct public inquiries to unravel the reasons for some public scandal or disaster. As such, they act as Commissioners of Inquiry. They perform the fact-finding exercise as a person with skills of testing the credibility and reliability of witnesses, but they do not do so as judges dealing with rival disputants and ordering a result. They do so at the behest of a Minister who asks for such assistance, without doing more than expressing gratitude to the judge for performing a political (with a small 'p') task.

There are undoubtedly traits that espouse the widespread view of the judge. The wearing of a wig (now only a gown, when sitting magisterially in a court of law) does not change the individual, or remove him from the same humanity as anyone else who is operating professionally under the eyes and ears of the public, or regulated civil servants. It is their own acceptance of disavowing equality that is desired. Judges must treat fairly all those affected by issues in and out of court. Nothing less will do in a modern society.

What precise status does the judge have in a modern democracy? Does the public really think that judges are wise, the rest of us otherwise? Clearly, in performing his judicial duties he has a special status adjudicating on disputes, but does his conduct otherwise, both on and off the Bench, preclude him from behaving differently in kind from his fellow citizen? What are the limits of a member of an independent judiciary? Or, to put it more clearly, does the ordinary citizen expect that the judge is set apart publicly from others? It often seems as if the judge is notionally on a pedestal erected by the society of judges in its daily affairs. The status should be otherwise: the pedestal is for statues and for prize-giving on sports day. The Consultation Unit at University College, London, recently (January 2014) issued a background paper on the changing nature of an independent judiciary. In that illuminating document, it posed the question whether the judiciary needs to isolate itself so much, or ought to increase its efforts to engage in public affairs.

The status of the judge is primarily dictated by the scope of his function. Ever since the Act of Settlement, the Crown's judges have been appointed for life, and so it was until the Pensions Act 1959 that a judge was irremovable so long as he acted with good faith. None in modern times has undergone parliamentary action, save for abortive motions by private members. The age-limit of 75 applied thereafter, until March 1995, when it was lowered to the age of 70 in conformity with public employment restrictions applied to public servants. An attempt in the House of Lords in 2012 to raise the limit back to 75, at least for appellate judges, was rejected by the Government, and it seems unlikely that there will be another attempt at reform. Thus, in employment terms, a member of the judiciary is treated like any other citizen in public service. But is there more to the judge's status than his work as a judge? Has an age-limit equated the judge with a commensurate pay for public servants? The incantation or mantra of an independent judiciary is that it implies something more than just the separate function of a judge from the other two arms of government. Should the judges be subject to some form of appraisal in order to maintain quality assurance in the legal process? These are contemporary issues that focus on judicial standards. Are there special reasons why the judiciary is to be treated as a class apart? I think not. As judges, they exercise a specialist function, adjudicating on issues within the framework of the established legal system, conducted almost invariably in open forum. Off the Bench, judges are publicly senior civil servants and entitled to their private lives when not engaged in public service. As Lord Bingham observed in a foreword to the third edition of *Judicial Review* by Supperstone, Goudie and Walker,[1] one should bear constantly in mind that Thomas Fuller's great injunction – 'Be you never so high, the law is above you' – applies to judges no less than ministers.

---

[1] M Supperstone, J Goudie and P Walker, *Judicial Review*, 3rd edn (London, Butterworths, 2005).

32

Judicial Heroes

VENERATION OF A member of the judiciary is intrinsically an attribute of the practising lawyer. And in these memoirs I am no exception to identifying my judicial hero, save that my selection is as much about the mark of heroism being made more complete by other virtues beyond juristic measureship or heroic decision. On account of being blessed with several other qualities, together with a first-class mind, humility in the art of decision-making, common sense about affairs generally, a flair for fairness, a consideration for fellow human beings and a sparkling wit, Lord Bingham of Cornhill (he insisted on being addressed as Tom Bingham) is my choice. Above all human values, he was quite outstandingly the best appellate judge of his generation. His equal is Lord Scott Reid, who, in an earlier age, would be Tom Bingham's fellow opening batsman in my first XI.

His extrajudicial qualities were manifest. Apart from scholarly works, such as his remarkable book *The Business of Judging*[1] (being a selection of essays and speeches), exhibiting an extensive intellectual range from professional journals addressed to law-makers and other opinion-formers, he was an admirer of Dr Johnson, himself an aspiring lawyer. Tom adopted Dr Johnson's apt quote, 'clear your mind of cant [prejudice, to be more precise]'. Tom Bingham's essay adopts likewise the claim in *The Campaign* (1794), by the literary figure and friend of Dr Johnson, James Boswell, to that complete heroism which was the reflection of the great tempest of 1703. Two impacts of that event were aspects of Tom Bingham's career. First, the cathartic politics of the ensuing years, and secondly, its historic meaning of democratic government that avoided anarchy, were both hallmarks of Tom Bingham. Nearly all his judicial pronouncements were fine-tuned and often embellished by historical allusions and development. No other judge had demonstrated the essence of the life of the law, both historically and logically. But it

---

[1] T Bingham, *The Business of Judging* (Oxford, OUP, 2000).

did not stop there. When he became, in 2000, president of the judicial House of Lords, he rescued the world-wide reputation of that institution after the maladministration caused by the initial non-disclosure about the composition of the Court in 1999 to hear the appeal of General Pinochet. It is no exaggeration that Tom Bingham's handling of the judicial House of Lords led to its successor, the UK Supreme Court, preserving intact the unwritten constitution. His manner, both in and out of court, was universally applauded. By his demeanour, the final court of appeal demonstrated Tom Bingham's claim for collegiality and an outstanding jurisprudence, no doubt influenced by his graduation at Oxford in English history. If Tom Bingham was impressed, if not persuaded, by the political argument for a written constitution (enforced by a Supreme Court), he expressed an alternative form to replace the parliamentary House of Lords (hopelessly negatived in 2013). His proposal was some institution along the lines of the Conseil d'Etat in France. This latter reference supplemented his vision of a 'new dawn of international-ism', replacing the traditional approach of the English judiciary which exhibited an excessiveness of detachment from the civilian system.

In September 2010 Tom Bingham died far too early, at the age of 76. But the memory of him as a judicial colossus, presiding over outstanding cases in the common law and the evolving declarations of civil liberties, is enshrined both in the law and by the country. In 2005 he was appointed a Knight of the Garter, a personal gift of the Queen, the first professional judge to be so appointed.

Lord Reid was a direct appointment to the House of Lords in 1948; he retired in 1975 having become Senior Law Lord in 1962. The retiring age was then 75, so that he spent 26 years as an appellate judge. He too was an historian, although he qualified academically in mathematics. His knowledge was brilliantly exemplified in the constitutional illegality of the unilateral declaration by Ian Smith in 1965. The main case touching on the right of a federal country to secede from the federation was an American Civil War decision of the US Supreme Court. There were in the course of counsel's submissions frequent allusions to the state of West Virginia, at the mention of which Lord Reid intervened with a neat explanation of the military and constitutional position of the seceding state of the Confederacy – much to the amazement of the historians!

Lord Reid did not expatiate a great deal on his judicial work, save for his memorable speech at an SPTL conference in Edinburgh, when he observed that nobody believes in fairy tales any more; amusingly he alluded to the classic words of Alice in Wonderland. More significantly, he adhered to reticence in public speaking, since he came to judgeship via a parliamentary and ministerial background (he had been Scotland's Lord Advocate). His judicial pronouncements were more than just workmanlike, if not intuitively juristic, although he was the prime mover of the Practice Statement of July 1966 removing the straitjacket of binding previous judgments. But, emphatically, he was an activist and also had a creative role in establishing a civilised system of public law.

Five cases in the 1960s under Lord Reid's impetus and classical judgments formed the essential foundation of the law of judicial review of ministerial decisions, and the creativeness of English public law, now embedded in a modern administrative law.[2] That alone qualifies Lord Reid as the other outstanding appellate judge of his generation and example to the judiciary 40 years hence. The judgments were scholarly: not landmarks of legal literature, but a wealth of logically immaculate statements of law that jurisprudentially found, and still find, acceptance by practising lawyers.

But the manner of his judgeship did nothing to detract from his judicial decision-making, even if the written product is less than pithily quotable. He told me once that the duty of a judge in writing conclusions was to be concise and clear. The result of a case should emerge during a probing interrogation of the rival parties, and only after the last word was spoken. Listening to argument was a vital pre-condition to rational judgment.

My appreciation is largely retrospective (although I did appear on a few occasions in the last days of Lord Reid's astonishing output – he delivered over 400 appeals with a high proportion of full judgments). His writings were always clear and concise, the latter a judicial model that nowadays is in short supply among the higher judiciary. Fact-finding is inevitably length-determined. Appellate judging should always avoid prolixity. My concentration in this appreciation is upon what judges do rather than engaging at length in the vitally interesting, if less stimulating question as to why and how they do it. In his oral history, *Final Judgment*,[3] Professor Paterson more than makes up for the deficiency in my own terms of reference. Yet Lord Reid tops my list of judicial heroes, as *proximae accessit*.

---

[2] For a detailed examination of the five cases, see L Blom-Cooper, B Dickson, G Drewry (eds), *The Judicial House of Lords 1876-2009* (Oxford, OUP, 2009) 219–26.

[3] A Paterson, *Final Judgment* (Oxford, Hart Publishing, 2013).

Inevitably one's heroes are former appellate judges, probably at the second tier of the judicial hierarchy, but they will normally have been High Court judges sitting at the first instance of the legal system. Many of their qualities of heroism will have been sufficiently evidenced as *puisne* judges. The High Court judiciary's primary function as fact-finders and declarers of law (they are bound by precedent and therefore rarely, if ever, law-makers) means that the qualities called for (where they sit, in civil cases, without a jury) are the capacity and facility to hear witnesses, to pass judgment on their cross-examination, and to give judgment (if necessary, reserved). I have great admiration for the general expertise of these judges, less than a hundred in number, working to a high, sometimes exemplary, standard. But, for me, the unsolicited guide to promotion to the Bench in my time came from Derek Hodgson, a Northern Circuiter of distinction, a prominent Law Commissioner in the late 1970s and a High Court judge in 1980. He told me that on his appointment, he placed, metaphorically, on the Bench in front of himself the following directive: 'Remember that the function you will be required to perform is of eminence to the parties in litigation in front of you, but that you personally are of no importance.' That is the clear implication of the judicial oath of office.

33

Lord Denning's Legacy: a Judicial Misfit?

ORD DENNING WAS Master of the Rolls for 20 years, from 1962 to 1982; he had been a judge since 1944 (38 years in total). Throughout those years he dominated the legal scene. Undeniably he was the master of court-craft, displaying all the attributes of a judge avoiding the aloofness of wig and gown, presentationally concerned to ensure that justice was seen to be done. Ever courteous to counsel and witness, he exuded all the appearance of a Solomonic wisdom of the English common law at its best. He appeared like some judicial colossus that is unlikely ever to be replicated. His style was Arcadian, exhibited by an affected Hampshire burr. Overall, he was admired – even adored – by a generation of law students and other non-lawyers of the immediate post-war period who felt inspired by a champion for reform of a legal system that had become ossified and needed refurbishment. Throughout the astonishing output of his judicial decision-making – it is said that as the presiding judge in the Court of Appeal, he invariably (literally) gave the first judgment, his two colleagues acting often as book-ends, occasionally daring to dissent – he was more than just *primus inter pares*. To the onlooker, he personified the image of justice in action, propelling his admirers to applaud the art of the possible.

If Denning's management of a reforming zeal was instantly attractive, both in and outwith the legal profession, his legacy in developing the law in a liberal, forward-looking way is decidedly questionable, and today is lost in the mist of a bygone age. Were the personal virtues of a legal luminary in any way justified in terms of a rational and logical jurisprudence for a modern democracy?

It is not as if, on his appointment as Master of the Rolls in 1962, Denning had not already demonstrated his waywardness, not to mention unorthodox judicial attitudes. In 1958, as the seventh member of the Judicial Committee of the Privy Council, he, along with six other Law Lords, decided an issue of parliamentary privilege involving the Labour MP George Strauss. Lord Denning was the sole doubter of the majority decision that there had been no breach of parliamentary privilege, preparing for his colleagues 'a memorandum of dissent'. The majority rejected his request to publish the dissent as an appendix to the decision, which at that time did not allow for any departure from the implied unanimity of the declared opinion addressed by the Court. Years later (after 1966) the Judicial Committee recognised the right of any member to publish a dissenting judgment. When approached by a House of Commons librarian who was writing an article for *Public Law* entitled 'Parliamentary Privilege and the Courts: The Avoidance of Conflict', Lord Denning gave permission for the memorandum to be published as an appendix to the essay:[1]

> The point was referred to the Privy Council. The majority (by 6 to 1) held that the word 'any' was to be limited by the circumstances. It did not include a privilege conferred by the Bill of Rights . . . the Privy Council construed their terms of reference very narrowly. They expressly *left open and undecided* the views of the Committee of Privileges to the effect:
>
> 1. That the 'defamatory letter of Mr Strauss to the Minister' was a 'proceeding in Parliament' within the Bill of Rights 1688; and
> 2. That the commencing of an action for libel was a breach of the privilege of Parliament.
>
> . . . I expressed my reasoning in a memorandum and appendices which I add hereto.

The incident displayed, at worst, an unprofessional nastiness, typical of a judicial maverick; it did not, however, impair the quality of the prodigious output over his memorable career, which continued for the next 20 years as head of the civil jurisdiction of the legal system, emerging from the common law's ossified condition, which he was quick to observe and reform in his own image. Moreover, it did not obscure a kindly and unspoken view from his colleagues, a testament to his capacity, engagingly, to win friends and influence the profession. But it was unwise, probably the innate decision of a self-publicist.

Denning pursued a uniquely personal vision of jurisprudence, in which the doctrine of precedent was readily side-stepped whenever he could not find the case law to his liking or where he disagreed with it whenever it did not accord with his own view of the justice

---

[1] [1985] PL 64, 82–83.

of the case. It was unsurprising, but exhilarating stuff. Earlier in his judicial career, as a Lord of Appeal in Ordinary in the House of Lords, he was roundly criticised by the presiding Law Lord, Lord Simonds, a conservative, black-letter lawyer of distinction, for 'naked usurpation of the legislature'. Outnumbered there as a maverick, Denning gladly stepped down in the judicial hierarchy (or rather took a step of equal judicial importance) to preside over the civil jurisdiction in the Court of Appeal. There, he proclaimed, he had only to contend with two colleagues instead of four in the Lords. In truth, he cannot be viewed, retrospectively, as an exponent of the law or as a creator of a modern legal system, although some decisions indicated a willingness to please the public. While, during his tenure of office, he appeared to be just that, it is significant that in the twenty-first century it is a rarity for any of Denning's judgments to be cited by counsel or by today's judiciary. Denning's fame lies firmly in antiquity. He will be remembered – fondly, it must be noted – as the protector of the underprivileged. He liked nothing better than to be regarded as the protector of the little man (not often, the little woman) having to face the trials and tribulations of living under the thumb of authority. Denning's judicial pronouncements were ever-present in the style of his judgments, too numerous for analysis in this essay. The style was deliberately idiosyncratic, with constant references to homely exordia that brought an unconventional, poignant and nostalgic flavour to the official law reports of the twentieth century. For one sample – and there are many examples – take the case of *Miller v Jackson*. Denning's judgment begins as follows:

> In summertime village cricket is a delight to everyone. Nearly every village has its own cricket field where the young men play and the old men watch. In the village of Lintz in the County of Durham they have their own ground, where they have played these last 70 years . . . yet now after those 70 years a judge of the High Court has ordered that they must not play any more. He has issued an injunction to stop them. He has done it at the instance of a newcomer who is no lover of cricket.[2]

Even if in his early days as Master of the Rolls his pronouncements were punctuated with such Arcadian allusions, and were appropriately appreciated as a judicially uncommon display of human activities, even foibles, the style became overdone and stale. By the end (then an octogenarian) he became insouciant in his undoubted scholarship; his memory displayed a weakness in legal reasoning

[2] [1977] QB 966

and professionalism (he was the last serving judge to escape the retiring age of 75 imposed in the Pension Act 1959). He stayed too long, and only retired under a cloud of extracurial writings that disclosed more than a hint of racism. His extracurricular activities should have alerted his supporters. In 1962, when he first became Master of the Rolls, he was asked by the Prime Minster to investigate, in private, single-handedly and with no cross-examination of witnesses, the case of and his report on the Profumo affair. If his unique method of public inquiry fell foul procedurally of the Royal Commission on Tribunals in 1966 before Lord Salmon (and thereafter for 40 years under the 1921 Act for public inquiries), the ultimate verdict largely escaped public criticism at the time. Only years later – in 2012 – was the whole episode regarded as a 'monumental whitewash' of the Establishment of the day, in which two young ladies were dubbed sluts and an alleged brothel-keeper committed suicide during his trial for living off immoral earnings. The author Richard Davenport-Hines in 2013, commenting on the Profumo affair, described Denning as a 'lascivious, conceited old man'.[3]

It was in fact only one aspect of a flawed personality that ultimately revealed his fundamentalism and old-fashioned prejudices and preconceptions. Here are some snippets selected from an impressive portfolio. But one case is fully cited with extracurial comments.

If one expected, or even hoped for, a new era of legal liberalism with the arrival of the new Master of the Rolls in 1962, one was not encouraged by his indiscreet utterances. Denning's 'justice' was always personally malleable. I was the most junior counsel in 1962 in the appeal of *Soblen*,[4] who had fled criminal justice from the USA as a convicted spy, but whose failed attempt to take advantage of Israeli status via his Jewishness led to his return via the UK to the USA. He lost his appeal in the courts against a deportation order, but committed suicide on his escorted journey to the airport. The comment on Lord Denning's judgment by Dame Rosalyn Higgins (then teaching international law, and ending her fine career as the President of the International Court of Justice at The Hague) undisguisedly queried the judicial approach. She said that the judgment had both blurred the traditional distinction between deportation and extradition, and gave the Home Office more protection than was legally necessary or politically desirable; the motivation for

---

[3] R Davenport-Hines, *An English Affair: Sex, Class and Power in the Age of Profumo* (London, Harper, 2013).

[4] *R v Governor of Brixton Prison, ex parte Soblen* [1963] 2 QB 243.

such tendency towards the Establishment was for the judiciary to allow administrators to act 'in good faith'.[5] This tendency was later exhibited in *Hosenball*[6] where, in the Home Secretary refusing successfully to produce further and better particulars to a potential deportee, Lord Denning insouciantly declared that a British Home Secretary's decision could always be framed in polite terms.

This fondness for the public administrator was amply demonstrated in his first decision in the field of social security. Students claimed Supplementary Benefit in respect of the payment by them to their landlord during the vacations under a term in their tenancy agreements. In rejecting their claim, Lord Denning said that there were areas of public administration where the law relating to landlord and tenant could not be applied. High Court rules, he proclaimed, could not interfere with the administrative tribunal's decision, 'even though it may be said to be erroneous in law'. Reference by counsel for the applicants (me) to the Yellow Books (the manual of the Supplementary Benefits Commission) was like listening to judicial fondness for the principles of the Poor Laws.[7] It was as if the welfare state had not yet arrived at the doors of the courtroom. The merger of the administrative tribunals and the law courts had extinguished any inapplicability of the legal system to decision-making by ministers and civil servants.

No better example of individual justice over Executive action was displayed than in Lord Denning's dissenting judgment in which he described my advocacy, on behalf of the Attorney-General as an intervenor in the case, as demonstrating the high constitutional status of the recognition of UDI in Southern Rhodesia, whereas it was clearly a case of 'simple justice'.[8] Lord Denning's inclination to favour the ordinary individual against the might of the State was subject to inbuilt malleability even towards less publicly attractive citizens. Twice, there are examples of such judicial attitudes.

First, the Church of Scientology (a constant litigant before the Master of the Rolls): Lord Denning said that it did not qualify as a religious body for the purposes of relief from paying rates as a charity. The decision was ultimately overturned in 2013 by the UK Supreme Court in *R (on the application of Hodkin and another) v Registrar-General of Births, Deaths and Marriages*.[9] Second, there

---

[5] R Higgins, *Themes and Theories* Vol I (Oxford, OUP, 2009), a collection of essays on international law, at p 439.

[6] [1977] 1 WLR 776, 783.

[7] [1975] 1 WLR 624.

[8] *Re James* [1977] Ch 41.

[9] [2013] UKSC 77.

was the referral in 1981 in Payne's case.[10] Here Lord Denning declined to order that a decision of the Parole Board refusing a recommendation for or against release should be fully reasoned; he declined the evidence of the Parole Board's chairman[11] which championed the prisoner's case for a reasoned decision; in all decisions nowadays there can no longer be any doubt that prisoners may argue that there is a legal obligation on the Prison Service to supply reasons for administrative decisions, including the duty always to act fairly.[12] Reasons are always supplied for a parole decision.

Most of the evidence is deliberate, although until he became an octogenarian he had amply displayed his undoubted scholarship; but as a scholar he became careless in his utterances, if not actively mischievous in his autobiographies, which ultimately led to his resignation. Denning's biographer (or, in this case, perhaps hagiographer) said that his 'unaccustomed vanity obscured his sense of judgment'. Sometimes his judgment was opaque; here is one example. It was in 1979, in *Lake v Essex County Council*.[13] My client was a part-time teacher in a primary school in the county of Essex. She had brought before the Industrial Tribunal a claim for unfair dismissal by the local education authority. At that time, the jurisdiction of the tribunal could be invoked only if the teacher could demonstrate that she (or he) could establish a requirement under the contract of employment to carry out teaching duties on the school premises for more than a stated number of hours a week. The contract was silent about the length of time that a teacher had to be at the school. My client argued, in the Industrial Tribunal, that the law implied in a contract of service as a teacher that the hours spent away from the site of the school should nevertheless include the time spent (in the evenings at home) marking students' scripts and preparing the lessons for the next day: in which case, it was possible for her to demonstrate that she far exceeded the basic number of hours a week physically at the school. The short legal question was: is a part-time teacher bound by the precise terms of the contract, or was it permissible to include in the hours of work, the time spent on school business but which was performed not at school but at home? The Industrial Tribunal found in favour of the

---

[10] *Payne v Lord Harris of Greenwich* [1981] 1 WLR 754; and see Livingstone, Owen and Macdonald, *Prison Law*, 4th edn (Oxford, OUP, 2008) 187 fn 45. In the two cases referred to here, as well as in *Lake* (below) I appeared in the capacity of counsel for the claimant, and witnessed Lord Denning's judicial attitude at first hand.

[11] In evidence, uniquely given to an appeal court, by me.

[12] See Lord Reed in *Osborn v Parole Board* [2013] UKSC 61.

[13] [1979] IRLR 241.

education authority, but the Employment Appeal Tribunal allowed her appeal because it thought that there was an implied term to the contract. Essex County Council appealed.

I should add that, to understand the litigation, it is necessary to note what lay behind the local education authority's appeal against the adverse finding that a part-time teacher could properly invoke the jurisdiction of the tribunal. Two factors featured in the background to the claim for unfair dismissal. First, my client was being financed in her legal claim by her trade union as part of its duty to support its members in such a claim. But the union was privately not too worried about the possibility of my client losing the appeal, the reasons being that at that time there were serious negotiations between the trade unions and the education authorities which were designed to achieve extra pay for those part-time teachers who had to prepare their work away from the school premises. If my client were to succeed in the argument, it would be a victory for the education authorities, who could resist the extramural claims because they would have been catered for within the existing contract. The requisite number of hours would have had to be performed exclusively at the school premises and not at home. Now for the hearing before Lord Denning and Lords Justices Lawton and Geoffrey Lane.

My opponent was Derry Irvine, later to become Lord Chancellor in the Labour administration from 1997 to 2003. He skilfully addressed the Court, deploying the case law to demonstrate that it was not permissible for the Court to imply any term into the contract that could allow for time spent working at home to be brought into the time count to exceed the limited number of hours at the tribunal's jurisdiction. By the time I was called upon to reply, the Court was attracted to my opponent's argument. The case was adjourned overnight and shortly before the luncheon adjournment on a Friday morning, Lord Denning delivered judgment in favour of Essex County Council, without too much reasoning. The two Lords Justices gave compelling reasons for allowing the appeal. As you will appreciate, my instructing solicitors and the union were not disappointed; in fact they were pleased to continue pursuing their argument for extra pay for homework!

It was Lord Denning's practice to lunch on a Friday at Middle Temple Hall, as a member *aliunde*, since his normal Inn of Court was Lincoln's Inn. It so happened that our paths at lunch crossed. In a thoroughly genial mode, he said he was sorry to have to find against me, but he was suitably (if over-generously) complimentary of my forensic efforts. But he emphasised that justice had to be done, according to the law. And he was almost certainly right, as the law stood then. When I replied that I was grateful to him, he looked puzzled. I had observed that my side were delighted, because it meant that the Court of Appeal had in effect put thousands of pounds into the pockets of part-time teachers, since the unions had preserved their powerful bargaining position. I should also add that, from past experience, Lord Denning had been hostile to trade unions; he did not like the teaching profession and women were not accorded priority in his way of thinking. When I responded by telling Lord Denning that he had not fully (if at all) appreciated the reality of the posture of the litigating parties, he instantly said – and I can almost repeat verbatim, 30 years later, his words – 'If I had known that, I would have decided the case differently.' And I was (and still am) convinced that he meant it. Justice, for Lord Denning, would have been in favour of my client, because the result would have denied the trade union on behalf of part-time teachers the strong claim to payment, over and above that provided in their contracts. The story is improved by the oral recounting of the event – together with an imitation of Lord Denning's 'Hampshire burr'.

Do I need to say more than this? Lord Denning had very strong views on the merits of any claim, and the courts, he considered, should come down on their side irrespective of the legal rules. It was a classic instance of one judge's pervading sense of justice that had to prevail. Was he in fact a judicial misfit, a man for his times when the law needed to be wrested out of its cocoon, protecting a Victorian vision of the law? Or should we revere a figure of such judicial prominence and effect on British society – a judicial misfit?

APPENDIX

Lake v Essex County Council

Court of Appeal CA (Civ Div)

Lord Denning MR, Lawton and Geoffrey Lane LJJ

Lord Denning MR

This case concerns part-time teachers and their position with regard to dismissal or unfair dismissal. It is to be remembered that any claim for unfair dismissal did not apply where the employment under the contract was for less than 21 hours a week. By recent legislation that has been reduced to 16 hours, but in this case we have to consider 21 hours.

The particular provision which says that a person shall not qualify for unfair dismissal is in the Trade Union and Labour Relations Act 1974, Schedule 1, paragraph 9(1)(f), which says:

'Paragraph 4 above [the right not to be unfairly dismissed] does not apply to . . .
(f) any employment under a contract which normally involves employment for less than 21 hours weekly.'

That provision must affect a large number of part-time teachers. We are told that there are 10,000 part-time teachers in the County of Essex. Over the whole country there must be a very large number.

Here we have to consider Mrs Lake who was a part-time teacher from 1973 onwards at Greensward School, Hockley. Her employment came to an end in August 1976. She would be entitled to compensation for unfair dismissal if she had been employed for more than 21 hours a week.

She was engaged on written terms. On July 24, 1973, the Essex County Council wrote to her, saying:

'I am required, on behalf of the Essex County Council to confirm the offer to you of an appointment as a part-time teacher at the above-mentioned school for 18 hours 20 minutes per week from September 1, 1973, until August 31, 1974, in the first instance. Your times of duty will be as follows: – Monday to Friday: 8.50 a.m. to 12.30 p.m.

Salary will be paid on a proportional basis of the full Burnham salary for each hour worked in accordance with the scales and regulations for the time being in force. . . .'

If she worked at the school for more or less hours, her salary was to be adjusted accordingly. That was the position under the initial contract in 1973. But there was a variation in September 1974 extending her appointment for a further academic year. The letter of September concerning her appointment said: '. . . Your hours of duty will be 19 hours 25 minutes for a six day timetable.' That is from Monday to Monday inclusive. During those six days 15 hours and 45 minutes were spent in the classroom and the other three hours and 40 minutes were 'free periods to be used at the teacher's discretion for preparation or marking.'

Those were the terms of the contract. The question is whether there was an additional term in the contract whereby Mrs. Lake was required to do extra work in the preparation of lessons or in the marking of pupils' papers and the like so as to bring the hours she worked each week to more than 21. The industrial tribunal held that there was no implied term in the contract requiring her to work more than the 19 hours and 25 minutes.

She appealed to the Employment Appeal Tribunal [1978] ICR 657. They allowed her appeal because they thought (p 660) there was an implied term whereby she was 'to do as much work outside the school hours specified in her contract as was reasonably necessary for the proper performance of her teaching duties in school hours.'

They therefore remitted the matter to the industrial tribunal to see whether, on the evidence, by reason of her out-of-school work Mrs Lake could prove that she had worked more than 21 hours a week. They said, at p 660:

'That tribunal will have to satisfy itself on evidence in the ordinary way about how many hours Mrs. Lake ordinarily worked outside her school hours in order to do her work in her school hours properly.'

Now there is an appeal to this court.

We have heard all the arguments in this case: and I must say that I prefer the decision of the industrial tribunal. It seems to me that the 'free' time of 3 hours and 40 minutes covered all that was required of her. That was the time allowed to her for preparation or marking. She was not required to do more. If she chose to do more, it was a voluntary act on her part outside her contractual obligations. This voluntary act was so unpredictable that it could not be regarded as contractual. One teacher might be able to do all the preparation and marking in the 'free' time of 3 hours and 40 minutes. Another might not. It would depend on the subject which had to be taught, on the qualities of the teacher, and the knowledge she already had in her particular subject. There is so much personal variation in regard to the subject matter, the teacher, the pupils and everything else that it is completely impossible to lay down any guidance for a tribunal to decide how much extra work an ordinary teacher would have to do. So much so that no implied term can be imported whereby Mrs Lake was required to work at any time over and above the 19 hours and 25 minutes.

There is also the question of payment. Mrs Lake was paid according to the number of hours she worked. She was paid for working 19 hours and 25 minutes a week. It is difficult to find any element in her salary which included her work out of school hours.

The recent fire brigade case is distinguishable. In *Bullock v Merseyside County Council* [1979] ICR 79 the fireman had to be on call for 102½ hours every week. He could not go away. During all those hours he had to be available within four minutes of the fire station. Being on call, he was on duty all that time. Contrast this with *ITT Components Group (Europe) v Kolah* [1977] ICR 740 *581 where it was held that voluntary overtime did not come into the calculation.

I do not think it necessary in this case to go into any more refinements. Suffice to say there is no implied term giving rise to any specific ascertainable or available hours of work over and above those specified in the contract. As the specified hours were less than 21 hours weekly, she is not entitled to compensation for unfair dismissal.

I would therefore allow the appeal and restore the decision of the industrial tribunal.

Lawton LJ

I agree. Under paragraph 9(1)(f) of Schedule 1 to the Trade Union and Labour Relations Act 1974, in the form in which it was at the material time, for the purposes of unfair dismissal the tribunal has to look at the contract under which the applicant makes his or her claim. The paragraph is in these terms: '. . . any employment under a contract which normally involves employment for less than 21 hours weekly' is excluded from the operation of paragraph 4 of Schedule 1. The tribunal has to look to see what the contract itself provides. Under various regulations, school teachers have to have written contracts. The written contract in this case provides for the period during which the teacher shall be employed, and goes on as follows: 'You times of duty will be as follows,' and they are set out. That is what the teacher is required to do under the contract.

Mr Blom-Cooper has accepted in the course of his submissions that the contract is the governing instrument, but he has gone on to say that the written contract does not contain all the terms of the contract of employment. He submitted that there must be added to the written terms an implied term, which he defined in these terms, as I took it down:

> 'A teacher is required by the nature of his employment as a teacher to do such work as will enable him properly to perform the task of teaching and to do so by way of preparing the lesson he will have to give, marking the books of his pupils and the essays he has set in class, and the like.'

Applying the well-known principles for the insertion of implied term in contracts, I ask myself the question: would any local education authority have agreed to any such term? At once questions of vagueness arise because the words 'preparing the lessons he will have to give' or some such like provision in the implied term would make it impossible for the local education authority to supervise, or measure for the purposes of payment, that which would be required for the preparation of lessons.

Mr Blom-Cooper has said that the difficulty of measuring for payment or supervising the period required for the preparation of lessons is one which is not insuperable for a tribunal. It may not be, but it is inconceivable, in my judgment, that any local authority would ever have agreed to any such vague term. With his usual forensic skill, Mr Blom-Cooper concentrated his submissions on such physical activities as marking essays, marking exercises in mathematics and the like. There are other kinds of preparation, such as background reading for history and English teaching, which would make accurate assessment virtually impossible. The written contract is what matters.

I would allow the appeal.

Geoffrey Lane LJ

I add a few words of my own in deference to the appeal tribunal from whose views we are differing. By a contract in writing Mrs Lake was engaged as a part-time school teacher by the Essex County Council. Her hours were specified to be (as later amended) 19 hours 25 minutes for a six-day week, which is, as the industrial tribunal found, equivalent to 16 hours 11 minutes for a calendar week. Of those 16 hours 11 minutes, no less than 3 hours 40 minutes were allowed for free periods to be used as Mrs. Lake's discretion dictated – for reading, marking, preparation of lessons, or whatever she might wish.

She worked under that contract from September 1973 until August 31, 1976, when her contract was not renewed. She wishes to claim now for unfair dismissal; but, before she can put forward an argument on the merits, she has to avoid the provisions of paragraph 9(1)(f) of Part II of Schedule 1 to the Trade Union and Labour Relations Act 1974 which provides that the right not to be unfairly dismissed does not apply to 'any employment under a contract which normally involves employment for less than 21 hours weekly.'

Counsel are agreed – both Mr Irvine and Mr Blom-Cooper – that the only hours which one is entitled to consider are those which the employee is obliged to work by virtue of the contract. Consequently the only live question before this court is whether there was an implied term in Mrs Lake's contract that she should work more than the hours stipulated in the agreement, namely the 16 hours 11 minutes. If so, the matter will have to go back to the industrial tribunal for them to consider for how many hours the employment was. That is necessary because the industrial tribunal decided against Mrs Lake on this preliminary point, but their decision was reversed by the appeal tribunal. The basis of the appeal tribunal's decision [1978] ICR 657 is at p 660 which I think it is useful to read. It runs as follows:

'Quite irrespective of the "free time," if a teacher found it necessary to spend time outside her on-duty-at-school time in preparation or in marking, essential elements in her job, there must in our judgment be a contractual obligation on her to do so whether it is written into her contract or not. If the headmaster had said, "Mrs, Lake, that lesson was quite insufficiently prepared" would she have retorted, "I don't have to prepare lessons outside school hours?" If he had said, "Why is that written work unmarked?" Would she have answered, "I don't have to mark papers outside school hours"? In our judgment obviously not.

Accordingly, in our judgment the employee was under a contractual obligation to the employers to do as much work outside the school hours specified in her contract as was reasonably necessary for the proper performance of her teaching duties in school hours, and that work outside school hours was employment normally involved in the performance of her contract which must be included in the computation of the 21 hours for the purposes of paragraph 9(1)(f) in order to see whether her right not to be unfairly dismissed was excluded.

Accordingly, the appeal succeeds, and the case must go back for rehearing before a differently constituted industrial tribunal. That tribunal will have to satisfy itself on evidence in the ordinary way about how many hours the employee ordinarily worked outside her school hours in order to do her work in her school hours properly.'

It is to be observed from that passage that there is a disparity between the way in which the judge expressed the reasons for the appeal tribunal's conclusion on the one hand and, on the other hand, the form of question which the industrial tribunal are requested to answer. It is said that she was obliged to do as much work outside hours 'as was reasonably necessary.' which is an objective test, but the industrial tribunal are required to find out how many hours she ordinarily worked, which is a subjective test. That perhaps indicates the difficulties in which the decision of the appeal tribunal leaves one.

It is quite impossible, it seems to me, to attempt to quantify in terms of hours the sort of work which might be done in preparation. Mr Blom-Cooper at one stage of his argument, at any event, said that only work which could physically be timed, like marking papers and writing examination questions, should be included, but it is difficult to see on what logical basis it could be so confined – and indeed on his argument I do not think that is logically correct.

Mr Blom-Cooper endeavoured, as Lawton LJ has already indicated, to set out the suggested implied term. It seems to me that that term, at least arguably, was void for uncertainty. It was certainly impossible of application. But are these circumstances circumstances in which it is justifiable to imply a term at all? If MacKinnon LJ's 'officious by-stander' (*Shirlaw v Southern Foundries (1926) Ltd* [1939] 2 KB 206, 227) had asked Mrs Lake and Essex County Council this question:

'Is Mrs Lake contractually required to work such hours out of school time as may be necessary to prepare her work so that if she does not do so she can be dismissed?'

neither would have replied either testily or otherwise: 'Of course.' Mrs Lake certainly would not and nor would the Essex County Council. It seems to me that this is not a circumstance in which it can usefully be argued that an implied term is necessary for business efficacy or would have been agreed by the parties.

For those reasons as well as those advanced by Lord Denning MR and Lawton LJ, I would allow the appeal and restore the judgment of the industrial tribunal.

Appeal allowed with costs. Leave to appeal refused.

34

Pilgrims' Progress: Academics and Practitioners

ONE OF THE more depressing aspects of joining a distinguished legal   profession as a barrister in 1952 was the gap – a glaringly one – between the coterie of those functioning in and around the Temple, and their co-professionals in academia. Law was in those days imparted to students as the qualities (if not the quiddities) of a developing legal system in a modern democracy. Legal training had been a traditional subject in tertiary education, but it was very much taught in isolation of the law in practice and allied disciplines. When I went in 1954 to Fitzwilliam House (not until 10 years later a full college of the University), I was contemplating a career in legal academia. After a year's experience under the brilliant tutorship of Dr Kurt Lipstein, the law dons at Cambridge seemed to me remote from the law in action, other than what they read and debated among themselves of the *ratio decidendi* of the case law. Professional contact was minimal; more specifically, the output from the courts of law disclosed little knowledge of what the theoreticians were producing in the literary world. When I began practice it was strictly permissible to cite in court a textbook as a legal authority only if the work's author was deceased! This absurd convention was blithely ignored, even if the effect was to acknowledge the dual operation of a viable legal system. Today it is quite different. Fusion has taken place. I cannot pinpoint the occasion when academic writings began to be cited in judgments, but I will try to trace the whys and wherefores of the fusion. Peripheral events, such as the influence of assistance from academically distinguished graduates in researching for the Law Lords, did much to infuse the judgments with quotations from academic articles. But not much more. I recall back in 1968, as the junior counsel for the appellant in *Madzimbamuto*[1] before the Privy Council, a range of

---

[1] *Madzimbamuto v Lardner-Burke* [1969] 1 AC 645.

historical and jurisprudential material was raised. The argument, after nine days of oral hearings, included a) the Statutes of Treason of Henry VII; b) the writings of Grotius from the early seventeenth century; c) the cases from the US Civil War of 1861–65; d) the defence of necessity; and e) most particularly, the theories of Professor Hans Kelsen, whose concept of Grundnorm has vast out-pourings from academia. Nothing like that has happened since, although the curial scenery has markedly changed in the composi-tion of both parties. The reason is, I think, underlying, if not simple; the common law of England has always prided itself on its pragma-tism. Usually it has turned its back on conceptualism. Has it remained as such, particularly since the Constitutional Reform Act 2005? But at least citations from legal journals seeped into judicial habit well before it became standard practice among appellate judges.

It suffices to quote the postscript of the judgment of Lord Goff of Chievely (himself an academic convert to successful practitioner and judge and eventually Senior Law Lord) in *Spiliada Maritime Corporation v Cansulex Ltd*.[2] He wrote:

> I feel I cannot conclude without paying tribute to the writings of jurists which have assisted me in the preparation of this opinion. Although it may be invidious to do so, I wish to single out for special mention arti-cles by Mr Adrian Briggs in (1983) *Legal Studies* 74 and in [1984] LMLCQ 227, and the article by Miss Rhona Schuz in (1986) 35 ICLQ 374. They will observe that I have not agreed with them on all points; but even when I disagreed with them, I have found their work to be of assistance. For jurists are pilgrims with us on the endless road to unattainable per-fection; and we have it on the excellent authority of Chaucer that con-versation among pilgrims can be most rewarding.

What, I wonder, does the legal pilgrimage indicate about the conse-quences for legal development in 2014?

WHY THE EARLIER SEPARATION?

The academic tendency of those destined to practise law was asso-ciated with the choice of university training in subjects usually unconnected with the law. If the tradition of English lawyers had been to attend one or more universities (usually Oxford or Cambridge), likewise it was rare for them to read topics (such as

---

[2] [1987] AC 480.

law) as an undergraduate or indeed as a graduate of an established legalistic course; law faculties taught occupational (rather than theoretical) subjects, initially as separate faculties of a university. The law only surfaced in studies of philosophy and jurisprudence, or in such subjects as Roman law, remote from action in the English courts. Too little assimilation took place with other faculties. Even medical jurisprudence was a late arrival on the academic scene, and even now makes little more than a nodding acquaintance with interdisciplinary teaching (one should observe the lack of understanding among medics and lawyers in the practice of expert witnesses in and out of court). Until the 1960s there was virtually no empirical research of the legal system in action. The publication of *Separated Spouses*[3] was the first to observe how the decision of magistrates in relation to cohabitation clauses in matrimonial proceedings was out of kilter with what was expounded in the textbooks on family law. As part of legal philosophy the law played its part in the development of social science, but it tended to be dominated by scholars from other disciplines than teaching law. It is often forgotten that the leading post-Second World War academic, Professor Herbert Hart, had spent many years before the war as a leading practitioner in the Chancery Division of the High Court. But he was a notable exception, and even then there was little evidence of close attachment to his erstwhile colleagues at the English Bar.

It is significant that the outstanding judicial voices of the last century (less so, now) all reflected their separate educational backgrounds, whatever may have been their personal inclinations towards the legal system that they entered. Most of the student topics sought by aspiring practitioners were generally either classics or mathematics. Lord Reid was an exponent of the latter (initially in Scotland), and a former Lord Chief Justice of England and Wales, Lord Parker, had read natural sciences. More recently, Lord Bingham had read history at Balliol College, Oxford, under the historian Christopher Hill, notably peppering his impressive judgments (1981–2008) with perceptible historical developments of the common law. The only account – possibly apocryphal – was that in the middle of the last century, it was rumoured that the Law Lords regularly consulted with the editor of the *Law Quarterly Review* about the decisions of the final court of appeal. The editor, Professor Arthur Goodhart, an American scholar and Master of University

---

[3] OR McGregor, L Blom-Cooper and C Gibson, *Separated Spouses: A Study of the Matrimonial Jurisdiction of Magistrates' Courts* (London, Duckworth, 1970).

College, Oxford, had a mystical effect over the law of England, which had stuck rigidly to the pragmatism of a case-by-case development, such that it happily eschewed any attempt at conceptual thinking. Similarly, the legal literature was sparse and was only spasmodically connected with practitioners – notably the nascent importance of civil procedure until the 1960s under Master (Sir Jack) Jacob.

The exception was the growth of specialism in legal practice. The development of public international law – more particularly the international law of human rights, stimulated by the European Convention on Human Rights, attracted to it exponents of global law in the wake of the impact of individual human rights. The work of Professor Hersch Lauterpacht in the interwar years has had a profound influence on bringing the English practice of law on to the European and world stage, with his classical book in 1933, *The Function of Law in the International Community*,[4] which is an academic study all on its own. The names of McNair, Waldock, Fawcett, Higgins and Bratza – mostly from academia – are some of the prominent English lawyers to have achieved eminence abroad. Civil servants from England, notably, had helped to set up the Council of Europe in 1948, but only as members of a team of international lawyers drafting chunks of the European Convention on Human Rights in the years after the Second World War. Their involvement in drafting the Articles of the Convention is often mentioned, but should not be over-emphasised in establishing its international input.

One ought to note one major change in judicial composition in recent years. Until the end of the last century, no academic lawyer had been appointed to the High Court Bench in England. Lady Hale's appointment – ultimately to the House of Lords in 2004 – was acclaimed, although belatedly. During more recent years, many academic lawyers have attained judicial prominence, outstandingly the late Lord Rodger of Earlsferry, uniquely a law don at Oxford, a Scottish Law Minister and judge (Lord Advocate, President of the Court of Session) and ultimately a Law Lord. Today, the higher judiciary features a large cohort of academics – in the Court of Appeal alone, we see Lord Goff in the 1980s and more recently Lord Justice Elias, Lord Justice Beatson and some others like Lord Sumption (a military historian) with part-time experience of law teaching (the newest High Court judge (in October 2013), Nicholas Green QC,

---

[4] H Lauterpacht, *The Function of Law in the International Community* (Oxford, Clarendon Press, 1933).

was also once a law teacher). There is perceptibly now no undue reaction to appointment from among teachers of law. It is almost expected that an academic can be appointed directly to the Supreme Court – but not yet! The transformation has not been due to any concerted legal attitudes within the profession. I venture to think that cultural attitudes have forced the change; indeed the prominence devoted to diversity in judicial appointments has not been attained yet. The lower echelons of the judiciary come mostly from practitioners – barristers and solicitors.

The reason for this sharp distinction between the practising and theoretical world of resolving disputes lay in the fundamental approach of the common law, distinct from Continental systems of Roman-Dutch law. To summarise: the English trial system of orality – that is, the resolution of litigious disputes, following oral testimony of the witnesses to the event – demands confrontational advocacy rather than legal expertise in written statements. On the other hand, the European system that relies principally on the written word (composed by the witness, together with legal assistance) relies more upon legal expertise than spoken language. Advocacy calls for skills of human communication and dialogue in the public forum. Evidence by way of documentary material calls for skills in written and interpretative composition. Legal services differ markedly in their exposition. I should explain further.

Trial by jury (until 1934, it included civil litigation) is quintessentially a system of procedure demanding the examination of live witnesses. The litigant seeks to persuade his case, invariably in the criminal jurisdiction before laymen, unqualified in the legal process, whether the magistracy (increasingly lay, but also professional district judges) or random jurors. Thus the leaders of rival disputes are involved in an interpretation of civil events by a qualified arbiter (a judge). The interpreters of the civil law in Europe are pre-eminently the leading academic lawyers – the professors of law are its leading practitioners. Hence the legal system instinctively produces a sharp divide between the professionals serving the litigant. They lean towards expounding the theoretical or conceptual aspects of the legal system.

The dichotomy is essentially induced when comparing the defence of the criminal offender with the claim made in civil proceedings. The attitude between the criminal practitioner and the criminal law is most marked, and continues to place criminal justice a system apart. Even in their procedural aspects, the criminal courts operate on a different basis: the mode of trial in Europe is a search for the truth of a criminal event; specifically it is not aimed to establish a level of evidential proof, which is labelled as adversarial. The prosecution's duty here is to prove its case beyond a reasonable doubt – whatever that phrase encompasses, it is a high standard of proof. The advent in the 1970s of judicial review – and its absence of oral testimony – began the shift away from the principle of orality. Other reforms in evidential procedure also tend to proffer testimony that limits or extinguishes evidence given in the witness box by live witnesses. The continuing protection of vulnerable witnesses – e.g. children in care cases – is designedly to avoid personal confrontation. There is another dimension to the legal services performed. Increasingly the two arms of practice vary through the handling of documentary testimony. Each requires a skill that has the same reference point. Developments in mediation and reconciliation, away from courts of law, attract practitioners from all quarters of life – not simply oral advocacy. The jury-advocate and the theatre of the criminal court are largely things of the past; even today he and the court are hardly discernible in a less punitive atmosphere. But the reform of the binary systems – adversarial and inquisitorial – is far from complete, although each tends to borrow details from the other.

JUDICIAL BIOGRAPHY

If that is a credible explanation for the coming together of the two branches of the profession, what, you might ask, have been the implications for the law? The interplay of legal commentary on the law in action is replete, but it defies exposition that calls for profound study. Suffice it to say, that no debate of a legal issue nowadays goes without reference to academic opinion. That interplay is certainly what Harold Laski had in mind when, at the beginning of the twentieth century, he wrote a personal letter to Justice Oliver Wendell Holmes saying that he wished people 'could be persuaded to realise that judges are human beings, and that it would be a great help to jurisprudence'. Richard Posner objects to the idea because he says that 'we did not learn much about the judicial process from judicial biography'. It may be so, but that depends on the quality of biography. Laski would have been commenting as much on the different views of English and US judicial pronouncements. At that time the disparity was even more evident. English judges (particularly appellate) were notably singled out for the clarity of expression in delivering their individualised judgments, either of assent or dissent. In 1925, Judge Cardozo of the US Supreme Court said this:

> For quotable good things, for pregnant aphorisms, for touchstones of ready application, the opinions of the English judges are a mine of instruction and a treasury of joy.

Justice Cardozo might have had in mind one of many examples that flowed from the pellucid pen of Lord Macnaghten, although he singled out for special mention Lords Blackburn, Esher, Bramwell and Bowen. Contemporaneous with Cardozo's praise, 'Q' (Sir Arthur Quiller-Couch), when compiling his *Oxford Book of English Prose*, included only three extracts from the Law Courts (in fact, short snippets from well-known pieces of elegance). But this is meagre fare, and it was not intended to promote legal debate. There was little evidence of what I call 'intellectual biography', either judicial or academic.

But apart from judicial opinions in judgments, English judges did little else extracurricularly. Infrequently they delivered public lectures (which appeared in legal journals). Their literary output rarely emerged outside of their judicial activity. Official opinion has, however, begun to move in the direction of greater openness. Only when the Kilmuir rules on judicial activity outside of court were finally removed by Lord Mackay in the 1980s did the transparency of judicial lives begin to emerge. It had the effect of openness about the judicial process, culminating only in the twenty-first century with the acknowledgment of radio and television playing a part in the publicity of court proceedings. It began, desultorily, with the televising of judgments in the Supreme Court in its past guise as the Appellate Committee of the House of Lords.

Academia was not directly involved. What was more significant was that books about the courts came mainly from academics, and even then bore a distinct mark of being politico-legal. There have been few judicial biographies, compared with the United States. Which of our great judges – I exclude the idiosyncratic autobiographies of Lord Denning and one hagiography from Irene Freeman – has been so treated?

There is a perceptible apathy to judicial biography. The biggest barriers at present seem to be those of academic, and especially legal academic, disapproval.[5] Such objections seem to be in principle a

---

[5] My knowledge on this subject is due to Professor Antony Lentin, an historian with a legal qualification who has given us a life of Lord Sumner and has turned his lively pen to Mr Justice McCardie.

typical outcome of example of *deformation professionelle*, no more valid in principle than academic objections to biographies of scientists, authors, composers or anybody else. The only distinction that matters is that between good biography and poor biography. Judicial biography is simply another branch of the tree of biography, potentially no less fruitful than any other. It deals with members of a particular profession with its own conventions and peculiarities, but inevitably it incorporates the traditional views of the professionals – ie academics and practitioners. With the publication in 2009 of *The Judicial House of Lords*,[6] I lay claim in a joint effort – with academics and practitioners – to a remarkable study of a remarkable institution. If not strictly a case of judicial biography it revealed a good deal of what lay behind the decisions of human institutions of the legal system. I should include the writings, in legal and non-legal journals, of Lord Justice Laws and Sir Stephen Sedley – both outstanding intellects in the judiciary, and *rarae aves*!

Few judicial lives reach a high level of drama; and it is also undeniable that judges in the English system are normally and necessarily middle-aged before they become judges, and the more so before promotion to the Court of Appeal or Supreme Court – 'elderly gentlemen', in Lord Haldane's description. Exceptions can be found. Mr Justice Williams, while on circuit in Nottingham in 1884, did not turn up in court one morning. After searches were set in motion he was found dead in a brothel; and in the 1920s the private life of 'the bachelor judge', Mr Justice McCardie, was adventurous by any standards, with a fondness for making the headlines, distressing to his judicial brethren, a mistress in London and a fatal addiction to gambling. Others have not escaped public notoriety. Take for example the unsuccessful prosecution of Lord Justice Richards. (As an aside, we need to encourage such writings, if only to minimise the unhealthy attitude of our judges behaving as citizens placed publicly on a pedestal, to be revered as a class above the rest of us.) Do I make a valid point when I think that the chairman of a public inquiry into press ethics under the Inquiries Act 2005 was Sir Brian Leveson, not Lord Justice Leveson, a judge of the Court of Appeal acting judicially?

---

[6] L Blom-Cooper, B Dickson and G Drewry (eds), *The Judicial House of Lords* (Oxford, OUP, 2009).

THE ACADEMIC CONTRIBUTION

If you accept the gist of my cases, that judges are no less fit subjects of biography than anyone else, how should their lives be written, and what has legal academia contributed? In terms of a long pedigree and a growth industry, America undoubtedly leads the way, with an average annual publication of three to four biographies of Supreme Court judges. Cardozo, Holmes, Learned Hand, Brandeis, Frankfurter, Brennan and others have been frequently studied. The American approach is impeccably scholarly. Judges' papers and correspondence are reverently stored in university repositories or published in sumptuous editions by university presses, as in the case of Justice Oliver Wendell Holmes. The judges themselves are the subjects of numerous well-regarded biographies, usually by their law clerks. Yet on the whole, American judicial biography is not just scholarly; it has been overwhelmingly the output of academics. It is 'intellectual biography', the analysis of a judge's rulings and the discussion of the particular ways in which he reached them.

Professor Posner has his sceptical counterparts outside the United States: Professor Girard at Dalhousie and Professor Richard Gwynedd Parry at Swansea both worry about the academic respectability of judicial biography. Gwynedd Parry's question 'Is legal biography really legal scholarship?' (2010)[7] implicitly has in mind the inhibiting constraints of modern academia – will legal biography pass muster at the REF or run the gauntlet of peer review? Where, he asks, with alarm, are its methodologies, its canons, its 'templates'? He believes that if it is to attain academic acceptance, judicial biography must formulate its own ground-rules, approved by 'a scholarly guild of legal biographers'. This sounds a dismal and horrifying prospect. But judicial biography has yet to pass the test of academic approval.

ACADEMIC STUDIES OF JUDGES

But if legal academia in the UK runs second best, one must imbibe Robert Heuston's monumental *Lives of the Lord Chancellors from*

---

[7] RG Parry, 'Is legal biography really legal scholarship?' (2010) 30(2) *Legal Studies* 208.

1885 to 1970,[8] the first of two volumes which he published when a professor of law. It is both a masterpiece of scholarship and a paradigm of good writing; but it may be wondered whether Heuston, a distinguished and stimulating teacher of constitutional law, would, in the conditions prevailing in British universities today, have been granted the leisure or the funding to complete those carefully researched and elegantly crafted lives. Of this triumph of what Heuston called the 'life and letters tradition of English biography', one is delighted that it is being carried on by Michael Beloff QC (a distinguished practitioner and at one time the Master of Trinity College Oxford – he is writing about the next batch of Lord Chancellors, up to the conclusion of the office of Lord Chancellor under the Constitutional Reform Act 2005). In place of the older English tradition, R Gwynedd Parry suggests the wisdom of 'intellectual biography', in other words the American tradition. And a first-rate instance of this approach is Professor Smith's study of Mr Justice James Fitzjames Stephen. The tradition of the English concept of *mens rea* was exemplified in his textbooks.

Ideally, the judicial biographer should also pay attention to the judge's style. There, if anywhere, is his crown of glory. As Lord Sumner wrote of Lord Macnaghten, his 'life is largely written in 26 volumes of the appeal cases', and wonderful judgments they are too, combining mastery of the law with wit and irony.[9] It was with posterity in mind that Birkenhead published a complete and literally monumental edition of his own judgments.

The Legal Biography Project was set up in 2007 by the Law Department of the London School of Economics as a forum for lectures and seminars for scholars with an interest in the subject. The outcome in terms of books remains to be seen. It was inspired by a publicly unknown solicitor called Cyril Glasser, who had a splendid collection of judicial scribblings. R Gwynedd Parry feels, somewhat coyly, that 'legal biography is on the verge of acquiring a degree of intellectual respectability'. I hope so. The judicial biographer must plunge boldly into the waters, not dabble his toe in them.

[8] R Heuston, *Lives of the Lord Chancellors from 1885 to 1970* (Oxford, Clarendon, 1964).

[9] This applied with equal force to Lord Reid, whose judgments were always clear and considered, but, not having been anthologised, their worth is undervalued. He deserves a biography, if only to state a case of Homer nodding. It was Alexander Pope who enjoined us all to study the works of Homer; even the worthiest of us, such as Cicero, nodded. As the Romans had it: *Quandoque bonus dormitat Homerus*. In *Dorset Yacht Co Ltd v Home Office* [1960] AC 1004 Lord Reid stated that English prison officers were made of sterner stuff than their American counterparts, and hence were liable civilly for the escape from custody of prisoners at large: see *Williams v State of New York* (1955) 127 NE 2d 545.

CONCLUSION

I began with the depressing experience 60 years ago of a divided profession that engaged in professional dialogue only intermittently and at arm's length. Today the picture is very different. If the pilgrimage of the two, developing a legal system in a modern liberal democracy, is a welcome sight, not all the vestiges of the past relationship have disappeared. The literary output among legal professionals still lags behind the Americans: one yearns for the publication of the biographies of, say, Lord Reid, Lord Wilberforce, Lord Scarman and, of course, Lord Bingham.

Index

Poacher's Pilgrimage

Poacher's Pilgrimage

An Island Journey

Alastair McIntosh

BIRLINN

First published in 2016 by
Birlinn Limited
West Newington House
10 Newington Road
Edinburgh
EH9 1QS

ISBN 978 178027 361 7

British Library Cataloguing in Publication Data
A catalogue record for this book is available
from the British Library.

Designed and typeset by Hewer Text UK Ltd

Printed and bound by Gutenberg Press, Malta

To the late Catherine MacKinven of
the Knapdale MacKinvens, Argyll,
tradition bearer, dear mentor:
le gach beannachd
mile taing

And of the upcoming generation, to my dear
daughter, Catriona, with Kevin,
and to Finley, their
wee one:
bless

Contents

PART 3

Hare

List of Illustrations

Artefacts from the journey on Harris Tweed
Christ of St Clement's Church, Isle of Harris
The Sun of Righteousness (tomb detail)
Red deer (tomb detail)
Rodel and St Clement's Church from Roineabhal
St Clement's looking towards Roineabhal
Lochan on the 'Golden Road', east Harris
The byre that was a boat, east Harris
Rediscovery of the Blacksmith's Well at Leac a Lì
The Golden Stag
Initials of J.M. Barrie at the Harris Hotel
The Harris Hills from Ardhasaig
On the trail to Loch a' Sgàil
The glen down towards Loch Langabhat, Isle of Lewis
My sheiling campsite, Glen Langabhat
Bannocks on the campfire
Loch Chleistir, towards the Atlantic Ocean off Uig
Deer prints and moult at Loch a' Sgàil
South wing of Both a' Chlàir Bhig, Harris-Lewis border
Planetarium effect inside the 'beehive' bothan
Kinlochresort and the river flowing from Loch Voshimid
Loch Resort, looking out towards the Isle of Scarp
Saint Bridgit's Sheiling, south central Lewis
Fern at the fallen lintel, Bridgit's Sheiling
The 'beehive' both of Loch a' Sguair, Isle of Lewis
The author at the Callanish Stones
Vérène Nicolas with the Campbell sisters at their family sheiling
Tobar Mhoire, St Mary's Well, at Shader
Tobar Brighde, St Bridgit's Well, at Melbost Borve
Dr Finlay MacLeod of Shawbost – 'Doctor Finlay'

Plainsong headstones at St John's Temple, Bragar
Holy Cross Temple at Galson
St Peter's Temple at Swainbost
Final campsite at Stoth Bay, Butt of Lewis
A foodie's guide to Poacher's Pilgrimage

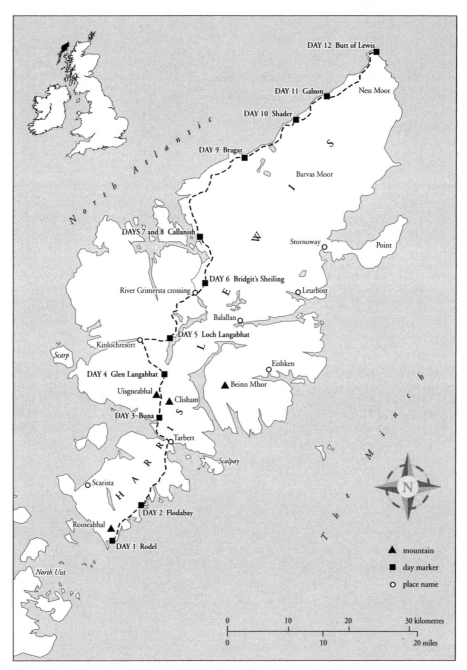

The Isles of Lewis and Harris: Trail of the Blue Mountain Hare

An Tobar ('The Well')

Tha tobar beag am meadhon a' bhaile
's am feur ga fhalach . . .

Resting in the village there's a little well
and the grass hides it,
green grass in sap closely thatching it.
I heard of it from an old woman
But she said: 'The path is overgrown with bracken
where often I walked with my pail
and the pail itself is warped.'
When I looked in her lined face
I saw the bracken growing round the well of her eyes,
and hiding it from seeking and from desires,
and closing it, closing it.

'Nobody goes to that well now,'
said the old woman, 'as we once went,
when we were young,
though its water is lovely and white.'
And when I looked in her eyes through the bracken
I saw the sparkle of that water
that makes whole every hurt
till the hurt of the heart.

'And will you go there for me,'
said the old woman, 'even with a thimble,
and bring me a drop of that hard water
that will bring colour to my cheeks.'
I found the well at last,
and though her need was not the greatest
it was to her I brought the treasure.

It may be that the well
is something I saw in a dream,
for today when I went to seek it
I found only bracken and rushes,
and the old woman's eyes are closed
and a film has come over their merriment.

By kind permission of the island bard,
Professor Derick Thomson, granted
shortly before his passing in 2012.
His translation, Gaelic original.

BEGINNINGS

I have a pocket compass on my desk. It is the simple sort that many of us kept as children, the kind for which the natural play is not damped down by viscous liquid like you have today inside more fancy models. When laid upon a map the needle swings and dances, for up to a minute, as it slowly settles to the steady pull of north.

We human beings, likewise. We too need time and times in which to settle our souls' compass. We too are pulled by north, and at the deepest level, I suppose that's why I set out on this pilgrimage.

It was back in 2009 and I was in my mid fifties. For several years before embarking, I had felt the island's winnowing call. Felt it tugging, like an umbilical cord that ran beneath the sea. The journey was an answer to that call, but it didn't end there. Ever since, the walk has kept on walking in my mind, and this chronicle describes the action, but as deepened by seven years of subsequent reflection.

I say, and will continue to say, 'the island', as if this land that lies some thirty miles west from off the northern Scottish coast is a single entity. However, you'll get an insight into the psychology of the place, on learning that this is where they give you two islands for the price of one. Lewis, where I was raised and the most populous part, is the low-lying expanse of waterways and shallow hills that slip down to the north. Harris, that even as a child entranced me with its grandeur, soars up rugged to the south. The boundary between the two is not a watery strait, but the stately Harris Hills.

The Outer Hebrides are world famous for their Neolithic standing stones – especially those at *Calanais* or Callanish. What's virtually unknown, even to many in the archaeological world, is that these islands host an astonishing array of sacred natural sites. Their sheer concentration is almost without parallel elsewhere in Britain. They include 'beehive' dwellings of corbelled stone, nestled into hidden glens. Some will go back to the Celtic era, or even to an elder faith that lingers on in the abundance of stories, and place names, that witness to a worldview based on 'faerie'. These are fertile ground for the imagination and, in my experience, can open out reflection on the structure of the human mind with insights, even, into space and time and consciousness.

Then there are the ruins of 'temples', chapels built for veneration in a time before the Reformation shifted gear towards the Protestant faith. Most of these are tiny structures resting by the sea, their tumbled stone-work bedding in, a little more with every passing year, to sheets of sand that drift in almost constant winds that blow along the shore. Often there are near-forgotten holy wells close by. Further afield, one might stumble upon Gaelic names that testify to sites of spiritual retreat, or to the elemental power of blessing – *beannachadh*. Most of these temples and the wells are consecrated to saints. Some remain familiar today. Others, half or long forgotten.

But 'religion is over', mused R.S. Thomas, in 'The Moon in Lleyn'. His poem was inspired by just such an abandoned chapel in North Wales, one that was being reclaimed by the sea. Impermanence is here to stay. Nature, in the end, humbles all the works of human hands. Yet which of us, the poet continues, can tell what might emerge 'from the body of the new moon'? As our city ways grow weary, 'people are becoming pilgrims again, if not to this place, then to the recreation of it in their own spirits'. We must remain kneeling. Hush! Remember! 'These very seas are baptised. The parish has a saint's name time cannot unfrock.'[1]

As for my approach to such matters, my writing can be too pagan for the Christians, too Christian for the pagans. However, we're living in a time when many might feel drawn by the Welsh poet's sense of turning to be pilgrims once again. There's something stirring in a lot of us that feels the urge to place that compass on the map, to let its needle swing – the wider and the wilder, the better.

I suppose that, at the deepest level, that was the force that pulled me north to make this island pilgrimage.

The geographical distance that I planned to walk was not going to be great. Only sixty miles as the crow flies, maybe double that with all the meanders, and a generous twelve days for completion. I'd be navigating by map and compass through eight hundred square miles of mostly uninhabited territory, crossing the fifty-eighth parallel, and probably experiencing all the weather that's to be expected when you're halfway between London and the Arctic Circle.

If the spiritual search was one motivation, another, and a closely related driving force, was my work on war and peace. It happened that I'd spent the month before my departure delivering guest lectures at military training institutions across Europe. That might not be what you'd expect of one who's been put on trial for protesting against Trident nuclear submarines at the Faslane naval base. However, in 1997, I'd received a letter from General Timothy Granville-Chapman, Commandant at the Joint Services Command and Staff College of what is now the UK Defence Academy. He was refining the new Advanced Command & Staff Course at Shrivenham. It was designed for up to four hundred senior army, navy and air force officers each year, mainly British, but also drawn from sixty or seventy other countries with which the United Kingdom has military alliances.

Junior ranks in the military are trained to follow orders. At senior levels, they also have to think independently. This requires exposing officers to 'the alternative point of view'. As one of those alternatives entails the questioning of war itself, a discussion had ensued in Shrivenham, as to where they might find a speaker who might mount the challenge. One of the course design team, then in a very junior capacity, ventured to mention: 'I happen to have a brother-in-law. It's a high risk strategy that might backfire, but . . .' That was me, signed up for the Queen's shilling, at least, to her shilling minted to nonviolent mettle. It went on to become an annual fixture, with spin-off invitations to staff colleges or military think-tanks in Ireland, France and Switzerland. These days the Defence Academy also sets me loose on a higher course, one that trains the next generation of admirals, generals and air marshals. The deal is the Chatham House Rule – I'm at liberty to reveal what was said, but not who said it. Anybody who wonders what I get away with saying can find an outline published as a chapter in their textbook, *Ethics, Law and Military Operations*.[2]

My brief has been refined over the years and, frankly, I find the swing that it permits my compass quite remarkable. I get set loose to:

> . . . explore the moral implications of conflict that exceeds military capacity to deter or contain it; and the application of nonviolence, including its religious basis, to achieve security in a complex world where the net results of conflict are not easy to predict.

As I was making final preparations for the pilgrimage that May, I'd just got back from an assignment in Switzerland. I'd been asked to address soldiers and diplomats on the NATO programme, 'Partnership for Peace', that had grown out of the Balkan wars that had so sadly soured the falling of the Iron Curtain. It had been a day-long session. There'd been a range of speakers tackling the theme 'God, War and the State'. The mad thought did cross my mind that a fitting rubric for my pilgrimage (if anybody asked) could be 'God, War and the Faeries'. However, thankfully my compass quickly dampened down on that one. I mean, it's nice to get invited back.

The night before the lecture I'd sat up late, discussing conflict and religion with the course's academic dean. We were billeted in Geneva's Hôtel InterContinental. Normally I'd be more used to camping, but at least it wasn't on the budget of the peace movement. Our lodgings were rendered all the more surreal by being seated next to a large family of piteously rich Arabic brothers. I say piteously, for each one of them looked bored to death with all that money could buy. One young man had a box of matches. He struck them, one by one, until the box was empty. He watched each match flare up, let it burn down to his fingertips, then dropped it onto a growing pile that smouldered, like a burning ruin, on the polished mahogany table top.

The scene felt curiously like a metaphor. At the time, our wars were smouldering on in Iraq and Afghanistan. I couldn't help but watch the solemn dropping of each match. It felt like witnessing a countdown. The lighting of blue touchpaper. The final stage, before ignition, of my pilgrim journey's launch.

On getting back to Glasgow, I went to Tiso's store, which sells outdoor equipment. It had attached to it a specialist map-printing shop. I was planning to walk from Rodel, at the most southerly tip of Harris, right up to Ness, at the Butt of Lewis. I knew that if I made it over the Harris Hills without breaking a leg, I'd come down into the rump of central Lewis, bang into a quagmire of deep peat bogs and tortuously twisting lochs. These might be very good for fishing – I'd be taking a collapsible fly rod with me. But they'd also be very good for getting lost amongst. Hardly anybody ever goes to this most lonesome haunt. Even the Ordnance Survey almost gives up. Their large-scale maps, that can be bought off-the-shelf, select the region, devoid of all inhabitation, to overlap three neighbouring sheets. Trying to piece that lot together when it's blowing a hoolie would have left me in a right flap.

Hence why I was in the queue at Tiso's. I wanted them to print me a bespoke single sheet, one that would be centred on my intended route's most treacherous meanderings. My mind drifted off as I waited for my turn. Curiously, I was wondering how best to give account of myself to people I might meet along the way. To say 'I'm on a pilgrimage' might merely seem quaint to folks of a secular turn of mind. But many native islanders are Presbyterians, and that, of a 'strict' leaning. Such an interpretation of the Christian faith rests upon the teachings of John Calvin of Geneva. He, in turn, stood on the shoulders of Martin Luther – a tempestuous monk who, in 1517, reputedly pulled off the grand slam of nailing his ninety-five theses of the Protestant Reformation to the cathedral door of Wittenberg.

In 1520, Luther had issued an address to the German nobility. This decreed that 'all pilgrimages should be done away with'. These, he asserted, only served to keep the common people off their work. They encouraged 'a vagabond life' that lay at the root of 'countless causes of sin', and so, those 'country chapels and churches . . . to which the new pilgrimages have been set on foot . . . must be destroyed'.[3]

But there was a caveat. Luther had to win over the nobles and the bourgeoisie to his cause. Then, as now, such social classes liked their travelling. He therefore made an exception. Excursions were allowed, provided they were emptied of all spiritual intent such as might treat them as beneficial for salvation, which was the gift of faith alone. As such, travel could be sanctioned only when conducted, 'out of curiosity, to see cities and countries'. Unwittingly, with those words, Luther canonised himself the Patron Saint of Tourism.

I doubt that many islanders on Lewis or Harris would have read Luther's *Address to the Christian Nobility of the German Nation*. We were raised as Calvinists, not Lutherans. Nevertheless, as children even into the 1960s, we were warned of 'Papist superstitions' that harked back to this early Reformation mindset. That's why, as I slowly shuffled up to the head of Tiso's queue, I was pondering how best to give account of myself. Into what groove might I quickly fit my story, such as might lubricate a fleeting wayside encounter? Pilgrimage, I mused, could be a dodgy gambit. But tourism! And with early Reformation sanction! Well, that might be a different matter. So it was, that with my mind now itching for temptation, titillated at the prospect of 'countless causes of sin', a mischievous solution to my predicament thumped home. *Poaching!*

Let me explain, if I might be excused for taking a rough cut at history. The rising of the clans – the indigenous Highlanders – against the fledgling British state was crushed by sword and musket at Culloden in 1746. It was the last battle on mainland British soil. Ever since, the 'lairds' or lords – the landlords on a massive scale – have presumed to hold as private property the land that once was the tribal patrimony. They were of a breed that had been born to rule; others, they presumed, born to be ruled. Often absentee, perhaps coming up from London for just a few weeks every summer, they guarded zealously their claim of sporting rights to deer and salmon. Set against the game protection laws that they've created on the one hand, there's a raft of Gaelic proverbs on the other hand that give succour to the humble poacher's soul. Lines like: 'A salmon from the pool, a wand from the wood, and a deer from the hill are thefts which no man was ever ashamed to own.'

Even the island churches, otherwise so quick to damn transgression, have traditionally soft-pedalled on 'the poaching'. The Reverend Professor Donald Macleod of the Free Church of Scotland once gave a sermon on the matter in his column in the *West Highland Free Press*.[4] 'Until I have a lobotomy,' he proclaimed, 'I will never be persuaded that poaching is a crime or even a sin.' The advantage of living in the City of London is that the Good Lord ordained you to make money. The advantage of living in Balallan on the Isle of Lewis – with the lochs and rivers of the Grimersta system out the back – is that the Good Lord ordained you to catch salmon. But, concluded the professor, the British Establishment has nefariously decreed that London should have both the money and the fishing. Balallan would have neither!

By now, I'd made it to the head of Tiso's queue. I explained my Ordnance Survey needs to the technician. With a few clicks of his mouse, the familiar kite-shaped outline of the Outer Hebrides leapt up on a ginormous screen. We selected a rectangle that ran from the foot of the Harris Hills in the south, over to Kinlochresort in the west, straight down the eight miles of Loch Langabhat that straddles the centre of Lewis, and up to where the Grimersta meets the sea near Callanish. We set the scale at 1:25,000 – two-and-a-half inches to the mile. It was then that he insouciantly asked: 'And what title would you like printed on the cover of your map?'

Little do I think he suspected anything, but those words were the trigger for *the vision* that fell upon me. Here, dropped from Heaven, was the muse by which I was bestowed my ruse: a cover story, that would delight the ears of every true-blooded islander. In my mind's eye, I glimpsed myself a-huffing and a-puffing over the hills, peregrinating from loch to loch, with my collapsible fly-fishing rod sticking up like an aerial from out of the camouflage green of my rucksack. It looked, for all the world, like the walkie-talkie of some clandestine military operation.

I whispered my instructions back to the man in the white coat, hoping he'd not notice the manic gleam that had most surely filled my eyes. With what seemed to be a conspiratorial nod, he pressed the coloured buttons on his console. A humongous printer whooshed to life. All lights were a-flashing. Noises, quite unspeakable, wheezed and beeped and burped and blew. Dr Who had done his darndest. The Tardis was in take-off. Space and time themselves were on the brink of going AWOL.

Steadily, the island's graven image stuttered forth. There was, for me, no going back. The myth had now been resolutely activated. The blue touchpaper – lit at Hôtel InterContinental – had burnt down to ignition. The countdown, at ground zero, signalled *lift-off!*

The journey lay stretched out on parchment. It waited only to be walked. Printed boldly on the cover was the proclamation:

Alastair McIntosh
Central Lewis
Poacher's Pilgrimage

PART 1

BLUE

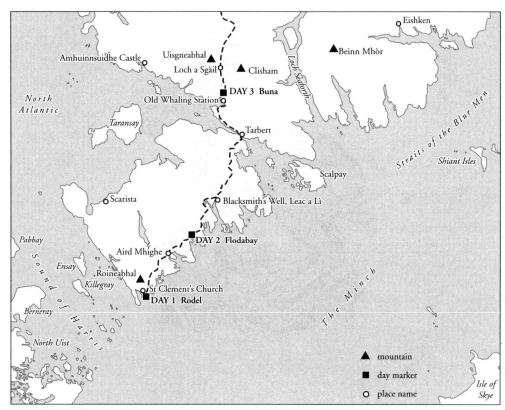

The Blue Trail: Days 1–2, South Harris

THE DEVIL'S DEBUT

An unseasonable hailstorm let loose as my wife Vérène and I set off from home in Govan, the part of Glasgow that had once built the ships of the Empire. It was Friday 9 May, and late afternoon. Winter had held a protracted grip that year. The distant peaks were icy dusted, flushed pink in the low-slung sun. We were stalked by rainbows of most startling iridescence, as we drove across the girth of Scotland, to what continues to be known as The Kingdom of Fife.

The philosopher and writer David Lorimer had asked me to give a talk in a series that he'd organised, called 'Café Spirituel'. These were held in the provincial town of Falkland, specifically at an organic farm called the Pillars of Hercules. The plan was for Vérène to take me thus far by car. We'd overnight with David and Jane. The next morning, I'd be dropped off at Ladybank railway station. I'd take the train to Inverness, then a bus for sixty miles, across the neck of the Highlands, to the fishing port of Ullapool. That's where I'd embark on the familiar three-hour ferry crossing of the Minch, this being the stretch of sea that separates the mainland from the Isle of Lewis.

In the port of Stornoway, I'd spend the weekend with my elderly mother. Then, on the Monday morning, I'd take a couple of bus rides down to the south of Harris. From there, at Rodel, I'd set out by foot on the long-awaited pilgrimage. That's the plan, but right now, it's to Falkland, and as we drive across the rich flat farmlands of Kinross-shire, the sun dips down behind the Paps of Fife, and leaves the little town that we're approaching to settle into dusk.

David is the grandson of Sir Robert Lorimer, a noted architect of the Scots Baronial and Gothic Revival styles, also an exemplar of the British Arts and Crafts movement. I've come to know him through his leadership of The Medical and Scientific Network, a group of physicians and academics, along with the occasional artist and left-field aristocrat, who take an interest in the interactions between body, mind and spirit. 'The Pillars', as the Herculean farm is fondly known, is already packed with people as we arrive. All are finishing their meal and deep in conversation. I enjoy speaking to such provincial groups. In rural communities of place, there's usually not the same social stratification that you tend to get with communities of interest, such as academic groups. That's not to say there's not a social order. It's just that everybody's there.

There's Ninian, the local laird, descended from the Stuart kings and passionate about Falkland's sense of place: its wood, water and stone. There's my old friend Tess, who wrote *The Scots Herbal*, gorgeous in one of her homespun cardigans of browns, reds and purples as if to make an autumnal protest at the spring's late arrival. There's Bruce, a gnarled organic farmer in a set of dungarees, the epitome of fashion now the industry's decided that the in thing is 'distressed'. There are several hard-up hippie couples, the kind of folks who don't ask for much but bring a bit of sunshine to the community. There are the retired professionals, the caravan, yacht and golf club scene, who bring a bit of money and hard-boiled expertise. And there's Marianna Lines, a spirited American artist, who works her Pictish pictures from the thatched cottage studio of a nearby medieval village.

I can't resist, whenever I see her, from calling out: 'All hail, the Great White Witch of Collessie!' At which, on one occasion, wondering whether I might have overstepped the mark and be in peril of getting thwacked by her broomstick parked outside, I followed up, more discreetly: 'Er, I do hope you don't mind my acknowledging your professional status in public?'

'I'm glad *somebody* recognises it!' she exclaimed.

The whole room's buzzing and the plates are being cleared away. I prefer to do my eating after speaking, so David cuts to the quick, introduces, and we're off. I'm billed to give a blast about climate change: about the need to forge *resilience* in communities, how this entails the outer work of cutting carbon footprints, but also the inner work of learning to live more with less. After the allotted twenty minutes I sit down and await questions.

I'm expecting some of them to feel quite challenged. I'd talked about the quest for meaning, about the experience of emptiness and the false satisfier of consumerism that transiently fills the gaps, but drives the cutting edge of climate change. But they're not challenged. Most don't even want to talk about climate change, and it's David's fault. He'd told them I'd arrived with a backpack and a fishing rod. They don't want to hear about climate change. They want to hear about the poacher's pilgrimage! So it's *tally-ho* and off we go, with a stalwart young man in a singlet first off the mark. 'What training have you done?'

'None,' I confess. 'I've been so busy. Only time for a few walks within Glasgow. But as I keep reassuring my wife, *the pilgrimage will be the training*.'

I sense the raising of a few unconvinced eyebrows. Mine too.

'What are you going to eat?' asks one of the organic volunteers.

'Three boxes of oatcakes, muesli, a bag of bread mix, pudding rice, milk powder, honey, marmite, butter, cheese, sugar, seasonings, tea, hot chocolate, bags of nuts and raisins, a huge slab of Cadburys and a bumper pack of Mars bars.'

The wave of right-on kudos, generated by the muesli and bread mix, crashes as fast as the dough had risen.

'And, perhaps a wee nightcap too?' suggests a lady of librarian precision, in that kind of 'I've got *his* measure' tone.

'A wee dram along the way would have been nice, but I can't be fuddling the mind.'

'And for fresh food?' asks a douce Earth Mother type, probably suspicious of my ratio of oatcakes to chocolate. 'How are you going to stay . . . *healthy*?'

'I'll buy some more bits and pieces at the last minute on the island. But fresh food's too heavy. I need a week's supply of stuff to go across the moors, and my bag's already tipping twenty kilos. Hopefully I'll supplement by foraging.'

To which I add, hoping that she's not a born-again vegan: 'Edible plants, for sure, but also fish and shellfish. I'm hoping to catch part of my diet. You see, I'll be crossing . . . *the Grimersta*.'

'Ooh! You'd better watch out if you're near the Grimersta!' interjects a hale and hearty English woman. She's chuckling away, laying on an eeh-bah-gum accent as if that's the way it would be spoken by the crofters, the island's small-scale farmers and fishers.

'My son's been a watcher during his holidays on the Grimersta, catching poachers all the summer long. You know what they do with poachers up there? They string 'em up, you know, like grouse in the larder, till their maggot-ridden 'eads drop off!'

Well, those might not have been her precise words, but they were her gist and gusto. I should say, before proceeding further, that all conversations related here are necessarily paraphrased from memory, and that, I hope, in ways that would find my conversationalists' approval.

Now, it was true enough, that were all to go to plan, I'd be crossing several rivers. It rains on the island for two out of every three days, fifty inches annually at Stornoway airport, but much more heavily in the mountain regions where the wind, sweeping straight in off the Atlantic, regularly tops the ton-up in winter. The Grimersta – a boiling force of nature that drains the island's centre – is a legendary watercourse. They used to say it was the third best salmon river in Europe. In 1888, a certain Mr Naylor set the British record, landing fifty-four salmon on one rod. Such were the days of the great white hunters. Poaching the Grimersta was a rite of passage when we were boys. It was also a political education. How come *they* claimed *our* fish? It got folks asking questions – about social class, about landed power – and precisely who the British Empire thought it had the right to colonise, and how come so, so close to home? It was the audacity of having a bash at the poaching that counted. Even if you weren't a Mr Naylor, just the derring-do of daring to throw a line out from the Grimersta's hallowed banks was enough; the thrill of lying awake at night, with visions of the gamekeeper looming up from the heather – his dog and his big stick – the unspeakable in hot pursuit of the all-too-beatable.

Alas, such was an initiation from which my all too 'respectable' upbringing as the doctor's son had shielded me. In those days, incomers to the island came to provide professional services, and were granted privileges. The local estates gave Dad all the fishing he could desire. The only time I ever had to drop my rod and run was when in hot pursuit by vicious clouds of biting midges.

Most pilgrimages go to strange and distant lands. Mine was to my own land, therefore I should share something of our family's island connections. Moreover, my approach to telling people about this remarkable part of the world, and the arguable importance of its insights to wider burning issues of our times, is necessarily discursive. I might seem to wander off on a wild goose chase now and then, but *trust me* (said the doctor's son), there's method in the madness. Hopefully the goose comes home to roost in ways that help to build up layers of mood and information, gradually to knit together to a greater whole.

Dad had left Edinburgh, newly qualified after the war, to take up a post in the West Riding, Yorkshire, town of Doncaster. There he met my mother, who was the nursing sister in the Royal Infirmary's children's ward. Her mother's people had Welsh roots, but all we knew was that 'they sung in choirs'. Her father ran the celebrated Ronnie Hancox Band for Dancers, and used to play *Come Dancing* in the early days of television. They were industrialists and squires, but he used to tell my mother, 'No-one teaches a Hancox how to ride a horse' – and it thrilled me when I found this out to be an old Gypsy name.

Dad had three parts Gaelic Highlands and one part Scottish Borders blood. Through these links, we have some very distant relations on Lewis. Moreover, his uncle, James Ewart Purves, was the superintendent of the Lewis Hospital in Stornoway in the 1920s.[1] To this day, an old woman, Mary Mackenzie, the widow of 'Sligo', lives in the village of Upper Bayble just a few miles outside of Stornoway. She has shown me the neat scar where 'Uncle Jim' had operated on a quinsy on her neck. It was on the kitchen table of her family's thatched house in Callanish, aided by a bottle of chloroform. She was just two years old at the time. 'I would be sorry for you if you'd left your child another night,' he'd told her parents as he headed off. Sometimes, the past seems very far away – yet there it is, just tissue-thin.

I was born in Doncaster in 1955, my sister in the following year, and my earliest memories are of the steam train that used to chug up from the Armthorpe coal mine to the slag heap. Dad, however, yearned to get back home to Scotland. He loved the outdoors, and especially yearned for a place that offered fishing. He said he wanted to be able to practice real medicine – 'medicine as both an art and a science' – but there had to be a salmon river. It was my mother who persuaded him to apply to an advertisement in the *British Medical Journal* for the North Lochs practice, midway between Stornoway and Harris. She, who was so into fashion and the modern life, and for whom the culture shock would be the greatest. She always had a feeling for the inner beat and ordering of things. So it was that we moved to the island in the summer of 1960. I was just four, but can still remember the excitement of that crossing on the old *Loch Seaforth*. At first, little Isobel and I were so urbanised that we called the Barvas hills 'the slag heaps'.

Being raised and educated on the island has shaped the person that I am today, yet I'll always think of Doncaster fondly, a place of holidays and grandparents. How easily my life could have configured differently! How easily, but for that winnowing compass call; the pull that Dad had felt on lifelines of the wild Atlantic salmon.

There was one last question at Café Spirituel that evening. 'Won't you get frightened, all alone, out in a tent at night in the middle of nowhere?'

'I don't see why,' I'd answered. 'I've camped out on my own, many times before.'

Yet there was a difference. Then it was just camping. This time it was pilgrimage; a conscious invitation to unconscious experience.

Once, when the Rev. Dr George MacLeod, later Lord MacLeod of Fuinary – a pacifist clergyman with double military decorations from the Great War – was praying in Iona Abbey, he was overcome with terror. It was his practice, like Jesus at the start of Mark's gospel, to rise and pray early in the morning. Before the world got going, he'd go alone amongst the Benedictine columns and arches that rest upon the probable site of the original Columban church. On this occasion, as he sat and opened inwardly, he was overcome by an overwhelming force of smothering malevolence. It was as if some quintessence of evil had risen up, perhaps to try and crush his work in setting up the Iona Community to recover Celtic spirituality.

'George was able to run out into the breaking daylight,' I had mused, lying in bed, pondering such matters in the wee small hours while planning my trip. But fear is an uncanny thing. We may not know it till the chasm opens.

'Where would you run to?' I'd thought to myself. 'Where, if it opened in the middle of a night, far out on the moors?'

Christ met the Devil in the wilderness. One doesn't, of course, believe in the Devil as such. But . . .

By now the hour was late and The Pillars of Hercules closing. Jane went off with Vérène in her vehicle. David put me into the passenger seat of his zippy little vintage sports car. It was very still outside. Both of us were quiet as we picked up speed. The country isn't like the town. The town maintains a never-ending buzz of normality that keeps reality stable. At least, a certain configuration of reality. That last question niggled slightly in my mind. It wasn't so much that it scared me. More, it intrigued me, like something to be picked up and examined.

David sped through darkening country lanes, lined with tousled hedgerow briars and the wilting pallid blossoms of the day's convolvulus.

'We'll just stop here – I'll show you something,' he announced unexpectedly, and pulled into a passing place.

Across the road was the pillared entrance to a grand estate. Beside it stood a Gothic gatehouse – a dumpy square residence, with a huge chimney rising from the centre. Seated astride the pot on top was a humanoid figure.

'Get out and take a better look,' he urged, turning off the headlights so that my eyes could get accustomed to the gloom.

'What . . . ?' I said. 'I can hardly make it out.'

'It is the Devil,' he replied, completely deadpan. Then, smiling to release the Peter Cushing tension: 'Rather splendid, don't you think?'

And there he was. A squat, cheeky-looking fellow, with cloven hooves, merrily tooting a bacchanalian pipe.

'It's called the Devil's Lodge. Designed for Balcarres House by my grandfather. He was into . . . many things mysterious.'

'Well!' said I, glad to have got off with making the acquaintance so lightly. 'I suppose that'll be me, now. Inoculated for the journey!'

2

A SACRED LANDSCAPE

There's a Calum Kennedy song that we all used to sing on bus trips: 'Make your way to Stornoway' where the town clock 'chimes its message every day.' This is where 'Heaven can't be far away'. Here, 'the folks are truly kind' and you 'leave the world behind'. Kitsch romanticism? And yet, there's something about a culture where such values are continually reinforced in patterns of song and story.

So here we are! I've arrived in Stornoway, and I've just spent the weekend with my mother. She's bright and well, but anxious at the prospect of my trying to traverse the island. At last, after all the preparations, it's Monday 11 May. Day one of my allotted twelve of pilgrimage. The bus is pulling away from its terminus on the pier, pulling away from Stjorn-Vagr as the Old Norse had it. Stornoway, as the Bay of Steering or Governing. Equally, it can be translated as the Bay of Stars. After all, steering is what stars were for in olden maritime cultures. They governed our passage and guarded our lives through cosmological connection. This sheltered inlet of the sea – this little port with its two-for-the-price-of-one inner and outer harbours, its fishing boats and its ferries – this is the centre of the island's governance, here in the Bay of Steering by the Stars.

The heart of Stornoway is a few criss-crossed streets of small-town shops, fix-anything garages and light industries. There's a library, a museum and a university college where you can study an enormous range of courses from marine engineering to Celtic languages, theology and hairdressing. There's the High Church on one hill. A castle on the other. Carry-out chip shops. Chinese, Thai, Indian and even Hebridean eateries. And bars. About ten of them. Nearly a pub for every church. No wonder Heaven can't be far away. No wonder, here's the place to 'leave the world behind', or perhaps to enter, with its lilting old-time motto, *God's Providence is Our Inheritance.*

These days, about nine thousand souls, a little less than half the island's population, live in or around the town. At this time of the morning, just at the back of ten on a gloriously sunny day, the bus is almost empty. Within minutes, we've reached the leafy outskirts, and at Willowglen slip past Uncle Jim's old house that stands, in faded glory, on the corner. Here pebble-dashed terraces of council houses yield to the prosperous villas of Stornoway's business and professional classes; their garages and their patios, their gardens and perhaps a boat outside. Next, we're into the crofting township of Marybank. Here it's rural but with signs of modest urban prosperity. The homes sit on several acres meant for the arable production of anybody who can be bothered these days, and out on the open moor, there's a much bigger share of common grazings for the sheep and cattle.

Another mile, we've sped past Tawse's quarry, and the road dips down to cross the River Creed. From here we come up into the moorland of a very different type of country. Now it's plain to see why a fond name for the island, popular in poetry and song, is Eilean Fraoich, the Isle of Heather. This is the road that leads to my home parish of Lochs, and from there, on down into Harris. All around, both visibly and dipped away in hollows, are shining lochs and smaller lochans. Each is threaded to a necklace by tiny burns that, according to their season's wont, trickle or churn a passage to the sea. And this is such a remarkably sunny day! Although I know the place so well, although I've crossed this Arnish moor so many times, I'm drinking it all in once more. Here, the rocky fortress of a *cnoc* or little hill. There, a puffed-out drifting sugar-candy cloud. Everywhere, these long and rusty heather ridges, that slouch to kiss their own reflections dipped in pools of liquid amethyst.

The change that's flipped since Marybank is geological. We shifted out of Stornoway's soft lime-rich and relatively fertile conglomerate, into the island's anchoring mass of hard, crystalline Lewisian gneiss. We're now bouncing over archaic beds of worn-down mountain stumps, these ground down to a low rumpled plateau over the aeons of the ice ages. Seen through the telescope of deepening time, glacial ice sheets are the default norm in these latitudes. Plant life is just a passing bloom of summer, one that flashes past in a blink, every hundred thousand years or so. In back-of-an-envelope terms, the last ice age ended ten thousand years ago. Since then, only thin peat soils have built up; these, from the remains of vegetation that wouldn't rot under such lime-impoverished acid-saturated conditions. These oozing beds of peat, resting on a spread of glacial boulder clay, are pretty much all that sustains the slender skin of life.

Pronounced 'nice', from an old German word that means sparkling, rocks of the Lewisian complex date to between two and three billion years, amongst the oldest in the world.[1] Known as metamorphic, which means 'changed form', they've been cask-conditioned deep within the Earth's crust, under enormous heat and pressure. This has caused their mineral composition to segregate into banded layers of dark and light, alternating every few inches. Add to this the fact that hot rocks bend as the Earth's crust slowly shifts over time, and it is common to see outcrops that have folded and contorted, like twisted bars of toffee.

Interpreting the island's place names is a further merry-go-round of Norse and Gaelic influences. Lewis, or Leòdhas, is thought to be cognate with the *Leod* of Macleod, and might suggest either *leodjus*, 'a place of lakes', or *ljóðhús*, 'the poet's home' or 'song house'. Harris – na Hearadh – probably comes from the Old Norse, *haerri*, meaning high ground, or possibly, 'the harries' where deer were hunted. Another Norse possibility is *hérad*, meaning a province ruled by a *hérsir*. The pioneering island historian W.C. Mackenzie said that such was 'not only the hereditary head of the community, but its "prophet, priest and king".'[2] The name Hebrides is a tougher nut to crack. The first written mention is in the *Natural History* of Pliny the Elder, a first-century Roman naturalist and geographer, who described the British coast. After mentioning Orkney, and what are probably the Shetlands, he moves south to 'the Haebudes, thirty in number'.[3] Quite what the name means is anybody's guess, but Mackenzie airs several suggestions, variously linked to Pictish kings, corn, habitation and Saint Bridgit.

The bus has just swooped up a hill. We're now on top of the Druim Dubh, the Black Ridge, and passing the little crofter's cottage where, for several years, we lived on first arriving in Lewis. Straight across the road from our garage there is a fallen stone circle. It was found by families cutting peat for fuel, and is visible partly excavated, just above the hollow where we had our rubbish dump. To think it was a sacred natural site, and that Isobel and I played there, never realising. To think that, even if we'd realised, we'd scarce have cared! To realise, moreover, that this whole chain of Outer Hebridean islands is so thickly freckled with places, stories and archaeological relics of sacred significance – both from the Celtic era and earlier – that it's quite extraordinary, and only superficially known about by most. What's more, it is documented that, from as early as the sixth century, people came from far and wide to these islands, specifically to pursue a spiritual life on the edge of the known world. Adomnán, the seventh-century biographer of Columba, speaks of one pilgrim, whose name wasn't Celtic, stopping at Iona, and asking 'the saint's blessing before setting out with others to seek a place of retreat in the sea'.[4] If there's such a thing as a spiritual gene, or even just a spiritual cultural meme, this is where it's been distilled. Furthermore, to use again that delectable term of maturity from the whisky industry – cask-conditioned!

It's not just what's above the ground or yet-concealed beneath the ever-growing depth of peat. It's also in the stories and the place names. A mile directly south across the moor from our house at Druim Dubh brings you to a loch, Àirigh an t-Sagairt, which translates as the Sheiling (or moorland hut) of the Priest. Go there, and in a sheltered cleft by its south-east end there are the foundation rings of several hut circles. My school friend, Rusty, took me to the spot. Next door is a huge ring of water with a large island in the middle, Loch Orisay. A patient told Dad that monks had once lived there, probably because the Arctic char, a mysterious fish that lurks in shoals deep in some of these waters, were (he thought) in good condition at Lent. The presence of a settlement like Àirigh an t-Sagairt lends credence to that theory. But there's another curious feature of this loch. Its name, *Orasaigh* in the modern Gaelic, suggests a causeway, probably one that once led out to the island. However, the name as printed in the first Ordnance Survey map conveys a very different sense. Completed for this part of Lewis in 1851, and based on local knowledge at the time, it renders it in large lettering as Loch Airidh Sìdeach. This suggests a green grove (or perhaps, a sheiling) of 'silkiness'. The word might be connected to the *sìdh* – meaning peace, or the faeries – thus linking, as we often see elsewhere, to the remnants of an elder faith with roots from times before the monks.[5]

The bus coasts down from the higher ground, passing a cluster of houses at the Leurbost road end. It swoops into a big dipper of a brae and runs past the house we moved to after living at Druim Dubh. Here, at Gleann Mòr, the Big Glen, is the parish doctor's surgery and what was, in our time, the doctor's official residence. In a flash, we career across the Abhainn Ghlas. Before the road was widened and the river straightened, there used to be two dry-stone tunnels carrying the flow underneath the bridge at this point. The one to the north was narrow; that to the south, very narrow indeed. We boys would dare one another to crawl through. It was scary, especially when it rumbled after a spate: dark in the middle, full of cobwebs, dripping moss and dangly things like a rural version of the Ghost Train. At the far end was a deep pool, where we'd spend hour upon hour with our bamboo rods, catching tasty little trout on dangled worms.

Some hold that Abhainn Ghlas means the Silver River. Others, the Grey, or Blue, or Green River. It depends who you ask and when. Why did I have to ask to try and clarify my confusion? The truth is, in those days we were told that Gaelic was a 'backward' and a dying language. An unintended consequence was that, apart from picking up a few words, I never learned the Gaelic when I could have done so. It's one of my few real regrets in life. The Abhainn Ghlas taught us many things as children. Today, I have found its very name to be a perfect illustration of what makes Gaelic such a difficult language to grasp. Or to be more accurate, a fascinatingly different language. To be told that one word can have several seemingly diverse meanings was scarcely an encouragement for a child used to the more prosaic rationale of English. It was only in adulthood that I came to appreciate that Gaelic is a poetic language, rippled through like metamorphic rock with metaphoric glides. A concept, or rather, a feeling like *ghlas* or *glas,* simply doesn't map directly onto Newton's spectrum of seven colours. Instead, the Gaelic reflects the shifting hues of a living and dynamic world. One definition of *Ghlas*, for example, might be: the colour of the moods of light from ever-changing skies, reflected on the surfaces of water.

Gaelic place names often derive from how a place might appear under certain distinctive conditions, or from a particular angle. From Dad's huge plate-glass surgery window, I would watch the upper reaches of the Abhainn Ghlas rise in the west and perhaps break its banks during a day of heavy rain. Later, if there was a ray of evening sun, I'd see the water shine like a mercurial rill from out of its raised position in the dark brown bosom of the moor. That, from my viewing angle, cements the name's translation as the Silver River. Silver-lined, too, after a spate, was my anticipation of a fresh run of little trout – up to quarter pounders – brought down from the stream's source in Loch Thobhta Brìdein. And there we go again! The Loch of Bridgit's Ruin. In the days when these moors were first baptised with names, the folklore tells that Bridgit was the guardian of the isles.[6] Whoever might have been the Bridgit of the ruin, the name points back towards an archetype. 'The parish has a saint's name . . .' – and if you pull in on the left, just before the Achmore road dips down to run along the waterside, you can still find traces of what look like hut circles, and the foundations of a rectangular stone building, on a little green ridge. We can but play a game of speculation if we so care to do, but looking back, the poet in me loves to think that Bridgit's fishes fed my fledgling bones.

Onwards rolls the bus, past the familiar villages of Dad's old practice – Keose, Laxay, Balallan and Airidhbhruaich – the latter meaning 'green grove on a bank', and too remote, in our day, to have been anglicised to something dreadful, like Ari-vrooak.

As Rusty, the red-headed Leurbost blacksmith, would call it, *stranglified!* My own use of these names is horribly inconsistent. I'm of that in-between generation, more immersed in how the English signposts used to be than in their new bilingual versions. Should I be saying Baile Ailein rather than Balallan, to show it means the Village of Allan? Probably, and yet, where to draw the line? It would feel pretentious for me, speaking English, to go round calling Stornoway, Steòrnabhagh, or to really play the trump, and take it back to Stjorn-Vagr.

Soon we're crossing the Aline or Ath Linne bridge that marks the Lewis–Harris border. It's not just the mountains looming up ahead that signal change. There's also a cultural shift, one that runs between two branches of a clan of dual ethnicity. Just over a millennium ago, the Norse came down from Scandinavia and melded with the Gaelic-speaking Celts, whose stock had much in common with the Irish. By the end of the ninth century, the resulting hybrid of the stranger and the heartland people caused them to become known as the *Gall-Gàidheil* (or 'GalGael'). To this day, one of the several names used for the Outer Hebrides, or Western Isles, is *Innse Gall* – the Island of Strangers, the irony being that these have now become the heartland people. Such is the power of fostership or adoption. The island's most common surname is *Macleod*. One branch, *Sìol Thorcaill* (the seed of Torcuil), inherited Lewis. The other, *Sìol Thormoid* (the Seed of Norman) was given Harris.

We've just sped past the head of Loch Seaforth. This huge fjord, gouged out by glaciers, runs like a tunnel for seven miles until it opens to the Minch. The water looks serene enough today, cradled by precipitous hills on either side; but out beyond the sea loch's mouth the Sound of Shiant is feared by mariners, as one of the most storm-stricken stretches of water of the British coast.

Now we're dropping gear, slowing as we grind a flagging way up Clisham, the island's highest mountain. Rising to just over 2,600 feet – some 800 metres – the Norse means Craggy. It commands the eastern flank of the dividing range that makes this island two-for-one. Here, we're into country where the land turns harsh and raw. I take a last glance backwards, out across the vast but soft expanse of Lewis, before we press into this yet more primal land that is the Isle of Harris. Gigantic boulders, ripped out from higher up during the Ice Age, squat like brooding trolls in lorry cabs. Gutters of shattered scree streak down from battered outcrops, into valleys that lie darkened by their depth. Landmarks have names like Creag na h-Iolaire – The Crag of the Eagle.

Along here there's a spot tradition calls the Leathad nan Clacha Mòra, the Slope of Big Stones. I can feel the churn of the story coming on, for these are places peopled through with legends. Here local folklore echoes universal themes that find a localised expression, whether as psychology that contours to the landscape, or landscape that contours the psychology. The tale that belongs to the Leathad nan Clacha Mòra was printed in 1900, by a renowned folklore collector, the Rev. John Gregorson Campbell of Tiree. He called it 'The Young Man in the Fairy Knoll':[7]

> Two young men, coming home after nightfall on Hallowe'en, each with a jar of whisky on his back, heard music by the roadside, and, seeing a dwelling open and illuminated, and dancing and merriment going on within, entered. One of them joined the dancers, without as much as waiting to lay down the burden he was carrying. The other, suspecting the place and company, stuck a needle in the door as he entered, and got away when he liked. That day twelve months he came back for his companion, and found him still dancing with the jar of whisky on his back. Though more than half-dead with fatigue, the enchanted dancer begged to be allowed to finish the reel. When brought to the open-air he was only skin and bone.

Here's far more than just a moral fable about alcoholism. What we're being shown is a portal to the unconscious and progressive depths of meaning. To tradition's ear, this discotheque beneath the ground was a *brugh*: the interior of a *sìthean* ('she-han') – the hollow-hill that's home to the *sìth* or *sìdh*. These are the faeries, the gentry of the countryside. Iron constrains their power of enchantment, probably because, ever since the Iron Age with its axes that hacked down the groves, it's been an element that represents the modern way of things.

Such Rip van Winkle tales are common across the world. I've even spotted one in Surah XVIII of the Qur'an – *Kahf* – The Cave. There, a group of young companions fall asleep for three hundred years inside a cavern. On awakening, they think that but a day has passed, yet find themselves now purified and worthy of the Gardens of Eternity. The Qur'an describes it as a paradise of flowing rivers and clear springs.

Here, the people dress in garments of green silk and brocade. They recline on couches in the gardens, wearing bracelets made of gold.[8] It sounds like Tìr nan Òg, the Celtic Otherworld, the land of the ever-young.

One can either brush aside such tales as child's play, fantasias that gave amusement in the age before TV – or one can seek to penetrate in ways that question the very structures of space and time, exploring consciousness and meaning in the deeper realms of life within the soul. This is what ethnographers call traditional cosmology, the study of the universe and worldviews. One person who would have loved the legend of the Leathad nan Clacha Mòra was the English anthropologist Gregory Bateson. In 1972 he wrote a book that continues to stir interest today, *Steps to an Ecology of Mind*.

Bateson had worked in New Guinea with his first wife, Margaret Mead, the celebrated anthropologist of child development. Their work suggested that to be psychologically healthy, children need to be supported by a rich web of loving relationships. That might not seem like rocket science today, but it was an eye-opener in the war-torn decades of the early to mid twentieth century, especially to the social classes of the stiff upper lip. Bateson's contribution was to suggest that diminished mental health – expressed in alcoholism and schizophrenia in particular – might have roots not just in the genetic make-up, but also in dysfunctional family relationships. The mechanism that he proposed to explain this was the 'double-bind' theory, those crazy situations where you're damned if you do, damned if you don't, and – here's the nub – with no prospect of escape from such damnation.

Although *Steps to an Ecology of Mind* had such a haunting title, Bateson never used the phrase between the covers. It appears as if it was an afterthought. The closest that he came to what might, with hindsight, be understood by way of definition, is in a single sentence where he wrote: '*Mind is immanent in the larger system – man plus environment.*'[9]

I had the opportunity to explore this gnomic statement with his youngest daughter, Nora Bateson, during a visit that she paid to Glasgow. She was previewing a film she'd made about her childhood and her father's life.[10] I was on the discussion panel, and took the chance to ask what she thought he had meant by 'ecology of mind'. She answered with a metaphor from biology. It draws on 'endosymbiotic theory'. *Endo* for within, and *symbiotic*, meaning life forms working together with other life forms. This is where certain cells are thought to have evolved by incorporating parts of other cells. If this is true, such cells are more than just the stand-alone building blocks of biological Lego. Rather, each could be said to be a composite living community within itself. The whole is greater than the sum of its parts. Nora suggested that her father had applied a similar principle to the structure of human consciousness. We're not just individuals, egos running about on legs of meat. We're part of something bigger. As she put it that night in her clinch phrase: 'I think perhaps my father was trying to say *that we don't know what we're inside of.*'

One of my questions to myself had been how to encapsulate what I hoped this walk would be. It helps to have a rubric to get started on. To be able to say to oneself: 'I'm off to try and find the lost Isle of . . .'

Like Bateson, I felt my quest was to explore the mind, but as an *immram* or *iorram* – a word that literally means a 'rowing'. It was used by the Irish monks to describe a pilgrim voyage, usually without a destination, and often with a tendency to slide towards the Otherworld. *Mind*, however, was not the nuance I was after. Mind, in today's mainstream culture, is too bound up with reason and cognition, too much a hall of mirrors that reflects its own consensus trance realities. I was yearning for something deeper. That night at Hôtel InterContinental had left me spooked. The matches burning down. The young man's stultifying boredom. The way that war becomes 'a force that gives us meaning',[11] and yet, when analysed by mind alone, can seem so very logical, all the way until you hit the double-bind of mutually assured destruction.

There must be more than mind alone in that so-very-reasoned sense of things, of Mr Spock's cold Vulcan logic. That was where Nora's words turned a key. That's what opened up a sìthean on the hillside – a connection to a greater and creative sense of living being. *We don't know what we're inside of!* I'll take it for the rudder of my immram: a voyaging through, and voyaging towards, *an ecology of the imagination.*

The bus shifts up a couple of gears as the road levels out now to cruise the contours of the Clisham's middle flanks. What was once so slow and single track is now so fast. Soon, we're cruising on the west bank of a long dark loch, from which a near-sheer wall of mountain rises straight up from the shores. I remember stopping there, as a child, to sail my toy yacht. Dad said there was a story that the water was as deep as the hill was high.

'Really?'

'Well . . . Probably not really, but a way of saying that it's very deep.'

Deep water fascinated me as a child. I'd lie down in the heather, and gaze into a black peat pool that lay behind our old house at Druim Dubh. Often, at night, I'd have a recurrent dream. It would start beside the pool, but somehow this morphed into an underground cavern, with a stream running through. I didn't know where it went, except that it was heading deeper. There'd be just me and little Isobel, the two of us, sitting on the rocks alone. That would be all. Not a nightmare, but slightly ominous, and me aware of having to protect her.

No doubt Freud would have had much to say on womb symbolism. It also shows that our approach to nature was not idealised. But more than that, when I think back to those times, I still feel within my belly a deep draw to nature's depth. It's not just landscape features that are held by places. They also hold human, and more-than-human, embedded presences. I don't mean like 'energies' attached to the rocks. It's a much more subtle basis than such physics-envy New Age literalism. It's something that just happens when space and time slip-slide. Something, more like Bateson's immanence of mind in nature, or Carl Jung's sense of the collective unconscious. I realise, now, that I was raised in a culture where such a reality was very real. Let me give an example that, for third party objectivity, I'll draw from the ethnographic literature:

> There were Gaels alive in the mid-twentieth century who . . . believed implicitly that the ancestral dead in the churchyard were in some sense all still alive there in another dimension of existence . . . I am thinking here of people I knew personally.

So wrote Dr John MacInnes, born on Lewis in 1930, now retired from Edinburgh University's School of Scottish Studies, and widely held to be the leading living authority on Scottish Gaelic culture. I shall be making frequent reference to him as I dip in and out of insights from traditional cosmology. But let me leave that hanging there for now. We've driven past the long dark mountain loch. We're now about to pace its tiny stream, and zoom back down to sea level and to everyday concerns.

Although I didn't know exactly what my walking route would be, I had thought through some options, and would decide according to the weather and my physical capacity. I had in mind to visit three special features of the cultural landscape. One was the island's stone *bothan* (singular, *both*), or 'beehive' sheiling huts. A few can still be found, intact, out in the remotest places. Second, the *teampaill* (singular, *teampall*) or 'temples', this being the name applied to the pre-Reformation chapels that dot the coastal villages, ruined and abandoned to the elements. And then, the *tobraichean* (singular, *tobar*), the drinking wells; and specifically, those reputed to have had associations with 'healing', or, before the Reformation, understood as 'holy' wells.

The bothan lend us, from the Scots and Irish Gaelic, the English words, booth and bothy. The oldest examples are domed, built up of inwardly circling stones. This 'corbelled' architecture led to their visual association with straw beehives. Nearly all such structures have long ago collapsed to tumbled rings amongst the grass and flowers. Be that as it may, their tales of sìth and sìthean echo down the generations, whether in story, poetry or song. Such sheilings sheltered the summer tenders of the cattle, but some would once have been permanent settlements. Others served as refuges for spiritual retreat. Often the place names give a clue, like as we saw with Àirigh an t-Sagairt between Druim Dubh and Leurbost – the Sheiling of the Priest. Tradition holds that some of these date back to the 'Druids'. Indeed, Martin Martin, a physician from the Isle of Skye with a reduplicated name, who wrote a key ethnographic account of the islands at the end of the seventeenth century, called them *Tigh nan Druineach* – Druids' Houses.[12]

A *drùidh* in the Gaelic context was a pre-Christian priest, an adherent of the 'Elder Faith' of our indigenous Old Testament. The Gaelic Bible variously translates the Wise Men of the East, in Matthew 2:1, as *Draoithe, Druidh* or *Druidhean,* and similarly, a fragment of poetry that is attributed to Saint Columba, speaks of Christ as 'my druid'. Many words in Gaelic take 'druid' as their stem. Again, and like with the colour *ghlas,* we see the metaphoric shape-shifting qualities of the language. MacLennan's dictionary links words like *drùdhadh* (pronounced *droo-u*) to qualities of essence, intimacy, influence and intimate penetration in the sense of moisture that seeps everywhere.[13] A wee dram of whisky is a *drùdhag,* the dew is *drùcht* and a teardrop, *drùchd.* The starling, a member of the crow family, is *druid-dubh* – the 'black druid'. There are also phrases like *cainnt drùidhbhteach* as the oratory of a bard or chieftain holding forth, with eloquence such as stirs the essence of a people's spirit, seeping through their bones, and binding them in spiritual, cultural and political cohesion.

My guide to bothan sites, with or without their Druids, was my old friend, the stonemason and antiquarian James Crawford. Seumas, as he prefers to be known. On the telephone before I left home, he'd given me the Ordnance Survey map references to a range of places that I might want to visit. These included The Major, a spectacular fallen standing stone at NB 27038:27875, and the site of a celebrated Last Battle at NB 15769:25169. I wasn't sure if I'd be going in those directions, but what most captured my imagination was a ruined both, one that he called Bridgit's Sheiling, at NB 21970:26890. This, as he described it, was a tumbled ring of stones in a lonely place of unadorned beauty. It was to be found at a rocky green ridge, the Rubha Leathann, that stood a mile north-east from the point at which he recommended that I try to ford the River Grimersta. It was right in the middle of the island.

Variously Bridgit, Brig, Brid, Bride, or most fulsomely *Brighde* – with a breathed *bree-jah* sound, in the Gaelic – she was the patron saint of poetry, healing and the blacksmith's art of purifying metals.[14] She was – and depending who you speak to, still is – a Christian saint, the foster mother of Christ, and a daughter of the Elder Faith, the *Tuatha Dé Danan* or people of the Celtic mother goddess, who in turn became the *Aos Sìth*, the faeries.

'That's where I've got to go and spend a night,' I'd said to Seumas with an almost startling rush of conviction.

'I thought you'd like that one!' he said, and though his voice was coming down the wire, it sounded like he said it with a knowing smile.

If my notes from Seumas Crawford were to guide me to the bothan, his counterpart, my lantern to the temples and wells, was to be the Gaelic broadcaster, educationalist and cultural historian Dr Finlay MacLeod of the village of Shawbost on the West Side of Lewis.

'Doctor Finlay', as he's affectionately known, is the island's most outspoken atheist. Atheists are an endangered species, rare amongst indigenous Hebrideans. Whatever Finlay's version of the irreligionist's creed may or may not be, it hadn't held him back from writing a reverential little pocket guide, *The Chapels in the Western Isles*.[15] It underscores the sheer concentration of these relics of devotion from an age that is no more.

These largely abandoned sites together build up a most intriguing network of locations throughout the length of the Western Isles; the fact that they still exist is surprising in itself, and the fact that they form such an unspoken part of the landscape and the history of the place contrasts with the more strident forms of belief which arrived in the islands during subsequent centuries.

In an equally exquisite companion volume, *The Healing Wells of the Western Isles*, Finlay's spirit again comes through, and that in a manner one might call *drùdhadh* – getting to the essence:

Through the wells we are able to see vestiges of customs which were at one time widespread throughout the land. Water was seen as a live and powerful element, and people were drawn to it although they were also in awe of it. The knowledge they had was knowledge of how they could attain health and wholesomeness through the power associated with water and wells. Although the nature of people's information has changed since those times, there are still some remnants of ancient knowledge in existence, and some of the wells are still known, bearing witness to thought processes that are today not easy to penetrate.

When I was at school, the story went around that Doctor Finlay had done his PhD on Rorschach ink blot tests. I think his studies were actually in wider aspects of educational psychology, but for us the label stuck, as did its improvised methodology. We boys would huddle in the back seat of the bus. We'd spray our exercise books with fountain pens, and use the blots to scry into each other's souls. Strangely enough, our adolescent psyches were configured in remarkably similar ways: exactly as would please old Uncle Freud.

But now my bus is coming down the Clisham. We're coasting to the little town of Tarbert. Here, the first leg of my southbound journey terminates beside the pier.

I buy some fishing tackle from the ironmonger's. It's one of those remarkable olde worlde shops that has everything. Boxes are piled up to the roof and ordered either by their weight, or archaeologically. Anchor chains are on the lowest shelves. Nails, a little higher up. Pity help you if you want a feather duster, unless an Edwardian one lurks behind the stob hammers.

Mindful of Earth Mother back at Café Spirituel, I get some apples and visit the butcher's. I'm not sure if the latter's what she had in mind by 'fresh food', but we've all got our weaknesses, even if for her, perhaps, for tofu. I'm worried about coping with my rucksack's weight as I build up a semblance of fitness. Thankfully, when I present myself to explain this additional, if minor weakness, the kindly woman in the tourist office lets me offload the camping gear that won't be needed this first night, and park it in a black bin bag behind a promotional placard. I pledge to pick it up tomorrow afternoon when walking back this way.

Within an hour I'm on a lively little bus, romping at a giddy rate up and down and all around the switchbacks of the single-track east Harris road. It's a merry banter. The driver shouts back and forth between his passengers, cracking jokes, sharing news, and flipping interchangeably from Gaelic to English.

It sets me thinking of a letter from a tourist that was published in the *Stornoway Gazette*. On one of these buses, halfway to one of the ferry terminals, the poor man realised that he must have dropped his wallet. The driver pulled up to a halt. He got out of his seat, and asked the passengers if anybody would mind if he did the decent thing. Doubling back, there was the wallet, lying in the grass where its owner had embarked. Doubling back again, they made the ferry just in time.

'That would never have happened on the mainland!' blurted the grateful tourist.

'Ah well, you see,' replied the driver, 'You're in the islands now.'

Forty dizzy minutes after leaving Tarbert, my bus re-enters orbit. With a shuddering halt, the door hisses open. I spill out into a lay-by with my now-reduced rucksack, and look up woozily, feeling queasy. There stands Saint Clement's Church of Rodel, my first temple, and the starting point for the journey.

Of all the island's three dozen or so pre-Reformation chapels, only two have been restored: Saint Clement's, here in the far south of Harris, and Teampall Mholuidh, dedicated to Saint Moluag (as it is anglicised), in the far north of Lewis at my walk's intended destination. The church sits beneath the cloud-fringed summit of an iconic mountain, Roineabhal. It sits with its square lookout tower, tight-pressed into a rocky knoll with views down to the southern Hebrides. This, to my eye, in its setting on a rise above the sea, is quite the most exquisite little gem this side of Tuscany. It has been called the Westminster of the Isles, but blessed would be Westminster Abbey were it worthy to be nominated the Rodel of London. I enter by the roadside gate, and leave my rucksack by the lichen-bearded wall. A winding pathway, inset with seashells in the cement between the paving stones, leads up to a heavy-studded oak-wood door. With a lazy creak, it yawns open to my push, and I step through into the half-light.

Gradually my eyes accustom to the dappled shafts of fluted sunshine from the narrow windows. The scent of stone is dank, yet rich like woodland loam. I still can't quite believe that I've arrived. This is somewhere that I've always loved. The walls are lined with grave slabs scrolled with foliage and knotwork, the symbols of both life and life's eternity. The air is reverently still, and, resting underneath the floor, the MacCrimmons: the hereditary pipers to the Macleods of Harris and Dunvegan whose spiritual stronghold this was. It is said that their gift came straight from out the hollow hill, the gliding _siubhal sìth,_ or 'faerie motion', of grace notes played in sheer quicksilver eloquence.

This might be embarrassing to contemporary secularism and to conventional religion alike, but you can't talk about the Sìol Thormoid Macleods without immersion from the outset into faerie lore. For generations, the 'Fairy Cradle Song' has been sung over the newborn sons of their clan chiefs. To this day, the Faerie Flag hangs, for visitors to see, in Dunvegan Castle on Skye, it having been the blanket with which the Otherworld wife of one of the first chiefs covered her little son on the day she was recalled to live amongst her own people. In 1922, the fabric was examined by a certain Mr Wace of the Victoria and Albert Museum in London. He offered his opinion that it was, in all probability, a relic brought back from the crusades.[16]

'Mr Wace,' said the clan chief of the time. 'You think that, but I know that it was given to my ancestor _by a fairy._'

'Sir,' replied Mr Wace, in a masterstroke of English understatement: 'I bow to your superior knowledge.'

Built in its present form in the early sixteenth century, the church's centre-piece is an ornate sculptured tomb, completed in 1528 for the eighth chief, Alasdair Macleod. On account of battle wounds with the Macdonalds of Clanranald, he was nicknamed _Crotach_ – Hunchback – but he eventually grew weary of war, and is thought to have lived out his days in spiritual reflection at Rodel.

Here is the finest piece of medieval sculpture in the Hebrides. A blazing heavenly sun shines out from just above the centre. Above that, stands Christ, crowned and crucified, with figures gathered at the foot of the cross. To the flanks are the four evangelists. Each is stylised with his totem mascot: Matthew's angel, Mark's lion, Luke's ox and the great eagle of Saint John. The scenes below include an exquisitely executed _birlinn_, a Hebridean longship, and a troop of deer, portrayed with all the natural poise of great cave paintings. Around the perimeter are effigies of the saints, with names or symbols to identify. James or _Jacobi_ has two. One is probably James the brother of Jesus and first bishop of Jerusalem, to whom the Epistle of Saint James near the end of the Bible is attributed. The other is unquestionably Saint James the Greater. This is shown by the scallop in his halo. I'd noticed an abundance of the shells of the scallop's smaller siblings, the cockle, in the pathway that led up to Saint Clement's from the gate. _La Coquille St Jacques_, as the scallop is called in France, is the symbol of pilgrimage. Its radial ribs converge towards the hinge, like pilgrim paths all leading to the sacred place. Returning back by those same routes again, the pilgrim spreads out blessing, far into the world.

A flight of steps leads up into the tower. I climb, and from the top the island-stippled Sound of Harris and beyond reveals itself. This is a sacred landscape, a rosary in geography. Few if any of these places, each one of them a little world and mostly uninhabited, do not boast at least one temple, holy well, standing stone, set of prehistoric cup marks hollowed into rock, or a place name that bears witness to some distant saint, portentous happening, or antique tradition of blessedness. Forty miles out lies St Kilda, a part of the parish of Harris, with temples dedicated to Saint Brianan, Saint Columba and Christ. In 1758, the Rev. Kenneth MacAulay wrote that one of its four holy wells, Tobar nam Buadh – The Well of the Virtues – was believed to cure distempers, deafness and every nervous disease. It was, he said, the people's 'constant practice to address the Genius of the place with supplication and prayer', and to offer tokens of the lowest monetary value, such as 'very frequently the whole expense of sacrifice was no more than one of the little common stones that happened to be in the Pilgrim's way'.[17] In other words, what mattered was not the monetary value, but what the people carried in their hearts.

Closer in is Pabbay – Priest's Island – with temples consecrated to both the Virgin Mary and Saint Moluag, he having been a Celtic saint who died in 592 and left his mark all over the West Highlands. Pabbay's people were famed for their illicit whisky. There's at least one Hebridean storyteller who still entertains his visitors with the tales, such as how the doughty wives of Pabbay would get the better of the excise man.[18] The earthiness of everyday life interwove intimately with these people's spiritual lives; but it was not to last. In 1846, the entire population of Pabbay was cleared away by the landlord, turning their pastures over to a commercial sheep farm.

South of Pabbay are the isles of North and South Uist, and these, the home to many wells and several temples. The most notable of the latter is Teampall na Trianaid, Trinity Temple at Carnish. This was built in the thirteenth century by a woman, Beathag, the daughter of Somhairle, the Lord of the Isles. A century and a half later, it was substantially repaired by another woman of formidable ilk, Amie NicRuairidh. It was also a medieval university. A modest plaque, pinned to the ruins, marks the local tradition that it was here the acclaimed philosopher, Duns Scotus (c. 1270–1308), had studied.

The little islands all around are similarly saturated in the twilight of sanctity. The Monach Islands or Heisgeir, for example, are known as Heisgeir nan Cailleach on account of their nunnery. It had a long association with Iona, and right up until the Reformation the sisters continued to pray for the world by the light of their lamps, fuelled by seal-oil. Today, there are no longer any people; but there's a lighthouse that, in its own way, prays for shipping. Boreray was the burial ground of Celtic monks from north of Eigg. Once when I was being driven in the taxi of Alda Ferguson of Lochmaddy, he stopped and pointed out this double emerald hummock that lounges in the surf some three miles out into the ocean. 'That island,' the old man announced, drawing on a local tradition, 'is the birth place of the grandfather of Neil Armstrong, the first man on the moon.'[19] I just thought to myself – if that's true, then these people know a thing or two about pilgrimage.

Coming back up into the Sound of Harris, four miles off Rodel sit a pair of islands, fringed with ivory sand, called Ensay and Killegray. The latter means the place of the monastic 'cell' or church. Again, place names bear enduring witness to sheer spiritual intensity. Teampall na h-Annaid – the Temple of the Monastery or Mother Church. Tobair na h-Annaid – the Well of the Mother Church. When I was a teenager, the South Harris doctor Angus MacKinnon took me out there in his boat. Some time later, he showed me a child's skull that he'd found washed out from the wave-encroached cemetery on Killegray. He placed the white sphere in my hands. I felt the sadness surging. For the first time in my life, I was looking into tragic death, straight through the eyes. 'It's all right,' Angus said. The shadow side of life was there, but also its absorption in some greater whole of being.

Tradition holds that the Druids were the first here at Saint Clement's, then the Columban monks from Ireland and Iona, and in their footsteps, the Culdees or *Céli Dé* – the Servants of God – who were noted for their simple lifestyles, their pastoral dedication to the poor and sick, their Sabbath observance, and for their love of sacred chant and hallowed song.[20] Then came change. The brutal Norman invasion of England in 1066 caused the Hungarian-born Margaret of Wessex to flee to Scotland. There she married the king, Malcolm Canmore, and this either made for, or coincided with, a turning point for the Scottish church. Gaelic liturgies started to be replaced with Latin ones. The localised basis of authority that had characterised the Celtic Church, with its nod to Ireland, began to bow distinctively to Rome. This wasn't all down to Margaret's personal influence. Similar changes were also happening in

Ireland, the driving force being the Gregorian Reforms that strengthened the hand of Rome.

In 1093, Malcolm was killed in battle. According to the Irish annals, Margaret died a few days later from her sorrow. A pious woman, she was later canonised. Their youngest son, David, was sent away, at the age of nine, to be raised in the Norman court of England. When his brother, Alexander I, died in 1124, the adult David returned and, in a bloody power struggle, seized the kingdom with the backing of Henry I of England, a son of William the Conqueror. David went on to introduce feudalism into Scotland. Land was given to Anglo-Norman friends who had helped him. These became the rootstock of many of 'Our Scots Noble Families'.[21] Their sense of underlying Christian cohesion as brothers in arms, notwithstanding all the internecine feuding, had been strengthened by the practice of 'taking up the cross' during the First Crusade of 1096–99.

So began the long erosion of Scotland's customary system of tenure, where the land, especially in Gaelic-speaking areas, was held by the chief on behalf of the clan as a whole. While he was consolidating his power and rendering Scotland a coherent nation, David radically accelerated his mother's innovation of introducing the European religious orders. While the facts are limited and much debated, this probably subsumed the Céli Dé and remnants of the original Celtic Church. David set up (in the course of making land grants to various European orders) some two dozen Augustinian priories. According to the Old (or First) Statistical Account of 1792, Rodel was handed to the Canons Regular of Saint Augustine in 1128.[22]

It would seem that this settlement settled down, and held sway until the Protestant Reformation took grip in Scotland in 1560. It was to the Reformation that Doctor Finlay had referred, when he dropped a mention, in his little book of chapels, to 'the more strident forms of belief which arrived in the islands during subsequent centuries'.[23]

Scotland's pioneering reformer, John Knox, had taken his lead from John Calvin's Geneva in implanting the Presbyterian version of Reformed religion. It was, at least until relatively recently in Scotland, a harsh approach. Calvin, for example, had denounced religious art as 'brutish stupidity'.[24] His best friend, the iconoclast William Farel, went around Geneva stirring up mobs that persecuted priests, harangued the nuns to marry, enforced attendance at their interminable sermons, robbed religious houses, smashed the statues of the saints and icons, whitewashed over the murals, and tossed the bells out of their belfries. The latter, according to the detailed chronicle of a Poor Clare nun, included melting down the fragments to make them into weapons.[25]

It is no longer possible to be sure what may or may not have happened to echo all of this in the Outer Hebrides. There is, I've heard it said, 'a black hole' in the post-Reformation oral memory. What is beyond dispute is that every one of the *teampaill,* the pre-Reformation churches, fell into ruin. Whether some of these were also racked – that is to say, wilfully destroyed – is a more variegated question.[26] But for now, I must take leave from this sacred place. I can hear voices, and as I alight from the tower's flight of steps, I nod a silent acknowledgement to a group of visitors who are wandering around with cameras flashing.

Turning towards the oaken door to take my exit, I glance up at a large white marble tablet that is set at head height into the wall. Its iron fastening studs have corroded, tarnishing the surface with a rusty stain. The inscription, discreetly couched in Latin, signalling only to the few, bears ominous testimony:[27]

> This sacred edifice, the very walls of which had been scarcely spared through the fury attendant upon religious change, which in its universal pillage devastated everything, and levelling the adjoining convent of friars and nuns to the ground, consecrate to the piety of his ancestors in former times, to God and St Clement, after having been for now over two hundred years roofless and neglected, was repaired and adorned . . . by Alexander Macleod of Harris in 1787 AD.

On the one hand, the eighth chief's tomb was left intact. At least that wasn't desecrated. But looking at the wider history of that era, what was such Reformation fury all about? What kind of problems in theology leave it vulnerable to associations with violence, and therefore, to ongoing problems within some religions? These are questions that I want to muse on as I walk. Questions that are not just historical, but also, and for our own times too, 'attendant upon religious change'.

I take a final glance down the length of Saint Clement's, then step outside to face the brightness of the daylight. The door draws slowly closed behind me. Its iron latch drops into place, a farewell clunk resounding to the ear.

3

BLUE MOUNTAIN HARE

I have a couple of respects to pay before leaving the churchyard, and a cemetery is a place of such unlikely bedfellows. Set halfway up the south face of the tower is one: an astonishing stone-crafted figure, the Sheila-na-Gig of Rodel. The lady crouches there, as if she's giving birth. Her womanhood is unconcealed in all its fullness. She nurses in her arms a heavily eroded figure that looks more like an animal, a lamb or seal, than the babe one might expect.

Only speculation surrounds the meaning of these peculiar features of medieval church architecture. They are found mainly in Ireland and the West of Scotland, including the isles of Eigg and Iona, and one suggestion is that they're like gargoyles, intended to frighten away the faithful from the allures of sexual love. If that's the case, then for me the Rodel 'Sheila' doesn't cut the bromide! Another suggestion is that they're fertility symbols. To me, she's just beautiful. Her presence tunes me to the note of mystical religion; to the way erotic love becomes a metaphor of Heaven. It's there in Hinduism, with the union of Shiva and Parvati, the Daughter of the Mountains. There, too, in Tantra, with Sky Dancer, Yeshe Tsogyel, whose consort, Padma Sambhava, carried Buddhism from the Swat Valley to Tibet. And although it is a matter about which few sermons are preached, it's in the Bible too. Voluptuously so, in the Song of Solomon. There's even a chapter in the Book of Job that, twice, pictures aspects of the Creation as breaking forth from out God's cosmic 'womb'.[1] Quite where that leaves the gendering of the deity, might well be pondered.

An inscription found above the entrance to some churches, reads: *This is the house of God and the gate of Heaven*.[2] Perhaps I'd better leave my speculations there. Suffice to say that the mystics, like the poets, have always been a risqué bunch, which brings me to my next stop. Underneath the south transept window rests the Rodel-born seventeenth-century bard, Mary Macleod, or Màiri Nighean Alasdair Ruaidh. It's said that Màiri was remembered into the early twentieth century as if she'd ambled through the village only yesterday, tap-tap-tapping along the road with her trademark silver-topped walking stick.

It was she who was chosen to sing the 'Fairy Cradle Song', or 'Cradle Spell', for a newborn infant son of Chief MacLeod. She rests in the church vaults, but lying face down. Why so, is much debated. The simple version is that she was a witch. However, that would be hard to square with such a sanctified place of burial. Locally, I've heard it suggested that she'd told too many lies in her poetry praising the chief of Macleod. She asked to be buried face down, 'so that her lying tongue would not be pointing to heaven'.[3] There are other views. Was it that her feisty nature had caused offence? The Gaelic scholar and singer Dr Anne Lorne Gillies points out that Mary was a powerful figure, a charismatic poet, but she was not a member of the elite bardic order. Indeed, 'she was not even a man'.[4]

Another, and a very lovely perspective on her, comes from the Rev. Dr Kenneth Macleod of the Isle of Eigg. His father's people had been from the north of Skye and were steeped in all the olden lore of clan Macleod. The Reverend Kenneth would have enjoyed some of today's scholars, who point out that Gaelic had no native word for a 'witch', and that women of such bearing as Màiri might better be understood as powerful shamans.[5] Indeed, Kenneth seized 'witch' from out of the mouths of churlish patriarchs, and gently cast it back, writing in 1927:[6]

> Such as wish to understand the Scottish Gael, what he is and what he is not, should study our witches as well as our saints. The responsible witches of Gaeldom were not the weaklings who are merely bad-hearted, or are trick-sters in self-defence. They were rather highly-gifted women who loved being alive, and who won their place by force of character, and by right of service . . . The only vice in them which would, perhaps, have shocked the saints was their keen sense of humour.

His book, *The Road to the Isles*, was an anthem to the old Hebridean ways. In taking special care to laud the spiritual élan of women, it devotes a full chapter to Màiri, this Daughter of Red Alastair. Kenneth concurs that the bard was buried face down, but not from any excess need for penance. Neither does he mince his words in what he goes on to say about her. Already, he would have been feeling the challenges to his style of 'romantic' Celtic 'twilightism' that set in following the disillusion of the First World War.[7] This accelerated through the century, often in a sceptical alliance between secular figures and the conservatively religious, who either hadn't experienced his world, or if they had, suspected it of being backward, pagan, and even Catholic, as are the southern Hebrides. This might explain the urgent tone of Kenneth's rallying call to hold the faith.[8]

> There is a bidding to which the Gael is never false, the bidding which puts him under the spells. An Islesman is under spells both to his heart and to his head to give love to Mary Macleod, the most fascinating figure in Gaelic poetry from the beginning of the seventeenth century to a century on which fate has not yet put a name. A woman not of the schools but of herself, and fond of taking her own way when her own way seemed the best . . .
>
> Mairi, Daughter of Alastair Rua, sleeps face downward, by the Church of Saint Clement, in Rodel of Harris, the Iona of her clan. 'Not on the clouds would my eyes be, O kinsfolk,' said she in the parting, 'but on Rodel of Harris.' Her thought was, perhaps, the thought of St Bride, the Foster-mother [of Christ], even as her blood was the blood: *Beautiful the cloud on high, my children, but more beautiful still the shower which falleth, giving growth to the corn and milk to the cattle, for little children.*

If this version is correct, it seems to me that Màiri is reminding us that Rodel is a place where Heaven grounds itself on Earth. 'Thy kingdom come . . . on Earth as it is in Heaven' – and those petitions of the Lord's Prayer, so cogent in these times of ecological predicament, preached by the post-mortem yogic posture of a so-called witch!

I'd like to feel that Kenneth will be one of my unseen companions on this walk. In the first half of the twentieth century he was considered to have been the greatest living authority on Gaelic traditions.[9] He was born on Eigg, and during the 1990s this island became the focus of my work with land reform, the residents eventually succeeding in bringing it into community ownership after a six-year-long battle with landed power.[10]

Kenneth ended his ministry at the Church of Scotland on the Isle of Gigha, and died in 1955. Both that island's parish church and Iona Abbey have stained glass windows to commemorate his life. When Vérène and I first visited Gigha, we marvelled at the wonder of this memorial, crafted in the manner of the Celtic Revival. Threaded in with knotwork symbols and a prominent white seagull, are the troika of Irish and Scots Gaelic saints: Patrick, the one-time slave, conferring blessing; Columba, in a birlinn on his immram voyage to Iona; and Brighde, Shepherdess of the Flocks, cherishing a lamb. The infant Christ has arms outstretched upon a cross ablaze with golden flames of love. The same rare portrayal of an infant crucified, yet glorified, also hallows the altar of the Catholic church on Eigg. An English inscription hails Kenneth as a 'preacher, pastor, poet'. Alongside, there is a treasured Gaelic saying:[11]

> *Thig crìoch air an t-saoghal*
> *Ach mairidh gaol is ceòl*
> (The world will come to an end
> But love and music will endure)

As we both soaked in the window's beauty that day, a beam of sunshine burst in through the glass. The colours quickened into vibrant life, and to Vérène's astonishment, and my embarrassment, I just burst into tears. It felt as if I'd seen a glimpse of all that has been lost from the deepest spiritual culture of the Hebrides. And yet – this was the strangest thing – those very tears were rippled through with joy. It was as if a silver pool had spilled and overwhelmed my disconsolation, lifting it to rapture.

I later learned of what tradition calls 'the carrying stream'. Not for the first time had I felt propelled along by its unending current.[12] John Lorne Campbell of Canna often said that that whereas the modern mind exists on a horizontal plane, 'dominated by scientific materialism and a concern with purely contemporary happenings', the consciousness of the Gaelic mind may be described as existing in a vertical plane, 'possessing historical continuity and religious sense . . . an ever-present sense of the reality and existence of the other world of spiritual and psychic experience'.[13] That was how it felt that day. The experience left me with a sense of calling to unspecified work ahead, an Otherworld path to walk and share into the world.

Well! Better be getting walking after all this talking. I'm going to spend tonight with my old friend John MacAulay of Flodabay or Fhleoideabhaigh, a boatbuilder and tradition bearer. His several books include a study of the birlinn as indigenous ship craft, not to be confused, he says, with Roman galleys; and *Silent Tower*, which is the definitive history of Saint Clement's. I'd said to him and Jane that I'd be there around six. I don't carry a watch, and my phone is off to save the battery, but judging by the sun it must by now have clocked three.

I lift 'Osprey', as I'm calling my rucksack, onto my back. That's the brand I'd purchased for the trip, not that I'd gone after sponsorship or anything. Thank goodness all my heavy stuff got left behind at Tarbert. This next twenty-four hours can be a gentle wooing of our new relationship.

The galvanised churchyard gate clanks closed – and finally I am walking.

'Just feel it,' I'm saying to myself. 'Just feel these footsteps. On the road. Actually walking!'

Rodel glen is rich and green, thanks to a seam of crystalline limestone that moderates the acidity of the peat. The road runs east, then sharply to the north, before narrowing to single-track with passing places. Spring is late this year. The heather's still in browns and greys and rattled from the winter gales. Today, it's breezing from the south-east. That's great. It cools the sunshine on my back and gives a gladness to my stride. That's also why I'm walking from the south to north. The position of the sun, and the prevailing southerly winds.

Across the Minch I can see the Isle of Skye, and, now and then, I maybe glimpse the Shiant Islands. Na h-Eileanan Seunta in the Gaelic – the Enchanted or the Sacred Isles. What a name – and where, you have to ask, would it have come from? And then, that crazy stretch of water! The Sound of Shiant in English, but in Gaelic, Sruth nam Fear Gorma. The Straits of the Blue Men – and they the oceanic faerie lads that dance to every storm.

One of these volcanic outcrops that comprise the Shiants is called Eilean Mhoire (or Mhuire). A late seventeenth-century traveller recorded that it had a chapel, 'dedicated to the Virgin Mary', and an early eighteenth-century map shows it as 'St Maries Isle'. [14] Mhoire (pronouned 'Vor-u') is the honorary equivalent of Màiri, used specifically for Mary as the mother of Christ. It makes me think of lines from Eliot's *Four Quartets*, to me the greatest mystical poem in the English language, though Hugh MacDiarmid's *On a Raised Beach* comes a very close second. [15]

> Lady, whose shrine stands on the promontory,
> Pray for all those who are in ships, those
> Whose business has to do with fish . . .

Good start, for a poacher's pilgrimage. I'll just leave out the verse that follows: '. . . and those concerned with every lawful traffic'!

There is such a lazy feel to this road. Only the occasional car slips by and even these go slowly. My pace is settling to a rhythm. My eyes are resting mainly on road. A road is such a physical thing. It flows towards me like a tarry river set with flotsam shards. The ubiquitous greys of Lewisian gneiss. The orange glints of feldspar and dirty-yellow stains of iron. The gemlike sparkle of black hornblende chips and snowy flecks of quartz.

MacDiarmid was supposedly an atheist. Whether or not that was so, I worship at his church.

> Let men find the faith that builds mountains
> Before they seek the faith that moves them . . .
> These stones go through Man, straight to God, if there is one . . .
> What happens to us
> Is irrelevant to the world's geology
> But what happens to the world's geology
> Is not irrelevant to us.

Climbing higher now, and the heather and the red deergrass yield to bare grey rocky beds, gnarled and wrinkled like pegged-out sheets of rhinoceros hide. I'm on the flanks of Roineabhal. The slope rises sharply upwards as a moonscape to my left. This peak, reclining out of view, has meant so much to me. We'd fought a battle in the 1990s. It stopped the mountain from being turned into the biggest roadstone quarry in the world. For sixty years, its belly would have been ripped out by thirty-six tons of explosive a week. Ten million tons of rock a year, crushed for paving motorways in the already over-developed south.

John MacAulay was the island's representative in the matter. He'd been elected to chair the Quarry Benefit Group, set up to look at the upsides – and the downsides – that the proposal might have brought to Harris. My part had been to bring the Mi'Kmaq War Chief of the time from Canada. He had stopped a similar superquarry on Kluscap, his people's sacred mountain in Nova Scotia. Stone Eagle was his name, and he told the government planning inquiry that we had to call a halt to such trashing of the planet. 'If we fail to do so, Mother Earth will cleanse herself of the offending organism that is killing her. This is our teaching.'

A leading environmental educator, Dr Robbie Nicol, who heads up the Institute for Education, Teaching & Leadership at Edinburgh University, emailed me out of the blue recently. He's one of a growing number that I hear from who'd been drawn, he said, to make 'a pilgrimage' to the summit.

> I say, *pilgrimage,* because I know how hard so many people worked to avoid the development of this mountain. It is achingly beautiful. The view down into the *coire* is unlike any other I've experienced, and I felt compelled to write.

Suddenly I freeze. A grassy gully runs up the side of Roineabhal, just past a solitary modern bungalow at the turnoff down to Lingerabay.

That looks like a *hare* amongst the rocks! Either that, or a huge rabbit.

The only island species is the Blue Mountain Hare, *Lepus timidus.* The habitat is right, but I've never previously seen one. 'Blue', they call it – said to be the tint the coat can take at certain times of year. Reminds me how the naturalist Frank Fraser Darling observed that mountains, too, 'become Highland blue, a deep ineffable shade.' Oh my! What a contribution to the artist's palette. Highland blue. Ineffable. That's how the mountains are today, the compass of the oceans too.

While brown hares came to Britain with the Romans, only the blue is truly native. Julius Caesar said the Celtic Britons held them to be sacred. *She* – as gendered in the folklore – is a witch disguised. She, true nature wild and free. She, the shape-shifting shaman – Is she human? Is she animal? Does it matter? – whose nest is called a 'form', and whose spiritual form is the walker between the worlds.

The quickest way for an amateur like me to tell a hare from a rabbit is by the long, black-tipped ears. I slowly reach to Osprey for my binoculars. But I'm spotted. She louches off, and disappears amongst a pile of boulders. But she's given me a metaphor. I've been thinking about the stages of this walk. Blue Mountain Hare. Here's *blue* along this smoky azure south-east Harris coast. Tomorrow night, into the *mountain* passes for several days. And if I get to next week, I'll play the mad March *hare* – well, maybe stretching it to May in these boreal parts – coursing through the villages of north-west Lewis.

I stand and peer through the glasses for several minutes. Not a movement. Nothing. Only Màiri Nighean Alasdair Ruaidh, a parting nod from hefted haunts on Roineabhal, nestling down into the crevices of my mind.

Here you'd hardly think that the Ice Age ended ten thousand years ago. The rocks are scored by great striations, etched like chalks on screeching blackboards trapped beneath the glacier's long-sliding gait. Hardy alpines – blue, white and yellow come the summer – have made their homes in soil-filled chinks that give their roots a stony toe grip from the gales. Everywhere are rills that seep from crumpled folds, deepen into pools, and, when the year warms up, will teem with water beetles, dragonflies and long-legged water skimmers.

I'm well into my stride now, and the road traipses down a long curved dip to pass across a bridge. I step aside and slip down beneath the hand-wrought layers of stone. Fast flowing water is my friend, and I lie down to sup my fill from Abhainn a' Coire – the Stream of the Cauldron. I love wild water's peaty taste – it's what we always drank as kids. Up and off again, climbing the hill, replaying all the switchbacks of the little bus in elegant slow motion. Goodness! How that seems like days ago, but scarce an hour or two's slipped past.

Now, I'm heading down from Roineabhal, slipping off the north end, and it leads into a very different scene. Coming up, I sight the staggered crossroads of the village of Aird Mhighe. Here, it's all change. Instead of the plant life struggling to hold on, the land is fertile. Either there's been a shift of underlying strata that's changed the soil type, or, more likely, it's the seaweed, blown up from the bay, and rotting to yield nutrients. The bare mountain, too, has fallen into relief behind me. A gentleness has settled into place. Instead of sheets of flayed rhinoceros, the ice down here has rounded off and polished the bedrock into strange humps. The French call them *roches moutonnées* – mutton or sheep rocks. In some parts of the world, the bigger ones would be called whalebacks. That's what I'm seeing as my mind, in playful mode, morphs the geology into animals of stone. I'm in amongst a pod of whales, fresh swum from out the studio of Henry Moore. They breach, and lounge, and lunge in sumptuous curves upon the surface of a bright green sea of short-cropped meadow grass.

I step aside from off the road again, and rest my back against one of these behemoths. It's been harpooned! A metal pin, staining the stone with rusty blood, anchors an iron ring. Of course! This is a crossroads from before the days of cars. This is where the youth would meet to dance away the evenings, maybe with a pony tethered. This is where you'd tie your cow while asking of a passer-by the perennial question: 'What's fresh?' And if there's nothing fresh, then there might be some sharing of the tales brought back from whaling fleets, or from the herding in the hills. And if the work is done, and leisure offers time to loaf at ease awhile, then maybe there'll be hoary tales of long ago. And if, instead of going north today, you went west. If you went not in a car, but by foot, or ever so gently on a bicycle. If you headed inland for a mile or two, past little lochs that shimmer in the summer's sun with water lilies, and the hoary dance of interstellar filigree of the bitter bog bean blossom, then you'd reach a loch called Langabhat. The Norse means 'lang-vat' or 'long water', but don't be confusing this Loch Langabhat with the other, even longer one, that stretches up through southern central Lewis. This is the Langabhat of Harris, more economical in scale, yet still quite long enough to span, from east to west, the middle half of southern central Harris.

A dearer little road that carries you there could scarce be found, and it was in *Crotal and White,* his homage to a crofting childhood, that the late BBC journalist Finlay J. MacDonald described a boyhood excursion to that very loch.[16] He speaks of the Isle of Harris as a place that 'wove a spiritual and physical magic as I grew up with it'. He adds, lest any latter-day churl be listening in: 'If it all sounds idyllic, it's because it was to the boy who I was.' And he tells of a tiny island on Langabhat called Eilean na Caillich.[17] Now, the *cailleach* – *caillich* being the possessive case – is an old woman. However, there's an older and more particular usage of the word that implies a *holy* old woman, and, according to tradition, there had been a nunnery attached to Saint Clement's. For whatever reason – some say she'd been banished, but maybe she just wanted peace from the priests – one of the sisters had built her hermitage on this wee island in Loch Langabhat. She'd get to it by a semi-submerged causeway. It's still there to this day, even shown on the oldest maps.

All through Finlay's childhood, he had been 'absolutely and firmly forbidden' to go to Eilean na Caillich. However, when boys reach a certain age – at least, the crofter boys in these parts – they get fired up with a kind of derring-do. So off he went one day, setting out two miles across the moor from his home at Scarista, supposedly on a fishing trip. Always be suspicious of a man you meet out in the wilds, who says he's 'only' on a fishing trip!

So, out he goes, gingerly edging his way across the causeway's rocking stepping stones, using his fishing rod as a steadying staff – and halfway over, what does he hear, but this long, slow, eerie whine . . .

Aaawwwooooo. . . .

And he's looking back, and it's his dog! The hairs of his tail and ruff are standing on end like the bristles of brush, and he's baying like a beast demented. *Demented,* I'll tell you, as if he's been touched by the Hound of the Baskervilles itself.

Well, Finlay can't turn back at this stage. If he did, he knew he'd only have to do it another time, or else he'd lose something in himself. So he presses on, and he gets to the island, and sure enough, there are the outlines of a hermit's cell, a doorway and its long lintel stone.

'And then I heard a voice,' wrote Finlay in his book. 'Or rather, felt a voice. It came from my ears but at the same time it came from within my head. It said, *Put off thy shoes from off thy feet for the place whereon thou standest is holy ground.*'

The boy dropped his fishing rod and bolted. He splashed back across the causeway, tore up the hills with his dog close to heel, and ran, non-stop, all the way home to Scarista.

Of course, everybody knew everything in those days. They didn't watch the television, they watched the sea and hills. They watched each other like they'd watch the weather, both on the outside and the inside.

That night at the dinner table, his father asked what he'd done with the day. But it wasn't anger that flashed in those eyes when he learned that his son had been to Langabhat. It was a twinkle.

'Did you go to Eilean na Caillich, by any chance?'

'Yes.'

'Well, you had to – some day!' said the old man. 'I suppose the surest way of making you go, was by telling you not to.'

As Finlay grew up, he learned that other villagers had also made their secret pilgrimages. Each tale of derring-do had its own circumstances, but:

> What was interesting – and why I wouldn't go back – was that one sentence was common to all the stories. *Put off thy shoes from off thy feet for the place whereon thou standest is holy ground.*

Beyond Aird Mhighe, leaving Roineabhal and the whales behind, I come into a genial and well-lived-in land. The road meanders over rocky bluffs. It skirts around the curves of little bays with causeways and box-girder bridges that span the frequent inlets of the sea. There are houses here, or rather, homes. Fields and gardens, old tractors kept for spares, boats pulled up and lobster pots, pastures grazed by sheep and pecked by flocks of hens and ducks, and sometimes a gaggle of hissing geese.

I pass a family couple, sitting on their veranda, a hundred or two hundred yards away. Their children all come running out and stare. I wave, and they return the gesture, giggling now. Oh yes, I know their game! I'll be the first of this new season's crop. We used to call it 'Spot the Tourist'.

Over the brow of a rise and a great gaunt shape looms up, another of those breaching whales, but just the whitened ribs and spine. Alongside stands a barrel-shaped shed. It's made from those curved sheets of corrugated iron, like the kind you see left over from the war, when Rodel was a pioneering early-warning radar base. And you know, I like that. My mind could play games with that one! Rodel still is an early-warning radar base; the spiritual life of Celtic times, not just a relic from the past, but missile incoming.

A Saltire, Scotland's flag, the cross of Saint Andrew – a fisherman, feminist and pacifist who convinced Roman soldiers to disarm – flutters idly from a pole above the shed.[18] A wooden sign over the arched doorway, reads 'Boatbuilder'. I have arrived at John MacAulay's workshop. And the roadside skeleton? That's his latest venture. An ocean-going sailing boat, set to an ancient design, taking shape in ribs of larch tongued into spine of oak.

It has taken me nearly four hours to go a mere seven miles. But so what? I'm here! John had seen me coming and, from his house across the other side of the road, stands beaming at an open door.

4

THE ELDER OF ROINEABHAL

Were there such a home as that of a seafaring Amish farmer, this stone cottage would be it. Built by his father, shared with his wife Jane and her teenage daughter, Ella, a blazing fire is the focal point, with armchairs and a sofa curled around its hearth, and not a television in sight to steal away attention. A fiddle hangs from the wood V-lining of one wall, a navigation chart of local waters on another, and, perched on a shelf, sits an old brass sextant. If it sounds set for *National Geographic* – too late – they've already been here.

He's a wiry, late sixty-something, my friend, arms like the hawsers of an ocean-going tug, blizzard-whipped white curls and a slight moustache. His piercing blue eyes convey a capacity to enchant that, according to Vérène, must have melted many a heart down the years.

'I've a bit of news for you, John,' I say, as we settle down to a massive pan of butter-fried scallops, dived for off the bottom of a local sea loch. 'I've been speaking at a conference of Lafarge, and I've got the inside story. From the horse's mouth!'

Lafarge is the biggest cement and roadstone company in the world. Based in France, they had swallowed up Redland, the smaller English company that had originally devised the scheme for blowing up Roineabhal. My having called Chief Stone Eagle over from Canada, inviting him to bring his sacred pipe (but to leave the AK-47 behind), had lent a bit of oomph to the campaign. But there'd been many hands to the pumps. Between the lot of us, we managed to stall the granting of planning permission to the point that Redland's share price had dived into decline. That was when the French swooped in with their predatory takeover. It felt like a masterstroke of karmic retribution. Redland lost all control of its ship. Through the intervention of a French banking executive, Thierry Groussin, I went to Paris and negotiated what we called the 'dignified exit strategy' – of withdrawing from the project.[1]

But there was a *quid pro quo*. Lafarge pointed out that we all use quarry products, even me, and therefore asked me to serve on their Sustainability Stakeholder Panel, 'to help us understand how to run our business better'. In consultation with my campaigning colleagues I'd agreed, but on an unpaid basis so as not to risk misunderstanding. So began a remarkable experience – I watched them radically cut their carbon emissions per ton of cement produced, build up expertise in conservation ecology for old quarry sites, recognise the UN Declaration on the Rights of Indigenous Peoples, and shift the axis of their business from an emphasis on resource extraction to what they called 'sustainable building solutions', based on developing efficient new materials and processes.[2]

'So what did you learn?' John asks, as we sit around the fire, and he pours us each a glass of wine. It was our first chance to talk in depth about it all.

'Well!' I say, with an almost boyish enthusiasm towards the older man. 'You know how our weakest link in the whole saga was all those unemployed guys who'd hoped to get a job for life on Harris?'

He stops me in my tracks. He says stiffly: 'I never saw that as a weak link.'

'I never, ever, trusted Redland's claims,' he continues, poking the fire.

'You know, Alastair. Those modern plants are so highly mechanised that they employ very few people. They'd have brought in their own specialists. All that Harris would have got is a few low-paid jobs for digger drivers and cleaners. The place itself – the place that our fathers and our mothers handed down to us in trust for the future – that would have been shipped away, from beneath our very feet.'

He pauses, visioning the scene.

'Shipped away . . . like the people themselves were shipped off in the Clearances.'

It hadn't been just the illicit distillers of Pabbay who were dispatched on emigrant ships, sent to feed the industrial revolution in emerging cities, or lined up as imperial cannon fodder. The Highland Clearances of the eighteenth and nineteenth centuries had had a very much wider geographical spread.

'I know,' I say. 'Lafarge's executives confirmed all that. Mostly low-grade jobs for the locals. But what's more, they never intended to open up a quarry in the foreseeable future anyway. They just wanted to get the planning consent *in principle*, so that they'd have it as a land bank on their balance sheet.'

'Just as we'd always suspected!' he said. 'But why did you say you thought the jobs argument had been our weakest link?'

'It was just . . . the thought of all the hopes and expectations of out-of-work folk being dashed by our campaigning. Such high unemployment in Harris. Their perception – and I agree that it was only ever a perception – was of economic salvation, forsaken at our doing.'

'Ah!' says John, broodingly. 'And that was the problem all along! You've put your finger right on the problem there, you have, my boy.

'Most of those who were pushing for the quarry were seeking precisely that. *Salvation*, as they called it!

'Salvation of the kind that went no deeper than their own hip pockets.'

There is a postscript. In my book *Soil and Soul* I'd referred to John MacAulay, anonymously, as 'the Elder'. It was he who had removed the summit rock of Roineabhal during the public inquiry in 1994, asking me to give it to Stone Eagle for symbolic safe-keeping. Under article seven of their 1752 treaty with the British, the Mi'Kmaq nation of Nova Scotia had agreed to 'use their best endeavours to save the lives and goods of any people shipwrecked on this coast'. Often, this was extended to helping distraught Scottish immigrants through the winters. Many of these were folk of crofting stock, forcibly cleared from their lands as part of the process that had released rapacious landlordism in the aftermath of the Highlanders' last stand at the Battle of Culloden.

As John saw it, having cleared the people, similar forces of greed, under the modern corporate guise, had attempted to clear even the very rocks themselves. This was what made such a powerful gesture of having Stone Eagle carry Roineabhal's sugar-bag-sized pinnacle of rock back to Nova Scotia.

In June of 2004, I went to Nova Scotia to retrieve our rock. There was a hand-over ceremony in the town hall at Pictou organised by Ishbel Munro, followed by a Mi'Kmaq sweat lodge ceremony for purification. Later that summer, a small procession of us climbed up Roineabhal. With immense dignity, John restored the summit rock – with the help of a small bag of Lafarge cement. Some of my old school friends from Leurbost had come with us. As we headed back down the slope, Alex George Morrison let out a whoop of surprise. From a cleft between some rocks, he pulled out a golden eagle's primary and, that night, gave the precious feather to John, the Elder of the Mountain.

At one point in the campaign, I'd been asked by the United Nations Environment Programme to write a contribution for their landmark volume, *The Cultural and Spiritual Values of Biodiversity*. I penned a piece that drew a parallel between the shooting of Scotland's 'last wolf' in 1743 and Culloden three years later. As part of this I'd needed to ask John's permission to quote from his closing submission to the public inquiry. I'd described him as *the community's* principal spokesperson on the superquarry issue. His reply, however, recast my framing to a wider perspective: to one that set things not in terms of a community of interests, but as community of place.

> I willingly endorse the inclusion of material from our submission to the public inquiry, with one proviso; that is, to alter your description of me as 'the *community's* principal spokesperson,' to that of 'the *island's* principal spokesperson.' This powerful sense of belonging goes infinitely deeper than that of the inhabitants of a built environment. The wolf and the mountain are one.

But by now, by this late hour in the evening, the living room fire has died down. John and Jane have gone upstairs. I've unrolled my sleeping bag. As we'd lingered with the embers, finishing off the wine, I'd asked Jane about her nursing work, in which her speciality was heart disease. She's originally from Yorkshire. She brings to the island an inside-outsider's eye. I'd asked why she thought our incidence of coronary illness is so high. Is it all down to our fatty mutton chops, salt herring, and frying scallops in the way Saint James intended, in butter?

'That's part of it,' she'd mused, 'but I can't help thinking there's something emotional as well,' and she went on to describe new research into the cardiovascular implications of anxiety and grief, the health consequences of raised cortisol levels in the bloodstream. 'And when you think about it, there's so much suffering here that's carried forward from the past.'

'Like? What kind of suffering?' I wanted to hear how she'd put it in her own words.

'Like . . . just so much . . . emotional burden. Look at their history. They had the Clearances. Then the Great War and the *Iolaire* going down . . .' that, having been the ship that hit the rocks just outside Stornoway harbour in January 1919, with more than two hundred of the surviving soldiers coming home from the trenches going down with her.

Then in the twenties and thirties there was the TB epidemic, hard times on hard times, and nearly three hundred of the young men, average age twenty-two, sailing off on the *Metagama* light-heartedly to seek a new life in Canada, not realising the all-round emotional consequences. Ironically, as the ship pulled away on 21 April 1923, the pipe band played *The Road to the Isles*, a tune that had been renamed thus after having been set to words by the Rev. Kenneth Macleod of Eigg and Gigha. It was a road that few would ever tread again.[3]

'It's like the life never stopped bleeding out of the place,' Jane continued. The Second World War followed. Many of the boys were on Atlantic convoys. Now the fishing's been all but wiped out, and crofting can no longer compete with industrial agriculture. 'It's just been the constant loss and battering of an ancient culture.'

'And do you really think they carry that inside?'

Her soft face grapples for expression.

'People just have such deep memories here. That's what I see when I go from house to house. If you're a fully feeling human being, you can't just grin and bear such burdens of the past and carry on unfazed.

'Not when the emotional currents run deep, so very deep, and run on between the generations.'

'So . . . you're suggesting,' I concluded, with a little too much of my own interpretation, 'that the weight of history *breaks the heart*, as it were?'

'Well don't get me wrong,' she'd said, with a slight jerk. 'It's not like everybody's miserable! There's plenty people living very fulfilled lives. But in terms of health, there's some pretty staggering statistics. It does make you wonder.'[4]

The night had drawn far in. We'd sat and gazed, all three of us, at the opalescent shimmer of the fading coals. Watching them shudder, one by one, like ruined castles that collapse and rattle down to ashes in the grate.

'And it's not just heart disease,' she'd concluded, getting up to straighten the sofa. 'You also see it in the Highland rate of suicide. The alcoholism too.'

The alcohol-related death rate is five times the national average, and everybody wonders why.

'It's a very west of Scotland thing,' she resumed. 'I really feel for some of the young men. They hardly know what their role is anymore.

'So I don't know. Is it the weather? The religion? Or something in the genes?

'Or is it just what happens when the ground's been pulled from underneath your feet, and you're stranded high and dry, cast up on rocks on which the past has left you?'

I awaken to the aroma of a heart-whacking fry-up in the kitchen.

'I thought you'd be needing something that would keep you going on the road,' John calls out cheerily, 'and it's another lovely sunny day.'

Day two it is, Tuesday, and Jane's going off to work. She's taking Osprey on ahead to dump him at the Tarbert doctor's surgery. This is the life! I'll be even lighter now. It means I'll only need to carry my skimpy day pack with a few essentials.

I chat with Ella as she's getting ready for school. She loves drawing. As I doubt I'll need both notebooks that I'd brought, and as they're of Moleskine art-grade paper, I take the opportunity to do the decent thing and lighten up my load a little further. She says she wants to be a vet. I say that, when I was her age, we all wanted to get off the island. Sow wild oats, get out of 'the dump' as we called it. *Familiarity breeds contempt* and all that. It sounds sacrilegious to say it, but me and many of my pals, we'd have been the adventurous ones, standing on the *Metagama*, waving goodbye forever. Until you lose that conviviality, you just don't realise, as an exile song has it, that 'there's no ceilidh on the prairie'. Ella concludes, however, that these things are changing. Many of today's teenagers have been there, done that. They've seen what's on offer elsewhere and, if they can, would rather spend the greater part of their lives at home.[5]

Over breakfast, I pick John's brains about my route and pilgrim stopping stations on the way. With no load to carry, I should be able to crack along at three miles an hour to make Tarbert by lunchtime. I'll then take the road back out towards Clisham, but cut up into the mountains at Bun Abhainn Eadarr – the River at the Foot of the Narrows – the glen and pass that runs between Clisham and surrounding hills.

Seumas Crawford, the stonemason who knows all about the bothan, had put me up to this route when we'd spoken on the phone. There were easier options, served by fishing tracks from Amhuinnsuidhe Castle further west along the B886. 'But you'd love going up from Bun Abhainn Eadarr,' he'd chuckled. 'The path withers out a mile or two beyond the village, then you're into wild land. If anything happens to you there, it'll take them long enough to find you!' It sounded like a very empty place, and, in my mind, I came to call it the 'Lost Glen'.

This east side of Harris, my route for this morning, had been sparsely populated until the early nineteenth century. The whole of Harris was inherited around 1818 by a thoroughly anglicised gentleman, one Alexander Norman (Hume) Macleod. The poor man – he'd probably been sent to one of those frigid boarding schools, where the sons of Highland aristocrats received the privilege of being cleansed of their cultural bearings, and 'educated' into modern mores. That's what happened to so many of them.

On acquiring the 'property', Alexander came back to Harris with his lady wife, hoping to create a huge sheep farm along the fertile south and western coasts. How else could the family maintain its new-found social standing in *polite* society? The Harris people had no idea what such 'politeness' might cost. They rejoiced, when they learned of their laird's return. In their trusting eyes, he was a long-lost son. This was like the return of a chief; perhaps the hope of bringing back the good old days that Culloden's social repercussions had diminished.

It is said that a group of village maidens met the couple on the road and danced an impromptu reel of welcome. But within a year, as testimony to the Napier Commission on the crofters' plight would record, 'these twenty women were weeping and wailing; their houses being unroofed and their fires quenched by the orders of the estate'.[6] In Rodel alone, one hundred and fifty hearths were swept bare. Seven hundred and fifty souls were evicted from the green glen where once the bells of monks and nuns had sounded. One old woman was dumped in the ditch while her home was physically dismantled, to ensure that she could never return. A young wife had just given birth, but her pleas for a few days' stay of execution were heartlessly rejected. These were no longer a people, a community with sense of place and dignity. These were now unwanted tenants, 'the surplus population' to be disposed of.

Many families were forced to flee to summer pasture sheilings in the hills until they came to terms with what had come to pass. An unknown number left Harris forever. Others squeezed in with relatives along this rocky east coast where John lives. When I asked him why there are so few sacred sites along this stretch, in comparison with the south and west of Harris, he said that it was probably due to the relative recency with which the people had concentrated there.

On my route this morning there is, however, one significant point of attention, noted in Doctor Finlay's guidebook. A well in the village of Leac a Lì called Tobar a' Ghobha – the Well of the Blacksmith – said to be named after Iain Gobha na Hearadh. This John Morrison (or Morison), the Blacksmith of Harris, had lived from 1790 to 1852. As I'd left Saint Clement's churchyard yesterday, I'd made a note of the inscription on his headstone.

> A great poet
> a saintly Christian
> an eminent evangelist.
> Erected by the people of Harris
> and other admirers of his genius
> at home and abroad.

The well named after him was said to cure stomach cramps and headaches. Its waters reputedly had their greatest efficacy at liminal times – either dawn or dusk – on the thresholds between day and night. But John is puzzled. According to Doctor Finlay, the Ordnance Survey grid reference is NG 134916.

'That can't be right,' he mutters, shaking his head as we push aside the breakfast plates and pore over the map together. 'Those coordinates would put it away up in the moor, near the old Mission Hall. The *Gobha* would never have had his well so far away from his house.'

'So where would it have been, then?'

'His croft was at the start of the village. Unless there's more than one tradition, or more than one well, that's where I'd start looking.'

5

ON THE GOLDEN ROAD

I head out the door, light of step, and onto the Golden Road. Strictly speaking, the name applies to a stretch that's further to the north. However, in these touristic days, it's often applied to the whole length of single-track carriageway that threads through the Bays of Harris. The tourists like to think it's so named for spectacular sunrises that set the Minch ablaze. Local humour is less romantic. The only gold involved was the construction cost of hacking through the adamantine folds of metamorphic rock and bridging numerous little inlets.

I've not even warmed up, but straight away I feel just so light and happy to be here. Not even any aches and pains from yesterday's endeavours. As I move slowly through the fields and scattered houses, I'm kind of watching myself, and observing that my senses are wired in to every detail. Especially the details. In this terrain, the older homes squat tightly on the bedrock. There's no need to have foundations, when the Earth itself is your foundation. The problem for building on Harris, is finding a patch that's flat enough. You can own a bit of land, but try developing it, and you'll need to call the boys with dynamite.

Most of the homes are traditional two-up two-down cottages, with chimneys built onto the sides. Always seems to me a waste of heat, but I suppose that, in the days before modern linings, it made for greater safety. Grander residences, that were built between the wars, stand gaunt and shivering in their declining majesty. Most of these have roofs of Ballachulish slate. You can spot it from the little cubes of fool's gold that, as boys, we'd chip out and play tricks on the unwary. A range of red-tiled bungalows and pre-fab kit houses give a nod to improved recent living standards. Here and there, the strangeness of some architect designs hint at either gold dug from elsewhere or, perhaps, a hippie with an inheritance.

Snaking down most of the hillsides are the wrinkled parallel curves of *feannagan* – the old raised beds, or 'lazybeds' – but lazy only in their languor of appearance. Thin soil had to be scraped together, literally made with sand, animal dung and creels of seaweed, hand-hauled from the shore, to eke out a meagre livelihood. Today, these ridge and furrow patterns on the land, like the dry-stone walls that perhaps enclose them, are settling slowly back into the ground. The same attrition of the past is true of much of rural Europe. The very features that lift a traveller's heart are turning into fossil landscapes. It takes a whole community to sustain an embedded way of life, but when your neighbours have forgotten how to milk a cow; or worse, if your neighbours have become a crowd of fleeting holiday-makers, who come and go as waving ghosts in revving 4x4s, it's you, and not the cow, that ends up feeling tethered to the rusty iron ring of antiquity. It's you, that in a short wave world is hefted to the long wave, with few remaining listeners to share your bandwidth – crackling and cackling for what's fresh.

In the early 1960s, at this time of year, I'd watch the feannagan in our part of the island being ploughed and harrowed by a proud white horse called Tommy. Some of us learned to ride him bareback, and to slide off down his side when he'd break into a canter. He'd overwinter in a field beside our house, and I'd scythe grass to pay him for the rides. We all made hay then, but when a company called Transatlantic Plastics started advertising its sacks in the *Exchange & Mart*, I switched to bagging it as silage. That way you weren't dependent on good weather for the drying. Tommy loved its sweet and musty richness. I can feel it in my nostrils now. On Berneray, which is off North Uist but counted as part of Harris, there's a crofter, Seonaidh Mòr, who used to do the ploughing as a boy. Today, he's the plague of mainland white van men, as he trundles round the island at twenty miles an hour in his car. 'Don't be blaming me, Alastair!' he called out one day. 'Remember – I learned to drive on a horse.'

The crofters planted potatoes, turnips, oats and *bere* – a native strain of barley, that had been bred to suit the harsh climatic conditions. Along with fish and shellfish, meat, eggs and dairy products, these were the staples of our diet. In my time I've enjoyed a feed of what, these days, would be classed as oddities, if not downright illegal. Dare I say it, roasted curlew, dried salted gannet (if 'enjoyed' was the right word), and regularly around this time of year, a boiled seagull's egg for breakfast, gathered from the nesting grounds on Loch Orisay island by one of Dad's patients.

Work was gendered in its braided rhythms. Women to milk the cow or treadle the spinning wheel. Men to plough the soil and set the long-lines to catch cod and haddock from the village boat. Grandmothers and children to bait the hooks with mussels gathered at low tide. And the old men? They told stories, tapped their pipes, and puffed out clouds of Virginia twist. From time to time they'd shuffle around the closer hills with walking sticks, keeping an eye on their wiry Blackface sheep and on the lads out at sea. You'd hear them go '*uaich, uaich, uaich*' as they'd come home and sit down, tired. They'd say it with that long guttural 'ch' that doubles up for clearing phlegm, and that only Gaels with words like *loch*, and Jews with names like *Chaim,* are properly qualified to pronounce: and even then, only with sufficient weariness of age.

A true peasant is of a nobility invisible to the urban effete. An old Catholic man from South Uist confided to me – I say confided, because he wanted to pass on the story, but did not want attention to be drawn to his person:

> We did not have fences on the fields until the Second World War, when timber came off the convoy ships that had been sunk. Before that, we boys had to constantly herd the cows, to keep them from eating our neighbours' crops. We grew up always with the cattle, and always with the old people, and we learned to be alive; to be humanity.

He gave me this example from his childhood, anxious to illuminate the dignity of that humanity.

> One day, an old woman caught a bee and drew from it a tiny drop of golden liquid.
>
> 'What is that?' I asked her.
>
> 'Taste it,' she said. And I tasted. It was a wondrous taste.
>
> 'That,' she said, 'is nectar. Only kings and royal people get to taste that. But we taste that; but we don't talk about it.'

Everybody says the same. They say, in contradiction of their own nostalgia: 'The old ways were so hard. We'd none of us be wanting to go back.' And yet, that very refrain heaves with strains of lamentation, and their eyes take on a near but distant look, as if they're seeing into something just behind. 'In the old days', they'll say, at the start of so many sentences, the fields and hills rang out with song. Working rhythms and laughter eased the weary aches of communal labour. Today, for all the gains – the television and the refrigerator; central heating and the incontinence tablets – they fear a loss of real education that comes from bonding into place and one another, a sorry pruning of the roots of character.

My father's retired practice manager, Agnus Maclennan from Achmore, must be round about eighty, but she goes every week to visit even older folks in a care home. 'How do they see the changes?' I asked, and did so, mindful that it is change, and not just loss. There are so many bright new openings – in renewable energies and high technology, in ecotourism and the arts, in fish and shellfish farming, and in agricultural products aimed at niche food markets, like the fabled Stornoway black pudding. It's not all gloom, just in case I'm sounding a tad . . . retro.

And yet: 'They feel confused,' was this dear woman's rueful answer. 'They cannot understand why nobody's keeping cows anymore. And why they're not planting the potatoes. And not putting out to sea together in their fishing boats.'

But what is this? O ho? Just look at this! Here I am, walking on the Golden Road, and I'm greeted by a Golden Stag. Where two fences meet at an acute angle, some joking artist has wedged a stag's skull with its antlers painted gold. A tad pantheistic, if you ask me!

I take a close look at the strainer in the corner – the post that takes the tension of the wires. It's cut from off a pine log in the round, and has rotted hollow at the top. Into this has grown an ecosystem of green mosses, creamy branching lichens, and blobs of weird transparent jelly, plus, when I give a poke, all manner of wee critters that creep and burrow, that linger and slither. The aroma is of autumn mushrooms in a Languedoc glade. Hmm. Maybe, Vérène would think I've gone a bit OTT there. The French do get rather fussy with their *appellations*, if less so with their husbands. How about: the aroma of a bubbling batch of botched home brew?

To most *normal* people this would be a picture of hell, an image from Hieronymus Bosch. But to an ecologist, it's heaven in a fencepost. My mind's mostly just been mellowing as I've walked, yet somewhere in the background, I've been mulling over what was said around the fire with John and Jane last night. We got on to Heaven and Hell and all that; indeed, I've yet to find the native Hebridean home where, late at night, the conversation doesn't turn to religion. We'd been talking, as one inevitably does in the islands, about John Calvin. About the straight line back from him, pivoting on Saint Augustine's interpretations, to some of the hard-line positions attributed to Saint Paul. John had said you get a very different impression from the New Testament if you read the gospels of Jesus first, than if you start with some of the epistles of Paul. 'It's as if,' he'd mused, 'Paul steps in and reinvents the very legalism that Jesus had thrown out.'

Augustine of Hippo – today, Annaba, a small city in Algeria – has been on my radar since leaving Saint Clement's yesterday. Augustinian houses, such as Rodel and the nunnery on Iona, may have settled into places of deep peace. However, it was he, more than any of the Church Fathers, who disrupted early Christian pacifism and substituted in its place what is now drawn together as 'just war' theory. In so doing, the original Christian message is abused and discredited.

For the first few hundred years, most Christians had tried to follow Christ in accepting suffering, but not fighting fire with fire. One example is in a second-century manuscript, *The Acts of [Saint] Andrew,* which portrays a Roman legionnaire telling his colleagues: 'You fools, do you not see what sort of man this is? There is no sword in his hand nor any instrument of war, yet these great acts of power issue from his hand.'[1] However, by the fourth century, Constantine had taken over the show, declaring Christianity to be the new state religion of the Roman Empire. This stopped its persecution but neutered its vision of nonviolent revolution and, by the year 418, Augustine was writing to Count Boniface – later the Roman Tribune of Africa – offering these words of comfort:[2]

> We do not seek peace in order to be at war, but we go to war that we may have peace. Be peaceful, therefore, in warring, so that you may vanquish those whom you war against, and bring them to the prosperity of peace.

Calvin's leaning on Augustine's interpretation of Paul provides the basis for the Westminster Confession of Faith. This remains a central influence on the Church of Scotland and, in variations of its themes, on many Presbyterian offshoots across the former British colonies. Drawn up in 1643, the Confession sets out the principle of predestination. God ordained the future of the universe in advance. Human beings are therefore powerless in the question of their own salvation. It's all been prearranged, 'before the foundation of the world was laid'. We are, as the Confession has it in the doctrine known as *total depravity*, 'utterly indisposed, disabled, and made opposite to all good, and wholly inclined

to all evil'.[3] As a consequence, said Calvin, God is 'armed for vengeance',[4] and Hell, our default destiny.

However, it's not all doom and gloom. Thanks to God's 'good pleasure', some will be saved. The Elect will go upstairs to Heaven. The
Damned, downstairs to Hell, and this is the doctrine of *double predestination* – the idea that God elects (or chooses) who will either be *saved,*
on the one hand, or *damned,* on the other.

However, in this cosmic schema, only the preordained Elect can be
saved – through God having sent himself, in the form of Christ his Son, to
take their punishment for them on the cross. According to the Calvinist
doctrine of *limited atonement*, this benefit of Christ's sacrifice is 'limited'
to the Elect alone. The Damned are, quite literally, the godforsaken. As
America's 'Godmother of Punk', the singer Patti Smith, summed up such
dogmas in her lyric, *Gloria*: 'Jesus died for somebody's sins, but not mine.'

On the Scottish Borders side of our family, a supposed ancestor is the
preacher, Thomas Boston of Duns and Ettrick. I'm sure that had I
mentioned him last night, John would have known all about Boston.
There won't be many pious homes in Harris that don't have, somewhere,
one of his books in either English or a translation into Gaelic. Here lies
a tale that draws together my interests in ecology, the imagination, hard-
line religion and its links to war.

Born in 1676, Boston became a foremost interpreter of Presbyterian
thought in Scotland and beyond. His books have remained continuously
in print to this day. Robert Burns described them as 'damned trash',
lampooning him in a poem to a 'brother sinner' as cause to 'grunt a real
Gospel-groan'.[5] To evangelical traditionalists, however, his writings
were, and remain, sweet music to the soul.

To start with the best foot forward, it is a little known aspect of early
Scots Calvinism that the emphasis on divine providence, illuminated by
a vibrantly extant rural life, lead to some sublime reflections on nature.
This was not *pantheism* – the idea that God *is* nature – and with it, very
easily, a denial of the transcendent. Rather, it was *panentheism* – the
sense of God being present *in* the material world of nature but not
limited to it. These are some of Boston's words upon the matter:[6]

> Here the goodness of God shines with a glorious lustre. All the varieties of the
> creatures which he hath made are so many beams and apparitions of his good-
> ness . . . Every creature hath a character of Divine goodness upon it. The whole
> world is a map to represent, and a herald to proclaim, this amiable perfection

of God . . . See how the Earth is kindly furnished with vegetables by providence, not only for men's necessity, but their conveniency and delight (Psalm
104) . . . Every pile of grass is a preacher of the loving-kindness of the Lord.

So far so good. Heaven in a fencepost, and I can imagine the Golden Stag
quite perking up at such a sermon. But have a listen to this, extracts from
a section of his writings with the subheading, 'The wicked shall lie for
ever under the weight of the curse in Hell'. Here, spread-eagled over four
pages, Boston relentlessly details the plight of *reprobates* – those poor
souls who, out of God's 'good pleasure' (and not even for any particular
sins of their own), have been irrevocably damned from before their birth:[7]

They shall be cast into the lake of fire, as death and Hell are, to be shut up
there without coming forth again any more . . . Yea, and to bind them in
bundles for the fire of God's wrath, that companions in sin may be companions in punishment . . . and there shall be weeping, wailing, and gnashing of
teeth. The curse shall enter into their souls, and melt them like wax before the
fire; it shall sink into their flesh and bones, like boiling lead, and torment them
in every part . . . No pity, no compassion to be shown any more, but fire-
balls . . . *Lastly*, the curse shall lengthen out their misery to all eternity.

Jeepers! You'd wonder what's the difference between God and the Devil
with such shuddersome dread from out the Hammer Church of Horror.
When I first encountered such passages I found myself asking: Was my
ancestor suffering from a condition, hopefully not inheritable? Then I
remembered something that my grandfather, with his mercifully merry
Ronnie Hancox Band for Dancers, used to tell my mother. He'd say: 'You
know, Jean, *I don't like that man*. I must get to know him better.' It
occurred to me that, just as psychologists have pondered Luther's harsh
parenting, and Calvin's loss of his mother at a tender age, so, too, I
should inquire into Thomas Boston's circumstances before being too
harsh in my judgement.
    What gradually pieced together was that the young Thomas had gone
through his most tender years in the Killing Times of the 1680s – the
religious civil wars of Charles II and his successor, James VII & II. Both
of the boy's parents were Covenanters. These were folk of a mostly
southern Scottish peasant stock. They had valiantly hunkered down and
dug in their heels for the right to practise their chosen religion –
Presbyterianism. Why would they have chosen the legacy of Calvin and
John Knox? One reason was that it answered to their need for religious

freedom. The Reformation had advocated a 'priesthood of all believers' – the right to read the Bible by oneself, to have a hotline up to God without the need for priests as intermediaries. Calvin saw no need for hierarchies of bishops. However, royal and other aristocratic power liked bishops as a medium through which to exercise their political control. 'No Bishop, no King,' James VI & I had said, meaning that a king needed bishops to sustain his divine right to rule.

In contrast, Presbyterianism meant church government by *presbyters*, from the Greek for elders. It was democratic insofar as these were drawn from the congregation, and Presbyterian congregations claimed the right to 'call' a minister of their own election rather than to have one imposed from above by church authorities, usually in league with the patronage of feudal landed power. As such, Calvin's epic *Institutes of the Christian Religion* has been described as 'the seedbed of democracy'. Like most religious radicals, the Covenanters paid the price of challenging the power structures of their age in suffering. Throughout the Killing Times they were tortured, rendered fugitive, and slaughtered in their thousands by the Episcopalian (or bishop-based) Royalist regime.

There are stories of how, when Thomas was a small boy, he voluntarily passed the nights in Duns prison to comfort his father, John, who had been jailed for his Covenanter preaching. Could it be, I wondered, that Thomas' theology took its excoriating vim-and-vigour from real-life trauma, that was always just around the corner? For example: in 1685, when he was nine years old, two Covenanter women, who had refused to renounce their faith, were tied to stakes in the Solway Firth and left to drown on the rising tide. The youngest, Margaret Wilson, was only eighteen. Later she was immortalised as *The Martyr of Solway* in a heart-rending painting by the Pre-Raphaelite artist Sir John Everett Millais. No less woebegone would have been the first- and second-hand accounts of such sufferings, moving from hearth to hearth in every Covenanter home.

In any war, each side amplifies the cruelty of the other, the better to energise and legitimise its own reciprocal atrocities. God – the deepest sense of inner sanction – must be co-opted to the cause. If not, it comes undone. That's why, across most faiths (and even nonviolent Buddhism), narratorial control is so vulnerable to capture by the violent religions of violent men of violent times. It leaves me pondering how far Thomas' lurid sense of Hell might have been linked to such exposure. I can imagine real-life images, that must have stormed the vaults of his unconscious, whirring in demonic flight through the magic lantern of his psyche; and then, in adulthood, beamed out to monstrous proportions on the silver screen of his theology.

I'm just wond'rin', that's all. And that silver screen, ministering both to those who knew the suffering from first hand, and those touched by its cold finger from afar. I am suggesting that it left them tinder-primed to believe in a system of cosmic apartheid. One that separated out the Damned (*them*) from the Elect (*us*). One that gave succour by the prospect of comeuppance for the reprobates.

Was such a system God-given? Or a plant from the other chap's department? Whatever, it would certainly have been an all-too-human response. It might have helped the people to process bitter experience. And who knows. For all that we, today, might think ourselves so clever, and so classless, and so free, might some of us still carry such psychohistories of bygone persecution within? And if so, how wide, and with what unconscious effects, their remit?

I have parted from the Golden Stag, gone through the villages of Beacrabhaic and Geocrab, and happen now upon a rocky bay. There are islets just a stone's throw off the shore. A colony of seals, maybe eight or ten of them, are lounging in the sun. But they're playing 'Spot the Tourist', and have seen me. They're flopping down into the sea on chutes between the rocks, festooned with dark green bladderwrack.

That's the kind of seaweed that pops. As kids, we used to chew it for the iodine. We'd be told that 'iodine's good for you'. Folk wisdom, with a dash of chemistry. We'd ruminate on a pod or two, especially when we'd take our buckets down to the head of Loch Leurbost to gather mussels. The right place – the furthest away from village septic tank outlets – was at the abandoned village of Crothairgearaidh. Goodness, that name looks pretty far out when you see it on old maps! We'd just say it something that sounds like 'Croi-gary'.

Alex George said that it was safe to pick the shellfish from one side of a particular fence, but not from the other. We'd be most punctilious about the matter. That was the 'done thing'. He was six months older than me, so he knew everything. Also, you were only supposed to take them in months with an 'r'. That way, with a dash of biochemistry, I suppose that we avoided any toxic summer algal blooms. It also meant this food source was conserved for winter. The best place for picking them is a little bay, right beneath the blackhouse ruins. There's a half-moon row of boulders, strategically laid out in the days of long ago. They're placed at just the right spot in the tidal range for mussels to prosper – not too high and not too low – and they grow huge, with shells that have the most lovely blue-green striations when held up to the light. When you lightly steam them, the tasty flesh falls out like golden egg yolks. Just mind you don't crack a tooth on the pinhead pearls that often lurk inside.

We'd yank them off in handfuls, and in no time we'd each get a haul to feed our families. Afterwards, we'd usually play awhile in the ruins. We'd be digging, turning over stones, looking to see if we'd find anything worth keeping. It might be me, Alex George himself, Derick, Calum Ian, Donald, Duncan Norman, John Neil, Murdie 'Plum'– that sort of crew, the boys from up the New Holdings and Cameron Terrace end of Leurbost. Our locus, mostly, was no further than a mile away from home. Before heading back, we'd scoop a wee *deoch*, a few slurps, from the little stream that comes down off the long low hill called Cailleach Crothairgearaidh. There she goes again! The feminine embodied in the landscape. This time, the old woman of the hills. You can even see her in recline from the roadside, though I only recently became aware of the fact.[8]

When done – when hungry, midge-bitten or seeing the rain threatening – we'd head back up to the road. We'd usually lift a few stones, looking for eels, as we'd wade across the estuary of the Abhainn Ghlas. We'd get onto our bikes, those of us who had them, and wobble home with the heavy buckets swinging from the handlebars. We'd say to one another that feats like this were 'good for the practice'. Quite what we were practising for, or who put that idea into our heads, nobody ever asked. There was just a sense in many of the things we did, that we were 'practising' for something. I suppose it was that kind of random readiness that fitted us to our surroundings.

The seals are through with playing 'Spot the Tourist' now. They've humphed back up onto their rocks, having figured out I'm just another bit of wildlife, not in predatory mode, so not enough to keep them off their sunbathing.

That's a sharp glare that's coming off the water. Time to don my Polaroids. A smear of sun cream too. Hmm – I've only brought a smidgeon. To save space and weight I'd decanted it from a bottle into one of those old black 35mm film canisters. One doesn't really come to this part of the world expecting good weather. However, if I've judged it right, there should be just enough to give precisely *half* protection, and that, enough to build up a protective tan. How so? Because, to really skimp on what I'm carrying, I only need sufficient to cover my east side in the mornings, and I'll swing round to the west in afternoons.

At this dawdle, I've only done two miles, but a good hour has slipped by. I've met absolutely no-one on the road. Cars and nine-to-five routines have killed off so much village life. I've not even seen a field planted with potatoes. Mind you, there'd be no point laying them out with this *rotach donn*, this dry and biting easterly wind. It leaves the seed lying cold and dormant in the ground, a meal for crows and mice before it gets a chance to germinate.

Round a bend, and now the road's rising steeply up a hill. On the right, and bounded tight by cliffs and ridges, lies a vale that spreads down towards a pair of lochs. In July, one of these fills up with water lilies, white with golden hearts, the lotus of the Hebrides. This glen would once have fed several families. The ridges of feannagan still freshly runnel its floor, each bed some six or eight feet wide, with a yard or so for drainage in-between. I love the way they vector down like herring bones, to meet the tiny burn that glimmers as a silver backbone through the middle.

A footpath slopes off through a field, a looping remnant from before the road was built. I follow, for I can hear the splash of running water. I'm thirsty. I've never made it my habit to carry a water bottle on this island. It's usually 'water, water, everywhere' and barrel-loads to drink. A tiny stream is falling over cliffs. I come to a kind of plat-form where the path crosses it amongst rocks. The stones are smooth from centuries of village use. It feels so good and right to join this ancient ritual. I kneel down and pout my lips, to draw directly from the flow.

The anxiously wary say: *But there might be a dead sheep upstream!*

My blasé thoughts reply: *At least you'll know it's been well washed.*

Yet, even as the devil speaks, the brakes slam on. Something's not right! Something's not quite . . . dancing with this water. There's not the sparkling scent I know of pristine purity.

I shudder to a jarring halt, ramming my motions into reverse. All senses raise to danger revs, as every instinct in me demands in outrage and repulse: *What is going on around here?* And there's the culprit! Tiny white flecks of *something* are caught up in the weedy margins of the stream. I shake my head, bewildered like a flummoxed sheep, and scurry on along the path to where it rejoins further up the road. And there's the explanation: A sign in blue and green that says 'UBC'. The burn runs right beside a heavy haulage parking bay of Uist Builders Construction. Dead sheep may be of nature's making, but I've just dodged a bellyful of lorry-washing suds.

Another half mile further on, and here's another stream. This time I take my fill, familiar and wholesome, whisky-tinted from its peat-infusing journey through the moors. I sit awhile and listen to its tinkling over shallow stones, its rumbling as it drops down into thunderous hollows. Marsh marigolds are blooming in the bank. I've always loved marsh marigolds. They're usually the first out in the spring; but still no sign of dainty blushing lady's smock, or raffish ragged robin flirting pink from boggy dips. Neither have I heard the out-of-nowhere chimes of cuckoo call: here today, gone tomorrow, coming back another day.

The road keeps lilting gently up, and it undulates again across an open moor. It winds past long dark narrow lochs, so tight between the cliffs that the verge drops, straight off, into deep water. A mountain lies ahead that's famous for its contours as a haggard woman's face. The guys just don't seem to get the same look in round here. It's getting very warm now, and I'm coming up to a bus shelter of all things, parked right out here in the middle of nowhere. I'll stop, take a layer off, and have a bag of fruit and nuts.

I sit down on the shelter's outer lip, and even as I do so, find myself interrogating myself: Why here? I mean, I've got the whole of nature, but without so much as thinking, I've chosen a concrete slab. Lafarge got me after all! I think it must be something in me seeking company, but company doesn't disappoint. Company comes, in the form of a colony of small black ants that stream like daubs of spilling ink from out the shelter's cracked foundations.

I chew a single raisin to a paste, spit the humble offering out, and push myself – just for the laugh – to shout aloud: *To the faeries!* Like Pharaoh's masons off they go, transporting massive chunks, from quarry to their den. I chuckle out aloud – *One more ant that believes in God!* – and I wonder if it's only me, or are they conscious too?

If we're conscious in our way, why not they in theirs? Could it be that our brains are radio receivers? Tuned to wavelengths we can handle? Ant to ant. Human to human. And *go, go, go!* said Eliot's bird, amongst the unheard music in the shrubbery. 'Human kind cannot bear very much reality.'

Or maybe, pace Thomas Boston, cannot bear the thought of loving-kindness preached from every pile of grass.

At Flodabay last night, we'd also discussed the Calvinist insistence on humanity's total depravity. It's not just Calvin who plays this tune. It's found wherever Augustine's teachings on original sin are emphasised including, some scholars argue, in versions of Irish Catholicism that got carried to America.[9]

As we sat round the fire, Jane was agreeing that none of our flames burn clean. We're all a bit of a mixed bag. 'But *total* depravity?' she'd asked, douce eyes agape. 'It just doesn't square with my experience. I see so much human goodness on this island as I go about my work.'

When the woman came to Jesus with her pot of precious oil, when she'd kissed his feet, massaging them with running tears and flowing hair, he didn't turn and tell the Pharisees what they'd have liked to have heard. He didn't say: 'She's done a *totally depraved* thing to me.' He said, 'She's done a beautiful thing to me' – or as the King James Version has it – 'She hath wrought a good work on me.'[10] Likewise, he never told a parable that posterity might have called: *The Totally Depraved Samaritan*.

What is it in us, we'd all three wondered, that disposes some of us, at least some of the time, to wallow in the pits of human nature, and maybe have our eyes dimmed? Could there be some sense in which, as my theologian friend Walter Wink put it: 'You get the Jesus you need'? Like Thomas Boston maybe got the vision of Hell he needed; and I mean that not pejoratively, but in seeking to understand.

The unyielding version of total depravity might be the currency of a Hebridean dinner party, but it also plays out, albeit in more unconscious ways, within wider society. Once, when I was debating on a military panel at a school of war, we hit on why it is that tiny Britain felt the need to have a level of military expenditure that, at the time, was fourth only to the United States, China and Russia.[11]

The analyst sitting next to me said: 'We must not forget that human beings are born to fear.'

'Born, or taught?' I replied. 'It makes a difference.'

One way invests in arms; the other way invests in trust.

One shoots from a presumption of depravity; the other hopes for the atomic power of love.

In Calvinism, to emphasise the point again, the doctrine of total depravity hinges on predestination. As the Westminster Confession of Faith puts it: 'God from all eternity did . . . of His own will, freely, and unchangeably ordain whatsoever comes to pass.'[12] Everything that happens is fore-ordained. We therefore have no free will, no human agency in life, no real ability to change the way we're born. Why? Because God's sovereignty – omnipotent, omniscient and omnipresent – trumps everything.

The trouble with such logic, so trapped within the head, is that human reason tries to trump the divine mystery. I've noticed, however, that the island has its ways of coming to terms with these unyielding aspects of its religious status quo. There's a book called *Lewis in the Passing* by Calum Ferguson. Some of his interviews with the older generation of islanders show these ways at play. One approach is to not confront things head on, but just to quietly let them fall away to the sidelines. For example, John MacDonald of Port nan Giùran, born in 1911, told Ferguson:[13]

> Today, Lewis has many religious denominations – even in the Christian Church. Some theologians argue about this and that. Is there a Hell? Is there a Heaven, even? Well, I never considered whether or not there is Hell. To me, my awareness is of the existence of God . . . [the] absolute certainty that there is God . . . because of things that have happened in my own life.

Another approach is through the telling of spiritual teaching stories that reframe a given situation to a bigger picture. Such a technique reminds me of the Sufi mystics of Islam. They'd gently trounce the heavy-handed clerics with their anecdotes, just like Jesus trounced the Pharisees with parables. An example that Ferguson recorded came from a crofter born in 1917, John the Miller of Habost.[14]

In his youth, John had known a woman living on the peninsula of Point, which runs east of Stornoway. It was during the poverty-racked 1930s. The woman was desperately poor, and her daughter lay dying in the house from *a' chaitheamh* – the 'wasting' or 'consumption' – as the tuberculosis was known. There was an epidemic at that time. Indeed, my father, who saw its tail end, suspected that it had been caused by strains of the bacillus, brought back by soldiers from the Great War, to which our insular population had piteously little resistance.

'Some of the most beautiful girls that I ever saw,' John said, suffered from *a' chaitheamh*. 'There was a certain kind of luminance in their countenances.'

And this woman on Point – her daughter was weakening by the day – and her mother heard her calling out for food.

'My *darling* girl,' she was forced to reply, using one of seventy or so terms in Gaelic to express endearment. 'There is nothing inside this house that I can offer you to eat.'

The mother then went and stood at her doorstep. She gazed out, across the moor and to the sky, and wept. After a while, she saw a man coming along the road. She stepped back inside so as not to let him see her tears. The man walked past the house, but turned round, retraced his footsteps, and came up the path and knocked.

'I wish you to have this,' he said, passing her a pound note. 'The Lord directed me to give it to you.'

And that's it. That's all there is to this deceptively simple tale. At least that's all there is on the rational plane. However, I've come to think of it in my own mind as 'The Parable of the Lord's Pound'. Only very slowly do such armour-piercing stories explode into the layers of the heart.

One can read it at a surface level. The man had simply found a ruse for helping. He had freed the woman from the burden of an obligation – one that she might have never been able to repay. It was no longer *he* to whom she owed gratitude. It was to *the Lord*.

But at a deeper level, who might be this *Lord?* Who, this ground of sovereign being?

It takes us to the heart of agency, to the question of free will, to the question: *who acts?*

On one side of the coin, it was, of course, the man who acted. On the other, it is the Lord.

Logically, it can't be both. But human logic stalls at celestial elevations. For me, this story points – as the apostle Peter put it – to our being 'partakers in the divine nature.'[15] To the level of mystical union.

Who said we can't transcend dichotomies? Who said *it can't be both*?

After I leave the bus stop of the swarming ants, another stretch of faded path leads me off-piste. Another of the olden ways dives sharply down a grassy brae. It allows me to short-cut the road's meanders. I rejoin the tarmac by the bridge at Liceasto, go wandering on around a corner, and there awaits an old friend.

I'd been looking forward to renewing this acquaintance. Normally, one whizzes past too fast. It is a small ruin, built of stone toed in to stone, without a touch of cement. Now, only these walls remain of what was once an outhouse byre, or shed, the larger blackhouse ruins themselves being higher up the slope. My memories are from its glory days of more than forty years ago. Then, it had a roof made from an upturned fishing boat. Whenever we'd come down this way on a family outing, I'd marvel at its striking ingenuity. I loved its frugal functionality, and though I didn't know the term for overlapping planks back then, I loved its curving lines of clinker elegance.

I peer in through the vacant doorway, and then turn to take a closer look at something lying to the side. You know what? There it is! The very boat that was the roof.

A twisted length of planks, criss-crossed with in-stepped ribs, is lying rotting on the ground. She's slowly growing back into the grass. Dust to dust. Wood to soil. The ministry of laying down. And copper nails that held her fast unto the last – *Hold fast!* – the boys would shout, as she rocked and rollicked to the pitch of nature's moods.

It's quite emotional, just being at this ruin, the lantern thoughts that flicker through my mind. Who built her? Who sailed her? Who worked beneath the upturned harbour of her shelter in this shed? Aye, the pang of long-lost secrets brought to mind. To think that I still know what these grey-brindled timbers once had been. Trivial knowledge, yes, and yet a vessel laden full with memory.

See those black splashes? They're her caulking tar. It was Archangel tar we always used. Distilled from roots of pine in Russia or Sweden. Aye, its thick aroma that would hang along the shoreline in the spring, before the boats went in. The kipper-scented wisps of smoke, that drifted from the pot that brooded over Finlay's small peat fire. The way the brush dripped hot black runs of treacle tears against the larch – and I'm feeling it quite viscerally – this cloying sense of presence now, so guttural and heavy in my chest.

Oh yes, it's 'just' nostalgia. But curiously I'm also feeling happy that it's come upon me. It opens up a deeper way of seeing. It reminds me that partaking is the fabric of experience, what sets the sail for seeing so much else. And that for all the hurly-burly of the world, I still have sentient capacity. And that nostalgia is *nostos-algos*, Greek words that mean 'returning home' and 'grief'. And that this great longing is what's called me here; this sailing home, this pilgrimage of slowly walking home.

From this point onwards, the road twists narrowly between the sea and landward cliffs. The cliffs press right up to the road, a reminder here that people fitted in to nature, not the other way around; yet this is what makes Harris such a very human scale of place.

I'm coming up towards another crossroads. One branch is a footpath that leads off to the left into the moors. The other turns right into the village of Leac a Lì. Here, if can I find it, is Tobar a' Ghobha, the well that John MacAulay and I had pondered over. The well of John Morrison, blacksmith, poet and healer – for they say the preacher gave out medicines as he went from settlement to settlement.

When understood as more than just a grocery chain, Morrison is a very great name. The Gaelic original is either *Moireasdan,* or *Mac Gille Mhoire,* the latter being anglicised as Gilmore. It means the Son of the Servant of the Blessed Virgin Mary. Such designations carry a packed payload in the old lore of the Hebrides. The relationships of who served whom, and how such service all went round in circles, is wonderfully interlaced by bonds of spiritual kinship.

The National Galleries of Scotland have a much-loved painting by John Duncan, an artist of the Celtic Revival. Called *Saint Bride* and completed in 1913, just on the eve of the First World War, it shows a sleeping, praying, island lass being carried by angels on the night of the nativity from Iona to Bethlehem. There she served as nurse to Mary. Out of this tradition, recorded the great nineteenth-century folklore collector Alexander Carmichael, Bride, Bridgit or Brighde became *Ban-chuideachaidh Mhoire,* Mary's aid-woman. Also *Muime Chrìosda,* the Fostermother of Christ, and even *Bana-ghoistidh Mhic Dè,* the God-mother of the Son of God.[16]

Christ himself is therfore *Dalta Bride,* the Foster-son of Brighde, and more fulsomely, *Dalta Bride bith nam beannachd,* the Foster-son of Bride of the Blessings, or *Mac Moire min, Dalta Bride nam buar,* Son of Mary fair, Foster Son of Bride of the Cattle.[17] As is often the case, even the animals get woven in. As Carmichael explains, the significance of fostership is that here was a culture where adoption counted for even more than blood lineage. Fostership chooses and is chosen, its conscious action lending it great spiritual significance. Brighde thus becomes 'the Mary of the Gaels', and in this way, a remote culture on the furthest fringes of Europe managed, most profoundly, to localise the nativity. This is not to marginalise the Bridgit of Kildare, the keeper of the sacred fire, with whom traditions overlap. It's just to say that, in the Hebrides, we've even trumped the Irish: and Duncan's painting is the living proof!

Alexander Carmichael also held *Eileana Bride* to have been an old name for the Hebrides. Whether or not 'Hebrides' itself pertains to Brighde is unproven and probably unprovable. What can be said with certainty – both from the oral tradition, and because I've found it written in an old legal title – is that the whole of pre-Reformation Harris was the Parish of *Kilbride.*[18] That is to say, this was the parish of Bridgit's *cille,* her hermit cell, or church; or at least, of ones named after her. In those words of the Welsh poet that keep on coming back to me: 'The parish has a saint's name time cannot unfrock.'

Brighde was a preacher and the patron saint of blacksmiths, poets and healers. I cannot help but notice that those qualities, too, were the attributes of John Morrison of Leac a Lì. It was she who, according to the Irish tradition, 'turned back the streams of war'.

Both she and John were passionate about salvation – the 'salving' of the human soul.

And why? To heal our *nostos-algos*, at an armour-piercing depth.

6

THE BLACKSMITH'S WELL

At the crossroads, a handmade sign points off in the direction of Leac a Lì. It proclaims 'The Bays Café', and in my mind on this bright day, it's California dreamin'. Who'd have thought such luck would chance my way, a coffee just in time to fix the old elevenses itch.

Inside the community hall, two women stand behind a counter. They're hard at work, preparing lunches. It's like I've walked back fifty years ago. They could be period actresses, dropped in from a more stately age. Actually, they're just the timeless island matrons that I've always known: the kind you'd always see, in flowery pinafores and knee-length dresses, starched blouses and ever-so sensible shoes, and mellowing locks bunched neatly back – what I always think of as a 'Presbyterian bun'.

These are a kind of people whom I almost feel I know without so much as knowing. There'll be a whole culture to them, and that, braided to distinctive individuality. In the villages of Harris, such wealth of what it means to be a person can still be very strong. The isles' poet, Iain Crichton Smith, wrote of what he called 'real people in a real place'.[1] That's my gut sense of who this pair will prove to be. Mind you, Smith's words leave some folks slightly edgy. So many have succumbed to the things that try to turn so many of us into plastic people. Happily, there's nothing plastic in what's spread out before me here. It's all home made. Their apple crumbles, and their sponge cakes packed with jam and cream. Their bulging sandwiches, and pies that ooze dark gravy out of earthquake fissures darting through the glazed brown pastry. Why, there's even quiche for those who don't eat meat – something that's still hard to fathom in a crofting culture where we caught or reared so much of it ourselves, as near organic as it comes.

'I can see *somebody's* been hard at work over the stove last night,' I say, as I request a slice of shortbread with my coffee. I'm signalling that I sense they're probably not just employees. It's most likely something that they're doing also, as they'd say, 'for the community'.

'And where will you be coming from today?' asks Jessie, introducing herself.

'From John MacAulay's at Flodabay, and Rodel yesterday.'

Not the usual tourist.

'Ohhh,' says Anne, searchingly. 'And where would your accent be from?'

'Leurbost, but with an English mother. You see, my father was Dr McIntosh. You might have heard of him?'

She thinks awhile. 'Oh yes, *a ghràidh*,' she says, with the familiar 'my dear', 'my love'. 'I think that I might remember the name, right enough. And where will you be walking to?'

'To Ness, but not all the way today! Today, I'm only heading for the hills above . . . urr . . . Bun-Avahhh-Eaddd . . .'

'*Oh yes*, a ghràidh. *Buna!*' she says, rallying to my rescue. '*Bun Abhainn Eadarra*. But we just call it Buna for short. You'll be wanting to see the old whaling station, are you?'

'I'll pass by that way, I'll see it from the road, but I'm hoping to spend tonight in the hills above *Buna*.' This time I thrust out the name with renewed confidence. 'Then tomorrow I'll go on to Kinlochresort, and from there, another nine days if I take it easy, up to Ness.'

'Oh well!' chips in Jessie, at the mention of Kinlochresort – *Ceann Loch Reasort* – the Head of Loch Resort. 'That will be some journey,' and she's looking at my pack. She'll be wondering how its slightness squares up to the story.

I explain that my stuff's straddled between the surgery and tourist office in Tarbert. As they ask more questions, I crack a joke about the poaching pilgrimage and a 'wee cast' on the Grimersta – at which they warn me, in a pretendy-finger-wagging sort of way, not to get caught.

'And your tent?' muses Anne, bemused. 'I suppose that it will have . . . *a flysheet?*'

'Oh yes, nothing but the best!' I laugh. She's obviously picked up the name and knows that it will keep the banter going. 'But at this time of year, more for keeping off the rain than flies.'

From there, it's down to business. I reach into my bag and take out the map and both of Doctor Finlay's books. The impending tourist influx will have to wait. The lunchtime preparations have been put on hold. All three of us gather round a table, and I point to the area that's up beside the mission hall. One half of me is musing that such halls were just a normal part of village life, especially for the mid-week meetings in the days when people lacked the cars with which to take their elderly a few miles to the nearest church. The other half of me thinks how very interesting that such a title throws back to a time when missionaries would come, just as they did in 'darkest Africa'.

I explain to them that, according to Doctor Finlay, there's a famous well '. . . that's called . . . now, how would you say it? Tobar a' Gughhh . . .'

Anne rallies to me again. 'We would say it *Toh-par-a-goh-a*, a ghràidh. That's how we would say it.'

Softly she repeats the phrase – *toh-par-a-goh-a* – and I mark her old-world politeness, the emphasis on *we would say it,* as if to bow to the possibility of 'superior knowledge'.

A possibility, but not this time. 'Toe-bera Go-er,' I repeat, in stranglified self-conscious clumsiness. Even as a child my hearing was poor. I struggle to catch the soft consonants. That's partly why I never picked up Gaelic. But only partly. Mainly, it's just the way it was in those days. I even remember feeling superior that I didn't speak Gaelic when visitors would ask. In the 1960s, the others were told to learn 'the English' from me and the only other two who had it in our class of nineteen. It was something that we all had 'to get' – as if it was a type of vaccination – a 'must' in order to 'get on' in life, and not 'fall by the wayside'. More like, 'get on and get out', for that's what happened in the fast lane. The island was no place 'to succeed'. And today? I feel as if it's left me almost with a psychological blockage. I can scrape my way along in French. Even in Papua New Guinea pidgin. But for some reason, or some complex constellation of reasons, not so in Gaelic. Even with the most basic greetings I feel a collapse of confidence, often underscored at the crucial moment by a frustrating inability to remember the words.

But this is not the time to go there. I just point to my hearing aids to show I've got a problem. Sometimes it helps to blame the hardware for the software.

'*Toh-par-a-goh-a*,' says Jessie, with painstaking slowness. 'You see, it is the well of Iain Gobha na Hearadh, John Morrison the Blacksmith of Harris,' and, between the three of us, we settle for something that sounds to me like *Tobar-a-go-er*.

'Oh, a ghràidh,' resumes Anne. 'That is a wonderful thing, that you have come here to find the well of the Gobha. You see, he was a very great Christian. *Very great*, my dear,' and she starts describing him, as if it was just the other day that he'd been spotted, going about his preaching in the village.

'You see, he brought so many people here to Christ.'

He cuts an enigmatic figure, this largely self-educated Iain or John Morrison. You'd wonder how a name like Ian maps onto John, but think of Jan, and you'll get a sense of how the sounds migrate. They say that he was descended from Roderick Morrison, *an Clasair Dall* – the Blind Harpist – who died in the early eighteenth century and has been called the 'last minstrel' of Gaelic Scotland. On the one hand, the Gobha was a party to all the usual Puritanical put-downs on secular music and dance, such as Calvin and his followers in Geneva had tried to squash. So much of the culture has been lost in this way.[2] On the other hand, he saw himself as dancing to a higher tune. Literally so. In 1830, when he heard that John Macdonald of Ferintosh, 'the Apostle of the North', had arrived with missionary fervour to preach on Harris, he wrote:[3]

> Some one came one evening to the smithy where I was hard at work at the anvil and mentioned that Dr Macdonald was come. I tried to subdue my emotion; and I longed for the absence of the messenger; and whenever the messenger had gone I ran to the smithy door and bolted it. I could then, when alone, give scope to my emotions. I danced for joy – danced round the smithy floor; for I felt a load taken from off my spirit suddenly. I danced till I felt fatigued; and I knelt down and prayed and gave thanks.

An anvil from his workshop still exists. It sits outside the house of his great-great-grandson, Alastair 'Alda' Ferguson, the Lochmaddy taxi driver who told me of the tradition that links Neil Armstrong to Boreray. Another time, Alda told me that his wife was looking out the window, when she shouted to him: 'Come and see this. There's five ministers in our garden, standing round the anvil.' To which I couldn't resist the quip: 'And were they dancing?'

The Gobha's poetry heaves with old-style evangelical effervescence. It's mostly not to my taste, at least, not as it comes through in English with its heavy, born-again theology. But that's me speaking, what they'd probably call an unreconstituted reprobate. That said, it has a spiritual integrity that can be moving. *An Nuadh Bhreith* – The New Birth – is said to be his greatest work. It depicts the 'old man', the Old Adam of the Gobha's unregenerate self, battling it out with the 'new man', the New Adam of Christ, struggling to be born from within.[4]

Tha mi bàtht' an cuan an t-seann duin',
Fo gheur fhuar-dhealt 's fuachd a' gheamhraidh;
Thig an t-òg na ghlòir gu theampall
Chuireas mis' a dhanns' lem chasaibh.

I am drowned in the old man's ocean,
under the sharp, chill dew and cold of winter;
the young man will come in glory to his temple,
which will set my feet to dancing.

The well that I was looking for, the women told me, would not be found up by the old mission house. They didn't know of any well up that hill. The well that I was looking for is right across the next fence. It's on what used to be the Gobha's croft.

What's more, 'You'll have to go and look for it!' they kept insisting – as if I needed any encouragement. When they were young, the village girls all used to go and take a drink. 'It was for the health, you see, for the health.' Not just the girls, but everybody in the village would go there, 'just to take a deoch' – a wee drink – 'for the health.'

'It had the sweetest water in all of Harris.' The spring that fed it rose from deep within the rocks. 'Rising water, we would always call it,' and no matter what the weather, it always came out very cold. These days, however, the well is all closed over. It hadn't been seen for easily thirty years. When not in use these little wells fill in, or grass over, so very quickly. About ten years ago somebody had come to the village on a search. Nothing was found. And yet, 'It must be over there, hiding somewhere in those boulders. Just you go and look! Go take a look.'

At that moment, a car came down the hill from the direction of Tarbert.

'Look!' says Jessie, pointing out the window. 'It's Morag. If anybody still knows where to look it will be herself. You sit down and finish your coffee. I'll give her a ring.'

Ten minutes later, and I'm off. Morag lives across the road and up a driveway. It's a long, modern house with three white dormer windows. Built, I'd guess, in that period of relative prosperity in the sixties and seventies.

Morag is a Free Presbyterian, these often being thought of as the islands' 'strictest' denomination. Their community on Harris has been described by a historian of religion as retaining 'that abiding, faintly Edwardian dignity'.[5] If that's the case, then she's the perfect picture. As erect in posture as, no doubt, in mind, she conveys the analytical, no-nonsense air of a woman who is well educated, but who takes her distance from the greater part of that which passes for the norms of worldly mores. Her pleated skirt itself speaks volumes, hanging almost to her ankles; and she's sizing me up, like I'm before the headmistress and have to give respectable account.

'So, that's why I'm here . . .' I conclude, daring to mention neither poaching nor pilgrimage. 'Doctor Finlay shows the well at one location. John MacAulay suggests another. Jessie and Anne said if anyone would know, it might be yourself.'

Her hand rests holding to the door, making up her mind, and with no slippage, prematurely, to *a ghràidh*. It's rare to feel so seen right through, and yet refreshing in its penetrating honesty. Her Westminster confessional worldview might not be mine, but still I feel a warmth for these, the type of folks who raised me. There's a kinship that goes deeper than the outer schisms of belief. These are, quite plain and simply, *good people*. And if she sends me packing, it'll only be because they've had enough of visitors who turn up – journalists from the south in the silly season, or the writers of flippant travel books – to find some aspect of their piety at which it can be easy to poke fun.

The hand drops slowly from the door.

'The Gobha's well . . .' she announces solemnly – and then speeds up her words, as if to get them out before a change of mind – '. . . is right over that fence.'

The gatekeeper has let me through

'It is on the croft of Dr Anthony Latham. That's where the well used to be when we were girls. But nobody has drunk from it for years and years. I don't know if it will ever be found again.'

'Do you think that Dr Latham would let me have a look?'

'Oh, I'm sure that he'd be very happy. Now, you climb over that fence. See if can find anything there. The well you're looking for used to be amongst those boulders. Go and see if you can find it.

'And if anybody passing by on the road asks what you're doing, just tell them that *Morag Macleod* gave you permission. And if you need a spade, you'll find one in that shed.'

I can't believe it. Not just permission, but aiding and abetting too! The fence is low, and with a hop, I'm over.

My mind's a-race. I have to still myself, and think about it logically. What signs might give away a hidden well? Old stonework, or the vestige of a path? Soak-ways, or rusty staining on the rocks? Plants like sundew and bog violet – the sorts that grow in boggy ground – compensating for the lack of nitrogen by trapping living insects on their sticky hairs. Oh! What a way to go!

I mosey through the boulder field, taking in every detail. There are maybe twenty rocks protruding from the sward. Each are the size of Fred Flintstone wheelbarrows, left over from the Ice Age. Only two of these have any sign of seepage from below. One has a massive wodge of sphagnum moss at its base. The other, a long depression running from it, perhaps a dug-out channel that's now partly filled. I take a photograph of both and, realising that I'll need the spade, take my camera back across the fence and knock on Morag's door.

'I think *that* will be the one,' she says, peering at the digital display and pointing to the channel. 'Have you tried digging?'

'Not yet. Are you quite sure it's alright?'

'Oh yes! Dr Anthony Latham will be *very* pleased if you can find water on his land.'

Apparently, the physician and his family came to Harris not just for work, but for its strong religion. I notice how she always speaks his name in full, and with respect, to say the least. My stark use of 'Dr Latham' sounds clinical in comparison.

'That well,' she adds, 'used to be about eighteen inches deep. It had stone walls, about eighteen inches square. Now, go and take the spade, and see if you can find it!'

I cross back over and begin to dig around the channel.

But nothing. Just dampness, and a slight trickle that comes to nothing. Maybe, I think to myself, the channel was cut by the person who searched ten years ago. It looks about that vintage. Maybe it's a red herring. I'll try the rock with the sphagnum moss instead. Come to think of it, that only grows in saturated ground.

I punch the spade down, but it bounces right back up. I try pressing with all of my weight, but it simply refuses to slice through. I even try bouncing on the spade, jumping up and down like one gone crazy on a pogo stick. Let's hope no passer-by calls Dr Latham on the 999! But still no joy.

Maybe it needs a little more intelligence. I probe in with my fingers to feel what's there. The moss is threaded through with toughly stringy roots of grass. It's got the texture of a sponge cake reinforced with wire.

Ah – there's a small hole going in by the side of the boulder. It's too narrow for rabbits, but maybe made by mink. Mink like water, but their razor teeth, like an overgrown shrew, are vicious if they're cornered.

Needs must, and so I lie down and slowly stretch my arm into the dark.

Oh wow! We have water! This must be a drinking hole for little creatures, right enough. What I can feel is not a depth of eighteen inches, but maybe three or four. I'm also feeling something long and smooth, a jar of some sort. It's an old Tennants' screw-top. So this'll be the well, right enough. They'd usually leave a cup or some container so that passers by could take their fill. It must be thirty years at least since beer was sold in these pint-sized brown bottles.

I try to yank at handfuls of the sponge, but the mass is just too tightly knit together. I'm puzzled, for sphagnum moss will usually pull out easily in tufts. As kids, we used yank out huge dripping clumps, and hurl them at each other in a prototype of playing paintball. During the First World War, vast quantities were gathered, dried, and sent off to the trenches for the soldiers' dressings. The plant can absorb as much as twenty times its own dry weight in liquid. Its chemistry creates an acid bog environment which gives it antiseptic properties. We used to use it for packing salmon, filling the gutted belly and surrounding spaces, but that's also why it worked for wounds. As a certain Mrs A.M. Smith rhymed in 1917:[6]

> The doctors and the nurses
> Look North with eager eyes,
> And call on us to send them
> The dressing that they prize
> No other is its equal -
> In modest bulk it goes,
> Until it meets the gaping wound
> Where the red life blood flows,
> Then spreading, swelling in its might
> It checks the fatal loss,
> And kills the germ, and heals the hurt
> The kindly Sphagnum Moss

Well! At least if Dr Latham intercepts me, I've got a talking point. *The Poacher's Contribution to Medical History*. But I'm mindful that I've got to get to Tarbert before five. Brain is failing in the task. It's time to try that Flintsone brawn.

Crouching down into a lifting position, I get both hands around the mossy plug. I'm hulking-up, Sumo style, locking into mythic battle with what morphs into the *Bog Monster*.

Leaning back with all my weight, I push as hard as I can with my legs, and pull with bulging arms.

No damned luck! I'm winded, and my finger nails are ripped and running red.

'So the Bog Monster demands *blood sacrifice*, does he?'

I've got to get cracking up the road, so it's the last chance. *Ahhrrggh!* I expire, in a long, wild, guttural growl. Here's hoping Morag's got her windows shut. Some pilgrim!

Come on! I'm saying to myself. *It's all or nothing. One more go at it. Heave! Heave! Heave boys, heave ho!* And it's like we're hauling out the boat before a storm, and it's *Come on boys! Put your bloody backs into it. Give it something. Go on, GIVE – IT – SOMETHING!*

My clothes are dripping with the green-jellied goo that squeezes out of sphagnum. But slowly, with a mighty sucking *Gloooooch* from out his lair, the monster pulls away. Back he comes, upwards, outwards, a slobbering mass of moss and roots all stitched together like a fothered sail. And there's the explanation. By growing down into the moss, the grass could trail its roots into a constant source of water. For there my beauty stands. There stands a rippling pool of icy water. All eighteen inches depth of it, the four-square stone surrounds – of Tobar a' Ghobha.

I climb back over the fence and knock again on Morag's door. There's no reply, then I hear she's talking on the phone. Probably the whole village has been ringing up, wondering what's going on.

I stand and wait, pondering what a well might mean in her worldview: the poetry of Psalm 104 that Thomas Boston leaned on for his sense of providence, where God 'sendeth the springs into the valleys, which run among the hills' and 'watereth the hills from his chambers' until 'the Earth is satisfied'.

But now she's coming to the door.

The woman looks me up and down. I'm dripping gobs of monster goo onto her step. Her face is deadpan. Words are hardly necessary.

'You've found it,' she says. 'You've opened Tobar a' Ghobha.

'Come on in.'

I reach down to untie my laces. 'Oh, don't worry about that! Come on in. You can take a wash at the kitchen sink over there.'

'Are you quite sure that Dr Latham's not going to mind?'

'Not at all! I'll tell him what has happened when he gets home.'

She passes me a towel. I mop my hands and eyes. Her eyes have softened to their kindness now.

'Did you take the water?'

'Yes, but only three wee sips. It's still stirred up and muddy.'

She slowly nods.

'We're very grateful to you,' she says.

It is written that Gobha na Hearadh was 'an aristocrat of nature's creation'. He would share 'with the needy and starving around him' his last morsel of the kail – the poor-man's cabbage.[7]

As such, he stood the test of the Gaelic proverb, '*Se càl a dhearbhas a' creideamh* – 'It is the kail that tests the creed' – and I feel that, mainly by her bearing, Morag too has nourished me on such a creed.

I step back out of her doorway. She catches my eye across the threshold.

'I haven't gone over that fence for several years,' she says. 'I'll give the water a couple of days to settle, and then I'll maybe put on my Wellington boots, and go and take a drink myself.' After all, it is written that even 'David longed, and said, Oh that one would give me drink of the water of the well of Bethlehem, which is by the gate!'[8]

'God bless,' I say, as I turn to part.

I surprise myself at such an utterance. Her face flickers too. Perhaps we're both surprised at just how deeply run the chambers of those stone surrounds.[9]

> 'And will you go there for me,'
> said the old woman, 'even with a thimble,
> and bring me a drop of that hard water
> that will bring colour to my cheeks.'
> I found the well at last,
> and though her need was not the greatest
> it was to her I brought the treasure.

Lunch was over by the time I got back down to the Bays Café. Here the tourist season measures more in hours than months. The guests had been and gone, and Jessie and Anne were wiping down the tables.

Unable to contain myself, I yelled out: 'I found it!

'Got it all dug out. Brimming to the top. Lovely!'

They could hardly believe me. I had to show them the pictures on the camera.

'Ohhh! We are very pleased!' Anne effused. 'So you are now *the discoverer* of Tobar a' Ghobha!' She looked at me and shook her head, as if I was a wonder to behold. And so I was, given the state of my clothing.

Had there been an anvil on the floor to circumnavigate, we'd have danced a little jig.

One of them suggested there should be a plaque erected at the roadside to mark the rediscovered spot. People would come to take a drink. They'd want to remember 'what he did for us'. Repeated Anne: '*Oh . . . to remember what the Gobha did for us!*' as if he'd been a figure of their childhood days, and not the century before.

'And did you leave the ground all neat and tidy?' Jessie asked, tilting her head with a coquettish tweak, as if about to launch another of her pretend reprimands.

'Tidy as your kitchen!' I assured her. 'I spread the mud down the feannagan, and covered it with a skin of turf.'

They both glanced at each other. A key had turned, a penny dropped.

'Oh, *ma tha . . .*' said Anne, her voice fading as she spoke, to a wistful remnant. 'So you spread it down . . . *the feannagan.*

'So . . . you know about . . . *the feannagan . . .*' and her words are lost in reverie. Those bygone days. Those days of laughter and togetherness when working on the land.

Her mind was rolling back through time to lifelines.

My mind was racing forward with the clock to deadlines.

It's now twenty to three. I've been in the village for a good three hours. Tarbert remains a full six miles away. I say I'd better dash. Jessie, realising the urgency, offers to run me there in her car. I could very gladly take up her kindness, but wish neither to consume her time nor short-change the walking. If I crack along at near three miles an hour, I should just make the 5 p.m. curfew at the tourist office. Three miles an hour, over hills, sustained! That'll be a pace, indeed, to test the kail.

We make farewells, and I hotfoot off and up the long and winding hill. Behind me, to the south, the silhouette of Roineabhal is fading in the haze, the grace of 'fair maid Harris' as I have it written by an old crofter living in her lee.[10] From here, her tresses sweep back to the west. They say you shouldn't 'anthropomorphise' nature. You shouldn't project human qualities onto the non-human. That's what I've heard some academics say. But others say that the mountains of the Hebrides were once a race of giant women who laid down to rest. I just give my scholarly colleagues a pretendy rattled look, and ask: 'But who are we to disregard such voices from the margins?'

Soon, my beloved Roineabhal is lost amidst a plethora of intervening hills. I'm high up on the level now, rejoining the main road, beating it along a winding way that runs amidst more beds of boulders interspersed with rank dark heather growing from the peat. To the north, a new horizon opens up. It spurs me on to see the tops of mountains that I'm heading for. Clisham's in the background, straight ahead. Big and Little Uisgneabhal, slightly to the left. Somewhere in-between them is the pass through which I hope to wend my way this evening and tomorrow.

I'm really pushing it hard, grinding in low gear up the steeper braes, then coasting down the far sides, sometimes breaking to a half apology for a trot. My radiator's overheating. Like this, I'll get to Tarbert looking like, and smelling like, a pig that's spent its day in muck. I come upon a stream, drop my bag, wade right in, and vigorously wash both body and my clothes. I wring them out as best I can and put them straight back on again. That'll cool the engine as they dry.

At last, I round the corner high above the Tarbert pier. I stampede full throttle down the precipitous hill, quite forgetting to mark any observance that, somewhere underneath the tarmac of this widened modern road, was once the Well of Mary – 'Tobar Mairi' – as a place sign on a corner house gently reminds me, as I breathlessly rush past.[11]

I hit the tourist office at precisely five past five. The notice on the door says: CLOSED.

Luckily, the lass is still inside and making up her till. Sometimes it's best to pull the tourist rather than the local card. The Joker justifies the eccentricity, for a crazed bog warrior is waving at her window. Unfazed, she lets me in. And I have to say it. You'd go unto the ends of the Earth before you'd find more kindly people than on Harris; and Harris – at least, the part for which I'm headed – is pretty much at such an end.

I get my bags, recover Osprey from the nearby surgery, and prompted by the screw-top bottle that I found at Leac a Lì, make for where I know I'll find salvation for the day's long drawn-out thirst.

7

MY OWN LOCHS NOW

The Harris Hotel in Tarbert is a wonder of the old world, a venerable fisherman's rest that is run to new world standards. The elderly proprietor, John Murdo Morrison, one of the last of a breed of Highland gentry, was not around. It's mostly his children, Sarah and Andrew, who run the place. When I told Andrew that I hoped to make it by tomorrow night to the abandoned village of Kinlochresort – the Head of the Red Fjord, possibly so-named because of sunsets, as it stretches out to the west – he answered with a longing smile: 'That is one of the most beautiful places in the world.'[1]

With a pint of ale in hand, I went out into the garden and the languid evening sun. I spread out all my gear on the lawn, arranged it into strata, and with not a nook or cranny to spare, repacked Osprey. An English lady, a tourist in her later years, came over to watch what I was doing. We struck up a conversation. It was one of those quite intimate exchanges that you sometimes get when both parties know they'll probably never meet again. She had come to the islands seeking something – she didn't know quite what – and was taken by my story of the well. It seemed to mean a lot to her, and telling it was also like telling it to myself. I suppose her listening ear and warmth helped me to process the day's experience. We both were pilgrims on respective paths. I told her where to find the writing on the hotel window: the swirled initials, etched in with a diamond ring – *JMB*. And there lies quite a story.

With books and plays like *Peter Pan*, Sir James Matthew Barrie probably did more than any other writer to bring alive the faerie genre to the British imagination of the early decades of the twentieth century. He was born in 1860 at Kirriemuir, a country town north of Dundee, that was seeped in *sithichean* – the faerie tales that the Scots and Irish 'Tinkers' or Traveller folks brought back each summer when they came to pick soft fruit. The son of a weaver, both of his parents were active members of the Free Church of Scotland, the doctrinally strict but very grassroots movement that broke away from the establishment Church of Scotland in a schism called 'the Disruption' in 1843.

Barrie had voyaged to Harris in the summer of 1912. He grandly rented Amhuinnsuidhe Castle for a fishing holiday with his friends. These included the orphaned Llewelyn Davies boys, as were depicted in the 2004 movie, *Finding Neverland*, where Johnny Depp played the tender if enigmatic Barrie.

At the height of his fame at the time, the writer had stayed at the Harris Hotel on the way to the castle, signing both the visitors' book and the window.[2] It was while fishing in the Harris Hills that he seems to have encountered local tales that contributed to a play that was at least fifteen years germinating in his mind – *Mary Rose*. His notebook for 1912 contains lines typical of Hebridean stories, one of which – 'the island that likes to be visited' – takes centre stage. Inspired by a tiny island on a salmon loch called Voshimid – Bhoisimid in the Gaelic – Barrie later wrote to the orphaned boys, in a dedication to the published version of *Peter Pan*, that this was '*where we caught Mary Rose*'.[3]

Although the work is rarely staged today, it was a massive box-office success when it first opened in April 1920. The initial staging in the Haymarket Theatre ran to almost four hundred performances, making it Barrie's longest-running play.[4] Behind what could be misread as a whimsical plot, the playwright masterfully explored the in-between states of life, death and consciousness. The emotions evoked would have spoken powerfully to his audience, recently afflicted as so many of them would have been by the traumas and the losses of the Great War. It would seem that the work also drew on a well-known ballad from the Scottish Borders, *Bonnie Kilmeny*. He had described it in a 1905 notebook as 'a sort of Rip Van Winkle'.[5] Young Kilmeny, in her bloom of innocence, had wandered up a wooded glen, where a faerie led her to 'a land of love and a land of light'. Her abductor from the Otherworld considered it a work of mercy, set against a harsh world for which she was too good. He had 'brought her away frae the snares of men/ that sin or death she never may ken'.[6]

Mary Rose is about a sensitive, pure-hearted little English girl, whose parents bring her on their holiday to the Hebrides. 'There's a whaling station,' said Mr Morland, her emotionally stuck, upright and uptight, upper-middle class father. 'We went because I was fond of fishing.' While sketching on an island while her father was in the boat, Mary Rose was spirited away by the faeries. Twenty days later she came back. Her distraught parents found her sitting, sketching, on the selfsame rowan branch from which she'd disappeared. The child was blithely unaware of any untoward happening or lapse of time.

She went on to grow up almost normally, but come her engagement to a young naval lieutenant, Simon Blake, nicknamed Simon Sobersides, her mother felt it necessary to explain why the little island in the loch 'became the most dreaded place in the world to us':

> I have sometimes thought that our girl is curiously young for her age – as if – you know how just a touch of frost may stop the growth of a plant and yet leave it blooming – it has sometimes seemed to me as if a cold finger had once touched my Mary Rose.

Three years after marrying, with a baby boy left back in England, where does Mary Rose choose to go for a delayed honeymoon, but back to the Isle of Harris, which held for her dim memories of some childhood paradise. Their boat on the loch is rowed by Cameron, a gawky youth from the village. Barrie's stage instructions pitch him 'in the poor but honourable garb of the gillie'. We're told that he is 'not specially impressive until you question him about the universe'.

The threesome land on the Island that Likes to Be Visited to have a picnic lunch. There, Mary Rose presses Cameron for a creepy story. Uneasily, he tells one about a little English girl. She had come to Harris ten years previously, and there she 'heard *the call* of the island'. It was a true story. Cameron's father had gone out looking when she'd vanished, they'd even dragged the loch. 'They searched, ma'am, long after there was no sense in searching,' and then she reappeared.

'I am glad,' Mary Rose responds, 'but it rather spoils the mystery.'

Simon, however, makes the connections and is now completely spooked. He tries to force a change of subject. 'You and your bogies and wraiths, you man of the mists,' he tells Cameron, patronisingly. He speaks disparagingly to Mary Rose in French, only to have Cameron reply in like tongue. It turns out that for all his humble appearance, the ghillie when not home for summer is studying for the ministry at university.

'It is not good to disbelieve the stories when you are in these parts,' he tells his social superior. 'I believe them all when I am here, though I turn the cold light of remorseless Reason on them when I am in Aberdeen.'

'Beware, Mr Cameron,' chides Simon, 'lest some day when you are preaching far from here the call plucks you out of the very pulpit and brings you back to the island like a trout on a long cast.'

At this, Cameron takes umbrage, and retires to bail the boat. Mary Rose seizes the opportunity of privacy to beg Simon to make love to her. He, however, in his sober emotional frigidity, has forgotten how. He takes his eyes off her to tend the fire on which they've cooked their trout, and as he does so, Mary Rose hears *the call* again, the unearthly music and the soft and furtive whisperings, as if from holes in the ground.

'How cold and grey it has become,' says Simon, and then sees she's gone.

Mary Rose, where have you got to? Please don't hide. Dearest, don't. Cameron, where is my wife?

Cameron, I can't find her. Mary Rose! Mary Rose! Mary Rose!

The scenes that follow swirl in and out of psychic twilight zones of the Great War. Bereft of his wife, Simon stoically worked his way up through the Royal Navy's ranks. In a second war that takes place twenty-five years later – prophetically anticipated by Barrie – he attains command of HMS *Bellerophon*. The allusion to this vessel would have pinged the sonar depths of Barrie's audience in 1920. Just four years previously, the dreadnought was one of the very few vessels to have sailed, like a ghost, unscathed through the Battle of Jutland. Within a few hours of maritime fury, six thousand British hands had been lost beneath the waves to the firepower of the Kaiser's fleet.

The play closes, as it had opened, in an English country mansion at the end of the second war. The house had long been lying empty, stuck on the market because of its haunted reputation. Hardly any of the neighbours could now remember the long-departed inhabitants, a certain Mr and Mrs Morland. A young Australian soldier, demobbed in London and with time on his hands, has turned up, posing as a prospective buyer. The housekeeper is suspicious, but he manages to fob her off to go and make a cup of tea. While she's away, he enters a forbidden room.

That young soldier turns out to be Harry Blake, Simon's estranged son. Semi-orphaned on his mother's loss, the boy had run away to sea, and in a deeply moving closing scene, he lays to rest his mother's ghost – the soul of Mary Rose.

*   *   *

It was my mother who first told me about *Mary Rose*. Even today, in her eighties, she vividly remembers watching it at the Birmingham Rep when she was a student nurse. It was in the late 1940s, just before she met my father. All that she can still recall is that it was about an island on a Hebridean loch, or maybe Lewis and Harris itself – an island that *liked to be visited*. When I think about it, that must have been her first encounter with the Outer Hebrides. It had then been she who had pushed Dad to apply for the vacancy for the North Lochs practice when it was advertised in the *British Medical Journal* in 1959. She'd pushed and pushed him, she told me, pushing to an almost irrational degree. He'd otherwise have thought the place too remote. I've therefore wondered whether Barrie's *Mary Rose* had played a role in us coming to the island, and to me being on this walk now. A little opening of the way, perhaps? A home-call from a place that welcomes visitors, and has something to say.

My mother was by no means on her own in having experienced such a sense of enchantment. Sir Walter Langdon-Brown was a regius professor of medicine at Cambridge in the 1930s. In a public lecture on the subject of 'Myth, Phantasy and Mary Rose', he offered the opinion:[7]

> I think in some respects *Mary Rose* is Barrie's greatest work. To deal with it fully is impossible . . . for it seems to me one of the completest expositions of the working of the unconscious mind to be found in contemporary literature.

But you could get carried away with such things! It has just clocked seven. The English woman has gone back inside for dinner, I've downed the last of my pint, and now must needs 'hard nose the highway'. This time, and for the first time, I'm as a fully laden pack-horse. I heave Osprey up over my shoulders and pull tight the straps. Wow! It's now going to be a four-and-a-half mile tramp along the road to Buna, then a further couple of miles up the 'Lost Glen' – the one that Seumas Crawford said would take them 'long enough to find you'. That's where I want to camp, beside a mountain lake called Loch a' Sgàil.

If the conditions underfoot are good, there's still a chance to catch the 'evening rise'. That's the witching hour when fish come on the take, just at the cusp of day and night. At these latitudes, and at this time of the year, the sun comes up around five o'clock in the morning, and it sets just short of ten. You've then another hour of decent twilight before night wins the day. But frankly, the odds on a sizzling trout supper are lengthening with the shadows.

It can be a sombre stretch, this length of road along the northern rim of West Loch Tarbert. A leaden flank of hills looms tightly to the south. They rob the ocean inlet of its due illumination. Further out, the sea loch brightens as it widens, until you get to Taransay. This four-mile stretch of island had its day on reality TV, when a group of strangers came and lived together for a year in space-age eco-pods – the so-called *Castaway 2000* 'experiment'.

More lastingly, as such residential experiments go, the island hosts two chapels side by side. These are Teampall Chè, dedicated to Saint Keith, and Eaglais Tharain, to Saint Tarran.[8] If *eaglais,* meaning 'church', sounds French, it's because Gaelic often drew from Latin. Indeed, the Celtic monks were bilingual. I've not been able to find out anything about Keith, but Tarran, Ternan or Torranan as he's variously named, may have been a missionary visionary who set up churches in the Hebrides. The truth is that no-one any longer really knows. The Celtic Church, like the early Christian church more widely, seems not to have made a great song and dance about canonisation. Even into medieval times in Scotland, saintly sorts were so declared by their communities – by 'popular acclamation'. I suspect the practice didn't entirely stop there, or with the Reformation. I'm thinking of the houses in our village that were especially pious. There'd be not a Catholic halo, or a statue to the Virgin in sight. But often, there'd be a table, or a mantelpiece, given over to framed photographs of black-suited ministers in their white dog collars. And then there was this morning. Our musings on the saint-like Gobha.

'Ah – *Saint Torranan of Taransay*', I'm saying to myself as I walk, picking the version of his name that packs the most poetic punch.

'Ah – *Saint Chè of Taransay*'; the only one this side of Cuba.

'I invoke you, patron saints of all we'd love to believe about the Celtic Church – but lack a shred of evidence to back it up!'

Vroom. Vroom. Vroom. The cars go jetting by, and I am truly famished. All day long I've thought of catching worms. Worms for catching fish. I've kept a weather eye out for turves along the verge, the sort that I could overturn and have a rake through. But there were no such useful spoil heaps. Time was, when men would clean the ditches out by hand with spades and shovels. Worms thrived amongst the rotting vegetation in the clods. But now, it's all gung-ho machinery. Good for neat-and-tidy. Bad for worms and fishing.

Wish I'd gone for fish and chips while still in Tarbert. Here I am, stalking the ocean, but not a fish to hand. It gets me thinking of something that I saw back at the Lorimers' house, after Café Spirituel. There was a print on their wall, a map that had been made in 1714 by the London-based cartographer, Herman Moll, showing: *The North Part of Great Britain called Scotland.*

For West Loch Tarbert, the legend reads: *Here is plenty of Cod, Ling and large Eels.* For the stretch of the Minch that I walked up yesterday, that which runs between Harris and Skye: *Abundance of herrings taken here.* For St Kilda, where the inhabitants live '. . . in their little Stone Houses, of which there are some hundreds': *Plenty of Cod, and Ling of a great size all Round these Ifles.* And for central Lewis, bang over the headwaters of the Grimersta system: *Here are many Frifhwater Lakes.*

The map was made just seven years after the 'parcel of rogues' – a bankrupt squad of aristocrats – acceded to the shotgun marriage between Scotland and England. So began a new joint venture, the 'British' rather than the English empire. Scotland had been too poor, and too preoccupied with its own struggles, to have had anything but a failed attempt to establish a trading colony in what is now a part of Panama. This, the Darien Scheme, had bankrupted her feudal overlords who, under such straitened circumstances, turned to their Anglo-Norman cousins for a helping hand and with it, the prospect of reaching new markets through England's grip on sea power and shipping lanes. The intent of Moll's map appears to have been to promote the natural resource wealth of 'North Britain' to a southern client group. Scotland had not come empty-handed to the marriage – it only needed investment. The script immediately beneath the title tells 'how easy it would be to settle the most advantageous Fishery in the World here', as well as to modify rivers for bringing timber down to the sea. 'If things were rightly managed' – whatever that means – there'd be no need any more to go to Norway for wood, or to Newfoundland for fish, 'seeing North Britain can plentifully furnish us with both'.

What we see here, then, is an exercise in political cartography; even, from the point of view of the isles, a coloniser's, or at least an adventurer's, charter.[9] To push the point, and only slightly tongue in cheek – *Here be the archaeology of poaching as a crime.*

Moll's inscription for the Hebrides' largest port touches on the backdrop of violence. It says: *Stornoway Castle was destroy'd by the English Garrison, kept there by Oliver Cromwell.* Within those words lies quite a story. Not content with having devastated Ireland, Cromwell's New Model Army invaded Scotland in 1650. The plan was to consolidate Great Britain as a specifically Protestant state. His Roundhead troops met stiff resistance on invading Stornoway. The clansmen eventually sent them packing, but not before a loss of life that was said, on both sides, to have been 'severe'.

In a reflection on the name of Stornoway's Cromwell Street and its links to a religious legacy, the historian, Dr Macdonald of Gisla, mused:[10]

> We behaved well under his stern Puritans, and must have picked up some good habits from them. We still retain a grim Calvinism, and a main shopping boulevard, called after the stern Protector.

As for Dr Johnson, who toured the Highlands and Islands with Mr Boswell in 1773, for him the stern Protector's colonising rationale was cut and dry.[11]

> What the Romans did to other nations was in a great degree done by Cromwell to the Scots; he civilized them by conquest, and introduced by useful violence the arts of peace.

I'm walking, on and on, and the road climbs gently up towards the strung-out settlement of Ardhasaig. Osprey sits comfortably across my back and shoulders – a growing heaviness – but the belt drawn tight around my hips is helping to spread the weight.

Everything around me here, and all the terrain that I'll be passing through tomorrow, is land that has been owned since 2003 by a community land initiative, the North Harris Trust. The people here – some seven hundred of them – now run the place. They manage its sixty thousand acres for such priorities as affordable housing, tackling fuel poverty, low-impact renewable energy generation, job creation and eco-tourism.[12] Their hope is to reverse the sharp population decline that, in the previous half century alone, had caused Harris to lose half of its people. The very thought of such a change of fortunes puts a spring into my step.

Coming into view, a mile ahead, is Buna. I can see the river threading through the pass that climbs between the Clisham and the other peaks. Shadows are creeping up the glen. Only the upper slopes remain bronzed, while out to sea the settling sun rakes down the embers of the day.

Below a line of houses sits the whaling station. I can just make out a slipway and a tall industrial chimney stack. They're all that's left. Once, I went into a Tarbert shoe shop that was run by a frail old man. He had only a few boxes on his shelves, none with contents that were in fashion, but it was his residual contribution to the community. He told me that he remembered the way Bun Abhainn Eadarra was back in the 1920s. Steam-powered whalers heaved into the bay with up to three carcases at a time being towed behind. They'd winch them up the slipway, flense the blubber off in strips, boil out the oil in vats and, lastly, grind the bones to fertiliser. The smell, he said, was like the Devil's kitchen; yet nothing could make leather softer, nothing burn a lamp's flame brighter, than pure sperm oil.

All of a sudden, a head pops out the side of a shed door, and hollers: 'Nice evening!'

I am about to be granted a very great pleasure: the acquaintance of Mr Samuel Macleod of The Anchorage.

'Where are you off to?'

'Camping at Loch a' Sgàil tonight,' I shout back, optimistically, given where the sun had got to, 'and then over to Kinlochresort.

'I don't suppose you'd know the best way up the glen?'

'Keep to the right, up from the village, and you'll be alright. They usually go by Miabhaig or Amhuinnsuidhe, but by the time you've walked along the road you'll be just as quick setting out from here.'

'Would you have any other *recommendations?*'

'Well, don't go along the river. It's full of bogs and gullies. Above the village, you'll come to what's left of a stalker's path. That'll take you on a mile, and after that, keep tight to the side of the glen. You'll find the ground's better drained on the slope.'

He's reading me, trying to put together the pieces and figure out the story.

'But why are you wanting to go there?'

'I'm on my way to Ness,' I say, throwing my thumb back at the walkie-talkie-like protrusion from the side of Osprey. 'Taking a few wee casts along the way.'

'Ahh! So you're a *poacher* are you?' His head tosses up and to the side, as if welcoming an old friend. 'I was wondering, when I saw you coming down the road with that rod. Well, you won't get much in Loch a' Sgàil. It's only full of tiddlers.'

'And yourself? A poacher too?'

'Poaching!' he spits it out in mock disdain.

'Well, I'll tell you something. My poaching days are over. Over and out! We don't need to be poachers anymore round here. You see, we've got the land. Anyone who lives here fishes for free.'

'And the rest?'

'They can buy a permit' – and he takes a breath, filling his lungs with pride – 'because, *these are my lochs now.*'

'Thanks to *the buyout?*'

'The buyout! *You said it*, my boy. The *best thing* that has ever happened round here.'

He emerges from the shed and comes down to the fence.

'You see, ever since I was ten years old I've wanted to control my own lochs. And now I do. We all do! How about that?'

'Since you were ten? Why ten?'

'Because . . .' and he points to a stream that runs down the side of the Clisham road: 'You know that chain of wee lochs up past the quarry?' He means where the water's as deep as the mountain's high.

'When I was a boy, the estate couldn't be bothered with those lochs. So we used to go there. We thought of them as our lochs. One day, I caught six little sea trout. *Lovely* little sea trout. But the keeper came and caught me. Red-handed, with my rod, and the fish. They were all dead, of course, but would you believe it? Wait till you hear this! He said to me, this keeper said to me: *Just put those back from where you took them out!*

'And I had to throw them all away. Every one of the six of them! Had to watch them swept down by the river to the sea.'

He shakes his head in dawning disbelief. 'That's how it used to be on these estates. From that day on, I just knew it. One day, I wanted to control our own lochs.'

'But who are you, anyway?' he asks, in an unexpected bark. The old Scots challenge. The demand to *Stand and give account!*

'My father was Dr McIntosh of Leurbost.

'I was involved in the buyout on Eigg.

'I write books.'

He looks at me, unsure what to make of it.

'What kind of books?'

'Best known is *Soil and Soul*. About the land reform.'

He shakes his head.

'Never heard of it. Never heard of it at all.'

I might as well bite the bullet.

'It wouldn't be so popular with everyone in these parts. It's also about the superquarry at Lingerabay.'

He jerks himself erect.

'For . . . or *against?*' as if enquiring: *Damned . . .* or *Elect?*

I gulp, sealing my fate.

'Against!'

He just stares at me. Dungarees and braces, chequered shirt, a big round balding bronzed head with reddish blotches bitten deep from years and years of working in the sun and rain. And he's got a gold chain hanging round his neck.

Might as well be for a sheep as for a lamb.

'I was the one who brought the Red Indian chief to the inquiry.'

He's shaking his head again, connecting streams of memory.

'Well, well, well . . .' he says, with slow-releasing relish.

'Just imagine that!

'You! Just you come on over this fence. Leave your bag beside the road. Nobody's going to touch it. Just step over at that post. I want to show you something.'

I follow him back into his shed. It's a workshop, stuffed with spare parts of this and that, and lobster pots and nets. He rummages through some shelves at the back, and pulls out a large cobweb-trailing picture frame. With a few rubs of his cuff it smears clean.

Pressed beneath the glass is a double-page article from the *Sunday Mail*. The date is 27 March 1994. It's about a Harris superquarry, but not the one that I'd been involved with. At the same time as Redland had been strutting around South Harris, another corporation had been eyeing up the cliffs of Loch Seaforth in North Harris, just a couple of miles over the hills from where the sea trout incident had taken place.

'You see *that*?' he says, as he jabs a fencepost of a calloused finger at the glass.

'That Ready-Mix quarry . . . that concrete mixing lot . . . that was very nearly our Lingerabay.'

'If they'd pushed Lingerabay through, then *she* – that *aristocrat,* who acted like *she* owned *us* . . .'

'Er – Mrs Panchaud, the heiress?'

'*That's* the very one. You named her. *She* was going to . . . well . . . you just read all about it here.'

And he stands to attention. Like a soldier waiting to be decorated.

'You just read what I told them.'

My eye falls on a yellowed quote ascribed to the 'local fisherman', Mr Samuel Macleod.

I've been here all my life. And there's something wrong when she dictates what is going on from Switzerland. It's not right that a hole can be blasted in the landscape without the people being consulted. The scheme was sprung from out of the blue. She's not the most popular person on the island.

'But we saw her off!' he resumes. 'We saw the lady off, and now we've got the land. We've got the Trust, the North Harris Trust, and with the Trust, we're the ones who call the shots.'

And he's off into stories that could run until the dawn.

'You see, one day she calls me up. *Herself* it is. She calls me up, and she's speaking to me in a *very nice* tone of voice. Very polite, indeed.

'*Sammy*, she says sweetly. *Sammy, I would like you to come down and talk to me at the Castle – please.*

'So I'm thinking to myself, *O ho! What's cooking here? This will be interesting* . . . and off I go in my van, down to see her there at Amhuinnsuidhe.

'Well, she takes me into the office, and she starts hunting around all over the place, opening drawers and cupboards, *f'ing* and *b'ing* like you'd never have believed the language that was coming out of the woman. And all just to find a pen!

'*You need a pen?* I say.

'*Why do you need a pen?* I ask her, because, you see, Alastair, I'm suspicious of her mind.

'*Oh*, she says, as if I was only there to do her bidding, *For you to sign something, Sammy* – and she finds a pen and brings it over to me with a sheet of paper.

'*I am not here to sign anything, Madam*,' I say to her. But she ignores me, the way she'd ignore anyone when it suited her.

'*Now Sammy*, she says in that grand tone of hers. *We have been noticing that you go backwards and forwards every day in your little boat, checking your lobster pots. And we have been thinking that while you're out there, you must see the poachers' nets. So we've been wondering whether, the next time you see one, you might lift it? Or at least, tell us where it is so that we can send in the estate boat.*

'Well, she nearly blew me out of the water, she darned well did!

'What was I expected to say? Did she really think I was going to shop the boys?

'So I said to her: *It's not for me, Madam, to be telling what I might be seeing, or what I might be not seeing, when I'm at the lobsters.*

'*Ohhh, Sammy!* she says, sounding so let down. *We thought you might say that, Sammy!*

'I mean, can you imagine? The cheek of it!

'*But Sammy*, she says, as if she was putting cream out for the cat to dip his whiskers. *There might be MONEY in it for you* . . .

'Now, I can tell you, Alastair,' and he draws in very close, dropping to a whisper. 'As soon as I heard that little word – *MONEY* – little wheels started spinning in my head. So I said: *So what do you have in mind, Madam?*

'And this is what she says to me. She says: *We have been thinking, Sammy* – meaning herself and the old *bodach*, of course; though he was all right, he and me got on alright when he'd want to buy lobsters. I'd give him the best, and he'd know it.

'She says: *We have been thinking, Sammy, that if you'd only like to sign this little agreement that my husband and I have drawn up, then we will pay you seventy-five pounds for every salmon net delivered to the Castle.'*

He grins, draws back, and stares at me, as if glazed by astonishment at his own story. My eyes, too, are bulging like a cod's caught in a lobster pot.

'So I say to her, *Madam, you are making a man an offer that he cannot refuse* – and I took the pen, and signed the agreement, right there and then, bang on the dotted line.'

'And then?' I ask. And though I'm mindful that the Buna glen has dropped down into half-light, this is just too good to hurry.

'And then, I get back home,' he says. 'And I get on the blower. And I say to the lot of them. *Boys! Guess what? See all those old nets you've got sitting up the back of the byre? All full of holes and good for nothing but the haystack? Well, just you bring them right round here to Sammy at The Anchorage!'*

'And she paid up?'

'Well, no.

'Because she went and told the factor. And the factor phoned me up.'

He shakes his head in sore disdain.

'He phoned me up, *on a Sunday afternoon*, I tell you. *On the Sabbath Day!*

'He was wanting to make his point, you see. And he said to me, he said: *Samuel Macleod. You may think that you can pull the wool over the old woman's eyes. But never over mine!'*

In a small community like this, even the factor, the estate legal agent, gets given his due for a bit of wit. Even so the old *bodach*, as with another tale that Sammy threw in about a nice connection in the course of trading lobsters. If I'd hung around for long enough, even Mrs Panchaud would probably have been left a redeeming chink through the eye of

Sammy's needle. He'd have had some little story secreted away of an unexpected kindness, or an endearing touch. Such counterpointing doesn't stop the hard truths from being spoken, but it does help to lubricate wheels for the times when people have to pull together, as well as rubbing sperm oil into the leather of one's own humanity.

As I made moves to continue on my way, Sammy apologised for not having invited me into the house. He was having to go out shortly. However, seeing as I was a writer, and he too, a writer of poetry, would I just come over, so that he could read me something that would be, as they used to say, 'one for the road'?

He led me into a boxroom office, and pulled a folder from the desk. From it he recited a tale, set to verse, about a crofter who was coming home drunk one day on a bicycle. While crossing the Clisham, and stopping to do a little business, he parked his bike amongst a cluster of boulders, perhaps somewhere on the Leathad nan Clacha Mòra. When he was ready to set off again, he couldn't for the life of him remember which cluster.

Eventually he found a bike. He grabbed it by the handlebars, swung into the saddle, and helter-skeltered down the mountain side – only to be paraded through the village on an angry Highland cow.

With the permission of the Bard of Ardhasaig, I copied down a couple of his lines into my notebook:

And you heard the fairies' laughter,
When you were looking for your bike.

And that was it. Time to hard nose the highway again. Osprey's waited safely by the roadside. The foot of Clisham lies at the bottom of the hill. There, I take my leave from retracing the bus route by which I came down this way from Stornoway yesterday, and take the turning to the west and into Bun Abhainn Eadarra.

I trot off into the settling mire of dusk, chuckling to myself. What poetic justice! For all their powers of capital, persuasion and modernity. For all their double-barrelled whammy, trying to take pot shots at both ends of Harris. For all that, neither Redland, nor Ready-Mix, had managed to blast out those whisky-reeling residents of hollow hills – the timeless gentry of the sìthean.

There's not a cat's chance of reaching Loch a' Sgàil tonight. By now, it must be after ten, so over to Plan B. While there's still an inkling of twilight, I'll try to get up through the maze of fences that criss-cross the in-bye crofting lands. I'll pitch my tent just far enough into the glen to lose sight of the village lights, and get a touch of proper darkness and of wildness. I've come into Buna, over the cattle grid and just beyond the whaling station, but the day's already so far gone that I simply can't make out where best to cut into the hills.

From up ahead, my ears pick up a rapid scuttling sound. I strain my eyes, and through the gloom three panting shadows surge towards me. They're collie dogs, and following on behind them looms a big man, paradoxically wearing a baggy pair of khaki cotton shorts and a body warmer on top. His animals look pretty local, but not his gait or dress code. Turns out that he's an incomer from England, one of a team of professional trappers that's employed by the Hebridean Mink Project.

The American mink had established and become a blight in the late 1960s. There had been a short-lived fur farm on the island, some of them escaped and went feral. Like many translocated species, they found plenty of prey but had very few predators. Their penchant for eggs and chicks wreaks wildlife havoc in the nesting season. To try and curb their numbers, even with the hope of eventual elimination, my new-found acquaintance tells me that there's a network of some seven thousand traps laid out in lines around the island. He works the Harris Hills. He goes out nearly every day, and his dogs help by sniffing out the minks' musky trials. He baits each cage, sets the trap door, and logs the exact position by GPS for regular checking. When he makes a catch, the animal's dispatched humanely with a powerful airgun pellet through the head.

A lonely road, a chance but warm encounter, can launch an avalanche of memories. I, too, once shot a mink with an airgun. It was back in Leurbost, around 1970, the first time we'd known such an animal to turn up at our end of the village. George and Kate Allen had spotted it a few days earlier while at work in their weaving shed. At first they didn't know what this strange creature was, skulking round their henhouse, casing out the joint. But soon word got around like wildfire.

'Have you anything fresh?' people would say, always on the hunt for news.

'Yes. George and Ceiteag *saw the Minx*!'

At first, that's how we thought it was called. We had in our minds a holy terror, Minnie the Minx from *The Beano*. It was a comic that we passed from hand to hand, until it fell apart and would be used to light the fire. In those days there weren't any Gaelic radio stations. People often picked up new terminology by listening with a Gaelic ear to English local news bulletins. Sometimes they'd hear it slightly wrong, and so the Minx hit number one in village chitter chatter. Dad had patients stopping him by the roadside to report sightings. One man even managed to catch it under a bucket, but when he came back later, it had managed to escape.

Dad, no doubt, would have discussed the matter with Ken Walker at the seaweed factory. He knew everything about wildlife. Quite likely, it would also have come up at the weekly meetings with John Murdo at the school, along with both the Church of Scotland and the Free Church ministers. Such was how social services operated in those days. The outcome of such counsel and deliberation was resolute. This mink, or Minx, or whatever it was, had to be executed. If it wasn't, and if it found a mate to breed, that would be the end of all our free-range hens.[13]

It was one afternoon in the thick of this, when us boys were all eyes and ears for anything untoward, that I heard a most terrible shrieking from Ceiteag, matched by an equally horrendous squawking from her henhouse a hundred yards away.

I grabbed my airgun off its holster on the wall. It was a *Diana* .177 with an engraving of the huntress by the rear sight. That would have been the only look-in that a goddess had in my upbringing. With Wink, my mongrel terrier, yapping rabidly at my heels, I ran across the road and leapt the fence.

Ceiteag had always been like a second mother to me and Isobel. In Africa, they say it takes a whole community to raise a child. This time, it was my part to comfort her. There she was – in her blue pinafore, arms held out wide, and everything a terrible *bùrach*. Before me was a murder scene, a mass killing, blood and feathers everywhere, and poor Ceiteag trying to shoo away this sleek black demon. The size of a large kitten, it hopped about between the clumps of heather. If anything, it seemed to resent more than fear her intrusion on a process of industrial killing that had just ripped out the living throats of half her flock.

Wink and I closed in. It was the kind of moment that is normally only dreamed about by boys and dogs alike. As we got within ten feet, it reared up on its hind legs and bared a spread of snarling needle teeth. I not so much as aimed, as pointed down a firing line of lethal instinct, and pulled the trigger. The creature half crumpled to the ground, but before it dropped completely, Wink had followed through in rearguard action. She got it by the neck, shook like crazy, and that was that. All before the astonished eyes of Ceiteag, who thereafter spent the remainder of the afternoon plucking for the stewing pot what had been six good laying hens.

Such could be the gory realities of a semi-subsistence rural way of life. It's called 'back to nature', except that, for us, there was nothing 'back' about it. Most of us were very close to our animals. Cows especially would be almost a part of people's families and genuinely loved. But when their time was up, we'd kill and eat without compunction. We understood that we were all part of a cycle that rotates the wheel of life and death.

The question for us was not whether it was right or wrong to kill living creatures for our staple diet. That would have seemed a stupid question. Rather, the question, one that was often discussed, was doing so in right relationship. We knew that managing the grazings, going at the fishing, gathering shellfish and so on had to be carried out in ways that would sustain the stocks. It surprised me when, in my late teens, I learned that 'ecology' was considered to be a subject. It was what we lived and talked about for much of the time. It was, quite simply, the balance of a nature in which, we too, had our place. I later learned that academics called this 'Human Ecology'.

The problem with mink lay in their disruption of that balance. These are beautiful, intelligent, playful and even very affectionate creatures in their proper place. But – location, location, location! Translocation, and the competitive advantage over native species that it provided, had turned the lithe American mink into the Greater Hebridean Minx. This was what had led to the government-funded Mink Project. A sad necessity, though even then, some people argue that we should just get used to translocation. It's just a part of nature's future. I've also heard it said that, without the mink, the rats come back more, and they're also hard on ground-nesting birds like arctic terns and waders.

There comes a point in such debates that I just know my knowledge has run out. Also, it has to be conceded that we could be harsh without intending so, or in a manner that was inured in rural life. Not for nothing did the little van of the 'cruelty man' – the animal protection society – drive around to check on problems like sheep being left without sufficient feeding in the winter. Suffice, however, to say that I've enjoyed this short encounter with my trapper friend. We may have overlooked exchanging names, but our shared interest in the mink gave a common handle to connect. I tell him where I'm trying to make for. He points me to a track running up between two houses. Go in there, he says, and go on through the field. Go this way, turn that way, across the reseeded grazing and out through the village gate. That'll land me in the unfenced wilds.

By now it's very dark. Much too much so for sensible adventure. Fear is for safety on the moorlands too, and not just for the sea. 'If you don't have your wits about you . . .' as they'd say. But I'm determined, and within another quarter hour, I'm scouting round the perimeter fence of the reseeding.

It proves impossible to pick out any gate. I've only brought a tiny flashlight, and that's too deep inside my pack to bother. I'm forced, instead, to clutch at fenceposts, wobbling a few until I find one good to take my weight. Precariously, I clamber over the barbed wire, managing not to get snagged.

And that's it. I've broken loose! I've crossed a threshold through both land and mind. I'm outwith the village bounds, and into what I've built up in my imagination as the 'Lost Glen'. Mind you, if the good folks of these parts ever get wind of that particular romanticisation – especially, pray, not Samuel Macleod – then it'll be me who'll hear the faeries' laughter.

Out here, it's mainly dark beds of heather interspersed with little greens of tough and spiky grass. Pools of water, mostly shallow some profound, lurk amongst the bare rock sheets.

It's now so dark you have to second guess each step. You have to walk with toes upturned to reduce the chance of stumbling. They used to say in Inverness that city dwellers could tell the country folk by their *ceum a' mhonaidh* – their 'heather loup'. Test every footfall with your heel before committing weight. Watch for hidden trips and dead man's drops. Watch, too, for wider patterns in the land – the flow of shadows that distinguish different types of vegetation, or the raised ground from the dips, or the dry from the wet. Let the eyes accustom to these mottled shades of grey and black, for here is 'relief and drainage' abstracted from the abstract school geography books. Here it is, all set out in the raw.

I remind myself (as if to give a pinch) that if I hear a sudden shriek, it'll just be some poor critter, startled from its slumbers, and more alarmed than me. But all is still. I haven't even heard the drumming of the snipe. The night has claimed the day, and cold itself stands watch and takes the helm. The moon is on the wane this week and won't be out 'til after midnight, but when she rises, there she'll ride. *Banrigh na h-oidh-che* – the Queen of the Night. *Lòchran àigh nam bochd* – the Joyful Lamp of the Poor.

It's written that, in both the Catholic and the Protestant districts of these parts, when folks would first catch sight of the new moon they'd greet her with the invocation:[14]

Siud agaibh a' ghealach ùr – Rìgh nan Dùl 'ga beannachadh!
'There is the new moon – the King of the Elements bless it!'

And I have to say, that kind of peasants' Christ attracts me more than the arid version of urban theologians. Give me any day the one who'd go and pray alone up mountains, who'd wander with the angels and wild beasts.

The village has dropped out of sight. I come up to a flattish spot of moss and grass. This will do to pitch my tent. Up it goes, more by a sense of touch than by the light of dithering torch. It looks a little kinked, but no-one will be looking. It's good enough to do the night, especially as the trapper said the forecast was for cold but calm. I feel my fingers numbing as I blow into a valve and roll out my mattress, fluffing up my sleeping bag to lay it down. At last, I crawl inside with a cosy sense of relief, zipping shut the flaps as if to roll a boulder across the entrance of my cave. Only then does it occur to me: I clean forgot to eat! Oh well – I'll just have to take recourse to childhood reading on survival training. *The Famous Five,* with their chocolate bars beneath the stars.

I'm lying here, aware the stars are out above the flysheet. When we were young, the old folks used say that on a moonless night, they'd move from house to house by just the light of a glowing peat taken from the fire. You could make a biography from those peats. Their great migration paths from hearth to hearth. Their kindling, dying and rekindling. The stories that they'd hear along the way.

Truly, so much has happened since I left John's place this morning. It's been a day without redundancy, a day when every tiny thing came filled replete with meaning, right through to the worms and even ants. Maybe that's what flysheets do – and, you know, that would have been a good laugh! To have said to Anne at the Bays Café: 'Oh yes, it's got a flysheet, sure enough. A magic sheet, on which to fly!' She'd have liked that one.

It would be fun to walk at night by just the moon. Not even with a compass, just going by the Pole Star. And no way, GPS! But satellites – now, they're a strange addition to the constellations.

I remember the first time I ever saw a satellite, transiting across a Hebridean sky. In those days, when the nights were mild, Dad and I would go out fishing once he'd finished with the evening surgery at seven.

It would be just him and me, out on a moorland loch. He'd be on the rod. Me, at the oars. We'd talk, and catch the evening rise. We'd usually land a few, then drive back home. He was kept so busy with his burden of responsibilities. It was probably the closest that I ever got to him, just a boy and a man, together in a boat.

I think it must have been September or October. Which, exactly, doesn't matter; but it must have been late in the season, for although the nights had not yet chilled, twilight had fallen fast. We were out on Loch na Craoibhe – the Loch of the Trees. It lay at the end of the peat cutters' road, up from the council houses at Balallan. It had an island full of rowans, safe where the sheep couldn't get at them. Dad and his good friend, Dan Smith of Sildinis, had stocked the water with a golden-coloured strain of hybrid trout, called Sunbeam. They'd been given the fry by the Highlands Board. This was in the experimental days of fish farming and restocking.

Dad was single-handed at the time, on call 24/7, with eighteen hundred patients for whom he had to be available. He held his patients like a hen would mind her chicks. The loch was up behind the police station. If needed, they would come and fetch him for emergencies. For a time, the Balallan folks called it 'the Doctor's Loch'. That's how places get or change their names. They knew he couldn't go and fish just anywhere out on the distant moors. Poachers, though some were, it's said they did the decent thing, and left the fish on Loch na Craoibhe to him and Dan alone – there is a poacher's honour.

That night, the evening rise had run far on into the dusk. Dad was reeling them in, and me, scooping them up with the landing net in virtual darkness. Nice half-pounders mostly. I asked how they could see his three tiny flies in such poor light. He said they felt vibrations in the water down the lateral line. That's why the twitching motion of the rod must be just right.

We filled the wicker basket with a hefty haul. Then the wind dropped. It went flat calm, and that was them, gone off the take. Usually we'd have packed in there and then. But this was such a 'glorious night', as Dad would say. That was his favoured turn of phrase. He laid his rod across the stern, lit a cigarette, and passed me back a chocolate bar.

I shipped the oars and crossed their butts beneath my knees. We drifted, pensively, out from the island of the berry-laden trees, off the headland where the water lay the deepest. The world had settled to a hush untroubled by the slightest ripple. The sky was settling down to midnight blue on charcoal.

Then we saw the fires come out. Odd embers blown ablaze at first but gradually, the speckled sheen of shimmered starlight right across the Milky Way. And we were there. Inside of all of this. Just the two of us.

A shooting star streaked by, and then another. You glimpse your life as held in cosmic splendour on such a night as this. Dad pointed out a satellite, a sight still rare back then. We watched the tiny speck of light, as if a distant carriage that was lantern-lit and pulled by pounding horses through the freckled constellations.

Such depths of silence let you feel another person's spirit. In ways I hadn't known before, I felt Dad's layers of being. His qualities of presence. His standing, in the sense of all he stood for. I was growing up, and he, it must be said, was growing older.

The satellite crept ceaselessly across the sky, and both of us were rapt, transfixed. Each knew it meant our world was changing. Such signs had not been seen before in Heaven or on Earth. We followed, wordlessly, like shepherds watching flocks by night.

For me, I have to say, I felt the surge of youth's excitement. It was Apollo's age when men from NASA reached out to the moon. We were in the space age, right here, right now; and there'd never been a thrill before quite like it – or, for that matter – since.

Dad sat straddled across the wooden thwart. His thick Harris Tweed jacket. His conspicuously Victorian plus fours and gartered socks. Back then, his white or chequered shirts would last a week. Their cuffs and collars were the olden sort, that could detach for daily washing and a dash of starch.

He was conservative in politics, as many country doctors those days were. That said, he was an ecologist of both planet and the body. A man who planted trees, who kept a tank of tropical fish for patients in the waiting room, who delivered a whole generation of babies with the district nurses, and who prided himself on having one of the lowest prescribing rates in the north.

He didn't believe in a pill for every ill. Instead, he'd make the time to sit with failing patients, to hold their trembling hands, to share about life's meaning and the future of the world.

That night, we watched the satellite go down on the horizon. I wondered when it would come round again. I wonder, now, what went round in his mind?

PART 2

MOUNTAIN

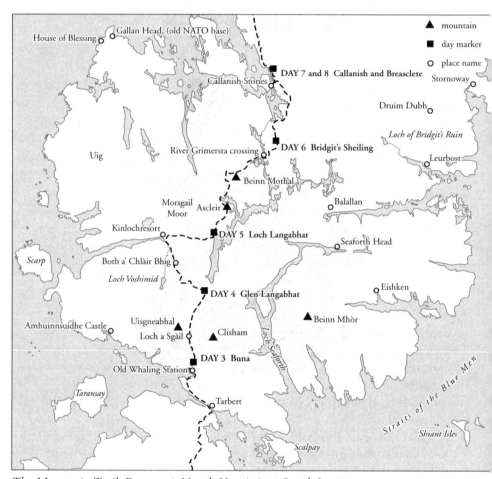

The Mountain Trail: Days 3–6, North Harris into South Lewis

8

THE RISING OF THE SÌTH

The sun is breaking over the peaks and already, as I peer from out my shakily-erected tent, the sky is radiant. It must be nearly eight o'clock. This is Wednesday, day three, and I've had a deep and dreamless sleep. Apart from fingernails that sting from the tussle with the old Bog Monster – to whom I feel a slight remorse for such a rude dislodgement – my feet feel none the worse for wear, and Osprey has been kind, indeed, to my back.

I draw the zip back fully along the flaps and shuffle out, like a slowly stretching cat. I fetch some water from the stream and, within a few minutes, have it bubbling on the hissing little gas stove. While my tea infuses, I overturn the tent and face it east to catch what gathering warmth there is, and dry the underside.

Some powdered milk made up with another splash of Adam's Ale does for the muesli, and I squat on top of Osprey, munching meditatively, scrying all around for the promised path built for the deer stalkers. There's not a sign of any trail in sight. Only the blue and silver glimmer of the river spilling down the slope. Only the tufts of purple moor grass speckled at random through the heather. And everywhere, a landscape strewn with boulders that ice once ripped from the towering mountains that surround me.

Down at this level, the valley is still broad, but higher up it tightens to a pass. That's what gives the meaning to the fully expanded name of Buna: the River at the Foot of the Narrows. Rising sharply up to my left are the slopes of Brùnabhal. Across, on the other side, loom the foothills of craggy Clisham. Beyond, and only just coming into sight, his horseshoe ring of sisters run with slides of jagged scree like laddered stockings dappled pink and grey.

I check my bearings with the compass, wanting to make sure that what I'm seeing squares up with the map. To reach Loch Langabhat, it looks like six miles up this glen then down the other side. I'd better allow four hours. When I get there, I'll maybe have a quick cast with the rod to see if I can land a trout, before heading west up a stalker's path that appears to run between the peaks of Stuabhal and Rapaire. From there, I'll probably head down a pathless glen along the Harris–Lewis border to Kinlochresort and come into a land of wide-spaced contours and a peppering with tiny lochs – a sign of boggy ground – before pitching camp for the night. Hopefully, I'll be there in time to gather a meal of mussels from the sea loch's Atlantic shore. I'd checked the tidal predictions before leaving Glasgow. The water will be low at around two o'clock. The shellfish – assuming that I find them there – should still be within reach for another couple of hours.

But it's going to be a slow start. I hadn't factored in that having packed Osprey so tight means that until I've eaten my way through some food, every time I repack will be a slow job. By the time I've got everything squeezed in and balanced just so, a full half hour has gone. Eventually, I swing him onto my shoulders. With a little shuffling jump, I pull the waist belt tight, and that's it. I'm off! Walking again. And it seems incredibly simple that all I have to do now, after all these weeks of thinking about it, is to walk, walk and walk – and this, with a rising sun on one side of my face and a chill wind like a helping hand on my back.

Very quickly, however, Osprey assumes the upper hand. I'm moving amongst gravelly beds of stone, weathered hunks of turf that have turned to mud, and innumerable little pools. The weight starts to feel like I'm walking in a deep-sea diver's leaded boots. Normally, you go across the moor in little leaps and bounds, a kind of ballet of the bog hop. Not so today. I'm much too heavy to jump, and whenever there's a patch of mire, I just have to clodhop through. This is going to slow me up a lot. Even the most modest slopes are forcing me to chug down into low gear. What's more, I keep on turning round every five or ten minutes to see how far I've gone. After a while, I get a grip, and tease myself by saying: 'You won't go forwards looking backwards!'

Gradually, I come more into the swing of things. It's as if my body was behaving like a stubborn nag. At first it kicked up a fuss, making out it was no longer up to the task at hand. Now it's knuckling down and getting moving, albeit surging with all manner of rare sensations. What's more, these twinges in my bones and muscles are, as it were, clicking hyperlinks within my brain. They're loaded with associations from other times like this of long ago, other times that I've carried heavy loads across the moor.

There was the time that we teenage boys were helping our dads to build dams on a stream above a trout loch. For several weeks running, we'd go out on Saturdays in one of those communal work projects that village groups would organise. This was the Loch Keose Angling Association, and our task was to make low weirs which were to catch the gravel and provide improved spawning beds for the fish.

It was nearly forty years ago, that must have been, and we'd be struggling with our sacks of cement – scarcely able to bear the weight that we'd insisted on taking on – when someone else's dad would ease alongside, like a gently docking ship, and without a word, drop his shoulder with a nudge to relieve you of your burden. There'd be the sheer relief to the neck, shoulders, biceps and even the gripping finger joints and nails as you'd roll your load off onto the broader set of shoulders. Then there'd be that half minute to follow, when you'd feel like you were floating – kind of walking on the air – as your muscle toning and deportment readjusted to the ease of relative weightlessness.

There was no humiliation in that yielding as you struggled to test your limits. Neither any hyped-up praise. At most, there'd be a passing comment, within earshot, from one man to another – 'The boy did good' – or some such other way of passing on between the generations what I've come to think of as the touch of blessing. The ethos wasn't one of competition. Like with gathering in the sheep or peats, or heaving stuff between the boat and shore, there was just a sense of common cause as everyone gave of their best and helped each other, likewise, to give of theirs. I've known men who'd take a sack across each shoulder blade. It sounds astonishing these days, but I emailed 'Jock' or Iain Mackenzie, an old school friend from Keose, to cross-check my memory with him.

'Were those really fifty kilo bags of cement – twenty of them to the ton?' I asked.

'Yes, indeed,' he replied, though email felt like such an incongruous technology by which to complete that circle of experience.

'A full hundredweight. One hundred and twelve pounds. Phew!'

Aye – those were the days, before the fuss of Health & Safety enforced the twenty-five kilo limit for a sack of building materials. The days we boys were raised with not a doubt of what it meant to be a man. The days we rippled through with fledgling brawn – though often, as we eased into our middle ages, a fledgling hernia too!

The ground is getting worse and worse, more heaved and churned by elemental forces as I climb up higher. I inch across a boulder field that's fissured through with break-leg crevices. What would it be like to slip, and twist, and with an inner crack of tensile shock, sustain a fracture? To have to crawl back to the village on my elbows – the pain and the disgrace – dragging the useless limb behind, like a maimed fox that's sprung the jaws of the gin, and praying to spot the mink trapper on his rounds, to summon his attention with blasts on my whistle, and an airgun shot of morphine to the veins to be put out of the misery?

God! You'd never go anywhere if you thought too much like that! We were always mindful when heading out alone, but we never let it worry us too much. 'Fear the sea' – for sure – but not enough to freeze it over.

It's taken maybe one and a half hours to get to the top of a ridge that's only half a mile from where I camped. But what a scene now opens out! Close by are two large pools, small lochans, rippling topaz in the strengthening sun. To the north-east are the Clisham's cliffs above Mò Buidhe – the Yellow Moss. North-west, the twin pyramids of Uisgneabhal. The name means either Ox Mountain by Norse derivation, or Water Mountain by the Gaelic. Either could be fitting, but John MacAulay thinks the Norse is more probable. The suffix *Bhal* or 'val', as he points out, is Nordic. It means a summit or 'abode of gods', as in the heavens of Valhalla.

But where's my Loch a' Sgàil? Where, my hoped-for destination of last night? Still hiding in the folds of rumpled hills, it seems. A mile or two is such a dawdle on the map when thought about from far away, with a coffee mug in one hand and a magnifying glass in the other, but it's not so much a dawdle out here. The notion that I'll be at Langabhat for lunchtime looks already like the pipe dream that the hope of a fried trout had proved to be. But here's the good news – I've actually hit on Sammy's stalker's path. Looking back, I can see now that I've been on it for a while, but such were the severity of the wash-outs lower down that I hadn't realised until in this better position to get perspective. Without its help unwittingly, I'd have been even more minced in the mash.

These Victorian trails are artefacts, for sure, of blood sport. And yet – if I might put in a special plea that might surprise – conducted well, the pursuit is of a character that binds the people to the land and to the deer themselves. Not everybody will agree, but to me it's like the Native American approach to hunting, the interlace of predator and the predated. But you don't have to be a carnivore to enjoy the stalker's paths. Many aren't marked on the Ordnance Survey maps, at least not on the older and most interesting ones. The estates didn't want to encourage walkers who'd unsettle the herds, especially in the shooting season – July to October for the stags, October to February for hinds. I've heard it said the estates would sometimes get their Ordnance Survey pals to forget to mark the tracks, as if they were military secrets. When you're in the know, however, or with a modern map, they're a joy to tread; though in the season I'd not go without first checking locally, not least by way of rural courtesy.

These thoughts set off another row of hyperlinks, clicked and popping open in my brain – windows on my teenage summers as a ghillie on the lochs and a stalker's pony boy amongst the hills. It surprises some folks when I say that I'm all for land reform *and* for responsible stalking. I even think that, if it's not lording it over the local people, or depriving them of a needed resource, a well-run private deer estate can be a service to environmental management. It's about maintaining the balance of nature, for the hard truth is that the stag has yet to be found that carries a condom. When deer exceed the carrying capacity of their environment – and that can happen in just a few short years of breeding – then it's quite the saddest thing to see them staggering around, on incredibly skinny legs, scraping at the seaweed along the shore to seek a bite worth eating. Better, a clean shot through the brains, or into the 'engine room' (as stalkers call the chest compartment with all its vital organs). From that quick ending, to be carried down from off the hill and to the larder; and from there, wild venison. Like the drop of nectar from the honeybee, such is food that 'only kings and royal people get to taste'. What's more, miserable indeed would be the larder from which there were no offcuts to the crofter's pot.

The men I've worked with kill the deer, but not by way of brutal slaughter. They also love them as a part of symbiosis between species, a fitting and well-fitted relationship. Sometimes it touches on the spiritual, even what might edge towards the psychic. Recently, I received a letter about something I'd written about relationship to the land from a Highland stalker, Iain Thomson of Loch Monar. His words turned my attention to his elegiac book, *Isolation Shepherd*, and there, to his tales – so common in the Highlands and Islands – of personal encounters with the seemingly paranormal. Why do such things interest me? Because of the light that they might shed, in Nora Bateson's sense, on what it is that we might be inside of. He correctly states: 'No Highlander has any doubt about the existence of *the second sight* or indeed simple prognostication.'[1]

That's quite a sweeping statement – 'No Highlander' – but it struck me because, in my experience, speaking of my own locale and formative era, it would be substantially true. These are parts of the world where the indigenous people have lived with one another, and their place, for a very long time indeed. I know families that can still trace their history back to Culloden, and, John Lorne Campbell maintains, even back to the Norse of a thousand years ago. This immense continuity creates a different set of relationships to space and time, and its implications for full human being, than is found in mainstream modernity, with its more shallow sense of temporality and its commodification of space. Campbell, one of the pre-eminent Hebridean folklorists and historians of the twentieth century, was well aware of the possible insights this might shed into the further reaches of human nature, for he rued: 'The scholar has not yet arisen who can apply Jung's ideas on the archetypes of the collective unconscious to Highland second sight or to Gaelic folklore: it would be well worth making the attempt.'[2]

Another stalking correspondent who reaches to this metaphysical hunting ground is Iain Thornber of Morvern, an old-school Highland gentleman, who doubles as an honorary sheriff and the deputy Lord Lieutenant of Inverness. He described to me the funeral, in the 1940s, of Rory MacLeod, who had been a head keeper on the Isle of Jura – 'a well known character, and a first class stalker, who had a great love of the deer'. As the mourners gathered in the cemetery, a hind came over the brow of a nearby hill. She moved in, so close, that everyone (being well aware of the timid habits of the deer) was quite astonished. The animal stood, and watched, until the coffin was lowered into the ground. At this point, and with a loud bark, she turned and ran back to the wilds.

In another of his letters, Iain told me how, in the days when he was never off the hill, 'I used to be able to sense where deer were; I could physically *feel* them in much the same way as a water-diviner does.' He described the *gralloching* – the shedding of the entrails that are usually left out on the heather for the birds of prey – and how:[3]

> It is a fine thing, after the gralloch, and the knife has been washed in the nearest burn and dried among sphagnum moss, to sit for a while with the stag. Usually not much is said among professional stalkers. To me, it is honouring the soul of that animal. I never shot, or have been involved with the killing of a beast, without coming away thinking I'd been at a funeral.

The same ethic was also very present in Tommy Macrae of Eishken, who kept the hills of south-east Lewis. Such men as these are *keepers* of the herd in more than any narrow understanding of a gamekeeper's profession. Such men, in my experience, are integral to the ecology and welfare of the deer. With skills honed sometimes from generations of handed-down experience, they will select and stalk the older, weaker, or diseased beasts; and when the kill is made, see that the deed is done in such a way as to try and avoid scattering the herds, or breaking up their family groups.

Tommy taught me how to handle a pony with a stag strapped to its saddle. We'd work a route home that would take us over bogs, through rivers, and sometimes up and down what seemed like terrifying gradients for a beast lumbered with such a load. On getting back to the larder, usually quite late in the evening, we'd hoist the carcase on a pulley to the rafters. From that eye-level working angle, I'd take my knife and flay the bristled hide, trying not to nick and thereby spoil the meat.

Since those days, I've been back once to my old job for a week-long sojourn at Eishken. This time it was with Christopher, who follows his late father's footsteps as the fourth in the Macrae lineage of keepers. When we'd finished for the day, Chris would pour out drams all round in the larder. Half jokingly, lest any think it quaint, but only half jokingly, he'd raise his favourite toast: 'To the Soul of the Stag'.

While on the matter of toasts, I am coming up to a gully, and hear the rushing of a stream. It's narrow and is partly hidden under heavy fronds of heather. The track dips sharply down and stops abruptly at its bank. This is Abhainn Thorabraidh – the Burn of the Wide Mound. I crouch amongst the stones, cup my hands, and sup.

In the lore of chemistry there is a silver-white metal that emits beta radiation, called strontium. It counts as number thirty-eight in the Periodic Table of the Elements, and it takes its name from Strontian, a tiny West Highland village, where the ore was first discovered. It happens to lie in the vicinity of Iain Thornber's stamping grounds. I doubt that many chemists will be aware of this fact. It might sit uneasily with the nuclear age. But the name, Strontian, is stranglified from Sròn an t-Sìthean – The Nose of the Faerie Hillock. As such, the lead mines that first yielded up this strange element – now used in power supplies for space stations, and in radiotherapy for bone tumours – were tunnelled deep inside a place where only those safeguarded with an iron needle jammed into the door hinge were safe to venture to and fro.

One glorious morning, as he recounts it, Iain was out in the nearby hills. It was the season for the culling of the herds of hinds. As he made his stalk, his ears picked up the sound of what, he believes, may have been the *oiteag shluaigh*. This phenomenon is also known as the *gaoth nan sìth*, for in the science of Gaelic, as in chemistry, there are often several isotopes, or subtle variations, of much the same thing. These terms pertain to the 'faerie wind', the 'hosting of the sìth' – the rallying and riding, mostly almost silent, sometimes raucous rollicking – of the Otherworld folk. In his journal entry for Monday, 4 December 1995, he wrote, as follows, of that glorious morning of the stalk:[4]

> At some stage as I was watching the deer, I can't recall exactly when, I became aware of the silence being broken by a sound which I initially took to be a little breeze picking up among the rocks above me. I paid little attention to it to begin with, but then it seemed to expand across the face of the hill. Although it grew in intensity, I found it impossible to say with any certainty where it was coming from, largely because I could not physically feel it on my face and neck. At times it seemed to start in Coire a Chuil Mhaim to my left, and then move over to Coire an Dubh-alltan and Coire nam Muc ahead of me. Much like the end of a rainbow, it was everywhere but nowhere.
>
> It is difficult to describe the sound. If one can 'feel' or 'see' a noise, it seemed cold, almost metallic and grey-blue in colour, like Payne's grey. Coming as it did on an otherwise fine winter's day, it felt strange, almost ominous. I was not aware that the deer reacted to it though. I don't know why, but I thought of the young USAF pilot (Capt Morris Reed, 28) who was killed in 1964 when the F101 Voodoo Jet Fighter he was flying crashed into the north side of Meall Odhar, a little way above. It was that sort of atmosphere.

There could, of course, be many interpretations of such an experience. What interests me is how Iain felt that something 'inner' was going on, and set it within a traditional framework of interpretation. His journal goes on to describe the callous commercial stalking practices that new foreign owners subsequently introduced to the area. Gaelic place names replete with meaning were mechanistically renamed as Corrie 1, Corrie 2, Corrie 3, and so on. Family groups of deer would be blown apart, the calves left with their 'pathetic human-like crying noise' as they searched in vain for their mothers, and wounded beasts left to wander, starving, with their lower jaws hanging off. He concluded, 'If the sound I heard was an *aisling* or a vision of something to come, especially concerning the deer, it could not have been more accurate . . . These people . . . should be dead themselves . . . but soon it will catch up with them.'

What interests me is how – at least in Iain's mind – the uncanny rising of the faerie wind spoke within his psyche to upheaval in his outer world.

And that, in full Voodoo drama. Whatever he might have experienced in Payne's grey, the old lore of the place – faerie lore or *sìthichean* – provided a framework of interpretation, together with assurance of comeuppance for the reprobates.

Suffice, for now, to say that each of these four stalkers – the Macrae father and son, Thomson and Thornber – are men whose proven skill involves spending prolonged periods of time on the cusps of the human and non-human worlds. As Christopher once told me, his work means 'thinking like the deer thinks' – and that requires a seasoned empathy. Each of these people is bound in with a sense of being grounded, homed, and belonging to a greater whole. This, at levels where the physical flows into the psychic. I want to reflect more on this as I go, but here we have started to glimpse a deep and very natural ecology.

Onwards from the Abhainn Thorabraidh, but no longer on any stalker's path, as I go up and over the shoulder of Mò Buidhe. A fresh panorama now stretches out and, at last, I see the shining of the fabled Loch a' Sgàil in a hollow half a mile away. To reach it means shifting diagonally back across the valley, while still gaining altitude. I'm getting more into my stride now. The ground up here is firm. That's probably why the path stopped. It's hardly needed, and I'm starting to enjoy swinging with my load. It's now the beauty more than the struggle that makes me keep stopping every few minutes. That blue haze still on the mountains, their wisps of iridescent clouds, the grandeur of this tapered amphitheatre – and to be here all by myself.

I'm making fun of myself. 'The Juggernaut of the Moors' I'm thinking, each time the gradient makes me chug and puff. 'The bog hop' I've already called it it, when I make what little jumps I can across the lurking lengths of morass. I'm creeping crab-like up the valley, traversing the neural networks of its watercourse way where seepages drain in to little rills, and these build up to burns that dash down to the river. I'm now onto a flat stretch of land that edges towards the lip of Loch a' Sgàil. In half an hour you could write a coffee table book out here called *Bogs that I have Known and Loved*. Here's one that shimmers with a rainbow iridescence that is caused, not by oil pollution, but by a molecule-thin layer of iron minerals that float on the surface and refract the light. Another, fed from an underground spring that issues from a pair of boot-sized holes that plummet down too deep to find the bottom. Pity help the one who might tread there when walking in thin winter ice! Next, a muddy moat around an island tuft of mosses, red and green, and bristled through with stems of last year's blossoms, resembling tiny flagpoles.

Give this moor just one more month, and the rusty swards of winter will dimple through with polka dots of colour. There'll be spiky quills of bog asphodel, bristling yellow to attention. Orchids, in every hue of pink and blue, white and sometimes yellow. There's even a subspecies of the common spotted orchid that's endemic to the isles – *Hebridensis* – with confetti petals etched in dainty loops that drape as if dropped down from out of dreamland. Along the river banks, there'll be starry paws of midge-devouring butterwort, its nodding pendant blossom winged and spurred, the dainty violet dancer on the breeze. And everywhere, in dryer parts, the foursome heart-shaped petals of the tormentil; sometimes as a single tiny plant, elsewhere raked in balls of tangled tumble.

My friend, the island artist Alice Starmore, was born a *Nic Mhathainn* – Matheson in English – the Daughter of the Bear. Even in the early 1960s, the family used to walk their cattle from east of Stornoway, through the town, and out to their summer sheiling that was situated just half a mile across the road from our place at Druim Dubh.[5] For her, the magic of the moor weaves memory, ecology and the imagination. She called one of her exhibitions *MAMBA – Miles And Miles of Beauty Astounding*. Its catalogue explained:[6]

> The moor is bound up in my very first memories, and that must be the reason why I associate it with my mother. The springtime smell, when everything is just starting to grow, particularly reminds me of her, and I cannot help but think of her whenever I leave the road and take a first step onto the moss and heather; the softness beneath my feet is somehow maternal and life-affirming.

One of her pictures in the exhibition that explored the infinite depths of green in sphagnum moss, was called *Eye of Creation*. That's the literal translation of *sùil-chruthaich*, the Gaelic for a quaking bog. Another, in a maelstrom of greens and blues, drew on local tales of worlds beneath the waves. It was called *The Water-Horse of Loch Mhisteam*. A wooden door portrayed *The Sheiling Remembered*, and while the door has lost its knob, it begs the question if it ever needed one.

And then there was *The Witch of Roineabhal*. Aye, there she was. My friend, the Blue Mountain Hare, seated in her winter coat upon a lichen-crusted rocky ledge. Woman wisdom in the sage astuteness of this spirit creature's haunting eyes. Nature fleeting free and wild, and love; oh yes, I saw the love that day in Alice Starmore's mountain hare of Roineabhal.

Above the sharp sides of a deep kettle pool, my eye catches a wispy haze. A freshly hatched-out swarm of mayflies dance a frenzied eightsome reel. A puff of wind, and off they flurry, back beneath the safety of the bank. Half a minute later, out they come again, whirling to some hidden bagpipe skirl until the next gust of *gaoth nan sìth* that shoos them back into their sìthean underfoot.

The *sì* or *sìth*: that twinkling sense of living laughing spirit danced through nature. I mouth the word and practice breathing out the 'h' – *shee-h* – drifting it off ineffably; playing too with the variations – *sìdh, sìd, sìdhe* – that have, or so I am instructed, more of a y-glide, making a *shee-y-e* sound that works the tongue and mouth, like the syncopated rhythms – the lilting and 'Scotch snap' – so characteristic of Celtic music.[7]

Such are the *daoine sìth*, the 'people of peace', the 'silently moving ones', the gentry or gentle folk of Scots, Irish and, I believe, the English tradition as well. But to be scientific about the matter, it is the male mayflies that dance while waiting for their lovers to hatch out. Waiting for their *ban-shìthichean*, their 'banshee' faerie wives. Moving with that gliding grace that classical pipers know so well, and speak of in their pibrochs as the *siubhal sìth*, the 'faerie motion'.

They're also called *daoine còir* – the 'honest folk'. Some have suggested that such honorifics were accorded only out fear, a kind of whistling in the dark, as if to ward off unwanted attentions. One who held this view was the late Dr Alan Bruford, a renowned archivist at the School of Scottish Studies at Edinburgh University. In the early 1990s, I was co-supervising a PhD student with Alan, and we met for lunch to discuss her progress and for me to pick his brains about the sìth. Unfortunately, I'd forgotten my wallet, I had only a pocketful of small change, and had to ask him for the loan of a couple of pounds. It was slightly embarrassing, not to mention the impending inconvenience of having to arrange repayment.

As we sat down to eat, we found that our tomato juice was sour, as if it had been diluted with vinegar. I got up and complained. The cashier was most apologetic. She didn't know what could have happened in the kitchen, but gave us back sufficient of a refund that allowed me, on the spot, to repay my debt.

As we settled down again to eat, I made a flippant comment about traditions of the faeries souring milk. Flippancy was compounded by folly in my conclusion: 'Whoever would have thought that the staff club of the University of Edinburgh is actually a *sìthean!*'

The elder scholar arrested his wayward understudy with a sharp and anxious gaze. 'Be careful of the faeries,' he said, grimly, and with every seriousness, as if something about what had just happened had left him slightly spooked. 'They can be *capricious,* you know.'

That said, there is a mitigating point of view. An eminent nineteenth-century authority on their behavioural sociology, the Rev. J.G. Campbell of Tiree, wrote down from an informant: 'They never took anything without making up for it in some other way.' W.B. Yeats recorded much the same from a woman in County Mayo: 'If you do good to them they will do good to you . . . They are always good to the poor.'[8] And then there is the way this genre of experience will often seem to pull down a notch those for whom, as W.Y. Evans-Wentz put it in his classic study, 'the outer is reality, the inner non-existent'.[9] As peasant informants told him, 'One does not have to be educated in order to see fairies' – the implication being that too much learnedness can get in the way. I could have patted such a statement on the head, were it not for a personal experience one night that still leaves me scratching my head.

During the six years that I taught at Edinburgh, I would usually take my human ecology master's degree students up to Lewis for field trips. We were in the Faculty of Science and Engineering. It was important that we should be empirical, or experimentally based, about matters that our colleagues in the humanities approached in a more relaxed manner. On the island we'd stay at Gearrannan (or Garenin), a conserved blackhouse village near Carloway on the West Side. It was 1995, and the further north we drove the more we felt a loosening of the faculty's constraints.

One of our number was Patrick LaViolette, now a respected professor of social anthropology. He was doing his thesis on the biodiversity of faerie hills in the Trossachs, the hills north of Glasgow. He combined a series of ecological surveys with interviews of local people. The conclusion was that old taboos about not removing anything from a sìthean – allowing dead trees naturally to rot away, and treating it as a haven – were still alive. This led to a richer variety of flowers, fungi, bird life and all the rest of it. In short, the sìthean are our residual indigenous equivalent of sacred groves, scattered little ecological islands, that sustain a wealth of biodiversity. Just to prove that such work was *scientific,* we jointly published his findings in *ECOS* – the Journal of the British Association of Nature Conservationists.[10]

Anyway, there we all were, a minibus of fourteen of us, happily heading north and playing the game of 'Spot the Sìthean'. 'There's another one, Patrick!' somebody would shout, as we'd pass a typical tree-fringed mound that mushroomed up from a farmer's field. It was dusk as we came upon a particularly fine example. I stopped the bus, wanting the students to experience the stillness that is often in such places, the softness of the uncultivated earth underfoot and, sometimes, such features as standing stones in the middle.

However, not all our crew were happy. That year we had an Irish lass in the class, a marine biologist from County Clare. She'd grown up with a sìthean out the back where she and her sisters played – except at dawn or dusk. Why that limitation? 'Because that's *their* time,' she told me forcefully, the threshold time of day, and I should be knowing better than to lead a study tour into a sìthean at the witching hour.

At this point, mindful of the faculty of which I was the representative, I stood in my superior knowledge, and proclaimed: 'Faerie is an imaginal world. It's more a metaphor than reality.'

'No!' she retorted sharply. The 'folk' to her were in no sense imaginary – and this was scarcely the right moment for me to introduce Henry Corbin, a French philosopher of Islamic mysticism, and his notion of *'le monde imaginal'* as the 'suprasensible' grounding of the soul, where prayer itself – interestingly – becomes 'the supreme act of the Creative Imagination'.[11]

'They're a different order of reality,' she insisted. Their world runs in parallel to ours, and quite frankly, she thought that my high-brow claptrap was disrespectful. If I carried on like that, she said, they'd withhold their revelations from me. So there! It was a strange rebuke. I confess it left me simultaneously bemused and slightly addled.

By the time we'd rolled off the Stornoway ferry the following day and had driven over to Gearrannan, it was dark. Some of our number were staying in the hostel. The rest pitched our tents. I placed mine on a little green promontory, just above the well at the end of the terrace of thatched dry-stone houses.

It had been to Gearrannan that my mother would come and do her oil painting in the 1970s. Three old women lived in the houses then, the last to do so. One of them led her to a well and dropped a pebble down. My mother heard its bell-like plop, and the old woman said: 'That is the finest water in the land.'

I got into my sleeping bag and lay awake, letting the busyness of the day settle down to sediment. Gradually, I became aware of a very strange sound. It was a like a sheet of tinfoil being shaken. Something high-pitched, tinkling and bright.

Viscerally startled, I shot bolt upright in the tent and found that I could see straight through its fabric walls. The land outside lay still and silver, clad by moonlight in unearthly beauty. Then I saw from what the sound was coming. It was a luminous disk, shimmering in lightening blue, moving down the winding path from higher up the hill. It was maybe two or three feet wide, a couple of inches in depth, and it gently rose and fell to the bumps and dips as it glided, just above the ground, at a slow walking speed.

What most alarmed me was a sense that this was something utterly other. As it approached my tent, I felt myself fill up with fear. But the fear was needless. The light went past, slipping between me and the well. As it did so, the thought came into my head from a place that was beyond intellectual censure: *That is their possé going down to the sea for the night. They'll head back up at dawn.*

Years later, when the island's first Ordnance Survey maps from the 1850s became available online, I discovered that a prominent hillock in the fields below which I had camped is marked – and in especially bold lettering – *Sithean*. I made enquires. It turned out that such had been the old village name.

Now, at last, I've reached the edge of Loch a' Sgàil, and it's created quite a stir. Little trout are darting V-lines through the sandy-bottomed shallows as they beeline for the middle, out of harm's way. I find a peaty bank on which to rest my back, get out a pack of oatcakes to eat for lunch, and feel as if I've reached a Himalayan holy lake. Its mirrored calms reflect the mountains that have closed in tightly all around.

Sgàil could mean a sheiling, covering, shade, shadow or a ghost. Rising precipitously above the west bank is Uisgneabhal Mòr. As seen from here, my mind elaborates the name to either Great Ox Mountain, or the Abode of Great Waters. No elaboration is required, however, to report that this is the very spot where Noah's Ark briefly ran aground, forcing its captain to unload some of the cargo, before refloating at high tide, and carrying on to Mount Ararat. That explains why Harris has blue mountain hares and red deer, while the Middle East got lions and camels. At least, so goes one of the many legends that were collected in the first half of the twentieth century by Otta Swire, a direct descendent of the South Uist-born Jacobite heroine, Flora MacDonald of 'Over the Sea to Skye' fame. Otta's granddaughter, Flora MacDonald Margaret

Swire, was a medical student whose life was taken in the 1988 Lockerbie bombing of Pan Am flight 103. Her father, Dr Jim Swire, went on, with a valiant sense of justice, to lead the campaign to exonerate the convicted Libyan, Abdelbaset al-Megrahi.

According to Otta's sources, Noah's mishap here on Uisgneabhal took place during the second of the Three Great Floods. The first flood was God's creation of the world's primordial oceans. The second was that of Noah, caused, we're told in the Book of Genesis, because 'the wickedness of man was great in the Earth . . . and the Earth was filled with violence'. The last, they say, has yet to come, yet:[12]

> Before the end of the world a great flood will sweep over and drown all the islands . . . but Iona will rise on the waters and float there like a crown; and the dead who are buried in her will arise dry and so be easily recognised at the Last Day.

There were so many stories like this. They conveyed a folk worldview and mindset, ones often folded in the twists of comedy or tragedy. Consider the golden hue to Loch a' Sgàil's sandy bottom. The effect of peaty water – or so you might think? Perhaps. But last night, after leaving Sammy's house, I glimpsed back in the direction of Luskentyre – *lys-kyntyre* – the Headland of Light. So it was that, once upon a time, according to Otta's sources, its miles and miles of sands were made of grains of solid gold. But a greedy man filled up his boat and sailed away to sell it in the markets of that source of sin, the mainland. A storm rose up around the Shiants. It did what storms are prone to do to overloaded boats. Why? Because *They* do not like greed. And *They* then changed the golden beach to sand. But once a year at sunset, *They* change it back again – so that we will not forget the truth of nature.[13]

I am noticing that the sand along this shoreline is banded dark and pale. Heavy grains of magnetite have been graded out from the lighter grains of quartz by the lapping action of the waves. And in this moment, I see my 'traces on the Rhodian shore' – for when the shipwrecked philosopher Aristippus was cast upon the sands of Rhodes, he saw some geometric drawings; and he comforted his crew, saying: 'We can hope for the best: for I see signs of men.'[14] But these are no signs of men. These are the signs that *They* have passed by, a-shepherding their herds. *They* with their *crodh-sìth* – the 'cattle of the faeries' – for what I see are footprints, the cloven hooves of deer.

I get down on my knees to take a closer look. The casts remain sharp-edged, and all the tiny scuffs and sprays still hold their pristine definition: dried, but not yet crumbled in the breeze. Probably the creatures watered here at dawn. And then I notice something else. The lake is fringed with brush strokes all around the water's rim. Or more precisely, a tide mark, scarce a finger's length, made up entirely out of bristles.

Ah! The washing of *Their* brushes after painting flowers all night. Such, it is said, throws light upon the striking hues of many a Highland loch. And spring is when the red deer shed their winter coats. And soon the buds of summer herbs will swell and burst to blossom.

I move on and upwards, and as the valley narrows and the gradient sharpens further, the stream begins to purr a tumbling song. I stop beside a pool to watch some bobbing water plants that weave from side to side, hypnotic in the current. There is a trout! It hasn't seen me. Must be getting on for several ounces, I'd say – and even as I say it, I note with a slight dismay the calculating measure of the angler's eye.

I drop down on my knees and edge close in. He's stalking round the stones, chasing after beetles, worms and all those May-time larvae – the naiads and the nymphs. Do fish have souls, have feelings? To watch this individual – this creature of intelligence, of loveliness and even personality – it scarce can be denied. If I have soul and feelings, the fish has too, as Schubert's quintet, *The Trout*, suggests with its portrayal of its purposeful movements through the water.

Should it be caught and eaten?

Well, should it catch and eat?

That symmetry noted, I think I'll leave my rod unpacked, this time.

I climb another fifty metres, and am standing now at around eight hundred feet. It's amusing if confusing how my generation muddles up the measures. All around the peaks exceed six hundred metres. But to say two thousand feet seems to proffer up a more munificent sense of justice. I'm nearly at the top, nearly reached the saddle of the pass. The valley has constricted to a funnel. The stream is petering out now. Its dulcet sighs have long since raised to xylophonic cadences, and now to quivering bells.

Here and there the water vanishes beneath some hollow ground. I seek the source, but, more and more, it eludes me. There is no single point of source. I'm on the watershed now.

And now is such a very thin place. Such a faraway place.

No planes or cars or fire engines. No fingers tapping texts on little screens, or kettles rumbling for another cup of tea. Not even moaning wind or birdsong. Only silence. Sheer silence.

The soil beneath my feet is firm but curiously soft. A short-cropped emerald fairway winds on through a cleft, past ghostly boulders strewn on either side. A few more paces, and behold. Beyond!

Far below, a faltering stream builds up momentum and then hurtles down a stair of cataracts en route to Loch Langabhat, and from there, the eight miles through to the Grimersta. Down I jaunt, and down and down and down, until within an hour the hillside flattens to a grassy plain, another country here, of crescent pools and gravel beds, the autumn spawning grounds of salmon and the sea trout.

Suddenly I see a movement, and now I spot the stalker's path that zigzags down from Stuabhal and Rapaire. Close on a mile away, an ant-like speck of camouflage brown is shifting rapidly from west to east. A hiker, or mink trapper? A crofter, minding sheep or cows?

And – oh, ohh! I am taken by surprise. A lunge from out my belly. A realisation that, for all my self-containment, a part of me is already pining for human company.

The figure goes as quickly as it came. I'm left with a yearning rawness within. A hand near-touched, but now withdrawn. Contact without connection. The crackle of the static when the radio has gone off-air at night.

I knew that this would be a lonely place, and . . .

Are . . . you . . . there?

Is . . . anyone . . . listening?

Does anybody remember that novel, *On the Beach,* by Nevil Shute? A thriller of the Cold War, just after I was born?

There was a movie. Created quite a stir at the time.

There'd been a massive nuclear exchange. When the submariners surfaced, they thought they'd picked up Morse code.

Took the bearings. Triangulated the source. Motored to a coastguard station on a cliff. But only a loose wire – tap, tap, tapping in the wind.

'They shall grow not old, as we that are left grow old.'

Only the loneliness.

The river passes through a lochan on its way to Langabhat. Its name shows on the map as Loch an Teine – the Loch of Fire.

Teine sìth. The faerie fire of in-between places. In-between states of being.

War leaves behind a very lonely sort of in-between world.
Few traces left upon that stark, Rhodian shore.

Lay down your hopes of making Loch Resort today.
Lay down your hopes of poaching Langabhat.
It's getting late, and cold, and as they say: *When the wind's in the east, the fishing is least.*
The famous 'they' who always have so much to say!
Know what? I'm going to give myself a break. Pitch camp and make a fire.

I've reached the stalker's path down which that walker came. Beside it runs a burn lined with ruined sheilings, just falling walls of stone, some four feet high at most. None has dimensions larger than a garden shed, but here's one with the remnants of a chimney and a fireplace. Time, I think, for me to warm it through again.

Further back, I'd found some fencepost offcuts. They had a greenish hue from being 'tanalised' with copper – an impregnation that prevents the rot. I set myself to work, gathering up an armful of dead heather stems to serve as kindling. I pile them into a pyramid, set up a chimney effect, and light a match at the base. Now we're in business! I've got three lamb chops from the Tarbert butcher's shop, plus a packet of Wright's ciabatta bread mix.

The wave of loneliness is lifting. The sheiling's coming back to life, as the heather crackles in the smoke. I watch the stems explode alight, the fenceposts slowly catch and then to pop and spit. They're blazing out in lovely blue-green *teine sìth* copper flames. Luckily, they don't add arsenic like they used to for the treatment.

I'll let the posts burn down to charcoal before I start the cooking. That'll drive off any toxic volatiles. You'd not want to be doing this every day, but as a once-off – *well* – there are clinics in California where you could pay a lot of money for such tonics of trace elements.

The flour contains its yeast already added to make the bread rise. I add sufficient water from the stream, and knead it into two small pats. The air is turning cold, but the stones that face south-west are still warm from the day's long sunshine. I should have warmed that water first to speed the yeast. Trouble is, when it comes to baking, as the prophet said, 'He that believeth shall not make haste.'[15]

My mixture's only puffed up slightly. Too bad. I'm too hungry to hang around. Within an hour I'm tucking in to Blackface chops and flattened if blackened bannocks. Were it in season, I'd have sprinkled the meat with wild mountain thyme. As it is, I'll just have to tell Vérène that I had to make do with an old Hebridean standby – the one we have to use when we can't get any better – *Herbes de Provence*.

So here I am. Dining out on Tanalised Lamb, seasoned with bitter herbs, and filling up with near-unleavened bread. An unwitting Passover meal. The evening is well advanced. Now is the time for reverence, and in the testimony that he gave to the Napier Commission in 1883, Alexander Carmichael spoke about the way of life that was followed by the people who came to such summer sheilings with their herds.

> When the grazing-ground has been reached and the burdens are laid down, the huts are repaired outwardly and inwardly, the fires are rekindled, and food is prepared.

He described their songs and prayers as: 'singularly chaste, beautiful, and elevated'. Many of them stretched back, he suggested, from evidence collected over several decades, 'to the time of bows and arrows'.

Never have I spent a night in a more solitary spot. And yet, I'm at this ancient people's hearth. The hearth that is the heart of home. What better a valediction? Nay, what better a *benediction* than what I have here? As Carmichael translates the Gaelic lines from an evening prayer of days that are no more, but which run on like a warp to which the future weaves its weft:[16]

> *Mhoire ghradhach! Mhathair Uain ghil,*
> *Cobhair oirnne ghlan Oigh na h-uaisleachd . . .*
> Mary beloved! Mother of the White Lamb,
> Shield, oh shield us, pure Virgin of nobleness.
> And Bride the beauteous, shepherdess of the flocks.
> Safeguard thou our cattle, surround us together.
> *Safeguard thou our cattle, surround us together.*
>
> And Columba, beneficent, benign.
> In name of Father, and of Son, and of Spirit Holy,
> Through the Three-in-One, through the Trinity,
> Encompass thou ourselves, shield our procession.
> *Encompass thou ourselves, shield our procession.*
>
> O Father! O Son! O Spirit Holy!
> Be thou Three-One with us day and night,

And on the back of the wave as on the mountain side
Thou our Mother art there with thine arm under our head.

And on the back of the wave as on the mountain side
Thou our Mother art there with thine arm under our head.
. . . 'S air chul nan tonn no air thaobh nam beann
Bidh ar Mathair leinn 's bidh a lamh fo 'r ceann!

9

TWO AIRMEN

Day four, Thursday, and another clear cold morning. The temperature during the wee small hours had sunk to around freezing point. As I peer out from the tent, my breath joins volleyed banks of hanging mist that fill this silent mountain amphitheatre. The heather is weighed down with dew, as if with tiny fruits, and every stem of grass stoops pregnant with a beady sheen. The mountains to the east remain in heavy shade, but the sky behind them has assumed a tungsten glow. West, the twin pinnacles of Stuabhal and Rapaire are soaking up the sun-line's warmth that's creeping down the slopes and causing them to steam.

I clamber out, take a token glacial splash in the burn, and fill the cooking pot with water for my muesli's milk and brewing tea. If it had been necessary, the condensation on my flysheet could have yielded up a cup of drips. It sags, dejected, like an old nag's back after a hard day's night. I spread it out to dry where it will catch the soon-arriving sun, and choose a mossy cnocan – a soft little hummock – on which to take my ease and write some notes.

The back pages of this Moleskine 'cahier' have a row of perforations, close to the spine, which makes it easy to pull pages out. That was what had clinched my choice at the stationery shop. But I'm disappointed by the cover. I'd thought it would be waterproof, but not so, I see, with this version. The quality of the paper, however, is lovely – smooth to the touch and creamy to the eye. Each day, I've been tearing out a sheet and folding it in four to fit into one of the pockets of Osprey's hip belt. These loose folios have become my daybooks, as I'm calling them; my place for scribbling notes while on the trot, or even just odd keywords that will later kindle memory. Right now, while the tent's drying, I want to write them up before their meaning sinks forever into jumbled bogs of tattered scrawls.

I have brought with me for the purpose, of all things, my fountain pen. Just for the ceremony! Back in the days of Leurbost School, our teachers – Miss Montgomery, Miss Graham, Miss Mackinnon – insisted that fountain pens were better for our writing. They hadn't bargained on a class that had a doctor's son. Yes, it seems to be hereditary, and in years to come a lecturer at Aberdeen University would write on my examination script – when lecturers could still have fun without being had up for traumatising their charges – 'Your writing, young man, is moronic. Your geology, it seems, is little better.'

The need to fill the pen, however, presented me with a problem. I had no wish to lug around a chunky ink bottle, and to have used cartridges, wouldn't quite have carried the pomp to match the ceremony. I'd therefore decanted just sufficient ink for the journey into one of those individual-sized jam pots that they give you in posh hotels. If it's jam-tight, I reasoned, it should be ink-tight – and what a splendid little jar this is! 'Baxters of Scotland, by Royal Appointment' it says, in gold lettering on the cap. I squint at it more closely. There's a royal coat of arms. The lion rampant. The unicorn in chains. And there's the motto of the British royal family. *Dieu et mon droit.*

'God and my right.' The heraldry buffs argue what it means. Some hold that *mon droit* signifies the right hand, the one that bears the sword. With spiritual power in the one hand, and secular in the other, you've got it made both ways. Others suggest that it refers to the 'divine right' by which medieval kings legitimised their rule of subjects they had conquered. Between the two interpretations, same difference, if you ask me. The truth is that *mon droit* has always tried to co-opt poor old *Dieu*. The world is oh so 'bright and beautiful' – both today, and in that dear old hymn – until you hit the verse that goes:[1]

> The rich man in his castle,
> The poor man at his gate,
> He made them, high or lowly,
> And ordered their estate.

I've now got a second cup of tea steaming beside me, and I'm slowly drawing back the plunger, filling up with ink from *Dieu et mon droit.* The moss goes turquoise as I dab the surplus off. That'll be fun for any earnest botanist that happens past this way!

Freed of the usual pressures of a day, I notice that I'm bestowing every act and observation with miniscule attention. My world is expanding to fill the space available in consciousness. Even such a tiny thing, as touching pen to paper, carries with it magic as I watch the flowing lines take shape in royal blue. In medieval monasteries, the scriptorium lay close to the sanctuary. Iona's monks, the ones who made the *Book of Kells,* knew about ink's alchemy as prayer. And now the sun has reached the valley floor. In its blaze, I watch the way my writing glistens on the paper – each letter as a mayfly, dancing in its momentary glory – before settling down into the pores and drying to a melanoid maturity.

Dieu et mon droit! God and war. All along, these past three days, I've dragged it in my mind. It's like a dream I had when the struggle with the superquarry was going tough. I was crawling along the side of the road at Roineabhal on all fours, dragging my satchel briefcase behind, at risk of being struck by passing cars, hypothermic and exhausted.

I've dragged war with me because I'd had it so much in my face before I left, just back from speaking to the soldiers and the diplomats. *Dieu* either gets the credit or the blame for wars. Nobody really wants to know that poor old *Dieu* got co-opted to the cause. 'Don't have a king,' said God to the Israelites, through the prophet Samuel. 'He'll only take your daughters to be perfumers and bakers, and your sons to run before his chariots of war, and levy on you all manner of tithes and oppressions.' But no. The Israelites replied: 'We want a king to be over us, like all the other nations. A king who'll go out before us, and fight our battles.' And God shrugged God's heavy shoulders. It's just so hard to be God sometimes. And God said, 'OK. I'll not stand in your way. You go and do it your way.'[2]

While the early followers of Christ were pacifist, the Roman Empire under Constantine became nominally Christian in the fourth century, and went on to crush the heathen with its battle cry *Nobiscum Deus* – 'God with us'. When colonisation is spiritual, as well as corporeal, the vanquished find it hard to process what has happened to them. They were meant to be grateful. They'd been 'given' God, after all. As such, the oppressed so often meld to join the next wave of oppressors. Pillage, rape and the scars of banal brutality run through the ancestral veins of everyone.

Warlords like William the Conqueror went on to dignify their act, paying their spiritual fire insurance by bestowing abbeys with the spoils of rack, ruin and serfdom. The Nazis didn't miss the trick either. For all their supposed paganism, German soldiers had the Roman motto stamped onto the buckles of their trouser belts: *Gott mit uns.* Goebbels read the New Testament with a jaundiced eye, concluding: 'Christ is harsh and relentless.' Erich Koch, the commissar of East Prussia who sent hundreds of thousands of Ukrainian Jews and Gypsies to the death camps, held that National Socialism was nothing less than 'Luther's unfinished Reformation'.

Why Luther's? Because in 1543 the reformer had said of the Jews that, as a deed of kindness, rulers 'must act like a good physician who, when gangrene has set proceeds without mercy to cut, saw, and burn flesh, veins, bone, and marrow'. Accordingly, German Protestants must 'burn down their synagogues [and] force them to work, and deal harshly with them'. Of such measures, Himmler remarked: 'No judgement could be sharper,' and asked that, after the war, his own contributions to such a Reformation cause should be remembered at the Luther Archive in Wittenberg. In the view of the historian, Richard Steigmann-Gall, the Third Reich developed a war theology that understood itself to be a 'favoured nation' where 'most Christian clergy condemned Germany's adversaries in harsh moral terms, elevating the war into a type of crusade in which God had chosen Germany to punish his enemies'.[3]

From such roots, Hitler's 'spiritual struggle' found inner cohesion and, therefore, outer legitimacy. The problem is not unique to Protestantism. Roman Catholicism and Orthodoxy have also been riddled through with violence and authoritarian religion. So, too, are some facets of other faiths, including the supposedly peaceful Buddhism of Burma or Sri Lanka. But those aspects of the Protestant tradition that entertain a binary division of the Damned and the Elect, and the ongoing God-sanctioned legitimacy of violence, arguably have a special problem at mission control. As Erich Fromm surmised: 'Calvin's theory of predestination has one implication which should be explicitly mentioned here, since it has found its most vigorous revival in Nazi ideology: the principle of *the basic inequality of men.*' That said, we should not make the mistake of imagining that this Nazi hijacking of the cause was true to the fullness of the faith. 'Hitler's ideology,' Fromm took care to point out, 'lacks the emphasis on freedom and moral principles which was inherent in Protestantism.'[4]

These issues surface in the military staff colleges whenever we debate the 'just war' theory of Saint Augustine: 'we go to war that we may have peace.' Why should the military entertain such theology? Why should such theory hold a central place in their curriculum and many of their debates? Quite simply, they understand that their values are their value. They have seen how otherwise decent people can, under compelling circumstances of social psychology, do the most terrible things to one another. They know how easily the moral anchor can drag if not well toed-in. They also know that we are living in a world where old certainties are gone. A world where, as my speaking brief from the UK Defence Academy puts it, 'the net results of conflict are not easy to predict'. Where the very 'utility of force', as they call it, is undergoing reappraisal.

In 1898, Winston Churchill rode into the Battle of Omdurman (in present-day central Sudan) on horseback, with a sabre by his side. By the end of his political career, it was Hiroshima and Nagasaki. Today the cutting edge of conflict has become 'asymmetric warfare' – the military's name for terrorism – the little guy's ability to paralyse the big, because technology has democratised violence. As General Sir Rupert Smith writes: 'Our opponents are formless, and . . . even if military action is on a big scale, and even if it is successful the confrontation will remain, to be resolved by other means and levers of power.'[5]

When I speak at staff colleges, I'll be in an auditorium with anything from thirty to four hundred serving officers. I'll pose questions like: *What might be those other means and levers?* To use a Quaker turn of phrase, *How might we seek to live in the virtue of that life and power that takes away the occasion of all wars?*[6] I'll maybe start by acknowledging that, so far, nobody has managed to rid the world of war with nonviolence. But neither so, with violence. We can proceed from the basis of such mutual deficiency, and nonviolent approaches have now built up an extensive track record of success worldwide – the revolutions in India, Portugal, the Philippines, Eastern Europe, to name but a handful. I find that there's a very thin line between the principled soldier and the principled pacifist. Both see peace as the end, but differ in the means. Both, in their own ways, are imperfect in an imperfect world. Said Martin Luther King: 'I came to see the pacifist position not as sinless but as the lesser evil in the circumstances.'[7]

'All life entails violence,' said Gandhi. 'Our duty can only be to minimise it.' As he taught it, nonviolence as *ahimsa* (literally 'not striking') is driven by *satyagraha* – a Sanskrit word that means 'truth force', 'soul force' or 'God force'. As such, 'The badge of the violent is his weapon, spear, sword or rifle. God is the shield of the nonviolent.'[8] Jesus never taught 'just war' theory. Jesus taught full-on *nonviolence*. 'Put away your sword,' he told Peter. 'We shall have no more of this.' And to Pilate at his trial: 'My kingdom is not of this world. If it was, my followers would fight to save me.'[9]

*   *   *

Killing is a very ultimate thing to do. Many are the occasions that I've heard fighting men privately express their ethical disquiet. It can be very humbling. One time, an RAF man came forward in the coffee break, just as I was about to go up on the podium. He had hovered in the background amongst all the buzz of activity until we could be momentarily alone, then closed in and announced, with an air of burning urgency: 'I just want to say that I'm just back from Afghanistan . . . and I feel . . . *defiled.*'

That was all. Those are the only words by which that airman etched himself upon my memory. But something in me shot into action. I told him that, whatever it was that he might have done or seen, it was forgiven. Point blank. Forgiven. 'Now, move on, and live the rest of your life – undefiled.'

The energy with which I said these words felt outlandish even as I spoke. I thought afterwards, 'What right have I . . . ?' But sometimes it's like that. The military have a good understanding of these moments. You only get one shot. If you pussyfoot around, the magic of the 'activist moment', as I call it, has moved on. We speak of 'baring the soul', and to experience it in such a way always feels a specially tender sort of intimacy.

I've not always caught such moments elegantly. Another time, a Brigadier at the Joint Services Command & Staff College, laterally a Lieutenant General, a man well-known for his bluntness but much loved by his colleagues for his fairness, came up to me the evening after my talk. He looked me square on, and said: 'Quite frankly, I think that you are mad.'

'Have you ever killed?' I retorted.

It took him aback visibly. He was one of the Pilgrims, as the SAS special forces call themselves, and he'd seen full-spectrum action, from Northern Ireland to Iraq.

'That's not a fair question!' he snorted, throwing back a thick set of martial eyebrows.

'Yes it is!' I said acerbically, throwing up a wall between the two of us. 'I am a taxpayer. You are a public servant. We are a democracy.

'Now: have you ever killed?'

'Yes,' he said, in a deflated air, and we parted, loose ends left hanging like raw flesh.

At first I felt quite proud of myself. Later, it came to me that all I'd done was play Smart Alex. It wasn't the validity or otherwise of the point I'd made that was the problem. It was how I'd made it. I'd gone on the attack rather than sitting down to listen. There'd have been a story, and bridgeheads, within that man if I'd understood the opportunity. As it was, I'd only fed the spiral of violence.[10] I'd flunked the Quaker test of 'seeking that of God in everyone'.

Another day, another lecture, and we're all relaxing in the officers' mess the night beforehand. We've had a couple of beers, and are thoroughly enjoying the challenges of one another's company. Tornado airman is on one side of me. Harrier airman, on the other. We're laughing, because they've noticed that my security pass indicates my status as *Unescorted*. How come such likes get set loose here? I must be part of the woodwork now. What's more, my mugshot on the pass has me saluting. A double-fingered V for peace.

'Lest we forget!' I tease them, adding that I'm still waiting for the index-linked pension and the medal.

Another round of ammunition has been ordered from the bar. Jolly good. Tally ho. We all three know its time for battle to commence.

'Gentlemen,' I say. 'You'll be aware that they only let me out of my box here to test your resolve under fire. And you'll observe that I'm not house-trained. Not even wearing a tie!

'So tell me,' and I turn to Tornado, and pop to him the question that I'd popped the brigadier, albeit in a more convivial spirit. 'Have you ever killed?'

These days, so many of them have seen death, or been its direct cause.

'I have,' he says, and starts to tell of dropping thousand-pound bombs on an Iraqi airfield in the First Gulf War. They'd been trained to fly low, but on this occasion were told to stay high. Lights off. Tight formation. Following each other's burners by the naked eye in the darkness to keep radio and radar silence.

The bombs were dropped on targets set entirely by their programmed instruments. Tornado had been troubled that he couldn't first eyeball what was down below. He couldn't double-check on manual control. When the payload hit the ground, 'it was like Armageddon lighting up'. Thankfully, when the recce pictures came back the next day, the strike had been spot on. Everything was fried. The runways would never run again. He was glad the raid had taken place in the middle of the night. Not so many people to be killed as there would have been in daytime.

'How did it make you feel?' I ask.

'Gut-wrenching.'

Long silence.

Over to Harrier.

'And you?'

He's a much younger man. He'd dropped cluster bombs on an Iraqi barracks.

'We wiped it flat.'

Longer silence.

'How did it make you feel?'

'Satisfied!'

And he's in for the kill. Newly back from Afghanistan, but smiling. I'm the one now in his sights, finger poised to zap the pickle button.

'Alastair – let me put this to you.

'Consider the reality in Afghanistan. You're at a checkpoint, and a civvy car drives up. A man gets out with two small children – arms blown off. They're dripping blood, too shocked to cry, just whimpering.

'Whatever's happened has only just happened, and in spite of all your training, you're completely thrown.

'All right!' the man shouts. 'I surrender! I confess. I am Taliban.'

They'd been making IEDs. Roadside bombs. One went off in the kids' hands.

'I give myself up,' he says. 'I renounce the Taliban! But please, please, help my children. Do what you want with me, but in the name of Allah, get my children to a hospital.'

The coalition's mission was to win hearts and minds. So what were the boys to do? They did what every decent instinct told them to do. They called in a medevac helicopter. Luckily, one was passing close by.

Just as it was lifting off, Daddy Taliban dives back into his car. He pulls out an RPG – a rocket-propelled grenade – and fires it at the chopper, with his own children inside.

'Now, *what do you say to that*, Alastair?' concludes Harrier. '*With his own little children inside.*'

Utter silence.

'You see,' he resumes, 'That's why! That's why – when they've got our boys pinned down in a fire fight. That's why – when I'm called in to take out a nest of Taliban. That's why I find the sound of cannon fire . . . *so satisfying.*

'What do you say to that? Alastair?'

And like an eagle, he circled around, climbing higher and higher in the silence. And when he was sure, he zeroed back in with one long thunderous blast on the pickle button.

'What does *pacifism* have to say to that?'

And, trapped in the crosshairs, it came to me the way that, once every few years, I'll have a recurrent nightmare. I'll be caught up in a savagely violent situation. Acting on instinct – before even having chance to think about 'my principles' – I'll have grabbed and used a weapon. It's as if the dream is to remind me not to be too self-assured.

'So?' Harrier asked, permitting no quarter.

Solemn pause.

'*Brutalisation,*' I replied. 'I would say that is what's happened to your Taliban man. That Taliban's whole culture has been brutalised.

'And guess who did the brutalising? Hardly cricket, was it? All the way back to 1839 – the first British occupation of Afghanistan – our power struggle with the Russian Empire, what we cheerfully called "The Great Game".'

'Hardly cricket, is it?'

And my mind was running in parallel with the presentation that I'd be giving in the morning. The images that I'd put up on the screen that spans the huge front wall of the auditorium of the Joint Services Command and Staff College.

A clipping from the *Daily Telegraph*. It had angered many readers at the time. Dr Muhammad Abdul Bari, the Secretary General of the Muslim Council of Britain, explaining the psychology of the making of a suicide bomber.

'I deal with emotionally damaged children. Children come to hate when they don't get enough care and love . . . It makes a young person angry and vulnerable.'[11]

And then the terrible images that I've gathered from the web that make even seasoned soldiers flinch.

'We don't get to see these in our media,' I say, 'but the Arab world sees them. In fact, this is how they've seen us for a very long time.'

The first is from *Al Jazeera*. A child's head exploded, his little face flowing in the dirt as if it has become a plastic mask that's melting in the fire.

'This is somebody's son.'

And then a man sitting in a truck, gone from the neck upwards, brain remnants dripping down his leather jacket; and in the final indignity, he has visibly wet his trousers.

'Somebody's daddy.'

Followed by an Iraqi woman. Her thighs are beautiful, her vulva neatly shaved, and hanging from below one knee are blackened drapes of tangled flesh and sinew.

'And this is what happened when Mummy went to the market.'
And now is such a very thin place. Such a faraway place.

Such a faraway place – where Harrier still circles – somewhere among the clouds above.

'Those Iraqis . . .' I say.

'We had to stop Saddam!' he interjects, throwing out distracting chaff.

'They chose to be there in those barracks. They chose to fight for his regime.'

'And the conscripts? Did your cluster bombs distinguish?'

His face twitches. Tornado watches like an old owl. I've made my point sufficiently. Time now to climb down from the tumult.

'But I invite you, gentlemen, to ask the same question of me. *Have I killed?*'

Both looked puzzled.

'You see, I'm a killer too. Every time I get into the car or on a plane, burning oil that's been fought for, poisoning the planet. Who can really tell?

'Goddamnit! Maybe even every time I don't do what you do.

'We're all complicit. All in this together. All so very human.'

10

RULE, BRITANNIA!

The morning dew has almost gone. It lingers only in the shady nooks, but even there it quickens to a rainbow sheen of pinprick diamonds for a while, then yields its iridescence to the climbing sun. My tent has now dried, my daybooks going back to Monday are written up, and I have lingered here for long enough. It's been a precious couple of hours. A time for settling into place, its utter stillness; and for taking stock, recalling all the reasons that have brought me here.

I tighten Osprey's straps, nod a ceremonial farewell to the sheiling's presences from which I am divided only by the veneer of time, and head off up the stalker's path. Compared with the one I touched on yesterday, this trail is in a reasonable condition. Perhaps it comes from having worked with stone, but I always love to walk on stonework that's been laid to last. What's right beneath my feet right now was made to take the pummelling of a pony with two hundred pounds of stag strapped to its saddle. You can see the quality of construction in the culverts and the cambered angles, as well as in the tightly packed mosaics of cobbles that are toed in deep to one another's heel, thus to give sure footing even on the steepest reaches. Those stones back on the road at Rodel – they'd been crushed by force to chips of standard size and grading. But these stones, uncut, range from a fist-sized pound in weight up to a hundred-weight and more. Of these, each lives out its service at a stone-paced rate of life – if such a thought is meaningful. Said MacDiarmid: 'I lift a stone; it is the meaning of life I clasp.'[1]

Here and there, every hundred yards or so, I pass the mossy pitted faces of tiny quarries. These were gouged out more than a century ago, for building up the foundations of much more ancient footpaths. I picture them being grafted at by men with picks and spades, and muscles knotted like Scots pine. Crofter men, in homespun tweeds and jerseys, an oilskin for the rain, who carted grit in baskets or on barrows while bantering in the Gaelic. The whereabouts of cattle, sheep or deer. The price per cran of herring landed on the Tarbert pier last week. The latest scrape of the Scalpay boys drift netting off the Shiants. The strength or weakness of the new minister's sermons. The who's who of shooting parties due up to the Castle next month. The furtive sharing of who got tipped by whom, fishing which loch, on what flies, and with what weight of catch. And from newspapers and letters read out by the literate, or from word of mouth from ships and those returning home: what's fresh from the shipyards of the Clyde. Or the whalers of the Arctic. Or the sheep ranches of the Falklands and Patagonia. Or the prairies of Canada. Or India and the Cape. Or whatever other fighting fronts were open in the name of God and Empire with the Cameron or the Seaforth Highlanders, who'd be recruiting, respectively, in Tarbert and in Stornoway.

There'd be the studied contemplation, too, as they'd sit and pare at liquorice slabs of plug tobacco, tapping ash from out the bowls of briar pipes, tamping down the aromatic flakes. The never-ending ritual of lighting up, expiry in the damp, asking round to see who's got another light, dispelling clouds of midges with the satisfying puffs, and smelling like the tar and tallow-seasoned toilers of the soil that they were.

Here the gradient sways and twists, in an easy-going switchback sort of way. It means you only get to see a little way ahead. The shorter lengths seem to shorten time. I scribble in my daybook: 'On the winding path no stretch is long'. There's a spring in my step. Even Osprey's lighter than yesterday. I feel so happy, and an hour soon idles by as last night's campsite slowly shrinks from sight.

I've come up to the pass, and another watershed. Rapaire is over on the right. On my left, the sheer black cliffs and chutes of scree of Stuabhal – the Abode of Staves, or of the Rocky Columns. You could trim that down to one word, metaphorically speaking. Fortress.

Just visible behind me, in the east, appears the summit tip of Beinn Mhòr. With it comes back Eishken, and those stalking days with Tommy. Ahead of me lounge the hills of Uig, and beyond, the two-toned Plimsoll line from where the pale blue of the horizon's sky meets richer hues from fathoms of the Atlantic's bounteous depth.

There is a headland somewhere over there that's called Am Beannachadh – The Blessing – and by it Taigh a'Bheannaich – the House of Blessing. It's part of Gallan Head, one of those old temple or related sites, a low stone ruin of some unknown antiquity. There used to be a spring, now just a muddy squelch, but you can still see rings amongst the grass of the foundations of their bothan dwellings, their little cells of prayer and spiritual retreat.

Right next to it, on the neighbouring promontory, is the Aird Uig NATO base. Some of the bunker-like buildings are still there, but the huge sweeping radar scanner and the six-hundred-foot-high mast with strobes that stabbed the Hebridean night have now been taken down. Rumours come and go as to whether less obtrusive structures have been set up elsewhere on the island to fight, they say, the War on Terror. Well, I've never quite seen Bin Laden getting this far north and west. But you never know. You just never know where the Devil's going to creep in next.

You just never know – and part of what I've been wanting to think about on this walk is the way that 'just war' theory locks religion in to an endless identification with violence. Christ, if we give him credence, was very clear. His world was not one to be fought for with the sword in any outward sense.[2] Paul, however, took a more pragmatic view, and with Augustine's influence, Calvin further ramped it up:[3]

> Hence we infer that empires did not spring up at random, nor by the mistakes of men, but that they were appointed by the will of God, because he wishes that political order should exist among men, and that we should be governed by usages and laws. For this reason Paul says, that all who resist the power are rebels against God, because there is no power but what is ordained by God (Romans 13:1, 2).

Such a theology of 'might is right' lies behind notions like 'American exceptionalism', 'favoured nation' status, the sense of being the 'chosen people', and the presumption of holding a 'manifest destiny' to order and command the world.[4]

In his book about predestination, the leading Reformed church theologian, Loraine Boettner, claimed that America represented 'one of the brightest pages of all Calvinistic history . . . Our forefathers believed in it and were controlled by it'. He quoted the renowned historian and US Navy Secretary, George Bancroft, that the Founding Fathers had been, 'Calvinists . . . according to the straightest system'.[5] The United States may proclaim a separation between church and state, but the underlying ideology, proclaimed in *The Star-Spangled Banner*, the national anthem, has these closing lines:

> Then conquer we must, when our cause it is just,
> And this be our motto: 'In God is our trust.'
> And the star-spangled banner in triumph shall wave
> O'er the land of the free and the home of the brave!

For some of those who draw depth and richness from Calvin's theology, it was a tragedy that the McCarthyite persecution of intellectuals in the 1950s inhibited America from evolving a liberal, mellowed-out mainstream Protestantism, such as came about in European countries like Scotland and Holland. Instead, the field was cleared for the business-friendly neoconservative gospel of evangelicals like the Reverend Billy Graham, with an obsessive focus on the privatised spirituality of personal salvation, and little by way of social witness.

Raised of Scots Presbyterian stock, Graham was ordained as a minister in the Southern Baptist Convention, a church that is, itself, of a substantially Calvinist disposition.[6] Every recent American president, right through to Obama, has found it expedient to sit in prayer with the preacher. Most strikingly, in January 1991, on the eve of launching Operation Desert Storm to initiate the First Gulf War, George Bush Sr called Graham in to pray with him at the White House. The evangelist later disclosed: 'Our prayers were for a short war and one that would be followed by a long period of peace in the Mideast.'[7] It was a short war, but war nonetheless, and with lasting ramifications.

As father, as son; and come the year 2000, George W. Bush drew on the ideology of American exceptionalism in his election campaign. 'Our nation,' he said, 'is *chosen by God* and commissioned by history to be a model to the world of justice and inclusion and diversity without division.' Bush had found his way to conservative evangelical Christianity. As he later put it, 'Reverend Graham planted a mustard seed in my soul.' With it came a heightened and very personal sense of manifest destiny.[8]

> I feel like God wants me to run for president. I can't explain it, but I sense my country is going to need me. Something is going to happen, and, at that time, my country is going to need me.

Something did indeed happen the following year, on 9/11. Within a month of the Twin Towers attack, America's neoconservative politicians had seized the chance to invade Afghanistan, albeit having promptly to rename 'Operation Infinite Justice' as 'Operation Enduring Freedom' to avoid seeming to appropriate an attribute of Allah.[9] The 'special relationship' between Britain and America fell into place and, starting from day one of these asymmetric hostilities, Tony Blair ordered British submarines to strike the poverty-racked landlocked country with Tomahawk cruise missiles.

Blair had been eased into power in 1997 as the UK prime minister with the godfatherly help of Rupert Murdoch, the Australian media magnate, whose grandfather and great-grandfather had both been Presbyterian clergy of the Free Church of Scotland.[10] His lead British newspaper, then with a circulation of nearly four million, had run a full-front-page headline before the May general election that announced: *The Sun Backs Blair: Give change a chance.* It was a sorry perversion of John Lennon's peace anthem. The following year, as ethnic conflict blew up in Kosovo, Murdoch's *Sun* ran another full frontal: *War in Europe: BOMB BOMB BOMB.* Not since the tabloid newspaper's famous *GOTCHA* when, in 1982, a British submarine sank the Argentinean *General Belgrano,* had the British nation been stirred up with such jingoism.

Come the Second Gulf War and the invasion of Iraq in 2003, George W. Bush's defence secretary was the arch-neoconservative Donald Rumsfeld. His Christian name is the anglicised form of *Dòmhnall,* Gaelic for The Ruler of the World. That perhaps befits one credited with the one-liner: 'Death has a tendency to encourage a depressing view of war.' Very little has been written about his religion, but in a 1962 campaign leaflet that is replicated in his memoirs, he described himself as attending a Presbyterian church.[11] In the early days of the second Iraq War, Rumsfeld allowed his military advisors to put jokes on the covers of his daily intelligence bulletins that were given to Bush. However, as American lives started to be lost, the jokes transmogrified into belligerent Bible verses. Alongside photographs of tanks and US soldiers at prayer, the chosen passages included:[12]

Put on the full armour of God (Ephesians 6:11)

Their arrows are sharp . . . their chariot wheels are like a whirlwind (Isaiah 5:28)

It is God's will that by doing good you should silence the ignorant talk of foolish men (1 Peter 2:15)

Ironically, it was the apostle Peter whom Jesus had explicitly disarmed.[13] Whether war was the kind of 'doing good' that Peter later had in mind with his epistle, is a moot point. The apologists for war repeatedly told the media: *this is not a crusade.* Such rhetoric was all very well. However, if anyone from al-Qaeda happened to switch on their television, and watched the crowd's annual rapture as they swayed to the chorus of 'Rule! Britannia' in London at The Last Night of the Proms, they might well have been forgiven for being fooled.

> When Britain fi-i-irst, at heav-en's command,
> Aro-o-o-ose from out the a-a-a-zure main,
> Arose, arose, arose from out the a-azure main,
> This was the charter, the charter of the land,
> And guardian a-a-angels sang this strain:
>
> Rule, Britannia! Britannia rule the waves
> Britons never, never, never shall be slaves.
>
> The nations, no-o-o-o-ot so blest as thee,
> Must i-i-i-i-in their turn, to ty-y-yrants fall,
> Must in their turn, to ty-y-rants fall,
> While thou shalt flourish, shalt flourish great and free,
> The dread and e-e-e-e-nvy of them all.

On the day after the session in the officers' mess with Tornado and Harrier, I was escorted down from the rostrum by a brigadier. He had that rather sweet, concerned manner, that is characteristic of a certain vintage of English gentleman, and he cleared his throat and asked me, almost shyly: 'Er, tell me, do the politicians ever have you come and say these things?'

'Never!' I said.

'The trouble is, I get the feeling that they can't believe they've made it until they've been blooded in a war.'

I had in my mind the way that a certain kind of guest at the sporting lodges will dip their finger into the entry wound of a freshly slaughtered beast, and daub a patch of blood on their foreheads. I had in mind, too, an article that had been in the *Daily Telegraph* about Lance Price, one of Tony Blair's spin doctors. Price said that he had felt the Prime Minister 'was relishing his first blooding' when he authorised air strikes on Iraq in 1998. Despite all the public hand-wringing about having had to act 'with a heavy heart', it was his sense that Blair had felt that dropping bombs was 'part of his coming of age as a leader'.[14]

The brigadier harrumphed. 'Yes,' he said. 'I feared that might be the case.

'Such a pity.'

We retired into an anteroom for a quick round of refreshments, then back into the auditorium for questions.

'So, what would you have done about inspecting Saddam's weapons?' asked a military policeman.

'Set a good example,' said I, cheekily. 'First send them up to Scotland to inspect our own weapons of mass destruction – Trident at Faslane.'

'And Saddam himself?' yapped an army major, as the tempo hotted up. I'm the fox, they're the hunt, and its *tally-ho* for the chase.

'A monster of our own making,' I retorted: 'But where were *you* when the West was arming him as he gassed his own people? What were *you* doing while the rest of us were writing our Amnesty International letters, getting fobbed off with Xeroxed replies from the Ministry of Defence who were in cahoots with the arms companies?'

'Pardon me, sir, but what would you do if somebody broke into your home?' inquired a punctilious Kuwaiti naval captain.

'I've been there,' I was able to say. 'They cleaned out the house while one of them held a knife to the throat of our friend who had been sleeping downstairs. If we'd had a revolver, like some expatriates kept under their pillows, she'd have got her throat slit.'

'And rape?' asked a USAF pilot, with that languid faraway air of having seen and heard it all before. 'Suppose they came for one of yours?'

So I told a real-life story.

It was in 1985, and I was working in appropriate technology in the capital of Papua New Guinea. One night, a young woman in our tiny Quaker Meeting – she was just seventeen – was dragged out of her car by fourteen disaffected young men, a so-called 'rascal' gang. Her boyfriend was beaten up. She was taken to a nearby hillside, where they took it in turns to rape her.

Normally the police would have gone in to their squatter settlement and administered indiscriminate rough justice. However, from her hospital bed, she said that she wanted no more perpetuation of the violence. Instead, she wanted something that might 'touch their hearts', that might have a chance of opening paths to empathy.

Her father, a university teacher, was friendly with the chief of police and sent a message to request restraint. A few days later, he asked me to accompany him to the settlement, so that we could talk with its leaders.

We walked in, unannounced, and sat down with the 'old' men underneath a tree. None of them would have been over forty. They told us straight out that they knew why we had come, and that they were deeply sorry about what had happened. They very much appreciated the police restraint, for they, themselves, had lost control of their youth. The old ways were in chaos. The bewildering new ways of rapid social change had broken down the customs and constraints. Their poverty contrasted painfully with the 'fruits of the white man's garden' and this generated frustration and alienation. Most of the boys in the gang had come from rural parts, hoping they might 'make it', but with not a hope. They'd fallen to a subculture of violent crime with all its brutalising rites of passage. The old men knew. They'd been there, done that, too.

We asked them a question. What, in their culture, would make for a fitting reconciliation with our community? They said that they would have to hold a compensation ceremony.

On the appointed day, the girl's father and I stood in ceremony, facing one another at the university gates. About a dozen of our companions witnessed in silent Quaker worship in the background. Processing down the main street, amidst much beating of drums and with all the bravado of a carnival, walked the entire squatter settlement. There were perhaps two hundred of them and of all ages.

We had said that we did not want any material compensation, that it was not our people's way. However, it was their way. The compromise was that the food would be sent up to the patients at the hospital afterwards. There they all were – a whole community – and pushing a cavalcade of six or eight wheelbarrows piled high with pumpkins, tapioca, yams, sweet potato, sago sticks, coconuts, pawpaw, chickens, tinned fish and betel nuts. Goodness knows where it all came from. One prefers not to ask. And right at the head of the procession, was a column of fourteen young men.

They had never expected to be treated in this way. Many were in tears. One by one, the lads filed between us. Each briefly looked us in the eyes, and said: *Mipela sori tru.*

'I'm truly sorry.'

That was it – and that was the end of that particular session with Harrier, Tornado and their colleagues. However, not all of the military with whom I have shared that story have been touched by it. Once, I was invited to speak to non-commissioned officers. These are the connecting link between the officers and other ranks. They're the spanners who use clout to make the army work at ground level. It was at the Army Training Regiment in Colchester.

I could feel their energy darken with a pensive hostility as I gave my lecture. Afterwards, in the mess, a wiry, moustached and fiery-eyed NCO came up to me.

'What you did,' he said, 'was to *prostitute* that girl! All you did was put a price on a white woman's rape.'

The mainstream expatriates in Papua New Guinea had said the same thing. There had been letters in the press saying that castration was the only answer: in Pidgin, *rausim bol bilong ol!*

'Then, what would you have done?' I asked the NCO.

'I'd have . . . *I'd have gone down to the market*,' he said, blurting out the words. 'And I'd have bought an AK47 . . . *and shot the bastards to Hell!*'

'And would that have made for a safer future?'

He held fire, fazed by the question. It seemed like for a long time. Then he shrugged his shoulders with a warming smile – and goodness, there is something that I love about the honesty and decency of these hard-bitten fighting men – 'Probably not. But what can I get you to drink?'

From here, the land dips downwards, and the view towards Aird Uig starts to slip from off my radar. The path winds on beneath a volley of looming cliffs. These rise so high and sharply that, for the most part, their lower faces hide inside deep shadows. At their foot lies a heart-shaped lake, Loch Chleistir. It means the Loch of the Cascading Rock. I stand awhile, and watch its surface billow with the gusts of breeze to sheets of rippling sapphire. I half think of getting out my rod to fish, but there's no point. The wind is still sat resolutely in the south-east. In any case, there is a sacrosanct feeling to this place. It should perhaps be left in peace.

The temperature can't be more than ten degrees, but that's been absolutely perfect for the walking. I've made it all the way up here, laden as I am, but shedding not a drop of sweat. Now, there's a choice of two route options down to Kinlochresort. Either I can keep to this path for another couple of miles, then strike directly north from the tail end of Loch Voshimid. Or I can turn off here and follow the stream that leaves Loch Chleistir and which defines the border between Harris and Lewis. Its name is Abhainn a' Chlàir Bhig – the River of the Little Plain – and it meets up with the river that flows out of Voshimid at a junction past the said small plain, shown on the map as Clar Beag. To go too close to Voshimid looks terribly boggy, even on the small scale map that I'm using at the moment to get more of a panoramic perspective. You can tell by all the tiny lochans and the spread-out contours. The Clar Beag route looks like it's on a steady gradient, and drier.

Hopefully, I'll dodge the marshes until much nearer to my destination.

Thus far, the ease of the path has made the day genteel, but very soon after leaving it I'm into rough and tumble. The ground comprises beds of peat incised by frequent flood path waterways. These chop it into little plateaus, rarely bigger than a tennis court. I have to keep on scrambling up the one side, and then skidding down the other with my boot heels on the slippery bare black 'hag'.

There is hardly any wind now, as I fall below the skyline. The silence ruptures only from the croak of ravens. I can make out three or four of them, somersaulting as black kites, playing in the thermals from the upper and now sun-soaked reaches of the cliffs behind. The deer have left their footprints in patches of the mud. Some, freshly flecked; others gone to mush. And although this is golden eagle country, I've seen but one so far, and that, far off on the horizon.

The lower down I get, the more the ground cuts up. Another half an hour on, and the tennis courts have shrunk to ping-pong tables – these, heaped up with clay and boulders that are the host to rank and thigh-high heather shrubs. This is where the retreating glacier forgot to tidy up. I'm in amongst the so-called 'hummocky moraine' of crushed rock debris. Its rugged chaos was laid down as blocks of ice, caught up within to melt away and leave behind the pits that are now kettle holes and sloshy bogs.

You could hardly say I'm walking; only a slow meander. I've given up on time, and just accept I'm near enough a day behind schedule. Ahead, I see Clar Beag, a grassy clearing as it were, about the size of a football pitch. It looks as if a flattening of the slope has caused the stream to braid, and spread out levelled beds of fertile sediment. I'm just ambling towards it, musing on nothing much, Osprey swaying this way and that way, up here and down there, maybe better go that way, when – as if whisked off by a gust of *gaoth nan sìth* – I'm into faerie land.

A miniature village! For such is what has come into my focus. Had I more carefully studied my bespoke map earlier, the large-scale one, I'd have been forewarned. They're marked clearly enough. Three times, at that: 'Old Sheilings'; 'Beehive Huts'; and 'Both a' Chlàir Bhig'.

In all my days out on the moors, I've never seen such likes before. It's a vision straight from Middle Earth. What I've stumbled on is a beehive sheiling settlement. Squatting on a grassy hump with the stream meandering around both sides, is a double both, in fact, two bothan, joined together like a castle with twin turrets. Each is conical, about a full-grown person's height, and wide enough at the base to be able to lie down outstretched inside. Each has its little doorway, an opening, square-set, with a lintel stone above, but only a couple of feet in height. The smaller structure is completely intact. The roof of the larger one stands open to the sky as if it is a cratered volcano, about to puff and blow.

I drop Osprey, kneel at the entrance, and pause for a moment. Then, lying down with my belly pressed flush to the ground, I wriggle through and slip backwards in time.

The ground inside is firm but filthy. Sheep have overwintered here, seeking shelter from the storms. Leaning back against the wall, a dappled splendour fills my eyes. Light is breaking through the cracks between the stones. The elements have stripped away much of the weatherproofing layer of turf outside. It's like I'm in a Stone Age planetarium. Pinprick stars are twinkling through the nooks and crannies. The dust raised by my entry is dancing in the hollow stillness. It makes the tapered shafts of sunlight seem to rotate, as if they're spiral galaxies at the birthing of creation.

The stones of which it is built are variable in size. They range from sacks of coal to bags of sugar. Each row steps in above the one below, spiralling to a cupola with the smoke hole at the top. There are several little recesses, 'cupboards' where they would have kept their things. This is an original eco-house. It was grown from out the moor, and now it settles slowly back from whence it came.

I crawl back out, back into a world that feels at first to be an overweening brightness. My stomach clock is chiming, and I settle down against one of the big foundation stones. Osprey gives soft padding for my back. I'm on standard lunchtime fare again. Oatcakes and cheese, freshly drawn stream water, and a bag of fruit and nuts. I'd thought they'd tasted slightly fusty back when I shared a pack with the ants on the Golden Road. Only now do I read what's written on the packet. '*Snack lovers rejoice. You are what you eat.*' And then the small print: 'Best before the end June 2006.' Oh well. Only three years gone!

Before I'd left home, Seumas Crawford had directed me to the writings of a certain Captain Thomas of the Royal Navy. In 1859 he'd made a formal notification of the existence of beehive structures on the island, sending it to the Society of Antiquaries of Scotland.[15]

> The general opinion is that they are very ancient. Martin, in his account of Skye, mentions them as *Tigh nan Druineach*, or Druids' houses . . . I consider

the relation between the *bothan* and the Picts' houses of the Orkneys (and elsewhere) to be evident . . . All the natives agree that no-one knows who built them, and that they were not made by the fathers nor grandfathers of persons now living.

In 1863 the captain returned to the island, this time with Sir Arthur Mitchell, who was the Professor of Ancient History at the Royal Scottish Academy. It was another double both structure that they'd found, one that (from the drawing) is nearly identical to mine, but located four miles north from here, at Larach Tigh Dhubhstail. In 1880 the professor published an account of the experience in his remarkable book, *The Past in the Present: What is Civilisation?*[16]

> I confess, however, to having shown, as well as felt, the effects of *the Wine of Astonishment*. I do not think I ever came upon a scene which more surprised me, and I scarcely know where or how to begin my description of it . . . We were in a dwelling in the construction of which neither wood, nor iron, nor cement had been used. Stone and turf, and nothing else had gone to make it. No tool had been used; scarcely even a wooden spade, and not a hammer of any kind . . . We felt that we had been almost introduced to the stone period without going either to far-off lands or far-off times to find it.

His astonishment was further amplified when he discovered nearby freshly broken fragments of what looked to be ancient pottery. Shortly afterwards, he made the acquaintance of the bothan's occupants. These were three sheiling girls who he found sitting on a cnoc. During the day, they minded and milked their cattle. At night, they slept inside the ancient shelter, just as their sisters before them had always done. The pottery was theirs. It had come from a seam of clay at Barvas, thirty miles away, worked by practices that had gone unchanged since Neolithic times. The women cut a touching pastoral picture:

> It was Sunday, and they had made their toilet with care at the burn, and had put on their printed calico gowns. None of them could speak English: but they were not illiterate, for one of them was reading a Gaelic Bible. They showed no alarm at our coming, but invited us into the *bo'h*, and hospitably treated us to milk. They were courteously dignified, neither feeling nor affecting to feel embarrassment. There was no evidence of any understanding on their part that we should experience surprise at their surroundings.

Sir Arthur speculated that some twenty or thirty such bothan remained in seasonal occupation on Harris and Lewis. However, 'it is not likely that a new one will ever again be built,' and he concluded: 'I leave this subject with the remark that the beehive-house certainly belongs to the man without a story, though the man without a story is still found clinging to it.'

VENISON AND HONEY

Perhaps Sir Arthur had to watch how deeply he drank of his Wine of Astonishment. Wearing another cap, he was also the Commissioner of Lunacy for Scotland. Captain Thomas had a more relaxed understanding that you cannot scratch beneath this landscape – into its place names and its people – without the stories stirring from their slumbers. He had enticingly entitled his 1859 missive to the Society of Antiquaries –

Notice of Beehive Houses in Harris and Lewis;
with Traditions of the 'Each-Uisge', or
Water-Horse, Connected Therewith

These are tales, like the one about the night a young man came to the sheiling door and asked if he might rest awhile from his weary travels. Of course, the lassie, being hospitable, offered him her lap to lay his head. As she stroked the sleeping man's hair, she realised that it was riddled through with waterweeds and gravel. He was the dread *each-uisge* in disguise, and when he awoke, he would change back into his true form, and hurl her onto his back, and gallop off into the depths of the loch – there to serve forever as his wife beneath dark waves. Picking up her sewing scissors, she carefully cut a circle in the fabric of her clothing around his head, and lifted it aside so that she could take her exit without causing disturbance. She ran non-stop all the way back to the village, and when she got there, the proof of the truth of the tale was the hole in her dress.

Stories like these continue to be handed down into the present generation. At one level they encode customary warnings. *Be careful of unwanted pregnancy* with the young man, or *be careful of the water's edge* if you're a child living by a loch.[1] At a deeper level, they open out into the old indigenous sense of Otherworld, into the realm of *sìthichean*, the *imaginal* realm, that overlaps with but should be distinguished from the merely *imaginary*. The imaginary is make-believe. The imaginal pertains to that which is in some sense 'there', because it arises out of the mythopoetic (or mythopoeic) realm.[2] This *Mythos*, as the Greeks called it, is the underlying ground of deep story or metanarrative. It is the realm from which the meaning-structures of our world arises; that which gives meaning to the meaning of meaning. The poetic 'making' of reality – that is what *poesis* means – and that as coming from beyond our conscious ken. Creation as the breaking forth from out the cosmic womb.

As Yeats described it, such is 'the soil where all great art is rooted [whether] spoken by the fireside, or sung by the roadside, or carved upon the lintel'. It is something, he goes on to say in *The Celtic Twilight*, that the western world has nearly lost 'in a society that has cast out imaginative tradition'. That is to say, in a society that, for the most part, no longer knows what it is that we might be a part of. One that has relegated the big picture – the frameworks of story, the values, the premises, the feelings and in a word, the spiritual – to a twilight world, for sure; but a far cry from the one of 'dew ever shining' of Yeats' poem, 'Into the Twilight', where 'God stands winding his lonely horn'.[3]

The Mythos pertains to the inner life, the soul and its imaginative intelligence.Its counterpart, the *Logos,* which frames the rational mind with its organising intelligence, pertains to the outer life of creation manifest. It is when it is uprooted from its grounding in the Mythos, that the Logos wallows in the monotonous materialism of its ever-so-logical positivism. This is the closed spirit that underpins Mark Twain's dire maxim: 'familiarity breeds contempt'. The only antidote to such life-retarding nihilism is mythopoetic reconnection. The reactivation of our creative spirits. It is why imaginal realities like faerie tales, miraculous Bible stories and epic legends, such as in the Hindu *Mahabarata* or Homer's *Iliad,* might seem like make-believe at one level, but reveal uttermost truths at another. Without such modes of knowing and being, the wellsprings of the soul run dry. We start to live a life that becomes, quite literally, soulless.[4]

The Angus and Aberdeenshire poet of the Scottish Revival, Marion Angus, was the English-born daughter of a Presbyterian minister. The latter qualification is almost *de rigueur* for writing in this metaphysical genre, and getting away with it. In 1928, she expressed the cultural and geographical significance of the imaginal realm in these terms:[5]

I myself would like to be the one (unfortunately I am not) to write a great poem on the spirit of place, *producing something born of myself and of the place,* which would be neither one or the other, but something very strange and beautiful. I should like to write of fairies, not the identical fairies of the old days, but the elusive glamour of the universe; and above all I would fain give voice to Scotland's great adventure of the soul. I never shall; some one may, perhaps.

Similarly, a decade earlier, in his book *Scottish Literature*, Professor G. Gregory Smith coined the corkscrew term, 'Caledonian antisyzygy', to capture what he saw as the quality of a culture that can entertain two seemingly contradictory worldviews, held together in creative tension. Like a battery with a high 'potential difference' or voltage between the terminals, this produces cultural energy. The antisyzygy, Smith said, is 'a strange union of opposites' in which rational reality on the one hand, and outrageous fantasy on the other – the realms of Logos and of Mythos as we might have it – become the 'two moods', the 'warp and woof', or the 'polar twins of the Scottish Muse'. On the one hand, you have the down-to-earth practicality of humble homesteads such as produced engineers, politicians and a breed of clergy who, in their more hidebound moments, could treat even theology as a dry rational pursuit. On the other hand, within the selfsame psyche there exists a counter-point capacity for such sobriety to be, as Smith put it, 'thrown topsy-turvy, in the horns of elf land and the voices of the mountains'.[6]

The function of the prophetic artist, a shaman of our times, is to sip the Wine of Astonishment: to be tossed high on the horns and wander amongst the voices. Provided that the good Commissioner of Lunacy is safely out of range, then that bardic function is to go a little crazy on behalf of others; on behalf of those who either lack the time, or whose 'sober wishes never learn'd to stray' far from the madding crowd, and yet whose lives would stultify without the winding horn of spiritual infusion, not least as received through the arts.

But stop! Practicality has come to claim me back. It's time to withdraw my iron needle from the door of Both a' Chlàir Bhig lest I wallow here for aeons, and to move on and hasten down to catch what's left of the low tide at Kinlochresort. Anything much past mid-water will be too late for the mussels. These can be found beneath the seaweed on the rocks of almost any sheltered bay in these parts, where a stream comes in. A touch of fresh water is said to deter their chief predator, the starfish. 'A good feed of the mussels' – that's how they used to say it back in Leurbost – and that's what's rumbling in my belly for this evening.

Down here, getting close to sea level, the ground collapses more and more to rough and tumble. The slope has slipped away. Everywhere is bog except for piles of rocks, dropped as if by parachute. The remnants of abandoned habitations? I don't know. My eyes are not informed enough to judge, and who knows what more might hide beneath the peat.

Now's the time for large-scale, and I check my bearings on my bespoke Poacher's map. Looks like all I need to do is keep on inching down until I meet the big river that flows out from Loch Voshimid. The wind has dropped right off, and Abhainn a' Chlàir Bhig has almost ceased the playful tinkling of its splashes as it starts to coil in a series of switchback meanders. I have to keep on leaping over squelchy soaks that mark out remnants of a former course. Even without Osprey on my back, this would be hard going, and I'm moving so very slowly that it feels like forever. Words like 'drudgery' and 'trudgery' dance mockingly around my head. 'God made the back for burden' – and I wonder where that one came from? The tiredness, oh a heavy tiredness, is coming over me. If it wasn't for the push to catch the tide, I'd curl up in the heather for a nap.

I stop to take stock, and stare up to the skyline. And there they are! Profiled on the shoulder of the hill. A herd of *their* cattle.

They're standing in a line, not yet seeing me, craning their stocky bristled necks and sniffing at the air. They're talking to each other with the twitching of their ears. This following wind has been why I've seen so little wildlife thus far. Up until this point, at which the valley base is broadening out, they'd have easily picked my scent up as it wafted tightly through the narrow glens. They'd have slinked away, before I ever had the chance to notice them.

Old stories suggest the existence of a deer-goddess cult in early Scotland. The herds were shepherded by the Cailleach as the wise old woman, the crone or hag, a seasonal face of the Celtic Goddess. The word for venison, the flesh of the deer, is in Gaelic *sithionn* or *sitheann* – almost the same as the *sìthean*. There are ancient songs and poetry about the 'darling deer', the 'beast of my love', and a lullaby called *Bainne nam Fiadh* – The Milk of the Deer:[7]

> On milk of deer I was reared,
> On milk of deer I was nurtured,
> On milk of deer beneath the ridge of storms,
> On crest of hill and mountain

Iain Thornber told me of an old stalker, with very little English, who used to say: 'I never once went to the hill but the deer didn't send me to university.' The Gaelic for the deer is *fiadh*, and I'm struck that one of the names in the old dictionaries for my friend, the Blue Mountain Hare, is *gearr-fiadh*, which means the 'short deer'. Fiadh is another of those words of a magnificently gliding semantic range, for it also means 'the wild'. John MacInnes of the School of Scottish Studies was born in Uig, the south-west parish of Lewis, onto which I'm presently bordering. Right now, I've probably got my left foot in North Harris and the right in Uig. He is – no surprises for such a preacher of the sìthichean – the son of a Church of Scotland minister. He explains:[8]

> Wilderness is a fundamental concept in Gaelic tradition . . . the distinction between humanised land and non-humanised land . . . The wilderness, being outside the normal boundaries of convention and order, was associated with the supernatural. The deer was the creature most strongly associated with the wilderness, as is suggested by its common name in Gaelic *fiadh* 'wild'. The deer were believed to be the livestock of the fairies, and the fairies themselves represent in many ways the powers and dangers of the wilderness.

John ends a pivotal essay, 'Looking at Legends of the Supernatural', with a personal memory that conveys a feeling for the depth and even the everydayness of the mythopoetic as it survived into his lifetime in traditional Gaelic communities:[9]

> I remember very vividly, when I was a little boy, seeing a wild hind grazing within the confines of the *baile* [the village]. Those who could read the signs realised that the natural order was being overturned and said: '*Se comharra cogaidh a tha seo* – 'This is an omen of war.' Not very long after the Second World War began. That sighting, that metaphor of order invaded by the wild, helped those who witnessed it to arrange their experience. The metaphor has a very long history behind it.

Similarly, John's colleague at Edinburgh University, Ronald Black, has described how the each-uisge, that lurked in every self-respecting Highland loch, also codified the invasion of order by the wild. In psychological terms, its sighting might be understood as an intrusion into consciousness of the archetypal contents of the collective unconscious; a superimposition, as it were, of inner vision onto the outer perception of reality. Like with John's wild hind as an 'omen of war', the tradition held that sightings of the water horse were harbingers of doom. That, in the full sense of destiny unfolding; of massive transformation, usually a disaster, impending on the clan. It is therefore no surprise, Black has argued, that reports amongst the indigenous population of the Loch Ness Monster attained epidemic levels in the 1930s. It was just as Hitler was rising to power, with consequences that would decimate many a Highland village.[10]

In John's opinion and life experience, 'Gaelic tradition implies that the distinction between wilderness and humanised space is mirrored in the human psyche.'[11] The sìthean – the encapsulation of wildness personified – is, he suggests, 'a metaphor of the imagination'.[12] It was (or is) an indigenous expression of the Jungian unconscious and not to be confused with the merely imaginary.

Such is why village bards whom he has known in person might, after composing their poetry or music, come out with such expressions as: *Bha mi 's a' Chnoc o chunnaic mi thu* – 'I was in the [fairy] Hill since I saw you'.

And the conclusion of this, from the greatest living Scottish Gaelic scholar, as if for any who might miss the full significance?

'From this shadowy realm comes the creative power of mankind.'

In his same essay on the supernatural, John MacInnes remarks that while Kenneth Macleod of Eigg and Gigha – the clergyman who wrote so warmly about Màiri, Daughter of Red Alastair, buried face-down at Rodel – has sometimes been taken for a romantic, the truth is that 'all the essential beliefs he draws upon are still talked about by bearers of Gaelic tradition'.

Once, Lord MacLeod of Fuinary was having dinner on Iona, with Kenneth as his guest, and it was old George's son, Sir Maxwell MacLeod, who gave me this story. Apparently, the two men had a terse relationship. There they were, sitting around the dining table, talking probably in that clipped manner of Presbyterian gentlemen whose prime fell in the first half of the twentieth century, but were truly of a much more ancient vintage. As the Winchester-schooled and metropolitan George struggled to make conversation with the Eigg-schooled and rustic Kenneth, he recalled a titillating sliver of local folklore that, he hoped, might make a suitably polite talking point.

'Er . . . we still have old Mrs So-and-So on Iona, and she *feeds the faeries.*'

'Oh? Really?' replied Kenneth, slowly. 'And tell me, at what time of the day does she feed the faeries?'

'I don't know!' said George, perfunctorily. 'Breakfast time? Dinner time?'

'Wrong time; wrong time,' said the Reverend Kenneth with a grave shake of his head.

'Then, what is the right time?'

'The right time to feed the faeries . . . is when the rain is still raining, and the sun is beginning to shine.'

Awkward silence.

'And tell me, on *what* does Mrs So-and-So feed the faeries?'

'Oh, I don't know!' said George, by now visibly irked that his olive branch of conversation had been taken up so seriously.

'Bread and butter, perhaps?'

'Ohhh!' exclaimed a pained Kenneth.

'Wrong food; wrong food!'

'Then what is the *right* food?' snapped George.

'The correct food on which to feed the faeries . . . *is venison and honey.*'

With a bounding turn, propelled as by a single motive force, the herd are off. Over the skyline I watch them go, bobbing their white rump patches as they run, back into the fiadh that is the sìthean of my mind. And when Gregory Bateson said, 'Mind is immanent in the larger system – man plus environment', he touched on a cultural carrying stream that is both human, and much more than just the human on its own. What the modern world calls the *supernatural,* says John MacInnes, is in Gaelic culture 'regarded by members of that society as part of the order of nature itself'. The 'super' is quite 'natural', a deeper ordering of reality that is made known through the second sight – *an dà shealladh* – literally, 'the two sights'. This, a stepping back of consciousness into what is normally unconscious, and with it, a corresponding loosening of the bounds of space and time.

The Gaelic term usually translated as the 'supernatural' is *anagh-nàthaichte*. My friend the American scholar Michael Newton, who takes a special interest in Gaelic metaphysics, tells me that it is pronounced like *ana-GRAAAA-eech-ah* – except with sounds that scarcely exist in English. It means the unusual, the uncanny, but these in a sense that is not completely of another world. Rarely do I come home to the island without receiving first-hand accounts of anaghnàthaichte. If I seem unusually open to such a contested reality, it is in part because I have experienced a dramatic case myself. When I was eighteen, I had the experience of watching helplessly as my father's beloved whippet crossed the road and was killed outright. My mother had left for Stornoway, seven miles away, just ten minutes previously. She went there nearly every day, but, on this occasion, she was just on the outskirts of the town when she was hit by an overwhelming compulsion to turn back. As I set about digging the dog's grave in the practical way one does in a rural society, I saw her car speeding down the hill. She skidded to a halt in the gravel of the driveway, jumped out, and looking racked with dread, demanded to know what was wrong. My answer was a relief. She said, 'I thought it might have been a child.'

In the island's traditions such experiences usually surround emotionally charged events like marriages, deaths and collective calamities. For example, in 2002, a retired policeman and lobster fisherman on Harris, Norman Macleod of Bridge House, wrote me a letter after reading *All in the Mind: Farewell to God* by Ludovic Kennedy. The broadcaster had pooh-poohed the idea of prophecy, to which Norman responded:[13]

> Even if I had never heard of a Bible or God, anyone as afflicted or gifted with the second sight as I am, to put it mildly, could not accept that. To give one tiny example, I could have written an account of the Falklands War and every stage of it, weeks or days before it happened, including being transported the 8,000 miles there in a split second and seeing . . . things that were to appear on TV afterwards, such as the warship HMS Sheffield with the metal superstructure going up in white incandescent flames.
>
> It actually happened. I could go on at great length, but as you are unlikely to believe a word of it, I will leave it at that. *My God*, Alastair, is the high and lofty one who inhabiteth *eternity*; whose name is *Holy* – not subject to any laws of man, mathematics, time or motion, and certainly not to be catalogued within the tiny mind of Ludovic Kennedy or any other mere mortal.

Dad's practice manager, Agnus MacLennan of Achmore, told me of an old man amongst her people on Great Bernera, who could locate the bodies of drowned fishermen – because he 'heard' the scream as they fell overboard.[14] 'Make sure you keep thinking about the stories I'm telling you,' she said at the end of one of my visits. I wrote her words of advice down in my notebook. They signified an importance that ran deeper than just superficial curiosity. Another time I asked her: 'Do you think that people experience the second sight these days as much as they used to?'

'No!' she harrumphed. 'Because these days, everybody is *too busy* and *too noisy.*'

In his record of the faerie faith amongst his seventeenth-century parishioners in Highland Perthshire, the Rev. Robert Kirk quotes at length from correspondence between his contemporaries, Lord Tarbett and Sir Robert Boyle. The former was a Highland judge of the Mackenzie landowning dynasty. The latter was the physicist who gave us Boyle's Law about the expansion of gases. Tarbett told Boyle of an observation made by a gentleman of his acquaintance, who had gone to Barbados. 'Several of those that did see with the Second Sight when in the Highlands or Isles, when transported to live in other countries, especially in America, they quite lost this quality.' Tarbett also noted: 'There were more of these seers in the Isles of Lewis, Harris, and Uist than in any other place.'[15]

Margaret Bennett is another of the School of Scottish Studies folklorists. She has observed that stories of the second sight have remained strong, to this day, wherever community and tradition remains strong in Hebridean diaspora outposts – including pockets in Newfoundland, Quebec, North Carolina and New South Wales.[16] Why, then, might it have been lost so quickly to those of Tarbett's near-acquaintance? Tarbett took a business interest in the 'African trade' – which is to say, slavery.[17] Barbados was a slave colony in his time; the Deep South that would one day become the stronghold of the KKK and the Bible Belt, much the same.

Could it be that violence to one's fellow humankind inflicts internal injuries upon oneself? That it violates a deeper psychic cohesion, the very basis of our interconnection through mind's immanence 'in the larger system'? And that the effects of war, its 'moral hazard', can therefore linger on, long after the outward guns have fallen silent?

I have tottered on, lurching and swaying through a deepening morass. My movements are ludicrous compared to the grace of the wild things I've just seen. This terrain is mired and jumbled, almost to the point of impassability. Thank God it's been dry weather. I am holding to the burn that winds like an Ariadne's woollen thread through the labyrinth. Again and again, I stop to check the map, wishing its large scale were even larger. There's got to be a better way through than this. I should have stayed up high, but if I'd done so, I'd have missed the Clar Beag bothan.

If I cut directly west for a quarter mile, I'll come to the Voshimid river. The map names it as the Abhainn Mhòr – the Big River of Loch Reasort. Perhaps it has carved out deeper banks that might make for better drainage and a firmer footing. I veer off on a compass bearing of 270° and this, surely, can't get any worse. But it does. The Bog Monster, my Minotaur, seeks vengeance.

I'm moving in amongst a vast expanse of black peat ooze. It is a surface that would, in more normal rainy weather, be mostly under water. Here and there on higher parts are polka dots of tufts of wiry grass. This may or may not present me with a problem to cross. Usually, when it's relatively dry like this, you can tread with care. You'll mostly sink in only halfway up your boots, more if burdened with a load, like Archimedes' Principle, but without the bathtub. But you never know. People do, rarely, fall through and flounder.

I advance, hopping from one patch of firm ground to the next. An eye for vegetation types is crucial. A tuft of grass – not to be confused with water plants – will have a safety net of roots that can support some weight. But clumps of rushes are the best. You'll never sink if you land your foot on one of them – and I'm just about to step into a stretch of stiff black porridge, that runs pretty much as far as I can see at this low angle – when I freeze.

It's like when the music stops in a statue dance, and your foot's left dangling in the air. Or in the jungle, when you spot the raised head of a snake. But here's no dance, no snake. Here's Ariadne's ball of woollen thread. Unravelled. Splayed out. Dissipating back into raw fleece.

Uh-uh, I'm thinking to myself. *I see the wool, but not the sheep.*
What has happened to the sheep?

I press my heel onto the gingerbread-like surface of the partly dried-out peat. It bounces up and down. Sùil-chruthaich! The Eye of Creation! The crust is just a couple of inches thick, and this, a quaking bog.

I pump my foot, but not too hard, and the whole surface wobbles like a waterbed. There must be a stream or spring running underneath. These things are death traps to the sheep, who spy a juicy tuft of grass, plough right in, and never quite manage to wallow out. It's as if the Bog Monster, like one of those insect-eating plants, can feed itself. Sometimes you'll see a patch that's grown bright green from where a sheep has been devoured. Plants thrive on the released nutrients, and their foliage attracts the next unwary grazing victim in a system of ecology that is, to say the least, dastardly.

'To be born is to be wrecked on an island,' wrote J.M. Barrie in 1913, always playing with the nexus of life and death. And when Peter Pan thought he'd met his end, stranded on Marooner's Rock, he only felt a single shudder, telling Wendy: 'To die will be an awfully big adventure.'[18] Not so, for the poor sheep. Sunk up to their bellies, thin legs churning in the mire, they starve and slowly weaken in their struggle over many days. Perhaps it's almost merciful when the eagles gather, and the ravens, hooded crows and greater black-backed gulls; and like Prometheus, punished for his theft of fire, they peck out the living eyes and tongue, and at the last, the liver.

There are other meanings, too, for *fiadh*. It also means 'barbarity' and 'cruelty'. The islander knows full well the beauty of their *dùthchas* – their heritage in the land. But like most other rural folks, they also feel disdain for urban myths of Bambi. Not for nothing did our forbears reject a direct pantheism – the worship of God as nature. They chose, instead, panentheism: that double sense of God as immanent in nature, but also out beyond, transcendent. That way holds the prospect of release from tortured suffering.

There is a famous passage near the start of *Missionary Travels*, where David Livingstone was seized by the shoulder and mauled by the lion.[19]

'It caused a sort of dreaminess,' the explorer wrote:

> ... in which there was no sense of pain nor feeling of terror ... like what patients partially under the influence of chloroform describe, who see all the operation, but feel not the knife ... The shake annihilated fear, and allowed no sense of horror in looking round at the beast. This peculiar state is probably produced in all animals killed by the *carnivora*; and if so, is a merciful provision by our benevolent Creator for lessening the pain of death.

In other words, it caused a sort of transcendence. A contraction from this world of pain, into the realm of soul. A drift from incarnation, towards disincarnation, and it makes me wonder, too, about some of the knock-on effects of war.

From where I've reached, it looks as if this sucking bog has arms that go in all directions. The weariness weighs heavily upon me, a bank of fog that's put a flannel on my senses. This place is leaching my morale, making me dismayed and disarrayed. I could retrace my footsteps, but then which way through such a soggy maze?

I suppose it comes from having grown to know terrain like this so well, that the eye is always tuned in to small signs. *What are those marks?* I'm wondering, as I peer to take a closer look at something in the mud.

It's *their* cattle. Right where I most need them! The *lorg nam fiadh*. The cloven footprints of the deer.

Where they can safely pass, then so can I.

Artefacts from the journey, on Harris Tweed by Norman Mackenzie, weaver of Carloway.

RIGHT. Christ of St Clement's Church, Isle of Harris, carved in the sparkling hornblende schist found locally. It was dug up in the churchyard during renovation works.

BELOW. Detail from the tomb in St Clement's of Alasdair 'Crotach', 8th chief of the Macleods of Harris and Dunvegan, completed 1528.

'The Sun of Righteousness', as St Clement of Alexandria called this symbol of perpetual resurrection.

The red deer, at once both the *fiadh* – 'the wild' – and 'the cattle of the faeries'.

Perched in the bright green glen of Rodel in south Harris, Tùr Mòr Chliamain – the Great Tower of St Clement – was my pilgrimage starting point. The site is linked to the Celtic monastic heart of Iona. (Photo 2005)

St Clement's Church is said to sit upon a Druid site on the lower slopes of Roineabhal. Shown here, obscured by clouds, the mountain narrowly escaped destruction for a roadstone 'superquarry'. (Photo 2003)

Day 2, on the Golden Road through the Bays of Harris. Originally the name belonged to the section north of Leac a Lì. Today the term is often applied to the whole of the east-coast route.

This byre (or crofter's cow shed) was roofed with an upturned boat when I was a boy. The relics of such memory now rest in the grass against the starboard wall.

The rediscovery of Tobar a' Ghobha – the Well of the Blacksmith – in the village of Leac a Lì. The remnants of my 'Bog Monster' with its bleaching of the boulder reveal the depth of moss that had caused the well's loss for 30 years.

The ecosystem of a rotting fencepost and the Golden Stag. But remember, it's pan*en*theism, not pantheism!

JMB – the initials of John Matthew Barrie – etched on a window of the Harris Hotel in 1912. Barrie drew on island faerie lore to explore the cultural psychology of war and its trauma. (Photo 2003)

Sundown at Ardhasaig. The chimney of the old whaling station down at Bun Abhainn Eadarra has lapsed to dusk. Higher up, my apocryphal 'Lost Glen' tracks north between the twin peaks of Uisgne-abhal and the Clisham horseshoe.

Day 3, entering the glen on my way to Loch a' Sgàil, using fragments of Sammy's stalker's path. This whole 'country' is now community owned in a partnership for people and conservation with the John Muir Trust.

It was a lonely place, here on the watershed of the 'Lost Glen', as I passed over into Glen Langabhat. The Isle of Lewis and the start of the 8-mile long Loch Langabhat is in the distance, Loch an Teine – the Lake of Fire – is on the river.

ABOVE. I pitched my tent beside a ruined sheiling and dined on tanalised lamb with bitter herbs.

LEFT. My semi-leavened bannocks cooking on the charcoal of the fencepost embers.

ABOVE. Day 4, heading over to Kinlochresort, down through the glen below Loch Chleistir, the Loch of the Cascading Rock. On the horizon, the Atlantic surfs with whales at Gallan Head with its old NATO base, and older still, the Blessing Place.

RIGHT AND BELOW. From the previous day, red deer traces on the shores of Loch a' Sgàil, and one of thousands of 'bogs that I have known and loved'.

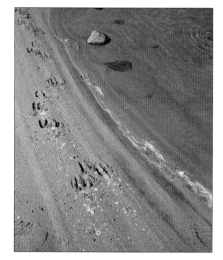

Both a' Chlàir Bhig, after following the stream down from Stuabhal and Loch Chleistir.

The planetarium-effect inside this double-chambered *both* or 'beehive' sheiling is exaggerated by the limited settings on my cheap camera. Originally, I had not intended to take photographs; I didn't want to filter the world through a digital lens. My wife Vérène persuaded me otherwise, but with just a single battery charge to constrain its use.

Ceann Loch Reasort (or Kinlochresort). The river with the watcher's cottage on the Harris side is the Abhainn Mhòr Ceann Reasort – the Big River of Kinlochresort – where I nearly came a cropper when fishing. It flows down from Loch Voshimid, where J.M. Barrie 'caught Mary Rose'.

Taken from the hill where I feasted on mussels, the 5-mile length of Loch Reasort, looking towards the Atlantic and the Isle of Scarp. The bank opposite shows traces of the *feannagan* raised beds. These shores were emptied of their people in the 19th-century Clearances.

St Bridgit's Sheiling at the Rubha Leathann, looking back across south central Lewis. There are two ruins – the main ring of stones is the one slightly further away. The mists have almost lifted from the distant Eishken hills that I love so much – one of the last wildernesses of the West.

A fern grows by the fallen lintel, here where Brighde's (or Bridgit's) memory is set in place. 'The parish has a saint's name time cannot unfrock.'

From earlier in Day 5 at my lunch stop, the little *both* of Loch a' Sguair. Brighde's would have stood like this, made wind-tight with a coat of living turf.

Day 6, Saturday, at the 5,000-year-old standing stones of Calanais (or Callanish). This, taken by my fleeting friend, the 'dead' American tourist lassie. My waterproofs were variously constricted by belts and puffed out by the brisk breeze.

This picture is from the previous summer when we'd walked out to the Campbell family's sheiling on the Barvas moor. Vérène (left), is with the sisters Catriona (who met me at Teampall Eòin), and artist-archaeologist Anne. Little Peigi Ann is hidden behind her dog. (photo 2008)

Tobar Mhoire, St Mary's Well at Siadar (or Shader). Tobar Brighde, St Bridgit's Well at Melbost Borve. These were visited over Days 9 and 10.

Dr Finlay Macleod of Siabost (or Shawbost) – the beloved 'Doctor Finlay' – sending me on my way to meet Catriona and Peigi Ann Campbell at Teampall Eòin, on the other side of the bay.

The close of Day 8 at Teampall Eòin, St John's Temple (or chapel), dedicated probably to John the Baptist and surrounded by the 'plainsong' headstones of a humble people, whose God 'is the high and lofty one who inhabiteth *eternity*: whose name is *Holy*'.

Day 10, at Teampall nan Crò Naomh at Ghabhsainn (or Galson), looking up past a series of headlands to my destination at the Butt of Lewis. The chapel lies mostly under windblown sand. Does its name mean simply 'Holy Cross', or is it more nuanced? Does it also mean 'the kernel of life', 'the pulsing heart of the holy'?

Day 11, Teampall Pheadair at Suainebost (or Swainbost). Most of the headstones in its ancient cemetery are 'plainsong'. As the modern fancy for more privatised memorials took hold, the community of the dead ran out of space and had to relocate over the hill.

Day 12, Friday morning, my final camping pitch at Stoth Bay, Butt of Lewis.

Cameos of wild food and other nourishment along the way. The mussels found at Kinlochresort. The sorrel that went into Doctor Finlay's sandwiches. The bread I made at Galson hostel, photo taken by Graham. As for the can amongst the seaweed, the less said the better.

Scarcely even bothering to test the sureness underfoot, I bound ahead and crunch across the crispy surface crust.

I follow their winding line of tracks, and pass from out the clutches of Bog Monster's arms. What's more, I think I hear the sound of waterfalls. It must be the Abhainn Mhòr, fresh flowed down from Loch Voshimid, where Barrie 'caught Mary Rose'. The weariness just washes from my eyes. A fresh excitement turns back on my senses. Higher up, and just before a long ravine, I catch a glint of dashing blue; and I have just spied . . . poaching!

It's like my fishing rod is twitching like a dowser's fork. For sure, there's still the underlying chill upon the breeze. But this is mid-afternoon. The water's temperature will be near its highest. Now's the day and now's the hour!

Sammy's face peers in. He's giving me a bright *aye-aye* with a cheery sideways nod. That the only permit I'll require for this once-off 'wee cast'. The community would never grudge the prospect of a fish to fill a pilgrim's pot.

I clamber down into the gully, carved out by the river's bed. The whisky-tinted water heaves and pitches down the chasm. I begin to shuffle cautiously along the sides. Now it narrows, then it widens, spreading gently like a sail, murmuring around the stones and tinkling over gentle weirs. The flow has slackened, backed up and held within a baggy lagoon that is too shallow for the fishing, but doubtless once a paddler's paradise for sheiling boys and girls.

A river of this nature, however, possesses fiadh as well as more bucolic properties. Lethargy soon irks its restive kelpie spirit. Fed up with going round and round in aimless eddies of recirculation, it pulls its act together, and with a martial roar, takes off in flight. A thousand elven hooves go cantering down an incline, thundering through the glen. They hammer at unwavering walls of solid rock until, at last, they burst into a boulder bed, and dissipate their laughter into blasts of spray that mist the air with dancing sheens of rainbow.

This time, the river draws into a spiralled coil. Shelving rocks have put a twist into a pool's bag end. It launches, hissing, on and through a lengthy worm-screw channel that reminds me of the confines of a bobsleigh run. It gathers speed until it hits a line of jagged fangs that guard the head of a most lovely, pear-shaped pool. Through the water comes, and through and through, churned into a spume of witches' spittle that skids onwards, reaching outwards, in streaks of marbled fingers. I watch them fizz, and dissipate; and halfway down the pool's blue length

I find a spot where sunlight fails to penetrate the olive depths. Here a flight of rocky ledges reaches down into a darkening underworld, and who knows the size of the fish that will have rested there.

The fiadh is on me, and with a slip of my shoulders I shrug off Osprey, and unpack my fishing rod. Suitably, for a pilgrimage, the brand name is *Bob Church*. Given my failure to find worms – the best lure – I'll have to act the proper sportsman and use a fly, but only one given the high risk of snagging on the rocks. Which one, I'm wondering, for these bright conditions? Perhaps the Teal Blue & Silver? No. It's an awfully tidy, suit-and-tie sort of a fly. I'll save it for more civilised conditions. For such a place as this, perhaps more of a Celto-hippie feel? I'll try a shaggy look-ing Blue Zulu with its punkish Afro-haircut, spiky beetle body, a twist of silver bling and a classy tail of Scarlet Ibis; only that the latter, in my budget edition, is a bit of red fluff.

I tie it on with a clinch knot and, with a few brisk flicks of the wrist to get the line out and flowing gracefully, I cast across the pool. It crumples with a splashy flop onto the water.

Too much line!

Salmon 1: Poacher 0.

I've spoiled my chances here, so I use the pool to practice casting, and then move on down. This leads me through a battlefield of vicious rocks, with water coursing fast and deep between their clefts. Another pool, this time a long deep stretch of perfect width. My knack with casting has come back. The fly lands perfectly, within a foot of the opposite bank. The current curves it gracefully downstream, and my eyes are keened for the swirl of a tail or the roll of a dorsal fin. Again, and again, I flick the fly out – and just as I'm about to move on, my line goes taut.

'Rod up and take in slack! Drop rod if he jumps! *Drop the rod,* before he smacks his tail down on the line and breaks you!'

But this isn't me, back as the ghillie, master of my boat, issuing instructions to a guest in need of help. This is me, right here. And it's only a tiddler, with rainbow fingerprints down either side; a cheeky little salmon parr that caught me by surprise. I wet my hands so as not to hurt his scales, let him off the hook, and away he goes with a quick tail wag.

By now I'm deep down in the gorge. These pools are such a thrill, so inaccessible I bet they're hardly ever fished. I'm just rock-hopping along, quite the dancer of the chasm, and this is such a gig. The sides are loom-ing high above me, cutting off the sunlight, and it's getting to a tumult in a bottleneck down here. Looks like there's no way through ahead. I'll need to climb up higher. Spiderman along an edge. Rod gripped in one hand, rocks and tufts of heather in the other. And I again freeze.

For God's sake, look at yourself!

Here I am. In the middle of MAMBA. Miles and miles of bugger all, and bugger all of a mobile signal this side of the nearest mountain top. And I'm swinging about like Tarzan with twenty kilos on my back!

A chill overcomes me. My movements jam. Can't see my footholds to get back down. Too vertiginous to carry on up. Knuckles locked and whitened onto what is now a crumbling rock face, with only loosely rooted heather.

If I stay like this, I'll just become exhausted. I'll further lose my nerve. I'd have to drop Osprey into the river, everything would get lost or soaked, and I'd have to end the trip.

Needs must, so, very slowly, I edge upwards, upwards, until I grapple sheepishly over the top.

Salmon 2: Poacher 0.

'Poacher's pilgrimage?'

Sammy shakes his head, another poem coming on. 'More like poacher's comeuppance.'

The end, however, is in sight. A further half a mile of easy going down the bank, and I reach my destination: Kinlochresort.

12

CATCHING MARY ROSE

Andrew Morrison was right about the beauty of this place, and the mussels were waiting here, sure enough. I made it just in time to grab some handfuls from amongst the greens, reds and browns of seaweeds growing on a rock, before they slipped beneath the whelming tide.

From my vantage point on top of this hill, the Abhainn Mhòr spreads gracefully out into the head of Loch Reasort, the Red Fjord. From there the brackish mix of waters curl their way five miles between low hills to the Atlantic. All that now remains of what was once a thriving village are a few stone walls, some blackhouse ruins, and everywhere, the ripples of feannagan that slumber back into the bog.

There are two boarded-up cottages. One is on the Harris side of the river, the other in Lewis, and an old map also reveals a shooting lodge. These days, only watchers stay in these to combat commercial poaching in July. That's when the shoals of salmon come into the bay, waiting for a spate to take them upstream to their spawning grounds amongst the hills.

My little gas stove is hissing in the early evening breeze. I've already boiled a cup of water for a pack of chicken soup, and now I've got another half cup on, just enough to raise a rapid head of steam to cook my mussels. They open within minutes, translucent shells of navy blue, some striped with dashing rays of green, and delicious is the creamy orange flesh inside. I always try to cook them very quickly, aware that even bivalves will feel pain in their own ways, and then there's all the little critters hanging on as collateral damage – the barnacles and the tube worms, the tiny sponges, snails and shrimps. I'm just another predator, and it could have been worse. The steady hack, hack, hacking of a seabird's bill until a fatal crack appears. The starfish arms wrapped round in death's embrace, secreting digestive juices slowly to suck out the goodness. Such is the fate of all wild things. Predation, pestilence or privation always get you in the end. I hope that David Livingstone was right about his anaesthesia. William Blake too, with 'The cut worm forgives the plough.' Even vegans have to deal with the maggot in the apple, the weevil in the flour.

I'm chewing on these mussels, softening my oatcakes in the cup of soup, and soaking up the splendour of this splendid isolation. And yet, I also feel great sadness in this place. It's coming over me in waves. The *nostos-algos* of that home pain. There is a Gaelic word, so onomato-poeic, that describes this soul-felt wearisomeness: *Cianalas* – 'Key-ann-a-lass' – and that, exhaled in anguished cadence.[1]

Truth is, that pretty much this whole western coastline of North Harris and South Lewis cries out, laconic in its emptiness. There are no longer any villages between Hushnish and Kinlochresort on the Harris side, and from here to Mealasta on the Lewis side. As an elderly historian who was born on the Isle of Scarp at the mouth of Loch Reasort wrote to me: 'Some of the most brutal evictions were in Harris, but little is known about the brutality as vast swathes of the population were evicted and they took their history with them overseas.'[2]

The Harris clearances hadn't stopped with Rodel glen. There were other waves during the nineteenth century. For example, in 1839, the Earl of Dunmore cleared some fifty crofting families, estimated to have been about 700 people. When these resisted his orders, he brought in from Fort George on the mainland the 78th Regiment of Foot – the Ross-Shire Buffs, also known as the Seaforth Highlanders.[3] It was imperial divide and rule. Many of these soldiers would have been recruited, or press-ganged, from neighbouring Lewis. The measures were reported to have been 'very severe'. According to *The Times,* the troops terrorised the local population, who thought that the Crown was about to re-enact upon them the Massacre of Glencoe. However, to be dispatched from such a 'rugged land' to live elsewhere, the newspaper suavely concluded, was surely a blessing.[4]

If the Crown was feared, it had form in its historic subjugation of the Hebrides. In 1599, Lewis was wrested from traditional clan control. King James VI of Scotland, four years later to become James I of the United Kingdom, granted a band of venture capitalists from Fife a colonial charter for 'the conquering of the Lewis . . . by rooting out of the barbarous inhabitants . . . void of all religion and humanity'. This, he hoped, would raise rents for the Lowland-based state authorities, and generate commerce from both land and sea. To such effect, the 'Fife Adventurers' were granted a Commission of Fire and Sword; namely, the authority to perpetrate 'slaughter, mutilation, fire-raising and other inconveniences'.[5]

When that endeavour failed due to clan guerrilla resistance, the Crown, in a further act of sowing division, gave the island to the Mackenzies of Kintail. Next came Cromwell's men. Then Deaf Mackenzie – Colonel Francis Humberston Mackenzie – who used it as a breeding ground for soldiers for the Empire. He is of considerable consequence to my story. 'The lads of this regiment will live and die together,' said his recruitment posters of 1793. 'Now for a stroke at the Monsieurs, my boys! King George for ever! Huzza!' It was Deaf Mackenzie who sent in the press gangs where volunteers were not sufficiently forthcoming. Whole villages saw their men scattered to the hills. Mothers and sweethearts were held with bayonets to their breasts as their sons and lovers were marched off to colonial wars across the globe and, in the case of one village that was perhaps not untypical, only one ever came back. Mackenzie was rewarded with the governorship of Barbados which, at that point, was still very much a slave colony. Living the Caribbean high life, he ratcheted up gambling debts. These required him to have the villages of south-east Lewis cleared of their native populations, and to be leased as a vast commercial sheep farm.[6]

That, in very general terms, is the kind of history that's laid before me here at Kinlochresort as I finish off my meal. I can't help wondering how much we carry of these things in our psyches; how much they might rub off and knock on down the generations. In my own case, I wonder if it influences my work in being so drawn to the confluence between landed power, militarism and religion? My twice-great-grandfather on my paternal grandmother's side was Murdo MacLennan, belonging to the Strathconon area of Ross-shire. He was a famous 'precentor' in the Free Church, a leader of the old 'long tunes', the drawn-out haunting way of singing Gaelic Psalms. Some of his tunes were set to pen and paper by Joseph Mainzer, the German ethnomusicologist. Murdo's grandparents had been cleared from elsewhere in the glen by the Balfour family. In his 1929 study of the making of the Scottish working classes, Tom Johnston mentions these evictions and, in so doing, touches on the spiritual depth of bonding between people and their places that the Highland Clearances violated:[7]

> The evictions of the Clan M'Lennan from Strathconon by the Balfour trustees were carried out in a most barbarous manner, and to this day the spot is shewn where the dispossessed men and women crouched together, praying rather for

a merciful death than that they should be driven farther from the strath of their birth. When the father of the late leader [Arthur Balfour, prime minister] of the Conservative party fell heir to the estates 'the gallows had succeeded the fever,' for he directed prompt eviction of another twenty-seven families, and today a parish, which in 1831 had a population of 2,023, carries only 445 people, mostly ghillies and their dependants on a London brewer's hundred square-mile deer forest.

The same had also happened in the making of the English working classes, but further back in history, leaving the English with less under-standing of their relatively untaught social history, and more in the grip of its resultant social class system. I just feel saddened to survey the rich-ness of community that has been lost. The resulting poverty, these days more psychological than material. That's the sense of *cianalas*, the melancholy that touches me now, as I gaze down the full length of this sea loch, thinking of its empty – cruelly emptied – little bays.

It touches me in just so many ways. Out there on the horizon, cradled on either side by the sea loch's widening hilly arms as it enters the Atlantic, I can see Scarp. As late as 1881, this island still supported more than two hundred souls. They had their own 'parliament' that was simi-lar to that of St Kilda. When the estate told the people that they were to be deprived of their vital summer grazings along the southern shores of Loch Reasort, their abject appeals for clemency were met with the stark response. 'Go to America!'[8]

These estates were run by, and for, an alien class of people who had a very limited idea of what it meant to be a connected human being. They behaved as if they neither knew nor cared that the sheiling way of life meant so much more than just the economics of a pastoral way of life. For the Scarp people, these grazings would have been their *geàrraidh* or 'garry', their pastoral garden of storied places soaked with time-enamoured famil-iarity. No wonder, that Carmichael had described the songs and prayers that emanated from such a way of life as: 'singularly chaste, beautiful, and elevated'. No surprise, that Sir Arthur Mitchell had encountered the sheil-ing girls from near here engaged in spiritual reflection. From such haunts as where I'd camped last night, or chanced upon with the Clar Beag bothan earlier today, the teenage girls, when done with their milking, made cheese and butter to take home at weekends. Sometimes they'd be quietly joined at night by village lads, home from the fishing. Marriages were known to follow. They'd become the mothers of the village, then the matrons, and that, in every soil- and soul-soaked richness of the word.

By 1971, isolated and with such a constricted resource base, there were only twelve people left on Scarp. They took the hard decision to evacuate to the 'mainland' of Lewis and Harris. Again, these things can rub off on one in such evocative ways. I was at school in Stornoway at the time. My passion was for geology. I'd read that Scarp was known for an outcrop of green-tinted rocks of an asbestos mineral. When I heard that a girl from Scarp had joined the school, I eagerly asked around. Helped by my female classmates, a meeting was arranged.

Funny how she's coming to me now. I haven't thought of her for years and years. It was such a small thing. We met in no-man's-land between the boys' and the girls' cloakrooms. She was maybe thirteen. Me, perhaps a year older. She said her father was a lighthouse keeper.

Funny how I'm seeing it so clear again, in my mind's eye. Seeing that way of life beyond the memory of words. Seeing her father, far away from home, on aching spells of duty. High above the churning surf of some half-sunken, devil-stricken skerry. And she, back home, brave smiling with him in her fretful dreams through nights of storm-tossed wakefulness.

These thoughts have grown in my imagination, but not as figments of imagination. They're from a very real meme in the culture. An old woman from Scalpay, an island on the other side of Harris, has told me how it was in her mother's time in the 1920s, when the father – my correspondent's grandfather – was at the herring fishing:[9]

> When it was a stormy night her mother, Peggy, could not settle in the house for worrying about him – there was no radio contact in those days. She used to wrap her shawl around her and take my mother, her eldest daughter, with her and go up the hill behind the house to pray for his safe return. Somehow being out in the elements she felt closer to God and returned home feeling calmer.

I asked my school friend of such fleeting acquaintance how she felt about having just left Scarp. She shrugged, and pursed an unrequited smile. As I see it in my mind now, it said more than she could ever have known nor I could then have understood. God! I never thought that lass had touched me so. Fair wispy hair that straggled to the shoulders of a standard issue blazer. A boyish slightness, still some way from womanhood. Such sweet demureness.

I doubt we talked for more than five minutes. She said she'd never heard of asbestos, but that there was a greenish stone to be found on the island. Well, that could have been any number of common minerals. I never looked her out again. But now she's come back into my thoughts. Following the herds. A woman nurtured down the generations 'on the milk of deer beneath the ridge of storms'. Roaming through wild gardens up the back-tracks of my mind. And there's something here, in all of this, that's gone but not gone out: and these words come to me –

> For she was the girl from off the moor
> She was the last of the sheiling line
> She the *cianalas* that pierces the soul
> yet her father kept a light

I could camp here at Kinlochresort for the night, maybe try the estuary for a sea trout. But the evening sky is showing signs of colder weather. It's settling in rarefied shades of astronaut blue. Instead, I think I'll use these last three hours of waning light to make up some lost time. I'll cut inland, directly east across the Morsgail Moor. That will bring me to the head of Glen Shandaig, and down to pitch camp halfway up the west bank of Loch Langabhat. From there, I'll be perfectly placed tomorrow morning to skirt the eastern slopes of a hill called Ascleit. Seumas Crawford had told me there are some great sheilings along its sides. Further north, he said, at Loch a' Sguair, there's a both that's in spectacular condition. After that, I'll promenade along the high Mothal Ridge. This, he'd added in his genial way, 'would give you a stunning walk on a fine day'.

Whether to go over or around the summit of Beinn Mothal is something I can decide at the time. Either way, it will bring me out at the Grimersta river. He'd told me where to ford it, a spot that's passable in most water conditions just by wading. Once on the other side, I'll walk another mile north-east, winding in and out around the little lochs until, if all is well, I see a bright green grassy bluff. This will be the Rubha Leathann – the 'Broad Promontory' – and by its side, Saint Bridgit's Sheiling. That's where I'd love to spend tomorrow night.

There's a conical little cnoc beside me called Tom Leatha. From its top, I manage to pick up just sufficient of a fleeting mobile signal to text my position to Vérène, and to say that all is well. I also take a compass bearing on a cleft between the hills that lead into Glen Shandaig. That will be vital if I lose my line of sight as I traverse this broad expanse of moor. I've packed up, and as I set off, the sun behind is slipping low across the sea. Scarp is now receding in a sparkling silver haze that shines from off the water. Overhead, I can't help but notice wisps of rippled cloud. Hmm. 'Mackerel sky/ mackerel sky/ never long wet/ never long dry.'

Out here, the year has hardly started. The heather is still stiff and brown and shows no yearnings for new growth. The *slèibh*, the fiery red bent deergrass of the bygone autumn, sways languid in tired tufts. All around are drifting curls of last year's moor grass. Here, in eddied swirls of drained-out golden locks. There, in lines combed out by the prevailing wind, aligned enough to chart a rough and ready compass course. Everywhere is vast and empty stillness. These parts, wrote W.M. Mackenzie, a local antiquarian, who had come to make a study of the bothan more than a century ago, are 'the scene of pastoral richness, quiet, and beauty, over which the shy deer boldly move among what were once the habitations of men'.[10] I see no deer, I see no habitations, but they're present in the place names. On my left, the rounded slopes of Sèilibridh or Shéilabridh are probably suggestive of the deer hunt. On my right, Beinn a' Bhoth, the Hill of the Both, is a nod to human habitations that predate the baptism of the land.

I'm turning over in my mind an epigram from Sorley Maclean.[11]

> *Tha tìm, am fiadh, an Coille Hallaig*
> Time, the deer, is in the Wood of Hallaig

Time is the deer, the wild, that moves in timelessness. The poet visits the clearance ruins at Hallaig, a Norse name that possibly means 'holy bay', on his native Raasay. While there, the people of the past – 'the Sabbath of the dead' – come back to life as woodland trees.

> And my love is at the Burn of Hallaig,
> a birch tree, and she has always been . . .
> a birch, a hazel, a straight slender young rowan.

The bard depicts a class of experience that just happens, sometimes, to the people of these liminal parts. What do I mean: *just happens*? Just that. You hear reports in private. I know of one, an eminent professor, a man grown from the rootstock, who told me of his visit to just such an abandoned village. While he wandered around amongst the stones, the voices of the dead awoke. 'What do you mean, *awoke?*' I asked. 'Just that,' he said, and he ran – terrified, he told me – back up to the present-day settlement, where a normal sense of time outwith the fiadh resumed its steadying hold upon his consciousness.

A breeze is getting up. What little warmth there was has left. I am nearing the cleft that has served as my landmark. The valley sides appear between the hills that head the glen. I can see them steepening to the stricture of the pass. Here, the ground is banked with hurdle after hurdle of suppurating peat hags. I clamber and I skid my way across each one. It's only my imagination, but they whisper to my footsteps' sucking sough.

'Alastair! Alastair! Step into your solitariness. *Within . . . within . . . within.*'

The sky above has dimmed from astronaut to cobalt grey. From behind me, the afterglow still squeezes through from under the horizon. Ahead, the east horizon has turned black. Night is almost on me, and a grim wind now hones its lonely edge upon a stone that runs too low and slow as yet to reach my hearing.

An hour ago, I'd warmed up enough to stop and take my fleece off. I had stood awhile, gazing back from whence I'd come, my mind awash with eddies and cross-currents from the day. The light had not yet faltered, and I had run my eye along the sharp relief of hills against the skyline that lay stretched out to the south. Distance had restored the smoky blue that mystifies such heights. I'd marvelled at Sron Uladail, an enormous prow of overhanging rock that breaches to the surface like a whale, with its belly full of legends. Eastwards, to its left, lay the valley of the quaking bog, and there, the chasm of the river that comes rushing from Loch Voshimid with the island that likes to be visited.

Sir Walter Langdon-Brown's perception of the psychological importance of J.M. Barrie's play was shared by Sir Alfred Hitchcock. In later life, the Master of Suspense was asked by an interviewer if there was any film that he regretted never having made. He replied:[12]

Mary Rose, which I really wanted to do, but they didn't want to let me. Do you know, it's written specifically into my present contract that I cannot do *Mary Rose*?

Hitchcock had been deeply taken by the play when, at the age of twenty-one, he saw a 1920 performance in the Haymarket. By 1964, he had got as far as commissioning a screenplay and had gone with his wife to the Isle of Skye to look for a suitable island-in-a-loch location. He desired to call the movie *The Island That Wants to Be Visited*, and *The Times* reported that his sponsors would want concrete evidence of where the island was, so as to appraise its tourist potential. His critics say that the script was dull, and that no further explanation is required for the no-no that was meted out by Universal Pictures. The Master, however, believed that their veto came from fear. The public lacked exposure, as he put it, 'to these twilight-zone stories'. The movie would have been 'too irrational'. This was what had made it too high a risk to pitch to the pragmatic spirit of the age.[13]

Hitchcock would have loved the Gaelic term, *àit uaigneach*. It means a solitary place – remote, forlorn, unsettling. To which cue, I have gone into the cleft between the hills, and have come up to the prow of the watershed. An icy blast strikes in from east-southeast. I had not realised how much shelter I was getting in the lee of the pass. Those peat hags, for all their slippery awkwardness, were doing me a kindness.

The dusk is well advanced. Here, a twilight star comes flickering out. There, obscured by clouds. I wander on along this fissure in the land. Down below, just coming into view, is the leaden face of Langabhat. The wind is coming straight from off its water. It's sweeping up Glen Shandaig, I feel it dragging at my body heat, and my inner voice is warning *don't get cold*.

There seems to be the semblance of a track heading down the way. A sheep or deer path? I carry on, and on a little further, but something in the gloom feels queer. The patterns of the ground are unfamiliar. Then I see a mound, and then, another, similar in size to what I'd found at Clar Beag. And so they are! Beinn a' Bhoth still has its *clachan* – a tiny village – depending on what to count in this near-darkness, of some four, five, or six *bothan*.

I climb on top of one, and yes: it is undoubtedly a beehive structure, sealed with a cap stone that crowns the corbel. There is no way inside because the peat has grown up around the entrance and sealed it off. Whoever may have once lived here has not been home, not for a very long time indeed.

I wish that Seumas Crawford were with me at this very moment. To me, he is the Keeper of the Bothan. Why? Because he cares so much about them.

'These bothan are not being taken seriously,' he once told me, fretfully. 'It's a disgrace! They've hardly been recognised since the days of Captain Thomas, Mitchell and Mackenzie.'

'How far back do you reckon they go?' I'd asked.

Some, to the days of the early Celtic Church. That's hinted at by place names suggestive of priests, blessing houses or tiny monastic settlements.

Others, well, who knows? Tradition holds as far back as the Druids. 'I would have no hesitation of putting an age of two thousand years plus to some of them – no hesitation at all,' he concluded, telling me that one structure on which he was working was seated on a Bronze Age site.

'They go back a long, long way, some of them do, Alastair. Back into the mists of time.'

I move on, and through a world now dimmed to silhouettes. They huddle by the valley sides, completely drained of colour, sometimes rearing up to etch their darker outlines against the sky. Loch Langabhat lies sunken in a brooding cauldron far below. The wind has backed a few degrees. It now blows straight from out the east. Cold, still low, but rising with a mordant grindstone growl.

'Yes. I feared that might be the case,' had said the gentle English brigadier, in his words of encouragement back at the staff college; his astute awareness of the dilemmas of his profession. 'Such a pity.'

Such a pity, 'and he knows he shouldn't kill/ and he knows he always will'. And when the Cree First Nations activist and singer, Buffy Sainte-Marie, wrote 'Universal Soldier', popularised by Donovan, she said that it was 'about individual responsibility for war and how the old feudal thinking kills us all'.[14] *Dieu et mon Droit* perpetuates itself precisely because violence cauterises the soul. It relies on trauma – psychic injury that cuts off empathy – to sustain an unjust social order. That is why many of the relatively powerful, as Hitchcock intuited, shun the 'irrational' twilight zones of the unconscious. To the Mr and Mrs Morlands of this world – 'more-land' – and the Simon Sobersides, these zones disrupt the rigid ego structures of their own controlled and controlling universe. They don't even see the limits of their own carefully schooled worldview. As is often said by locals about a certain kind of incomer, who comes in to the island with unseemly avaricious attitudes – 'they can't help it'. The Universal Soldier, and his counterpart in the proxy warring worlds of finance, property and speculation, 'never sees the writing on the walls'.

Revealing the emotional impacts of a culture that cultivates the stiff upper lip of emotional blockage is part of what Barrie achieved with *Mary Rose*. More importantly, he opened out fresh insights into why war represents a failure of the imagination, marooning the imaginal world. This sheds crucial light on avenues of cultural healing for the future.

Writing *Mary Rose* when he did, it is likely that Barrie would have been familiar with the work that Captain A.J. Brock and Captain

W.H.R. Rivers were pioneering at the Craiglockhart War Hospital in Edinburgh with such war poets as Wilfred Owen and Siegfried Sassoon. Around 1917, Brock corresponded with Sigmund Freud about their mutual interest in 'battle neurosis' or shellshock. Today, it is better known as post traumatic stress disorder (PTSD). Brock told the psychoanalyst that the condition's most characteristic symptom was a 'lack of solidarity' brought about by a 'segregation of the parts' within the mind. Elsewhere, he explained that such patients become 'like the fragments of their minds, isolated units, *unrelated in space and time*'. This state of splitting and dissociation manifests as a 'childishness' by which 'the ordinary progress of the individual's life appeared to halt; he ceased to grow up . . . or he might partly fall back into childhood'.[15] In a nutshell, Captain Brock described the syndrome demonstrated by Mary Rose.

In 1919, the same year as Barrie was writing his play, Sigmund Freud published an influential essay, *Das Unheimliche*, The Uncanny. He noted that the German term, *das unheimliche,* means 'the opposite of that which is familiar'. Also, that its etymology is *heimlich*, 'home', which links to *heimisch* ,'native'. As such, 'the unheimlich' (as the term is usually rendered into English) is literally the sense of uncanniness that results from a profound 'un-homing', or overturning of a person's native sense of place. It represents a disembedding, or eviction from reality; quite literally, an unhinging of the mind from its environment. The German concept has a close parallel with the Gaelic, àit uaigneach, 'a forlorn place', derived from *uaigneachd* – meaning 'loneliness', 'remoteness' or 'moroseness'. That, in turn, is rooted in *uaigh,* which is a grave, tomb, or home of the dead. The experience of nostalgia derives from this unhomed experience.

Strikingly, in the biblical gospels, the Gadarene or Gerasene demoniac or madman lived amongst the tombs of the dead. He self-harmed, using sharp stones, and named his demons 'Legion'. Jesus cast this legion out into a herd of pigs, which ran down the hill and drowned themselves in the Sea of Galilee. Liberation theology asks questions like: who ate pigs in that society? Not the Jews, but the Roman legionaries. How did the empire exert control? By getting around in ships. Scholars think it likely that Mark's gospel, which has the earliest version of the story, was written just after Vespasian's troops had slaughtered the youth of the demoniac's region in reprisals for the Jewish Revolt.[16] One can read the story literally, or as a parable. It names and unmasks a demonic spirit: the spirit of colonisation, that drives an unhomed people into tombs of living death. It engages that spirit. It casts it out and back from whence it came.

Around the same time as Freud was developing his thought on *das unheimliche,* he was also working on the 'death instinct', or Thanatos. This too, in response to what he had seen of psychological suffering from the terrors of the Great War. He came to view Thanatos as the counterpoint of Eros, his sense of the life instinct, and he concluded: 'We came to recognize sadism as its representative.'[17]

Back home, I have a collection of papers in a book from Cambridge University Press, called *Cultures under Siege.* Several chapters explore the unheimlich from contexts in which wars have rent the fabric of normality, and ripped the psyche open. The cover picture was taken in 1948 at a Polish residence for traumatised children. Its US Army war photographer was David Seymour, whose own Jewish parents had been slaughtered by the Nazis six years earlier. His image shows a little girl, Tereska, who had grown up in a concentration camp. Maybe eight years old, she stands beside a blackboard covered with a white chaotic scrawl, after being asked to draw the meaning of 'home'. Tereska wears a velvety black dress. Ash blonde hair sweeps back in wisps around her emotionally pummelled brow. Her eyes gaze out, uncannily wide, with the 'frozen awareness' of a child who has seen it all, but can respond very little. As Mrs Morland said, 'It has sometimes seemed to me as if a cold finger had once touched my Mary Rose.'

A key chapter is by Professor Yolanda Gampel of the University of Tel Aviv. Her life's work has been with children born in death camps, looking at how unresolved psychic injury knocks on to the children and the grandchildren. She speaks about the 'radioactive identification' of 'transgenerational indigestible trauma'. She explains that, 'when one experiences the uncanny or *unheimlich,* what has been hidden becomes visible, what is familiar becomes strange and frightening'. This takes the sufferer into 'the zone of the unthinkable and the unspeakable'. Here is a world where 'they can no longer fully believe what they see with their own eyes; they have difficulty in distinguishing between the unreal reality they have survived and the fears that spring from their own imagination'. It induces 'a break, a cleavage between the "me" and the "not-me", which can become an unstoppable wellspring of uncanniness'. Such a world now pivots on the cusp of anxiety and terror. The psyche invokes defence mechanisms, in particular 'psychic numbing'. It inhabits 'a world of estrangement', where the central characteristic is a blockage 'to the *articulation between internal and external worlds*'.[18]

Like Mary Rose, Bonnie Kilmeny attempted to come back into 'normality'.[19] She attempted to articulate or connect again between the worlds –

> But all the land were in fear and dread,
> For they kendna whether she was living or dead.
> It wasna her hame, and she couldna remain;
> She left this world of sorrow and pain,
> And return'd to the land of thought again.

Disarticulation between the inner and the outer life invites two possibilities. One, as we've just seen, is to withdraw from outer life into the sìthean of the inner life. To go back 'to the land of thought again'. This was the response of the Biblical demoniac, or 'the bleeding hearts and the artists' of Pink Floyd's *The Wall*. It is what happened to the alcoholic man who failed to place a needle in the sìthean door. Lost in the Mythos, unsorted in the Logos practicality of the outer life, he became emaciated. The cost of this response is self-harm.

The opposite possibility, one that equally hinges on psychic numbing, is to withdraw from the inner life and put all of one's expression into the outer life, into the world of ego. This is the response of the bullies who have been bullied, the hyper-competitive, the hard-line authoritarians and sociopaths. It is what happens to the one who never ventures into the sìthean in the first place. Validating only the things of Logos, the Mythos is kept at arm's length and she or he becomes brazen. The cost of this response is harming others.

Our wars in Afghanistan, Iraq, and elsewhere, argues the American philosopher and playwright, Professor Walter Davis, must be understood in their psychological depth if we are to have a hope of exiting the spiral of violence. These recent wars expose an 'underlying psychosis' of national narcissism, a doggedly rigid collective egotism, where the psychological function of George W. Bush was 'to cover the void at the centre of American society'.[20] Gampel said that if trauma carries on, undigested and not understood, we will find proxy 'chosen' traumas in a desperate bid to reach assimilation and closure. At both individual and collective levels, trauma can be likened 'to indigestible stones, that rattle around the belly of the world'. What's not dealt with in our history will literally stay on to haunt us, harming or self-harming, or both.

That is why we need the magic of the sìthean, but with the grounding of the iron needle from our plaid. The type of person who is qualified to heal the violence of our times is the one who can mediate between the inner and outer worlds, able to unblock the wellsprings of life's energies. It was in helping to fulfil that role that J.M. Barrie's shamanistic genius lay. His work is pooh-poohed – of course – by the sophisticates. These dismiss him as the king of 'kailyard' – writing of the populist and rural cabbage patch. But in his time, people sensed his consequence. From 1930, until his death in 1937, he was the chancellor of Edinburgh University. In the same year as he completed *Mary Rose*, the students of St Andrew's University elected him to be their rector.

His Rectorial Address, delivered in May 1922, showed the difficulties of carrying such a calling. The speech got off to an uncomfortable start. He shuffled, tongue-tied, at the podium, and when he finally broke the long, embarrassing silence and got going – his voice inaudible, fingers fidgeting with a paper knife – he was heckled from the floor. At that, a transformation came about the man. He struck out in a bardic register. He spoke about his prophecy, alluded to in *Mary Rose,* about the likelihood of a second world war.[21]

'You must excuse me,' he told the students, 'if I talk a good deal about courage to you today . . . the rib of Himself that God sent down to His children':

> [The] youth have for too long left exclusively in our hands the decisions in national matters that are more vital to them than to us. Things about the next war, for instance, and why the last one ever had a beginning . . . Do not be too sure that we have learned our lesson, and are not at this very moment doddering down some brimstone path.
>
> The war has . . . taken spring out of the year . . . The spring of the year lies buried in the fields of France and elsewhere. By the time the next eruption comes it may be you who are responsible for it and your sons who are in the lava. All, perhaps, because this year you let things slide . . . Courage is the thing. All goes if courage goes.

He illustrated courage with a letter that Captain Scott had written to him as he and his companions lay dying in the Antarctic. 'We are in a desperate state – feet frozen,' Scott had said, 'but it would do your heart good to be in our tent, to hear our songs and our cheery conversation.'

Barrie then turned to Nansen, the Norwegian explorer, who was awarded the Nobel Peace Prize that same year for having, as the citation put it, saved 'the remnants of the Armenian people from extinction', setting up a system to re-home refugees. With a lurch to unexpected psychological depth, allowing the rhetorical question suddenly to descend, the playwright asked – '*What is beauty?*'

'Sometimes,' he answered: 'beauty boils over.' Sometimes, the sheer trip-you-out epiphany of it all just blows the circuits of the mind, and shifts you from the organising frames of Logos to the poetic quicksilver of Mythos. And, at this point in the speech, he shared a legend that he'd heard from Nansen. It was about a monk, who'd wandered into fields and heard the lark begin to sing – and to sing and sing until its song had joined the heavens. On returning to the monastery, he found that he no longer recognised the doorkeeper. The other monks asked who he was. He said that he was Father Anselm. Eventually, they delved into a book. They realised there'd been a Father Anselm there a hundred years or more before.

Barrie took from Nansen's tale that time itself 'had been blotted out' in listening to the lark. The inner life had been restored from some unfathomed depth of being. 'That,' he told the students, 'was a case of beauty boiling over, or a soul boiling over; perhaps the same thing.

'*Then spirits walk.*'

The clachan of Beinn a' Bhoth has been left far behind me. Although my eyes are straining, I see the going's easier now. This path is more than just a deer track. It must be a footpath, made perhaps in olden times by people of the bothan plying to and fro from Langabhat.

The ground is levelling out. I am down onto a grassy plain with little ox-bow lakes. A burn, whose banks the path had followed, weaves in broad meanders on its way towards a sandy bay, from which Glen Shandaig takes its name. It must be getting to eleven. Were the skies clear, there'd be sufficient starlight to see reasonably. But the wind has come up strong and bitter. What specks of light had peeked out earlier have lost themselves behind thick clouds. I'm losing body heat and I need to pitch my tent soon – but where? Where to find sufficient shelter on a night like this is brewing up to be?

I'm afraid that when I bought my tent, I traded weight for flimsiness too far. I'm just not seeing any place that's suitable to make a pitch. The plain is much too windswept. The ox-bow hollows are tempting, but flood-prone. Short of struggling back into the hills, or lying very low with just the flysheet wrapped around me, I can't see where to go. My pack is dragging heavily, and I'm weary, weary; oh, my weary mantras from the afternoon are teasing me again. I feel so very much alone, yearning for refuge from this closing in of night.

Ahead I see a mound emerging from the murk. Another of those Ice Age dumps of sand and gravel. It's maybe ten foot high, I guess, grassed over. I've already skirted several, none of which afforded any shelter equal to the slicing of this wind. I just feel cold and yearning to lie down. A voice of low alarm is exhorting caution. I'm well aware that this can be the way you start to lose the plot. I'm shuffling slowly on towards the mound – when something stirs, and I stand rigid in my tracks.

Is that . . . *movement?*

My eyes scry out the last few photons of the dusk. Standing there, just near the hillock's base, are two red deer, a pair of hinds. I've walked head on into the wind. They've neither heard me nor picked up my scent. The poor things, startled, stare bewildered.

They hold motionless for maybe ten or twenty seconds, toss their heads, and without so much as a warning bark, gird their haunches into pounding piston strokes. I watch them glide across the turf, the elegance of wild things, lost in seconds to the folds of darkness.

I'm standing here before their mound, a pang of guilt at having stirred these gentle creatures from their rest.

'What will the sìth be making of all this?' I'm musing to myself, so far from Aberdeen, from cold remorseless Reason. Pulled now as on a long cast into Cameron's native world.

Then the pieces drop together to a pattern in my mind.

The brushstrokes rippled round the loch side yesterday.

The trail that led me through the bog this afternoon.

Where they had sought their shelter, no better quarters shall I find.

I struggle with the gusts, and manage to erect some semblance of a tent. At last, and staying fully clothed, I slip down inside the sleeping bag.

My unease at my transgression has calmed down, overtaken by a drowsy sea of gratitude. For ever since that stop for lunch at Loch a' Sgàil just yesterday, I've herded with the deer, the fiadh, the shy and fleeting cattle of the wild.

13

SMOKING OUT THE DEVIL

It was a night of wild and fretful sleep. The tent walls billowed out as if to burst, and then snapped back to give a ghostly pummelling. I pulled Osprey close in beside me as a bed mate, sheltering behind the bulk to fend off the worst of the battering, dozing, and then being shaken back awake again until, at last, exhaustion claimed the night and seemed to quell the tempest's force.

It was the dawn light that woke me on day five, Friday. People who study wilderness experience say that civilisation is only four days deep. The trappings fall away and we open to a world more primal.

I draw back the zipper and peer east. It looks Baltic out there. The sky's a hodden grey. Is it earlier than I'm thinking, and this, just the first glimmerings of dawn? I fire up the phone. The clock shows seven. Thankfully, there's no signal and so no beep-beep of messages. John Muir said that we don't go out to nature, we go in, but on a day like this I'd rather just be staying in. Deep ecology sounds fun until you're in the thick.

I clamber out into a porridge of low mist that cuts off the hilltops. The wind has backed north-east, and I can smell the freshening sharpness that signifies impending rain. Better get packed up while everything's still dry. I light my stove for a quick brew-up of tea. What little heat there is gets blown away before it hits the bottom of the pan. I make do with a lukewarm cup, and then the spits come on, and soon the splats. For the first time, I put on my waterproofs and pull up Osprey's red protective hood to keep my stuff dry. Thankfully I'm warm, and don't need to wear the fleece. It's comforting to know there's something in reserve.

The mist is creeping lower. I'd better take a route that hugs the lochs and streams. That way, you've always got a thread to follow if it drops right down. I'm going to walk along this sandy bay and then go up the next glen, heading west a while to skirt the shores of Loch Lomhain. From there, I'll curve around the eastern flank of Ascleit. I'll keep a look-out for the sheilings Seumas mentioned, then dip down towards Loch Coire Geurad, a coiled offshoot of Langabhat. From there, the map hints at a footpath running north to Loch a' Sguair. I'll go and try to find the both he said was nestled in the rocks above its north-west corner. Then after that, depending on the visibility, either over or around the Mothal Ridge, and from there, to the Grimersta.

I make a ceremonial little bow to thank the lodgings of the deer – very good Mythos; very dodgy Logos – and off I lumber. In contrast to the stalker's path of yesterday, the ground round here is heavy-going – spongy underfoot, from hummocked clumps of last year's ungrazed growth that have yet to settle down and rot. It forces me to stomp a lumpy heather loup, and as I reach Loch Lomhain, the heavens fully open. I stop and watch the smothering force of raindrops quell the waves, muffling down their agitation to a sullen surge that slaps against the rocky shore. The mist is sinking lower on the Harris Hills behind, and as I round onto the eastern face of Ascleit, the rain beats drum rolls on my hood. It forces me to pull the drawstrings tight, leaving – like one of those narrow church windows – just a leper's squint for vision under siege.

I know I must keep moving, keep the effort going, and take care. If the wet gets in, the balmy fug will soon become a clammy hand of cold, lifeless and life-draining. If there are sheilings here, they're not on this trajectory. I'm probably down too low. The mist has robbed me of a sense of altitude. The wind has now wound up to gale force. At times I have to lean so sharply forwards that I'd keel right over if it suddenly dropped off. The rain comes hurtling down in banded sheets. They lash across my shoulders, and any higher up, their icy flecks would turn to stinging hail. Probably it's snowing right up top.

I've been battling for an hour now, my pace has slowed, and my body temperature dropped. The low alarm is going off inside again. Nothing serious. It's just the 'getting cold' of the peripheral circulation closing down. The grip of chill in hands and feet that is, they say, stage one, mild hypothermia. It's at stage two, 'moderate', that the brain gets addled. 'Blue with cold' you'll notice first the coordination going. Before that happens, you need to heed the full alarm, put up the tent while still you can. Stage three is when the body's temperature has dropped by four degrees or more. Then – as I've heard them say – it's like a nice warm bath. You want to fall asleep, a nice long sleep, but no awakening seven years later from such a hill as that.

As youths, when we'd be bailing out the boats or pulling up the lobster pots, we'd sometimes touch the boundary of two and three. Our speech would slur like drunks. We'd wobble, dizzy, on our feet. We'd give each other knowing nods for home that, in their very understatement, warned 'we'd better pull like hell, boys!' In such effort, hauling on the oars, we'd be warmed up by the time we'd get back to the mooring. But that was in our youth. We had the energy reserves and stamina to prevail.

The worst thing would be the crushing pain that comes on as the circulation kicks back in. I've inquired of doctors, but never had its causes satisfactorily explained. It's just 'what happens when'. The pain comes on from out of nowhere, endures for several minutes, and feels as if your hands and feet are clamped into the screws of some medieval inquisition dungeon. You wouldn't want to go there. Yet, somehow, I pity those whose only chance to live an exercised outdoors life these days, is tugging on an outboard motor's starter cord.

A man-sized boulder looms ahead. I take the shelter of its lee, quickly yank my jacket off and put the fleece on underneath. Now I'm fully armed against the elements, wearing everything I've got. A chocolate bar completes the pit stop, and it's strange how quickly it revives my energy. I've noticed that quite often. As if before it's even melted in my stomach, the Numskulls in my Metabolic Department are shouting to each other: 'Ah! He's paying us attention now. Relax!'

Down below, the folds of Ascleit spread their stubby toes into the twists of Loch Coire Geurad. There's a gentle rise down by the water's edge that the map names as the Sìthean Mòr na Liana – the Big Faerie Hill of the Meadow. A couple of miles north-east are the dark cliffs of Sìthean Mòr Beinn a' Chuailein. Probably it means the Great Faerie Hill of the Mountain of the Cattle. Alternatively, of the Hair-ringlet or possibly the Hunting Hound. Even the experts find it hard to figure out many of these names. Most of them were first shifted from the oral to the written tradition by Irish sappers – military engineers – who made the first Ordnance Survey maps to a generous six-inch scale in the early 1850s. They would have spoken Irish Gaelic, but in transcribing from local Hebridean informants, all manner of strange spellings slipped in.

From where I hope to cross the Grimersta, the sapper map shows, within just half a mile of one another, no fewer than five sìthean place names. Names like the magnificently daunting Sìthean Dubh Ghèarraidh Dhubh Bheag – the Black Faerie Hill of the Little Black Garden of the Grazings. If the Eskimos have umpteen names for snow, the Arabs similarly for sand, then in Dwelly's Gaelic dictionary alone I've counted seventy-nine words or phrases pertaining to the sìth. There's one that says it all – *Sìth-bhrughach;* 'Abounding in fairy hills'! Reflecting on the double meaning of sìth as both 'peace' and 'faerie', Ronald Black points to the word's likely etymology as cognate with the concept of being 'settled' in a place, or, one might say, 'homed'. As such, the sìth were 'the peace people'. The were the gentry of the land who 'enjoyed peace when the main activity of the Celtic tribes was war'. Black cites the work of Tomás Ó Cathasaig, professor of Irish Studies at Harvard University, who conjectures that the homely sense of sìd or sìth refined over time to 'abode of the gods' and to 'hollow hill', because, 'for an unsettled, or migrant people, the notion of abode or settlement might readily be linked with that of peace'. To wit, in early Gaelic tradition, 'the concept of peace was closely linked to the otherworld'.[1] To set the unheimlich of *Mary Rose* into faerie as the psyche's refuge from war, is to sit very comfortably in this tradition.

When Torcuil MacRath, the bard of Grimshader in North Lochs was still alive, I asked if he thought that sìthean always means a *faerie* hill. He answered by telling me of a bodach in the village, an old man by then deceased, who'd peer out when the sun was rising on a dewy summer's day, and as every hillock steamed in the warmth, he'd solemnly announce: 'They've lit their fires early this morning.' 'Mind you,' Torcuil quickly added, drawing back from being tossed too high in the horns of elfland, 'he wasn't quite right in the head.' And yet, my friend's poetic sensibility was picking up something. The ecology of the imagination, the realm of faerie as the spirit of nature personified, comes alive through living in the stories; and this is what it means to be connected to the Mythos.

Whatever happened to the island's faeries? One explanation is that a strain of evangelical clergy, brought in from the mainland in the nineteenth century, introduced a different disposition. A herds boy on the Lochs road was asked by a passing gentleman if there were still faeries in the parish. 'No,' said the boy, 'they all left when Mr Finlayson came.' Ironically, prior to that, their Lewis nickname had been 'Finlay's people'. Thus the Gaelic saying, 'As numerous as Finlay's people.'[2] But to blame it all upon the clergy is to take an easy swipe. It's mainly through the writings of the clergy that the tradition was conserved. And then, there's living testimonies connected with the second sight. Not that I'd be wanting, in this age of Aberdeen, to be persuading anybody about anything wacky. Just that I'm intrigued by Nora Bateson's comment, about what we might be inside of.

Invigorated by my bar of chocolate, I'm off again – and coming up now to a sharp slope that leads down to the western tip of Loch Coire Geurad – the Loch of the Sharp-edged Cauldron. With such limited visibility, this hellish weather unrelenting, my mind finds little stimulation from 'outside'. Right now, it's like I'm banged up 'inside', away in the land of thought: and if from here you soared as like a bird across Loch Langabhat, six miles directly east to Eishken, you'd come to a haggard spike of mountain crag called Sidhean an Airgid – the Silver Faerie Hill.[3]

If you come down that mountain, past the Crag of the Ravens to the head of Loch Seaforth – the Faerie Port, or Port of Peace, if we venture to go by *Sithphort* as the sappers called it on their 1854 map[4] – you'll come to a hill marked as Sìdeabhal. At its foot, right beside the sea, there lies a soft spread of emerald turf, and on it, a substantial dry-stone ruin. Uniquely, as far as I'm aware, the walls incorporate part of a prehistoric stone circle. This was probably a residential quarter belonging to the nearby first stronghold of the Mackenzies of Kintail when they seized Lewis under the Crown's Commission of Fire and Sword in 1610. The circle's incorporation to such a utilitarian purpose has led it to be said that Mackenzie 'could not have been very reverent or superstitious', or he'd never have usurped a 'Druid' place of worship.[5]

These fertile south-facing slopes run riddled through with feannagan. They remained hand-worked for potatoes, turnips, oats and barley well into my lifetime. The last person to tend them in the old ways was Mary Kate Maclennan – *Ceiteag*, to most people. However, in the anglicised formality with which she'd address me as the son of her doctor, 'Katie' was the name by which, in a letter that I treasure, she explicitly invited me to call her.

As the night closes in I sit in her kitchen at Seaforth Head by an oil lamp burning from a wick of braided cotton. Being off-grid in such a remote part of the island, she does have a diesel generator, but disdains its hammering racket. In any case, why waste drums of diesel when a little cup of paraffin gives quite enough flame by which to read a book, or a visitor's face?

Were she living in the East, Katie would be treated as a God-intoxicated holy woman. There'd be a queue of western pilgrims knocking at her door, hoping that by sitting at her feet they might 'get the *cùram*' – as the Gaelic calls sudden spiritual enlightenment. However, because she's a fully paid-up member of the Free Church of Scotland, prone to handing out sutras from the Westminster Shorter Catechism of 1647 – well – let's just say that I'm the lucky one. I get to sit at her feet all by myself.

'How is it for you these days, Katie?' I ask. 'How is it being the last person, left all alone in the village? Don't you get lonely?'

'Oh a ghràidh!' she exclaims – literally 'oh my love' – with a radiance that breaks through an intense hawk-like intelligence. She's in her late eighties, her ashen hair drawn back in the old Presbyterian manner. She's sitting there in a working pinafore over a long dark skirt, and now and then her spectacle rims catch an amber fire from the lamplight.

'Oh a ghràidh,' she repeats: '*How can I be lonely* . . . when I'm with God?

I protest that she's living at the end of this long dark sea loch, several miles from the next nearest neighbours, surrounded by bleak mountains. Since her husband died, she's continued to run the croft pretty much single-handed.

'Don't you ever get frightened?'

'Oh a ghràidh, *how can I be frightened* . . . when I'm with God?

And she laughs, with a most infectious giggle, enjoying the sight of my wavering incredulity, then adding: 'Mind you, the Devil was in here recently.'

'The Devil.' I repeat. Deadpan. Eyebrows no doubt rising.

'Oh yes! You see, a ghràidh, the Devil is always on your back. But God is in your heart. So you have to fix your eyes upon your heart to stop the Devil getting in.'

We all have a stone in our hearts, she said. If we don't let God take it out, the Devil finds his way inside, then all we're left with is a stony heart.[6]

As for the Devil's visitation, she'd been hearing him in the house for some time, going *chirp-chirp* like a bird. Jane MacAulay, John's wife from Harris, had dropped in on a nursing visit. She'd heard the chirping too, and neither could figure out where it was coming from. After she had left, Katie scoured everywhere. Eventually she found where he was hiding. 'In the smoke alarm!'

She removed the device and threw it outside. 'I wasn't going to be giving house space to the Devil!' The next night, she opened the door and there were seven faeries dancing in a circle on the grass.

'You saw . . . seven faeries?'

'Oh yes my dear – and they were horrible!'

'Like, how?'

'Oh, they were about this high' – she holds her hand at chair height off the ground – 'and they had little short pleated skirts, and horrible skinny legs; oh, *horrible* legs. They were dark. Repulsive!'

'So the faeries are not . . . pretty?'

'Oh no, a ghràidh,' and she leans in closer. 'You see, the faeries are in league with *himself*.'

'All of them?'

One of the traditions is that the sìth were angels who were discontent with God's way of running Heaven. God said that they could leave, but as they were not wicked enough to join Lucifer in Hell, they settled the middle regions of the Earth. For three days and nights they fell like snow, until God got worried that he'd have a labour shortage. As an old woman from the Uists told John MacInnes, 'With the voice of a sergeant major of the English army, he shouted *Halt!*' – slamming shut the trapdoor, and establishing the cosmic order.[7]

'You see them all as demonic?'

'The whole lot of them!' she insisted. 'You see, they are not of this world. They are in – how would you say it? – another sphere. An invisible world.'

And that was Katie's very straight Protestant take on the sìth. Such was what had led Yeats to write 'A Remonstrance with Scotsmen for Having Soured the Disposition of Their Ghosts and Faeries' because, he opined, 'In Scotland you are too theological, too gloomy.'[8] Katie wouldn't have seen it like that. She'd have seen her focus as being on the higher realms.

At one level, one could dismiss her story of the Devil's visitation as the confusion of an elderly person, not attuned to the wizmo-gizmo of electrical gadgets, living too much in a place of isolation. While true up to a point, it would miss the inner richness of her worldview. She had no television, no soap operas or adverts to generate a spurious sense of meaning. Instead, reality for her was elemental, based on raw experience, and self-evidently God-ordained. The fleeting changes in the weather, the weaving in and out of rainbows in the sky, even the vexed question of the rabbit population on her croft were all part of the give and take, the ebb and flow, of divine providence. When I'd sit in her company I'd encounter, carried through into the twenty-first century, a woman who held Thomas Boston's sense of 'every pile of grass . . . a preacher' of God's loving-kindness. Like with Barrie's Cameron, you could think that you had encountered a simple soul, and in some ways you maybe had, 'until you question him about the universe'.

She adhered, of course, to the Calvinist doctrine of predestination with the Damned and the Elect. But when I protested; when I asked how a God of love could damn anyone – and suggested that, in the very end, all might be 'saved' – she conceded through pursed lips: 'You might be right, but that would be *His* business.'

I asked how she had arrived at her spirituality. Was it something that had always been there? I was particularly curious as to why her emphasis was not just on God, but on the Devil, and why such belief in, and yet disdain for, the sìth. She told me a very personal story, a sequence of events that had entailed profound trauma in her life. Suffice to say, she'd lost her only son when he was five days old. That and its consequences broke her in both heart and mind. She'd had a vision that had warned her of upheaval. One night, well before going into labour, she had seen a 'blue man' standing on the stairs. In Gaelic lore, the 'blue men', the *fir gorm,* are the faeries of the sea. The Sruth nam Fear Gorma, the Straits of the Blue Men, lie out from the mouth of Loch Seaforth towards the Shiants. He had pointed to a pile of money that was in the house, and told her: 'Keep that . . . you will need it for the funeral.' In the agonising grief that followed, compounded by a further medical cause for suffering, her mind was stretched beyond the normal limits of endurance. It was then God opened to her.

The rational question would be: 'Does the Otherworld, the spiritual world in whatever its culturally-coloured permutations, exist?' But the mythic question is very different. That would ask: What *function* do these experiences and beliefs fulfil in the ecosystem of the mind? What *meaning* attaches to this sense of God and the Devil, or the angels and the sìth. What is the meaning that gives meaning to meaning? What, for that matter, gives meaning to anything? If we're all Mythos, we get lost in a dream world. If all Logos, we lose the symbolic world of meaning. Then the distinction between the angels and the faeries would reduce down to a single word: altitude.

As for the smoke alarm, neither Jane nor I had the heart to ask if she'd thought to change the battery. But in one of those funny ways of things, it got me thinking. I thought: that's actually the trouble with the Devil, if we might talk metaphorically. There he goes. As the opening of the Book of Job tells us, 'up and down upon the face of the Earth', like the long straight lines upon a map that signifies a lawyer's pen – the claim of 'property', and evictions.

And he's always going *chirp-chirp,* always trying to draw attention to himself, because he only runs on battery power. Can't get no satisfaction – though he tries, and he tries, and he tries. Too proud to get wired in, to the mains supply of God, 'whose name is *Holy*'.

Forgive my treading on such ground, but I know that's where Katie would like me to rest her memory.[9]

I must for sure have been too low to find the Ascleit sheilings, but on the cauldron's rim at Loch Coire Geurad I'd tried for signal on my mobile phone, and managed to get through to Vérène. Hearing her, set loose a burst of joyousness in me. I took off, skipping and whooping down the ludicrously sharp gradient, braked by the up-blast of the gale that sustained me like a parachute. I called my mother too. She could hardly hear my voice against the storm, but such are island micro-climates that Stornoway, she said, was bright and sunny, with only a stiff breeze.

The hint of a footpath that I'd seen on the map turned out to be an old turf boundary dyke. However, the ground around it was so choppy that, for a while, I walked along the top like on a tightrope. The mist had closed right in. One by one I'd watched the landmarks fail. I hugged close to the dyke until, from out of the mists, the little Loch a' Sguair emerged, huddled up against a wall of rocks. The both, a single dome, was even better preserved than what I'd found at Clar Beag, and I'm sitting now inside a nearby sheiling ring of stones. Another lunch of cheese and oatcakes. Musing on what happy times this sheltered corner must have seen. The days spent with the cattle. Evenings fishing on the loch. The smoke-cured tales around the hearth at dusk. No doubt there'd be a share of tears as well, and yet, as an island doctor friend who had been born in a blackhouse told me: 'We never needed therapists because we had each other.'[10]

It's out of the question in this visibility to traverse the Mothal Ridge across a line of three summits. I'll have to skirt Beinn Mothal's flanks instead. Ideally, I'd have gone the southern route, above Gleann Marstaig. There, within a two-mile stretch, the old sapper map shows ten places marked as *àirigh* – sheiling, or *gearraidh* – the grazings that were germane to sheiling life. That way, however, would have brought me to the foot of Sìthean Mòr Beinn a' Chuailein, which was not the place to cross the Grimersta that Seumas had recommended. With this rain, I can't be taking chances. I'll therefore take the northern course, ford a small river, then the Grimersta, and come at last to the 'crag and tail' formation of the Rubha Leathann. There, I hope, I'll find Saint Bridgit's Sheiling, and there I'll spend my fourth and final night out on the moors, before re-entering village sociability.

The rain is picking up again. I pack up lunch and quickly take a compass bearing. Already, from this morning's use, the map is slightly damp. The hi-tech inkjet colours are at risk of smudging. Vérène had said to buy a plastic map holder – the kind you loop around your neck. For some stupid reason, I'd not done so. Too bad. Prophetic confirmation of the scripture written on our fridge magnet: 'If at first you don't succeed, try it your wife's way.'

The bearing that I've taken points me on a wayline, a line of sight, that runs twenty degrees east. I've set my eyes on a rock some several hundred yards in that direction. Once there, I'll take another bearing on another waypoint, and so on, landmark by little landmark through the mist. However, very quickly, the steepness of the climb proves greater than I'd reckoned from the contours on the map. This can't be right. I'll change course, just slightly. Head directly north a while, up a slope that feels more like my expectations.

On, and on and on. Plodding through the wind and rain. Pretty miserable. Just meandering along. Drifting in a moistish sort of meditative mope. Can't expect to have it good every day. Hit so lucky with the sunshine earlier. But what's that funny noise?

At first I'm thinking it's a plane, but then a break comes in the mist. A mile away, a tiny speck, a van is speeding on a road that shouldn't be there. Civilisation cuts in with a thump. I pull the map back out, align it north-south with the compass, and face my error. Elementary! Never trust the naked eye in mist. What I had thought to be Beinn Mothal in my veer to north, was just the puny foothill of Cleit Mothal Mòr. I've gone and put myself an hour off course. 'If at first you don't succeed . . .'

I change tack and climb, recovering position. Gradually, I work my way along the flank and then down onto lower ground. Here the small river I'd noticed on the map straddles the moor. I cross it without difficulty, yet I'm troubled by its vigour after just one morning of rain. I'm now into a flat land, a zone that flows with bogs in all directions. The Grimersta is a mile away, but the mist has dropped back down again with vengeance. I can't see any hills at all. Even the lochs are dipped right down into the hollows, remaining out of sight until you're standing on their rims.

The land is quite devoid of any texture. It creates that slightly weird feeling of mild sensory deprivation. I'm having to micro-navigate, sometimes only seeing seventy or a hundred yards ahead and stopping all the time to take another bearing. The map is squelching to a Jackson Pollock quagmire. I inch along, seeking boulders, knolls, even big tufts of heather that stand out as waypoints. What can't be predicted are the tentacles of branching pools. These lead me in and trap me in their maze. It's like *The Lord of the Rings,* the Mere of Dead Faces in the middle of the Dead Marshes. Tolkien said it was an old battlefield, 'dreary and wearisome', where 'rotting reeds loomed up in the mists like ragged shadows of long forgotten summers'. That heaviness has settled onto me again. The same cianalas feeling that I had last night at Kinlochresort. A gnawing burden of . . . unspecified emotion.

I come upon a little rise, a tiny cnoc a few feet higher than the swamps that fester all around. Perched on top are two or three haphazard rings of bygone bothan sites. There are no sheilings left intact around the Grimersta. I've heard it said they were destroyed when the estate was set up, to stop them from harbouring poachers.

I perch to rest, and from this misty cnoc the whole world goes drifting by. And I know what has brought the *nostos-algos* back. These moors – these *are* old battlefields. These sheiling ruins – these *are* the ragged shadows, of long forgotten summers.

In January 1815, Deaf Mackenzie – Colonel Francis Humberston Mackenzie of Kintail, Seaforth and Barbados – passed away. His four sons had predeceased him and the whole of Lewis fell to his eldest daughter, Mary Elizabeth Frederica Mackenzie, whose mother had been the daughter of the Very Reverend Baptist Proby, Dean of Lichfield. Lady Mary had been married to an elderly admiral, Sir Samuel Hood, who had commanded the British fleet out of Madras. He had died just three weeks prior to her father's passing. It was as a doubly bereaved young widow that she returned to Scotland.

A doyenne of the Raj, Mary had led a dashing life in India. She claimed she was the first British woman to have shot a tiger. However, tales of her intrigues with diplomats, the literati and native princes set the tongues of polite society wagging. Remarks were made about her 'roving propensities'. She was dubbed a 'Tom boy', and even her paternity was questioned with her sultry 'Gypsy' beauty. When she remarried, only two years after losing her husband, the Whig politician, T.B. Macaulay, described her to his sister as a 'wicked woman'.[11]

In contrast to such disapproval, Sir Walter Scott eulogised her in his heroic poem, 'Farewell to Mackenzie, High Chief of Kintail'. Here was a 'gentle dame', to be addressed in reverential terms. Elsewhere, he hailed her 'warm heart and lively fancy', with 'the spirit of the chieftainess in every drop of her blood'. I think of her as something of a feminist ahead of her time, a woman whose sense of liberty and, it seems, sometimes of taking liberties, curled the upper lips of stiff patriarchs. I can't help warming to Lord Teignmouth's story that, on her way back home from India, a strange sail was sighted. As the crew leapt to battle stations, the passengers were ushered below deck. However, the captain noticed what he took to be a skulking sailor hiding underneath a sailcloth. In ejecting the miscreant, he revealed Herself, hoping for a bit of the action.

Her second husband was a minor Galloway landowner, James Alexander Stewart of Glasserton, later to become the governor of Ceylon. Chronically short of cash, he ran an advertisement in the Inverness Courier in 1830 offering '. . . very extensive Sheep Grazings, of the best quality'. These would 'be arranged by removing to other parts of the Island all the smaller Tenants at present dwelling thereon'. This venture, the text continued, was 'well worthy of the attention of Capitalists'. It was, he wrote elsewhere, a 'grand improvement . . . the introduction of mutton in lieu of man'. For the people of Uig in south-west Lewis, it meant families being crowded together on insufficient remaining land. As a village elder told the Napier Commission half a century later: 'The rest were hounded away to Australia and America, and I think I hear the cry of the children till this day.'[12]

As her husband got on with being the Capitalist with a capital C – attempting such ventures as printing his own banknotes, and setting up a whisky distillery in Stornoway – Lady Mary seems to have become absorbed with religion. For reasons not so far researched, she became an ardent advocate of Puritan evangelicalism. She used her powers of patronage as the landlady to hand-pick evangelical clergy from the mainland, and appoint them over Church of Scotland island parishes. So began the hardline Calvinist strand of island religion. As the Uig historian, Donald Macdonald, puts the matter, albeit in simplified terms: 'One must remember the Calvinist type of religion did not start in Lewis till 1824.'[13]

The significance of 1824 was the arrival of the first, and most influential, of Lady Mary's hand-picked appointees, the Rev. Alexander Macleod. He was posted to Uig, a parish that had earlier been decimated by her father's press gangs, and where her husband's clearances were to include evictions from some of the best land to create the minster's glebe – his larder.[14] It was, says an Uig historian, Donald J. Macleod, a creed of 'hellfire in the pulpit, sheep on the glebe, and Seaforth's lucre in his back pocket'.[15] Macleod was horrified to find a parish where, as a biographer puts it, he 'witnessed with his own eyes their homage morning and evening to the sun and moon'. His sermons generated 'a sense of fear, amounting to well-nigh terror', and he never failed to raise 'his silvery voice against all those pleasures and practices that seemed to him to impair the spiritual life . . . dancing, cup-reading, ceilidhs, gay clothing' – even – 'galloping on broomsticks'. Such abominations 'opened the vials of his wrath', and he 'denounced them in unmeasured speech'.[16]

Macleod's own diaries describe his conscious use of the pulpit to warn that 'fears and terrors, terrors unspeakable, would never terminate through the rounds of eternal ages, if the offers of salvation were rejected'. He petitioned Lady Mary for funding to circulate Thomas Boston's works in Gaelic translation, as well as seeking grants from the Royal Bounty. This was the missionary fund of the British state, started by George I in 1725 to convert the Highlands to Protestantism, thereby hoping to quell rebellions. When Macleod saw – in his own words – that 'every heart was pierced, and general distress spread through the whole congregation' as a result of his preaching and refusal to baptise the children of waverers, he concluded, with utmost satisfaction: 'May it bear forth fruit!'

Macleod was far from alone in celebrating the achievements of authoritarian religion. As Dr John Kennedy of Dingwall – the town next door to the Mackenzies' mainland seat of power at Brahan – proudly summed up the achievements of such Ross-shire preachers in 1861: 'The power of the pulpit was paramount in Ross-shire and the people became, to a great extent, plastic to its influence.'[17]

The Mackenzies had already mastered fear as a mechanism for colonising social control long before Lady Mary's time and her evangelicalism. Between 1577 and 1706 twenty-three members of the dynasty had been commissioners in prosecuting witchcraft. While the records are scanty, it is established that two women were burnt as witches in Stornoway in 1631 by authority of the Privy Council, led by the Mackenzie gentry. One historian of the era remarks that the 'religiously orthodox' would certainly have had plenty to bother themselves about, given superstitions as trivial as 'practices connected to holy wells and the pouring of milk on fairy knolls'.[18]

The same religious tactics that the British Empire deployed in its colonies abroad had been pioneered at home as part of the 'internal colonisation' or consolidation of the British Isles. Sustained colonisation of the land requires colonisation of the soul, what I call inner colonisation, where religion is structured to control the spiritual life. As Deaf

Mackenzie had said in his 1793 regimental recruitment poster, the name of the game was 'the defence of his Glorious Majesty . . . and the preservation of our happy constitution in Church and State'. In his era, the north-west frontier lay in the string of forts that straddled the Highlands to keep the clans in good behaviour. There was, and continues to be as an army base, Fort George, in the east near Inverness. Fort Augustus was in the middle and Fort William in the west, as well as lesser wild west garrisons. What the sword had achieved at the Massacre of Glencoe in 1692 and again at the Battle of Culloden in 1746, a Protestant reading of the Bible would help to sustain, with its focus on personal salvation. As many an African freedom fighter would say: 'They gave us the Bible, and we closed our eyes to pray. We opened them, and they'd taken the land.'

Paulo Freire of Brazil called such tactics 'cultural invasion'. Here, 'it is essential that those who are invaded come to see their reality with the outlook of the invaders rather than their own; for the more they mimic the invaders, the more stable the position of the latter becomes.'[19] Stigmatised and inferiorised, the colonised are thrust into a double-bind. They're damned to internalise their own oppression if they go along with the coloniser's norms. Or they're damned to the sword, hellfire, or just the privations of being a subordinate social class, if they don't.

Religions that make binary distinctions between people – whether as Elect or Damned, Mu'min or Kafir – are wide open to such political usage. A type of Stockholm Syndrome sets in, where a hostage group can enter into 'traumatic bonding' with their captors. As Alice Walker put it in *The Color Purple*: 'Some colored people [are] so scared of whitefolks they claim to love the cotton gin.'[20] Likewise, some folks are so scared of God that they buy into the notion of all hell to pay and play for others. Augustine even taught that those in Heaven will be well aware of the eternal sufferings of those in Hell. How else might they count their blessings, and 'for ever sing the mercies of God'?[21]

The only trouble is, the theology of fear discredits any god of love. It shrivels up the wells of spiritual life. It leaves the wounded neurotically seeking salvation from their wounds. No wonder growing numbers feel that atheism is a purer creed.

Such is the world that drifts past me, sitting on this cnoc amongst these fallen sheiling stones, surrounded by dead faces in these meres that morph amongst the mists of the Grimersta's headwaters.

A skylark rises straight up from the heather. I love to watch the way they sing, and slowly drop, and then rise on high to sing all over again.

Fosgag-Mhoire they're called in Gaelic – Our Lady's Lark – or as Alexander Carmichael had it, the Songster of the Virgin Mary. In Luke's gospel, the Song or Magnificat of Mary proclaims a very different god; one who stands in solidarity with the poor, who 'has brought down the powerful from their thrones, and lifted up the lowly; he has filled the hungry with good things, and sent the rich away empty'.[22] The Buddha was a prince who found enlightenment while contemplating suffering underneath a tree. Krishna was a god who spent his spare time chasing after the gopi cowherd girls at their Himalayan sheilings. All of these are eminently worthy pursuits. What for me distinguishes Jesus is that he was born in the most humble of circumstances, in a country under military occupation, and spent his life amongst and suffering with the poor. That alone is too great a gift to neglect, just because it has been twisted, and to fail to bring it to the table of world faiths.

Such are the qualities that distinguish liberation theology – theology that liberates theology itself from the boxes into which it has been shut. Not all of the clergy sided with landed power. One who did not, the Rev. Donald MacCallum, preached a liberation theology on Lewis and elsewhere. The Church of Scotland censured him. His denunciation of 'the vices of the rich', his likening of the crofters' plight to the Israelites under Pharaoh, and his urging them to 'resist the Devil and he will flee from you' were deemed to be a part and parcel of 'inciting violence and class hatred'. In 1886 on Skye, the Royal Navy sent in two gunboats to suppress a rent strike. MacCallum was arrested, albeit later released. He is remembered by the people as *Caraid an Duine Bhochd* – the Friend of the Poor.[23] As the proverb says, it's the kail that tests the creed.

But now I must get moving. I ease myself up and trudge on again – more and more of the same enervating territory – steering only by the map and compass, hoping that I haven't goofed the route again. At last, a breakthrough. The mist starts rapidly to clear. Where there had been only drifting drapes of whiteness, a pitch black rectangle looms. As I move in closer, I see it is a boathouse, made watertight with lashings of Archangel tar. A wind vane, shaped as a salmon, gutters from a pole above the roof. What's more, the wind has dropped down to a gentle breeze.

A gravel path leads on ahead and puts the spring back into my step. My mood has lifted with the mists. To wit, I feel a tightening of the vise of *sin* within my entrails. I've got everything I need to fish – except permission – but some words assemble as a poacher's proverb in my mind:

A sin not enjoyed is a sin wasted,
and a sin wasted is a double sin.

The dainty little footpath traipses round some knolls. It glides towards a whisper, that murmurs to a roar.

And there it is, a wildly foaming torrent. The Grimersta, that bellows from the island's heaving heart and surges to the sea.

14

SAINT BRIDGIT'S SHEILING

After such dry weather, I'd have thought the chain of lochs that are up above would have taken longer than a day to fill up. But that's the trouble when the moor has gone so crisp. It takes several days to restore its absorbency. Initial rainfall runs straight off. What's before me now is startling. Seumas had clearly lacked the second sight when he'd suggested this should be an easy place to ford.

I'm standing at a short stretch of broad stream that links two lochs. At the upper end, it issues through a weir, built to hold back water for the fishing. At the lower end it comes out beside a boathouse. The darkness of the surface there tells me that the channel must be deep.

I'm walking up and down the bank, checking out my options, and nowhere offers easy passage. What's more, the temperature's not helped by molten hail that's drained down from the heights. Right now, my body's warm enough, but I'm mindful that this is not the day to chance it with heroics.

There seem to be three options. Plan C would be to accept defeat, walk a mile down the side of Loch Faoghail Charrasan, and then join a footpath that eventually meets the B8011, the road where I saw the van go speeding across to the coastal villages of Uig.

Plan B would be to ford at the widest part, with the slackest water. The problem is, the river runs lopsided. The far side would be easy. There the force is broken by a line of stones that stretch out from the bank. The challenge would be on this side. Here the torrent's raging at thigh depth, and at a speed that could easily sweep me off my feet.

Plan A – the one I'm going to try for – is to wade into the top loch, and walk a broad arc round above the weir. Whether that can work depends on whether I can get out far enough to escape the suction as the water gathers in a V-formation, to funnel through the weir.

It's worth a try, plus I've got a bright idea with which to circumvent the icy cold. Osprey is fitted with removable elastic straps for tying on loose tackle. I fit a couple of these over my waterproofs, tightly around the ankles, and thereby improvise a dry suit. At the same time, I unhitch the rucksack's waist belt, lest I'm forced to ditch him in a hurry – poor thing.

The water's freezing, sure enough, but as I wade in deeper, the dry suit takes effect. I can feel the pressure pressing round my legs, but with no icy leaks. My fishing rod doubles up as a walking stick. Yet it's hard going. A mushy peat bottom is strewn with large angular rocks. Their sharp edges suggest a relatively recent date of quarrying. I'd guess they've been dumped there to create a salmon lie, and to snag poachers' nets. The truth is that Grimersta has suffered poaching on a truly reprehensible industrial scale. No wonder they protect their stock. As for the poachers – 'string 'em up like grouse . . .'!

As I move towards mid-flow, the water's lapping up my thighs and the suction from the weir is getting stronger by the footstep. What I hadn't reckoned on is that the deeper in I go, the more buoyed up I become. That makes me lighter on my feet, with less and less traction to the bottom the more and more I need it. I'm caught in a devil's calculus. Either, I can wade out even deeper, to reduce the suction. Or, I stay in the speeding shallows, and try to keep a grip. Time to switch off Mythos, turn on Logos. A cubic metre of water weighs a ton. Where it crosses the weir, it's easily a metre deep and the weir's about a metre-and-a-half wide. It's pounding through at, very roughly, five metres a second, so that's a giddy eight tons of water every second, nearly five hundred tons, half a million litres, a minute. If I lose control, I'll be catapulted through in flailing helplessness which, for a pilgrim, would be very bad karma.

Well, it's been an honourable effort. I beat a retreat back to the bank.

Over to Plan B, but with diminished gumption. I munch a Mars bar to summon up fresh energy, and select the stretch where the river is most wide and shallow, choosing a spot that's just above a deep pool. If I lose my footing, I'd rather be swept to where I can swim out, than to be bounced about the rocks amongst the rapids.

I take some time to read the water – looking for where surface smoothness hints at hidden depth, where swirls and boils suggest a lurking rock with fast water flowing round the sides, and observing from their colour which stones might offer a decent grip, and which are maybe treacherous with slime.

I step in, initially just over ankle deep, but immediately the force of flow surges to my knees. Turning to face upstream, I lean with both hands on my fishing rod, creating a tripod effect like Highlanders would do with their staffs back in the days before the bridges were built. I bend near-double, spreading my legs wide, partly squatting to keep the centre of gravity low, and forcing each foot down against the bulwark of a stone to block it from being thrust downstream.

Shuffling sideways like a crab, I move on outwards. The water shoots up to my knees and then surges almost to my waistline. It's not the depth, it's more the force that counts; yet I'm managing to hold ground. There's no returning now. I'm inching closer to the line of boulders, and as I come in beneath their welcoming lee, the torrent drops right off.

From this point on, it's just a dander to the bank. And this is Bridgit's country.

From the west, an unexpected burst of evening sunshine slants through a brief parting of the clouds. Be that as it may, the mist still lingers on the hills, and the wind has veered defiantly back east – where 'the fishing is least'. But to poach the Grimersta is a ritual, a patriotic duty. Like John Buchan's character making a similar point, this is my John Macnab moment. Were there even a remote chance of catching anything, I'd tie something serious. In this heavy water it would be a Muddler, a bushy Hairy Mary or a Stoat's Tail. If the sun came back, a Blue Zulu on a dropper for the sea trout; otherwise a Bloody Butcher, or even a spidery Black Pennell if the light got worse. It's the way that a fly moves in the water as much as what it looks like that matters. But these conditions are a joke – so, just for the fun of it, I'll choose a fly with poaching *attitude*. A solitary Jock Scott – the tartan soldier of the fly box – rarely one we used in my day, though no doubt some would swear by it.

I tie it on with eight-pound nylon – rather light. On the Eishken lochs, Christopher would say, 'always double figures'. But this is just a wee trout rod, and with a trumpet fanfare running through my head, I cast it out upon the glorious Grimersta. I'm a dab hand now from yesterday's practice, and with a few flicks of the wrist, I'm reaching to the other side. The line arcs to a graceful curve as I draw it back across the current. Beautiful! You could argue that fly fishing is perfected spiritual practice. The one-pointed awareness, as you attend a rise. The vigilance of kundalini, coiled to strike. And every cast, a mantra. Yes, here I am! Standing on these banks that the very Masters of the Universe, the men who built the Empire, have dreamt of as their earthly compensation – albeit prior to karmic retribution kicking in. And the solitary burden on the conscience of yours faithfully – a mere half hour of *poaching* – is one that the island's foremost men of the cloth have assured us is no sin.

We used to get them coming to the house, the shooting and fishing set. Dad specialised at drawing hooks from out of thumbs and ears. The trick is to press down and depress the barb, before you tweak. Anaesthesia is handy too – both for patient and, especially, doctor – at seventy per cent proof. We had a couple of guests drop in every year from Grimersta. 'Drinks-before-dinner', as they'd say. The Farlow-Joneses, they were called, and I think that Claude was 'in the Stock Exchange', as they'd say, like we'd say we were 'at the peats'. I remember Virginia's description of the old Grimersta Lodge – its rusty bedsteads, fusty counterpanes, peeling wallpaper and clanking lavatories – never 'toilets' – flushed by chains with swinging truncheon handles, and ball-cocks that would hiss and splutter from on high, all night long.

My mother was incredulous. These were the richest people in the land. Why such affections of impecuniousness?

'But that's what they love about it!' said Virginia. 'It reminds them of their days at boarding school.' It reminded them of all that many of them ever had as a home.

Apparently, the place was riddled through with petty rules. A particular chair was reserved for some old buffer, with hell to pay for trespass. Meal times were strictly regimented, and after dinner, the ladies would withdraw while the 'boys' settled down to port, cigars and telling 'damned good stories'.

'You see, Jean, they like being told what to do. They want to know exactly where they stand.'

There were tiny shibboleths, codes of conduct that communicated in-group norms and status, in the most understated ways. You'd have to be in the know, to know; and those who don't know, simply don't know any better. Never do up the bottom button of your waistcoat, especially not Etonians. One never tips one's soup bowl towards one; and if one dribbles, one dabs it with a napkin, never a serviette. Some gentlemen came faithfully each year, with their fishing wife. Others, it would be quietly noticed, brought their fish wife.

I cast my way down the best stretch of the river. Not a rise to Jock Scott. Half an hour is quite sufficient. The dastardly deed is done. That's me good enough initiated. I'll now await my summons from Grimersta Lodge. Mind you, there's a sporting charm I rather like about these folks. As like as not, 'Drinks-before-dinner?'

My adrenalin surge has lost its oomph and the weariness is creeping back. Although the lower ground has cleared of mist, the weather's showing signs of closing in again. The wind is rising, tugging at my jacket in that lonesome manner. I guess it must be mid-evening. The sky is darkening, and I sense another stormy night ahead. With only Seumas' brief description to go by, it might be challenging out here to find the Rubha Leathann.

I dismantle the rod, and wander on. The semblance of a path leads me past the boathouse that is on the opposite bank, and, from there, I veer off on a compass bearing north-east. The lochs and land round here are aligned in troughs and wrinkles that mostly run north-west to south-east. I cut across them at right angles, up and down, making for Loch an Earbaill as the next main landmark.

Walking, walking, and inwardly I'm wrestling with this island. The heavy tangle of religion that takes its accent from imperialism. That violent religion, again, of violent men of violent times. How can any supposed Christian preach fear, I'm wondering, when Jesus said so often: 'Fear not'? Or when John, the beloved apostle, said that 'Perfect love drives out fear, because fear has to do with punishment. The one who fears is not made perfect in love'?[1]

Oh yes, there are countervailing texts in the Old Testament, but Jesus – if one wants to give him any credence in the matter – made an explicit point of sidestepping these. Early on in Luke's gospel, he reads his mission statement from Isaiah.[2] It's all about the liberation of the oppressed and those who life has bruised. What's rarely noticed is that he stops, dead, halfway through Isaiah's second verse. Had he carried on, the very next line would have proclaimed 'the day of vengeance of our God'. But he didn't carry on. Luke records: 'And he closed the book . . . and sat down.'

How, then, could Calvin have portrayed a God 'armed for vengeance'? How, then, could Alexander Macleod have taken such delight in kindling the fear of divine retribution amongst his Uig parishioners? How, then, under the *Dieu et Mon Droit* that every British citizen carries on their passport cover, can the United Kingdom justify a fleet of Trident nuclear submarines with names like HMS *Vengeance*? One wonders, sometimes, if angry men project onto the world an angry god; and if so, at what price to love?

The poet Derick Thomson, like so many Hebrideans of the twentieth century, wrestled with this legacy of a wrathful representation of god. His short poem, 'Although Calvin Came', testifies to an underlying island spirituality; to a love that maybe still runs deeper than the injuries.[3]

> Although Calvin came
> he did not steal the love out of your heart:
> you loved
> the tawny moor, and suffered pain
> when that land and the flower were taken from you,
> and a coffinful of songs was laid in the earth.

But now the Grimersta has dropped far out of earshot. I shuffle on amongst the heather, over hillocks and down through little hollows. An old tune known as *French* comes humming through my head. And with it, words from a Scots paraphrase of the Psalms that was written down in 1615 – ironically, straight from the tradition of John Calvin and John Knox.[4]

> I to the hills will lift mine eyes,
> From whence doth come mine aid.

From whence, indeed. And there's the question: *How, today, might we sustain the love not stolen from the heart?* How, given the traumatic scarring that we carry, and that they in their time also carried, even more so? How, when often it would feel so very much more *satisfying*, just to go down to the market, buy that AK47, and *shoot the bastards to Hell?*

Sometimes only stories, preferably real-life stories, can point a way to hope beyond dehumanisation. Around 1911, the Rev. Kenneth Macleod of Eigg wrote 'An Clachan a bh' ann' – 'There Was a Village'. To the best of my knowledge, it has never been published in English, but my dear friend and Gaelic cultural mentor, Catherine MacKinven, made me a partial translation.[5] It starts with a reference to the Act of Proscription, the so-called 'Disarming Act'.

After the defeat at Culloden in 1746, the Clachan, the village, was like the rest of Gaelic-speaking Scotland, 'in a stir and troubled.' The 'wise men of London' decreed to strip the Highlanders of their traditional kilted attire, saying: 'We'll put trousers on the Gael, we'll take every sword and musket from them . . . so these wild men will become as meek as lambs.'

Troops of English redcoats were sent to implement the new laws. A contingent was posted to the Clachan, the village, about which this tale is told, 'and by their way of it, because of their love for the people . . . they were in no hurry to leave.'

However, in the course of his duties, the second in command fell down a cliff while searching for hidden treasure. His commander knew that there was a custom in the clachan to sing *tuireadh*, elegiac laments, over the dead. He called for those who performed such ceremonies.

The three women came, politely, seemingly respectfully, and with tears in their eyes. But the song they sang in Gaelic had the words:

> The Englishman has gone.
> He's covered in fire that will never be quenched.
> We'd be happy if the rest went the same way.

This pleased the commander, for he could not understand their language. He could only understand their tears, and gave them each a silver coin.

But as the women left, conscience struck them. Their position had been terribly conflicted. They had loved the Englishman, but deplored what he represented. 'God forgive us,' said the first woman. 'This is no night for mockery and our beloved man in deadly danger.'

'Hurry,' said the second. 'It would hurt me all my life if our beloved man (*fear ar gaoil*) should go without a *tàladh* (a death lullaby) in his ears or heart. It would be our loss, not his – the blessings of the poor are a *tàladh* and a pillow for him.'

They hastened back up the hill to the big house where the body was laid out. '*Gu Shealladh an àigh!*' said the third woman, who had the double sight. 'The door is closed – the soul is still within the body!'

They went in softly, sat by the bed, and began to sing:

> You are going home tonight to the everlasting home,
>   to the house of autumn, spring and summer.
> You are going home tonight on the sounds of the chant,
>   white angels awaiting you on the banks of the river -
> God the father at your sleeping,

Jesus Christ at your sleeping,
God the Spirit at your sleeping.
Sleep softly. Sleep softly. Sleep softly.

His eyes were closed, the door of the soul was opened, his spirit took the road of the fathers to the sea and to the other side of the horizon.

'I will go,' said the first woman, 'and in the name of the Trinity I will bake a *bonnach* that will keep him right on this journey.'

'I'll do the same,' said the second. 'I'll prepare a lantern that will brighten his steps.'

'And I will take the three coins that we were given to the *Gobha*,' said the third, 'and he will make of them a key that will open the door of Paradise for our beloved man – *och nan och èire* – I grieve that he is no longer with us.'

The women took the contradictions of their lives, melded them to the contradictions of their oppressors' lives, and through redemptive sympathy, fashioned them to food, and light and to the Gobha's holy key.

Here is the triune weave of smithcraft, poetry and healing – the qualities of Brighde – she who 'turned back the streams of war'. Alexander Carmichael wrote:[6]

Bride with her white wand is said to breathe life into the mouth of the dead Winter and to bring him to open his eyes to the tears and the smiles, the sights and the laughter of Spring.

So beauty boils over. So spirits walk. So articulation is restored between the inner and outer worlds; and the spiral of violence, thrust into reverse.

I must press on. Her sheiling should be close by in these moors.

Because the land is corrugated in long ridges, it forms a row of dipping bays along the shores of Loch an Earbaill. I pick a listless way across their sand and stony beaches. The wind is gaining force again. Rain clouds closing in. Dusk begins to settle. I want to get the tent up while it's still dry. Getting cold and weary – weary, weary. Come to think of it, not had a drink since Loch a' Sguair. I kneel down, cup hands to sup, and feel the run of water through my fingers, its cold trickle down the backs of my wrists. Such a very basic thing to do. Such animal survival.

I'm musing how I've morphed the meaning of this place; how I've assumed it to be Saint Bridgit's Sheiling. But Seumas never mentioned any saints. All he'd said, was *Bridgit's Sheiling*. I asked him how he knew. He said the sappers' map showed the ground beside the ruin as Gearraidh Ghill Bhride – the 'garden' pastures of the sheiling of her *ghillie*, her servant. This area is littered through with hints of sanctity. It's not just all the sìthean place names. There's also a small hill where I crossed the Grimersta – Airde Gille Mhicheil – the Heights of the Servant of Michael. There's a loch of the same name. Gille Mhicheil is Carmichael in English – as with that latter-day saint by popular acclamation, the collector of the *Carmina Gadelica*.[7] In the Celtic Church, Michael was important as the patron of protection. Here he is next door to Bridgit. What's more, the flooded stream that I encountered before the Grimersta flows out from Loch an Fhir Mhaoil – the 'tonsured man' – which is to say, the Loch of the Monk.

I count along to Earbaill's fifth bay, then cut up directly north into the moor. I'm trying to figure out which of several grassy bluffs might be the Rubha Leathann. These little cnocs are special places. To me, they're stupas of the moors. The dung of cattle seeking breeze has built into the soil a deep fertility. In the high summer, they're spangled through with sky blue flecks of speedwell, wild pansy or 'heartsease', and tiny eyebright with its flares of seashell-white that burst from out of a golden yellow nucleus.

I make my choice of crag, and start to climb. There is a kind of ladder, made of bedrock rungs, that ripple through the tight-set sward and give me a sound footing. On Iona, Saint Columba saw the angels going up and down between the Earth and heavens from a little hill like this. Unusually, it has two names that bridge between traditions: Cnoc an Aingeal, the Hill of Angels, and plain simple Sìthean.[8] Adomnán, the seventh-century biographer of the saint, said that, 'One should take notice of this story', for the angels 'generally came to him as he remained awake on winter nights or as he prayed in isolated places while others rested'.

Such gems show why it was that Celtic anchorites – the anchors of the soul between the worlds – would place their sheiling hermitages in lonely spots like this. Places of just God and Nature. They say that Brighde would awaken on spring's laughter, and spread her flowery mantle out across the Earth. The cattle yielded milk, the maiden filled to motherhood, and after harvesting the fields, perhaps the *cailleach*, the last head of standing corn, would be left alone as if a kind of offering back. There was, too, the corn dolly – the *maighdean bhuana* or Maiden of the

Stubble. Her virtue, on being fed to the animals, was passed on to the following year's crop. Then there'd be the weaving of the Bridgit's Cross, the ears of which would sometimes go into the next year's seedcorn. These traditions varied with locality, most of them are overlapping. Through them we glimpse the triune principles of life, death and rebirth; of the Maiden, Mother and the Holy Crone – the turning, through the ages, of the feminine face of God.[9]

A decade or so into the twenty-first century, an old Catholic priest from one of the southern isles said quietly to me:

> I don't have to go to a church as a Hebridean. I only have to go down to the shore, pick up a piece of the tangle, listening to the birds and talking to the sea. Brighde was at the heart of our religion. The tide coming in was bringing her gifts. She is in charge of all that. We don't worship her – we wouldn't use the words 'to worship' for Brighde – but we go pretty near it.

And I'm scanning everywhere for ruins. Walking, sunwise, around the top of the ridge, wondering if I've got the right one. In 1883, when Carmichael told the Napier Commission about the 'joyous life' once lived around the sheilings, he lamented that 'the smoke of the whole people, nuns and all, now ascends through the chimney of a single shepherd'. He added: 'Should not these places be marked and held sacred for all time coming?'[10]

There's nothing to the south, or west, or north. East?

I peer over the edge, and – ohhh! ohhh! – *there you are, my beauty*.

I have found the ring of fallen stones. Saint Bridgit's Sheiling.

From here, the land slopes gently down towards the misted hills of Eishken that loup across the bottom of the horizon. I have clambered down the cliff, and crouch beside the formless blocks. These have lain here, undisturbed, for a very long time. Their once-sharp edges have now rounded down to softness, and mottled white and grey with lichen shrouds.

I am gazing at the lintel stone, so long and flat and very thin. This would have carried all the weight above the door. It rests, reclining in the grass, retired amongst the other rocks, unharmed by any force of human hand.[11]

> And God said unto Moses: *If you use stones to build my altar, use only natural, uncut stones. Do not shape the stones with a tool, for that would make the altar unfit for holy use.*

Once, all but the little children would have bowed their heads on crossing underneath. Visitors would have paused, to call a blessing on the house.

I likewise bow my head, ask blessing, step inside the ring and kneel.

Such sweetness. Tenderness. Holy, holy, holy.

And then I notice. A fresh-sprung fern is pressing through a cleft against the lintel. Not bracken, but a flush of verdure such as I have not seen elsewhere in all my walking.

A line from a John Martyn song comes willowing across my mind.

You curl around me, like a fern in the spring.

And in George Bernard Shaw's *Joan of Arc,* the inquisitor puts it to the lass that God's voice sounds only in her imagination.[12]

'Of course,' she answers. 'That is how the messages of God come to us.'

The rain is coming on. I pull my hood in tight.

'I'm with you always,' says the voice in my imagination.

'Do what you have to do with people, but try to keep your heart open.

'Go easy on rocky old Calvinism.

'Don't use hard tools on rocks that need their time to smooth.

'Never forget . . .

'*I curl around you, like a fern in the spring.*'

And it's just me, Alastair, alone out here. At Saint Bridgit's Sheiling as the night sets in. Absorbed in skeins of textured mist that drift in folds across the far south-east.

Only the rain, a rising tide that whelms the quilted lichens.

I watch it trickle down in dribs and drabs through tiny written runnels.

Kneeling at the lintel in this ring of unhewn stones.

PART 3

HARE

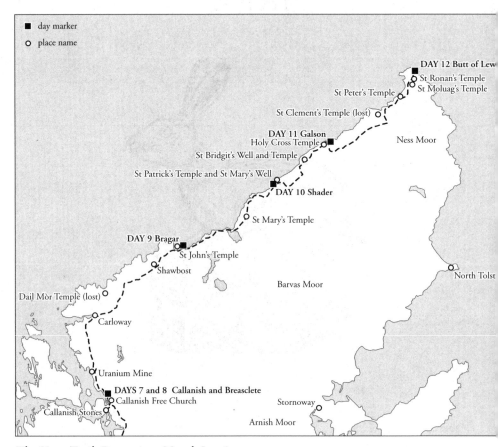

The Hare Trail: Days 7–12, North Lewis

15

THE BAPTISM OF THE GODS

I am lying in a bed. Nights in white satin sheets that smell so freshly laundered. The walls too, ever so white. I am looking at an Artex-coated ceiling, mind floating in and out amongst its swirling scallop shells; drifting from one to the next, seeing shapes and patterns in the gaps that fall between.

I become aware that my fingertips are pulsing. They're puffy and ragged round the damaged nails. That wrangle with the Bog Monster was only five days back but seems so very far away.

My legs feel set in plaster, but slowly sleep is lifting from their deep fatigue. I become aware of flu-like aches, and then the fireworks show begins – racking my whole body with shooting pains that race up and down the veins like piranhas tearing clumps of jellied muscle.

'This is how it would be to wake up in hospital,' I think. 'How do I know I'm not?'

I stand up, and sway from side to side. It's like I'm drunk, or in a minor earthquake, or when you're back on land from days and days at sea, and think the boat's still moving underneath your feet. But it's only waves of bouncing bogs that I've been sailing on, albeit with a similar effect.

I lie back down, let the world steady, and as my mind more fully comes to, take stock by counting on my fingers. Days one and two were threading through the azure bays of Harris. Days three to six were over mountain trails that brought me into Lewis. Now it's the seventh day, Sunday, and my totem mountain hare is about to take off on its final lap, darting north amongst the people, wells and near-forgotten temples of the villages of what we call the West Side.

On Friday night, at Bridgit's Sheiling, I'd camped beneath the lee of the Rubha Leathann, close to the Sithean of Murdo's Loch. The rain and wind came hammering in with a refreshed vengeance. It blew in under the flysheet, and soaked the line of dirty clothes that I'd laid out as a defensive bund to protect my sleeping bag.

I'd been swithering about the weekend, about the Sunday. The question had come up when back at Café Spirituel. Somebody had asked how I planned to spend the famous Hebridean Sabbath, when everything 'grinds' to a halt. 'No,' I'd suggested. 'That's the wrong idiom. It is *rested* to a halt.'

It put me on the spot. I didn't want to seem peculiar, afflicted by a rigid touch of fundamentalism, and yet, I had to tell them that I'd not feel comfortable to spend a Sunday marching with a rucksack through the villages of home. The good people of Falkland looked politely quizzical. David Lorimer rallied to my rescue. He said, in his sprightly way, 'That's interesting. It's because he's in the island's mental field.'

Both in the sense of organised religion, and in its sense of what it means to be a community, this island is a religious community. In one of his commentaries on Gaelic poetry, Ronald Black makes an observation, very true for Lewis and Harris, that, 'Throughout the twentieth century respect for the Sabbath, rather than for the language, remained the principal marker of Gaelic identity.' Professor Macleod of the Free Church put it this way in a newspaper column: [1]

> It's not Sunday ferries that will eventually undermine us. It's the loss of Sunday itself, the one day in the week when we might have time to reflect on where we came from and what we ought to be. Such a Sunday made metaphysicians of crofters and fishermen. Today's Sundays turn lawyers and accountants into football hooligans.

You have to grant this to Lady Mary of the Seaforth Mackenzies. The strict observance that her evangelicals brought in was felt by some of the more lowly as a liberation. It was their employment protection policy. No longer could labourers and domestic servants be made to work seven days a week. Today, the native islanders accept that many tourists either don't care, or don't know any better. But for me, being from here, it's different. Folks would feel it kind of wrong if I went clamouring past their doors, regaled with all my clobber. The more devout would feel it cut across their sanctuary, as if I'd tramped through their gardens. At its worst, the island's Sabbath can be obsessive legalism, like stories of the cock being covered with a basket on the Saturday night to stop him getting at the hens until the Monday. At its best, however, it creates a sense of collective retreat. It punctuates the week by setting aside time for fallowness of mind and family togetherness. It shields against the pressures and bland sameness of a 24/7 world. What's more, some incomers and tourists are its staunch defenders too. These days, there's even a growing creed of militant atheist Sabbatarians.

For me? I try to mark some rhythm to the week. I don't fuss overmuch when away in 'Aberdeen'. But here? Well, I've not come back to bust the island's code.

Yesterday, Saturday, I had walked out from Bridgit's Sheiling. I'd laid the compass on the map and found my wayline slotted perfectly along the wrinkles in the land. All I had to do was follow in their folds.

After an hour, I came to undulating swathes of feannagan, densely overgrown with heather. They laced both sides of a little glen as V-lined wheals, just east from where the Grimersta had joined the sea. Once, there was a village there on Cnoc an Ruagain, the hill directly overlooking Grimersta Lodge. Today's map marks it as a sheep pen. The people had been cleared when Sir James Matheson set up his sporting estate. The baronet had made his fortune in the Chinese Opium Wars. He purchased Lewis following the death of James Stewart-Mackenzie in 1843. Disraeli launched a scarce-disguised broadside at him in *Sybil*: 'A dreadful man! A Scotchman, richer than Croesus, one McDruggy, fresh from Canton, with a million of opium in each pocket, denouncing corruption, and bellowing free trade.'[2] One can imagine the type.

It had felt weird, when the time came, to step from the moor back onto a tarmac road. I had crossed another threshold. A rumbling lorry bounced past, with clanking chains that dangled off the back like a portcullis. A car whistled by, too fast to make eye contact with the occupants. Then another, and another. *A-zippp . . . a-zippp . . . a-zippp* they went, like fleeing blobs of colour launched from a firework. It felt like all the world was out of kilter, but it was only me.

I felt unsettled, slightly vulnerable, and I did up Osprey's scarlet rain hood to be more visible. I hadn't fully realised at the time, but on the moor, every step had been a dance of shifting balances. In contrast, every step along the road plodded off a Henry Ford production line. On the moor, it was a rhythmic world; my movements contoured to the shape of space around me. Time slipped by in no time, which was why I'd felt that on the winding path, no stretch was ever long. On the road, however, especially on the long straight stretches of a Roman ilk, the monotony of sameness put the brakes on half an hour to drag like half the morning.

Where a finger of the sea pokes in at Loch Ceann Hulabhig, I'd dropped my bag beside a gate and climbed a short, unsurfaced track, that leads up to Cnoc Dubh – the Little Black Hill. From there, two miles away on the horizon, the naked eye can just make out the Callanish Stones, like a brooding field of chessmen. Although these were set in place some three thousand years before Christ, they take the sun-wheel pattern of a Celtic cross. Close by, immediately back across the road, there's another ring of stones with only five remaining menhirs, transfixed as if in never-ending prayer. These are off the tourist route and clad in thickly bearded tufts of a creamy lichen. They're encrusted, too, with lightly hammered silver flakes of *crotal* – the symbiosis of a lichen and a fungus that was used to dye the Harris Tweed.

I sat down and faced the huddled congregation. There must be about a dozen of these outliers from Callanish. They keep discovering more beneath the peat. Perhaps the people then were like us now, with breakaways of breakaways from the established kirk. Being out, alone, upon the moors had been a time to stand apart. But by this time, I could feel the welcome pull of people coming back into my mental field.

Running through the exposed crags of Cnoc Dubh is a massive vein of snowy quartz. Seumas Crawford, who lives nearby at Garynahine, had shown me the evidence that it had been quarried thousands of years ago. You can clearly see the stepped ledges, pitted with opaque impact scars on an otherwise translucent rock. They look like whitened rings, the size of peas or lentils, where people from the age of stone and bronze had chipped away to get their knives and arrow heads.

My friend's pride and joy at this site is a both, on which he's worked for several years. The original had fallen prey to vandalism. A man who'd feared its reputation as a 'Druid's house' had linked it to the Devil, and wrecked it with a crowbar. Seumas had carried out the restoration. He'd used archaeological photographs to identify and number each stone, and return it with precision to its rightful resting place.

One afternoon, in the summer of 2003, I'd dropped by to offer a hand. There he was with his archaeologist's trowel, built like a shotgun cartridge and ministering to the stones with hands of wrestled leather. He has that gnome-like demeanour that is often seen in men who work mostly on their own, with elemental forces. I had come to see him as an elder figure; one whose qualities of presence speak as deeply as their purely technical skills.

He set me working, digging out the matted turf that concealed a stone pavement leading up to the dome. We'd laboured together for several hours, mostly in silence. At the end, he said he'd been surprised by how much I'd achieved, and at my deftness with the spade.

'I never thought you'd be up to it!' he said, in the voice of overdone flattery and the wry smile by which such outdoors men will often pass backhanded compliments.

'Me neither,' I conceded. 'Thought I'd been too long on the computer.'

I was struck by how much I'd felt that this was *wonted* work – work that is our 'wont' – deeply fitting to our nature. I'd hardly thought that the skill to wield a foot-spade like a hand-trowel – that delicate matching up of brain with brawn – remains ingrained from years and years of early experience. I had felt forgotten muscle patterns sliding back to harmony. It was my body, itself, in homecoming.

A funny thing happened as I dug, and pulled, and cut the twisted roots from out amongst the cobbles. Gaelic words and phrases, even images of people from the past, came flooding through my mind. It felt like a reversal of the long ebb tide of childhood. Returning on the flow were echoes of the Old Folks, still here and all-accepting. The feeling carried on into the evening. It was like when you've seen an epic movie, and it keeps on running in your mind, long after you've left the cinema.

There's a passage in the *Tao Te Ching,* the teachings of Lao Tzu, in which the sage observes:

> The myriad creatures all rise together and I watch their return. Returning to one's roots is known as stillness. This is what is meant by returning to one's destiny.

That was what it felt like. Roots and stillness, back to destiny. And when we downed our tools that day, it was an ancient path that stood revealed, the stones still tightly interlocked.

Some years later, I mentioned it to Seumas – the way I'd felt a sense of voices of the Old Folks awakening in my imagination. All he said was, 'I know what you mean' – and that was quite sufficient. I haven't asked him, but I think he too would share in Nora Bateson's observation that *we don't know what we're inside of.*

On that morning of day three, when I'd walked up the 'Lost Glen' on the way to where I'd seen the mayflies dance, I'd briefly stopped to sit down on a mound. Some twenty minutes later, I realised that I'd left my sunglasses behind. I considered retracing my steps, but as my eyes by then were two full days habituated, and the sunshine was falling mostly on my back, I reckoned – rightly as it proved to be – that I could manage without. But it set me on a path of thought. It seems to me that the eyes, like the skin, become accustomed to strong light. It's as if they too take on a tan, though whether that has any medical basis, I cannot say. The loss had put me on alert for photokeratitis – a painful night-time scratchiness, that is caused by ultraviolet damage to the cornea – and in so doing, it set me thinking of how the Inuit made goggles to prevent snow blindness. They'd craft the shoulder bones of reindeer, the thin flat scapulae, incising them with narrow slits to limit the low and reflected sun's intensity.

It's hardly an original thought. Just one that's shaped from such experiences. But could it be, I'd wondered, that we limit down reality in much the same way?

Could it be that memory – the means by which we hold our place in time – resides in more than just the electro-chemical networks of the brain? That the deeper realms of memory and meaning are not so much like data on a hard drive, as accessed by the server of the brain from a web beyond constraints of space and time? That even notions from neuroscience and the new physics – such as the quantum brain, quantum mind or quantum consciousness – are perhaps just early inklings of a whole new flight of understanding, that joins up to theology?

Time, said Plato, is 'a moving image of eternity'. Could it be that memory is a peering in on what's already there?[3] And the second sight, a widening of the slits in mental reindeer bone; and that this is why the seers will say it's like 'remembering the future', and that it can go both forwards and backwards?

In short, could it be that everything that ever was, or waits to be, *just is*? Is that what we're inside of; we who, perhaps, also 'inhabiteth eternity'?

Just as E.F. Schumacher only used the term 'small is beautiful' twice within his book of the same name, so Gregory Bateson's *Steps to an Ecology of Mind* hinges on its title and that single line: 'Mind is immanent in the larger system – man plus environment.'

When I asked Nora that night in Glasgow why she thought that her father had not developed the concept further, she said she thought that he had been discouraged. He was in his last decade of life when his book was published. She thought perhaps his friends and colleagues had wanted to protect his memory. To have gone further down a mystic road would have challenged the dominant scientific view of what it meant to be a human being. This was based on the mechanistic biology of 'value free' science. Indeed, it had been none less than Gregory's own father, William, who had both founded and named the modern science of genetics.[4] One can imagine, too, that the implications of interconnection might have been unsettling for some of Gregory's upper class social circle, for whom empathy might not have been at top rank in the comfort zone. Einstein had shown that space and time are fluid. If the human mind was to be entertained as somehow 'immanent' – inner or intrinsic – to such a universe of relativity, then what might be the implications for prevailing mechanistic and materialistic theories of reality? The very notion of an ecology of mind would have lifted the lid on a sìthean into which few, with reputations worth not losing, would have wanted to take a tumble.

Just as Bateson's studies of schizophrenia and addiction explored dissociation from the world under the pressure of trauma, so traditions of the sìthichean do much the same.[5] However, the tradition does not stay stuck only at the level of mental illness. If we might take *Mary Rose* as standing in its carrying stream, the 'call' that she heard whispering from the holes of the ground on her island had two elements. On the one hand, there were sounds of tempestuous fury, 'horrible' and 'unholy'. On the other hand, vying with them was 'music of an unearthly sweet-ness' that sought 'to put a girdle of safety round her' and which, at the end of the play, carried her 'into the empyrean'.[6] She reaches, at last, the healing depth from which, as John MacInnes commented, 'comes the creative power of mankind'.

The function of the sìth and sìthean, says Michael Newton in a study of the bardic process, is 'a way of speaking about the creative process [that] can take our consciousness into a realm beyond the mundane constraints of time and space'.[7] In Celtic myth, this empyrean is vari-ously the green world, Tìr-fo-thuinn (the land-under-the-waves), or Tìr nan Òg (the land beyond the setting sun). Across the great water, such realms belong to the ever-young, a cosmic homecoming, the end of all our *nostos-algos*. Here life's full bloom, its fullness of potential, its beauty, is reconstituted.

A good example from the early Gaelic literature is the *Immram Brain*, the Voyage of Bran. It was first written down in Ireland in the late seventh or early eighth century. A woman 'in strange raiment' mysteriously appears inside Bran's locked-down fortress. She brings a silver bough, a sure sign of her Otherworld provenance, and sings of mythic isles across the western wave.[8]

A branch of the apple-tree from Emain
I bring, like those that are familiar;
Twigs of white silver on it,
And crystal-fringed with flowers.

There is an island far away,
Around which sea-horses glisten;
Pillars of white bronze are under it,
Shining through aeons of beauty.

Without sorrow, without grief, without death
Without any sickness, without weakness;
But sweet music striking on the ear,
That is the character of Emain.

A quality of many of these early texts is their articulation between the 'pagan' worldview of the Elder Faith, and Christianity. The 'old' Testament is bridged to the new. In the *Immram Brain* the sìth are a heavenly host whose 'colours glisten with pure glory'. They minister from out of timelessness to a human world decayed 'by greed and lust'. Far from being in competition with Christ, they anticipate a Christian redemption of the world. The *Immram Brain* continues:

We are from the beginning of creation
Without old age, without consummation of earth;
It is a law of pride in this world,
To believe in creatures, to forget God.

A noble salvation will come
From the King who has created us;
A white law will come over seas,
Besides being God, He will be man.

He will delight in the company of every fairy-knoll
He will be the darling of every goodly land;
He will be a stag with horns of silver,
A speckled salmon in a full pool.

Professor John Carey, an Irish-American who is a leading Irish-Welsh medievalist, holds that such texts achieved a remarkable 'imaginative reconciliation' between the traditions. Here the sìth and all their pantheon reflect 'not devilish trickery and evil magic, but the perfection of human nature as God had first created it'. As far as he is aware, this defence of the old religion is unique in the literature of medieval Christendom: 'an idea of brilliant originality, startling boldness, and beautiful simplicity'.[9]

Carey calls it 'the Baptism of the Gods'. Here, 'eternity is always present at the heart of time – or, to express the same thought in other language, Eden is always present at the heart of the fallen world'. The literature puns consciously on the double meaning of *sìth* and *sìthean*. It points towards 'the peace that passes understanding'.[10]

Why, in the greater scheme of things, does any of this matter? It matters, because the imaginal realm *is* the greater scheme of things. The pagan Celts were, as one of the early texts puts it, 'faithful to the truth of nature'.[11] Only too much narrowing of the slits in reindeer bone; only an excess of separation, of disarticulation from the inner life, or of 'sin' in traditional vocabulary, has closed the eyes of mortals and closed us to the underlying truth of Eden – thereby perpetuating violence in the world.

Human beings and the cosmos, the tradition tries to show, 'are portions and versions of one another'. That is what becomes visible as the slits open, the light gets in, and time starts to fall away in the course of 'the world's passage into eternity'. As such, Carey concludes, the ecology of the planet and the soul of humankind cannot be separated. 'If we hope to escape from spiritual death, this hope must be indissolubly bound to the survival of the world of which we are a part.'[12]

And that is where I left it at, as I came back down the track from the restored 'Druid's house' at Cnoc Dubh. Ecology emanates from the cosmic imagination. Imagination leads back to ecology. That's the ecology of the imagination, and it differs from what Gregory Bateson had tried to say about mind only in the reach, and the cultural antecedents, of its conception. Perhaps, too, in its implicit sense that the imagination is the counterpoint of materialism. Imagination is much more than neural pathways in the brain. It works with them, channels through them, but is ultimately born of soul.

I climbed back over the gate, heaved Osprey into harness, and carried on along the main road towards the first of the West Side villages. I had only gone a little way when I came across a wondrous sight – a *sgiobadh* – a communal work crew, cutting peats for the next winter's fuel. Half a dozen men and women were on the moor, chattering and laughing as many hands made light. As one would slice a square of tar-black ooze with the *tairsgear* – an L-shaped peat iron – another would hurl it up from the trench onto the heather bank to dry.

I thought of going over for a blether. Very likely, around here, they'd be some of Agnus' cousins. But I felt a shyness on me. I wasn't ready yet for social immersion. I carried on, over the Blackwater bridge and up to the white expanse of Garynahine Lodge. As I went, so many things were clicking hyperlinks of familiarity within my brain. My mother told me the story that when the Stornoway contractor, Willie 'Bucach', had completed our new surgery in the early 1960s, the work had been to a very high standard. Dad therefore recommended his firm to Captain Neil and Betty Perrins of the lodge, and of the family that made Lea & Perrins Sauce.

When the work was finished, the Captain said: 'Look, Willie. I know that you're a poacher. But to thank you for all you've done, I'm going to send you to the hill with a keeper and let you bag a legal stag.'

So, off went Willie with the stalker; and when he came back with a stag in the bag, the Captain said: 'So how did it feel, not to have to be a poacher for once?'

'Ach!' said Willie, 'To be honest, Captain, it wasnae the same at all.

'You see, if when you're going out, every rock doesn't look like a stag; and if when you're coming back, every rock doesn't look like the keeper – then there's just nae the same fun in it.'

Two miles on from the lodge, I reached the Callanish Stones. Been there, done that, so many times before, so I made a beeline for a hot meal in the Visitor Centre. I went into the gents, glanced in the mirror, and, *Oh my, oh my! That is some weirdo!*

My hair that hadn't seen a comb for days was whipped to a storm of curls, and my beard gnarled like lichen. My face had lost the muscle tone that social interactions normally compose. I looked as if I'd just been pulled from out of the Hill. When I went back out and nobody was looking, I quickly snapped a selfie so I'd not forget.

I headed on, up through the Stones, and there in the central circle was a woman from America, who asked if I would take her photograph. She wanted to be lying down, inside the burial crypt, pretending to be dead.

I took the camera and she lay down in her slacks and red shell jacket, grinning in the way that archetypal American tourists are archetypally meant to do.

'Stop smiling!' I chastised. 'You don't look dead enough!'

She grimaced. I snapped. We laughed at our tomfoolery. It was just ships passing in the night, but pleasing in its fleeting human warmth.

I walked on, through Callanish, towards Breasclete; and by now my legs were seizing up with gravity of lassitude. A dreary ache was in my bones as if a bout of flu was coming on. At Zimmer speed, I passed some modern buildings by a war memorial. There was a belfry with no bell – common in the Hebrides, an architectural throwback to when the Calvinists threw them down in Geneva to melt into weapons[13] – and a sign outside, that said: 'Callanish Free Church'. Further on along the road, beside a children's swing park that has no lock on the gate, there's another sign:

> Welcome to Breasclete
> Play area
> Open: Mon. to Sat.

At the Stones, I'd finally made up my mind to take the Sabbath as a day of rest. Conveniently so, given how my body's giving up the ghost: but as they say, 'The Sabbath was made for man; not man made for the Sabbath.' The Visitor Centre staff had been very kind, and had helped me to track down the one and only remaining bed and breakfast room in the area for the weekend.

I turned off, right, at the foot of a hill. It seemed to take forever, grinding up the brae in bottom gear. My attention flagged, I went into a daze, and only when I neared the top did I realise that I'd walked right past the gate when halfway up.

A welcoming local woman showed me to my room. And that was how I came to wake up here this Hebridean Sabbath morning – with these satin sheets, these snowy walls, and the pilgrim scallop shells that swirl across the ceiling of the Loch Roag Guest House.

16

THE GREAT COSMIC POACHER

I'm just lying here in this comfortable bed, having a long lie on this, day seven, and watching how the Artex patterns shimmer into one another. I've come nearly two-thirds up the island since setting off from Saint Clement's. As for Saint James of the scallops, what providence it was that, after being martyred at Herod's sword, his scallop-encrusted body washed up on the shores of Galicia in north-west Spain. What beauty that they call his pilgrim paths, the *Camino de Santiago de Compostela* – the Pilgrim Path of Saint James of the Field of Stars. Where else, but in the Celtic world, might a suitably qualified sgiobadh of bards have been found to weave such a story together? And to think that it all starts off in Harris, with the emblematic shell to prove it, carved into the hunchback warrior's tomb!

I care little if these stories are embellished, as might be so for so much of religious tradition, including parts of the scriptures themselves. Unless we're in an academic mode, we miss the mythic point if we try to drive too sharp a wedge between fact and fable. I care mainly that they speak truths of the heart. There are at least four Jameses in the gospels and the distinctions tend to blur. Our scalloped friend is James the Greater, patron saint of pilgrims. However, in my state of reverie he jogs me on to James the Just, brother of Jesus. Tradition holds that he authored the *Epistle of James* that appears near the end of the New Testament. I love that little book, and the Dalai Lama loves it too. In a rousing commentary, the Tibetan leader writes:[1]

As I read the lines of this *Epistle of James*, I am struck by the similarities between this beautiful letter in the Bible and some of the texts in my own Buddhist tradition . . . It teaches us how to bring our spiritual vision to life at the highest level . . . It reminds us to relate to fellow human beings at a level of basic humanity . . . What matters most is basic warm-heartedness.

Strangely, for one who otherwise promoted the unerring authority of the Bible, Luther wrote James off as 'an epistle of straw'. He said that it has 'nothing of the nature of the gospel about it'.[2] The epistle is all about spirituality, the life of the soul. Luther, like Paul before him, was trying to structure a religion, a collective and even a politicised expression of faith. For Luther, 'justification' (or being made good in the eyes of God) is *sola fide*, by faith alone. This he held to be 'the article with and by which the church stands'. However, possibly to rein in some of Paul's slight excesses, Saint James tweaked a spanner in those works. 'Show me thy faith without thy works, and I will show thee my faith by my works,' he said, adding for good measure, to put it in the vernacular, 'Faith without the kail is dead.'

Neither did James teach eternal suffering for the Damned. Instead, he said, with crisp compassion: 'Anyone who has committed sins will be forgiven.' That didn't mean he let the selfish off the hook. Mean-mindedness attenuates the soul by self-destruction. It follows that, 'As the sun rises with its scorching heat and withers the flowers of the field, so the rich, in the midst of a busy life, will wither away.'[3] As for conflict, James the Just gave no quarter to 'just war' theory. He went directly to the roots of violence, asking: 'These wars and fightings among you, where do they come from? Do they not come from your cravings that are at war within you?'[4]

And I'm lazing in this Sabbath morning's easy peace. I'm musing – *do they not, indeed* – while far away, war in God's name is waging all around.

'It's very simple to explain the idea of Blair the Warrior,' said John Burton, the author of *We Don't Do God: Blair's Religious Belief and Its Consequences*.[5]

'It was part of Tony living out his faith.'

Burton had been Tony Blair's local political agent for more than two decades. He knew him very well, and saw the Prime Minister's motivation in leading the country to war as disarmingly self-evident. 'Tony's Christian faith is part of him, down to his cotton socks. How can you understand his thinking on any front if you don't understand his core beliefs?'

Blair 'believed strongly,' continued Burton, 'although he couldn't say it at the time, that intervention in Kosovo, Sierra Leone – Iraq too – was all part of the Christian battle; good should triumph over evil.'

It is as if Blair, for all the avuncular exterior, shares what the historian, Richard Hofstadter, called 'the paranoid style in American politics', a trait of 'heated exaggeration, suspiciousness, and conspiratorial fantasy'. In contrast to the clinical paranoia of an individual, a leader's political paranoia is 'directed against a nation, a culture, a way of life whose fate affects not himself alone but millions of others'. In America, it has been argued that it goes back to the siege politics of the early Puritan settlers – battling with the Indians, with the witches at Salem, or with Catholics, Communists and all manner of un-American activities. It is as if, suggests Richard Parker of the John F. Kennedy School of Government, the violent religious politics of late seventeenth-century Britain continued to play out on in the amphitheatre of the New World.[6] Sometimes, you have to wonder – like the picket-fenced obsession with property rights, and the need to carry guns – if unresolved anxiety lurks at the heart of it all.

Be that as it may, on 15 February 2003, one million of us marched in protest at the impending war on Iraq. The police described it as the UK's 'biggest ever demonstration'.[7] It failed to have any impact on the launch of Operation Iraqi Freedom, with US and British forces spearheading the invasion. One month into the war, I happened to be invited to a dinner with two serving generals of the British Army. I'd known both for a number of years. There could have been no other topic of conversation; but what riveted me was how the more senior man shared, with complete candour, his feelings that had come about once the political decision had been made to substitute diplomacy with war. It had torn at his conscience as he had set about ordering massive assaults, inflicting heavy enemy casualties.

'I have not seen the intelligence that Blair claims to have seen,' he told us. 'If it turns out that Saddam has no weapons of mass destruction, then Blair will have led us up the garden path.'

Out on the battle front, even as we were finishing our dinner, his men were killing and being killed. But this was no callous calling 'Forward!' from the rear, 'as the front rank died'. This was just one human being living out the Mythos of his time; caught up in the Myth of Redemptive Violence – the idea, perpetuated by any 'domination system', that violence can redeem violence. That petrol can put out the fire.[8]

'*Up the garden path*,' I whistled. 'But would that not make you – a war criminal?'

Our poor hostess visibly flinched. Chatham House Rule, for sure, but I'd stepped on the edges of decorum.

'That is something I take very seriously,' the general said, in a premeditated tone that put the table back at ease. It was as if he welcomed an opportunity for shared reflection. This man was of a military vintage that had a deep respect for the Nuremberg Principles; a generation that had been born into the world of a time when German officers were being hanged by allied forces under Nuremberg's provisions.

> Principle I: Any person who commits an act which constitutes a crime under international law is responsible therefore and liable to punishment.

> Principle IV: The fact that a person acted pursuant to order of his Government or of a superior does not relieve him from responsibility under international law, provided a moral choice was in fact possible to him.

He had therefore gone in person to see the Attorney General to seek assurance that the orders handed down from Number 10 were legal. Neither was he alone, at his level of command, in having knocked on Lord Goldsmith's door.

'But you still felt ill at ease,' I said. 'So *why* did you issue the orders? Why did you not . . . resign your commission?'

'Because . . .' said this dear man, wrestling with an enormity of events that left him humbled, 'I was placed in a position where I had to make a moral decision. Did I obey my own gut feelings? Or did I obey orders from my own democratically elected Prime Minister?'

In my experience, the military's use of 'just war' theory is more than merely a mechanism to justify war. The military strategist Carl von Clausewitz famously gave the definition that 'war is thus an act of force to compel our enemy to do our will'.[9] Without constraints, war would become 'absolute war'. Such is the ever-so-logical endgame that Saint James understood to be the outcome of unrestrained 'cravings that are at war within you'. The military are acutely conscious of the need to limit war. They hold nuclear keys. Time and again when I've spoken at defence institutions, I've been told afterwards: 'You remind us of the limits.'

I'm happy to play along with that, but I also suggest that there is a spectrum of power's expression. Spiritually speaking, the name of the game is to shift along that spectrum. It starts with hard force, or as the military would say, the 'kinetic' expression of power by weaponry. It moves to the soft force of persuasion by sub-lethal measures such as sanctions. From there, it moves to the psychology of convincement – the process of 'winning hearts and minds' (and even being open to being won). Lastly, and what I seek to point towards, the spectrum gets to the spirituality of transformation. That is where the full power of nonviolence comes into play. But the process has a ratchet. You can't just say, 'We'll try nonviolence, but if it doesn't work, we'll slip back to pulling a gun.' It has to work from an inner place of integrity, if need be to the point of sacrifice. Such is the mystery of the cross.

Here, at the end of the spectrum, the aim 'to compel our enemy to do our will' dissolves into a two-way process. The endgame becomes one of building relationships based on respect, fairness and helping one another to satisfy, not cravings, but fundamental human needs. This can only happen in a spirit of cultivating empathy. Power shifts from 'power over' to 'power with' to the deep 'empowerment' of spiritually-resourced power from within. Here is where the teachings of Jesus become such a rich contribution to the table of world faiths. 'Love your enemies, do good to them which hate you.' When Peter swiped his sword at the high priest's servant's ear, Jesus stuck it on again, symbolically restoring the enemy's capacity to hear.[10] There is transformative method, not just incredulous magic, in the seeming spiritual madness.

What about the few passages where Jesus appears to countenance violence?[11] When he said that he came to bring 'not peace, but the sword', he is warning, using metaphor, that his teachings will unsettle the Roman peace of those who guard the status quo, especially within families. When he turned over the money-changers' tables and fashioned a whip to drive 'them' out, the Greek is ambiguous, but modern translations point towards it having been the animals lined up for sacrifice that were driven out (thereby saving them). Their owners would have naturally followed. When he told the disciples to go out and buy swords, telling them that it was sufficient when they produced two, the passage that he quoted from the Hebrew Bible reveals it was explicitly to fulfil the prophecy that he would be perceived as a common brigand, the lowest of the low.[12]

All of these passages show that Jesus was challenging power, to the point of direct action in civil disobedience. None suggest that he endorsed violence against the person, not even framed as 'just war'. The nonviolent witness of early Christians became central to how the faith was spread through the Roman Empire. Even while in prison awaiting their tortured executions, the martyrs looked for every opportunity to forgive and convert their captors. In their willingness to follow Jesus in bearing but not reciprocating violence, they taught the way of transformative love. Like my friend who suffered in Papua New Guinea, they confronted their assailants in a way that sought to 'touch their hearts'. The hope was to catalyse *metanoia*, a Greek word that is usually translated as 'repentance', but actually means the radical transformation of the mind from within.

The co-option of Christianity into 'just war' theory rests on later interpretations of what the cross was all about. Was the God of Christ violent, or nonviolent; and if the former, in what ways does that legitimise our use of violence? Here the crucial question is – *Why did Jesus die?* The pivotal gospel text in answering this, is Mark 10:45 – 'For the Son of Man came not to be served but to serve, and give his life *a ransom for many*,' or as a text from Paul had it, 'as a ransom for all'.[13] This is called the Ransom Saying. In Christian theology, the million dollar question has been this. If human souls are *ransomed* – and if Christ died to pay the *ransom price* as 'an offering for sin' as Isaiah had prophesied – then precisely who might be the Ransomer of Souls?[14]

The question might seem arcane, but for its importance in understanding the religious dogmas (or teachings) that came out of trying to make sense of Jesus' death, and from there, to questions of how we should live, including 'just war' theory. Over each of the past two millennia, mainstream western Christian thought has come up with a different line of answering the Ransom Question.

The first millennium's answer was the 'Classic' or *Christus Victor* view. The Devil is the Ransomer of Souls, and Christ, the ransom on the cross. Saint Gregory the Great likened it to a fishing trip. When Jesus died, the Devil, like a great sea monster, seized the tasty morsel thinking it an ordinary human soul, and plunged into the depths. As the Apostles' Creed has it, Christ 'descended into Hell'. At that moment, the Great Cosmic Fisherman struck. Only when it was too late did the Devil feel concealed within the barbed and burnished hook of God. In Gregory's own words: 'The bait tempts in order that the hook may wound. Our Lord therefore, when coming for the redemption of humanity, made a kind of hook of himself for the death of the Devil.'[15] The Devil, though not yet destroyed, is thereafter played out on a long cast. His power, though twisting and leaping, is at least held in check until the final showdown of end-times.

As for Gregory the Great, in my book that makes him the *Patron Saint of Poachers*. Which, joking apart, was precisely the problem. Come the second millennium, the *Christus Victor* theory of *why did Jesus die?* was facing two criticisms. To God, it attributed deception. To the Devil, too much power. Where might be found an alternative theory of 'the atonement' – the idea that Christ, in offering himself as the ransom payment, had 'atoned' or paid the price for human sin?

Enter Anselm, a monk from a noble family in Lombardy who, in 1093, was appointed Archbishop of Canterbury by William II, the brutal son of William the Conqueror. If the Devil was no longer to be Ransomer of Souls, who else was qualified to take the vacancy? There was only one other candidate in town. It had to be . . . old *Dieu* himself.

Anselm was a deeply pious man, but his framing of reality was profoundly feudal. To sin, he wrote, is 'to fail to render to God what God is entitled to'. God is entitled to our 'righteousness, or rectitude of will'. Our failure, since Adam, to deliver such fealty 'robs God of that which belongs to God, and thus dishonours God'. Without an honour code, the authority of the feudal hierarchy would collapse. Without fealty to God, the cosmic order would collapse. The only way to hold the show together, is that 'punishment should be inflicted'. However, God being a loving god, says: 'Receive my only Son, and offer him for yourselves.'[16] Through the sacrifice of Christ, humankind was thereby spared eternal torment, and God's honour duly 'satisfied'.

This is therefore called the Satisfaction Theory of the atonement. If one goes into a church, and asks why a cross is on the wall, that would be the most doctrinally correct answer that most doctrinally correct western Christians would give. It is why many hymns contain lines such as these, which were sung in 1947 at the wedding service of the future Queen Elizabeth II:

> Praise, my soul, the King of Heaven
> To His feet thy tribute bring
> Ransomed, healed, restored, forgiven
> Evermore His praises sing.

Anselm's theory was pushed to its logical conclusion in the sixteenth century by the legally trained mind of John Calvin. 'We are all,' he said, 'offensive to God, guilty in his sight, and by nature the children of Hell.' Not one of us can examine ourselves 'without feeling that God is angry and at enmity with him', thus the context of God's being 'armed for vengeance'. For the benefit of the Elect alone, however, Christ was sent to 'the bar of God as a criminal in our stead'. He 'interposed, took the punishment upon himself and bore what by the just judgment of God was impending over sinners.'

This, concluded the reformer, is 'what is meant and implied by *ransoming* us from the justice of God.' In this way, Christ's sacrifice 'satisfied and duly propitiated God the Father . . . appeased his anger . . . and by this tie secured the Divine benevolence.'[17]

Calvin's ramping up of Anselm's Satisfaction Theory is known as the Penal Substitutionary Atonement Theory. Such blood atonement theories remain at the core of most Catholic and Protestant dogma. They let God off the *Christus Victor* hook. God is exonerated from the charge of being the Great Cosmic Poacher. Unfortunately, especially in modern eyes and in the light of modern criminal cases, it puts God foursquare back into the dock, as the Great Cosmic Child Abuser. It normalises violence. Whether as crusader, jihadist or other holy warrior, such a psychology gives the political classes a sense of legitimacy in using violence to sort out a rotten world. Such a god must be a patriarchal hierarchy or else maternal wires might short-circuit the system. You'd only get some Brighde somewhere, turning back the streams of war. As for Mary – keep her as the patron saint of silent servitude, but not of no full-on Magnificat.

Is this what Jesus tried to teach? The theology of penal substitutionary atonement only adds up if the carriage of Christianity is drawn by an Old Testament warhorse.[18] However, Christianity is still a very young religion. There might be mileage further down the road, by which 'then spirits walk'.

At which point, it's time for me to walk. I rise, and with my land legs still awash, sway down the stairs and into the Loch Roag's dining room. Soon there's a rack of toast and two huge Stornoway kippers staring at me bug-eyed from a plate. I dig into one, and ask the waiter if he would be so kind as to wrap the other in foil for later. He obliges, with a 'Who would eat a cold kipper?' sort of courtly smile.

I'm wrestling with how to spend the day. It's one thing to respect the local Sabbath, to choose to take a welcome day of rest. But the done thing in these parts would be to go to church. I'm not sure I'd fancy the menu. There's no Quaker Meeting round here. The only option in the village is the Free Church – marked by the empty belfry.

Mind you, for all its conservativism these days, I can't help but feel a soft spot for the Free Church. It was the home of my Highland ancestors and the main denomination of the island folks who raised me. I cannot help but admire its origins. Donald 'Sligo' MacKenzie – the husband of Mary, on whose quinsy Great Uncle Jim had operated in Callanish in the 1920s – describes it in this way:[19]

Until 1843, there was only the Church of Scotland. Unfortunately, the Church of Scotland in those days was governed and controlled by the landowners and ministers were appointed by them. Ministers said from the pulpit what the landowners wanted them to say – the very landowners who were driving the people off the land. That, of course, was the era of the Clearances, a time of great hardship for the people of the Highlands and Islands. Our oppressed people at that time decided to form their own church – the *Free Church of Scotland.*

And yet, they're called the Wee Frees, because of their insistence on Westminster Calvinism with its limiting sense of the Elect. Do I really want to spend the morning immersed in that?

Maybe it's just fall-out from the kipper – red herrings and all that – but wafting through my mind appears a red-robed Buddhist nun. We'd met when seated beside one another on an interfaith discussion panel that the Bishop of Edinburgh had chaired. Her name was Sister Candasiri. Her affiliation, the Amaravati Buddhist Monastery.

'I'm sorry,' I had to say, 'I've never heard of the Amaravati order.'

'Theravada tradition,' she said, and realising the trigger, said it with a twinkle in her eye.

'Theravada!' I said. 'You mean . . . the Wee Frees of Thailand?'

'I know!' she laughed, 'I know.

'But you see, when I first met them – ahhh – they were just such lovely people. I've been with them now for twenty years.'

She had grown up in Edinburgh. Like the bishop, she'd been a Scottish Episcopalian, a part of the Anglican family. However, Theravada had come to be her calling.

'You Buddhists!' I said, teasingly. 'You have this sense that everything's joined up. That we're all one, all part of the Buddha Nature. But tell me: where does that leave your prior belief in *God?*'

'*God?*' she asked, in feigned puzzlement, as if the answer wasn't blindingly obvious.

'It leaves me in . . . *total immersion.*'

O come on! I'm saying to myself, as I polish off the toast. *This walk is meant to be a holy pilgrimage. How about a bit of . . . total immersion?*

Better get a move on, then. The service starts in twenty minutes flat. I run upstairs, grab my coat, rush out the front door and almost bump into a dark-suited elderly man. He is, I think, of the family of the Loch Roag's owners. Evidently heading off to church, he looks me up and down. His demeanour tells me that he's wondering whether he should offer a lift to his near-assailant.

I'm too embarrassed to ask. Don't want to seem all 'holy' like. He doesn't want to cause embarrassment by asking. These days, you can talk about sex more comfortably than religion. In any case, I'm dressed more like a walker. He nods a little smile, gets into his little car, and trundles off down the hill at a suitably Sabbathly *vitesse*.

I've now got fifteen minutes, and near enough a mile to go. Off sets the hare, coursing at a suitably un-Sabbathly *vitesse*.

Pity. He'd have just loved it if I'd asked. Acceptance of, and acceptance by, the community and its ways. Had my plan been to go walking, then as likes as not he'd have gone out of his way to drop me off. 'Ah well, you see: you're in the islands now.'

Full speed, full stomach. A lift just lost to pride. And the kipper burps the way that kippers on the trot are prone to do. Up comes a sutra from Saint James' epistle.

Verse 4:10: 'Humble yourselves in the sight of the Lord, and he shall lift you up.'

Ouch!

It's such a lovely morning. The hills are veiled in rising wisps of vapour. The sun is almost breaking through.

Burp!

Verse 4:14: 'What is your life? For you are a mist that appears for a little while and then vanishes.'

And I'm vanishing as I go, full scarper down the road, kipper vapour in my train.

What had been a little flurry of slow-moving cars has passed me by and parked. The road's gone quiet and everyone's inside. The church that's by the war memorial, the church that has the belfry with no bell, now looms just several hundred yards away. And in a crazy flight of kippered fancy, Sister Candasiri's at my side. Her red robes hitched up high above her knees, she's hirpling along at quite some giddy rate.

She wants to know the story on the bell-less belfry. But part of me's not wanting to let down the side. Not wanting to push old friends into a corner, to leave no quarter for redemption from bygone violence, or ongoing reformation – even for rocky old Calvinism.

'Well you see, Sister, it's just where the past has left us stranded. I suppose the trick is to find new light by which to see new meanings.

'Perhaps to look up through the empty space, and see the sky, the moon, the sun and other stars.'

'Ah, so!' she says, quite breathlessly. 'I hear what you are saying.

'I have heard about this Hebridean Zen.

'I see you have . . . an architectural *kōan!*'

She means those gnarly riddles that the Roshis ask beginners. Questions that set up a clash between realities, supposed to trip the rigid mind out into deeper frames of knowing.

'Oh yes, Sister! Very nice way of putting it!

'Like – *what is the sound of one hand clapping?*'

'Ah, so!' she says. 'Applause! Applause!

'So now I think I understand, this Free Church *kōan* of yours . . .

'*What is the sound of an empty belfry chiming?*'

'Well maybe, Sister, maybe. Perhaps you'd better go and ask the minister . . .'

'Ah, so!' she says. 'But I like it very much.

'What church should need to have a bell, an empty bucket rattled?

'When God sounds from the Belfry of Creation.'

The doorman peers from out the porch. He takes a little walk around the car park, then takes a second look more pointedly in my direction. He's wondering if I'm walking to them, or past them. I raise an arm as if half-heartedly to hail a taxi. He returns a little wave, and draws back halfway out of sight in doorman's dignified decorum.

I stride in through the gates, shake the doorman's hand, and fast decelerate to seem at ease, if not a little odd, amidst the thirty or forty parishioners lined out on varnished wooden pews.

Oh dear, it's really not my scene. The Bible is carried in by a cohort of elders, all men in dark suits. The minister follows and takes up his place, not in a pulpit but at a lectern. But then Psalm 103 is first-off. I know it from the version that is sung by the Iona Community, derived from Taizé.

> Bless the Lord my soul,
> and bless his holy name.
> Bless the Lord my soul,
> he rescues me from pain.

The minister moves into an extemporary prayer. Not a script or note in sight. I have to admit, he has a fresh and cheerful manner. His words are simple, deep, and speak directly to the heart.

Next, Psalm 104. Verses eight to fourteen. Here is a God of Katie's world of immanence in all creation, the life force that unfolds into the grass that feeds the birds, the people and their beasts. A God of village wells, of Morag's world who 'sendeth the springs into the valleys, which run among the hills' and 'watereth the hills from his chambers'. And I'm starting to think – wait a minute – give me more such *total immersion!*

Then comes the sermon. Spotting that the congregation has a stranger in their midst, the minister explains that he's been working, week by week, through the Book of Job. It just so happens that they've got to chapter twelve – and I'm nearly jumping out of my seat. This is pretty much the most ecological, the most pantheistical – I beg your pardon – *panentheistical* chapter in the Bible. 'The tabernacles of robbers prosper' and those that mock God get rich. That's Job's sorry observation of the world that he was living in.

> . . . but ask now the beasts,
> and they shall teach thee;
> and the fowls of the air,
> and they shall tell thee.
> Or speak to the Earth,
> and it shall teach thee . . .

. . . because 'the soul of every living thing, and the breath of all mankind' is held in God's hands. The minister laments the fact that Job's full power of Hebrew poetry is lost in the translation. The prophets often turned into poets when doing their most full-on stuff. Here, he explains, is a book that explores unwarranted suffering at poetic depth. Prosperity, he tells his congregation – what the robbers store up in their tabernacles – is not to be equated with virtue. Neither is suffering to be equated with sin.

It's just too good to lose. This might be conservative evangelicalism, Hebridean-style, but it's certainly no American-type 'prosperity Gospel'. With probably a vain hope that I'll not be noticed, I whip out my pen and scribble down some notes – kind of a literary pinching of oneself.

'You must not judge a man's piety by his plenty, by what is in his hand, but by what is in his heart.' God is not a watchmaker who winds up the universe and leaves it to run down. Job shows that God is utterly involved in the unfolding of the Creation. 'By him all things consist.'[20]

Global warming, the financial crash of the past year, the scandal of the fraudulent expense claims of British politicians – *oh yes* – the tabernacles of robbers may prosper for a season; but in the end, God pours forth 'contempt upon princes, and weakeneth the strength of the mighty'.

We have neglected compassion for the orphan, the widow, the alien and the poor. The environmental crisis is a self-inflicted 'judgement' on our hubris. It is time that we faced up to spiritual bankruptcy. The God of love is *ravenous* for justice. God who, concluded Job, 'discovereth deep things from out of darkness'.

The service ended with Psalm ninety-two.

> How great are your works, O Lord!
> Your thoughts are very deep!
> The dullard cannot know,
> The stupid cannot understand this.

And I'm left pondering – who might have been the dullard? Who? Had I judged them only by their dogmas, only by the head and not the heart; and by my absence, missed such a sermon.

And I'd have missed lunch too! It had been Margaret, the wife of the Rev. Calum Macdonald of Callanish Free Church, who had welcomed me at the Loch Roag last night. She works there part-time as a waitress. After the service, they invited me with three of the elders back to their manse. We feasted on heaped plates of roasted island lamb, followed by a trifle, and sat around a peat fire and talked theology.

I'd raise a point. As often as not Calum would put the question to one of the elders, so everybody was kept on their toes. Atheism is a hot topic on the island, but we hit some rocky ground over the 'gay' issue. It was in the air because the Church of Scotland were debating it at their general assembly in Edinburgh that week. I said that we who are heterosexual should acknowledge difference, and in any case, Jesus had never said a single word about the issue. They said that Paul had carried the injunction over from the Old Testament to the New. I said that if we followed Paul's grounds for so doing, then we should also ban the island delicacy, the *marag dhubh* or Stornoway black pudding. The same Council of Jerusalem that had decided, after the death of Jesus, that Christians should uphold the sexual prohibitions of the Law of Moses had also carried forward the ban on eating products made from blood.

We could have gone on and on. We could have built it up into the *Marag Dhubh Controversy*. But it was a lovely fire that was blazing in the grate. I was mindful that the Law of Moses had also forbidden gathering sticks and the kindling of a fire on the Sabbath day. The penalty was death. However, Rabbi Abraham Heschel, one of the great modern

Jewish liberation theologians, said that this means that, once a week, we should refrain from stirring up the fires of controversy. Just give each other a break. Listen for the voice of a deeper calling. Failure to do so leads to slow spiritual death. Good teaching, I thought, very good teaching. I drew back, from the head into the heart.[21]

There's something about spiritual energence that I call the First Love syndrome. Just like they say you never forget your first love, so it can be with how we first encounter religious doorways. For me, it's having a soft spot for the Hindu scriptures and the writings of Carl Jung, even though I've probably got blind spots to their foibles because of what they've otherwise given me. I suppose it's no different for Presbyterians with their Reformed faith. Calum would probably defend Calvin to the hilt. He'd probably think that I just get a little over-obsessed with sticking points like the Westminster Confession, or the Free Church's all-male ministry. For him, what led to convincement might have been some of Calvin's more sublime writings. For example, where the Genevan reformer said: 'Mankind is knit together with a holy knot . . . we must not live for ourselves, but for our neighbours.'[22] Raw spirituality may be God-given, but religions, at least in part, are fashioned through apprentice human hands.

'The old people of the island,' Calum told me, 'often say that there is only one quality in the human heart that the Devil cannot counterfeit.'

'The Devil?' I said, raising a liberal eyebrow.

'Yes. I've heard it several times. The old people in this community would say that there's only one thing he cannot fake.'

'And what's that?'

'We call it in the Gaelic, the *miann*. M-i-a-n-n.'

'Mee-an,' I echoed back. 'And what might that mean?'

I feel like I'm now cast as the stiff and starched George MacLeod, and that he's the Reverend Kenneth, on the brink of coming up with venison and honey.

'You could translate it as *ardent desire*,' he said. 'The ardent desire for God.

'The one thing in the human heart that the Devil cannot counterfeit, *is the ardent desire for God.*'

When the time came to leave, he asked where I was bound for in the morning.

'Up to Shawbost,' I said. 'To have a blether with . . . Doctor Finlay.'

To name the Atheist in Chief felt almost like a raising of the local demon.

'Well, he's been very busy recently, right enough!' smiled Calum. 'He's been on the radio this past week, arguing in favour of Sunday ferry sailings.'

'But I'll tell you something about Finlay,' he said, lowering his voice. 'There's more to Finlay than meets the eye.'

He explained that when he had got the call to the ministry, he'd been working in the Harris Tweed mill at the spinning machines. He'd lacked an academic background and didn't have the entry qualifications for the Free Church College. He tried to fill the gap, but failed some of the exams. He'd asked around for help, but needed lots of tutoring, and no-one had the time.

'But it was Doctor Finlay . . . and he didn't really have the time either . . . who came to my aid.

'If it hadn't been for Dr Finlay MacLeod, I wouldn't be the minister in Callanish today.'

17

SAGES OF SHAWBOST

Monday morning, day eight. It is dry outside with bright cloud and patches of sunshine. The wind is cold, having gone back into the southeast, but perfect for the twelve-mile hike north to Shawbost.

I've spent half the morning writing up my journal at the Loch Roag. Now, back on the road again, the cars are zipping past and Osprey's hood is blazing red for visibility. It takes me half an hour to get beyond the houses of Breasclete, then out onto a stretch of moorland that is etched with bygone peat workings. As I come up to the junction with the Tolsta Chaolais road a flood of lovely memories come in. This village was the birthplace of my old friend John MacGregor. He used to be the warden at the Gearrannan hostel when I'd bring my human ecology students there. He'd take us round, show us the ruins of the blackhouse where he was born, and explain the ways the village worked, the intricacies of interconnection. We'd drive on in the minibus to a lay-by. There, he'd impose a reverential silence, and with a chortle that was half in jest, half deadly serious, proclaim, 'How now, brown cow?' – and tell us of the dear old family friend that he'd buried there on the spot where she'd died.

People would be so attached to their cows. They were essential for the dairy economy, a gift of providence. A Scalpay seaman, Kenny Macleod, told me, 'I remember coming across a neighbour, who was an elder in the church, praying in his byre a couple of hours after we had buried their cow which had died in the field.' He added that people would have 'praying points' in the moor to which they'd go regularly, and that people of the generation to which John had belonged, those born in the early decades of the twentieth century, were immersed in a sense of 'total dependence on God and prayer to help with everyday things like food, safety and general activities'.[1] With some, this would play out in a very 'strict' way. Theirs could seem to be a joyless faith, thrawn with anxieties about salvation and devoid of 'worldly' song or dance. However, John was one who took things deep but with a joyous touch. The roadside shed in which he wove his Harris Tweed had a sign up outside: 'MacGregor's Boutique'. Inside, the walls were lined with whisky miniatures, and a placard that read:

> *Be not forgetful to entertain strangers: for thereby some*
> *have entertained angels unawares – Hebrews 13:2.*

One day, in the early 1990s, the stranger who came unawares was Kenneth Clarke, the Chancellor of the Exchequer in the Conservative government of John Major. He chose his length of tweed for a suit, but only after John had cut it from the roll did the politician hit that endearing hazard of Hebridean holidays: he'd left behind his wallet.

John later said to me: 'Every time I see him on the telly wearing my tweed, I turn to Pat and say: *There's the man who balances the nation's books, but comes to my Boutique for credit.*'

I miss his cheery cherry-red face, his love of stories and of passing on traditions. And I miss his generous sharings of an Islay whisky called *As We Get It* – straight 'as we get it' out of the cask, undiluted. Such was his means of bootstrapping strangers unawares into angelic orbit, and that at 103° proof.

'How now, John MacGregor?' I utter, as a toast beneath my breath, and lay down Osprey by the road end: for this was where I had my very own uranium mine.

I was sixteen at the time, doing Higher physics at school in Stornoway. One day a geology PhD student came into the lab and asked to use the Geiger counter. He'd found a chunk of extremely dense black rock, with a dull metallic sheen and some yellow encrustation. The teacher, Donald MacKay, called us all round. He held the Geiger tube above the specimen. Sure enough, the radiation meter went three-quarters up the scale. It was pitchblende. Uranium ore. And as geology was my passion, I arranged to meet up with the impending PhD the following Saturday, and took the bus to exactly where I'm standing now.

The lode lay in an exposure of coarsely crystalline quartz and feldspar pegmatite. Near on forty years have passed, but I wonder if – just for old time's sake – I can still find the spot? I jump the fence, head up to one of several bare white outcrops on the hill, and there it is! The very spot. A neatly chiselled cubic hole, some several inches square. Material evidence for what had otherwise long since taken mythical flight in my fancy. I'd not left any of the pitchblende behind, but there are still some distinctive yellow traces of gummite, a secondary mineral of uranium. Here would hardly be the spot on which to sit for over long and rest the family jewels.

These days, an ethical geologist would never countenance such vandalism of 'a find'. But that was those days, and I have to say, what fun it gave me! At least, before the day it met its end in a municipal landfill site. I made my very own nuclear safe storage facility from a sheet of lead that I'd pulled off a disused sheep dip in Keose, and melted down in one of my mother's saucepans when she was out shopping. I made a mould out of two tin cans, one inside the other. Between these, I poured the mercurial liquid; and when it hardened and I'd stripped the cans away, I was left with a cylindrical encasement that proved thick enough to block even the release of gamma rays. It worked, just pure dead brilliant.

I proudly took it with me when I went off to study geology at Aberdeen in 1973. Barrie's Cameron never had such likes to supplement his Aberdonian studies! By then, to prove the claims of my very own Manhattan Project – the making of the Hebridean bomb – I'd bought my own ex-army Geiger counter. I'd bring 'the specimen' out at parties to liven things up. I kept it in the only storage drawer we had in our tiny hall of residence bedrooms at Hillhead. We'd sit up half the night listening to music – Mike Oldfield, Moody Blues, Pink Floyd and Barclay James Harvest – the latter with those lines to 'please lay down your pistols and your rifles' and to 'concentrate on what you ought to be'. And yet, for some reason, I was being very slow at finding any girlfriends.

One day, the lass I'd spent the best part of a year trying to coax, made a solemn announcement. 'I am never coming back into your room again!

'Not until you empty the drawer beneath your bed – of that *THING*.'

A little further on, I reach a loch with a herd of Highland cattle grazing by its side, and fish farm cages floating in the middle. There's a pickup by the roadside and I recognise the number plate – *TO 1 STA* – as in Tolsta Chaolais. Sure enough, from over the brow of a hill above a hatchery shed, appears an old school acquaintance, Alastair Fraser and his son Ranald.

Their weather-beaten faces convey the seasoned character that a life spent out of doors can impart. The youth must be in his twenties, and I can sense from his bearing that he doesn't suffer from confusion as to what it means to be a man, or just a human being, and to be finding his place in the world. Their business is to raise salmon fry in fresh water, then have them lifted out by helicopter for bringing on at sea.

'How are you surviving against the multinationals?' I ask.

'No problem,' Alastair replies. His father was 'Doc Fraser' – one of the best science teachers I'd ever had.

'We don't use chemicals. Never used them. Chemicals always let you down in the end. Good water flow and moderate stocking levels is the answer.'

The big companies, he explains, are greedy. That's why they get trouble. As far as possible his operation is organic. That gives a niche cost structure that makes it pay.

The two of them get back to work, I move on, but I'm struck by how the young man, who'd hardly said a word, had been so attentive to every nuance that had passed between us. I hear the old folks lament that the spirit of the past is dying out. Even we of my generation, after every village funeral we'll say to one another: 'There'll soon be no more of them left.' And we're right. There won't be. Not unless we pick up the baton and pass the spirit on, pass on the touch of blessing.

'How now, brown cow?' Don't forget what ground you're standing on. The game's not up quite yet.

I pass through Carloway, and up a long slow hill towards the Dalmore junction. Once the village in the glen down there hosted Teampall Dail Mòr. Its stones were robbed to build a house, sometime after the start of the Great War. Doctor Finlay's guidebook says: 'Between the two wars visitors came to seek it out, but the man next door told them, *Gone . . . Gone . . .*'

'Gone indeed,' adds Finlay, laconically.

Aye, Teampall Dail Mòr. Sacred to the memory of what was.

Onwards, and I'm coming in to Finlay's village, *Siabost* or Shawbost. A quick check on the phone, and its only half past four. There's time enough to drop in on my old friend, Kenny 'Leather'. He's an artisan, by his original trade, in all things made from hide.

It's always such a joy to visit Kenny, that I half skip down the brae and into the dip beside the bridge where he lives. His croft is a patchwork of feannagan. The West Side has a better microclimate than where I've come from. Everywhere is planted out with cabbage drills, potato plots, flower beds and native tree nurseries. Threaded through them all is an eat-your-heart-out-Donald-Trump nine-hole golf course. On Google Earth it's even visible from space.

I knock three times upon the cottage door. There's some slow shuf-flings, the latch lifts, and a sleepy Kenny squints out through a narrow chink into the daylight. The poor man's been working the milk run on early morning shift, and I've woken him up.

'Alastair!' he roars, his beard wagging ivy trails. 'It'll be yourself! Wait till I get some clothes on. You go in and sit down by the stove.'

Soon the Raeburn is stoked up with peats and a whistling kettle set to boil. By many standards, Kenny lives in semi-poverty, surrounded by his tools and a few sturdy handbags and satchels for sale to passing tourists. But the leather-man doesn't do poverty. He does dignified frugality. Sufficiency without the need for surplus.

He offers me his best reclining seat. It's an antique dentist's chair with all the wheels and levers working. You have to mind out what he presses, especially – as I know from experience – when you're raising a tumbler of the amber liquid to your lips.

'And your pack?' he asks. 'You're hitch-hiking?'

'No. Walking. The sheilings, the temples, and the holy wells. You see, Kenny, I'm on a *holy pilgrimage!* Immersed in *God, war* and the *faeries*, the way one does, as you'll so eminently understand.'

Kenny wouldn't have much time for the Manhattan Project, but all the time of day for a mad hatter. 'I'm on my way to Doctor Finlay's, then this evening, up to Bragar to meet Catriona Campbell at the temple of Saint John.'

He lowers his voice to ceremonial register and sagely strokes the ivy. 'Ah . . . Teampall Eòin . . . or Cill Sgàire they also call it, from the Norse. You've not been there? I think that you will find it a very special place.

'And the wells, Alastair? You have been visiting the healing wells?'

'Only one so far,' and I tell him of the tussle with the Bog Monster.

'A rare privilege. A rare privilege, indeed! But it does not surprise me. You see, we have reached a time in history for the old wells to reopen. And they will be reopened. And some of them are *already* being reopened.'

The kettle starts to coo. He makes the tea, draws his chair more closely in, and shares experience.

In the 1970s, more than thirty years ago, he'd been an auxiliary nurse in the Lewis Hospital. In those days a special fridge of industrial propor-tions was kept in the duty room. It stored all manner of local delicacies: *Marag dhubh* – black pudding made from oatmeal and sheep's blood; *ceann cropaig* – from oatmeal and a cod's liver, stuffed inside its head; salted *guga* – from when the Ness boys would come back ashore with their haul from the annual gannet hunt. Most of the in-patients had come in from the country. Their convalescence happened quicker when they could have their own kind of food. But the fridge was also full of lemonade bottles. Each was labelled with the patient's name, and filled with water from their favourite spring or well.

'These days, they'd have rules and regulations, and we'd never get away with it,' he says. 'But the country people wanted what they thought of as the *beneficial qualities* of the water. That was always their expression. The 'beneficial qualities' for 'the health'.

It had taken just a single decade – from the late 1970s to the late 1980s – for the most recent wave of modernity to sweep the island. Television, that came in the decade before, would have had a lot to do with it. You'd see people chopping up beautiful old furniture for firewood. In the place of bespoke pieces that had been handed down through the family for generations, they'd buy a three-piece suite from a catalogue.

'It all happened so very quickly,' he says. 'As if they just flicked off one switch, and turned on another.'

I mention the island proverb: *A lot went out with the horse.*

'Absolutely, Alastair! People thought they'd just exchange the horse for the tractor. They never realised all the linkages they'd lose.

'They'd get a loan to buy the tractor. Then a job to pay the loan. And now we're wondering why we've no longer got the same time for each other.'

Nobody, he's careful to say, would want to go back to the hard old ways again. 'But we all know that something isn't right. We see it in the kids. A change has come about that we hardly understood before it was too late. You'll still find plenty here that's lost elsewhere, but there's not the same connections any more. People think it hasn't hit them: until one day, they might find they're standing very much alone.'

It's time now for me to leave Kenny alone, to move on up to Finlay's.

'But, the wells,' I ask. 'You said they're coming back?'

'It's a remarkable thing,' he replies, 'but in this last five years, as I've gone from door to door on my milk round, meeting a complete cross-section of the island, I've heard more people talk about old wells than in the whole of the rest of my life.

'You see, people are yearning for a connection with the past. Wanting to bring back control into their lives.

'So, yes. There's been people opening up their wells again and drawing water. Some want it for making their tea without all the treatment chemicals. And I'll tell you something else. I'm noticing, these days, that whenever people hear about a neighbour reopening a well, they get excited.

'Very excited indeed.'

Leaving Kenny's cottage, I cross the bridge and make my way uphill past hayfields edged by dry-stone walls. Twenty minutes further on, I turn up to the left, and a familiar stout figure strides out from a bungalow to greet me in the middle of the road.

'Welcome, pilgrim traveller!' hollers a beaming Doctor Finlay.

'A little *dance*, perhaps?' And then, dropping his voice to a wickedly conspiratorial tone: 'Let us dance *deiseil* around one another . . . and make sure that everybody in the village . . . is watching!'

We perform a little sunwise jig, just to show that paganism is alive and well. And we're laughing at our own ridiculousness. In my mind, at least, we're imagining the twitching of net curtains. For while God sees everything, the neighbours miss nothing.

Finlay's eyes play impishly behind the glasses of his full and rounded face. Recently retired from a career pioneering Gaelic television – helping the community to swing with change, but not to lose its footing – his much-feted atheism is expressed in a sticker on his car. The fish symbol of early Christianity is sprouting legs. It sports the caption: *Darwin*.

'Come on inside for something to eat,' he says, 'then we'll go and walk the land.'

The kitchen table is set with a ham salad and a bottle of red wine. His wife, Norma, is heading over to Callanish for a community gathering. I eat ravenously, and without lingering for a second glass, we step back out and into the softly settling mood of an early summer's evening.

The wind has fallen to a whisper. Children's voices jingle through the village and mingle with the lowing of cattle and the yakking of a sheep dog. Now and then we hear a mother's call, or the dying phut-phut-phut of a tractor being rested for the night. You feel that everybody's either here, or coming home. A sense that the village is complete, like the stillness when the flood tide reaches its high water mark.

We wander slowly through a flower-filled maze of pocket handkerchief pastures. These have supported human life for nigh on nine thousand years, yet still retain their soil in best of heart.

All around us are the markings out of time. The wire-mesh fences that go back for up to fifty years, and a thrush singing from the strand of twisted barbs that run along on top. The easygoing dry-stone walls, long sagged into the contours of the land. Rabbits have their warrens there and starlings tend their nests. Everywhere are heaps of rock and ruins tracing outlines under turf. These rest anonymous, except to those who carry their keys of meaning.

We wander over wobbling stiles and through ramshackle creaking gates. Finlay doesn't say a lot. He shows, and knows he's opened quite sufficient doors for me to walk through in this passing hour.

After a while, I tell him about the rediscovery of Tobar a' Ghobha at Leac a Lì. He's intrigued by the ambiguity of the map reference. It might be an error on his behalf, but it could also be cross-currents of tradition. His informant had been an old man in the village. Whatever the historical truth of the matter, he delights at the thought that the confusion had led to my encounter with the 'three wise women', as Jessie, Anne and Morag have become to me.

'You see,' he says, 'these wells grow over and close up so very quickly if they're not kept clean. The decade that Kenny Leather spoke to you about – the seventies through into the eighties – that alone was enough for many to have been lost. And yet, they mean such a lot to people.'

'How come?' I ask. 'If they mean something, people let them fall into neglect?'

'Because they'd not have wanted to take on the maintenance themselves,' he says.

The fashions of this day and age would have made them feel self-conscious. They'd be afraid of people wondering why they were digging around on somebody else's croft. In the past, people weren't so proprietorial. It would have been quite normal.

'But today?'

'It would be thought of as a strange obsession.' And he looked down to the ground, and shook his head.

'The women who you spoke to, they'd have felt a need within themselves, but they'd have lacked the justification of necessity to do what you could do.'

'So . . . you're saying that they were able to hide behind me?'

'Quite so – because you're a stranger to the village, but not a total stranger since you have island connections. When you turned up, you could be the key to unlock something that was already in the background of their minds.

'And just you watch . . . they'll probably be over that fence when nobody's looking . . . with a cup in hand to take a *deoch*!'

I'm curious as to why Finlay has it in for religion. He seems to me bestowed with such spiritual acuity.

It's not so much religion in itself, he says. 'It's more the psychology by which, on this island, it was used to manipulate the people's minds and maintain social control.'

In the past, his people would have considered the characters in the Bible to have been completely historical. They had no concept that large parts of the story might best be understood as metaphor. They heard the stories, and made sense of them in ways that they could interpret through their own lives.

'For them, the fear of Hell that Lady Mary's hand-picked evangelicals played on was very real indeed.' It had trampled over the simple sensitivity of what had been before.

We come up onto the brow of a hill. Here the evening light slings our shadows far across the grass, like men with standing stones attached. This is the eighteenth day of May, a mere five weeks from solstice. The sun is setting almost due north-west. At night it dips for just seven hours beneath the sea, and only when it's due full north is total darkness fleetingly achieved.

He raises up his arm, and points across the bay. Above the boulder beach, I see the walls around a vast village cemetery. I'm due to meet Catriona Campbell by its gates in half an hour.

The thin light catches face-on to the lichen-whitened headstones. Even from this distance, they shine like ruddy navigation beacons.

'There it is,' Finlay whispers, as we focus on a huddle of illuminated walls and gable ends that have survived against the winter gales.

'There is Cill Sgàire or Teampall Eòin. Some say Saint John the Evangelist, but in Ronald Black's view, the dedication is probably to Saint John the Baptist.'

The archaeologists, he says, reckon that it's fifteenth century. However, there is so much work still waiting to be done. What we can see today will rest on layers and layers of what was there before. 'Layers and layers of meaning and interpretation, that say different things to many different people.

'Layers and layers and layers,' he muses.

'Sometimes in these places, all that's left are the places themselves.' The history has otherwise all gone. 'We'll never get to the bottom of it all. Never at all.'

What matters, he suggests to me, is what comes into the mind. The imaginative possibilities. 'The layers of stories that weave through time, and how these speak to us today.'

The wind has dropped away completely. It leaves only residues of ripples, fading on the ocean's surface.

'*Teampall Eòin.*' He rolls the Gaelic sounds beneath his breath. '*Teampall Eòin,*' he repeats, so tenderly.

I'm thinking of that wild man of the desert, John the Baptist.[2]

If you have two coats, give one to whosoever has got none.

And John the Evangelist.

God is love.

A flock of oystercatchers rise and cut across our line of vision.

Red bills, white crosses flashing on their backs when veered in flight.

The servant bird of Bridgit – *gille-brighde* in the Gaelic.

They're shifting over from the shore to evening fields.

U-vil, u-vil – I hear their winnowing call.

U-vil, u-vil – a blessing on the wing.

U-vil – u-vil – u-vil.

18

FLÉCHETTES IN THE SOUL

The island's pre-Reformation *teampaill* or 'temples' probably had much the same purpose as similar tiny chapels across Europe. They would be repositories for chalices, perhaps an icon, the cross or a statue of the Blessed Virgin. In France, Vérène and I have seen them used by peasant folk who might drop in for solitude and prayer. On the feast day of the patron saint, or at times of regional pilgrimages, mass might be celebrated on the grass outside as there would rarely be sufficient room to fit everyone under the roof.

Teampall Eòin is only some ten paces in length. Martin Martin, writing around 1695, confirms that such Hebridean sites were, indeed, the focus of pilgrimages and special festivals. These continued until the Presbyterian clergy were able to introduce a more instructional basis of religious observance. This had the sermon as its focal point, being of the preaching rather than the contemplative tradition. However, the old ways were deep rooted. Even as late as 1630, an English naval captain who had been sent to map Lewis and Harris was able to report to the Privy Council of Charles I:[1]

> In theire religion they are very ignorant and have been given to the idolatrous worship of divers saints as doth appeare by theire Chappells which are yet to bee seene.

In other words, he had yet to see these saintly apparitions, and didn't harbour any great expectations. But I'm in luck. Catriona Campbell with her daughter, Peigi Ann, were to be seen appearing as I'd trudged across the beach and onto the *machair* – the sandy coastal pasture that is characteristic of the West Side.

I first met Catriona in association with Doctor Finlay, through their opposition to the proposed wind farm in north Lewis. The issue had split green groups down the middle. It had divided me within myself. On the one hand, our society desperately needs to decarbonise its energy supply. Think of Bangladesh. Think of parts of the Hebrides, so vulnerable to the sea level and storm surges. On the other hand, Great Britain is an energy-profligate country. We're bloated by consumerism and entertained by wars. Do we have to wreck the very beauty that can inspire a little care for the world?

In the midst of all this hand-wringing, Catriona put a powerful letter in the *Stornoway Gazette*. It spoke about indigenous identity and belonging. About the people and their place. Their *dualchas,* or cultural heritage, and how that rests upon their *dùthchas* as heritage in the land. I was very moved. I sent her a copy of *Soil and Soul*. She wrote back and said, 'Come and let me show you why the moor means so much to us.'

Last summer, with Anne, her artist and archaeologist sister, and little Peigi Ann, Vérène and I had hiked for several hours into the heart of the Barvas moor. We'd been taken to see their family sheiling. It was a small stone hut on a piece of raised and drier ground. Where the turf and rafter roof had partly collapsed, an incongruous blue tarpaulin could be temporarily pulled over improvised bare rafters. We made a peat fire in the middle of the floor, brewed tea in a chipped enamel kettle, and were enraptured listening to the sisters share their memories.

By their childhoods, around the 1970s, the family no longer had to go there for their cattle's summer grazings. Instead, and in the era before flying off to the sun, they went purely for the love of it. Catriona showed us a picture of their father, Kenneth, crouched outside the door, taken when the roof was still intact. His face was weathered with the rills of kindness. His whole bearing, of one substance with the stones.

Peigi Ann made Vérène and me lie down on the ground beside the door jamb, and examine its foundation stone. Chiselled on its surface was a deer with antlers, simple, like cave art. They knew not its story nor its age. Catriona just smiled, and said: 'We've been here for hundreds if not thousands of years.'

We talk very little as we walk, the three of us, amongst the ruins of Teampall Eòin. It sits within a partly walled enclosure. There is a nave, where the people would have stood, and a chancel for the altar. If you didn't know otherwise, you'd think it just another blackhouse ruin, although some of the stonework is superb. To Catriona and Peigi Ann, it evokes mystery and contemplation, a sacred place; and that, for all that their Free Church backgrounds might query such a notion.

The child leads me to the headstone of her twice-great-grandmother. Cut to an arched shape, it reflects what was by then the emerging modern mode. She describes it to me, coyly but observantly, as a 'rich one'. It stands out, but not sufficiently to be out of place, amongst its neighbouring uncut and unmarked stones. Many dozens of these poke above the grass, mostly less than knee height. Row upon humble row, they huddle round the temple, like figures warming round a hearth. The first time I ever saw such abject simplicity was at a famine cemetery in a field in County Mayo. To myself, I call them 'plainsong' headstones. Each speaks with such a rawness that they rend the heart. They're like notes dropped out of nowhere in those monophonic chants that the Gregorians revitalised, but which have Galician connections from the Celtic world of Santiago de Compostela. Links back to the underlying undivided church.

Set further back, and slightly higher up the slope, stands another wave of stones. These, too, are heartrending, but this time crisply cut from silver granite. These are the war graves that leave their footnotes in so many island cemeteries. Those with an Admiralty anchor mark a seaman's loss. To islanders, the symbol brings to mind a text from Hebrews: 'There is a hope both strong and steadfast which is the anchor of my soul.'

One bears the inscription:

> A sailor of the
> 1939–1945 War
> Known Unto God

It brings a tear into my eye. When you stop and think about it, what life is any life, if not so known in some way?

Most have laconic epigraphs, chosen by their families and inscribed along the bottom. Often these are lines of scripture, but Catriona calls to me – 'Come over and see this one.'

It is the resting place of Private Colin MacDonald of the 28th Seaforth Highlanders. Deaf Mackenzie's regiment. Killed in action – 1916 – in God-only-knows what hell-hole of that European tribal war. The inscription?

> To the memory
> Of my beloved son
> Whose death I deeply deplore

And all Catriona says is: 'How's that, for a statement about war?'

The island author, Calum Ferguson, who was born midway between the world wars, has written: 'From a very early age, I was conscious of having entered a world grief-stricken and still reeling from the war's seemingly never-ending punishment.'[2]

That world continued into my childhood. It was normal for us to see village women, and not particularly elderly, clad constantly in black. The wars, the sinking of the *Iolaire* and the departure of the *Metagama*, had left behind a generation of widows or spinsters. The world had, indeed, as J.M. Barrie warned in 1922, doddered down the brimstone path. Their sons or lovers in the lava had had the spring ripped from their year. It is salutary to remember that, even to this day, some of the eldest in this community turn out their lights each night with thoughts of how it might have been. How it might have been to have lived their lives with those whose lights went out forever. Lest we forget.

When the time came for my friends to leave, Peigi Ann handed me a brown paper bag with two freshly laid eggs. 'They're for your breakfast, from our own hens,' she said, and said so ever so brightly. 'We'd have brought you more, but thought you wouldn't want to carry much.'

They left me there, refreshed of spirit, at the Temple of Saint John. They left as soft at foot as they had come. I stood awhile, and watched them go. Meandering up the track beside a field fresh sown in sandy soil with barley. I stared, until they dipped below the brow, these people of the sheiling of the deer. A doe that sauntered between worlds, her calf following.

I turned, leaned on the cemetery wall, and watched the dying of the day. The sun dropped down across the bay and melted to a blazing Celtic cross. It stretched a golden shaft towards me at the temple, then slowly slipped between the covers of the sea.

I pitched my tent outside the cemetery walls. Soon I was fast asleep. Every other night had been completely dreamless. This night was different. I dreamt a dream that strangely had no images. Just words, and those, a single phrase that echoed on and on, like waves that flopped and lapped around the caverns of my mind.

There is a lot of love in this community.

Tuesday, day nine, and my next destination is Teampall Mhoire – the Temple of the Blessed Virgin Mary. I am making breakfast, sheltering snugly in the lee of Teampall Eòin. I'm boiling the Campbells' eggs in water that I'll then use for the tea, when, who should pop his head around the wall, but Doctor Finlay.

'I thought you'd like some sandwiches for the day,' he beams, so happy to have found me, and holding out a package wrapped in greaseproof paper. 'Also, if you've time before you go, I thought you might like to see the site of Fuaran Buaile Dhòmhnaill.'

We wander up the side of a stream, really more of a ditch, until we come to a spring line. It shows as a boggy zone with reddish-yellow staining where iron-rich water has seeped to the surface.

'Here was the Yellow Spring of Donald,' he said. It would probably have served the temple, and was said to cure toothache, but around 1980 somebody unwittingly ran a digger through the site.

'And now it's gone, Alastair. Gone, gone . . . just like so many of them.'

We wander down to the seashore. He stoops beside a boulder, and pulls aside the seaweed. It's partly hollowed, scooped out like the bowl of a lute.

'And what do you make of this?'

It was a Stone Age quern for hand-grinding corn, washed out from the soil by the encroaching sea in a storm a few years back. 'You see, Alastair,' he says, bringing back Catriona's words, 'people have been living here for a very long time.'

I ask him about Teampall Mhoire. He says, 'It's wonderful!' But I shouldn't expect to see anything. Remarkably, for such a remote edge of the western world, on 27 May 1403 the Pope in Rome addressed a letter 'to all the Christian faithful'. It was for 'granting an indulgence to visitors of the church of Saint Mary in Barvas in the Isle of Lewis, diocese of Sodor, on certain feast days and those who contribute to its reparation'.[3]

The walls and the baptismal font were still visible when visited in 1803 by the sheep farmer, James Hogg – the 'Ettrick Shepherd', or as Wordsworth had eulogised him, 'the mighty Minstrel'. He, whose *Bonnie Kilmeny* pulled together and preserved such a rich mélange of the old faerie lore, and to whom the temple was 'an ancient place of Popish worship'. By the time that T.S. Muir arrived in 1861, everything had disappeared beneath the sands of drifting dunes.

'And do you think, one day, the sands might *un-drift* themselves?' I asked, ever hopeful.

'They might,' Finlay said, with a prankish twinkle to his eye.

'You know, it would make a *great project* for an *archaeological dig*.

'Yes, that would bring it back.'

*   *   *

It's half an hour off noon, and only now am I heading up across the hill, towards the phantom of Saint Mary's Temple. Last night, Catriona had advised me to follow a line of posts that the community had put in to mark the coastal way. Eventually, you come to a little river. It cuts deep through the sand. The bed is always changing shape and the sides, sharp and slimy. 'Be careful,' she had warned. Looking at the map, I couldn't say which of several possible candidates she'd meant, but in my mind it had become Slime River.

I'd loved it, that intense flurry of human company, but now it's good to be alone and out in nature once again. Today's a day of sparkling seas and puffy white clouds. It's a wee bit darker on the far horizon. The weather is warmer here, by the ocean, than it was in the hills. The machair is bright green from the lime-rich shell sand that's carried on the wind. Everywhere is carpeted with yellow buttons of 'spring messenger' – the lesser celandine. There's even clumps of primrose breaking into flower on some of the more cloistered banks.

More than anything, today I've moved into a world of birds. The air's alive with eider, mallard, cormorant, guillemot and fulmar. The wind, that has returned since last night's calm, is singing with the mew of curlews and the long drawn-out pee-wit of lapwings. Below the cliffs, on sandy beaches spread between jutting rock outcrops, I see flocks of waders – redshanks, sandpipers and goodness knows what else – running up and down at every wave. They teeter, trill and pipe, excited as they dash to grab their fill of tiny crabs and sprats.

Far out to sea, the saffron-throated gannets climb, and plane, and plunge as headlong thunderbolts that spear into the shoals of fish beneath the great Atlantic's ceaseless swell. And everywhere, those wheeling gulls. So many different seagulls. These are, said Kenneth Macleod, 'the carrier between the Land-under-Waves and the Land-of-the-Living.' That explains the white gull on his stained glass window in the Gigha church. The fishermen of Barra call the Western Ocean, *Cuile Mhoire*, the Virgin Mary's Treasury.[4] He deeply loved that sense of feminine divinity, not sentimentalised, but as the tradition saw it, a living truth of nature.

Some of these cliffs are maybe sixty foot. I'm feeling blissfully happy as I almost bounce along their tops. It was the same on the road yesterday. It came upon me several times, fleeting but distinctively. I'd find myself, as it were, looking at myself with a transcendent clarity. It was as if the me was watching me, but from a place of more than me. Neil Gunn, the Highland writer, described the same when shelling hazelnuts as a boy. He was sitting on a river boulder and, 'I came upon myself sitting there.'[5] His experience was 'transitory, evanescent'. Mine too. I'd feel an expansive warmth come on, reach out to clutch for more, and in so doing snapped the ego self back stolidly in place.

I drop down towards a brackish lagoon, Loch Arnol, and crunch along the narrow bank of pebbles that are all that separates it from the sea. A rapid change has come into the air. Those earlier hints of darkness on the horizon have thickened up to heavy cloud, fast closing in. Looks like it's going to be a squally patch. Up I climb again, on to the next headland and over rows and rows of old feannagan. The strips of crofts of Arnol stretch inland to my right. These days, the village's conserved blackhouse is a honey pot for tourists and historians. I stop and watch four camper vans nosing around each other. They're all trying to get parked, or unparked, on the single-track road, like over-fed dodgems in a fairground. As I'm smiling to myself, a man comes out of the museum. He strides down to the road's end and strikes out across the headland in front of me. He's got the heather loup – not walking like a tourist – and his cap's more flat than woolly.

The first drop of rain splats my cheek. Out come the waterproofs and up goes Osprey's hood. Half an hour further on, I meet the man returning. By now, it's bucketing. He doesn't have a hood, but seems not at all put out. We stop to make acquaintance. He works as a guide in the visitor centre. Slightly built, silvering hair, this is Donald Morrison. Come rain or shine, he always likes to take a lunchtime stroll.

Where am I going? Teampall Mhoire, I reply – as if such a destination is just the done thing – and then, another three miles on to camp for the night at the foot of his own village, Siadar or Shader in the English. There I want to visit Teampall Pheadair, Saint Peter's Temple. According to Finlay, some of the old people knew it as Teampall Phàdraig after Saint Patrick. He said that Peter and Patrick are equivalents in Gaelic. I'm going to follow the old folks with Phàdraig. Not least, that will help to differentiate it in my mind from another Teampall Pheadair that I hope to visit further north, at Swainbost.

Oblivious to the downpour, evidently genetically programmed to withstand 'total immersion', Donald settles in and starts telling me all about this ancient sacred site on the edge of his village. You must have water at places where people will gather, and Phàdraig once had three sources. There was Fuaran an Dèididh, right down by the shore. 'That one was the cure for the toothache,' he says, 'and you would not drink from that well unless you really needed to go there for *the treatment*. It was only used for that purpose.' Unfortunately, it has now collapsed into the sea. Thank God, I think wryly to myself, for dentistry.

Then there was Tobar Anndrais – Saint Andrew's Well. That's also, sadly, past tense. It was on a croft just north of the temple, and was believed to have the power to predict whether a sick person would live or die. If a wooden dish was floated on the surface and rotated sunwise – rejoice, rejoice! If, however, it spun in the opposite direction – alas, alas. But that's all gone now. Andrew's watering place was lost when somebody – he'd rather not say who – used it for a fencepost socket, and filled it in with stones.

The last surviving of the three is Tobar Mhoire, Saint Mary's Well. That's immediately across the road, just where it comes down from the village and bends sharply, passing closest to the temple.

'A little while ago,' he says, 'we restored it for the village. It was for the *historical* interest.'

I nod, in understanding at the rationale. They made a stone tablet to display its name, 'for the visitors'. Some of the village men go down from time to time to keep it clear of weeds.

'And how are these wells thought of in the village today?' I ask.

'The present generation . . .' he says, making a careful choice of his words, '. . . would mostly view them . . . *as superstitions.*'

'And the generation before the present?'

'Oh, that was very different! My father's generation held them . . . *in reverence.*'

I've now moved on, and come upon another beach, just before you get to Barvas. I'm hungry, looking for a nice spot to enjoy Finlay's sandwiches as the weather starts to lift. I'd dropped his name, of course, to Donald. That led us on to *atheism.* It kind of fitted with the pouring rain, and I was amused by his parting words: 'Finlay's more a Christian than he's pretending not to be.'

Well, I'm not quibbling. As far as I'm concerned, with his ham sandwich in hand, Finlay's just about to feed one of the five thousand. The only trouble is, after all these days of abstinence, I'm starting to crave greens. Sometimes when your body needs it, you yearn for the kail in ways that aren't just metaphorical. He and Norma can't have had any lettuce in the house.

But oh my, oh my! – I just can't believe what I've just stumbled on. Here I am. Walking through a bed of sea-tossed pebbles, the size of cricket balls. Each is varnished by the drizzle. With the light now perking up, it's bringing out their mottled whirls of quartz on grey and black, their little flecks of pink and green. And there. Right there, before my very eyes – sprung like Brighde's fern back at the sheiling, from out amongst the stones no less – is *manna* from the heavens. The elongated heart-shaped leaves, the succulent fresh shoots, of a wild-grown clump of sorrel.

Wow! Give it just a thousand years, and see how they'll tell that one of Saint Finlay.

The 'cuckoo's meat' it's called in some parts – an early sign that summer's come. Before doing anything else, I take out the camera and snap a picture. If I didn't have the evidence, but was asked to give another talk in Falkland, then woe betide! Earth Mother would not otherwise believe that stones had turned to veg.

Leaf by leaf I pluck a bunch, layer it in amongst the ham, and munch upon the crispy lemon tang. Blessed be! The saint of Mary's Temple would appreciate that grace. Then off again – on across another narrow shingle fringe that leads to Barvas beach and Loch Mòr Bharabhais. The rain's gone off, the wind's swung round south-west, and the cemetery that marks the temple site is coming into view. I see its wall above the grassy plain, about a mile away. There's a sand quarry in the dunes, and two lorries trundle lazily to take their fill. A solitary digger nods its brainless head.

The machair here is absolutely flat. It doubles as a part-time army firing range. At school, the West Side boys impressed the rest of us by turning up with live rounds that they'd scavenged. They'd tell of lurid practical jokes that typically resulted in some poor victim's peat fire going bang.

The firing points step back, a line of mounds across my path. Each is exactly a hundred yards apart, extending for about a third of a mile. The cadets would aim at cardboard human cut-outs on the target butt. Red flags when firing signify a two-mile marine exclusion zone. If nothing else, the lobsters get a break from being potted.

In our day, the firing would be all with open sights. You had to have a steady hand to hit a human engine room from full six hundred yards. We were raised to consider telescopic sights unsporting. These days, however, they're all the rage – and not least so, for seeing God.

No kidding! In America, the ABC news channel has had under investigation precisely such a capability in standard issue rifle sights. *Trijicon*, a Michigan arms manufacturer, was founded by a devout Christian from South Africa. The catch line of the company is *Brilliant Aiming*

Solutions™. 'That's mine!' They supply the Pentagon alone with 800,000 sights a year for the troops in Iraq and Afghanistan. Somewhat to the horror of the military, once it was found out, each is engraved with a Bible verse coded into its model number.[6] Number ACOG6X48PSA27:1 is currently on issue to the British infantry. Those last seven characters, refer to Psalm 27:1.

'The Lord is my light and my salvation. Whom shall I fear?'

And whom, indeed? *Chirp-chirp.*

I'm now right in the range's line of fire. It's late afternoon, the rumbling lorries and the weary digger are calling it a day. I go up to inspect the butt. It's burrowed through with rabbits, and looks as if it might be now disused. I, too, do a little burrowing in the sand. Half wondering if I might unearth a spent bullet, or a brass cartridge case for a souvenir, for old time's sake – and then – for goodness sake!

Why should I even think of wanting such a souvenir?

War worms its way so readily into the minds of boys and men. A while ago, I was speaking at a military base and my host, let's call him Tom, was a half-colonel who'd just come back from duty in Iraq. He had some family connections to Lewis. We'd chewed the cud the night before and, while waiting to give my lecture, we had a bit of time to kill. He asked me if I'd like to see the museum of munitions.

He got the clearance, got it unlocked, and inside was every manner of warhead and projectile. Each was – in the engineering sense of the term – 'exploded', so as to show the brilliant logic of their ballistics, their vehemence of kinetics. Many of the lighter units of ammunition – not least, the cluster bombs – were filled with tiny barbed arrows, the size of fountain pen nibs, called *fléchettes*. These lacerate soft tissue in every way that cruelty could imagine.

One type of shell, the 'beehive round', contains hundreds of fluted fléchettes that emit a spooky drone when zipping through the air. The idea is that those it doesn't kill are left instilled with shell-shock. Another, the 'pyrophoric' fléchette, is coated with phosphorus to ignite in flight by atmospheric friction. Then the DIACBA: Direct Injection Antipersonnel Chemical Biological Agents. This was developed by the US Army in the 1950s, grooved to carry such pathogens as anthrax spores or Botulinum toxin into a soldier's shredded flesh.[7] The US has unilaterally ended its biological weapons programme, but the Taliban have cottoned on. They lace the shrapnel for their roadside bombs with dog shit, or pus squeezed from septic wounds, to spread infection to the mained.

The museum had a table where a cocktail of fléchettes were displayed in little bowls, like nibbles at a party. I ran my fingers through them. They felt like fish hooks, but with an Orc-like aura. Lustrous alloys – black, bronze, and where rich in titanium for super-penetrative hardness, Payne's grey.

I drew out a pinch between my thumb and index finger. I felt their skewer points, their skiver edges, their jagged little daggers. 'This is the reality of war,' I thought. But what struck me most disturbingly, was their quasi-pornographic vice. They held a grip of fascination, even on my so-called pacifist mind.

I released my fingers. Let them drop. They plinked back into the bowl.

It was Tom who broke the silence.

'I thought you were going to ask if you could take some as a souvenir.'

'I nearly did,' I admitted, 'but then I thought, a souvenir of what?'

I knew he understood. We'd struck a common chord.

'Actually, Tom, I've been wondering if there's something I might ask. 'Did you ever kill when in Iraq?'

It had been in the Euphrates marshes. Clearing out remaining pockets of Saddam's men. He'd not done so directly, but had administered commands to guys who pulled the triggers and pressed the lethal buttons.

'Same difference, really.'

'And, can I ask? How does it leave you, now?'

In my mind I had the soldier who has come back home, and everyone at the party is grooving to Echo and the Bunnymen, but his mind's back into the firefight. Back to what was oh so very *real*. And nobody else quite understands. And his children know he's different: where's Daddy?[8]

'I notice three things . . .' began Tom. And God knows – I can't help but feel an admiration, indeed, affection for these men. Their sense of community. Their ethic of looking out for one another. The research that shows that most don't want to kill, they want to protect, and that's a form of love. Even young Harrier. Maybe, especially, Harrier.

There's something happens when a man comes face to face with Hell. It burns away the bullshit. It betrays the plastic world that passes for normality in all its crass vacuity.

'I notice,' repeated Tom, 'that I don't sleep so well. I get irritable more quickly. And I *feel the cold* more easily than I used to.'

Dante had described Hell's inner circle not as hot, but frozen.

I asked him what had been his proudest moment.

A pocket of the enemy was dug into a foxhole, hiding in the reed beds. The lads had itchy fingers and wanted the green light to blast them out. But the reconnaissance had suggested that such a lethal course of action might be avoidable.

Tom stopped them from opening fire. He said that he was glad to have that memory. It left him with a souvenir of those whose lives he could have taken, but chose otherwise.

We all take up positions on a long front. None of us can quite see how it looks from the next person's post. That's how I reconcile my differences with the military. Rarely does a human being get to glimpse full compass of the battlefield of life.

'Sounds to me, Tom,' I said that day as we parted, 'like you opted for the God's-eye view.'

I've left the rifle range and am edging towards the end of the plain. A stream meanders sluggishly to the sea along the base of the sand dunes. I can see some dried-out ox-bow arcs where it must have changed its course from time to time. And I know where I've got to. Slime River.

I'm not feeling great. Hope it's not a bug coming on. I'd felt a touch of something much the same this morning when coming up to Loch Arnol. A changing not just of the outer weather, but of the inner too. A kind of icky rawness, as if my stomach's being lightly sucked at by a pump.

When crossing the river that came out of Loch Barvas, I'd stopped and had a few casts, since the wind had changed. Hooked a salmon parr straight through the eye. Killed it, rather than to throw it back like that, and then there was another that I wrongly kept, just to help make up a meal – quite forgetting that I already had my cold kipper. On Voshimid, Cameron had told Simon that the trout landed in his boat had 'given themselves'. Mine didn't feel that way. 'It was as though some crime lay on my soul,' wrote Dostoevsky.[9] So much for the poacher! Left me musing that, in a way, we're all poachers in the flow of life. None of us, or very few at any rate, complete the cycles of gratitude and right relationships that open up to greater depths of being. That's what Jung was getting at when he said we've all got a shadow side. But the problem, said this visionary son of a Swiss Calvinist preacher, isn't that the shadow's there. The problem's when we deny it. When we fail to understand it as our psychological compost, our karmic burden, 'sin' as work-in-progress, and so we trip up on the bucket.

Set in this light, 'The fire of Hell,' says one of the many awesome Russian Orthodox thinkers, 'is the fire of love that gives remorse a terrible clarity.'[10] It only burns off encrustations of the ego, only strips away what's not most truly us.

That's the paradox that I see in many of the military too. They've been there, seen and even done terrible things, but mostly don't deny complicity. It can open up a truthfulness, a forgiveness, even, a re-articulation to the inner life.

In *The Brothers Karamazov*, Dostoevsky's saintly Father Zosima says we're all responsible for one another's crimes. 'No man on this earth can sit in judgement over other men until he realises that he too is just such a criminal.' We can't just carry on projecting shadow onto others – good state or bad state; with us or against us; the Elect or the Damned. The truth of interconnection is that we're all bound in with one another, with everything. 'However mad this may appear, it is the truth,' insists the Russian monk. 'Believe this, believe this implicitly, because therein is contained all the hope and all the faith of the saints.'[11]

I had taken out the stove, cooked and ate the two little fish, just to close the circle. Truly, all this walking, walking, walking. The fishes were just the coin that edges up the lid on things one hardly knows are there. Old fléchettes, long buried in the soul, that now and then turn in their cocoons, and leak a little toxin from their grooves.

And I'm standing by Slime River now. The green is just the algae that attaches to its white sand sides. It's just another little river, doing what a little river does when pushing to the sea. The digger has scooped out the dunes across the other side. The wind has finished off the job and left them flayed, like winding sheets that drape across the machair's edge. I climb up to the top, beyond the excavations, and walk towards the temple's cemetery. This ground was used for burials until perhaps a century ago. The grass is speckled through with plainsong headstones.

A young man from the village is out walking with his dog.

'Where is Teampall Mhoire?' I ask.

He has the softest energy. 'Probably, it's right beneath your feet.'

I wait until he's left, and sit down beside two headstones. Both are oblong, flat and have an eye the thickness of a finger through the top. Finlay had said he thinks they may be roof slabs, recycled from the temple. If so, they're all that still remains of it in sight. From here, I have an open view, north towards my final destination. I'm moving to the pilgrimage's end. I'm thinking of a man I once met in Sami land, up beyond the Arctic Circle of Finland. He told me that he came from Archangelsk, where they make the tar that caulked our boats. He told me that, in Russia, the further north you go the holier it gets.

The heavy clouds that brought the rain have nearly lifted. What few are left are drifting by in widening shrouds of blessed blue. In the Eastern church of Russia and Greece, the title that they often use for Mary is *Theotokos*. It means God-bearer, hence why she's also called the Mother of God. It nods towards a love that's very incarnate, the spirit one with matter, the re-articulation of the inner and the outer.

I used to fret about the song and dance around the literal 'virginity' of Mary. That may be how it's meaningful for some to understand. For me, however, a living myth speaks in kaleidoscopic ways to deep reality. I've come to see such 'virginity' as the archetype of transformation. As 'Our Lady' of perpetual renewal. That, of social justice as is shown by the Magnificat. That, too, in John Carey's sense of Eden ever-present in a fallen world. Like the first morning. 'Like a virgin . . .'

Mary transformed the terrible predicament of being pregnant, out of wedlock, in a harshly patriarchal and judgemental society. She gave expression to the truth that the Psalms had proclaimed. The truth that Jesus later underscored – that all of us are 'gods', all are 'children of the Most High'.[12] So her son was also, regardless of paternity. 'Be it unto me,' she told the angel. Let go into the life of God. 'Let it be, let it be.' Let it come to pass. 'There will be an answer.' Let go into the answer.

And I'm just sitting here as evening falls, at Saint Mary's in the forgotten diocese of Sodor, where once, it's said, indulgences were granted. Where people found conviction that the baggage that they carried was laid down, forgiven.

The cemetery is overhead the temple, as if the dead are lifted up on high. Transformation comes from somewhere hidden deep within. That's a symbol that can speak to me, and to many of the most broken people I know.

19

THE TEMPLE OF CRÒ NAOMH

Wednesday, day ten. I have just come up from viewing – and from underneath – the huge foundation slabs that are a part of the Teampall Phàdraig complex. They jut out from the cliff that overlooks a pebble beach, Mol Éire, at the foot of Siadar village. Nearby is Rubha na h-Annaid – the Headland of the Mother Church – and several other local names also point to what must once have been a major spiritual centre.[1]

One by one, as the coast gets gnawed away by storms, the masonry that was set in place by saintly hands crashes down onto the shore. I had raked around amongst the debris at the water's edge. I'd wondered if there might be anything to find. But apart from remnants of the temple walls – a low rectangle, settled in the grass above – there isn't very much remaining for the novice eye to see. There is, however, on the west face of a little inlet, a crack down through a sheet of rock that spouts a spring that's fast enough to drink from. It has a sulphurous metallic taste, musty and mephitic. Could that, I wonder, be what's left of the erstwhile Fuaran an Dèididh – the Fountain of Toothache? Is that medicinal savor why it was only used for toothache? If so, I'll tell Earth Mother that it granted me an indulgence – for the Cadburys and Mars bars.

Yesterday evening, after leaving Teampall Mhoire, I'd crossed a headland thick with old peat workings. There was what seemed to be a ruined village, and a solitary menhir – Clach An Truiseil. At nearly nineteen feet tall, about six metres, it is said to be the tallest standing stone in Scotland. It leans, like a human figure, at an angle. Some have interpreted the name to mean The Stone of Compassion, though Doctor Finlay thinks it might more likely be a person's name from long ago. I'd sat there for half an hour, dined like a king on my cold kipper that had, by a miracle of incorruptibility, not gone off, and then crunched across the pebbles to Saint Patrick's. I got my tent erected just as the rain was coming back for yet another stormy night. Now, dreich and rainy morning that it is, I'm sitting by the temple's well. I've drawn a cup of water, but take just a token sip, as it's somewhat green with algae fed by surface water runoff. As Donald Morrison had described, its capstone is of pinkish-grey Lewisian gneiss. Perched on top, a small arched block of sandstone, like a bookend, that proclaims in flowing Celtic script: Tobair Mhoire.

All around, the luscious meadow grass is set with wildflower herbs. Close to the rim, marsh marigolds are blooming – 'Mary's gold', the 'winking Marybuds' of Shakespeare's *Cymbeline*. 'Hark, hark! the lark at heaven's gate,' the bard sang out, 'my lady sweet, arise, arise, arise.' And so must I! My mission for the morning is heartened with an ulterior motive – the smell of coffee beans.

Back at Café Spirituel, what seems like so very long ago, a 'lady sweet', the renowned artist, Marianna Lines, had pressed one of her acclaimed spells into my hand. It was an original drawing – something I must frame for posterity – a map inked onto a paper napkin.

'Take this,' she'd said, like all the best faerie godmothers, 'and go and have a cup of coffee with Sue and Alex Blair at the Borve Pottery.'

I set off along the old unsurfaced road. It runs beside a row of black-house ruins that used to be the village. Once the A857 was constructed, the settlement moved inland – pragmatic if less elegant.

As I reach the main road the rain goes off and, having warmed up, I stop to take some clobber off. A vehicle pulls up in front of me. Guess what? The sticker on the back is sprouting legs.

'Good morning!' beams the ever-cheerful Doctor Finlay. 'I was hoping I might catch you before you disappeared across the moors again. I was wondering whether, to start the day, you might like some *coffee,* and some *freshly-baked* scones?'

Wow! The Great White Witch of Collessie had never promised scones as well.

'I knew that you'd be looking out for Bridgit's place, the well and temple. But they're both so hard to find. How about I take you there and drop you back here afterwards?'

You betcha! We motor off, down to the turning circle at the road end in Melbost Borve, and stop there beside a bungalow called Sundown. Through a gate we go into an undistinguished field.

'See anything?' Finlay asks.

'Err – grass?'

'Clear it away from around those,' he says, pointing to several little hummocks at our feet. I do so, and there are the stumps of plainsong headstones. We're in an unmarked cemetery.

'Can you see anything more?'

'Nothing. Just that wee ridge.'

'Take a closer look.'

Gradually, I pick out an oblong shape under the grass, about the size of a crofter's cowshed.

'That's Teampall Brighde for you,' he says, with a flourish.

'Now, see if you can find the well.'

I look around, but absolutely nothing. The only visible feature is a heap of old posts, up by the fence that's north-east of the temple.

'Take a look under those fenceposts.'

They had been placed for dryness on top of a small concrete mound. It turns out to be the capstone of the well, and bears the imprint of a horseshoe, a mark of smithcraft.[2] The cap gives shelter to an exquisite grotto of lichen-mottled stones, one of which can be lifted in and out as a little entrance door.

Ever so gently, as if he is a priest officiating at a ceremony, Finlay moves it sideways. The daylight struggles to reach all the way inside, but there it is. We gaze into a casket formed of interlocking blocks of unhewn stone. An emerald jewel. The algae-fringed but crystal waters of the Tobar Brighde.

A large white slug has found its heaven, sleeping underneath the lintel. We sit down upon the grass and settle into wordless contemplation.

A cup is lying to one side. After several minutes, Finlay nods towards it. He gives a little smile, and whispers: 'Be careful of the spider's web.'

We each sip several mouthfuls of the icy water. He sets back the stone and, slowly, we retrace our footsteps to the car. There we share his coffee and home baking.

'My *atheism*,' he told me, 'can be put very simply: compassion for all living beings and for the Earth on which they move. Everything else flows from this.'

And that would be the last that I would see of him on this pilgrimage. He dropped me back to where he'd picked me up from. I stood and watched him drive away, off back down the road to Shawbost. And I was thinking, almost saying to myself, with a twinge of sadness as he disappeared: Farewell and adieu, my Darwinian Druid guide. *Le gach beannachd*.

*   *   *

I venture into an Aladdin's cave of the Borve Pottery's handmade mugs and lamp stands. Alex noses out from behind the firing kiln, wearing an apron and an umber smock that's reinforced with heavy elbow pads. He's a gentle giant of a man, probably around sixty, a bushy moustache with soft black curly hair, and muscled arms of such hirsute splendour that they must have spared the need for a few winter shirts in his lifetime. He's in the middle of preparing a firing, hands clarted with clay, but he yells to Sue, who's making lunch. In no time, I'm sitting in their kitchen with a flock of happy hens clucking at the window.

They'd come from Lancashire to Lewis with two other families in 1973, attracted by the Highlands and Islands Development Board.

'I was always the sceptical one,' she concedes. 'We were back-to-the-landers, you know, grow your own vegetables and all that.'

She'd been the one who'd kept on saying that it wouldn't work out. The island doesn't even have a Marks & Sparks! But in the end, probably because they had the lowest expectations, they're the ones who lasted out the winters. Now the hopes for which they came are far surpassed.

'And the culture? Did you find that very different when you came here?'

'Oh completely!' and she laughs and laughs in reminiscence. 'The thing is, that when you first arrive you just can't understand how much at odds it is. People would tell you things like not to hang your washing out on a Sunday. Back then, most of them wouldn't watch TV on the Sabbath either. But no advice could have prepared you for just how great the difference really was.'

'And how would you describe that difference?'

'Well, it's the depth of what is found here. Their culture . . . it's like a deep, deep geological seam. It's there in the language . . . the music . . . the religion. You've no idea! Simply no idea until you've really lived in it. Until people start to open up and accept you.'

'Do you feel accepted now, thirty, forty years down the line?'

'Oh yes! I would never say that we're the same as them. But they make us feel very welcome. Lots of our business these days is from locals buying gifts. It's not just the tourist trade. That's very touching, very heart-warming.'

Lunch is on the table, and she gives a shout to Alex. 'The truth is, I've never come across a community anywhere with such a generous spirit. It's not the Scots who are mean here. We're the mean ones in comparison.'

'And the religion? How do you sit with the Free Church and all that?'

'Well . . . it's so hard to fathom. But underneath there's something very, very profound, something very lovely and connected, that's always been here. It's as if – whether they think of themselves as Calvinists or whatever – they're all drinking from a source so deep and so ingrained, they hardly know they've got it.'

I leave the pottery, heartily stuffed with cheese on toast and a clutch of four freshly-laid eggs to top up Osprey's larder. All I'm left with is a little flour, a single pack of oatcakes, some drips of honey and dregs of the muesli. I'd only meant my food to last a week. Now I'm almost out and it's a slightly funny feeling, but I don't want to have to go and find a shop.

The Abhainn Bhuirgh passes underneath the road on its way to the sea. There's a track that runs alongside. I saunter down a flight of dry-stone raceways that had once fed a string of Norse mills. They continued to be used into the nineteenth century. The stream flowed through the lower part of each mill hut. A wooden paddle – 'undershot' in that the water goes beneath rather than over it – turned one millstone against another by means of a shaft to the upper chamber. So the crofters ground their corn. Finlay told me that he'd just sent off a book about their history and locations to a Stornoway publisher. The illustration on the inside cover is by Seonaid Crawford, Seumas' daughter. It'll even include classical paintings of similar mills from Persia, Kashmir and the Punjab, not to mention classic Doctor Finlay sutras on such both-like stone huts: 'And they stand and ask themselves: *Where from, and when, and who, and why – and what now?*'[3]

I reach the sea near Bridgit's church and wander up the brae, past *Sundown*. A hundred yards ahead, an old man emerges from a working croft, strewn with agricultural implements. He dawdles over the road and seems to tinker with his rubbish bin. I can tell from his deportment that he's local, and think I guess his game. I'm right. In no time, it's back around a kitchen table, kettle on the boil, a huge plate of biscuits, cheese and baking, in the home of James and Peggy Morrison.

'I saw you walking down the burn, and thought I'd just come over,' James confesses, stretching back into an armchair that commands the corner by the window. He'd spotted me, like a stray sheep in the village, and was curious to enquire as to my earmarkings. Where am I from? Who are my people? Where am I going?

'Leurbost – Dr McIntosh's son – poaching.'

'Isobel's brother!' he shouts in delight. She once managed the catering at the oil rig fabrication yard near Stornoway. He was a welder with BP. Before that, weaving the tweeds and now, retired, he runs a few sheep.

They gave me such a happy hour, a constant stream of stories, leg-pulling and laughter. Why no poultry on the croft? 'The hen has not been born that didn't die in debt.'

As in the old ways, Peggy asked if I would say a grace before she poured the tea. Here, the pilgrim was caught slightly short. Quakers do it quietly. I said a few brief words – could have done much better – to which she said, 'Well – if *that* will be your grace!'

As for traditions of the local saint, well, James said he didn't know of any. But poaching, that's a different matter. The stream I'd just come down used to run with salmon when he was a boy, back before the factory ships sucked clean the sea.

'Now, you see, the salmon is a very clever fish. The wisest in the water. When you're at him in a pool, you'll feel him bump into your Wellington boots, trying to escape. But if once he feels your net, he'll never touch it again.

'What you do, is lay two nets in a V shape. Drive him up the pool and trap him in the cleft. And *that's the way we did it*, my boy. Oh yes, *a bhalaich*! That's the way it was done when we were young.'

'You'll be very welcome back here anytime,' he hollers, as I set off on my way.

'Always very welcome – unless I'm *on the watch below*.'

'The what?' I stop, and turn to catch his words again.

'That was in the merchant navy. You'd either be on watch on the deck above, or sleeping on the watch below.

'You'll always find me here, *a bhalaich,*' and he's chuckling to his parting shot. 'Always here. Until the day they lay me six feet under – *on the watch below.*'

My next destination, Teampall nan Crò Naomh, is usually translated, rather squarely, as Holy Cross Church. But this misses out on Doctor Finlay's 'layers and layers of meaning and interpretation'. *Naomh* means sacred, consecrated, or held in sanctuary, so 'holy' is good enough. Normally, however, the Gaelic for cross is *crois*. But *crò* has in fact a much wider semantic range. It suggests an enclosure. A circle, a needle's eye, a cattle fold, a hut-like cell and even, the heart and the blood that circulates.

Moreover, Ronald Black points out that 'the differences between *cnò* "nut" and *crò* "blood" are of gender and nasalisation only'. The night that succeeds *Féill Ròid* – Roodmass, the Feast of the Exaltation of the Cross – was in the old ways called *oidhche na cnò, na Cnò Naomh* – 'the night of the nut, the Holy Nut'. On this day, according to the Rev. J.G. Campbell of Tiree, people went out collecting hazelnuts. Even 'the devil goes a nutting'. The feast also marked the start of the rutting season for the stags. Campbell notes that 'the belling of red deer among the hills on this night is magnificent'.[4] *Crò*, or *Cnò*, therefore suggests a sense of the cross in a way that brings to mind, for me, the circled Celtic cross. It also suggests a sanctuary, the kernel or essence, and the heart with all its pulsing of the life force. Crò Naomh is thus both holy cross and temple of the sacred heart.

Out on the open moor again, another kind of *crò* was on my path. Dun Bhuirgh or Dun Borve is a prominent stone ring, a prehistoric *broch* or fort some thirty feet across. Its walls are some eleven feet in thickness at the base, and once they held within them seven beehive cells. Down the centuries, most of the smaller stones were carried away, quarried for walls and houses, thus robbing it of what would once have been a most impressive stature. When Captain Thomas documented the site in 1890, he quoted at length from an antiquarian, the Rev. Malcolm Macphail of Shawbost. Happily for posterity, the minister had placed on the written record the following facts:[5]

> Though neither history nor tradition are associated with Dun Bhuirgh, the fairies have long made it their residence. They used to be seen with their big black dogs, with large iron chains round their necks, going about like ordinary men in their *Bruithean*. They were of great assistance to the Borvians, often helping them out of their difficulties, and even performing apparent impossibilities.

At the pottery, Alex had warned me that the forecast threatened heavy rain. Sure enough, within a short time of having left the Morrisons' house, the clouds had thickened. Thinking that I'd better plan for another stormy night, but lacking the sun to tell the time by my compass, I'd reluctantly turned on my phone. All I'd wanted was to see the clock, but with capricious forces hanging round the bruithean, it grabbed a signal too – and *chirp-chirp*.

Normally, I only use this phone when travelling and don't give out the number. It was a text from Gehan Macleod. She had founded the GalGael Trust in Govan with her late husband, Colin, building boats to reconnect the hand, head and heart. My involvement on the board is why Vérène and I live there. The text was terribly apologetic, but could I call her urgently? Some trouble with *The Sun.*

I sat down on a stone inside the broch's enclosure. My call was answered by Helen, the office manager. It will suffice to say that, before we managed to recruit her, she was the king-pin in the running of a Glasgow demolition company.

'Alastair! How's it going? Still out on the moors *finding yourself?*'

Gehan rallied to the rescue. Turned out that one of Rupert Murdoch's hacks had slapped three hundred quid on the table of one of our volunteers – a man whose daily life battles with the bottle. He wanted him to help concoct a story about one of our young female heroin addicts. The commission was to write a piece about 'sex, drugs and the charities that mug the taxpayer'.

'It's horrible,' said Gehan. 'They're making up lies out of people's misery just to sell newspapers.'

The volunteer – who had served fourteen years in jail back in his gangster days – threw the money back, and came in to tip us off. Gehan had only needed reassurance that she'd handled things in the best way. But for a while, it drew me back into another world; that of those whose forebears had been uprooted from the land, the end-products of such intergenerational poverty. And yet, as Colin used to say, 'You can hold a person down for long enough, but sooner or later, they'll resurface. It's the buoyancy of the human soul.' We simply try to hold a space where folks can seek to re-articulate between their inner and their outer lives.

The full uncanniness of unheimlich, of deep un-homing caused by such structural violence, is an everyday reality for many of our people. Joseph Jones was born in Wine Alley, a now-demolished Govan slum. An exquisite musician, he'd seen hostels, prisons, hospitals, the lot. One night, he told me that his problem was he had the Devil in him.

I'd suggested maybe not taking 'the Devil' too literally. A useful metaphor, perhaps?

But Joe held me in his big soft puppy eyes. He said he wouldn't want to disagree: 'Not with yourself, Alastair.

'It's just that, you see . . . I can only make sense of my life with the Devil and God.'

It was just one of those funny little encounters. One that left me feeling, 'Who am I to argue?' That was all. But the following week, I was seated beside an army chaplain at a luncheon function. He'd just returned from active combat in Afghanistan.

'You said, *active* combat?' I asked. 'A chaplain?'

He explained that it's not widely known, but in some of the special forces units the chaplains don't just go along to say the prayers. They're an integral part of the fighting unit. He wondered: could he use Joe's story for a forthcoming sermon?

'I'll just need to check back with him,' I said, 'but there's not a lot to go on, is there?'

'I'll tell you why it speaks to me,' he said. 'In my branch of the Commandos, I helped to run the course that trains the boys what happens if they're tortured.

'I'd tell them that if captured by the enemy, you may have everything stripped away. Your uniform, your health, your identity. Not even the family bonds of those you love may be enough to help you hold together.

'You may find yourself broken – quite beyond imagination – by the demonic forces brought to bear upon you. You may find yourself stripped down to where the only thing that's left . . . is God.'

Out here, north beyond the broch, I come to swathes of thick dark heather sweeping down towards the sea. Like back at Cnoc an Ruagain, it's growing over rows and rows of long-forgotten feannagan. They reach the edges of storm-bitten cliffs then drop, truncated, off the end.

Joe too dropped, truncated, from this world before his time. It's said the proud will ask: *If there's a God, how could this happen?* The humble say, and Joe would have said: *This has happened, God is with us.*

These coastal trails play hide and seek. The evangelicals could call them 'faith trails'. You have to keep on going in the hope they'll reappear. I'm just walking, walking, walking. On and on and on. Another step, another and another. Walking, to the Teampall nan Crò Naomh. Making for the Holy Cross. There used to be a ridiculous saying, 'It's X that marks the spot.' In my mind's eye, the temple up ahead exudes a golden glow, as if it is a gently flaming Celtic cross. I think I know why. It's probably a memory, or after-image, from that night at Teampall Eòin. The way I'd watched the sun drop down into the land-under-the-waves. Its refraction and reflection on the water. And how, in that low light, I'd watched devoid of sunglasses, not even slits in reindeer shoulder bone. That's the burning image that I'm seeing, where X marks the spot. The *cnò*, the kernel, and echoes of *sùil-chruthaich*, Creation's Eye, that sets the very Earth a-quake.

What is the cross? I'm saying to myself.

First millennium – *Christus Victor Theory* – ransomed to the Devil.

Second millennium – *Satisfaction-cum-Penal Substitutionary Theory* – ransomed to God.

What now – I'm wondering – *if anything?* Anything, that wouldn't be ridiculous, incredulous, to see us into this, the third millennium? If Jesus hadn't been such an activist for loving justice in the world – if he'd not been like one of us strung out to dry – I'd hardly even bother asking. I even know a church where they've taken down the cross, such was the creeping Christian cringe it caused.

So – *what is the cross?* 'What do you say to that, Alastair?' echoes Harrier, coming in upon another gyre, some higher mission drawing me when under fire to clarity.

'What does *pacifism* have to say to that?'

What, indeed?

I'd say, *nonviolence is the cross.*

Abbé Pierre was a radical French priest who, when the poor were dying on the Paris streets in the bitter winter of 1954, led *L'insurrection de la Bonté* – the Uprising of Kindness – and awoke the conscience of a secular nation.

All his life, the Abbé had struggled with the Ransom Saying. It was through hard-pressed folks like Joe, that a whole new vista opened to him:[6]

> It has been while living for a long time amongst drug addicts that another explanation came to me. The addict is, in effect, at the same time his own executioner and the victim. He is both the ransomer and the hostage. Based on this observation, I realised that it is the same with all human beings. Because we are disconnected from our authentic divine source, we have become our own executioners. We are slaves to our disordered desires, to our egotism.

The Greek for 'ransom' in the gospels is *lútron*. It means 'to loose', as in the freeing of a captive's bonds. It means, as Walter Wink points out, to *liberate*.[7] Jesus was saying – and in ways that need not exclude other faiths based on love – that he came to give his life *as liberation* for humankind. That puts a slightly different angle on the cross. Therefore:

Third millennium – *Liberation Theory* – ransomed to ourselves.

'Only forgiveness breaks the law of karma,' said the great Hindu-Christian scholar, Raimon Panikkar, in *Nine Sutras on Peace*.[8] Only *for-give-ness* – the power of love that melts the power of violence in its golden fire. A love to which resurrection is intrinsic, for this is love that cannot die, its greater part never having been born into the confines of space and time.

'Now, move on, *and live the rest of your life*.'

That, to me, is why the cross shines out, a supreme transformative symbol of nonviolence. Far from being past its sell-by date, the wrapping paper's hardly off the gift. We're still in the early days of what might be thought of as three eras of emergent Christian understanding.

'I have even heard people say,' said Gorky, 'that the Earth itself is a pilgrim in the heavens.'[9] All of us are walking on the pilgrimage of life. We're moved and beckoned by an inner light, the fire within the *crò*, the power that turns the stars around, the very 'atom of delight' – as Neil Gunn called his 'hazelnut experience'.[10]

That's what I sense an opening of upon this pilgrim pathway to the Teampall nan Crò Naomh. 'I have come to set fire to the world,' said Jesus, speaking both as a human being and as the archetypal principle of divinity incarnate. Not the fire of hell. Not in any sense of punishment. But as the fire of love.

I'd better take the greatest care. The moor has given way to fields. They're fenced down to the water's edge in narrow strips of in-bye crofting land. Some are fewer than a hundred yards across, and while the cliffs have dropped away to just some twelve-feet high, they're still enough to make a nasty fall.

Worldwide, the level of the sea is rising by an inch in every decade, and accelerating. Add storm surges and some natural subsidence, and that's the reason why this coast is getting undercut so rapidly. One moment I'll be on the path. The next, it drops away. Fences dangle off the end, giving crude measure of the loss of land. I cross from field to field by grabbing each last standing post with both my hands, and swinging round across the yawning chasm to the other side.

The temple is now coming into view. I see its outline, low upon a green cnoc, close against the sea. The council have put up a wall to stop it getting washed away.

In 1815, the artist William Daniell came and made an aquatint that now sits in the Tate. It's called *Remains of a Temple at Galston, Isle of Lewis*. Already, by his time, the roof was off and just the walls were standing proud. A shepherd sits bucolic by the plainsong headstones with his dog. A sailing ship is out at sea. That's what was, but all that still remains today are three deep-sunken walls. Only the upper third of a doorway pokes above the sand.

I enter, lie down in the long green sward, and press my face into the ground. I'm here, within the fold, the sacred heart of Holy Cross.

In a vision, Christ came to Julian of Norwich. He showed her something, round as a ball, the size of a hazelnut, and it nestled in the palm of her hand.[11] He said: 'It is all that is created.'

'What can this be?' she wondered. 'How could it last?' So fragile and so small.

'And the answer in my mind,' she wrote, was that 'it lasts, and will last forever, because God loves it.'

God is the primal atom of delight. Early evening, and the sky has darkened. Leaden, laden, and the sea has turned a heaving black. A cold wind rises once again, away up here, in holy north.

20

THE HEART OF THE SUN

Slowly, I draw away from the Teampall nan Crò Naomh. The wind has taken on a mean bite and flags me up a yellow card for body temperature. I set off again along the track. From here, it squeezes in between the sea and a robust stone wall that marks the boundary of Galson Farm.

Ahead, lies another lonely hillside. A series of long stone walls traverse its contours like a flight of ever-higher hurdles. There is a river at its foot, no wider than a road, but heavily in spate from last night's rain. Add to that an impending cloudburst, and it looks grim, grim, grim.

I should maybe raise the tent right here and now, in the shelter of the wall while everything's still dry. It feels, however, like an awfully early hour to hunker down for nightfall. There's nothing worse than being banged up, sleepless for hours on end, in a sack of stormbound flysheet.

The farm wall meets the river at a right-angled bend. From round the corner comes a teenage girl. She must be of the village. She's heading in the direction of the temple, wandering in a pensive dream with a shock of golden hair that tosses on the wind. She seems not to have noticed me, but as the wall and coastline funnel us together, she lifts her head in a shyly murmured greeting.

'Excuse me,' I say, with a genial formality, to put her at her ease. 'Would you know the best way to cross those walls up there?'

She brightens, stopping short of smiling. 'Just climb over them.'

'There's no way through – by stiles or gates?'

'There aren't any. It's alright just to climb them.'

We pass, but the thought of climbing walls with Osprey seems a Herculean effort. There is an inn five miles away at Cross. Maybe, a hot pub meal? Even a bed for the night? I'm going to give myself a break from leaping hurdles. What's more, that swollen river's looking pretty deep. Don't fancy getting swept down to where it fans out on the shore.

I weave a weary way, up through the fields and to the steadings of the farm. As I come into a courtyard, I see a sign that says 'Galson Hostel'. A man and woman are sitting there inside a 4x4, just about to drive away. They'd seen me coming, thought that I might be a customer who'd booked, and waited to provide a welcome. Yes, they've got plenty of room at this time of year. There's just one guest at the moment, another's coming later. Yes, it's warm and quiet, and a bed can be mine for a tenner. Done deal!

With a surge of relief I scurry in the door. Literally, as I cross the threshold, the skies let loose their volley in a monsoon overture. After a few minutes it stops as quickly as it started, but with a violent grand finale, a whiplash tail of pea-sized hailstones. By the time I've got my clobber off, the ground outside has turned half-white.

Graham is an electrical engineer from Durham. As I enter, he sits stoically at the kitchen table with a bottle of wine beside him.

'I can offer you a glass of red,' he says, matter-of-factly, as his opening words, 'but no food. I've been cycling all day. There's no shops and I'm out of supplies.'

'I've got plenty of eggs,' I say, happy to find such company, 'and a little bread mix – though it's hardly enough for two.'

'There's some stuff left in there,' he suggests, pointing to a cupboard by the cooker.

Our luck is in. Somebody has remaindered half a bag of self-raising flour. I've never tried baking a loaf with a mix of yeasted flour and self-raising before, but needs must. I warm a little water, work it in with a smattering of salt, and a couple of teaspoons of sugar. If the yeast's going to go, that should set it off like a rocket. Tally ho.

Graham watches curiously, partly sceptical, partly intrigued, but willingly investing in the venture with a generously proportioned glass of wine. I knead the mix on the sideboard until the dough pulls out, all long and stringy. After half an hour, it's achieved a partial rise. Hopefully, the self-raising bicarbonate will do the rest. With biology and chemistry joining hands, into the oven it goes.

We've been chatting about electrical engineering in the way men do when flexing expertise, and checking out shared ground. In Papua New Guinea, a quarter of a century ago, I'd set up a couple of small village hydro schemes. I was an amateur and therefore find it fun to pick an expert's brains. Arcane stuff – like power factors, three phase voltage curves, and how induced currents with inadequate earthing can give an unexpected shock from the neutral wire.

'So, what brings you here?' he asks.

'Pilgrimage,' I say, slightly embarrassed, sensing that the poaching gambit isn't going to wash.

'Pilgrimage!' he guffaws. 'So you believe in Him-Up-There, do you?'

'Not like that! Not a *Him*. And not quite *Up There* either.'

'So, what *do* you believe in then?'

'It's not about belief. More, about experience. Ways of seeing. The ground of being from which our deepest selves emerge. The further reaches of consciousness – both as individuals, and cosmic consciousness – like the Hindu scriptures describe so well.'

He's landed a right one here, so I might well ramp up the voltage.

'You see, it's about the very *source* of life and underlying unity. Life as love made manifest. This whole spiritual . . . *shebang!*' At which I clap both my hands together, just for a bit of fuse-blowing panache.

He laughs incredulously. My wine is kicking in very nicely on an empty stomach. We're both enjoying this stand-offish rapport.

'Look!' he says. 'I'm a Geordie. I'm from the north of England. Where I come from, if you talked like that, people would say: *Don't think about it, and drink plenty of beer.*'

'But that's the problem,' I retort. 'If they don't look, they won't see. They'll get all froth and no beer.'

Oh, he is enjoying this! Getting as good as he gives. What's more, emanating from the oven is an aroma that, back in the days of proper sacrificial offerings, would have been 'pleasing unto the nostrils of the Lord'.

Graham tops our glasses up again. Jürgen Moltmann, the German theologian, says he loves the company of atheists. By the second glass, all they want to talk about is God.

'So what's your *evidence*?' he asks. 'How are you going to *prove* to people that this *God* of yours is real?'

That's not, actually, the greatest of my worries. I'm more thinking to myself: *Better not let on about the faeries!*

'Spirituality!' he says, shaking his head. 'You know what? Where I come from, some people would get angry about *spirituality*.'

'Angry?'

'O-o-o, I don't know. I really don't know. But I'll tell you what they'd say. Some of them, they'd say: *Eee . . . ye'r doin' my head in!*'

There's a rattling at the outside door, and in comes Peter from the Isle of Barra.

He's been travelling the length and breadth of Lewis, knocking on doors for the Mori polling company, canvassing views about local government services. I kick off by asking what he thinks is his decisive skill in carrying out such work.

'Much of it,' he muses, 'is just getting people to converse. The trouble is, people no longer know how to have a chat across the garden fence. They're all so caught up in their computers and TVs.'

'Even on the islands?'

'Even here.'

Turns out that he's the founder of a fledgling Isle of Barra distillery.

'Read about it just two weeks ago, in the *Stornoway Gazette*,' I tell him. 'Is it true that you've already sold the entire first year's production run?'

He gives a satisfied nod. 'Every single bottle.'

'Any samples in the car?' quips Graham, optimistically.

'Not yet. We've still to build the place.'

Graham's struggling to add this up.

'Hang on,' he says. 'If you've still to build the distillery, how come you've flogged the first year's output?'

'Cask sales! In advance. You see, there's a huge premium on the first batch from collectors. That's how you build the finance base for a new distillery.'

'If it's not too nosy,' I ask, 'how much to set one up?'

'About two million.'

'So, let me get this right,' I say. 'Your day job's doing door to door social research. At night, a backpackers' hostel. And you're trying to pull a couple of million for a . . .'

'That's the way you start a business!' he said, with a swish of entrepreneurial verve. 'What's more, you don't find wee communities that talk religion and philosophy in most hotel rooms.'

Graham's now getting his head done in from another direction.

'You're planning a distillery,' he coos, 'on the strength of *non-existent* whisky?'

'That's what the man said!' I chortle, as I swing the oven door open, with a swish of debonair élan.

'How's that for faith in spirits invisible!'

And if I have to give the dénouement myself – *Risen to perfection!* Crisp, golden, rounded – all astounded.

But now it's Thursday – day eleven of my twelve – and the rain is heavy, heavy, pounding on my back and shoulders. I've got my head huddled down, walking like the outer door is bolted fast and I'm going to stay inside. These last three miles of inland road, up to the Butt of Lewis, must be the bleakest stretch in Lewis. No houses. No vistas on the sea. Not even a decent river's saving grace. No wonder they say it's haunted. Just acre after acre of drab moorland, dripping peat hags, hardly even any traffic once the morning rush hour down to Stornoway is past.

I plan to head up to Teampall Pheadair, Saint Peter's Chapel, in the old cemetery at Swainbost. From there, on to Teampall Mholuidh and Tobar Rònain – Saint Ronan's Well – also known as Tobar an Teampaill, in the village of Eoropie at Ness. Tomorrow, my last day, I'll see if I can find Fuaran Stoth, a spring said to be good for the stomach and to confer feelings of wellbeing. Also, to visit the most northerly sacred site of them all – a little rise with what remains of Teampall Rònain. Finally, there will be the small matter of a closing ritual that's been shaping up in my mind. Then, the bus back to Stornoway, and from there, the ferry, train and Glasgow.

If I'd taken the route of the hurdled walls this morning, I'd be passing through North Dell by now. Somewhere there, in a field long since ploughed over, is the lost site of Teampall Chliamain. There's nothing any more to see. The very thought brings up a sutra, chiming like a messaged text from the Empty Belfry School of Hebridean Zen.

> The less there is to see
> the holier a place it be

Three sacred sites are consecrated to Saint Clement in the Outer Hebrides. The others are at Rodel, from where I started off, and Teampall Chliamain in the old graveyard at Tigharry – Taigh a' Ghearraidh – on North Uist. Clement is the patron saint of the Macleods of Harris and Dunvegan.[1] No-one can be sure which Clement it is, as there was more than one. Generally, he's assumed to be Clement of Rome, a first-century pope who was martyred in the Black Sea – tossed in with an anchor stone around his neck – the punishment for opening up a miraculous spring to relieve his thirsting fellow quarry slaves.[2] He thus became the patron saint of quarry workers. It was a nice thought in the Harris superquarry campaign.

That said, John MacAulay points out that the church in Rodel lacks his trademark symbol of the anchor. Could it be then, that the Clement in question is that of Alexandria, or both, in one of those classic saintly fusions? I'm thinking of the blazing heavenly sun that is carved into Macleod's tomb, and the old island practice of walking sun-wise round the church. The Alexandrian Clement loved solar imagery of the resurrection.[3]

> Hail, oh light for he who rides over all creation is the *Sun of Righteousness* who has changed sunset into sunrise, and crucified death into life.

There are other possible Clement candidates, including obscure Celtic saints who took the name. Maybe it's not the questions that matter. Musing on an English country chapel, T.S. Eliot said:[4]

> You are not here to verify,
> Instruct yourself, or inform curiosity
> Or carry report. You are here to kneel
> Where prayer has been valid. And prayer is more
> Than an order of words . . .

This, he said, is where we meet 'the intersection of the timeless moment'. For me, such timelessness unveils the deeper mysteries. 'Do this in *memory* of me,' said Jesus at the Last Supper. The bread, the body, as the fabric of the universe. The wine, the blood, its animating spirit. Here *anamnēsin* as 'memory' in the original Greek infers the calling back of real presence. And that, from outside of space and time, as the *apocatastasis* – the revelation of the true underlying nature of all things. That too, as the *parousia* – being 'alongside' the 'presence' or the 'essence' – the so-called 'second coming' of the Cosmic Christ that always is, always was, and always will be if we just *wake up*, which is 'enlightenment'.[5]

Hey! That mouthful would have been a cracker for Graham in our bread and wine party last night. They're just other ways to talk not just about the 'deep time' of geology and physics, but deepest time. The stilling point – 'be still and know' – at which, John Carey said of the early Celtic poetry, 'eternity is always present in the heart of time'. The world touched on in *Mary Rose,* by tradition's deepest realms of faerie, and Nansen's tale of Father Anselm's sojourn in the monastery garden. Therein the cosmic homecoming, the resolution and the healing of our deepest *nostos-algos*.

More peat. More moor. Just sufficient passing cars to keep the ghosts at bay. This weather's blotting out all sounds and has me muffled in white noise. There's nothing else to do but watch the rain in pitted craters boiling at my feet. Drops that splash and splash again with droplets from their splashes. The Celtic monks, like those across North Africa, sought out their places of retreat in deserts but *in oceano desertum* – in oceanic 'desert' hermitages.[6] This sea lane that I'm on is running as an endless shining stream. If I started on the Golden Road from Harris, I'm ending on the Silver Road to Ness. What's more, the verge round here is lined with bouquets of sea pinks. The soil is suited to them, thanks to ocean spray and added salt that the council spreads on winter ice.

Three churches jostle on the horizon as I come up to the village of Cross, the heart of Ness, both port and district. 'Eee . . . ye'r doin' my head in!' – I could imagine Graham saying if he saw them all. Mind you, it was a touching thing this morning. When we divided up the remainder of the bread and rinsed out the wine glasses, he'd asked me for the reference on William James – a classic piece of research on religious experience.

I can feel the hardness of the road taking its toll. Shooting pains are coursing through my knees. With little else for distraction, I watch each ache come on, linger, fade and then another takes its place.

That clarity of being, that sense of me observing me, is on me once again. Walking in that same vague sense of golden light as yesterday. Walking into Cross, the village, you could say that marks the spot. I'm glad I didn't take the headland route but chose instead this mono-toned monotony. Glad that it's still raining, and that I've spent the morning, as it were, inside. So glad about this *gladness* in my life that keeps on breaking through – as I keep on walking, walking, every next step.

'To what are you walking?'

Into the heart of the holy.

'Do you remember "Set the Controls for the Heart of the Sun"?'

The tune's been running in my head. Roger Waters borrowed lines from a book of Chinese poetry – Li Shangyin – Tang Dynasty, ninth century, same time as the Celtic saints. Yes, I remember the chant-like chords, the synthesiser glide.

'Watch little by little, the night turn around.'

The heart of the Sun. The heart of the Sun.

'Over the mountain, watching the watcher.'

The heart of the Sun. The heart of the Sun.

'Making the shape of, his questions to Heaven.'

The heart of the Sun. The heart of the Sun.

'Love is the shadow, that ripens the wine.'

The Heart of the Holy, the heart of the sun.

'The ancients considered the Sun to be a living entity, part of a divinely animated universe' – or so Rupert Sheldrake said to me, once upon a time.

And now, *Ladies and Gentlemen* – courtesy of Gerald Scarfe animations – we have the Satanic pleasure of presenting you with, *A DEMONIC VISITATION!*

Creeping towards me, cacophonously, at little more than a walking speed, and flaunting great revolving wings from out of the sides of its fat wasp-yellow carcase, crawls a council road-sweeping machine.

I step aside in abject disbelief. This road is haunted after all.

Here we are – in a world that's trying to reduce its carbon emissions – on an island that is closing schools because it can't afford to pay the teachers – and this *behemoth* comes sweeping rain from a surface clean enough to eat off!

'We don't draw our tea water out of wells anymore. We get it out of road sweepers.'

O woe, woe, bring on Saint Anthony the Great of Egypt.[7]

> A time is coming when men will go mad, and when they see someone who is not mad, they will attack him saying, *You are mad, you are not like us.*

A side road leads me off down to the coast. I escape onto an unpaved path that comes out above Tràigh Chrois, the Beach of the Cross. The grass is luscious here, with banks of primrose breaking into flower. The rain goes off, I sit and picnic on the end-crust of bread, dipping it into the last drops of the lovely honey that had been given to me by a Muslim friend in Glasgow. That's what a place called Cross should be – a crossing place; and down on the beach, I cross another flooded stream, this time over wobbly stepping stones that only just permit my boots to stay dry. Fantastic boots they've been. Berghaus – *from the north of England, Graham!* Gratitude.

The headland on the other side is wimpled with feannagan. Further on, the land dips down into a stretch of wind-scourged machair. Here the grass again is white with drifting sands. Another river, this time with a footbridge, and just beyond, a hillside with a big hexagonal enclosure. In the bottom corner stands a single gable end. There is a long narrow window facing east. Somebody has cared. It has been temporarily reinforced with a simple wooden frame. This is Teampall Pheadair.

Carmichael tells that Peter is *us righ nan iasgair, Peadair treun* – 'the King of the Fishers, brave Peter'. The Christmas catch from boats on Uist was given to the poor, and known as *deirce Pheadair* – Peter's trib-ute. The haddock, with black fingerprints behind its gills, is *iasg Pheadair runaich* – 'the fish of loving Peter'. And the petrel is described as *peadaire-ach* – Peter-like – because it flies so low above the waves it nearly seems to walk upon the water.[8]

The air is preternaturally clear, the way it goes when cleansed of dust just as the rain stops. There is no question. This whole place heaves with sanctity. Between it and the sea is Teampall Thòmais, and somewhere there's a hillock, Cnoc an Annaid. Serried rows of plainsong headstones face east with the gable window. None of them are more than kneeling height. Set further back, there are some larger monuments of more recent provenance. Lank lengths of last year's herbage lie flayed and tangled all around.

I push the gate and step inside. A freshly varnished plaque, mahogany I think, is set there on a plinth. An inscription reads: 'Over four hundred old Bibles were buried here on Friday 30th June 2006.' Most families didn't want to throw their careworn tattered pages out for dumping in the landfill. It's like rural Russians will often prefer to hang old icons in the forest, or float them down the river, and thus with veneration give what had been given back to providence. The plaque bears a passage from Isaiah: 'The word of our God will stand forever.' The kind of islander who'd visit here would mostly know the context. 'The grass withereth, the flower fadeth: but *the word of our God shall stand forever.*'

Down at the river, the wind has gusted hollows in the sand. As can happen in these ancient cemeteries, it has scattered out the bones. I kneel, and lift a human finger bone, its joints fused solid by arthritis. An old woman comes to mind, one of many from my childhood, their bodies racked with pain, their beings wrapped in prayer. John MacInnes tells about an old Skye woman who he knew when he was young. In her belief, the dead lie waiting in the village cemetery, 'longing until the last of the future generations should join them, whereupon their society would be complete'.[9]

I hold the finger for awhile, then gently put it back amongst the other relics of the saints. Here rest a humble people. Here, the consummation of the soul to soil. Ashes to ashes. Dust to dust. The ministry of laying down. And this is holy ground. 'Be still and know that I am God.'

'Be still and know . . .' the Psalmist urged; and thirty years ago, when I was travelling in the Himalayas, an old man from Sikkim knocked upon the door of where I stayed. He spun his prayer wheel, and when I asked him for the meaning of his utterance – *Om mani padme hum* – he gave to me the purest invocation: 'God come to my heart.'

I kneel again, this time within the walled confines of brave Saint Peter's temple.

Be still and know . . . come to my heart.

Be still and know . . . come to my heart.

That Psalm, that old man's wheel, they just keep spinning on.

'I'm with you always. Like a fern in the spring.'

And my eyes are on a level with the congregation of the plainsong headstones. The wind has settled down to calm. The smell of rain still lingers fresh upon the air, but the sun is now beginning to shine through. Before me is a quite remarkable sight. Hundreds of snails, with big striped shells, have risen from the tangles of dead foliage. They're clinging to the stones, and doing what God's creatures do when comes the merry month of May.

Love is living in the midst of death, and from my gut a song breaks out – a strange but old familiar song – and I can feel my eyes are filling.

Angus Smith, the minister of Cross Free Church, once told an interviewer:[10]

> You see, when you sing in Gaelic . . . you use so many grace notes and everybody can be slightly different but it all merges together into a kind of shimmer. And, to me, it's like the sounds of the sea, or the sound of the wind, or all the sounds of nature merging into one.

But stop! Ego cuts in and cuts me dead, in sheer embarrassment.

What if you are being heard?

I look around, but here is far from anywhere. The rain has kept folks shut indoors. There's just a herd of cows, lined up and watching from the hill. A rabbit pops out from a hole beneath a slab, noses around, and ducks back down again.

A voice fills my imagination.

THERE IS NOBODY HERE . . .

And freed from inhibition, I let the song resurge. I hurl myself upon its waves, dissolving into tides of tears that stream as holy unction down my face.

Everything is just . . . so beautiful.

And the voice – that is both of me and beyond me – says:

THERE IS NOBODY HERE, BUT EVERYBODY IS HERE.

There is a lot of love in this community.

At which the main switch trips. The fuses blow and melt the logic circuits of my mind. I throw away the reindeer shoulder bone and the sand is blown completely off the Hill.

'I will go down to Hallaig,' said Sorley Maclean. 'And when the sun goes down behind Dun Cana' – behind the sìthean of the bards – 'a bullet will come from the gun of Love.'

'And will strike the deer . . . sniffing at the grass-grown ruined homes.'

'Tha tìm, am fiadh, an Coille Hallaig.'

And time itself, in time will die, but die into the arms of Love.

> . . . *'s nuair theàrnas grian air cùl Dhùn Cana*
> *thig peilear dian à gunna Ghaoil . . .*
> I will go down to Hallaig,
> to the Sabbath of the dead,
> where the people are frequenting,
> every single generation gone.
>
> They are still in Hallaig,
> MacLeans and MacLeods,
> all who were there in the time of Mac Gille Chaluim
> the dead have been seen alive . . .
> . . . and their beauty a film on my heart
> . . . *'s am bòidhche 'na sgleò air mo chrìdhe.*

21

THE WOMAN AT THE WELL

I slowly pull away from Teampall Pheadair and climb the hill. It overlooks a vast expanse of machair that, with the change of weather, is blanketed with rabbits. Less than a mile away, the last horizon starts to shrink before me as I walk. Here is the Butt of Lewis and the tight-packed homes of Eoropie, each with a narrow strip of croft land streaking up the back.

In the middle of the village, just above the line of houses, stands Teampall Mholuidh – Saint Moluag's. The name probably means 'monk', or perhaps 'promontory' or 'patience'. This contemporary of Saint Columba floated over from Ireland on a rock (that is to say, sitting on the ship's ballast!) and set up his church on the Isle of Lismore, later the birthplace of Alexander Carmichael. From there, he is said to have evangelised the Picts, and to have had the power to cure insanity. I've heard that, even into the present era, if somebody in Ness acts a bit daft people might joke: 'Watch out, or we'll take you to the Temple.'

On picking it out from amongst the other buildings, I ceremonially drop to my knees. That, according to Martin Martin, is what peregrinating pilgrims did when first a temple entered into view. 'They were in greater veneration in those days than now,' and one of his informants in the late seventeenth century could remember witnessing it at Saint Moluag's when he was a boy. These days, the building is restored and cherished by the Scottish Episcopal Church.

Martin also tells about the temple's jolly reputation. At Halloween and Candlemas – the latter equating with the feast day of Saint Bridgit at the start of February – the villagers engaged in what he felt obliged to call 'this ridiculous piece of superstition'. Pilgrims from all over the island would converge on the nearby beach. They brought a special ale, brewed with a peck of malt from every home. A cup was poured out on the waves in sacrifice to Shony, their sea god, with the hale and hearty incantation: 'Hoping that thou wilt be so good as to send us plenty of seaware for enriching our ground during the coming year.'

Afterwards, everyone would head off to the temple. They'd stand in reverential silence by a candle burning on the altar. As soon as it expired, 'all of them went to the fields, where they fell a-drinking their ale, and spent the remainder of the night in dancing and singing'. The historian W.C. Mackenzie has it that they all converged upon the church 'with lights in their hands' where 'they worshipped the saint all night long' in 'drunken orgies'. Although the people were nominally Protestant, 'the real religion of the people was simply saint-worship'. Instances of Shony veneration, he said, endured into the nineteenth century. The clergy, 'by means of argument, warning, and threats,' induced the people 'to give up their idolatrous practices'.[1] Thankfully so, of course.

I leap across a deep little stream, its width just inside the limits I could cope with, and, to my astonishment, find that I am standing at a ring of menhirs. There aren't supposed to be stone circles in Ness! It takes a minute or two of wandering about before I realise I've emerged inside a kiddies' theme park. I toss my head and mutter: *You're gone! gone! gone!* Snap, snap! It's time to pull the needle out and shut the sìthean door. Time to bring the Tardis back to earthbound orbit.

I amble up towards the houses. There is a tourist sign – 'Eoropie Tearoom – Not Open on Sunday'. But this is only Thursday, and I quickly find it does a tempting line in bacon butties. Oh well – 'A sin not enjoyed . . .'

Tobar Rònain should be somewhere by the roadside. I wander to and fro, peering through the long grass and the buttercups that line the verges. It's one of those sedately mellow evenings that often follows heavy rain. A woman with a little girl at heel comes idling up towards me. I notice there's no ring upon her finger. Perhaps a single mother.

'What are you looking for?' she asks.

'I am looking for Saint Ronan's well.'

She drops her voice, as if to make a personal apology. 'You won't find it any more.' She points down to an ugly concrete culvert. 'It used to be right there, but the digger knocked it in when they were widening the drain.'

I stutter in disbelief. Finlay had told me it was damaged, but not completely gone.

'Is this what has become of Ronan's Well?' I ask, indignantly. 'Holy water, running down the drain?'

'There are other wells,' she says, trying to console.

'What about Fuaran Stoth? Would that still be intact?'

'Oh, you should find it up the road. Look out for the streaks of iron coming from the spring. They say it used to be a cure for stomach ache.'

'And any others?'

'There's plenty. They used to be on nearly every croft. One had such good water that people kept on going to it until recently. But the man who owns the ground . . . he decided that he didn't want them walking on his land. And he . . . blocked it.'

'Blocked it?'

'Well . . . he put a dead sheep down. It was a bad thing to have done.'

We're both looking at each other wordlessly. The child is hugging tightly to her arm. I must seem to be a strange man.

'To poison a well . . .' I say, slowly. 'That is to destroy the flow of life that runs within a community.'

She nods, but refrains from commenting. The child is tugging at her dress, anxious to get moving.

'And Ronan's Well? Has there been any talk of restoring it?'

'A man from the village wanted to, but somebody from Health & Safety said he couldn't.'

Again, we look at one another in a shared sense of bewilderment.

I watch them wander slowly back along the road from where they came. I feel like I've been blessed by one whose inner well is always springing up.

A narrow path leads through the crofts, up to the staunch grey temple. There is a seagull sitting on a stubby stone finial. They punctuate the easternmost extremity of a mottled slate roof. There is a low-sunk doorway with an arch. Alongside, a high Celtic cross of silver granite, a memorial to those who fell in the Great War.

I sit down beneath its interwoven knotwork, and draw what little warmth I can from the thin evening sun. An epitaph is written on the plinth. To my surprise, it is a passage from the Apocalypse of Saint John, one that Tom Forsyth of Scoraig would often quote, stirring up our fledgling courage in the early days of the land reforming work on Eigg. He'd gone there with his wife, Djini, and camped for several days amongst the ruins of the cleared village of Grulin – the aptly named Stony Place. There, as a sign and portent, they had restored the Well of the Holy Women. The passage reads:

> To him that overcometh will I give to eat
> of the Tree of Life, which is in the midst
> of the paradise of God

'We have got to face the Angel with the flaming sword,' he'd often tell me. 'The fire of God that guards the Tree of Life in Eden.

'That's what it means to *overcome* – to overcome self-centredness that dims our eyes, and blinds us to eternity within a grain of sand.'

'What is the Tree of Life?' I'd ask.

'Been there all along. Concealed within this very world of brokenness. Its leaves are for the healing of the nations. That's what our deeper work is all about.'

Through the arched door, inside the church, the scene is set for services. There are pews and prayer books, children's artwork, and a Bible on the lectern. But it's getting on. I must take my leave. I want to pitch my tent above Stoth Bay, the local beach.

I take a last look back as I go out the door. There are a pair of candles standing by the altar, their holders garlanded in flowers. Apart from that, I see no hint of preparations for a bit of sea god revelry. What a pity. To think – I could have called up Doctor Finlay.

'A little dance, perhaps?'

Friday 22 May, and the year is 2009. It is, finally, day twelve. I wake up, and can scarce believe I've made it here. Once packed, I head back down the road and look, but to no avail, for Fuaran Stoth. I'll just have to draw my wellbeing from elsewhere today. When I get to the back end of the in-bye strips of crofting land, I break off to the east, and solemnly proceed towards a fence that corresponds to reference NB 524654 on the map. Up here should be the site of Teampall Rònain.

It takes some minutes searching, but there it is, for all that it is. A few foundation stones protrude from an eroded grassy ridge. Oh well – 'The less there is to see . . .'

I lie down on the turf beside them. It had rained in the night, but now the sun's come up and it's turning out to be a balmy island day. Candy clouds drift lazily through powdered tones of pastel blue, and I'm gazing southwards, back through all the horizons I've traversed. All those West Side villages, the Uig moors and Grimersta, the mountain passes of the Harris Hills, the whaling station and hotel at Tarbert, the Bays Café and John's boat shed – the whole array, like flights of locks all stepping down to meet the sea at Rodel.

The Butt of Lewis lighthouse stands behind me. A dozen leagues out north to sea lies the tiny island of North Rona, where Saint Ronan built his final temple. After bringing Christianity to Lewis in the seventh century, the monk decided that the people of Ness were too busy and too noisy for his prayer life. An angel sent the *cionaran-crò*, the leader of a pod of whales – with 'his great eyes shining like two stars of night' – and so the saint was spirited across the water.[2] On North Rona lived a people, of whom Martin Martin said, 'They take their surname from the colour of the sky, rainbow and clouds.'[3]

Some of the legends of the Hebrides go back, it is said, to the *Cailleach Bheag an Fhasaich* – the Little Old Woman of the Wild. She, 'whose age even tradition failed to account'. Her maiden days were spent in Glen Corradale, South Uist. Her words described a kind of golden age, one where 'the little brown brindled lark of Mary bounded to the ear of heaven to herald the dawn', and where all the islands of the Hebrides were joined up into one.

Then came Culloden, followed by the Clearances, and in Carmichael's words, 'The whole of these faithful people of Corradale, and hundreds more, were evicted and driven to all ends of the earth – many of them to die moral and physical deaths in the slums of Glasgow and other cities.'

In 1869, a South Uist woman recited to him a poem of coming cataclysm. She prophesied a continuation of the 'overflowing of the Atlantic and the submerging of certain places'. In the end, there will come a time in which:[4]

> The walls of the churches shall be the fishing rocks of the people, while the resting-place of the dead shall be a forest of tangles, among whose mazes the pale-faced mermaid, the marled seal and the brown otter shall race and run and leap and gambol – *Like the children of men at play.*

Flood legends don't need second sight in the era of climate change. The folk memories of many coastal peoples in the world look back to inundation after the Ice Age, when the global sea level rose by some 120 metres.[5] What intrigues me about the Hebridean legends is Otta Swire's account of three great floods. That of Creation, that of Noah, and that which has yet to come – but with the latter, 'Iona will rise on the waters and float there like a crown'. This, so that the dead 'will arise dry' to ease their recognition on the Last Day.[6]

To me, these places that I've visited, this spirit represented by Iona that rolls on into the present day, is a crown no inundation can wash away. This path to keep our feet dry – its old ways preserved by collectors like Carmichael, its new ways embedded in real-life communities – is nothing less than a heritage of world importance.[7] That crown is the *crò*, the heart or kernel of the places that I've visited, the people that I've met, and what it means to be a human being. Come what may, that might help us face what comes to pass.

We don't know what we're inside of. So far, the 'children of men' have only glimpsed at an ecology of the imagination, but the changes happening in our world are a basic call to consciousness.

But the walk is not quite over yet. The Stornoway bus isn't due until 11.40. I've one last duty. The closing ritual. The sacrifice.

I scramble down the rocks and onto Stoth beach. Kneel beside a stinking pile of rotting seaweed. Take from my pocket a strange cylindrical object. This, I shake with vim and vigour, in a manner that anybody watching would consider quite fanatical.

I don't have a copy of Martin's book with me. His version, anyway, was rather terse – too much on the 'short wave', to satisfy his metropolitan intended readership. So, needs must. With a furtive glance to make sure the tourists with their fancy camera phones aren't out yet, I raise my head unto the heavens, pull the silver popper from the sacred chalice – and as a golden fountain spurts across the famished waves I yell, in foghorn tones that send a flock of seagulls skirling from their nests –

Ho *Shony*! I invoke the tides of your benevolence!
May you send us your waves of providence
May we conduct ourselves in . . .
(Oh bugger, what else rhymes with *ence*?)
That this dear ocean be sustained:
And so I *sacrifice* to you –
This splendid can
Of *Irn-Bru*.

> P.S. The bacon butty teashop didn't have a licence, so I thought you'd like a shot of Scotland's other national drink.

> P.P.S. I gave you the literary version – on the long wave.

> P.P.P.S. Doctor Finlay says hello.

I cavort back to the village. An old man sees me coming, and sidles slowly over. He's in his late seventies, a thin Norse face, wry native intelligence, and he speaks hesitantly, double thinking from the Gaelic into English for my sake.

What has brought me here?

I talk about the poaching pilgrimage, about my failure to catch anything admissible. I leave unsaid the gift of landing everything.

'Did you spend the night in the village?'

He's looking for my earmarkings.

'No. I camped out at the bay. Was trying to find Fuaran Stoth, but couldn't see a spring or well of any kind.'

The surge of water turns some near-forgotten millstones in his mind.

'It was there when I was last that way,' he says. 'We used to go and clean it.'

'You did? And do you think it might get cleaned again?'

The mills of God are grinding very slow. For myself, I feel as if I'm dropping gently back to Earth inside a capsule. Little by little, I'm waking up from aeons of voyaging through space and time.

'I might . . .' he utters, falteringly. 'I might go up and have a look.'

The bus pulls in, and I sit down with Osprey by my side. The villages flit by as if a movie's running in reverse. The air's alive with Gaelic, but the further south we go, the more the balance shifts to English. I note the costly thoughtfulness, more costly than the norms out there can mostly understand.

By the time we draw up to the pier in Stornoway, they're chatting and they're laughing such a lot the driver has to shout to get them off. Within an hour I've crossed the world. Now, there will be shops and newspapers – and mountains not of stone, but of emails to catch up on.

I have arrived back at the Bay of Steering by the Stars. Back to this dear fishing port, whose motto – *God's providence is our inheritance* – runs as liquid sapphire through the veins. Like nectar from the honeybee, 'only kings and royal people get to taste that'.

Twelve days I've been away. Time now get back on the ferry and to take the music home. I pull the needle from the sìthean door. I lay it down, and watch it settle back: the compass needle of my soul.

Acknowledgements

The walk just kept on walking in me for the seven years that it took for this book to find its final shape. There are so many people I could thank. Perhaps it will suffice to say to all those with whom I met on my journey: it was a blessing. Especially so, however, my thanks are due to the gate-keepers who so deeply structured my experience – John MacAulay of Flodabay, Seumas Crawford of Garynahine and Dr Finlay MacLeod of Shawbost.

My wife, Vérène Nicolas, may have had a break for twelve days in May 2009, but then endured a further seven years of living with an author. As I've slogged away at my computer, she's still not convinced about my fitness training. The other day at breakfast, the following formula came up:

$$\frac{7 \times 365}{12 \text{ days}} = ???$$

I'm not sure what it means, but I'm told the answer comes out somewhere north of two hundred. Furthermore, 'Other great explorers achieved the reverse ratio.' Oh well. But thank you – for so much – my dear love.

Many friends and colleagues helped by reading over key portions of the text. These are in no way responsible for my errors. They include (in alphabetical order): Professor Timothy Gorringe of Exeter, John 'Rusty' Macdonald of Leurbost, Iain MacKinnon of Isle Ornsay on Skye, Jennifer McCarry of Glasgow, Maire McCormack of Linlithgow, Alex George Morrison of Leurbost, Andrew Morrison (Viscount Dunrossil of Vallaquie in North Uist) of Texas, Hilly Raphael of Oxford and David Thomson of Lossiemouth.

I also thank my literary agent, James Wills of Watson Little, for cajoling me to work complex material into a more accessible form, paring down the layers of paint to reveal the underlying picture on the canvas. Similarly so, Roger Smith, the indexer, my editors at Birlinn in Edinburgh,

Andrew Simmons and Barbara Simmons, and its proprietor, Hugh Andrew, one of those rare surviving independent publishers with a flair for the Socratic arts of literary midwifery. For help in ways that that helped to keep my thinking, writing and hearing on track, special thanks to John and Fiona Sturrock of Edinburgh, and to Professor Michael Northcott of the School of Divinity at Edinburgh University. Michael involved me in his three-year Arts & Humanities Research Council Project, *Caring for the Future Through Ancestral Time*, which helped to deepen my thinking about time and climate change as I wove them softly into this book.

In using Gaelic, I had to live within my own limitations. My friend, Babs Nicgriogair of the Bay of Stars, gave the Gaelic a dusting off when Cath MacKinven could no longer continue with the task, and Iain 'Jock' Mackenzie of Keose helped me to sort out some of the Gaelic pronunciations in the glossary. Even then, there are difficulties, especially with place name spellings from maps, changing conventions and the vagaries of quoted texts.

Readers might notice my double dedication of this book. I hold a huge debt of gratitude to Catherine MacKinven. She was a Gaelic-speaking native, a widowed lady of the manse, who held a vast but quietly-stated cultural and theological knowledge. She took it on herself to become my cultural mentor as I wrote, most weeks sending letters filled with photocopied articles, or her own translations from Gaelic lore. She pressed me to press deeper into the tradition, and not to shy from expressing what was coming through. Old age took its toll just as we were due to run a week together – *The Pilgrimage of Life* – at Iona Abbey in 2014. Without her, this book would have been finished very much more quickly, and very much more poorly. At times, what will come through as my voice is really hers behind me. Such is the beauty and the braided richness of a living culture's carrying stream.

Now, one of the advantages of an 'acknowledgements' page, is that they're read by only the most dedicated. They can therefore be a hiding place to share things only for the most determined. The writing of this book was a very difficult process. It took me back into the Hill for seven years. I'd get lost down rabbit holes, and later have to delete most of my diggings in the sand. However, I was helped to bear the process by several major dreams along the way. The last will be enough to share, and that, by way of closure.

I was in an island church where I'd been asked to preach the Sabbath morning sermon. But I'd only brought a New Testament. The tiny huddled congregation, mostly dressed in heavy black coats, were expecting a lesson from Amos, but that's Old Testament. All that I could remember from the prophet off by heart, were the lines:

> Let justice roll on like a river
> And righteousness, like a never-failing stream

Somehow, magnificent though such sentiments are, they weren't quite sufficient for those I was charged to address. I stood before them, tongue-tied, cringing with embarrassment, and this spasm of anxiety went on and on for very near the full allotted hour.

With only minutes to the end, I stared in desperation at the wooden board on which the numbers of the Psalms were set out. As I gazed, the lettering began to fade. It never went away. The Psalms endured – my Presbyterian friends will be relieved to know – but it was like watching an old photographic plate developing. As if from out of a wash of silver nitrate in the dark room, the backdrop of an image slowly came to view.

And there she was again! Crouched, vigilant, amongst the rocks of Roineabhal.

The Blue Mountain Hare. My pilgrim guide along the way. Ancient, wild, eyes full of love.

And I have returned from out the Hill now, but never fully so.

Walking, walking, every next step.

Deeper, ever deeper.

Into the *Crò Naomh*.

Gaelic Glossary and Pronunciation Guide

This rough guide to some of the key terms used in the book is not definitive. The spellings and approximate pronunciations (in italics) vary with context, locality and the era out of which I might have quoted. As such, my usage is not always consistent.

Abhainn river or burn (a small fast-flowing river) – *a-vane*.

A bhalaich my boy, my lad, term of endearment from an older to a younger man – *a val-aich*.

A ghràidh my dear, literally 'my love', one of dozens of terms of endearment – *a-graii*.

Àirigh a 'sheiling' or hut made of wood or stone at the summer grazings in the moors – *ar-ai*.

Aisling dream or vision – *ashling*.

Àit uaigneach a solitary place – remote, forlorn, unsettling, grave-like – *ayt u-uayg-nech*.

Anaghnàthaichte the extension of the natural into the realms of the 'supernatural' – *ana-gra-eech-ah*.

An dà shealladh 'the two sights', second sight, ESP – *an da shall-ach*.

Baile, bal village – *bal-uh*.

Beannachadh blessing (**le gach beannachd** – with every blessing) – *bee-ann-ach*.

Brighde one of many variations of Bride or Bridgit, Celtic goddess and Christian saint – *Bree-jah*.

Bodach old man – *bod-ach*.

Both, bothan (plural) a hut or bothy, usually applied to the corbelled stone 'beehive' structures out on the moors – *bo-th, bo-th-an*.

Broch prehistoric circular stone fort – *broch* (rhymes with loch).

Brugh, bruithean interior of a faerie 'fort' or sìthean – *broo, broo-an*.

Bùrach a grand muddle – *boo-rach*.

Cailleach, caillich (possessive) old woman, holy old woman – *cal-ea-ach*.

Cianalas wistful longing, nostalgia, soul-felt weariness, sometimes translated as 'the terribleness' of being cut off from one's land and people – *key-an-a-lass*.

Cille small church or cell for spiritual retreat, anglicised as 'kil' as in Kilbride, the cell of Saint Bride – *keel-u*.

Clachan small, usually clustered, village settlement – *clach-an*.

Cnò nut, especially the hazelnut – *cn-ooh*.

Cnoc small hill – (a **cnocan** is even smaller) – *knock, knock-an*.

Crò sometimes translated as cross, but literally an enclosure, sheep or cattle fold, cell, centre, the heart or the blood – *kr-awe*.

Crodh-sìth the 'cattle of the faeries', the deer – *kr-owe-shee-h*.

Crotach hunchbacked – *crow-tach*.

Cùram sudden religious conversion, Gaelic equivalent to the Greek *metanoia*, also means 'care' – *coo-ram*.

Deiseil sunwise, as to process deiseil on entering a cemetery, also means 'ready' – *dee-sel*.

Deoch a drink (of water, etc.) – *joch* (rhymes with loch).

Drùdhadh pertaining to the Druids, the essence, that which is penetrating, also means a 'soaking' – *droo-ugh*.

Dualchas cultural heritage – *doh-ul-chas*.

Dubh black – *dooh*.

Dùthchas heritage in the land – *dooh-chas*.

Each-uisge mythical water horse (sometimes rendered 'kelpie') – *eh-ch uis-gah*.

Eòin name anglicised as Ian or Iain – *ee-in*.

Feannagan lazybeds (raised cultivation beds) – *fea-an-agan*.

Fiadh the wild, wilderness, the red deer – *fee-agh*.

Fir gorm the 'blue men', the sea faeries – *fir-gorm*.

Fuaran a spring, often used synonymously with a well – *foor-an*.

Gaoth nan sìth gust of wind stirred up by a passing faerie host (see also **Oiteag shluaigh**) – *Ga-oth nan shee-h*.

Geàrraidh the 'garden' or in-bye grazing area close to a sheiling – *gee-arr ay*.

Gearr-fiadh the 'short deer' or blue mountain hare – *gee-arr fee-agh*.

Ghillie a boy, a male servant, an oarsman at the boat or pony boy on the hill – *gilly*.

Ghlas hues of green, blue, silver and/or grey – *glass*.

Gobha, ghoba (possessive) blacksmith – *go-a*.

Gralloch to gut, to disembowel, the intestines – *gralloch*.

Iorram (Scots Gaelic) or **immram** (Irish Gaelic) – a rowing (of a boat), a long sea journey that may lead to the ocean of the soul – *yor-am* or *im-ram*.

Irn-Bru a post Bronze Age faerie fortification (see **Brugh**), an intoxicant recipe of which was stolen from the **Sith** by a Glasgow soft drinks manufacturer – *the bru*.

Loch a Scottish lake – *logh* (with a deeply guttural *ch* like the Jewish name *Chaim*).

Machair alkaline soil formed from wind-blown shell sand along the coast, creating grassy flower-rich pastures – *machhh-ar* (there's that guttural *ch* again).

Marag dhubh black pudding, trademarked to Stornoway, made of blood and oatmeal – *marag dooh*.

Mhoire the name Mairi or Mary specifically as the Virgin Mary – *Vor-u*.

Mholuidh name anglicised as Moluag or variations thereon – *maol-u-aie*.

Miann ardent desire, used by the old folks for the ardent desire of God – *mee-an*.

Mile taing a thousand thanks – *meala-tang*.

Naomh holy, sacred, consecrated, sanctuary – *nuh-v*.

Oiteag shluaigh faerie wind (see also **Gaoth nan sìth**) – *oitag sl-ua*.

Phàdraig or **Pheadair** name anglicised as Patrick or Peter, equivalents to each other – *far-draig* or *fay-dar*.

Sgiobadh a communal work team – *skip-agh*.

Sìth, sì *or* **sìdh, sìd, sìdhe** the faeries, 'the gentry', the Otherworld inhabitants – *shee-h* or *shee-y-e*.

Sìth-bhrughach abounding in faerie hills – *shee-h vr-ooh-agh*.

Sìthean small hill or **Cnoc**, often inhabited by the faeries – *shee-han*.

Sìthichean faerie lore and belief systems – *shee-iu-han*.

Siubhal sìth 'faerie motion' of gliding eloquence in music – *soo-hal shee*.

Sùil-chruthaich literally, 'the Eye of Creation', a quaking bog – *sool kr-ooh-ich*.

Tàladh a death lullaby, to send the soul on its journey – *tahl-ugh*.

Teampall, teampaill (plural) the pre-Reformation 'temples' or chapels of the Outer

Hebrides and a much smaller number of Inner Hebridean and West Highland sites – *tea-am-pall, tea-am-pill*.

Teine sìth faerie fire – *tina-shee-h*.

Tobar, tobraichean (plural) a well for drinking water – *tobar, tob-rach-an*.

Tuireadh elegiac laments sung over the dead – *tour-ugh*.

Bibliography

URLs are shortened, and valid as of first going to press.

ABC (2010) 'U.S. Military Weapons Inscribed with Secret "Jesus" Bible Codes', *ABC News*, 18 January, http://goo.gl/R4CzpM.

Adomnán of Iona (1995). *Life of St Columba* (ed. Richard Sharpe), Penguin Classics, London.

Ayres, Peter (2013) 'Wound dressing in World War I – The kindly Sphagnum Moss', *Field Bryology* 110, 27–34, http://goo.gl/V8QoHm.

Barrie, J.M. (1922) *Courage: The Rectorial Address Delivered At St. Andrews University May 3rd 1922*, Hodder & Stoughton, London, http://goo.gl/WOaCYX.

—(1925 (1920)). *Mary Rose*, Hodder & Stoughton, London, http://goo.gl/JTsMvK.

—(1928 (1904)). *Peter Pan, or The Boy Who Would Not Grow Up*, Project Gutenberg, http://goo.gl/YK83eb.

Barrowman, Rachel & Hooper, Janet (2006). *Lewis Coastal Chapel-Sites: Topographic Survey 2005*, University of Glasgow, Glasgow, http://goo.gl/j8DYD6.

Barrowman, Rachel (2008). *Lewis Coastal Chapel-Sites Survey 2007–8*, University of Glasgow, Glasgow, http://goo.gl/wnXVR6.

Bateson, Gregory (2000 (1972)). *Steps to an Ecology of Mind*, new edn, University of Chicago Press, Chicago.

Bateson, Nora (2011) DVD. *An Ecology of Mind*, Bullfrog Films, Oley, PA.

BBC (2001). 'Infinite Justice, out – Enduring Freedom, in', BBC News, 25 September, http://goo.gl/FJgkSg.

—(2003). '"Million" march against Iraq war', BBC News, 16 February, http://goo.gl/2a8Nko.

—(2016). 'Donald Trump and the politics of paranoia', BBC News Magazine, 24 January, http://goo.gl/n2oYD9.

Bennett, Margaret (2009). 'Stories of the Supernatural: from Local Memorate to Scottish Legend'. In: Henderson 2009, pp. 167–84.

Birkin, Andrew (2003). *J.M. Barrie and the Lost Boys*, Yale University Press, New Haven.

Black, Ronald (2005). See Campbell 2005.

BMJ (1928). 'A Surgical Outpost in the Hebrides', *The British Medical Journal*, 2 June, pp. 954–5, http://goo.gl/VXSyj3.

Boettner, Loraine (1932). *The Reformed Doctrine of Predestination*, Christian Classics Ethereal Library, Grand Rapids, MI, http://goo.gl/EQTL64.

Boston, Thomas (1852). *The whole works of the late Reverend and learned Mr. Thomas Boston, Minister of the Gospel at Etherick*, George & Robert King, Aberdeen. Vol. I, https://goo.gl/MMEjLo; Vol. XI, https://goo.gl/RHXomh.

Bradley, Ian (2003). *The Celtic Way*, 2nd edn, DLT, London.

—(2009). *Pilgrimage: a Spiritual and Cultural Journey*, Lion Hudson, Oxford.

Brock, Rita Nakashima & Parker, Rebecca Ann (2008). *Saving Paradise: How Christianity Traded Love of This World for Crucifixion and Empire*, Beacon Press, Boston.

Burton, John & McCabe, Eileen (2009). *We Don't Do God: Blair's Religious Belief and its Consequences*, Continuum, London.

Bush, George W. (2000). 'Remarks at the Simon Wiesenthal Center in Los Angeles, March 6', *The American Presidency Project*, http://goo.gl/ootLjt.

Calvin, John (1553). *Commentary on John*, Christian Classics, Grand Rapids, MI, trans. William Pringle, http://goo.gl/TB7m6R.

—(1555). *Commentary on Acts* (Chapter 13), Biblehub, http://goo.gl/xoLo1z.

—(1559). *Institutes of the Christian Religion*, trans. Henry Beveridge, Christian Classics, Grand Rapids, MI, http://goo.gl/i66I92.

Câmara, Hélder (1971). *Spiral of Violence*, Sheed and Ward, London, http://goo.gl/7HwGXL.

Campbell, Angus Peter (2012). *An T-Eilean: Taking a Line for a Walk Through the Island of Skye*, Islands Book Trust, Kershader.

Campbell, Iain D. (2011). 'Viewpoint', *Stornoway Gazette,* June 23, p. 17.

—(2012). 'Viewpoint', *Stornoway Gazette*, February 16, p. 9.

Campbell, John Gregorson (2005), ed. Ronald Black. *The Gaelic Otherworld*, Birlinn, Edinburgh.

Campbell, John Lorne & Hall, Trevor (2006). *Strange Things: The Story of Fr Allan McDonald, Ada Goodrich Freer, and the Society for Psychical Research's Enquiry into Highland Second Sight*, Birlinn, Edinburgh.

Carey, John (1999). *A Single Ray of the Sun: Religious Speculation in Early Ireland*, Celtic Studies Publications, CSP-Cymru Cyf, Aberystwyth.

Carmichael, Alexander (1883). 'Statement by Mr Alexander Carmichael as to the Farming Customs in the Outer Hebrides' (pp. 213–16) and 'Grazing and Agrestic Customs of the Outer Hebrides' (pp. 451–82) in *The Napier Commission: Report with Appendices* (sometimes called Vol. 5), The Crown, Edinburgh, http://goo.gl/Uo2sbH.

—(1900). *Carmina Gadelica: Hymns and Incantations . . . orally collected in the Highlands and Islands of Scotland*, Vol. 1, T. & A. Constable, Edinburgh. These, vols. 1–3, can be found in PDF by searching www.archive.org.

—(1900b). *Carmina Gadelica*, Vol. 2, T. & A. Constable, Edinburgh.

—(1940). *Carmina Gadelica*, Vol. 3, (ed. James Carmichael Watson), Oliver & Boyd, Edinburgh.

Chamberlaine, John (1716). *Magnae Britanniae Notitia: Or, the Present State of Great-Britain*, (publisher unspecified), London, https://goo.gl/Kor56v.

Charlton, Noel (2008). *Understanding Gregory Bateson: Mind, Beauty, and the Sacred Earth*, SUNY, Albany.

Clausewitz, Carl von (2008). *On War*, Oxford University Press, Oxford.

Clément, Olivier (1993). *The Roots of Christian Mysticism: Texts from the Patristic Era with Commentary*, New City Press, New York.

Clough, Monica (1994). 'Early Fishery and Forestry Developments on the Cromartie Estate of Coigach: 1660–1746', in Baldwin, John R. ed. *Peoples & Settlement in North-West Ross*, Scottish Society for Northern Studies, Edinburgh, pp. 227–42.

Corbin, Henry (1969) trans. Ralph Manheim. *Creative Imagination in the Sufism of Ibn Arabi*, Bollingen Series XCI, Princeton University Press, Princeton.

Crossman, A.M. (2003). 'The Hydra, Captain A.J. Brock and the Treatment of Shell-Shock in Edinburgh', *Journal of the Royal College of Physicians of Edinburgh,* 33, pp. 119–23, http://goo.gl/ZgGkw4.

Davidson, Hilda Ellis (1998). *Roles of the Northern Goddess*, Routledge, London.

Davis, Walter A. (2006). *Death's Dream Kingdom: The American Psyche Since 9-11*, Pluto, London.

Disraeli, Benjamin (1845). *Sybil or The Two Nations*, Baudry's European Library, Paris.

Dostoevsky, Fyodor (1998). *The Karamazov Brothers*, Oxford Word's Classics, Oxford.

—(1991). *Crime and Punishment*, Penguin, London.

Draper, Robert (2009). 'And he shall be Judged', *GQ.COM*, June, pp. 84–94, http://goo.gl/lPH9Cv.

Dressler, Camille (2014). *Eigg: The Story of an Island*, Birlinn, Edinburgh.

Dunbar, Janet (1970). *J.M. Barrie: the Man Behind the Image*, Collins, London.

Duncan, Angus (1995). *Hebridean Island: Memories of Scarp*, Tuckwell Press, Phantassie.

Dunn, Douglas ed. (1992). *The Faber Book of Twentieth-Century Scottish Poetry*, Faber & Faber, London.

Dwelly (1911), *Scots Gaelic – English Dictionary*, online searchable version, http://goo.gl/3RENHU.

Dymes, Captain John (1630). *Description of Lewis by Captain Dymes*, State Papers published as Appendix F in Mackenzie 1903 (below), pp. 591–5.

Eagle, Raymond (2014). *Seton Gordon: the Life and Times of a Highland Gentleman*, Neil Wilson Publishing, Castle Douglas.

Eliot, T.S. (1959). *Four Quartets*, Faber and Faber, London.

Evans-Wentz, W.Y. (1994 (1911)). *The Fairy Faith in Celtic Countries*, Carol Publishing, NY.

Fanon, Frantz (1967). *The Wretched of the Earth*, Penguin, Harmondsworth.

Ferguson, Calum (2007). *Lewis in the Passing*, Birlinn, Edinburgh.

Follett, Westley (2006). *Céli Dé in Ireland: Monastic Writing and Identity in the Early Middle Ages*, Studies in Celtic History, Boydell & Brewer, Rochester, NY.

Fossard, Lee (2014). *La Vieille dans la toponymie du Royaume-Uni et de l'Irlande: trace d'un ancien culte voué à la Nature?* (The Old Woman in the toponomy of the United Kingdom and Ireland: traces of an ancient cult dedicated to Nature?), Linguistics, HAL Id: dumas-01080422, http://goo.gl/hmq6jV.

Freire, Paul (1972). *Pedagogy of the Oppressed*, Penguin, Harmondsworth.

Freud, Sigmund (1997 (1919)). 'The Uncanny', *Writings on Art and Literature,* Stanford University Press, Stanford, pp. 193–233.

—(1984 (1923)). 'The Ego and the Id', *On Metapsychology,* Vol. 11, Penguin Freud Library, London, pp. 339–407.

Fromm, Erich (2001). *The Fear of Freedom*, Routledge Classics, Abingdon.

Funk, Robert W., Roy W. Hoover & The Jesus Seminar (1993). *The Five Gospels: What Did Jesus Really Say?*, HarperCollins, NY.

Gampel, Yolanda (2000). 'Reflections on the prevalence of the uncanny in social violence', in Robben, Antonius C.G.M. & Suárez-Orozco, Marcela M., eds, *Cultures under Siege: Collective Violence and Trauma*, Cambridge University Press, Cambridge, pp. 48-69.

Gillies, Anne Lorne (2010). *Songs of Gaelic Scotland*, Birlinn, Edinburgh.

Glacken, Clarence J. (1973). *Traces on the Rhodian Shore*, University of California Press, Berkeley.

Goodenough, Kathryn & Merritt, Jon (2011). *The Outer Hebrides: a Landscape Fashioned by Geology*, Scottish Natural Heritage, Battleby, http://goo.gl/38XaNf.

Gordon, Bruce (2011). *Calvin*. Yale University Press, New Haven.

Gordon, Katherine ed. (2006). *Voices from their Ain Countrie: the poems of Marion Angus and Violet Jacob*, Association for Scottish Literary Studies, Glasgow.

Gottlieb, Sidney ed. (1995). *Hitchcock on Hitchcock: Selected Writings and Interviews*, University of California Press, Berkeley.

Gunn, Neil M. (1986). *The Atom of Delight*. Polygon, Edinburgh.

Hedges, Chris (2003). *War is a Force that gives us Meaning*, Anchor Books, USA.

Henderson, George (1896). *Dain Iain Ghobha: the Poems of John Morison (Collected and edited with a Memoir)*, Knox Press, Edinburgh.

Henderson, Lizanne, ed. (2009). *Fantastical Imaginations: The Supernatural in Scottish History and Culture*, John Donald, Edinburgh.

Hennessey, Patrick (2009). *The Junior Officers' Reading Club: Killing Time and Fighting Wars*, Allen Lane, London.

Heschel, Abraham (2011). *Abraham Joshua Heschel: Essential Writings*, Orbis, Maryknoll.

Hietala, Thomas R. (2003). *Manifest Design: American Exceptionalism and Empire*, revised edn. Cornell University Press, NY.

Hofstadter, Richard (1996). *The Paranoid Style in American Politics*, Harvard University Press, Cambridge, http://goo.gl/cqJ7cV.

Hogg, James (1919). 'Kilmeny', *The Oxford Book of English Verse*, No. 514, http://goo.gl/rPIa7R.

Hooper, Janet (ed.) (2008) (see also Barrowman 2006). *The Papar Project – Hebrides*, www.PaparProject.org.uk, http://goo.gl/cT255D.

Hunter, James (2014). *On the Other Side of Sorow: Nature and People in the Scottish Highlands*, Birlinn, Edinburgh.

ILC (International Law Commission of the UN) (1950). *Principles of International Law Recognized in the Charter of the Nuremberg Tribunal*, https://goo.gl/oozxSq.

Jack, Ian (2011). 'Will Rupert Murdoch end up like Citizen Kane?', *The Guardian*, 22 July, http://goo.gl/RKPxm9.

Jack, R. D. S. (1991). *The Road to the Never Land: A Re-assessment of J. M. Barrie's Dramatic Art*, Aberdeen University Press, Aberdeen.

James, Saint (the Just) (2000). *The Epistle of James, with an introduction by the Dalai Lama*, Canongate, Edinburgh.

Johnson, Samuel & Boswell, James (1984). *The Journey to the Western Islands of Scotland*, Penguin, Harmondsworth.

Johnston, Thomas (1909). *Our Scots Noble Families*, Forward Publishing, Glasgow.

—(1929) *The History of the Working Classes in Scotland*, Forward Publishing, Glasgow.

Jones, George (2005). 'Blair "relished" sending troops into Iraq', *Daily Telegraph*, 19 September, http://goo.gl/1O1fWy.

Jussie, Jeanne de (2006). *The Short Chronicle: A Poor Clare's Account of the Reformation of Geneva*, University of Chicago Press, Chicago.

Kennedy, John (1979). *The Days of the Fathers in Ross-Shire*, Christian Focus, Inverness, http://goo.gl/d9stA.

King, Martin Luther (2000). 'My Pilgrimage to Nonviolence', in Wink 2000, pp. 64–71.

Langdon-Brown, Walter (1938). 'Myth, Phantasy, and Mary Rose'. In his *Thus We Are Men*, Kegan Paul, London, pp. 123–51.

LaViolette, Patrick & McIntosh, Alastair (1997). 'Fairy Hills: Merging heritage and conservation', *ECOS* 18 (3/4), pp. 2–8, http://goo.gl/h9Li82.

Lawson, Bill (1991). *St Clement's Church at Rodel*, Bill Lawson Publications, Northton.

Livingstone, David (1870). *Missionary Travels*, Harper, New York.

Longley, Clifford (2002). *Chosen People: the big idea that shapes England and America*, Hodder & Stoughton, London.

Lugar, Richard (1999). 'President Bush's 75th Birthday', *Congressional Record – Senate*, 12 July, pp. 15497–502, https://goo.gl/9Cc1h5.

Luther, Martin (1520). *Address to the Nobility of the German Nation*, Modern History Sourcebook, Fordham University, https://goo.gl/bB5GD2.

—(1543). 'On the Jews and their Lies', in Lund, Eric ed. (2002). *Documents from the History of Lutheranism 1517–1750*, Fortress Press, Minneapolis, pp. 76–8.

—(1546). 'Prefaces to the New Testament', *Luther's Works*, Vol. 35, Fortress Press, Philadelphia, https://goo.gl/FkyqJ7.

MacAulay, John (1993). *Silent Tower*, Pentland Press, Edinburgh.

Macaulay, Rev. Murdo (1980). *Aspects of the Religious History of Lewis*, John G. Eccles, Inverness, http://goo.gl/qrOMYq.

MacCoinnich, Aonghas (2015). *Plantation and Civility in the North Atlantic World: The Case of the Northern Hebrides, 1570–1639*, Brill, Leiden.

MacColl, Allan W. (2006). *Land, Faith and the Crofting Community: Christianity and Social Criticism in the Highlands of Scotland, 1843–1893*, Edinburgh University Press, Edinburgh.

MacDiarmid, Hugh (1985). *The Complete Poems of Hugh MacDiarmid*, Vol. 1, Penguin, Harmondsworth.

Macdonald, Donald (of Gisla) (1990). *Lewis: a History of the Island*, Gordon Wright Publishing, Edinburgh.

—(2004 reprint). *Tales and Traditions of the Lews*, Birlinn, Edinburgh.

Macdonald, Finlay J. (1984). *Crotal and White*, Futura, London.

—(2003). *Crowdie and Cream*, Time Warner, London.

MacDonald, Fiona (1994). *Island Voices*, Canongate, Edinburgh.

MacFarlane, Norman C. (1995). *Apostles of the North*, The Gazette Office, Stornoway.

MacInnes, John (2006) ed. Michael Newton. *Dùthchas Nan Gàidheal: Selected Essays of John MacInnes*, Birlinn, Edinburgh.

—(2009) 'The Church and Traditional Belief in Gaelic Society', in Henderson 2009, pp. 185–95.

Mackenzie, W.C. (1903). *History of the Outer Hebrides*, Simpkin, Marshall & Co., London.

Mackenzie, W.M. (1904). 'Notes on Certain Structures of Archaic Type in the Island of Lewis – Beehive Houses, Duns and Stone Circles', *Proceedings of the Society of Antiquaries of Scotland*, VOL. XXXVIII, pp. 174–204, http://goo.gl/xXknkk.

Maclean, Calum I. (1964). 'The Last Sheaf', *Scottish Studies*, Vol. 8, pp. 193–207.

Maclean, Magnus (1925). *The Literature of the Highlands*, Blackie & Son, Glasgow.

Maclennan, Malcolm (1979 (1925)). *Gaelic Dictionary*, Acair, Stornoway.

MacLennan, William Murdoch (1976) recorded by Emily Lyle. 'Childhood Memories of Lewis', *Tobar an Dualchais*, Edinburgh, http://goo.gl/zx2koA.

MacLeod, Alexander (of Uig) (1925). *Diary and Sermons of the Rev. Alexander Macleod*, Robert Carruthers Printers, Inverness, http://goo.gl/VI7ta8.

MacLeod, Donald J. of Bridge of Don (2015) ed. Alastair McIntosh. *The Highland Clearances on the Isles of Lewis and Harris*, web published, http://goo.gl/vQlRj5.

MacLeod, Finlay ('Doctor') (1997). *The Chapels in the Western Isles*, Acair, Stornoway.

—(2000). The *Healing Wells* of the Western Isles, Acair, Stornoway.

—(2009). *The Norse Mills of Lewis*, Acair, Stornoway. (All three listed here are also available in Gaelic editions from Acair).

MacLeod, John (2008). *Banner in the West: A Spiritual History of Lewis and Harris*, Birlinn, Edinburgh.

Macleod, Kenneth (Coinneach MacLeoid) (1908) 'Sea-Poems', *The Celtic Review*, Vol. V, pp. 146–8.

—(1911). 'An Clachan a Bha ann'. In: MacKay, David N. (ed.), *Leabhar a' Chlachain: Home Life of the Highlanders, 1400–1746*, Maclehose, Glasgow, pp. 135–45.

—(1927). *The Road to the Isles: Poetry, Lore & Tradition of the Hebrides*, A & C Black, London.

MacQueen, Angus (Canon) (2008). 'Under the Mantle of Holy Bride', in Domhnall Uilleam Stiùbhart (ed.), *The Life and Legacy of Alexander Carmichael*, Islands Book Trust, Port of Ness, p. 183.

Mansfield, Stephen (2004). *The Faith Of George W Bush*, Tarcher/Penguin, NY.

Marsden, John (1995). *Sea-Road of the Saints: Celtic Holy Men in the Hebrides*, Floris Books, Edinburgh.

Martin, Martin (1994 (c. 1695)). *A Description of the Western Islands of Scotland*, Birlinn, Edinburgh.

McGinty, J. Walter (2003). *Robert Burns and Religion*, Ashgate, Farnham.

McGrath, Alister E. (1995). *The Christian Theology Reader*, Blackwell, Oxford.

—(1997). *Christian Theology: an Introduction*, Blackwell, Oxford.

McIntosh, Alastair (2000). 'Saint Andrew: Non-violence & National Identity', *Theology in Scotland*, University of St Andrews, VII:1, pp. 55–70, http://goo.gl/648Umk.

—(2001). *Soil and Soul: People versus Corporate Power*, Aurum, London.

—(2008). *Hell and High Water: Climate Change, Hope and the Human Condition*, Birlinn, Edinburgh.

—(2011). 'A Nonviolent Challenge to Conflict', chapter 3 in Whetham, David (ed.), *Ethics, Law and Military Operations*, Palgrave Macmillan, Houndsmill, pp. 44–64, http://goo.gl/5Fd27C.

—(2012). 'O Donald Trump, Woe Donald Trump', *Earthlines,* Issue 1, May 2012, pp. 43-6, http://goo.gl/1CBcjv.

—(2013). *Island Spirituality: Spiritual Values of Lewis and Harris*, Islands Book Trust, Kershader, http://goo.gl/QNu759.

—(2014). 'Foreword' to the new edition of James Hunter, *On the Other Side of Sorrow: Nature and People in the Scottish Highlands*, Birlinn, Edinburgh, xv–xxxix, http://goo.gl/khtYKd (extract).

—(2014b). 'Lost lexicon of piety recovered', *The Herald*, 23 June, p. 16.

—(2015). *Canoe Pilgrimage to the Isle of Boreray*, http://goo.gl/bk8rpi.

—(2015b). *Spiritual Activism: Leadership as Service* (with Matt Carmichael), Green Books, Cambridge.

McKay, J.G. (1932). 'The Deer-Cult and the Deer-Goddess Cult of the Ancient Caledonians', *Folklore* 43:2, pp. 144–74.

Meek, Donald ed. (2003). *Caran an t-Saoghail: The Wiles of the World: Anthology of 19th Century Scottish Gaelic Verse*, Birlinn, Edinburgh.

Merton, Thomas ed. (1965). *Gandhi on Non-Violence*, New Directions, NY.

Meyer, Kuno (trans.) (2000). *The Voyage of Bran (Imran Brain)*, In Parentheses Publications, Medieval Irish Series, Ontario, http://goo.gl/sxHlp7.

Mitchell, Arthur (1880). *The Past in the Present: What is Civilisation?* David Doublas, Edinburgh.

Moral, Tony Lee (2013). *Hitchcock and the Making of Marnie*, revised edn. Scarecrow Press, Lanham, chapter 'Mary Rose', pp. 197–221, not in earlier edition.

Murchison, T.M., ed. (1988). *Sgrìobhaid Choinnich MhicLeòid. The Gaelic Prose of Kenneth MacLeod*, Scottish Gaelic Texts Society, No.16, Edinburgh.

Napier, Lord (1884*). Report of Her Majesty's Commissioners of Inquiry Into the Condition of the Crofters and Cottars in the Highlands and Islands of Scotland, in 1884*, The Crown, Edinburgh, https://goo.gl/OsnE4S.

Neat, Timothy (2013). 'Hamish Henderson – the Art and Politics of a Folklorist'. In: Chambers, Bob (ed.), *The Carrying Stream Flows On*, The Islands Book Trust, Kershader.

Newton, Michael ed. (2006). *Dùthchas Nan Gàidheal*, see MacInnes 2006.

—(2006b) '*Bha mi 's a' chnoc*: Creativity in Scottish Gaelic Tradition', *Proceedings of the Harvard Celtic Colloquium*, 18/19: 1998 and 1999, Harvard University, https://goo.gl/1gJ2dg.

OCA (2016). *Hieromartyr Clement the Pope of Rome*, Orthodox Church in America, http://goo.gl/vRheVC.

O'Cathain, Seamus (1995). *The Festival of Brigit: Celtic Goddess and Holy Woman*, DBA Publishing, Dublin.

Ó Crualaoich, Gearóid (2003). *The Book of The Cailleach*, Cork University Press, Cork.

Oppenheimer, Mark (2014). 'Evangelicals Find Themselves in the Midst of a Calvinist Revival', *New York Times*, 3 January, http://goo.gl/HStZfq.

Ormond, Leonee (1987). *J.M. Barrie*, Scottish Academic Press, Edinburgh.

Panikkar, Raimon (1991). 'Nine Sutras on Peace', Interculture XXIV:1, pp. 49–56, Montreal, http://goo.gl/eIawm.

Pierre, Abbé (2005). *Mon Dieu . . . Pourquoi?* Plon, Paris.

Roberts, John L. (1999). *Feuds, Forays and Rebellions: History of the Highland Clans, 1745–1625*, Edinburgh University Press, Edinburgh.

Rumsfeld, Donald (2011). *Known and Unknown: a Memoir*, Sentinel, NY.

Sainte-Marie, Buffy (1964). 'Universal Soldier', *It's My Way!*, album website http://goo.gl/FQz727.

Shaw, George B. (2001). *Saint Joan*, Penguin, London.

Smith, G. Gregory (1919). *Scottish Literature*, Macmillan, London.

Smith, Iain Crichton (1986). *Towards the Human: Selected Essays*, Macdonald Publishers, Loanhead, http://goo.gl/edwEWO.

Smith, Rupert (2006). *The Utility of Force: the Art of War in the Modern World*, Penguin, London.

Starmore (née Matheson), Alice (2008). *Mamba – the Exhibition* (exhibition catalogue), Windfall Press, Gress.

—(2012). 'Isabella's Crag: Language, landscape and life on the Lewis moor', *Earthlines*, Issue 1, 4–9.

Starr, Mirabai (trans.) (2014). *Julian of Norwich: The Showings*, Canterbury Press, London.

Steigmann-Gall, Richard (2004). *The Holy Reich: Nazi Conceptions of Christianity, 1919–1945*, Cambridge University Press, Cambridge.

Stewart, R.J. (1990). *Robert Kirk: Walker Between Worlds – A New Edition of The Secret Commonwealth of Elves, Fauns and Fairies,* Element, Longmead.

Surtees, Virginia (1984). *The Ludovisi Goddess*, Michael Russell Ltd, Salisbury.

Swire, Otta (1966). *The Outer Hebrides and their Legends*, Oliver & Boyd, London.

Sylvester, Rachel & Thomson, Alice (2007). 'Dr Bari: Government Stoking Muslim Tension', *Daily Telegraph*, 10 November, http://goo.gl/aTPQpD.

Thomas, F.W.L. (Captain RN) (1859). 'Notice of Beehive Houses in Harris and Lewis; with Traditions of the "Each-Uisge," or Water-Horse, Connected Therewith', *Proceedings of the Society of Antiquaries of Scotland*, Vol. III:1, pp. 127–44, https://goo.gl/bPoBf6.

—(1867). 'On the Primitive Dwellings and Hypogea of the Outer Hebrides', *Proc. Soc. Ant. Scot.*, Vol. VII:1, pp. 153–95, http://goo.gl/jMlqdL.

—(1890). On the Duns of the Outer Hebrides. *Archaeologica Scotica*, Vol. V, pp. 365–415, http://goo.gl/y3hX6D.

Thomas, R.S. (1996). *R.S. Thomas* (anthology of poetry), Everyman, London.

Thompson, Paul (2009). 'Donald Rumsfeld's holy war: How President Bush's Iraq briefings came with quotes from the Bible', *Daily Mail / Mail Online*, 20 May, http://goo.gl/H8u7wo.

Thompson, Paul & Drury, Ian (2010). 'Shot in the foot: Propaganda fear as our troops are given U.S. guns carrying secret Bible codes', *Daily Mail / Mail Online*, 20 January, http://goo.gl/8naCIk.

Thomson, Derick (1982). *Creachadh na Clàrsaich: Plundering the Harp*, Macdonald Publishers, Edinburgh.

Thomson, Iain R. (2001). *Isolation Shepherd*, Birlinn, Edinburgh.

Truffaut, François (1985). *Hitchcock: A Definitive Study of Alfred Hitchcock*, Simon and Schuster, New York.

Walker, Alice (1983). *The Color Purple*, The Women's Press, London.

Ward, Benedicta (trans.) (1984). *The Sayings of the Desert Fathers*, Liturgical Press, Collegeville.

Watt, Eilidh (1989). 'Some Personal Experiences of the Second Sight'. In: Davidson, Hilda Ellis, ed., *The Seer in Celtic and Other Traditions*, John Donald, Edinburgh, pp. 25–36.

WCF (1647 (1986 edition)). *Westminster Confession of Faith* (with introductory statement of the Church of Scotland's partial dissociation in 1986), http://goo.gl/ZCWQR.

—(1991). *The Shorter Catechism*, Knox Press, Edinburgh.

Weaver, J. Denny (2001). *The Nonviolent Atonement*, Eerdmans, Grand Rapids.

West Side Historical Society (undated). *List of emigrants from Arnol, Bragar and Shawbost on the Metagama*, http://goo.gl/qO4uWU.

WHFP – West Highland Free Press (2011). 'Donnie Foot – "the People's Theologian" – and the West Highland Free Press', 27 May 2011, p. 20.

—(2011b). 'Island men can expect to die earlier than most', *West Highland Free Press,* 28 October, 1.

—(2015). 'Survey shows youth attachment to the Isles', 13 November 2015, p. 7.

Wink, Walter (1992). *Engaging the Powers: Discernment and Resistance in a World of Domination*, Fortress Press, Philadelphia.

—(2000) ed. *Peace is the Way: Writings on Nonviolence from the Fellowship of Reconciliation*, Orbis, Maryknoll.

—(2002). *The Human Being*, Fortress Press, Minneapolis.

Winthrop, John (1630). *A Modell of Christian Charity*, Collections of the Massachusetts Historical Society, http://goo.gl/y5fA7f.

Wynne-Jones, Jonathan (2009). 'Tony Blair believed God wanted him to go to war to fight evil, claims his mentor', *Daily Telegraph*, 23 May, http://goo.gl/DSWsuh.

Yeats, W.B. (1990 (1893)). *The Celtic Twilight*, Prism Press, Bridport.

Endnotes

To minimise intrusion in the text, I often group nearby references into a single note. See www.AlastairMcIntosh.com/poacherspilgrimage/ for this book's web page with additional resources.

Beginnings

1. 'The Moon in Lleyn', Thomas 1996, 82.
2. McIntosh 2011.
3. Luther 1520.
4. WHFP 2011.

1 The Devil's Debut

1. BMJ 1928, for a swashbuckling account of the following story.

2 A Sacred Landscape

1. Goodenough & Merritt 2011.
2. Various sources, mainly Mackenzie 1903, xxxvi–xxxix. All of this is fairly speculative.
3. Pliny, first century, IV:30.
4. Bradley, 2003, 2009. Adomnán 1995, p. 127 (I:20). Sharpe's commentary to this passage (his endnotes 108 and 109) states that the pilgrim in question had a Pictish, not a Celtic name. Sharpe also discusses manuscript claims that, by the eighth century, Irish clerics wanting to live an eremitic life had reached as far as the Faeroes and Iceland, before being driven out by the 'heathen' mores of 'Northmen pirates'. Adomnán stresses that the mission from Iona stretched out across the known world. Columba's destiny, from before birth, was to 'become famous through all the provinces of the ocean's islands, and he will be a bright light in the last days of the world' (p. 105, Adomnán's 2nd preface). In this he was 'predestined to lead the nations to life' (p. 207, III:3).

   Right at the end of the hagiography, Adomnán affirms that Columba had, indeed, 'earned a reputation that is famous not only in our own Ireland and in Britain, the largest of the ocean's islands, but has also reached the three corners of Spain and Gaul and Italy beyond the Alps, and even Rome itself, the chief of all cities' (p. 233, III:23). In the Celtic era the Hebrides and western seaboard of Scotland formed a Gaelic-speaking cultural continuum with Ireland, united (not divided) by the information superhighway of the Irish Sea and Sea of the Hebrides. Then the big dividing barrier was Druim Alban – the Ridge of Scotland – the name given to the mountain ranges running down the middle of the mainland, to the east of which were the Picts that Columba evangelised. It is to such geography that we might look for the earliest origins of Scotland's east–west divide.

5. Ordnance survey, Ross-shire (Island of Lewis), Sheet 27, 1851, http://goo.gl/zB8iTi. This shows the name as Airidh na'n Sagart, but Rusty, the blacksmith (John Macdonald, 31 Leurbost) considers that it should be Àirigh, consistent with the presence of the sheilings.

6. Discussion in *Soil and Soul*, McIntosh 2001, 18–19, citing John MacAulay of Flodabay.

7. Campbell 2005, 33–4. Campbell notes that this story is also localised in Ferintosh (Black Isle, Ross-shire), and he gives similar examples from Iona and Mull. In the latter instance, the faeries speak English, to which the narrator remarks: 'It is well known that Highland Fairies who speak English are the most dangerous of any.' Ronald Black's commentary (p. 319) suggests this is 'the steep slope negotiated by the Tarbert-Stornoway road where it descends to Scaladale in North Harris', or I think it may be a little higher on the same mountainside, above where *Lochan nan Clach-Mòra* is marked on the OS map by the roadside.

8. The Qur'an, XVIII:31, Yusuf Ali edn. ('The Cave').

9. Bateson 1972, 317, my italics. The chapter was first published in the journal, *Psychiatry*.

10. Bateson 2011. In this book I have sometimes used literary licence with the sequencing of time, projecting thoughts or incidents that happened later on back into my thoughts during the walk. While actually walking, my mind was empty for much of the time. I even came back and told Vérène that I wasn't sure if I had material for a book. Much of the conscious reflection took place later, interwoven with dreams, subsequent events and conversations that connected with the pilgrimage in a continuum in my mind that felt outside of strict time boundaries, as if the walking, reflecting and writing became a continuous process. The encounter with Nora is an example. The panel did not take place until 17 February 2012 by which time I was well into writing the book. Her event was fittingly called *Remembering the Future*. Her words that night helped me to constellate ideas I'd been working on from well before the walk. In particular, I had been stimulated by a paper on creativity and the Celtic mind, delivered at Harvard University by my friend, the Gaelic scholar Michael Newton (Newton 2006).

    Apart from such occasional loose playing with the sequencing of time when telling anecdotes, and apart from the need sometimes to protect sources by disguise and to reconstruct conversations from notes and memory, I have not assumed literary licence. Any magical realism is for real.

11. 'War is a force that gives us meaning' – Hedges 2003.

12. Martin 1994, 207. He gives it as *Tey-nin-druinich*, but as that is antiquated, I have used Captain Thomas's version in referring to Martin, as quoted later.

13. Maclennan 1979, 136.

14. The most scholarly study of Brighde is O'Cathain 1995. Black (in Campbell 2005, 586) states: 'The saint's name is in the nominative *Brighid*, in the genitive Brìghde or, for short, Brìde.' I have gone for the simple but poetic for my mainly English-speaking readers.

15. MacLeod 1997. For archaeological surveys of the ecclesiastical sites see Barrowman 2006 & Barrowman & Hooper 2008. Also, the Papar Project compiled by Hooper 2008.

16. Eagle 2014, Chapter 7.

17. In MacLeod 2000, 75–7.

18. Shonny 'Mhòr' Macdonald of Berneray. Just don't ask him to tell the one about the

wife of Pabbay climbing high onto a cliff in exchange for a shilling, to show the excise man her husband's *poit dubh*!

19. Alastair 'Alda' Ferguson gave me his source as the late Berneray tradition bearer, Roddy MacAskill. Hansen's biography of Armstrong leaves just enough genealogical wriggle room for the story possibly to have foundation, and Neil is a very island name, not otherwise in the Armstrong family. See discussion in McIntosh 2015. On the monks, Martin 1994, 138–9.
20. Follett 2006. A modern Scottish movement, that understands itself to be continuing the spirit of this tradition, is www.ceilede.co.uk
21. Johnston 1909. Tom Johnston, initially brought to prominence by Ramsay MacDonald, became the wartime Secretary of State for Scotland under Winston Churchill.
22. Statistical Account of 1792 quoted in Lawson 1991, 7.
23. MacLeod 1997, 9.
24. Calvin 1559, 1:11:1 (p. 95).
25. Jusse 2006, 122. See Gordon 2011 on Farel's iconoclasm and close friendship with Calvin.
26. See discussion in McIntosh 2013, 20–3; 100–1.
27. Translation as in MacAulay 1993, 10–12. I have added a comma after 'former times'.

3 *Blue Mountain Hare*

1. Job 38:8, 29. Another face of the Rodel tower has an equally sexualised male figure, said in tourist guides to be known locally as Suemas a'Bhuid, translating into the vernacular as 'Jimmy the Willy'.
2. Genesis 28:17.
3. This is what John MacAulay of Flodabay said. He also told me that her tomb was originally just to the right of the entrance door and raised above the floor. However, it was moved by Historic Scotland because of a recurrent problem with dampness. It now lies (out of sight and mind), 'underneath the floor of the church, and directly below the window in the south transept' (MacAulay 1993, p. 15).

    John also pointed out that the Sìol Thormoid are known as the Macleods 'of Harris and Dunvegan', the stress being on Harris, although Dunvegan Castle is located on Skye.
4. Gillies 2010, endnote to her Introduction.
5. MacInnes 2009, though he is not writing specifically about Màiri.
6. Macleod, Kenneth, 1927, 223.
7. I discuss such, including the satirical attacks of Hugh MacDiarmid, Sorley Maclean and the 'Celtosceptic' leanings of Donald Meek, in McIntosh 2014.
8. 'One Who Sang *The Cradle Spell of Dunvegan*', Macleod 1927, 169–78.
9. This high regard was expressed by both Professor Donald Mackinnon and Professor James Carmichael Watson – each of them pioneering holders of the chair in Celtic at Edinburgh 'There is only one man, Kenneth Macleod,' Mackinnon told Mrs Kennedy-Fraser in the 1920s. 'None now living can match his understanding,' wrote Carmichael Watson in his Editor's Note to Vol. 3 of the *Carmina Gadelica* in 1940. See McIntosh 2013, 146.
10. Dressler 2014 (1998). McIntosh 2001.
11. Thanks to the ethnomusicologist, John Purser, for this translation of what is a common Gaelic epitaph.
12. Neat 2013 states: '*The Carrying Stream* is an old "folk" phrase' that was given new

meaning by Hamish Henderson of the School of Scottish Studies. I have recorded a similar palpable experience of being swept up in the stream at the height of the Eigg land reform campaign in McIntosh 2001, 185–6. (If we don't talk about such experiences, our silence becomes the voice of complicity in contributing to their delegitimisation by materialistic worldviews.)

13. Campbell & Hall 2006, 7.

14. Martin 1994 (1695), 105. Herman Moll's map of 1714, http://maps.nls.uk/view/74417584, see also my Chapter 7. Curiously, other English language maps do not reflect Moll's explicit association with sainthood. The 1850s OS six-inch series, like the present day version, shows it as Eilean Mhuire, which requires a Gaelic understanding to decode the spiritual import. John MacAulay tells me that early cartographers and writers often spelt Mary's name as 'Mhuire' (e.g. Rev. Macphail in Thomas 1890, 366), but that most Lewis and Harris people today would render it as Mhoire. He adds that the isles: 'all have individual names, but are locally known collectively as "Na h-Eileanan Mor" which is generally accepted as meaning the Big Islands, which does not really make good sense. My own thoughts are that this was meant to be Eileanan Mhoire, or, Mhuire – the Virgin Mary's Islands, and the local name is a corrupt form of that. The north-easterly island in the group is called Eilean Mhuire' (pers. com. emails 2015).

    Martin says of the Shiants, 'Island-More hath a chapel in it dedicated to the Virgin Mary . . .' (p. 105). This infers but does not directly state John's view. He then says of Eigg's kenning name (the name by which it is known by mariners when at sea): 'The natives dare not call this isle by its ordinary name of Egg when they are at sea, but island Nim-Ban-More, i.e., the isle of big women' (p. 304). However, I have heard a Roman Catholic opinion on Eigg that this is a Protestant misnomer, and that it should properly be translated as Island of the Holy Woman Mary, 'nim' being a corruption of *naomh* (holy, sacred).

    John MacAulay's opinion of this (pers. com. 2015) is: 'I'm fairly certain that Martin Martin's *More* [in the Shiants] is the Virgin Mary's island. Likewise, Eilean na'm Ban *More* [for Eigg] is also the Virgin Mary's island. Had it been 'big women' it would be Eilean na'm Ban *Mor*. MM was supposedly a Gaelic speaker, but I'm often surprised at some of his writings.'

15. Eliot 1959, 42; MacDiarmid 1985, 422 ff.

16. 'Boy I was', Macdonald 2003, 10. Eilean na Caillich story, Macdonald 1984, 149–60

17. Unfortunately, the early Ordnance Survey maps for Harris lack the rich detail of those for Lewis, where the landowner (Matheson) helped finance the operation. However, the maps of both the 1843–82 and the 1888–1913 six-inch series show an island at the NW head of Langabhat with 'stepping stones' leading out to it, as well as a Dun (or fort) on a nearby island. John MacAulay has confirmed to me: 'I have always been led to believe that Eilean na Caillich was the one with the causeway.' Google Earth (which I had not used to look at the territory before going on the pilgrimage) shows markings that may be sheiling settlements and traces of feannagan (raised bed cultivation) near Eilean na Caillich, and what could be the ring of a collapsed both on the island. The OS maps also mark the remains of a dun (or fort) on a smaller island nearby. Half a mile to the north-west there's a loch in the hills called Loch na Caillich (Loch of the Old/Holy Woman), and just over a mile to the east, at Holasmul, the tiny Lochan Bhrighde (Little Loch of Brigit), with a long line of nearly a hundred small cairns, of evident spiritual significance, that Seumas Crawford (with John's local expertise) documented and surveyed in 2012.

    In reviewing my manuscript, John wrote: 'Maybe you could add that about halfway along the eastern shore of Loch Langabhat there is a small bay inside a string of small islands. On an ancient map this area is called A Chomraich (the sanctuary, or, a place of sanctuary). There is also a cairn – Carnan a'Chomraich. It all adds to the spiritual significance of this place.' This raft of spiritual associations, as John has emphasised many times, is substantially feminine, in a way that he feels to be associated with the ancient traditions linking Brighde to the Hebrides generally, and Harris in particular. The parish church at Scarista was originally consecrated to Saint Bride, and Harris itself was the pre-Reformation Parish of Kilbride (see note on Kilbride at the end of Chapter 5).

18. McIntosh 2000.

4 *The Elder of Roineabhal*

1. See material added to the 2004 edition of *Soil and Soul*, http://goo.gl/WKFoJm.
2. Full details of this engagement are on my website at http://goo.gl/hZZTbK. Lafarge has now merged with Holcim, and I came off the Sustainability Stakeholders Panel in 2013, after serving for ten years.
3. West Side Historical Society, undated.
4. WHFP 2011b – Island women have a life expectancy of 82, one of the best in Scotland; but on average men die at 74, ranked as the eighth worst in the UK, along-side deprived urban areas like Glasgow, Manchester and Belfast.
5. WHFP 2015. This youth survey suggests 40% want to be living on the island in five years' time, and 48% to be back by the age of 35.
6. Napier 1884, 1176. Professor Donald MacKinnon, a friend of the Rev. Kenneth Macleod, was one of the six Napier commissioners.

5 *On the Golden Road*

1. *The Acts of Andrew*, in McIntosh 2000. In the Orthodox tradition, Andrew is the *Prōtoklōtos*, meaning 'first-called'.
2. Augustine's *Letter 189 to Boniface*, http://goo.gl/1Z2eJF, using the translation in Aquinas' *Summa Theologica, Question 40: War*, http://goo.gl/3fJGz2.
3. WCF 1647, 6:IV.
4. Calvin 1559, 2:16:1. For further discussion of these points, and in an island context, see McIntosh 2013.
5. McGinty 2003, 41–43. The poem naming Thomas Boston is Burns' 'Letter to James Tennant, Glenconner'.
6. This is from Boston's commentary on the Westminster Shorter Catechism, of which question eight answers: 'God executeth His decrees in the works of CREATION and PROVIDENCE.' Boston 1852, Vol. I, 129, 223.
7. From *A View of the Covenant of Works from the Sacred Records,* Boston 1852, Vol. XI, 317–320.
8. While writing this, I entered Crothairgearaidh into Google, and to my astonishment, the single reference that came up is to an academic thesis, in French, by one Lee Fossard (Fossard 2014). He describes having visited Lewis to be shown the shape of an old woman in this hill, his informant being 'Doney Martin'. (Wait till I get hold of that old milkman and ask what tales he's been telling to the poor French tourists!) I'd never noticed this shape myself nor heard of it talked about, though when shown in Fossard's photographs (taken from the place beside John-Neil Montgomery's house, where we'd leave the road to get the mussels), it stands out sure enough.

9. Some scholars have argued that, during the era of the Penal Laws imposed by English colonisation, Irish Catholic priests were forced to seek training on continental Europe where some fell under the influence of the Dutch theologian Cornelius Jansen (1585–1638). Like the Calvinists, Jansen emphasised original sin and total depravity. Jansenism was subsequently declared heretical by the Catholic Church. Other scholars refute this as a major influence, suggesting that the 'strictness' of Irish-American Catholicism is better explained by the knock-on of Victorian English morality on its Irish subjects, as well as by asceticism from religious orders rubbing off on lay society. It should be noted that Presbyterians were also persecuted under the Penal Laws in that they sought to impose a very Anglican version of Protestantism and thus, in part, the explanation for Irish Presbyterian emigration to America.

10. Luke 7:36-50; Mark 14:6.

11. The ranking varies from year to year. In 2014, the most recent at my time of writing, the UK had slipped to 6th place, SIPRI, http://goo.gl/zBQOhI.

12. WCF 1647, 3:I. The theological parallels between some expressions of Calvinism and Wahabbism in Sunni Islam are striking, as is the historical penchant of both towards authoritarian psychology and enforcement.

13. Ferguson 2007, 101–110.

14. Ferguson 2007, 50–61.

15. Peter 1:4, KJV. Other translations say 'participants', both being true to the Greek.

16. Carmichael 1900, 166. I have left the spellings in his original forms.

17. Carmichael 1900, 166; Carmichael 1900b, 114–5.

18. Carmichael 1900, xv. The present-day Church of Scotland at Scarista was consecrated to Brighde, and in its vestry, John MacAulay (who is an elder there) has framed a *Record of Serving Ministers*, going back to 1542. This states: 'Originally, the Parish of St. Bride, which included Barra and St. Kilda; was later known as the Parish of Harris.'

    The legal document to which I refer is one that I stumbled upon by chance, pertaining to the disposal of the estate of Alexander Hume in the *Edinburgh Gazette* of 24 February 1832, p. 64. This states: '. . . the following Subjects as included in the said Process of Ranking and sale, viz – The Patronage of the Churches and Chapels of the whole Lands of Harris, lying within the parish of Kilbride, commonly called Harris, and Sheriffdom of Inverness.' It is revealing that even church patronage – the right to confer a minister on the population – was, in those days, something to be bought and sold.

    Another angle on Kilbride is from Otta Swire, who cites Miss Ada Goodrich Freer as maintaining that, during the first half of the eighteenth century (i.e. before the arrival of Protestant evangelicalism), Harris was not called Na Heradh or The Herries, but Kilbride (Swire 1966, 61). Freer was commissioned by the Society for Psychical Research in the 1890s to conduct a survey of the second sight in the Hebrides. Her work, published in *Folklore*, was later discredited as having been substantially plagiarised from Fr Allan MacDonald of Eriskay. How much of it was valid, nonetheless, would be difficult now to appraise, as she appears to have been a woman who played loose with the truth. Her biographer, Trevor Hall, explores the implications of her having lost both parents in childhood, and while I have not read his book, I suspect that she might be an example of Barrie's Mary Rose syndrome.

6 *The Blacksmith's Well*

1. Crichton Smith, 1986.
2. Calvin had his opponents summoned to the Consistory (Geneva's religious court) to answer charges of dancing at a wedding in defiance of his preaching – a matter that threw him into fury. In other inquisitions, it seems probable that he participated in torture by the rack of his opponents to procure confessions of heresy. He was also instrumental in the execution, by live burning at the stake, of Michael Servetus for heresies of which pantheism was prominent (Gordon 2011, 140–1, 215, 217–32). The suppression of dancing was, in places, undoubtedly carried into the Highlands and Islands (McIntosh 2013, 54, 100. Carmichael 1900, 4–5).
3. Henderson 1896, xliii.
4. Trans. Meek 2003, 281–7
5. MacLeod 2008, picture caption facing p. 174: There is a lovely energy to this picture, which includes Morag. It reminds me of traditional Mennonites or Amish, albeit with a different theology but probably no difference in the underlying piety.
6. Cited in Ayres 2013.
7. Henderson 1986 (biographical sketch), xlix–l. Henderson (p. xlv) describes him as 'An aristocrat of nature's creation.'
8. 2 Samuel 23:14–16.
9. This poetry is a reprise from Derick Thomson's 'An Tobar' / 'The Well', the first three verses of which are quoted at the start of this book, from Thomson 1982, 48-9. The theme is continued as a separate poem, but of the same title, on pp. 240-5.
10. The late Norman Macleod of Bridge House, Leverburgh, crofter, lobster fisherman and retired policeman, pers. com. (letter) 21 November 2001.
11. John MacAulay says the well was on the sharp hill leading south out of Tarbert, but was lost when widening the road.

7 *My Own Lochs Now*

1. Kinlochresort – Ceann Loch Reasort – *ceann* = head; *ruadh* = red (Old Norse); *fjord* shortened to *ort* – thus, The Head of the Red Fjord (John MacAulay pers com., 2010; though an alternative etymology has it as the Boundary Fjord, bounding Lewis and Harris).
2. Sarah Scott (née Morrison) of the Harris Hotel says that at the time, both the hotel and the castle were under the same ownership, and that it was usual for visitors to stay at one while on the way to the other: a journey made in Barrie's era by pony trap. The dining room has now been double glazed, but the JMB pane has been conserved and is on display in the hallway.
3. Dunbar 1970, 246–50. The dedication was to the five orphaned Llewelyn Davies boys (Barrie 1928). Birkin 2003, 203–6, includes a photograph of the island (or rather, tiny island cluster) on Loch Voshimid. There was also Norwegian inspiration based on what was probably a true-life child abduction story, see Moral 2013 (new edn), 197–205. All quotes from *Mary Rose* that follow are from Barrie 1925.

   The expression about the island liking to be visited is close to a saying that Kenneth Macleod (1927, 54) renders as: *Dh' iarr a' mhuir a bhi 'ga tadhal*, 'The sea likes to be visited'.

   A local source on the Voshimid connection to *Mary Rose* was the Rev Angus Duncan of Scarp who died in 1971 (Duncan 1995, 151–3). In 1966, Nicolas Llewelyn Davies wrote to Duncan, saying that he had more or less ridiculed the idea of a

Voshimid connection to the play until, in 1964, he returned to the lochside and sat down just opposite Mary Rose Island (the capitalisation of the name is his). He wrote: 'Strange as it may seem, I had the most vivid recollection' of sitting with Barrie by the waterside, looking across to the island, and Barrie recalling an old legend 'which I think first sprang from Scandinavia' (Duncan 1995, 151–3, 200–1). The Rev. Duncan's memoirs are compiled by his eponymous son, Angus Duncan, who added this correspondence in an appendix.

As seems to befit Presbyterian clergy, Duncan observed in his writings that the Scarp of his childhood was full of sìthean, faerie hills. 'Island children had implicit faith in fairies.' The dog would pick their presence up and show alarm, even when humans couldn't see them. 'We did not regard the fairies as either friendly or hostile. They were neutral, keeping to their own company and not likely to interfere with us unless taken by surprise' (Duncan 1995, 115).

4. Moral 2013, 205.
5. Ormond 1987, 133–5.
6. Hogg 1919. James Hogg (1770–1835) compiled his version of Kilmeny from what was already in the Borders ballad tradition. *Kil* = church of; and *meny* is thought possibly to relate to Eithne, the visionary mother of Saint Columba. This creates lovely resonances and interweaving of traditions.
7. Langdon-Brown 1938.
8. MacLeod 1997, 51 & 71. MacLeod also cites the tradition, from Martin Martin, that women were buried in St Tarran's and men at St Keith's. It seems to be through Martin that the association between Keith and Chè is presumed. However, in Twitter discussion (of all things) with the Irish scholar, @VoxHib, *Vox Hiberionacum*, another possibility is invited. He pointed out (24 Nov 2015) that there is also a standing stone of the same designation on North Uist, Clach Mhor A'che. Menhirs often marked burial. He suggests that Chè might be a corruption of the Old Irish *caí*, meaning lamenting, weeping or keening (death song) – http://edil.qub.ac.uk/9072. Thus, Teampall Chè would make sense as Teampall of the Keening, this fitting with its male designation and therefore the place at which the women would keen for their departed menfolk.
9. Martin Martin, John Chamberlayne and Daniel Defoe all recognised the value of Hebridean fisheries to the newly fledged Union of England and Scotland. Moll had been the maker of Martin's new map of the Western Isles (Martin 1994, 2–3). Two years after the publication of Moll's map of all Scotland, John Chamberlayne FRS, citing Martin as his informant, wrote in *Magnæ Britanniæ Notitia* that, with English investment, these fisheries which were the best in Europe would become 'one of the Blessings which this Island will reap by the late Happy Union', and that, 'the Settling of a Fishery in those Parts, will raise a Nursery of stout and able Seamen in a very short time, to serve the Government on all Occasions' (Chamberlayne 1716, 384). In other words, the fishing grounds would be good recruiting grounds for the Royal Navy and building up the Empire. See also Clough 1994, and a major new study of the colonisation of the Hebrides published as this book was undergoing its final edit, MacCoinnich 2015.
10. Macdonald 2004, 220.
11. Johnson & Boswell 1984, 51.
12. The purchase of the land by the North Harris Trust involved a private partner who bought the parts of the estate in which the community were not interested, namely, Amhuinnsuidhe Castle and its associated salmon fishing. The funds required for the land purchase were received from a multitude of private donors, the John Muir Trust (JMT), Comhairle nan Eilean (the Western Isles Council) and Scottish Natural Heritage, plus local fundraising events and such statutory sources as the Scottish

Government's land fund. David Cameron, the inaugural chair of the Trust, has asked me to mention that the JMT, which is dedicated to the conservation of wilderness areas, put no conditions on the community in making its contribution. The relationship with JMT operates by mutual respect, similar to the pattern established with the Scottish Wildlife Trust's community partnership on Eigg.

The Trust's board is elected by local residents, the area having a population of about seven hundred people. Its guiding goal is adapted from the definition of 'sustainable development' from the Brundtland Commission of the United Nations: namely, to further 'forms of progress that meet the needs of the present without compromising the ability of future generations to meet their needs'. Further information from http://www.north-harris.org.

13. The incident with the bucket might have been a separate occasion, I don't remember clearly. There was more than one such scare, as polecats also made an appearance in our part of the island at about the same time.

After the shooting, I skinned the poor beast, tanned its hide with a chromium product called Sheeptan, and proudly presented it like ermine to my mother. She was underwhelmed, pointing out that she'd need rather a lot to make as much as a stole. According to my sister's friends, I also had a penchant for presenting prospective girlfriends with tanned mice and rabbit skins. Apparently, the story of the uranium, told in Chapter 17, was not an isolated instance. Casanova never knew the likes!

14. See Dwelly's Gaelic dictionary entry for 'moon'. The old names for the moon are from the South Uist poet, Angus Peter Campbell, https://goo.gl/lzKDnN.

8 *The Rising of the Sìth*

1. Thomson 2001, 86.
2. Campbell & Hall 2006, 7 (Vikings), xiii (Jung).
3. Email from Iain Thornber, 25 November 2011.
4. Same Thornber email as above, with attached extract from his stalking journal, entitled: *Glengalmadale and the Oiteag Sluagh*.
5. See her elegiac account of this transhumance, Starmore 2012. Alice is best known for her books of knitting designs.
6. Starmore 2008, 60.
7. This is Cath MacKinven's view. For discussion of spelling variations and nuances between sìth and síd, and the relationship between faeries and peace, see Black's commentary in Campbell 2005, especially p. 293. I should emphasise that, as one who does not have the Gaelic other than a smattering of words, I should not be considered an authority on these matters.
8. Campbell 2005, xxxiii, 41; Yeats 1990, 38.
9. Evans-Wentz 1994, 8, xxxiv.
10. LaViolette & McIntosh 1997.
11. Corbin 1969, 248. *Le monde imaginal* = the imaginal world, or realm. See also (in French) www.amiscorbin.com.
12. Genesis 6:5, 11. Swire 1966, 63-65. Otta Swire was writing for a popular readership and usually fails to give her sources. They seem to be a mixture of existing writings such as Martin Martin, and personal experience. As a child, her family would be guests of the Mathesons at Lews Castle in Stornoway. While her writings do not attain the standards of modern folklore studies, the ethnographer Ronald Black, in his introduction to her book on Skye, warmly praises her achievement none the less.
13. John MacAulay pers. com. suggests, *lys* = light; *kyntyre* = headland. The sands of gold story is from Swire 1966, 74.

14. This quote is the context of the illustration on the cover of Glacken 1973.
15. Isaiah 28:16, KJV.
16. Carmichael 1900, 190–195, '*Laoidh an Triall* – Hymn of the Procession'. I have omitted two verses, and the last verse is specific to the version collected from the Barra fishermen.

9 *Two Airmen*

1. Mrs Cecil Frances Alexander, who wrote 'All Things Bright and Beautiful', was born in colonial Ireland but had a deep spiritual sensitivity and a concern for the poor. However, her politics in this verse may have been shaped by her English father having been the land agent (factor) for the Earl of Wicklow.
2. Paraphrased, partly in my own words, from 1 Samuel 8.
3. Luther's 'On the Jews and their Lies' (1543) reproduced in Lund 2002, 76–78. Steigmann-Gall (2004) quoting Goebbels (p. 21), Koch (p. 2), Himmler (p. 235), 'favoured nation' etc. (p. 15).
4. Fromm 2001, 77 & 32, my emphasis. Fromm explores both the Lutheran and Calvinist backdrops to Nazism in his chapter, 'Freedom in the Age of the Reformation' (pp. 33–88).
5. Smith 2006, 25 & 237.
6. McIntosh 2011.
7. King 2000, 70. For a more complete exposition of the case I put to the military for nonviolence, see my paper in the textbook edited by UK Defence Academy staff, McIntosh 2011.
8. Like many sayings attributed to Gandhi, this is loosely based on translations from the Hindi, but is consistent with material in such anthologies as Merton 1965.
9. John 18:11; Luke 22:51; John 18:36–37.
10. Câmara 1971.
11. Sylvester & Thomson 2007.

10 *Rule, Britannia!*

1. MacDiarmid 1985, 422 ff., 'On a Raised Beach'.
2. John 18:36–37. It may be objected that twice in the gospels, Christ appears to raise the sword – Matthew 10:34 and Luke 22:36. However, in the first case this is clearly as a metaphor, and in the second, it is symbolically to fulfil a prophesy of Isaiah's that he would be seen as a brigand.
3. Calvin 1553, commentary to John 10:35.
4. Longley 2002; Hietala 2003. In contrast to Calvin's interpretation of power in Romans, Walter Wink (1992) holds that, in human hands, power becomes fallen, can be redeemed, and must therefore be called constantly back to its higher, God-given vocation.
5. Boettner 1932, 275–281.
6. Oppenheimer 2014. Calvinistic Baptists are often known as 'strict' or 'particular' Baptists because of their sense of being a 'particular' or Elect people.
7. Lugar 1999.
8. Mansfield 2000, 68 (my emphasis), 109.
9. BBC 2001.
10. Jack 2011.
11. Rumsfeld 2011, 59.

12. Thompson 2009; Draper 2009.
13. John 18:11; Matthew 26:52.
14. Jones 2005.
15. Thomas 1859. I have corrected 'boths' to *bothan*. See also Thomas 1867 and Mackenzie 1904.
16. Mitchell 1880, 58–72.

11 *Venison and Honey*

1. My contemporary, Rusty (John Macdonald) of Leurbost, tells me that as children they'd be told not to go out to the loch alone, 'in case the each-uisgue gets you'.
2. My use of 'mythopoetic' is based on the more correct 'mythopoeic'; however, the latter is usually used to suggest a *fictional* narrative. I consider that there is nothing fictional about poetry. Poetry is primarily the heart's mode of direct perception of reality. It is engagement with *poesis* as 'the making' of reality. My usage overlaps with, but does not imply any necessary connection to, Robert Bly's use in the context of the Men's Movement, where the mythopoetic means the use of myth specifically to aid self-understanding. The sense of myth as being something that is untrue, is a usage that dates only to the mid nineteenth century.
3. Yeats 1990, 120–1.
4. From a Biblical perspective, Jesus never promised us the letters of Paul, or Hebrews. If we go by Saint John's gospel (e.g. 14:16–18), he only promised us the Paraclete – the discerning power of the Spirit – and that is the standard to which all subsequent scriptural exegesis should be subordinate.
5. In Gordon 2006, 12, my emphasis.
6. Smith 1919, 19–20.
7. McKay 1932. See also Ó Crualaoich 2003, 124, about Ireland, and Ronnie Black's discussion in Campbell 2005, 306–8. The Gundestrup cauldron suggests a shamanic relationship with the deer.
8. MacInnes 2006, 500. This is from the abstract, prepared by Michael Newton, of John's paper, *Am Fàsach ann an Dùthchas nan Gàidheal*.
9. 'Looking at Legends of the Supernatural', MacInnes 2006, 459–76. John MacInnes draws explicitly on Jungian psychology in this essay. Although born in Uig in 1930, his family moved to Raasay, off Skye, before he was eight.
10. Black (in Campbell 2005, lxxx) alludes to this line of Loch Ness Monster interpreta-tion, but his promised Note 151 turns out to be about something else. My memory of his thesis is from one of his columns in the *West Highland Free Press* in the 1990s. Black also draws attention to Campbell's view that, properly speaking, the each-uisge is of the loch and the kelpie of the river (p. 372).
11. MacInnes 2006, 500.
12. MacInnes 2006, 459–76, including remaining quotes, this section.
13. This was Norman's letter of 21 November 2001, five pages of typescript, written about two years before his death. It said: 'I thank you above all for the dogged perse-verance with which you resisted the rape of fair maid Harris by corporate powers and the help you enlisted from such unlikely quarters as Chief Sulian Stone Eagle Herney. I like his conclusions: *If we fail to find the solution and cure for Mother Earth, Mother Earth will cleanse herself of the offending organism that is killing her.*' However, Norman took issue with some of my interfaith appreciation, saying: 'Your theology as far as I can follow it, leans too much towards the New Agery that is sweeping the world, a mish mash of all faiths and deities male and female stirred into one unholy *brochan* in the belief that it cannot do you any harm as there is no

God anyway (Psalm 14).' So – that was me, fair told! It's a good example of how the island way of mentoring between an older and a younger man will proceed with praise in the one moment, and reprimand in the next.

14. For typical examples of the second sight from the records of Fr Allan McDonald of Eriskay, see material reproduced in Part 4 of Campbell & Hall 2006. The degree to which these stories continue to circulate in local culture is remarkable. Literally as I was final-editing this passage, the '60 years ago' section of the *Stornoway Gazette* reproduced a report of 20 December 1955 about the 'Benbecula seer' who stopped his work, and announced: 'The minister's son has been drowned on Loch Langavate and they cannot find him; but I "see" the body.' The man went to join the search party, they dragged the loch at the place of his vision, and recovered the body. This story was at least third hand and could be considered indicative of a genre but not reliable – though were it untrue, locals would quickly say. Others come first or second hand. The case with my mother and the dog is written up in full in McIntosh 2008, 200–3.

15. Kirk in Stewart 1990, 39–45. Tarbett, also spelled Tarbat.

16. Bennett 2009. For an insight into the degree to which the second sight continues in modern times, see Watt 1989.

17. Clough 1994.

18. 'To be born . . .', from Barrie's introduction to the 1913 edition of my favourite childhood book, R.M. Ballantyne's *The Coral Island* (cited in Moral 2013, 201). 'To die . . .', from the end of Act III, Barrie 1928.

19. Livingstone 1870, 12.

12 *Catching Mary Rose*

1. Campbell 2011: 'Of course the past awakens a sense of nostalgia . . . *Cianalas* – that Gaelic sense of wistful longing – is a great word but a horrible feeling.'

2. Donald J. Macleod of Bridge of Don, see Macleod 2015, 15. I use his estimate (below) about the 700 souls. Most of the households would have been extended families with elderly maiden aunts etc. as part of the typical household.

3. The designation, Seaforth Highlanders, was used in Mackenzie's recruitment campaign of 1793 (see below), but it was not until 1881 that the Seaforth Highlanders were formally created within the British Army, following merger of the Ross-Shire Buffs with the Duke of Albany's Own Highlanders.

4. 'Very severe' – from Napier 1884 (Vol. 2), 859. Reports from *The Times* of 1839 in Macleod 2015, 31.

5. Roberts 1999, 142–147. Mackenzie 1903, 187–188.

6. Sources and discussion in McIntosh 2013.

7. Johnston 1929, 203.

8. Duncan 1995, 74. In contrast, the present proprietors of Scarp, the Bakewell family (hello Petra!), have always been welcome on Harris, the more so now that they have brought in investment to open up the Isle of Harris Distillery at Tarbert – the world's first commercial 'social distillery', as it proudly calls itself.

   Kinlochresort itself continued to be sparsely occupied into relatively recent times, but clearances of the villages to the north and south meant that no road was ever put in, leading to the settlement's complete abandonment in 1963.

9. Pers. com. from Maureen Russell of Bridge of Weir, 4 May 2015. Her mother, the daughter of Peggy and William, was Morag MacKay of Ardnacille, of Scalpay.

   Commenting on this, Kenneth Macleod, a mariner of Scalpay, has said (pers. com. email 23 April 2015): 'People of that generation were very strong spiritually and would have regularly prayed outdoors . . . I remember coming across a neigh-bour, who was an elder in the church, praying in his byre a couple of hours after we had buried their cow which had died in the field. There are similar stories of people having praying points in the moor which they would go to regularly. Sometimes I think we have lost that total dependence on God and prayer to help with everyday things like food, safety and general activities.'

10. Mackenzie 1904.
11. Sorley Maclean's 'Hallaig', in Dunn 1992, 129–33. Web version http://goo.gl/hJoCDG. For commentary, see MacInnes 2006, 418–21. At the end of this book, where I return to Hallaig, my source for Dun Cana (or Dun Caan) as a sithean of bards, into the present, is Newton 2006b, 329 (footnote). I did not want to place the footnote there as it would have disrupted the emotion.
12. Interview with John Russell Taylor, Gottlieb 1995, 59–63.
13. Moral 2013, 44, 209–18 (on *Times* and non-commercial prospects). Truffaut 1985, 307–9 (on irrationality). Moral's chapter, 'Mary Rose', became available in a later edition of his book only when I was at a late stage of editing. It offers a comprehen-sive overview of the scattered sources.
14. Sainte-Marie 1964.
15. Crossman 2003, my emphasis.
16. Mark 5:1–20; Luke 8:26–39. The account is in Josephus, Book 3:7.
17. Freud 1997. Freud 1984, 380–381. Freud did not use the term Thanatos (after the Greek god of death). Rather, it was later applied to his concept of the 'death instinct'.
18. Gampel 2000, my emphasis.
19. Hogg 1919.
20. Davis 2006, 13 & 35, xiii.
21. Barrie 1922. Dunbar 1970, 271–6. One critic who appreciates Barrie's dramatic importance and refuses to have him relegated to the kailyard, is Jack 1991, 21–4.

13 Smoking Out the Devil

1. Black in Campbell 2005, 293. These quotations are Black summarising Ó Cathasaigh's thoughts.
2. Herdsboy in Macaulay 1980, 97. Finlay's people, Maclean 1925, 151.
3. This peak is the reclined woman's nose of the so-called 'Sleeping Beauty' complex. There is an archival recording in the School of Scottish Studies of an old man of nearby Airighbhruthach telling how, when he was a child, it was pointed out to him as being 'the Silver of the Faeries' (MacLennan 1976).
4. Often, today, a purely Norse derivation is suggested – *sja-fjörör* – 'sea firth'. However, the sapper maps, surveyed in the early 1850s, used variant spellings. These included *shithford* and *sheaford*. Their intention does seem to have been to convey *sith*, but perhaps in the sense of *peace*, as this highly contorted loch was long renowned for providing safe anchorages in any direction of the wind.
5. Macdonald 2004, 85. There is some question as to the exact site at Seaforth Head. Macdonald (2004, 84–6, 89–90) holds that it was at the stone circle site on Croft 6, but Christopher Macrae (pers. com, telephone, 2 March 2016), the present Head Keeper and grandson of Macdonald's source, Duncan Macrae, tells me that he always understood it to be a few hundred yards to the east, at the point on the road below where the present-day memorial to the Seaforth Highlanders was erected by Mr Ian Mitchell of Stornoway. This view would be consistent with the presence

there of a mound with substantial stone foundations. Seumas Crawford thinks that it was a on a nearby island in the sea loch.

6. Katie would, of course, have been thoroughly versed in passages like Ezekiel 11:19.
7. John MacInnes, Saint Bride's Day Lecture, University of Edinburgh, 1 February 1996, oral delivery.
8. Yeats 1990, 92–5. Margaret Bennett has remarked that, within her own island family and locality, traditional belief had no need for labels to separate one category of experience from another, as 'the entire system is simply taken for granted'. This can 'range over an extensive continuum of belief in God, the Holy Spirit, the Devil, angels, saints, fairies, ghosts, spirits of the dead . . . and so on' (Bennett 2009, 179).
9. Mary Kate Maclennan of Seaforth Head died on Sunday 13 May 2012. Although I mentioned her in *Soil and Soul* (p. 25), it was only in the last two years of her life that I had the opportunity to spend several evenings with her, and a subsequent wonderful visit with my son, Adam. I have back-written this aside into the pilgrimage story by way of a reflection on a rainy morning. I also used part of my story with her in *Island Spirituality*. In March 2015 I sent a copy of this to her sister, Mary Ann Mackenzie of Totescore, Skye, who I had chanced to meet on Harris as they were a Luskentyre family. She wrote back saying: 'The book will be a forever reminder of how dear Ceiteag was to the family and the people she met and held dear.' I mention that, because it would be easy, in today's world, to doubt the very existence of such a person; or to question how they might be esteemed within their own families and communities. For more on this theme, see McIntosh 2013, 81–2 and Watt 1989.
10. 'Never needed therapists' was the late Dr Donald Murray of Back, laterally of Crossbost.
11. For referencing of these and following remarks, see Chapter 3 of McIntosh 2013 (now free online at the web link). Also, biography in Surtees 1984.
12. Again, references and more detail in McIntosh 2013.
13. Macdonald 2004, 99. Calvinism had been the religion 'by law established' in Scotland since 1560, but Macdonald is referring to its hard-line expression on Lewis, to which I have applied the loose term hyper-Calvinism. I use that term in its more traditional sense of holding a belief in 'limited atonement', though it could be argued that such is just plain *Calvinism*, and such is what Macdonald means.

   The paradox of most island Calvinist preachers, including Alexander Macleod, is that they adhere to the Westminster Confession's doctrine of limited atonement – 'Neither are any other redeemed by Christ . . . but the elect only' (WCF 1647, 3:VI) – but, at the same time, teach justification by faith through freely-offered grace, *as if* anyone so choosing 'to turn to Christ' can be 'saved'. Quite how this sits with the Arminian heresy that they otherwise repudiate, is complex to fathom.
14. Macleod was well aware that these clearances, two years after his arrival, reflected poorly on him. In one of his begging letters to Lady Mary, he requested that his sheep might graze land other than that which she was in the process of clearing for his benefit, 'as some of them are foolishly disposed to blame me for their removal'. He worried, lest 'this circumstance may render my gospel ministration unsuccessful' (Macaulay 1980, 182).
15. Macleod 2015.
16. MacFarlane 1995, detailed citations in McIntosh 2013.
17. Macleod 1925. His letters to Lady Mary in Macaulay 1980, 181–4. Kennedy 1979, 98. Again, see McIntosh 2013 for a more complete exploration of these themes.
18. MacCoinnich 2015, 243.
19. Fanon 1967. Freire 1972, 122.

20. Walker 1983, 225. The gin, a hand-cranked machine for teasing out cotton fibres on the plantations, epitomised forced labour.
21. Augustine, *City of God*, XX:22, http://goo.gl/FMEYd8, and XXII:30, http://goo.gl/1wBgWu.
22. Luke 1:51–3, NRSV.
23. MacColl 2006, 169–78.

14 Saint Bridgit's Sheiling

1. 2 John 4:18.
2. Luke 4:17–20, reading from Isaiah 61:1–2, KJV.
3. Thomson 1982, 172–3, used with the late poet's kind permission.
4. Scots Psalter of 1615, the paraphrase of Psalm 121.
5. Macleod 1911. With Cath's approval, I have abridged her translation, placing some of Kenneth's original turns of phrase in quotation marks to better catch their nuances. Cath died in October 2014.

    Macleod's story could be an account of the *bardo* journey of the dying process, straight from *The Tibetan Book of the Dead*. The women start off in what I would describe as the *shamanic function* that mediates between the worlds, there to perform 'keening' songs that ease a soul's transition through the watery veils of death. However, tempted by revenge for their sufferings, their gift of blessing turns to venom. They slide into the *malefic function* of becoming sorceresses of the dark arts. It is one thing to withhold blessing, but quite another to curse. Later, as their consciences awake, they rise to the *prophetic function*. Compassion leaves them as the handmaids of redemptive love.
6. Carmichael 1900, 172.
7. At an ecumenical service held in Griminish Church in 2006 as part of an academic conference, Canon Angus MacQueen of South Uist and Barra said of Alexander Carmichael: 'I realised that [as children] we were still living in the world of Carmichael, moving gently to the rhythm of the passing seasons, conscious of the hand of God guiding our path . . . I realise how sensitive his approach to our prayer life was, as if he were eavesdropping on the private life of those old folk who included their God in every passing moment of the day' (MacQueen 2008). What Carmichael saved in the six volumes of the *Carmina Gadelica* endures, in part, as a continuous living tradition and not merely as a burnished fossil.
8. Adomnán 1995, 200, 218, and Sharpe's commentary on the place names (p. 368).
9. Ó Crualaoich 2003, 139–40; 184–5. Davidson 1998, 67. Maclean 1964.
10. Carmichael 1883, 460.
11. Exodus 20:25, NLT. The Hebrew *chereb*, usually translated as 'tool', literally means a sword. As such, this passage metaphorically says that the altar of God should not be built on a foundation carved out by violence.
12. Shaw 2001, 59. The late Walter Wink alerted me to this in his discussion of imagination, Wink 2002.

15 The Baptism of the Gods

1. Black 1999, 719. The Macleod quote is from one of his 'Footnotes' columns in the *West Highland Free Press* from around 2009, but I have lost the original cutting.
2. Disraeli 1845, 43.

3. Plato's *Timaeus*, 37d, trans. Jowett. 'Wherefore he [the Father creator] resolved to have a moving image of eternity, and when he set in order the heaven, he made this image eternal but moving according to number, while eternity itself rests in unity; and this image we call time.'

4. Charlton 2008, 13.

5. Scholars of folklore have explored faerie as a set of 'retrieval codes' to talk about borderline issues, including mental illness, disability and child abuse. See Black 2005, li–lxvi.

6. Barrie 1925, 93, 139.

7. Newton 2006b. On Tír-fo-thuinn (below) see Macleod 1927, 59–63.

8. Meyer 2000. This choice of verses are a medley of my own compilation. Emain Ablach is the land of apples, of which Avalon is another version, both overlapping with if not the same as Tìr nan Òg.

9. Carey 1999, 11–12, 32. This John Carey, the medievalist, is not to be confused with the Oxford literary critic.

10. Carey 1999, 34, 29.

11. Carey 1999, 38.

12. Carey 1999, 106, 91, 106. Blake: 'To the Eyes of the Man of Imagination, Nature is Imagination itself.'

13. See, for example, Jussie 2006, 122. Also www.re-soundings.com.

16 The Great Cosmic Poacher

1. James 2000, viii, xv.

2. Luther 1546. However, he dropped this dismissal, and other judgements on James, in the 1522 edition.

3. Epistle of James 2:18–26, 5:15, 1:10–11.

4. Epistle of James 4:1. I have used both the KJV and NRSV to combine both poetry and clarity.

5. Wynne-Jones 2009 quoting mostly from Burton & McCabe 2009.

6. Hofstadter 1996, 3–4. I hit on Parker, BBC 2016, just as this was going to press and in the same context of Donald Trump's psychology. The presidential runner self-identifies as Presbyterian and attributes his religious values to his mother, who was an émigré from the Isle of Lewis (at a time when it was mainly the men who emigrated). I have explored aspects of this relationship in a poetic work, McIntosh 2012; see also McIntosh 2013 on island religious psychohistory. Trump's narcissistic psychology fits the thesis of this book concerning disarticulation between the inner and the outer life. He appears to be a man for whom everything is on the outside, with little empathy and high narcissism. This might connect with any family trauma that he himself carries from both parents' separation from their home countries, but also, especially given the Hebridean Calvinist backdrop, with the trauma arguably carried by America's Protestant conservative evangelicals with their often binary world-view. An irony is that Hebridean evangelicals are mostly evangelical and socially conservative, but not politically conservative, because they have retained the strong and empathetic links to community that an émigré loses – see my discussion in Chapter 11 on Lord Tarbett, Sir Robert Boyle and the second sight.

7. BBC 2003.

8. Wink 1992.

9. Clausewitz 2008, 13.

10. Luke 6:27; Matthew 5:44. The ear – John 18:10-11; Luke 22:49–54.

11. Because, within my own community on the Isle of Lewis, there is little mileage to be had in arguing about the authenticity of what has been handed down in the Bible, I tend to argue from face value, and therefore metaphorically. However, there is now a vast literature on authenticity based mainly on textual analysis. An accessible synopsis of scholarly thought are the findings of the Jesus Seminar (Funk & Hoover 1993), though I think sometimes they miss the metaphorical possibilities in some of the texts that they consider improbably attributed to Jesus.

12. Matthew 10:34; John 2:12–22 where the ambiguity is mainly around the Greek, *te*, and which the NIV translates as: 'So he made a whip out of cords, and drove all from the temple courts, *both* sheep and cattle; he scattered the coins of the money changers and overturned their tables'. Luke 36:38, 'And he was reckoned among the transgressors' quotes Isaiah 53:12. In exploring such texts I roam between the multiple translations now available on sites like www.BibleHub.com, especially looking at the Greek and Hebrew originals and the semantic range of key translated words.

13. Also in Matthew 20:28. Paul (or attributed to him) in 1 Timothy 2:6.

14. Isaiah 53:10.

15. Saint Gregory in McGrath 1997, 397–8. The line in the Apostles' Creed probably hinges on 1 Peter 3:9 – Christ 'preached unto the spirits in prison.' Catholic and Protestant traditions differ in their interpretations. On atonement theories and nonviolence, see Weaver 2001.

16. Anselm in McGrath 1995, 182–3.

17. Calvin 1559, 2:16.1–2.

18. Like with predestination, penal substitution is pivotal to the Calvinist worldview. In his newspaper column, one moderator of the Free Church – a man for whose ministry I nevertheless have much respect – called for, 'a healthy emphasis on the central tenet of the Christian faith: the penal, substitutionary atonement of Christ' (Campbell 2012).

19. 'Sligo' in Ferguson 2007, 187.

20. Colossians 1:17.

21. Council of Jerusalem, Acts 15:20 (where Paul and Barnabas were the messengers). Numbers 15:32–36 (sticks) & Exodus 35:3 (fire). Heschel 2011, 150–4 (essay on 'The Sabbath').

22. Calvin 1555.

17 *Sages of Shawbost*

1. Kenneth Macleod, a seaman of Scalpay, email pers. com. 23 April 2015.

2. Quotes that follow – Luke 3:11; 1 John 4:16. *U-vil* is Kenneth Macleod's rendition of the oystercatcher's call, see 'St Bride's Bird' in Macleod 1927, 101–2. Also, for the bird in less plaintive mood he suggests *Fal liu o* (p. 48).

18 *Fléchettes in the Soul*

1. Dymes 1630. On Dymes and the English 'planters' (i.e. colonisers) of Stornoway, see MacCoinnich 2015, 321–5.

2. Ferguson 2007, 2. The Hebrews quotation, above, is 6:19.

3. MacLeod 1997, 18. The diocese of Sodor was formed in the Norse era and extended down the Hebrides and West Highlands to the Isle of Man, where the name is still retained. Kenneth Macleod mentions the 'Sodor Isles' in poetry (Macleod 1927, 49).

4. Macleod 1927, 101, 40.

5. Gunn 1986, 20.
6. ABC 2010. Thompson & Drury 2010. The Psalms verse is confirmed on a (transient) soldier web forum, 'British 3 Rifle Infantry MTP' at https://goo.gl/qF1xoy.
7. In my brief time in the museum I did not have chance to pick up on this detail. What is written here has been filled in by later research into fléchettes in general. Also, the ABC news story did not break until a year after my walk. I have back-written it in as the pilgrimage continued to take shape in my mind during the years that I wrote this book.
8. Inspired by a passage in Hennessey 2009, 252–3.
9. Dostoevsky, *Notes from Underground*, as in the editorial extract used by McDuff in Doestoevsky 1991, xvii.
10. Clément 1993, 303. Where Jesus said he came 'to bring fire to the earth' (Luke 12:49), this can be read as Hellfire, the fire of the Spirit, and/or the fire of love. What reading might the overall spirit of Jesus suggest?
11. Dostoevsky 1998, 402–4 (see also 206).
12. Psalm 82:6, quoted by Jesus to defend himself against blasphemy in John 10:34. 'Let it be' (below) – Luke 1:38 KJV – which other translations render as, 'Let it be . . .', including the famous version according to Saint Paul of Liverpool.

19 *The Temple of Crò Naomh*

1. See Barrowman 2008. Her work was not readily available until 2014, but it now adds rich context and factual information to the temple sites discussed here. For my purposes, I've held to a folk focus with Dr Finlay MacLeod's handbook, and not tried to be an archaeologist.
2. I didn't see the horseshoe because of the fenceposts. I was later given this information by Jill Smith, author and artist of Aird Uig, who regularly attends the well. In the early noughties, she was told by an old woman who lived in the nearby house that her brother-in-law had set the horseshoe imprint into the cement cap 'for luck'. She added that the lady – who had looked her in the eyes, grasped her by the arm, and taken her to see the well – 'told me how she and another lady cleaned the well, by filling it with stones, then taking them out and while the water was low, scouring it with heather. She said it never ran dry, and people came from miles around in times of drought (from Carloway) and would sit for an hour waiting for their pail to fill. Oh the pace of life then.' Pers. com. emails 12/13 November 2015.
3. MacLeod 2009, quote below from p. 47.
4. Campbell 2005, 558, with Black's commentary on p. 598. See also Dwelly's and Maclennan's dictionaries.
5. Thomas 1890, 374. Captain Thomas credits Sir James Matheson with stopping the destruction of island archaeological sites (p. 375). Many of these would be robbed for building stones once the old superstitions had worn off with the advent of modernity and evangelicalism. Doctor Finlay writes: 'An Old Norse word for fort is Borgh, and Bhuirgh is the genitive' (email 26 January 2016). In Ireland, sìthean are commonly referred to as 'faerie forts', these being to where the original mythological inhabitants of the land retreated when the Milesians (us) arrived, bearing weapons of iron, such as would have chopped down the forests and destroyed the primordial ecology.
6. Pierre 2005, 69–70. My thanks to Joëlle Nicolas, my mother-in-law, a theologian of French Huguenot (Calvinist) extraction, for drawing my attention to this passage and helping me to translate it.

Orthodox theologians, and probably also J. Denny Weaver (Weaver 2001) with whom I have discussed this matter, would argue that Liberation Theory is only a new representation of *Christus Victor,* and that a liberationist praxis is what the Church Fathers were always trying to express with their imagery of the Devil. Perhaps, but such imagery needs dusting down and rendered fit for future purpose, which is what Walter Wink has done with his Jungian exegesis of the Powers that Be.

7. Wink 2002, 109–10. Walter Wink's critique of blood sacrifice atonement theories here are of huge future importance.

8. Panikkar 1991. I have tided up the quote into the version that my colleague Alastair Hulbert, myself and others used with Panikkar when we hosted an event with him in Govan, Scotland, in 1990 – http://goo.gl/Rnikab.

9. Maxim Gorky, *The Lower Depths,* 1903.

10. Gunn 1986. 'Inner light' is based on John 1:9, known as 'the Quaker text'. Consider also Luke 12:49.

11. Starr 2014, 13.

20 *The Heart of the Sun*

1. Macleod 1908, footnote.

2. OCA 2016.

3. In Brock & Parker 2008, 173. Clement of Alexandria came out with pithy statements, like: 'Everything belongs to the God of beauty; everything subsists in the God of beauty' (Ibid., 167). Although venerated as a saint in the Eastern church, the Western church (or Rome) bumped him off its list of saints during the sixteenth century purge of the aptly-named Cardinal Caesar Baronius. Just possibly, Clement was ahead of his time. In 'The Rich Man's Salvation', he insisted on the spiritual equality of women, and had a penchant for gender-bending statements, like: 'God . . . to us became feminine. In His ineffable essence He is Father; in His compassion to us He became Mother' (Chapter 37, http://goo.gl/DhyGuH).

4. Eliot 1959, 51.

5. Luke 22:19 (*anamnēsin*); Acts 3:21 (*apocatastasis*); 2 Peter 3:12, James 5:7, etc. (*parousia*). These mystical Greek words of the New Testament resonate with Plato's concept of time and eternity that was touched on in Chapter 15.

6. Marsden 1995.

7. Ward 1984, via *Orthodox Church Quotes,* http://goo.gl/kXmjON.

8. Carmichael 1900, 322–5.

9. MacInnes 2009, 186. Apparently she was Presbyterian too, but sometimes the old ways linger.

10. MacDonald 1994, 63–69. This remarkable interview includes: 'Gaelic has its own culture. How will I put it? It's bardic. Gaelic songs are full of love and feeling and passion and emotion. Take the word "dear" or "darling" . . . Gaelic has about 70 words for that.' Not bad for one of the most hard-line Calvinists of my childhood! Shows what richness can lie behind the stereotypes.

21 *The Woman at the Well*

1. Martin 1994, 106–8. Mackenzie 1903, 524–7.

2. Carmichael 1900, 126–7. The identification of the *cionaran-crò* with the pilot of a pod of whales comes from Professor Donald Meek.

3. Martin 1994, 100–104.

4. Carmichael 1900b, 270–2. 'Children of men' – the italics are Carmichael quoting within the quote, I'd guess, as a reference to the apocalyptic imagery of Psalms 90:3 and 115:16 KJV. Campbell 2012, 63–4, recounts a similar version of this legend from his own South Uist background, observing that it speaks to 'a very different ecological environment to the one we have today ... it creates a wholly different aesthetic – indeed a wholly different cosmology.'

   Dòmhnall Uilleam Stiùbhart, who headed the Carmichael Watson Project at Edinburgh University until recently, tells me that he thinks the poem Carmichael refers to will be the one archived at CW150/56 – 59 at http://goo.gl/YW6mNO (pers. com. 2015). The text appears to be fragmentary and mostly not (yet) translated into English. Its source was Mary MacMillan, a domestic servant from Lionacuith, South Uist.

5. See my chapter in McIntosh 2008, 107–39.

6. Swire 1966, 63–65.

7. In 2014, it was my great pleasure to be asked by Dr Domhnall Uilleam Stiùbhart to serve as a referee with his application to have the Carmichael Watson Collection at the University of Edinburgh granted *Memory of the World* recognition by UNESCO. See *The Herald*, Glasgow, 19 June 2014, and my subsequent Letter to the Editor, McIntosh 2014b. The application was a success. The world has recognised the deep spiritual heritage of the Hebrides. The rest is over to us.

Index

Note: Topographical names are generally given using the most common spelling. Where this is English, the Gaelic equivalent (if appropriate) is given in brackets. Entries such as 302n refer to the endnotes.